POSTMODERN

AMERICAN

POETRY

A Norton Anthology

POSTMODERN AMERICAN POETRY

A Norton Anthology

edited by **PAUL HOOVER**

COLUMBIA COLLEGE, CHICAGO

W • W • NORTON & COMPANY

New York   London

Copyright © 1994 by W. W. Norton & Company, Inc.

Printed in the United States of America

First Edition

The text of this book is composed in Caledonia with the display set in Rockwell and Park Avenue.
Composition and manufacturing by the Haddon Craftsmen, Inc.
Book design by Jack Meserole.

Since this page cannot legibly accommodate all the copyright notices, the pages preceding the index constitute an extension of the copyright page.

Library of Congress Cataloging-in-Publication Data
Postmodern American poetry : a Norton anthology / edited by Paul
  Hoover.
     p. cm.
  Includes bibliographical references (p.) and index.
    1. American poetry—20th century. 2. Postmodernism (Literature)—
United States. I. Hoover, Paul, 1946–
PS615.P669 1994
811′.540801—dc20   93-22753

ISBN 0-393-31090-6

W. W. Norton & Company, Inc., 500 Fifth Avenue, New York, N.Y. 10110
W. W. Norton & Company Ltd., 10 Coptic Street, London WC1A 1PU

1 2 3 4 5 6 7 8 9 0

To my parents

Opal Catherine Hoover and Robert David Hoover

Contents

Poetics

Acknowledgments

I would like to acknowledge the help and encouragement of Julia A. Reidhead, who supervised this project at W. W. Norton, as well as the insight of the late Barry K. Wade, who first welcomed the proposal. I am also grateful to Robert Creeley, Susan Howe, Charles Bernstein, Bob Perelman, Michael Davidson, Art Lange, Ron Padgett, and Jerome Rothenberg for their counsel in selecting a title to this volume. As always, I would like to thank Maxine Chernoff, my wife and fellow editor of *New American Writing*, for her love and support. Thanks are due to my children, Koren, Philip, and Julian, for their patience.

I am grateful to Columbia College, Chicago, for a Faculty Development Grant given in recognition of my work on this project.

Introduction

1

The poet Charles Olson used the word "postmodern" as early as an October 20, 1951, letter to Creeley from Black Mountain, North Carolina. Doubting the value of historical relics when compared with the process of living, Olson states: "And had we not, ourselves (I mean postmodern man), better just leave such things behind us—and not so much trash of discourse, & gods?"[1] Over the years, the term has received increasing acceptance in all areas of culture and the arts; it has even come to be considered a reigning style. As used here, "postmodern" means the historical period following World War II. It also suggests an experimental approach to composition, as well as a worldview that sets itself apart from mainstream culture and the narcissism, sentimentality, and self-expressiveness of its life in writing. Postmodernist poetry is the avant-garde poetry of our time. I have chosen "postmodern" for the title over "experimental" and "avant-garde" because it is the most encompassing term for the variety of experimental practice since World War II, one that ranges from the oral poetics of Beat and performance poetries to the more "writerly" work of the New York School and language poetry.

Avant-garde art, according to critic Peter Bürger, opposes the bourgeois model of consciousness by attempting to close the gap between art and life. However, "an art no longer distinct from the praxis of life but wholly absorbed in it will lose the capacity to criticize it."[2] Vanguardism thus collaborates with nineteenth-century aestheticism in the diminishment of art's social function even as it attempts to advance it. The risk is that the avant-garde will become an institution with its own self protective rituals, powerless to trace or affect the curve of history.

This anthology shows that avant-garde poetry endures in its resistance to mainstream ideology; it is the avant-garde that renews poetry as a whole through new, but initially shocking, artistic strategies. The "normal" way of writing, such as the contemporary habit of free verse, is first the practice of a few innovators. By this reasoning, recent postmodern aesthetics like performance poetry and language poetry will influence mainstream practice in the coming decades. However, because centrist practice is hostile to change, belatedness is also a feature of avant-garde poetry in terms of publishing opportunities and literary prizes. It was not until the mid-1950s, when William Carlos Williams was in his seventies, that he finally received significant recognition.

1. *Charles Olson and Robert Creeley: The Complete Correspondence*, Vol. 8, Santa Rosa, 1987, p. 79.   2. *Theory of the Avant-Garde* (1974), trans. Michael Shaw, Minneapolis, 1984, p. 50.

Until then, his work was considered "antipoetic." Yet much American poetry since that time has been written on the Williams model.

The critic Fredric Jameson argues that postmodernism represents a break with nineteenth-century romanticism and early twentieth-century modernism. In his words, postmodernism is characterized by "aesthetic populism," "the deconstruction of expression," "the waning of affect," "the end of the bourgeois ego," and "the imitation of dead styles" through the use of pastiche.[3] In Jameson's opinion, postmodernism is the perfect expression of late capitalist culture as dominated by multinational corporations. If Jameson is correct, "deconstruction of expression" would be symptomatic of the loss of individuality in a consumer society. The reputed death of the author would reflect the decline of colonialism and central authority in general. As history finds its "end" in liberal democracy and consumerism, it loses its sense of struggle and discovery. This results in an affectless or "blank" style. Similarly, Jameson's "aesthetic populism" would reflect the triumph of mass communications over the written word.

An opposing argument to Jameson's is that postmodernism is an extension of romanticism and modernism, both of which still thrive. Thus what Jameson calls pastiche is simply a further development of modernist collage—today's cultural pluralism can be identified in *The Waste Land*, *The Cantos*, and Picasso's cubist appropriation of the ceremonial masks of Benin; the self-reflexiveness of postmodern art can be found in *Finnegans Wake* and as far back as *Tristram Shandy;* performance poetry is simply the most recent of many attempts, including those of Wordsworth and William Carlos Williams, to renew poetry through the vernacular. The poetry of John Ashbery is quintessentially postmodern, yet it is influenced by the modernist romantic Wallace Stevens and the modernist Augustan W. H. Auden. John Cage's use of the "prepared piano" and his emphasis on indeterminacy in language represent high postmodernism, yet they can also be situated, along with the aeolian harp, in the history of romanticism.

This anthology does not view postmodernism as a single style with its departure in Pound's *Cantos* and its arrival in language poetry; postmodernism is, rather, an ongoing process of resistance to mainstream ideology. In the 1960s, in opposition to the impersonal, Augustan poetry encouraged by the New Criticism, the postmodern revolt was primarily in the direction of a personal, oral, and "organic" poetry. Frank O'Hara's injunction, "You just go on your nerve,"[4] called for an improvisatory poetics of the everyday that was essentially neoromantic. Yet, in its intense casualness, his poetry also argued against the romantic concept of self; in its disdain for the metaphysical, it broke with the "transcendental signified." By the late 1970s, a new generation of postmodernists had either challenged a speech-based poetics by means of language poetry or extended spoken poetry into performance poetry. Despite their differences, experimentalists in the postwar period have

---

3. *New Left Review*, No. 146, July/August 1984, pp. 53–92.   4. "Personism: A Manifesto," in *The Collected Poems of Frank O'Hara*, New York, 1972, p. 498.

valued writing-as-process over writing-as-product. They have elevated the pluralistic, which Charles Olson called "the real biz of reality," over the singular, which Olson called "the whole ugly birth of the 'either–or.' "[5] Postmodernism decenters authority and embraces pluralism. It encourages a "panoptic" or many-sided point of view. Postmodernism prefers "empty words" to the "transcendental signified," the actual to the metaphysical. In general, it follows a constructionist rather than an expressionist theory of composition. Method and intuition replace intention. With the death of God and the author, appropriation becomes a reigning device. Having no conclusion to come to, narrative doubles back on itself with overlapping and sometimes contradictory versions. For example, Italo Calvino's novel *If on a winter's night a traveler* (1979) consists of the first chapters of ten novels, none of which is developed or concluded. What a text *means* has more to do with how it was written than with what it expresses. As Robert Creeley has written, "Meaning is not importantly *referential.*"[6] Quoting Charles Olson, Creeley continues, " '*That which exists through itself is what is called the meaning.*' "[7] Thus the material of art is to be judged simply as material, not for its transcendent meaning or symbolism. In general, postmodern poetry opposes the centrist values of unity, significance, linearity, expressiveness, and a heightened, even heroic, portrayal of the bourgeois self and its concerns. The poetry in this volume employs a wide variety of oppositional strategies, from the declaratory writings of the Beats to the more theoretical but fiercely political work of the language poets. The empty sign, like the use of transgressive material or aleatory composition, is but one means of that resistance.

2

In his poem "The Rest" (1913), Ezra Pound alluded to the United States as a culturally backward country: "Artists broken against her, / A-stray, lost in the villages. . . ."[8] But by the end of World War II, the United States had become the primary exporter, as well as market, for advanced ideas in the arts. Today the young Ezra Pound would leave his Philadelphia suburb of Wyncote not for London and Paris, but rather The Poetry Project at St. Mark's Church in the Bowery, San Francisco's New Langton Arts, or the Nuyorican Poets' Cafe. His work would be published in such magazines as *Sulfur, Conjunctions, New American Writing, O-BLEK, Temblor, The World,* and *Hambone,* and his books would be published by such presses as Black Sparrow, Coffee House, North Point, The Figures, City Lights, Kulchur, The Jargon Society, Burning Deck, Sun & Moon, and Roof, which have joined New Directions in their commitment to avant-garde writing. In short, since 1950, the year Charles Olson's essay "Projective Verse" appeared, innovative poetry in the United States has flourished.

5. Letter to Robert Creeley, October 20, 1951, in *Charles Olson and Robert Creeley: The Complete Correspondence*, Vol. 8, p. 73.   6. Introduction to *Selected Writings of Charles Olson*, New York, 1966, p. 9.   7. The same.   8. *Personae: Collected Shorter Poems*, New York, 1971, p. 92.

In analyzing American poetry after 1945, it is traditional to point to the so-called battle of the anthologies that occurred with the publication of *New Poets of England and America* (1962), edited by Donald Hall and Robert Pack, and *The New American Poetry: 1945–1960* (1960), edited by Donald M. Allen. The former put forth a literature that was more traditional, formal, and refined. Its contributors were schooled in the assumptions of the New Criticism, which held that poems are well-made objects to be judged independently of the author's intentions or personal experiences. Cleanth Brooks's *The Well-Wrought Urn* placed emphasis on the poem's craftsmanship and traditional subject matter, as well as, implicitly, its white, upper-middle-class constituency. To use Robert Lowell's terminology, the poetry of the Hall/Pack anthology was more "cooked" than "uncooked." Trusting in tradition, its contributors were not eager to reject the influence of British letters in favor of a home-grown idiom. Yeats was preferred to Williams, the mythical to the personal, the rational to the irrational, the historical to the contemporary, learnedness to spontaneity, elitism to populism. However, the early confessional poems of Sylvia Plath and Anne Sexton were included in the Hall/Pack volume, an indication that New Criticism's demand for objectivity and critical distance was already under question. Robert Pack's introduction to his section of American poets under forty (Hall selected the British poets) shows his distaste for spontaneous poetry:

> The idea of raw, unaffected, or spontaneous poetry misleads the reader as to what is expected of him. It encourages laziness and passivity. He too can be spontaneous, just sit back and respond. A good poem, rather, is one that deepens upon familiarity. . . . It is not enough to let a poem echo through your being, to play mystical chords upon your soul. The poem must be understood and felt in its details; it asks for attention before transport.[9]

Pack sides here with the formalism of the New Criticism, which required consistency of structure and poetic detail. Positioning himself against the romanticism of Beat poetry, he emphasizes "attention" (the close-reading style of New Criticism) and "familiarity" (tradition). He implies that the only worthwhile poems are those which lend themselves to study. His disdain for the "laziness and passivity" of certain readers comes perilously close to a social-class distinction. The overall defensiveness of the introduction suggests that the new poetry had already begun to make its mark.

It was in 1955, five years before publication of the Donald Allen anthology, that the San Francisco Renaissance burst on the scene with a single momentous reading at Six Gallery. Jack Kerouac described the event in *Dharma Bums:*

> Anyway I followed the whole gang of howling poets to the reading that night, which was, among other important things, the night of the birth of the San Francisco Renaissance. Everyone was there. It was a mad night. And I was the one who got things jumping by going around collecting dimes and quarters from the rather stiff audience standing around the gallery and coming

9. *New Poets of England and America*, Cleveland, 1962, p. 178.

back with three huge gallon jugs of California burgundy and getting them all piffed so that by eleven o'clock when Alvah Goldbrook [Allen Ginsberg] was reading his, wailing his poem "Wail" drunk with arms outspread everybody was yelling "Go! Go! Go!" (like a jam session) . . .[1]

In fact, as poet and critic Michael Davidson points out, there had been earlier activity in San Francisco. As early as 1944, Robert Duncan had begun to set the stage for a publicly gay role in literature by publishing his essay "The Homosexual in Society." In 1949, Jack Spicer wrote, "We must become singers, become entertainers," a prophecy of the Beat movement's return of poetry to its bardic roots.[2] Since the 1920s, Kenneth Rexroth had been a significant avant-garde figure in the Bay area, organizing "at homes" for writers and artists and reading poetry to jazz long before the Beat poets made the activity popular. The Six Gallery reading galvanized media interest in a variety of alternative poetries. It also introduced the concept of poetry as public performance, one that is increasingly dominant in an age of television and rock and roll.

If Robert Pack's model poet "deepens upon familiarity," Donald Allen's model poet deepens upon strangeness, preferring the irrational and spontaneous to the decorous and well made. In the tradition of Walt Whitman and William Carlos Williams, the poets in Allen's anthology also emphasized the American idiom and landscape. Although predominantly male, many of these poets were Jewish, Irish, Italian, black, and gay—that is, from "new" ethnic and social groups. They lived primarily in New York City and San Francisco, where they were influenced by the other arts, especially jazz and painting. None of them taught at a university. The distinction between bohemia and academia was clear in 1960. Today that difference is harder to establish, as many avant-gardists make their living by university teaching. The radicalism that inspired many poets of the 1960s has found expression in critical approaches such as feminism, post-structuralism, and multiculturalism that are increasingly central to the study of liberal arts.

The most public of the new poetries was the Beat movement led by Allen Ginsberg, Jack Kerouac, Gregory Corso, Gary Snyder, and Lawrence Ferlinghetti. The word "Beat," suggesting exhaustion, beatitude, and the jazz improvisation that inspired many of its writers, was first used by Jack Kerouac. Kerouac's novel *On the Road* (1957), written on a continuous roll of teletype paper, provided the Beat model of spontaneous composition. "Not 'selectivity' of expression," Kerouac insisted, "but following free deviation (association) of mind into limitless blow-on-subject seas of thoughts."[3] In Ginsberg's *Howl*, this verbal improvisation and jazz sense of measure can be heard in lines such as "ashcan rantings and kind king light of mind." According to Ginsberg, Kerouac believed that "the gesture he made in language was his mortal gesture, and therefore unchangeable."[4] It could no more be revised than the act

---

1. New York, 1958, p. 13.   2. "The Poet and Poetry—A Symposium," *One Night Stand and Other Poems*, San Francisco, 1980, p. 92.   3. "Essentials of Spontaneous Prose," in *The Moderns*, ed. LeRoi Jones, New York, 1963, p. 343.   4. *Allen Verbatim*, ed. Gordon Ball, New York, 1974, p. 145.

of walking across a room. Spontaneous composition is not, however, without discipline. "What this kind of writing proposes," Ginsberg once said, "is an absolute, almost Zen-like, complete absorption, *attention* to your own consciousness . . . so that the attention does not waver while writing, and doesn't feed back on itself and become self-conscious."[5] With its roots in the poetry of Blake, Whitman, and William Carlos Williams, Beat writing is public, direct, performative, ecstatic, agonized, oral, and incantatory. It is both irreverent and spiritually aware. Ginsberg's "angelheaded hipsters burning for the ancient heavenly connection to the starry dynamo in the machinery of night" search for meaning high and low. Ginsberg experimented with drugs, was expelled from Columbia University for writing an obscenity on the window of his dorm room, and spent time in the psychiatric ward of Rockland State Hospital. At a time that demanded form, decorum, refinement, and impersonality, Ginsberg's poetry was vivid, direct, profane, personal, and declamatory. The "secret hero" of *Howl* is Neal Cassady, also immortalized as Dean Moriarty of *On the Road,* who lived the exuberant and ultimately self-destructive life the bohemian tradition so admires. In 1968, Cassady died in Mexico at age forty-one from a lethal mixture of alcohol and sleeping pills; Kerouac died the following year. By 1975, the Beat influence had been largely subsumed by the Hippie movement. Nevertheless, poets like Ginsberg and Snyder continue to enjoy a wide following. The thriving presence of performance poetry on the current scene has also helped sustain interest in the Beats.

Central figures of the New York School are John Ashbery, Frank O'Hara, Kenneth Koch, and James Schuyler. Most attended Harvard; all but Koch were gay; and all lived in Manhattan. Strongly influenced by French experimental writing, especially the novels of eccentric amateur Raymond Roussel, they founded the magazines *Locus Solus* and *Art and Literature* and set upon the most self-consciously nonprogrammatic program of the period. However, something of a general stance can be found in O'Hara's essay "Personism: A Manifesto," a parody of Charles Olson's "Projective Verse." O'Hara stated that one day in 1959, while writing a poem for a specific person, he realized that he could "use the telephone instead of writing the poem, and so Personism was born."[6] Personist poetry speaks with immediacy and directness of everyday experience, in everyday language. O'Hara's statement, "You just go on your nerve," is reminiscent of the spontaneity and antiformalism of the Beats; his insistence that Personism "does not have to do with personality or intimacy"[7] suggests an affinity for the poem as a work of art rather than a means of expression. But the Personist mode is not characteristic of all New York School poetry. John Ashbery's use of the novel, sestina, and pantoum combines traditional forms with an innovative impulse and tone. Kenneth Koch wrote his comic epics *Ko* and *The Duplications* in ottava rima, the stanza of Byron's *Don Juan.* Like Byron, Koch and the rest of the New York School poets admire wit,

5. The same, p. 147.   6. O'Hara, p. 499.   7. The same.

daring, urbanity, and an offhanded elegance. As courtly eccentrics, they set a tone that is distinct from the earnest bohemianism of the Beats. A characteristic New York School project is Harry Mathews's sestina "Histoire," the end words of which include "militarism," "Marxism-Leninism," "fascism," and "Maoism." Awed by the oddness of the project, the reader shares the author's triumph over the formal problem. Form becomes, in effect, the primary content of the work. New York School poetry reveals a fondness for parody (Koch's "Variations on a Theme of William Carlos Williams") and pop culture (Ashbery's Popeye sestina, "Farm Implements and Rutabagas in a Landscape"). It also works within the avant-garde tradition of the "poet among the painters." As a curator for the Museum of Modern Art and organizer of major exhibits, Frank O'Hara was the Apollinaire of New York painting in the late fifties and early sixties. John Ashbery was editor of *ARTnews,* and James Schuyler was a frequent contributor to *Art in America.*

It is important to note the leading role of John Ashbery in American poetry since the publication of *Self-Portrait in a Convex Mirror* (1975). Perhaps because his poetry expresses the period's most important theme, indeterminacy, Ashbery has become a "major poet" in an age suspicious of the term. Indeterminacy means the conditionality of truth, as well as a compositional tendency away from finality and closure; the text is in a state of unrest or undecidability. Characterized by sudden shifts of tone and a wide range of reference, making frequent use of the self-canceling statement, Ashbery's poetry has the capacity, to quote Frank O'Hara, for "marrying the whole world."[8] Through circuitousness and obliqueness, Ashbery alludes to things in the process of avoiding them; in saying nothing, he says everything. In the words of critic and poet David Lehman, "Ashbery's poetry points toward a new mimesis, with consciousness itself as a model."[9] Mimesis refers to representation in art—for example, the ability of a painter to make an apple look like an apple. Ashbery paints a picture of the mind at work rather than the objects of its attention. Ashbery has remarked, "Most reckless things are beautiful, just as religions are beautiful because of the strong possibility that they are founded on nothing."[1]

In the late sixties a second generation of New York School poets, including Ted Berrigan, Ron Padgett, Anne Waldman, Tom Clark, Bernadette Mayer, and Maureen Owen, came into their strength. Through readings at St. Mark's Church on the Lower East Side and through journals such as *The World, Telephone,* and *C,* they brought a more bohemian tone to New York School "dailiness" and wit. As self-appointed pope of the scene, Ted Berrigan influenced a large number of younger poets. His book *The Sonnets* (1964), a classic of the period, applied the cut-up method of Dada (and of Beat novelist William Burroughs) to the sonnet form. With Ron Padgett, Berrigan wrote the nota-

8. "Poem Read at Joan Mitchell's," *The Collected Poems of Frank O'Hara,* New York, 1972, p. 266.   9. "The Shield of a Greeting," in *Beyond Amazement: New Essays on John Ashbery,* ed. David Lehman, Ithaca, 1980, p. 118.   1. "The Invisible Avant-Garde," in *Avant-Garde Art,* eds. Thomas B. Hess and John Ashbery, London, 1968, p. 184.

ble *Bean Spasms* (1967). As a result, collaborative writing, which challenged and extended the concept of authorship, was popular in the late sixties and early seventies. Other significant books produced by this generation are Padgett's *Great Balls of Fire* (1969) and Alice Notley's *How Spring Comes* (1981). Anne Waldman, with her skills as a performer, organizer, and anthologist, provided much of the energy that made the St. Mark's scene a powerful literary force.

Projectivist or Black Mountain poetry evolved under the leadership of Charles Olson at Black Mountain College in North Carolina. The leading alternative college of its time, Black Mountain was home to an extraordinary number of major figures, including painters Josef Albers and Robert Rauschenberg, composer John Cage, dancer and choreographer Merce Cunningham, and futurist thinker Buckminster Fuller, creator of the geodesic dome. The poets Robert Creeley, Ed Dorn, Hilda Morley, John Wieners, and Robert Duncan were in residence. Black Mountain poetics, which is more programmatic than that of the Beats or New York School, depends primarily on the essays and teachings of Charles Olson, especially "Projective Verse" (1950). In the essay, he calls for an "open" poetry, in which "FIELD COMPOSITION" replaces the "closed form" of the past. Field composition means that the poet "put himself in the open," improvising line by line, syllable by syllable, rather than using what Olson called "an inherited line" such as iambic pentameter.[2] He quotes the young Robert Creeley as saying that "FORM IS NEVER MORE THAN AN EXTENSION OF CONTENT."[3] Form and content are therefore inextricably linked. Quoting his mentor Edward Dahlberg, Olson writes, "ONE PERCEPTION MUST IMMEDIATELY AND DIRECTLY LEAD TO A FURTHER PERCEPTION."[4] To this he adds the injunction that "always one perception must must must MOVE, INSTANTER, ON ANOTHER."[5] This compositional pressure includes close attention to the syllable, which is "king."

> Let me put it baldly. The two halves are:
> the HEAD, by way of the EAR, to the SYLLABLE
> the HEART, by way of the BREATH, to the LINE[6]

Attention to the line as a unit of breath is a major principle of Black Mountain composition, though as a technique it was flexible rather than prescribed. Each breath is a unit or measure of utterance; this is reflected in the length of the line, and, with Creeley's work especially, how the line is broken. Recordings of Olson and Creeley, whose speech patterns are quite different, reveal the importance of the line and breath to their spoken words. The line becomes an extension of the body itself. A similar emphasis is found in Ginsberg's statements that each strophe of *Howl* is ideally a unit of "Hebraic-Melvillean bardic breath."[7]

Another important aspect of Olson's essay is his concept of ego: "get-

2. *Charles Olson: Selected Writings*, New York, 1966, p. 16.   3. The same.   4. The same, p. 17.   5. The same.   6. The same, p. 19.   7. "Notes for *Howl and Other Poems*," in *The Poetics of the New American Poetry*, eds. Donald Allen and Warren Tallman, New York, 1973, p. 318.

ting rid of the lyrical interference of the individual as ego . . . that peculiar presumption by which western man has interposed himself between what he is as a creature of nature . . . and those other creations of nature which we may, with no derogation, call objects."[8] Olson's goal is to avoid the self-congratulatory elegiac mode, with its inevitable drift toward pathos. This is not to say that Projectivist poetry is impersonal. Olson's "The Librarian," among other poems, deals with his own life; the same is true of work by Robert Creeley, Denise Levertov, Robert Duncan, and Hilda Morley.

Significant developments of the period 1950–1975 include Jerome Rothenberg's study of ethnopoetics, prophetic of multiculturalism; his early interest in performance poetry; and his invention of the term "deep image." The deep image, as seen in various phases of the work of Diane Wakoski, Robert Kelly, Clayton Eshleman, and Rothenberg himself, is inspired by the Andalusian *cante jondo*, or "deep song," surrealist-influenced Spanish poetry, including that of Federico García Lorca, and Lorca's essay "Theory and Function of the *Duende*" (a Spanish word denoting ghosts and magic but in the poetic sense a deep knowledge, as of beauty and death). Strongly felt and resonant, the deep-image poem is as heroic in mood and stylized in execution as the flamenco. Rothenberg wrote in a letter to Robert Creeley:

> So there are really two things here, conceivable as two realities: 1) the empirical world of the naive realists, etc. (what Buber and the hasidim call "shell" or "husk"), and 2) the hidden (floating) world, yet to be discovered or brought into being: the "kernel" or "sparks." The first world both hides and leads into the second, so as Buber says: "one cannot reach the kernel of the fruit except through the shell"; i.e., the phenomenal world is to be read by us; the perceived image is the key to the buried image: and the deep image is at once husk and kernel, perception and vision, and the poem is the movement between them.[9]

Fraught with the symbolist theory of correspondences—that nature may be read by means of its external appearances—the passage expresses the desire to see deeply and capture truth in a moment of mystical enlightenment. The Rothenberg passage above was written in 1960. As major influences on postmodern poetics, Wittgenstein and indeterminacy still wait in the wings.

Deep-image poems of any length tend to be organized as catalogues of self-sufficient images. Diane Wakoski's "Blue Monday," included in this volume, is an example of such a work. But practice of the deep image was so short-lived and unsystematic that it cannot be fully represented as a school. Moreover, many of the above poets were also associated with other aesthetics, especially Projectivism. Eshleman's work can be said to have descended through the deep image into the chthonic or underwordly.

Influenced by Zen Buddhism and Dada, the poetry of John Cage and Jackson Mac Low reflects an interest in the use of aleatory, or chance, procedures. Cage's *Themes & Variations* depends on a "library of mesostics on one hundred and ten different subjects and fifteen differ-

---

8. "Projective Verse," p. 24.   9. "Deep Image & Mode: An Exchange with Robert Creeley," in *Pre-faces & Other Writings*, New York, 1981, p. 57.

ent names to make a chance-determined renga-like mix."[1] Cage used *I Ching* operations to focus his project, as well as to link a notebook of ideas (to be found in the Poetics section of this volume) with the names of friends. The purpose was "to find a way of writing which though coming from ideas is not about them; or is not about ideas but produces them."[2] By employing mesostics, a form of word puzzle in which emphasized letters spell out words vertically at the center of horizontal lines of poetry, Cage attempts to free the language from syntax. This "demilitarizes" it. "Nonsense and silence are produced, familiar to lovers. We actually begin to live together," he writes in the foreword to *M: Writings '67–'72*.[3] In the preface to his book *The Pronouns*, Jackson Mac Low explains that the series of poems involved a "set of 3-by-4-inch filing cards on which there are groups of words & of action phrases around which dancers build spontaneous improvisations."[4] Due to a "correspondence of format to syntax, each verse line, *including its indented continuation*, if any, is to be read as one breath unit."[5] Thus the series of poems not only stands as script for the dance, but also provides its own instructions for oral performance.

Aleatory poetry is not widely practiced by the generations of avant-gardists to follow Cage and Mac Low. Yet in its emphasis on the indeterminate and accidental, its reliance on rigid structures and methods to achieve randomization, its use of appropriation and found materials, and its willingness to lend itself equally to performance and to language poetry theory, it is the essence of postmodernism. Cage's work also bridges the earlier European avant-garde, especially Dada, and more recent American developments such as conceptual art.

By 1975 a new generation had begun to assert itself. Andrei Codrescu, Russell Edson, and Maxine Chernoff, among others, made use of Surrealist influences. It was also a period in which the prose poem, founded by the French poet Aloysius Bertrand as early as 1842, came into prominence. The prose poets went in two directions: some, like Chernoff and Edson, wrote narratives, fables, and metafictions; others associated with the budding language poetry scene—Ron Silliman, Lyn Hejinian, and Carla Harryman, for example—used the form to redefine the "unit" of attention from the line to the sentence, sentence fragment, and paragraph. Hejinian and Harryman, among others, used the prose poem to experiment with related prose forms such as autobiography, the essay, and fiction.

In the first postwar generation, only a few women, such as Denise Levertov, had risen to importance within the avant-garde. However, the 1970s saw the arrival of a number of significant women poets, from Anne Waldman and Alice Notley among the New York School to Susan Howe, Mei-mei Berssenbrugge, Rosmarie Waldrop, Rae Armantrout, Diane Ward, Lyn Hejinian, Leslie Scalapino, and Carla Harryman, among others, associated with language poetry. Implicit in the language poets' break with traditional modes such as narrative, with its emphasis on linearity and closure, is a challenge to the male-dominant hierarchy.

1. John Cage, Introduction to *Themes & Variations*, Barrytown, 1982, p. 8.   2. The same, p. 6.   3. Middletown, CT, 1973, p. 2.   4. Barrytown, 1979, p. viii.   5. The same, p. ix.

In her essay "The Rejection of Closure," Lyn Hejinian quotes Elaine Marks regarding the desire of French feminist writers to "use language as a passageway, and the only one, to the unconscious, to that which had been repressed and which would, if allowed to rise, disrupt the established symbolic order, which Jacques Lacan has dubbed 'the Law of the Father.' "[6] At the same time, Hejinian sees the limit of complete openness: "The (unimaginable) complete text, the text that contains everything, would be in fact a closed text. It would be insufferable."[7] Jayne Cortez's "Inez Garcia, Joanne Litte—Two Rape Victims of the 1970s" and Wanda Coleman's "Brute Strength" refer to sexual conflict directly, using narrative elements to intensify the drama of the poem. Because they are more rhetorically forceful, the poems may seem more political than the work of women language poets. Yet the comparatively oblique work of Leslie Scalapino frequently alludes to the intrusive power of the male gaze over women as objects of desire.

In the last decade, two relatively marginal influences of the seventies, language poetry and performance poetry, have become increasingly the dominant postmodern modes. The first emphasizes textuality and therefore a degree of difficulty. Strongly based in theory, it requires an initiated reader. In its difficulty and literariness, language poetry is reminiscent of the High Modernism of T. S. Eliot and Ezra Pound. Yet language poetry is Marxist and feminist in theory and disdains Pound and Eliot for their politically conservative themes. Performance poetry, especially as it has evolved into poetry "slams," has its chief appeal with the popular audience. Its interest is not in the "poem as poem," but rather in using the words as script for spoken word performance. In its verbal intensity, it recalls the Beat coffeehouse readings of the 1950s.

Language poetry finds its disparate precursors in Gertrude Stein's *Tender Buttons* (1914); the writings of Russian Futurist Velimir Khlebnikov, inventor of *zaum*, or "transrational language"; Louis Zukofsky's *A* (1959/1978) and the Objectivist movement in general; John Ashbery's most radical book, *The Tennis Court Oath* (1962); the early work of Clark Coolidge such as *Polaroid* (1975); and the chance procedures of Jackson Mac Low as seen in *The Pronouns* (1964/1979). Some aspects of Black Mountain poetics, especially Olson's statement against the individual ego, are also of interest to language poets, though they disassociate themselves from what Charles Bernstein calls the "phallocentric syntax" of Olson's poetry.[8] Seeing a poem as an intellectual and sonic construction rather than a necessary expression of the human soul, language poetry raises technique to a position of privilege. Language poets see lyricism in poetry not as a means of expressing emotion but rather in its original context as the musical use of words. Rather than employ language as a transparent window onto experience, the language poet pays attention to the material nature of words. Because it is fragmentary and discontinuous, language poetry may appear at first to be automatic writing; however, it is often heavily reworked to achieve the

---

6. *Writing/Talks*, ed. Bob Perelman, Carbondale, 1985, p. 282.   7. The same, p. 285.
8. "Undone Business," in *Content's Dream: Essays 1975–1984*, Los Angeles, 1986, p. 329.

proper relation of materials. This approach is consistent with William Carlos Williams's definition of a poem as a "small (or large) machine made of words. When I say there's nothing sentimental about a poem I mean there can be no part, as in any other machine, that is redundant."[9]

However, the principle of plenty often found in language poetry tends to frustrate the economy of phrase, and its suggestion of organic form, inherent in Williams's model. Ron Silliman's *Tjanting* (1981) consists of 213 pages of prose poetry, the last paragraph of which starts on page 128. It begins, "What makes this the last paragraph?" The sprawl of such work is designed to communicate the democratic principle of inclusiveness. Its form is located in what Silliman calls "The New Sentence," sentences being "the minimum complete utterance" according to linguist Simeon Potter.[1] Favoring the prose poem for its formal freedom and exhaustiveness, the language poet builds up a mosaic structure by means of seemingly unrelated sentences and sentence fragments. This progression of non sequiturs frustrates the reader's expectation for linear development at the same time that it opens a more complete world of reference. The emphasis in language poetry is placed on production rather than packaging (beginning, middle, end) and ease of consumption. Gertrude Stein gave the credit for this egalitarian theory of composition to her favorite painter: "Cezanne conceived the idea that in composition one thing is as important as another thing. Each part is as important as the whole."[2]

The author cedes his or her false authority as individual ego; broadly distributing wealth in the form of words, the author acquires a more trustworthy authority. Because the words are so freely given, they may seem scattered and disorganized. It is therefore necessary for the reader to participate actively in the creation of meaning. Charles Bernstein states in his essay "Writing and Method":

> The text calls upon the reader to be actively involved in the process of constituting its meaning. . . . The text formally involves the process of response/interpretation and in so doing makes the reader aware of herself or himself as producer as well as consumer of meaning.[3]

A poem is not "about" something, a paraphrasable narrative, symbolic nexus, or theme; rather, it is the actuality of words.

Language poetry's resistance to closure, which infuses meaning throughout the poem rather than overlaying it in lyrical and dramatic epiphanies, may prove to be one of its most lasting effects. It has also revealed the limits of a "natural" or "organic" concept of poetry. In language poetry, as in Marshall McLuhan's theory of television, the medium is the message. Words are not transparent vessels for containing and conveying higher truth; they are instead the material of which

9. Author's introduction to *The Wedge* (1944), in *The Collected Poems of William Carlos Williams*, Vol. II, New York, 1988, p. 54.   1. *Modern Linguistics*, New York, 1964, p. 104.   2. "A Transatlantic Interview 1946," in *A Primer for the Gradual Understanding of Gertrude Stein*, ed. Robert B. Haas, Santa Barbara, 1976, p. 15.   3. *Content's Dream: Essays 1975–1984*, Los Angeles, 1985, p. 233.

it is shaped. Gertrude Stein said that she was interested in two aspects of composition:

> . . . the idea of portraiture and the idea of the recreation of the word. I took individual words and thought about them until I got their weight and volume complete and put them next to another word, and at this same time I found out very soon that there is no such thing as putting them together without sense. It is impossible to put them together without sense.[4]

In much the same way an artist might view paint and stone, Stein conceived of words as the plastic material of her compositions in language. Each word has its own "weight and volume." It exists from an artistic viewpoint for its own "recreation." Such a view disinvests the language of metaphysics and returns it to the physical realm of daily use. Like Stein, language poets shatter the assumption that poetry is necessary and deep; it is, instead, arbitrary and contingent. Language poetry, too, rejects the idea of poetry as an oral form; it is written. To use French critic Roland Barthes's terminology, it is more "writerly" than "readerly." Indeed, language poetry could be seen as fulfilling Barthes's prophecy of a "neutral" mode of writing:

> . . . writing thus passed through all the stages of progressive solidification; it was first the object of a gaze, then of creative action, finally of murder, and has reached in our time a last metamorphosis, absence: in those neutral modes of writing, called here "the zero degree of writing," we can easily discern a negative momentum . . . as if Literature, having tended for a hundred years now to transmute its surface into a form with no antecedents, could no longer find purity anywhere but in the absence of all signs . . .[5]

Early workers in what is now called language poetry—Jackson Mac Low, Clark Coolidge, and Michael Palmer—remain among its leading practitioners. However, much of the critical theory and organizational energy have been the work of Charles Bernstein, whose books of essays *Content's Dream* (1986) and *A Poetics* (1992) most effectively express the group's thinking. Among other important points, Bernstein rejects reading as an "absorption" into the text, wherein the reader is imprisoned by the author's mimetic devices. Like many other postmodern theorists, he also opposes the heroic stance, which "translates into a will to dominate language rather than let it be heard."[6]

Also of note are Barrett Watten's essays, collected in *Total Syntax* (1985); *Code of Signals: Recent Writings in Poetics,* edited by Michael Palmer (1983); Ron Silliman's *The New Sentence* (1987); and *Writing/ Talks* (1985), edited by Bob Perelman, a collection of talks given at New Langton Arts in the late seventies and early eighties.

The work of Allen Ginsberg and Amiri Baraka has always lent itself to performance. But in the early 1970s, with David Antin's creation of the "talk poem," Rothenberg's performances of Native American chants, John Giorno's early electronic choruses, and the growing importance of performance as an area of conceptual art, performance poetry

4. "A Transatlantic Interview 1946," p. 18.   5. *Writing Degree Zero,* trans. Annette
Lavers and Colin Smith, New York, 1967, p. 5.   6. "Undone Business," p. 329.

entered a new phase. It was no longer based on reading to an audience from a printed text, but rather in extending the prepared text, if one existed, through theater and ritual. This returned poetry to its communal roots (if gallerygoers can be said to constitute a community) and gave words a hopeful uncertainty as well as oracular sweep and confidence. Performance poetry implicitly challenged the preciousness of the page and the concept of a poem as a closed system. Always provisional, living and dying dramatically in the air, the spoken word is also unconditionally public, and therefore frequently political or persuasive in character.

If language poetry seeks to invent a future through the written text, performance poetry bears nostalgia for a more perfect past when orality was primary. David Antin says in his talk poem *what am i doing here?* (1973):

> the past had a lot more
> talking than it had writing   i'll make a bold hypothesis before
> there was talking   before there was writing   before there was
>   talking there wasnt talking   before there was writing there was
> talking   this may not be an immense hypothesis   but its
>   certainly true   and   it has its consequences   there are
> certainly consequences i can draw from this   that before there
>   was writing down   and looking up   there was remembering[7]

In his talk poems, which appear in print as transcripts of unrehearsed talk before an audience, Antin goes into the instant of speech, when the "writing" of the thought and its utterance are nearly instantaneous. The haltingness and repetitiveness of the above fragment are part of the project's allure, as is the risk that his utterance will be ill-conceived or intellectually thin. Present at the very moment of creation, the audience observes the fragility of invention in every pause and stammer.

The early performance poems of John Giorno, one of the form's pioneers, used multiple voices and repetitions, sometimes by adding additional tape tracks to the spoken word in performance. This echo converted each line of the text to its own refrain and gave a ritualized, almost choral, character to the work. Giorno often shouts his lines in an insistent cadence, which gives a disembodied universality to his assertions. The poems are not improvised, but written in advance and rehearsed. In recent years, Giorno has memorized his work, which gives it an even more oracular quality.

Other leading performance poets include Jayne Cortez, who sing-shouts her work in a piercing voice; Anne Waldman, who follows Rothenberg and Ginsberg in her use of the chant; Kenward Elmslie, whose work is dense with wordplay and often sung in a handsome baritone voice; Ed Sanders, who makes use of homemade electronic devices, including a musical tie; Miguel Algarín, founder of the Nuyorican Poets' Cafe, a center for performance poetry; Jimmy Santiago Baca and Victor Hernandez Cruz, winners of the Taos Poetry Circus competition; and the fiery Wanda Coleman, one of the best political poets now writing.

7. *talking at the boundaries*, New York, 1976, pp. 4–5.

The multiculturalism of performance poetry is no accident. According to Gary Snyder, "Of all the streams of civilized tradition with roots in the paleolithic, poetry is one of the few that can realistically claim an unchanged function and a relevance which will outlast most of the activities that surround us today."[8] The activities that the multicultural poets resist are cultural genocide, the political and economic fallout from imperialism, and the homogenizing forces of modern technology. Orality, the primary means of communication among pre-industrial societies, enables the artist to achieve a ritual connection with his or her community, disparate as it may be. The effect of performance poetry has been to devalue the "poem as poem," a self-contained object, and to reinstitute its instrumental function as communication. The dilemma of performance poetry lies in a paradox of commodity. While performance art began as a way to decommodify the art object, its inherent theatricality quickly reinvests it with commodity value.

In *The Poetics of Indeterminacy*, Marjorie Perloff traces the avant-garde from its infancy in symbolist poetry, especially that of Rimbaud: "it is Rimbaud who strikes the first note of that 'undecidability' we find in Gertrude Stein, in Pound, and Williams . . . an undecidability that has become marked in the poetry of the last decades."[9] This inheritance includes futurism, Dada, surrealism, modernism, and the varieties of postmodernism we are now experiencing. The *fin de siècle* position of postmodern art suggests to some that it is in a state of exhaustion; in *Has Modernism Failed?*, art critic Suzi Gablik argues unpersuasively that "innovation no longer seems possible, or even desirable."[1] In fact, the poetry now being produced is as strong as, and arguably stronger than, that produced by earlier vanguards. As history remains dynamic, so does the artistic concept of "the new." The period since 1950 will be seen as the time when the United States finally acquired its full share of cultural anxiety and world knowledge, and thereby its most daring poetry.

8. "Poetry and the Primitive: Notes on Poetry as an Ecological Survival Technique," in *The Poetics of the New American Poetry*, New York, 1973, p. 396.   9. Evanston, 1983, p. 4.   1. London, 1984, p. 11.

POSTMODERN AMERICAN POETRY

A Norton Anthology

CHARLES OLSON ■ ■ ■ ■ ■ ■ ■ ■ ■ ■ ■ ■ ■ ■
1910–1970

In the winter of 1944–1945, in his mid-thirties, Charles Olson rejected a promising political career in the Roosevelt administration and turned to writing prose and poetry. His study of Herman Melville, *Call Me Ishmael*, appeared in 1947, followed shortly by his first book of poetry, *Y & X*, in 1948. The same year, Olson began a series of lectures at Black Mountain College, an experimental institution in North Carolina, where his success led to his replacing his mentor Edward Dahlberg as a visiting lecturer. Olson wrote his best early poetry at Black Mountain, including "In Cold Hell, in Thicket" and "The Kingfishers," as well as his manifesto "Projective Verse," published in *Poetry New York* in 1950. From 1951 until its closing in 1956, Olson served as rector of Black Mountain College, inviting poets such as Robert Creeley and Robert Duncan to teach. By 1960, the year in which he published *The Distances*, Olson was recognized as a major figure of American poetry.

If Allen Ginsberg was the popular and spiritual leader of the postwar experimental poetry, Charles Olson was its leading thinker and strategist. Like Ginsberg, he reconnected poetry with the body, emphasizing what he called the "proprioceptive," or inward, character of human speech. For Olson, each line of poetry was both idiosyncratic and "necessary" as a result of each speaker's particular breath.

The first sentence of *Call Me Ishmael* is "I take SPACE to be the central fact to man born in America, from Folsom Cave to now." The poetics of place is basic to Olson's thinking. In *The Maximus Poems*, his epic poem, that place is his hometown of Gloucester, Massachusetts. Also important to Olson's poetics is what the philosopher Alfred North Whitehead called "presentational immediacy." Art and life fail, Olson stressed in his essay "Human Universe," when the passive replaces the active, for it is not in "spectatorism" that culture is earned but rather in work. The descriptive and the metaphysical fail because they "crowd out participation" in the same way "monopolies of business and government . . . protect themselves from the advancement in position of able men."[1] Summarizing perception rather than presenting it, the symbolic also falls short. "Art does not seek to describe but to enact," Olson writes.[2] Emphasizing poetry as process, the postmodern poet replaces what Olson called the "Classical-representational" with the *"primitive-abstract."*[3] Thus Olson predicts the shamanistic poetries of Ginsberg, Jerome Rothenberg, and Gary Snyder, among others, as well as the current trend toward cultural pluralism.

1. *Selected Writings*, New York, 1966, p. 58.   2. The same, p. 61.   3. "Letter to Elaine Feinstein" (May 1959), in *Selected Writings*, p. 28.

In Cold Hell, in Thicket

In cold hell, in thicket, how
abstract (as high mind, as not lust, as love is) how
strong (as strut or wing, as polytope, as things are
constellated) how
strung, how cold
can a man stay (can men) confronted
thus?

All things are made bitter, words even
are made to taste like paper, wars get tossed up
like lead soldiers used to be
(in a child's attic) lined up
to be knocked down, as I am,
by firings from a spit-hardened fort, fronted
as we are, here, from where we must go

God, that man, as his acts must, as there is always
a thing he can do, he can raise himself, he raises
on a reed he raises his

Or, if it is me, what
he has to say

1

What has he to say?
In hell it is not easy
to know the traceries, the markings
(the canals, the pits, the mountings by which space
declares herself, arched, as she is, the sister,
awkward stars drawn for teats to pleasure him, the brother
who lies in stasis under her, at ease as any monarch or
a happy man

How shall he who is not happy, who has been so made unclear,
who is no longer privileged to be at ease, who,
                                        in this brush, stands
reluctant, imageless, unpleasured, caught in a sort of hell, how
shall he convert this underbrush, how turn this unbidden place
how trace and arch again
the necessary goddess?

2

The branches made against the sky are not of use, are
already done, like snow-flakes, do not, cannot service
him who has to raise (Who puts this on, this damning
                                        of his flesh?)
he can, but how far, how sufficiently far can he raise
                                        the thickets of
this wilderness?

            How can he change, his question is
            these black and silvered knivings, these
            awkwardnesses?

            How can he make these blood-points into panels,
                                        into sides
            for a king's, for his own

for a wagon, for a sleigh, for the beak of,
                                    the running sides of
a vessel fit for
moving?

How can he make out, he asks,
of this low eye-view,
size?

And archings traced and picked enough to hold
to stay, as she does, as he, the brother, when,
here where the mud is, he is frozen, not daring
where the grass grows, to move his feet from fear
he'll trespass on his own dissolving bones, here
where there is altogether too much remembrance?

                            3

The question, the fear he raises up himself against
(against the same each act is proffered, under the eyes
each fix, the town of the earth over, is managed) is: Who
am I?

Who am I but by a fix, and another,
a particle, and the congery of particles carefully picked
                                    one by another,

                as in this thicket, each
                smallest branch, plant, fern, root
                —roots lie, on the surface, as nerves are laid open—
                must now (the bitterness of the taste of her) be
                isolated, observed, picked over, measured, raised
                as though a word, an accuracy were a pincer!
                                                this
                        is the abstract, this
                        is the cold doing, this
                        is the almost impossible

So shall you blame those
who give it up, those who say
it isn't worth the struggle?

                            (Prayer
Or a death as going over to—shot by yr own forces—to
a greener place?

                        Neither

    any longer
    usable)

By fixes only (not even any more by shamans)
can the traceries
be brought out

II

ya, selva oscura, but hell now
is not exterior, is not to be got out of, is
the coat of your own self, the beasts
emblazoned on you   And who
can turn this total thing, invert
and let the ragged sleeves be seen
by any bitch or common character?   Who
can endure it where it is, where the beasts are met,
where yourself is, your beloved is, where she
who is separate from you, is not separate, is not
goddess, is, as your core is,
the making of one hell

where she moves off, where she is
no longer arch

(this is why he of whom we speak does not move, why
he stands so awkward where he is, why
his feet are held, like some ragged crane's
off the nearest next ground, even from
the beauty of the rotting fern his eye
knows, as he looks down, as,
in utmost pain if cold can be so called,
he looks around his battlefield, this
rotted place where men did die, where boys
and immigrants have fallen, where nature
(the years that she's took over)
does not matter, where

that men killed, do kill, that woman kills
is part, too, of his question

2

That it is simple, what the difference is—
that a man, men, are now their own wood
and thus their own hell and paradise
that they are, in hell or in happiness, merely
something to be wrought, to be shaped, to be carved, for use, for
others

does not in the least lessen his, this unhappy man's
obscurities, his
confrontations

He shall step, he
will shape, he
is already also
moving off

      into the soil, on to his own bones

he will cross

      (there is always a field,
      for the strong there is always
      an alternative)

          But a field
      is not a choice, is
      as dangerous as a prayer, as a death, as any
      misleading, lady

He will cross

      And is bound to enter (as she is)
      a later wilderness.
               Yet
      what he does here, what he raises up
      (he must, the stakes are such

               this at least
      is a certainty, this
      is a law, is not one of the questions, this
      is what was talked of as
      —what was it called, demand?)

      He will do what he now does, as she will, do
      carefully, do
      without wavering,
      without
         as even the branches,
         even in this dark place, the twigs
                 how

        even the brow
    of what was once to him a beautiful face

as even the snow-flakes waver in the light's eye

        as even forever wavers (gutters
        in the wind of loss)

        even as he will forever waver

precise as hell is, precise
as any words, or wagon,
can be made

1953[4]

I, Maximus of Gloucester, to You

Off-shore, by islands hidden in the blood
jewels & miracles, I, Maximus
a metal hot from boiling water, tell you
what is a lance, who obeys the figures of
the present dance

1

the thing you're after
may lie around the bend
of the nest (second, time slain, the bird! the bird!

And there! (strong) thrust, the mast! flight

                              (of the bird
                              o kylix, o
                              Antony of Padua
                              sweep low, o bless

the roofs, the old ones, the gentle steep ones
on whose ridge-poles the gulls sit, from which they depart,

                                        And the flake-racks

of my city!

2

love is form, and cannot be without
important substance (the weight
say, 58 carats each one of us, perforce
our goldsmith's scale

                              feather to feather added
                              (and what is mineral, what
                              is curling hair, the string
                              you carry in your nervous beak, these

[4]Poems in this volume are dated according to their first appearance in a book by that
author; these dates are located at the right margin following the poem in question. Dates at
the left margin or in proximity to the title indicate time of composition as given by the poet.

make bulk, these, in the end, are
the sum
(o my lady of good voyage
in whose arm, whose left arm rests
no boy but a carefully carved wood, a painted face, a schooner!
a delicate mast, as bow-sprit for

forwarding

3

the underpart is, though stemmed, uncertain
is, as sex is, as moneys are, facts!
facts, to be dealt with, as the sea is, the demand
that they be played by, that they only can be, that they must
be played by, said he, coldly, the
ear!

By ear, he sd.
But that which matters, that which insists, that which will last,
that! o my people, where shall you find it, how, where, where shall you listen
when all is become billboards, when, all, even silence, is spray-gunned?

when even our bird, my roofs,
cannot be heard

when even you, when sound itself is neoned in?

when, on the hill, over the water
where she who used to sing,
when the water glowed,
black, gold, the tide
outward, at evening

when bells came like boats
over the oil-slicks, milkweed
hulls

And a man slumped,
attentionless,
against pink shingles

o sea city)

4

one loves only form,
and form only comes
into existence when
the thing is born

born of yourself, born
of hay and cotton struts,
of street-pickings, wharves, weeds
you carry in, my bird

of a bone of a fish
of a straw, or will
of a color, of a bell
of yourself, torn

5

love is not easy
but how shall you know,
New England, now
that pejorocracy is here, how
that street-cars, o Oregon, twitter
in the afternoon, offend
a black-gold loin?

how shall you strike,
o swordsman, the blue-red back
when, last night, your aim
was mu-sick, mu-sick, mu-sick
And not the cribbage game?

(o Gloucester-man,
weave
your birds and fingers
new, your roof-tops,
clean shit upon racks
sunned on
American
braid
with others like you, such
extricable surface
as faun and oral,
satyr lesbos vase

o kill kill kill kill kill
those
who advertise you
out)

6

in! in! the bow-sprit, bird, the beak
in, the bend is, in, goes in, the form
that which you make, what holds, which is
the law of object, strut after strut, what you are, what you must be, what

the force can throw up, can, right now hereinafter erect,
the mast, the mast, the tender
mast!

> The nest, I say, to you, I Maximus, say
> under the hand, as I see it, over the waters
> from this place where I am, where I hear,
> can still hear
>
> from where I carry you a feather
> as though, sharp, I picked up,
> in the afternoon delivered you
> a jewel,
>   it flashing more than a wing,
> than any old romantic thing,
> than memory, than place,
> than anything other than that which you carry
>
> than that which is,
> call it a nest, around the head of, call it
> the next second
>
> than that which you
> can do!

1953

Letter 3

Tansy buttons, tansy
for my city
Tansy for their noses

Tansy for them,
tansy for Gloucester to take the smell
of all owners,
the smell

Tansy
for all of us

> Let those who use words cheap, who use us cheap
> take themselves out of the way
> Let them not talk of what is good for the city
>
> Let them free the way for me, for the men of the Fort
> who are not hired, who buy the white houses

Let them cease putting out words in the public print
so that any of us have to leave, so that my Portuguese leave,
leave the Lady they gave us, sell their schooners
with the greyhounds aft, the long Diesels
they put their money in, leave Gloucester
in the present shame of,
the wondership stolen by,
ownership

Tansy from Cressy's
I rolled in as a boy
and didn't know it was
tansy

1

Did you know, she sd, growing up there,
how rare it was? And it turned out later she meant exactly the long field
drops down from Ravenswood where the land abrupts,
this side of Fresh Water Cove, and throws out
that wonder of my childhood, the descending green does run
so,
by the beach

                where they held the muster Labor Day, and the engine teams
                threw such arcs of water

                                      runs with summer with

tansy

2

I was not born there, came, as so many of the people came,
from elsewhere. That is, my father did. And not from the Provinces,
not from Newfoundland. But we came early enough. When he came,
there were three hundred sail could fill the harbor,
if they were all in, as for the Races, say
Or as now the Italians are in, for San Pietro,
and the way it is from Town Landing, all band-concert,
and fireworks

So I answered her: Yes,
I knew (I had that to compare to it,
was Worcester)

As the people of the earth are now, Gloucester
is heterogeneous, and so can know polis

not as localism, not that mu-sick (the trick
of corporations, newspapers, slick magazines, movie houses,
the ships, even the wharves, absentee-owned

they whine to my people, these entertainers, sellers

they play upon their bigotries (upon their fears

these   they have the nerve
to speak of that lovely hour
the Waiting Station, 5 o'clock, the Magnolia bus, Al Levy
on duty (the difference
from 1 o'clock, all the women getting off
the Annisquam-Lanesville,
and the letter carriers

5:40, and only the lollers
in front of the shoe-shine parlor

these, right in the people's faces (and not at all as the gulls do it,
who do it straight, do it all over the "Times" blowing
the day after, or the "Summer Sun" catching on pilings, floating
off the Landing, the slime
the low tide reveals, the smell
then

                                    3

The word does intimidate. The pay-check does.
But to use either, as cheap men

o tansy city, root city
let them not make you
as the nation is

I speak to any of you, not to you all, to no group, not to you as citizens
as my Tyrian might have. Polis now
is a few, is a coherence not even yet new (the island of this city
is a mainland now of who? who can say who are
citizens?

Only a man or a girl who hear a word
and that word meant to mean not a single thing the least more than
what it does mean (not at all to sell any one anything, to keep them anywhere,
not even
in this rare place
                                                          1953

Maximus, to himself

I have had to learn the simplest things
last. Which made for difficulties.
Even at sea I was slow, to get the hand out, or to cross
a wet deck.
                    The sea was not, finally, my trade.
But even my trade, at it, I stood estranged
from that which was most familiar. Was delayed,
and not content with the man's argument
that such postponement
is now the nature of
obedience,

                    that we are all late
                    in a slow time,
                    that we grow up many
                    And the single
                    is not easily
                    known

It could be, though the sharpness (the *achiote*)
I note in others,
makes more sense
than my own distances. The agilities

                    they show daily
                    who do the world's
                    businesses
                    And who do nature's
                    as I have no sense
                    I have done either

I have made dialogues,
have discussed ancient texts,
have thrown what light I could, offered
what pleasures
doceat allows

                    But the known?
This, I have had to be given,
a life, love, and from one man
the world.

                    Tokens.
                    But sitting here
                    I look out as a wind
                    and water man, testing
                    And missing
                    some proof

I know the quarters
of the weather, where it comes from,
where it goes. But the stem of me,
this I took from their welcome,
or their rejection, of me

      And my arrogance
      was neither diminished
      nor increased,
      by the communication

2

It is undone business
I speak of, this morning,
with the sea
stretching out
from my feet

1956

The Librarian

The landscape (the landscape!) again: Gloucester,
the shore one of me is (duplicates), and from which
(from offshore, I, Maximus) am removed, observe.

In this night I moved on the territory with combinations
(new mixtures) of old and known personages: the leader,
my father, in an old guise, here selling books and manuscripts.

My thought was, as I looked in the window of his shop,
there should be materials here for Maximus, when, then,
I saw he was the young musician has been there (been before me)

before. It turned out it wasn't a shop, it was a loft (wharf-
house) in which, as he walked me around, a year ago
came back (I had been there before, with my wife and son,

I didn't remember, he presented me with insinuations via
himself and his girl) both of whom I had known for years.
But never in Gloucester. I had moved them in, to my country.

His previous appearance had been in my parents'
                                bedroom where I
found him intimate with my former wife: this boy
was now the Librarian of Gloucester, Massachusetts!

      Black space,
      old fish-house.

Motions
of ghosts.
I,
dogging
his steps.

He
(not my father,
by name himself
with his face
twisted
at birth)
possessed of knowledge
pretentious
giving me
what in the instant
I knew better of.

But the somber
place, the flooring
crude like a wharf's
and a barn's
space

I was struck by the fact I was in Gloucester, and
                                        that my daughter
was there—that I would see her! She was over the Cut. I
hadn't even connected her with my being there, that she was

here. That she was there (in the Promised Land—the Cut!
But there was this business, of poets, that all my Jews
were in the fish-house too, that the Librarian had made a party

I was to read. They were. There were many of them, slumped
around. It was not for me. I was outside. It was the Fort.
The Fort was in East Gloucester—old Gorton's Wharf,
                                          where the Library

was. It was a region of coal houses, bins. In one a gang
was beating someone to death, in a corner of the labyrinth
of fences. I could see their arms and shoulders whacking

down. But not the victim. I got out of there. But cops
tailed me along the Fort beach toward the Tavern

The places still
half-dark, mud,
coal-dust.

There is no light
east
of the Bridge

Only on the headland
toward the harbor
from Cressy's

have I seen it (once
when my daughter ran
out on a spit of sand

isn't even there.) Where
is Bristow? when does I-A
get me home? I am caught

in Gloucester. (What's buried
behind Lufkin's
Diner? Who is

Frank Moore?

1960

JOHN CAGE ▪ ▪ ▪ ▪ ▪ ▪ ▪ ▪ ▪ ▪ ▪ ▪ ▪ ▪ ▪ ▪ ▪
1912–1992

Born in Los Angeles, John Cage was the son of an inventor who developed an explanation of the cosmos called "Electrostatic Field Theory."[1] This history predicts Cage's own innovations in music, a field he chose after early ambitions as a writer and painter. In 1933, he became the student of Arnold Schoenberg, who later called Cage not a composer but "an inventor—of genius."[2] Committed to experiment, especially the Dadaist example of Marcel Duchamp, Cage went on to pioneer a new conception of music based on the use of chance and other nonintentional methods. In this, he was aided by his study of Zen Buddhism and a pacifist social philosophy based in the writings of Thoreau. As William Carlos Williams had done in poetry, Cage expanded the definition of music to include all categories of sound, such as random everyday noises. As he writes in "The Future of Music": *"Klangfarbenmelodie* has not taken the place of *bel canto*. It has extended our realization of what can happen."[3]

In the 1960s, following his own example in music, as well as the work of Clark Coolidge and Jackson Mac Low, Cage turned his attention to poetry, using both nonintentional and intentional methods. He soon discovered the use of mesostics, a form of acrostics, as an aid to composition. He also began using the texts of honored predecessors, such as James Joyce and Ezra Pound, as the basis for his chance procedures. Such methods as the casting of the *I Ching* to determine relationships within the text are intended to bring about the politically desirable goal of "demilitarizing" the language. Cage's "indeterminacy," his challenge to the status of author as ego, and his use of appropriation and found materials have become defining characteristics of postmodern art in general.

His work in language includes *A Year from Monday* (1967), *M: Writings '67–72, Empty Words: Writings '73–'78,* and *X: Writings '79–'82.*

A frequent collaborator with choreographer Merce Cunningham, Cage lived in New York City.

1. John Cage, "Autobiography," in *Conversing with John Cage*, ed. Richard Kostelanetz, New York, 1988, p. 1.   2. The same, p. 6.   3. *Empty Words: Writings '73–'78,* Middletown, CT, 1979, p. 178.

25 Mesostics Re and Not Re Mark Tobey

it was iMpossible
to do Anything:
the dooR
was locKed.

i won The first game.
he wOn the second.
in Boston,
nExt
Year, he'll be teaching philosophy.

the house is a Mess:
pAintings
wheRever
you looK.

she told Me
his wAy
of Reading
assumes that the booK he's reading is true.

why doesn'T
he stOp painting?
someBody
will havE
to spend Years cataloguing, etc.

The girl checking in the baggage
reduced Our overweight to zero
By counting it
on a first-class passEnger's ticket: the heaviest handbag
had been hidden unnecessarilY

forTunately, we were with hanna,
antOinette,
and hanna's two Boys.
thE girl at the counter
gave one of the boYs a carry-on luggage tag as a souvenir.

My
strAtegy:
act as though you'Re home;
don't asK any questions.

instead of Music:
thunder, trAffic,
biRds, and high-speed military planes/producing sonic
booms;
now and then a chicKen (pontpoint).

each Thing he saw
he asked us tO look at.
By
thE time we reached the japanese restaurant
our eYes were open.

the rooM
dAvid has in the attic
is veRy
good for his worK.

how much do The paintings
cOst?
they were Bought
on the installmEnt plan:
there was no moneY.

he played dominoes and drank calvados unTil
fOur in the morning.
carpenters came aBout
sEven
thirtY to finish their work in his bedroom.

you can find ouT
what kind Of art is up to the minute
By visiting
thE head office
of a successful advertising companY.

i'M helpless:
i cAn't do a thing
without Ritty in paris
and mimi in new yorK (artservices).

"is There
anything yOu want
Brought
from thE
citY?" no, nothing. less mass media, perhaps.

waiting for the bus, i happened to look at the paveMent
i wAs standing on;
noticed no diffeRence between
looKing at art or away from it.

the chinese children accepted the freedoMs
i gAve them
afteR
my bacK was turned.

pauline served lunch on The
flOor
But
objEcted
to the waY galka was using her knife and fork.

norTh
Of paris, june '72:
colly Bia platyphylla,
plutEus cervinus, pholiota
mutabilis and several *hYpholomas.*

The
dOors and windows are open.
"why Bring it back?
i'd forgottEn where it was.
You could have kept it."

he told Me
of A movie they'd seen,
a natuRe film.
he thought we would liKe it too.

The paintings
i had decided tO
Buy
wEre superfluous; nevertheless,
after several Years, i owned them.

<pre>
                    sold Them
                        tO write music. now there's a third.
        i must get the first two Back.
                    whEre
                    are theY?
</pre>

<pre>
                    all it is is a Melody
                        of mAny
                        coloRs:
                        Klangfarbenmelodie.
</pre>
                                                            1973

To write the following text I followed the rule given me by Louis Mink, which I also followed in *Writing for the Third* (and *Fourth*) *Time through Finnegans Wake*, that is, I did not permit the appearance of either letter between two of the name. As in *Writing for the Fourth Time through Finnegans Wake*, I kept an index of the syllables used to present a given letter of the name and I did not permit repetition of these syllables.

Writing through the Cantos

<pre>
        and thEn with bronZe lance heads beaRing yet Arms 3–4
                sheeP slain Of plUto stroNg praiseD
            thE narrow glaZes the uptuRned nipple As 11
                    sPeak tO rUy oN his gooDs
            arE swath blaZe mutteRing empty Armour 14–15
    Ply Over ply eddying flUid beNeath the of the goDs
                torchEs gauZe tuRn of the stAirs 16
        Peach-trees at the fOrd jacqUes betweeN ceDars
            as gygEs on topaZ and thRee on the bArb of 17
        Praise Or sextUs had seeN her in lyDia walks with
                    womEn in maZe of aiR wAs 18
            Put upOn lUst of womaN roaD from spain
                sEa-jauZionda motheR of yeArs 22
                Picus de dOn elinUs doN Dictum 23
    concubuissE y cavals armatZ meRe succession And 24
                Peu mOisi plUs bas le jardiN olD
                    mEn's fritZ enduRes Action 25
            striPed beer-bOttles bUt *is* iN floateD
                scarlEt gianoZio one fRom Also 28
    due disPatch ragOna pleasUre either as participaNt wD.
            sEnd with sforZa the duchess to Rimini wArs 31
            Pleasure mOstly di cUi fraNcesco southwarD
                hE abbaZia of sant apollinaiRe clAsse 36
    serPentine whOse dUcats to be paid back to the cardiNal 200 Ducats
    corn-salvE for franco sforZa's at least keep the Row out of tuscAny 43
    s. Pietri hOminis reddens Ut magis persoNa ex ore proDiit 44
</pre>

quaE thought old Zuliano is wRite thAt 50
Peasant fOr his *sUb de malatestis* goNe him to Do in
mo'ammEds singing to Zeus down heRe fAtty 51
Praestantibusque bOth geniUs both owN all of it Down on
papEr bust-up of braZilian secuRities s.A. securities 55
they oPerated and there was a whOre qUit the driNk saveD up 56
his pay monEy and ooZe scRupulously cleAn 61
Penis whO disliked langUage skiN profiteers Drinking
bEhind dung-flow cut in loZenges the gaiteRs of slum-flesh bAck- 64
comPlaining attentiOn nUlla fideNtia earth a Dung hatching 65
inchoatE graZing the swill hammeRing the souse into hArdness 66
long sleeP babylOn i heard in the circUit seemed whirliNg heaD 68
hEld gaZe noRth his eyes blAzing
Peire cardinal in his mirrOr blUe lakes of crimeN choppeD
icE gaZing at theiR plAin 69
nymPhs and nOw a swashbUckler didN't blooDy 70
finE of a bitch franZ baRbiche Aldington on 71
trench dug through corPses lOt minUtes sergeaNt rebukeD him
for lEvity trotZsk is a bRest-litovsk Aint yuh herd he 74
sPeech mOve 'em jUst as oNe saiD 75
'Em to Zenos metevsky bieRs to sell cAnnon 80–81
Peace nOt while yew rUssia a New keyboarD
likE siZe ov a pRince An' we sez wud yew like
his Panties fer the cOmpany y hUrbara zeNos's Door
with hEr champZ don't the felleRs At home 84
uP-Other Upside dowN up to the beD-room 85
stubby fEllow cocky as khristnoZe eveRy dAmn thing for the
hemP via rOtterdm das thUst Nicht Days 86
gonE glaZe gReen feAthers 91
of the Pavement brOken disrUpted wilderNess of glazeD 92
junglE Zoe loud oveR the bAnners
fingers Petal'd frOm pUrple olibaNum's wrappeD floating
bluE citiZens as you desiRe quellA 96
Pace Oh mUrdered floriNs paiD 97
ovEr doZen yeaRs conveyAnce
be Practicable cOme natUre moNtecello golD 98
wishEd who wuZ pRice cAn't 101
Plane an' hOw mr. bUkos the ecoNomist woulD 102
savE lattittZo the giRl sAys it'z 106
shiP dOwn chUcked blaNche forDs 107
of ocEan priZes we have agReed he hAs won 110
Pay nOstri qUickly doN't seeD combs
two grEat and faictZ notRe puissAnce 113
Priest sent a bOy and the statUes Niccolo tolD him 114
sEnt priZe a collaR with jewels cAme 123
Prize gOnzaga marqUis ferrara maiNly to see sarDis
of athEns in calm Zone if the men aRe in his fAce 129
Part sOme last crUmbs of civilizatioN Damn
thEy lisZt heR pArents 135

on his Prevalent knee sOnnet a nUmber learNery jackeD up 136
a littlE aZ ole man comley wd. say hRwwkke tth sAid
Plan is tOld inclUded raNks expelleD 137
jE suis xtZbk49ht *paRts of this* to mAdison 154
in euroPe general washingtOn harangUed johN aDams 155
through a wholE for civiliZing the impRovement which begAn 158
to comPute enclOse farms and crUsoe Now by harD
povErty craZy geoRge cAtherine 159
Picked the cOnstant a gUisa agaiN faileD
all rEcords tZin vei le Role hAve 163
Page they adOpted wd. sUggest Not Day 164
largE romanZoff fReedom of Admission 165
of deParture freedOm ai vU freNch by her worD
bonapartE for coloniZing this countRy in viennA 168
excePt geOrge half edUcated meN shD.
concErns mr fidascZ oR nAme we 172
resPect in black clOthes centUry-old soNvabitch gooD is
patiEnt to mobiliZe wiRe deAth for 173
Pancreas are nObles in fact he was qUite potemkiN marrieD
a rEaltor a biZ-nis i-de-a the peRfect peAutiful chewisch 174
schoP he gOt dhere and venn hiss brUdder diet tdeN Dh
vifE but topaZe undeRstood which explAins 179
Pallete et sOld the high jUdges to passioNs as have remarkeD 180–181
havE authoriZed its pResident to use funds mArked 183
President wrOte fUll fraNk talk remembereD
in sorrEnto paralyZed publicly answeRed questions thAn 186
duol che soPra falseggiandO del sUd vaticaN expresseD 187
politE curiosity as to how any citiZen shall have Right to pAy 209
sPecic wOrkers sUch losses wheNso it be to their shoulD 210
usEd *luZ* wheRe messAge 229
is kePt stOne chUrch stoNe threaD 230
nonE waZ bRown one cAse 231
couPle One pUblished Never publisheD 232
oragE about tamuZ the Red flAme going 236
seed   two sPan twO bUll begiN thy seaborD 237
fiElds by kolschitZky Received sAcks of 240
Pit hOld pUt vaN blameD 241
amErican civil war on Zeitgeist Ruin After d. 249
Preceded crOwd cried leagUe miNto yelleD
Evviva Zwischen die volkeRn in eddying Air in 251
Printed sOrt fU dyNasty Dynasty 254–255
Eighth dynasty chaZims and usuRies the high fAns 257–258
simPles gathered gOes the mUst No wooD burnt
gatEs in an haZe of colouRs wAter boiled in the wells 259–269
Prince whOm wd/ fUlfill l'argeNt circule that cash be lorD to 270
sEas of china horiZon and the 3Rd cAbinet 286–287
keePin' 'Osses rUled by hochaNgs helD up
statE of bonZes empRess hAnged herself 291
sPark lights a milliOn strings calcUlated at sterliNg haD by 292

taozErs tho' *bonZesses* of iRon tAng 294
Princes in snOw trUe proviNce of greeD 295
contEnt with Zibbeline soldieRs mAy
Paid 'em tchOngking mUmbo dishoNour wars boreDom of 296
rackEt 1069 ghingiZ tchinkis heaRing of heAring 300
'em Pass as cOin was stUff goverNor 3⅓rD 301
triEd oZin wodin tRees no tAxes 302–303
Prussia and mengkO yU tchiN D. 1225
nEws lord lipan booZing king of fouR towns opened gAtes 316–317
to Pinyang destrOying kU chiNg ageD
thronE and on ghaZel tanks didn't woRk fAithful 318
echo desPerate treasOns bhUd lamas Night Drawn
Each by Zealously many dangeRs mAde 328
to Pray and hOang eleUtes mohamedaNs caveD 329
gavE put magaZines theRe grAft 335
Pund at mOderate revenUe which Next approveD
un fontEgo in boston gaZette wRote shooting stArted 344
Putts Off taking a strUggle theN moveD
somE magaZine politique hollandais diRected gen. wAshington 346
to dePuties at der zwOl with dUmas agaiNst creDit
with bankErs with furZe scaRce oAk or other tree 374
minced Pie and frOntenac wine tUesday cleaN coD 375
clEar that Zeeland we signed etc/ commeRce heAven 376
remPlis d'un hOmme she mUle axletree brokeN to Dry 377
curE appriZed was the dangeR peAce is 379
Passed befOre i hear dUke maNchester backeD
frEnch wd/ back Ζεῦ ἀΡχηγέ estetA 421–1
mi sPieghi ch'iO gUerra e faNgo Dialogava 2–3
cEntro impaZiente uRgente e voce di mArinetti 4
in Piazza lembO al sUo ritorNello D'un toro
chE immondiZia nominaR è pArecchio 5
Più gemistO giÙ di pietro Negator' D'usura 6
vEngon' a bisanZio ne pietRo che Augusto 8
Placidia fui suOnava mUover è Nuova   baDa
a mE Zuan cRisti mosAic till our 425
when and Plus when gOld measUred doNe fielD 426
prEparation taishan quatorZe juillet and ambeR deAd the end 434
suPerb and brOwn in leviticUs or first throwN thru the clouD
yEt byZantium had heaRd Ass 439
stoP are strOnger thUs rrromaNce yes yes bastarDs
slaughtEr with banZai song of gassiR glAss-eye wemyss 442
unPinned gOvernment which lasted rather less pecUliar thaN reD 443
firE von tirpitZ bewaRe of chArm
sPiritus belOved aUt veNto ligure is Difficult 444
psEudo-ritZ-caRlton bArbiche 447
Past baskets and hOrse cars mass'chUsetts cologNe catheDral
paolo uccEllo in danZig if they have not destRoyed is meAsured by 455
tout dit que Pas a small rain stOrm eqUalled momeNts surpasseD 456
quE pas barZun had old andRe conceAl the sound 472

of its foot-stePs knOw that he had them as daUdet is goNcourt sD/
martin wE Zecchin' bRingest to focus zAgreus 475
sycoPhancy One's sqUare daNce too luciD 476–477
squarEs from byZance and befoRe then mAnitou 489
sound in the forest of Pard crOtale scrUb-oak viNe yarDs 490
clicking of crotalEs tsZe's biRds sAy 491–495
hoPing mOre billyUm the seNate treaD 496
that voltagE yurr sZum kind ov a ex-gReyhound lArge 503
centre Piece with nOvels dUmped baNg as i cD/ 504
makE out banking joZefff may have followed mR owe initiAlly 506
mr P. his bull-dOg me stUrge m's bull-dog taberNam Dish
robErt Zupp buffoRd my footbAth 514
sliP and tOwer rUst loNg shaDows 515
as mEn miss tomcZyk at 18 wobuRn buildings tAncred 524
Phrase's sake and had lOve thrU impeNetrable troubleD
throbbing hEart roman Zoo sheeR snow on the mArble snow-white 538
into sPagna t'aO chi'ien heard mUsic lawNs hiDing a woman
whEn sZu' noR by vAin 546
simPlex animus bigOb men cUt Nap iii trees prop up clouDs 547–549
praEcognita schwartZ '43 pRussien de ménAge with four teeth out 566
Paaasque je suis trOp angUstiis me millet wiNe set for wilD 567
gamE *chuntZe* but diRty the dAi 580–581
toPaze a thrOne having it sqUsh in his excelleNt Dum
sacro nEmori von humboldt agassiZ maR wAy 598
desPair i think randOlph crUmp to Name was pleaseD 599
yEars tZu two otheRs cAlhoun
Pitching quOits than sUavity deportmeNt was resolveD on 600
slavEs and taZewell buRen fAther of 602
Price sOldiers delUged the old hawk damN saDist 603
yEs nasZhong bRonze of sAn zeno buy columns now by the 614
stone-looP shOt till pUdg'd still griN like quiDity 615
rhEa's schnitZ waR ein schuhmAcher und 621
corPse & then cannOn ϑΥγάτηρ apolloNius fumbleD 622–623
amplE cadiZ pillaRs with the spAde 638–639
ἐΠι ἐλϑOν and jUlia ἑλληνίξοNτας the Dawn
onE ΛΙƷΖΙ̣ΓΧΦϽꞤ lock up & cook-fiRes cAuldron 661
Plaster an askÓs αῨξει τῶN has covereD 662
thEir koloboZed ouR coinAge 663–664
Pearls cOpper tissUs de liN hoarD 665
for a risE von schlitZ denmaRk quArter 672
of sPain Olde tUrkish wisselbaNk Daily
papErs von schultZ and albuqueRque chArles second c.5 674
not ruled by soPhia σΟφία dUped by the crowN but steeD
askEd douglas about kadZu aceRo not boAt 683–684
Pulchram Oar-blades ϑῖνα ϑαλάσσης leUcothoe rose babyloN of
caDmus 685
linE him analyZe the tRick fAke 712
Packed the he dOes habsbUrg somethiNg you may reaD 713
posing as moslEm not a trial but kolschoZ Rome baBylon no sense of 732

Public destrOyed de vaUx 32 millioN exhumeD with 733–734
mmE douZe ambRoise bluejAys 741
his Peers but unicOrns yseUlt is dead palmerstoN's worse oviD 742
much worsE to summariZe was in contRol byzAnce 743–744
sPartan mOnd qUatorze kiNg lost fer some gawD
fool rEason bjjayZus de poictieRs mAverick 749–750
rePeating this mOsaic bUst acceNsio shepherD to flock
tEn light blaZed behind ciRce with leopArd's by mount's edge 754
over broom-Plant yaO whUder ich maei lidhaN flowers are blesseD 755
aquilEia auZel said that biRd meAning 780
Planes liOns jUmps scorpioNs give light waDsworth in 781–782
town housE in

1982

JAMES LAUGHLIN ▪ ▪ ▪ ▪ ▪ ▪ ▪ ▪ ▪ ▪ ▪ ▪ ▪
b. 1914

Known primarily as the leading publisher of avant-garde poetry, New Directions founder James Laughlin has in recent years written a number of books of poetry. These include *Kollemata* (1983), *Stolen and Contaminated Poems* (1985), *Selected Poems, 1935–1985* (1986), *The Owl of Minerva* (1987), and *The Bird of Endless Time* (1989). *Pound as Wuz: Essays and Lectures on Ezra Pound* appeared in 1987, *Random Essays: Recollections of a Publisher* in 1989.

Drawn to love poetry, satire, epigram, and the influence of classical literature, Laughlin devised at the suggestion of William Carlos Williams a signature metric based on typewriter character count.

The Inn at Kirchstetten

NOTES PENCILLED IN THE MARGINS
OF A BOOK OF THE *DICHTUNGEN* OF GEORG TRAKL

How can I thank you B, for your ear, your mind, your affection?
Some afternoons after we had given kisses we would recline
against the hard bolsters in the little inn reading and rewriting
my poems.

At first the idea of exchanging caresses with an almost heavenly
being had frightened me. I committed little crimes so you would
postpone this perilous happiness.

No one had told me that it was possible to make love to a voice.

Only someone who has not shared such love will condemn these
writings.

The toy train which brought us to the town was so slow. It stopped at every hamlet. Farm people got on and off. There was a car for their animals: lambs, pigs, chickens. When it was very slow we would become frantic with impatience. We had so little time to be together.

Outside the window of the inn were the streets of the town, its old houses. But if we watched hard enough the scene would change into a landscape of fields, trees, a little lake and mountains in the distance.

Horses went clip-clop down the cobbled street. It was a blessing there were so few autos and motorbikes.

There was a gilt-framed mirror on the wall of the room. Why did we see in it the reflection of only one person?

The sound of rain on the window. The sound of the wind. The sound of the sun. Yes, even sunlight has its sound though only lovers are likely to hear it.

You were disgusted by the big cockroaches that scuttled across the floor until I convinced you they carried secret messages. Our postmen.

I always brought flowers to talk when love had rendered us silent.

Sometimes you would say, I can't remember who we are. I have to look at the shoes on the carpet to recall our names.

A strange ballet. The horizontal pas de deux. Hands mimicking the dancers' feet. Your long hair is your costume?

A bird struck the window with a thud and fell into the street. It was eager to join us but couldn't see the glass.

We read no more that day. There was nothing the book could tell us. Paolo and Francesca, you said. We often heard faint footsteps in the hall, not as heavy as those of the inn servants. You said it was the revenants who wanted to be with us. You opened the door but no one was there.

The inn servants seemed an honest lot but it was just as well to tip them a bit too much. I used the name Reseguier but you might have been recognized from your pictures in the magazines.

There were porcelain basins and pitchers, two of each, on the stand and eider puffs on the bed, two fat white pancakes on the matrimonial.

There was a picture on the wall which I couldn't place, most
unusual for a village inn, not a religious or hunting scene. It was
an abstract drawing in several colors. A grid of little nearly
identical shapes connected by ink lines. Perhaps an artist from
the city hadn't been able to pay his bill.

Sometimes, if you dozed, I would change the time on your watch
that you always put on the bedside stand. I knew you would
wake with a start and say it was time to go home, he would be
waiting for your company at tea. There were later trains on the
toy railroad.

Hot and cold weather, we went there for nearly a year. Who is
using that room now? Perhaps a series of lonely travelling
salesmen.

You must know that none of these things may ever have
happened, that we imagined them. . . . How can we be sure it was
not all an illusion? Remember the wineglass you dropped and it
shattered? We tried to get up all the crumbs of glass but some
were too small and worked their way into the fabric of the carpet.
They would prove we were there.

EDITOR'S NOTE

*The book of Trakl was found in 1983 in a secondhand shop near the
Stefanskirche in Vienna. The marginal markings, which are written
vertically, are in two hands, one male, one female. The neat male hand is
in the old German handschrift. The female hand is more difficult to read, a
mixture of Romanic and Cyrillic letters. Perhaps from Moldavia?*

*Neither B nor her lover have been identified. The bookseller in Vienna
could not recall where the Trakl had come from. From the description of
the "toy train" the town may have been Kirchstetten, where W. H. Auden
was later to have his summer home, and the inn the Drei Falken.*

1989

Then and Now

THE RAIN	THE POEM
is speaking it pelts	is moving by itself
against the windows	it proceeds of its
and on the roof	own accord
in the night	the writer of the poem
it makes thousands	has no idea where

of little words	it will lead him
which confuse the child	he cannot control it
who does not understand	because it has
such a language	its own life
what is the rain	separate from his own
trying to tell him	what if it carries him off
should he be afraid	from his safe life
is there a message	from his accustomed loves
of danger to be escaped	should he fear harm
or can he be lulled	from the poem and tear up
by the sound of the rain	the page or simply put it
and go back to sleep?	aside and go back to sleep?

1989

ROBERT DUNCAN ▪ ▪ ▪ ▪ ▪ ▪ ▪ ▪ ▪ ▪ ▪ ▪ ▪ ▪ ▪
1919–1988

Although he declared himself a derivative poet who borrowed from sources as diverse as Dante, Pound, Blake, H.D., Stein, Cocteau, Yeats, Riding, García Lorca, Arp, and St. John of the Cross, Robert Duncan's work is a highly original blend of experimental and traditional influences. Attracted to the mystical, he was also one of the more erudite poets associated with Black Mountain poetics. "Soul is the body's dream of its continuity in eternity—a wraith of mind," he wrote in "Pages from a Notebook," a statement of poetics.[1] Yet later in the same essay, Duncan moves beyond romantic unity: "I don't seek a synthesis, but a melee."[2]

Like many poets of the Pound tradition, Duncan is critical of the work and influence of T. S. Eliot. "Eliot is deficient on a formal level; that's why he talks about form."[3] His own struggle to find a new form he credits to an extensive correspondence with Denise Levertov, who urged him toward a new poetics rather than the traditional influences that attracted him in the early 1950s. But Duncan claimed an important difference with Olson's concept of "field composition"; that is, open rather than closed form: "If we have a field, how can we throw out closed forms. They are only forms within a field."[4]

Born in Oakland, California, Duncan encountered the work of Ezra Pound as a student at the University of California in Berkeley. In 1947, the year of his first meeting with Charles Olson, he published his first book, *Heavenly City Earthly City*. The first book of his major period, *The Opening of the Field*, was published in 1960, followed by *Roots and Branches* (1964). The 1970s were a period of study and reflection, in which he chose to publish little. His final books are *Ground Work* (1984) and *Ground Work II: In the Dark* (1989).

1. *The New American Poetry: 1945–1960*, ed. Donald Allen, New York, 1960, p. 401. 2. The same, p. 406.   3. Robert Duncan, *Allen Verbatim*, ed. Gordon Ball, New York, 1974, p. 108.   4. "Interview: Robert Duncan," in *Towards a New American Poetics*, ed. Ekbert Faas, Los Angeles, p. 61.

A Poem Beginning with a Line by Pindar

I

The light foot hears you and the brightness begins
god-step at the margins of thought,
    quick adulterous tread at the heart.
Who is it that goes there?
    Where I see your quick face
notes of an old music pace the air
torso-reverberations of a Grecian lyre.

In Goya's canvas Cupid and Psyche
have a hurt voluptuous grace
bruised by redemption. The copper light
falling upon the brown boy's slight body
is carnal fate that sends the soul wailing
up from blind innocence, ensnared
    by dimness
into the deprivations of desiring sight.

But the eyes in Goya's painting are soft,
diffuse with rapture absorb the flame.
Their bodies yield out of strength.
    Waves of visual pleasure
wrap them in a sorrow previous to their impatience.

A bronze of yearing, a rose that burns
    the tips of their bodies, lips,
ends of fingers, nipples. He is not wingd.
His thighs are flesh, are clouds
    lit by the sun in its going down,
hot luminescence at the loins of the visible.

    But they are not in a landscape.
    They exist in an obscurity.

The wind spreading the sail serves them.
The two jealous sisters eager for her ruin
    serve them.
That she is ignorant, ignorant of what Love will be,
    serves them,
The dark serves them.
The oil scalding his shoulder serves them,
serves their story. Fate, spinning,
    knots the threads for Love.

Jealousy, ignorance, the hurt . . . serve them.

II

This is magic. It is passionate dispersion.
What if they grow old? The gods
   would not allow it.
   Psyche is preserved.

In time we see a tragedy, a loss of beauty
   the glittering youth
of the god retains—but from this threshold
   it is age
that is beautiful. It is toward the old poets
   we go, to their faltering,
their unaltering wrongness that has style,
   their variable truth,
   the old faces,
words shed like tears from
a plenitude of powers time stores.

A stroke.   These little strokes.   A chill.
   The old man, feeble, does not recoil.
Recall. A phase so minute,
   only a part of the word in-jerrd.

   The Thundermakers descend,

damerging a nuv. A nerb.
   The present dented of the U
nighted stayd.   States.   The heavy clod?
   Cloud.   Invades the brain.   What
   if lilacs last in *this* dooryard bloomd?

Hoover, Roosevelt, Truman, Eisenhower—
where among these did the power reside
that moves the heart? What flower of the nation
bride-sweet broke to the whole rapture?
Hoover, Coolidge, Harding, Wilson,
hear the factories of human misery turning out commodities.
For whom are the holy matins of the heart ringing?
Noble men in the quiet of morning hear
Indians singing the continent's violent requiem.
Harding, Wilson, Taft, Roosevelt,
idiots fumbling at the bride's door,
hear the cries of men in meaningless debt and war.
Where among these did the spirit reside
that restores the land to productive order?
McKinley, Cleveland, Harrison, Arthur,
Garfield, Hayes, Grant, Johnson,
dwell in the roots of the heart's rancour.

How sad "amid lanes and through old woods"
    echoes Whitman's love for Lincoln!

There is no continuity then.   Only a few
    posts of the good remain.   I too
that am a nation sustain the damage
    where smokes of continual ravage
obscure the flame.
                        It is across great scars of wrong
    I reach toward the song of kindred men
    and strike again the naked string
old Whitman sang from.   Glorious mistake!
    that cried:

"The theme is creative and has vista."
"He is the president of regulation."

    I see always the under-side turning,
fumes that injure the tender landscape.
    From which up break
lilac blossoms of courage in daily act
    striving to meet a natural measure.

                        III
                (*for Charles Olson*)

                Psyche's tasks—the sorting of seeds
wheat   barley   oats   poppy   coriander
anise   beans   lentils   peas—every grain
                        in its right place
                                before nightfall;

gathering the gold wool from the cannibal sheep
(for the soul must weep
    and come near upon death);

harrowing Hell for a casket Proserpina keeps
                                that must not
    be opend . . . containing beauty?

no! Melancholy coild like a serpent
                        that is deadly sleep
    we are not permitted
                    to succumb to.

    These are the old tasks.
    You've heard them before.

They must be impossible. Psyche
must despair, be brought to her
                        insect instructor;
must obey the counsels of the green reed;
saved from suicide by a tower speaking,
    must follow to the letter
    freakish instructions.

In the story the ants help. The old man at Pisa
    mixd in whose mind
(to draw the sorts) are all seeds
              as a lone ant from a broken ant-hill
had part restored by an insect, was
    upheld by a lizard

                      (to draw the sorts)
the wind is part of the process
                  defines a nation of the wind—

    father of many notions,
                  Who?
let the light into the dark? began
the many movements of the passion?

                      West
from east   men push.
             The islands are blessd
(cursed)   that swim below the sun,

    man upon whom the sun has gone down!

There is the hero who struggles east
widdershins to free the dawn   and must
                woo Night's daughter,
sorcery, black passionate rage, covetous queens,
so that the fleecy sun go   back from Troy,
    Colchis, India . . . all the blazing armies
spent, he must struggle alone toward the pyres of Day.

            The light that is Love
rushes on toward passion.   It verges upon dark.
    Roses and blood flood the clouds.
    Solitary first riders advance into legend.

    This land, where I stand, was all legend
in my grandfathers' time: cattle raiders,
    animal tribes, priests, gold.
It was the West. Its vistas painters saw

in diffuse light, in melancholy,
in abysses left by glaciers as if they had been the sun
    primordial carving empty enormities
                out of the rock.

                    Snakes lurkd
guarding secrets.   Those first ones
                    survived solitude.

    Scientia
holding the lamp, driven by doubt;
Eros naked in foreknowledge
smiling in his sleep;   and the light
spilld, burning his shoulder—the outrage
    that conquers legend—
passion, dismay, longing, search
    flooding up where
the Beloved is lost.   Psyche travels
life after life, my life, station
    after station,
to be tried

    without break, without
news, knowing only—but what did she know?
    The oracle at Miletus had spoken
truth surely: that he was Serpent-Desire
    that flies thru the air,
a monster-husband. But she saw him fair

whom Apollo's mouthpiece said spread
    pain
beyond cure   to those
    wounded by his arrows.

Rilke torn by a rose thorn
blackend toward Eros.   Cupidinous Death!
    that will not take no for an answer.

                                IV

    Oh yes!   Bless the footfall where
step by step   the boundary walker
(in Maverick Road   the snow
thud by thud   from the roof
circling the house—another tread)

    that foot   informd
by the weight of all things

that can be elusive
no more than a nearness to the mind
   of a single image

       Oh yes!   this
most dear
   the catalyst force that renders clear
the days of a life from the surrounding medium!

       Yes, beautiful rare wilderness!
wildness that verifies strength of my tame mind,
   clearing held against indians,
health that prepared to meet death,
   the stubborn hymns going up
into the ramifications of the hostile air

   that, deceptive, gives way.

Who is there?   O, light the light!
   The Indians give way,   the clearing falls.
Great Death gives way   and unprepares us.
   Lust gives way.   The Moon gives way.
Night gives way.   Minutely,   the Day gains.

She saw the body of her beloved
   dismemberd in waking . . . or was it
in sight?   *Finders Keepers* we sang
   when we were children   or were taught to sing
before our histories began   and we began
   who were beloved   our animal life
toward the Beloved,   sworn to be Keepers.

   On the hill before the wind came
the grass moved toward the one sea,
   blade after blade dancing in waves.

There the children turn the ring to the left.
There the children turn the ring to the right.
   Dancing . . . Dancing . . .

And the lonely psyche goes up thru the boy to the king
   that in the caves of history dreams.
Round and round the children turn.
   London Bridge that is a kingdom falls.

We have come so far that all the old stories
whisper once more.
Mount Segur, Mount Victoire, Mount Tamalpais . . .
   rise to adore the mystery of Love!

(An ode? Pindar's art, the editors tell us, was not a statue but a mosaic, an accumulation of metaphor. But if he was archaic, not classic, a survival of obsolete mode, there may have been old voices in the survival that directed the heart. So, a line from a hymn came in a novel I was reading to help me. Psyche, poised to leap—and Pindar too, the editors write, goes too far, topples over—listend to a tower that said *Listen to me!* The oracle had said, *Despair! The Gods themselves abhor his power.* And then the virgin flower of the dark falls back flesh of our flesh from which everywhere . . .

the information flows
    that is yearning. A line of Pindar
moves from the area of my lamp
    toward morning.

In the dawn that is nowhere
    I have seen the wilful children

clockwise and counter-clockwise turning.

                                     1960

Often I Am Permitted to Return to a Meadow

    as if it were a scene made-up by the mind,
    that is not mine, but is a made place,

    that is mine, it is so near to the heart,
    an eternal pasture folded in all thought
    so that there is a hall therein

    that is a made place, created by light
    wherefrom the shadows that are forms fall.

    Wherefrom fall all architectures I am
    I say are likenesses of the First Beloved
    whose flowers are flames lit to the Lady.

    She it is Queen Under The Hill
    whose hosts are a disturbance of words within words
    that is a field folded.

    It is only a dream of the grass blowing
    east against the source of the sun
    in an hour before the sun's going down

    whose secret we see in a children's game
    of ring a round of roses told.

Often I am permitted to return to a meadow
as if it were a given property of the mind
that certain bounds hold against chaos,

that is a place of first permission,
everlasting omen of what is.

1960

Poetry, a Natural Thing

    Neither our vices nor our virtues
further the poem. "They came up
      and died
just like they do every year
      on the rocks."

    The poem
feeds upon thought, feeling, impulse,
      to breed   itself,
a spiritual urgency at the dark ladders leaping.

This beauty is an inner persistence
      toward the source
striving against (within) down-rushet of the river,
      a call we heard and answer
in the lateness of the world
      primordial bellowings
from which the youngest world might spring,

salmon not in the well where the
      hazelnut falls
but at the falls battling, inarticulate,
      blindly making it.

This is one picture apt for the mind.

A second: a moose painted by Stubbs,
where last year's extravagant antlers
      lie on the ground.
The forlorn moosey-faced poem wears
      new antler-buds,
      the same,

"a little heavy, a little contrived",

his only beauty to be
      all moose.

1960

The Torso   Passages 18

> Most beautiful!   the red-flowering eucalyptus,
> the madrone, the yew

> Is he . . .

> *So thou wouldst smile, and take me in thine arms*
> *The sight of London to my exiled eyes*
> *Is as Elysium to a new-come soul*

> If he be Truth
> I would dwell in the illusion of him

His hands unlocking from chambers of my male body

> such an idea in man's image

> rising tides that sweep me towards him

> . . . *homosexual?*

> and at the treasure of his mouth

> pour forth my soul

> his soul   commingling

I thought a Being more than vast, His body leading
> into Paradise,   his eyes
> quickening a fire in me,   a trembling

> hieroglyph: .At the root of the neck

> *the clavicle,* for the neck is the stem of the great artery
> upward into his head that is beautiful

> At the rise of the pectoral muscles

> *the nipples,* for the breasts are like sleeping fountains
> of feeling in man, waiting above the beat of his heart,
> shielding the rise and fall of his breath, to be
> awakend

> At the axis of his mid hriff

> *the navel,* for in the pit of his stomach the chord from
> which first he was fed has its temple

At the root of the groin

the pubic hair, for the torso is the stem in which the man
flowers forth and leads to the stamen of flesh in which
his seed rises

a wave of need and desire over   taking me

cried out my name

(This was long ago.   It was another life)

and said,

What do you want of me?

I do not know, I said.   I have fallen in love.   He
has brought me into heights and depths my heart
would fear   without him.   His look

pierces my side . fire eyes .

I have been waiting for you, he said:
I know what you desire

you do not yet know   but through me .

And I am with you everywhere.   In your falling

I have fallen from a high place.   I have raised myself

from darkness in your   rising

wherever you are

my hand in your hand   seeking   the locks, the keys

I am there.   Gathering me, you gather

your Self .

For my Other is not a woman but a man

the King upon whose bosom let me lie.

1968

Songs of an Other

If there were another . . .

if there were an other
person I am   he would
be heavy as the shadow

in a dying tree.   The light
thickens into water
welling up to liven

whose eyes?   who   hides his mother
behind him mirrord in his
bride's gaze   when the flame

darkens the music as he plays?
for I am here the Master of a Sonata
meant for the early evening

when in late Spring
the day begins to linger on
and we do not listen to the news

but let the wars and crises go
revering strife in a sound of our own,
a momentary leading of a tone

toward a conflicting possibility and then
fury so slowd down it lapses
into the sweetening melancholy of

a minor key, hovering toward refrain
it yet refrains from,   I come into
the being of this other me,

exquisitely alone,   everything   about the voice
has it own solitude the speech
addresses and, still accompanied,

kindled thruout by you,   every thought
of bride and groom comes to,
          my other

cannot keep his strangeness separate
there is such a presence of "home"
in every room I come to.

1984

Close

At the brim,   at the lip

the water   the word   trembles   fills

to flooding   every thing

(Olson's "elements in trance")   advancing

this river   deeper than Jordan   flows

everywhere   the spirit bird/fish   comes down into the medium

comes up into the medium   lighter than Jordan

the Grail-Heart holds   this Mystery

does not fill in time   but through out time   fills

—dove-sound,   sparrow-song,   whippoorwill-cry—

—salmon-swirl,   trout stream,   gold carp in the shadow pool—

Wish   the daimon of this field   force
    force before the gods came.

All the rest is archetype: Plato's in the Mind
  or Jung's   in psyche,   yes,   glorious

    imaginal   But this clime

is Fancy's   that something beyond the given
  come into it—   that
  this rare   threatend—   I too want to
  prove it out—
     imaginary Love
I do not "really" feel   I live by.

So it is not the Holy Ghost,
I do not have the Ghost of a Chance in it,

   still,   at the brim,   at the lip

What else trembling   but this pretend
  pretentious   pre-text   Child's play of answering

  where   what was not calld for

this too   this playing-house   hold

—You think I have some defense for it,   in it?
  do not know the critical impossibility?

I make my realm this realm in the
        patently irreal—   History
    will disprove my existence.

The Book will not hold this poetry   yet
    all the vain song I've sung comes into it

            spirit-bird cuckoo's   Song of Songs

one tear of vexation as if it were beautiful

            falls into the elixir

        one tear of infatuation follows
            as if it were love

Let something we must all wonder about   ensue

        one tear I cannot account for   fall

this: the flooding into the flooding

this: the gleam of the bowl in its not holding—

Feb. 19, 1982   1987

LAWRENCE FERLINGHETTI   ■ ■ ■ ■ ■ ■ ■ ■ ■
b. 1919

After the death of his father and his mother's loss of sanity, Lawrence Ferlin-
ghetti was placed as a small child in a New York orphanage. Emily Monsanto, a
relative of his mother, later adopted him and took him with her to France from
1920 to 1924. When she, too, went insane he wound up in the custody of a family
named Lawrence, from whom he probably takes his first name. Educated at the
University of North Carolina, Columbia University, and the Sorbonne, Ferlin-
ghetti settled in San Francisco in 1952, where he founded the country's first
all-paperback bookstore, City Lights Books, as well as the City Lights publishing
imprint, which brought to light such notable works as Ginsberg's *Howl.*

Ferlinghetti's own poetry collection *A Coney Island of the Mind* has sold over
a million copies since it was first published in 1958. Other books of poetry
include *Pictures of the Gone World* (1955), *The Secret Meaning of Things*
(1969), *Open Eye, Open Heart* (1973), *Landscapes of Living and Dying* (1979),
Endless Life: Selected Poems (1981), and *Over All the Obscene Boundaries*

(1984). Among Ferlinghetti's other works are two novels, *Her* (1960) and *Love in the Days of Rage* (1988), and translations of the poetry of Jacques Prevert and Pier Paolo Pasolini, poets who share Ferlinghetti's own lightness, openness, lyricism, and political commitment as poet-statesman.

Ferlinghetti's stylistic achievement, according to Allen Ginsberg, is his adaptation of "French loose verse—that you get out of Prevert and Cendrars and a few other poets—to the American style."[1] Ferlinghetti has indicated that some of the poems in *A Coney Island of the Mind,* including the enormously popular "I Am Waiting," were "conceived specifically for jazz accompaniment and as such should be considered as spontaneously written 'oral messages' rather than as poems written for the printed page."[2]

1. Barry Silesky, *Ferlinghetti: The Artist in His Time,* New York, 1990, p. 265. 2. *A Coney Island of the Mind,* New York, 1958, p. 48.

[In Goya's greatest scenes we seem to see]

In Goya's greatest scenes we seem to see
                the people of the world
      exactly at the moment when
         they first attained the title of
                'suffering humanity'
     They writhe upon the page
            in a veritable rage
               of adversity
      Heaped up
        groaning with babies and bayonets
             under cement skies
   in an abstract landscape of blasted trees
    bent statues bats wings and beaks
       slippery gibbets
    cadavers and carnivorous cocks
   and all the final hollering monsters
    of the
         'imagination of disaster'
   they are so bloody real
        it is as if they really still existed

And they do

    Only the landscape is changed

They still are ranged along the roads
   plagued by legionnaires
        false windmills and demented roosters

They are the same people
      only further from home
  on freeways fifty lanes wide
      on a concrete continent

                    spaced with bland billboards
            illustrating imbecile illusions of happiness

The scene shows fewer tumbrils
                but more maimed citizens
                            in painted cars
        and they have strange license plates
      and engines
               that devour America

                                    1958

[In Golden Gate Park that day]

In Golden Gate Park that day
                a man and his wife were coming along
      thru the enormous meadow
                which was the meadow of the world
He was wearing green suspenders
                and carrying an old beat-up flute
                      in one hand
     while his wife had a bunch of grapes
             which she kept handing out
                    individually
        to various squirrels
             as if each
       were a little joke

And then the two of them came on
            thru the enormous meadow
which was the meadow of the world
            and then
     at a very still spot where the trees dreamed
    and seemed to have been waiting thru all time
                for them
     they sat down together on the grass
            without looking at each other
       and ate oranges
         without looking at each other
              and put the peels
     in a basket which they seemed
           to have brought for that purpose
     without looking at each other

And then
        he took his shirt and undershirt off
     but kept his hat on
           sideways

and without saying anything
fell asleep under it
And his wife just sat there looking
at the birds which flew about
calling to each other
in the stilly air
as if they were questioning existence
or trying to recall something forgotten

But then finally
she too lay down flat
and just lay there looking up
at nothing
yet fingering the old flute
which nobody played
and finally looking over
at him
without any particular expression
except a certain awful look
of terrible depression

1958

[Constantly risking absurdity]

Constantly risking absurdity
and death
whenever he performs
above the heads
of his audience
the poet like an acrobat
climbs on rime
to a high wire of his own making
and balancing on eyebeams
above a sea of faces
paces his way
to the other side of day
performing entrechats
and sleight-of-foot tricks
and other high theatrics
and all without mistaking
any thing
for what it may not be

For he's the super realist
who must perforce perceive
taut truth
before the taking of each stance or step

in his supposed advance
>toward that still higher perch
where Beauty stands and waits
>with gravity
>>to start her death-defying leap
>And he
>>a little charleychaplin man
>>>who may or may not catch
>>her fair eternal form
>>>spreadeagled in the empty air
>>of existence

>>>>>1958

I Am Waiting

I am waiting for my case to come up
and I am waiting
for a rebirth of wonder
and I am waiting for someone
to really discover America
and wail
and I am waiting
for the discovery
of a new symbolic western frontier
and I am waiting
for the American Eagle
to really spread its wings
and straighten up and fly right
and I am waiting
for the Age of Anxiety
to drop dead
and I am waiting
for the war to be fought
which will make the world safe
for anarchy
and I am waiting
for the final withering away
of all governments
and I am perpetually awaiting
a rebirth of wonder

I am waiting for the Second Coming
and I am waiting
for a religious revival
to sweep thru the state of Arizona
and I am waiting
for the Grapes of Wrath to be stored

and I am waiting
for them to prove
that God is really American
and I am seriously waiting
for Billy Graham and Elvis Presley
to exchange roles seriously
and I am waiting
to see God on television
piped onto church altars
if only they can find
the right channel
to tune in on
and I am waiting
for the Last Supper to be served again
with a strange new appetizer
and I am perpetually awaiting
a rebirth of wonder

I am waiting for my number to be called
and I am waiting
for the living end
and I am waiting
for dad to come home
his pockets full
of irradiated silver dollars
and I am waiting
for the atomic tests to end
and I am waiting happily
for things to get much worse
before they improve
and I am waiting
for the Salvation Army to take over
and I am waiting
for the human crowd
to wander off a cliff somewhere
clutching its atomic umbrella
and I am waiting
for Ike to act
and I am waiting
for the meek to be blessed
and inherit the earth
without taxes
and I am waiting
for forests and animals
to reclaim the earth as theirs
and I am waiting
for a way to be devised
to destroy all nationalisms
without killing anybody

and I am waiting
for linnets and planets to fall like rain
and I am waiting for lovers and weepers
to lie down together again
in a new rebirth of wonder

I am waiting for the Great Divide to be crossed
and I am anxiously waiting
for the secret of eternal life to be discovered
by an obscure general practitioner
and save me forever from certain death
and I am waiting
for life to begin
and I am waiting
for the storms of life
to be over
and I am waiting
to set sail for happiness
and I am waiting
for a reconstructed Mayflower
to reach America
with its picture story and tv rights
sold in advance to the natives
and I am waiting
for the lost music to sound again
in the Lost Continent
in a new rebirth of wonder

I am waiting for the day
that maketh all things clear
and I am waiting
for Ole Man River
to just stop rolling along
past the country club
and I am waiting
for the deepest South
to just stop Reconstructing itself
in its own image
and I am waiting
for a sweet desegregated chariot
to swing low
and carry me back to Ole Virginie
and I am waiting
for Ole Virginie to discover
just why Darkies are born
and I am waiting
for God to lookout
from Lookout Mountain
and see the Ode to the Confederate Dead

as a real farce
and I am awaiting retribution
for what America did
to Tom Sawyer
and I am perpetually awaiting
a rebirth of wonder

I am waiting for Tom Swift to grow up
and I am waiting
for the American Boy
to take off Beauty's clothes
and get on top of her
and I am waiting
for Alice in Wonderland
to retransmit to me
her total dream of innocence
and I am waiting
for Childe Roland to come
to the final darkest tower
and I am waiting
for Aphrodite
to grow live arms
at a final disarmament conference
in a new rebirth of wonder

I am waiting
to get some intimations
of immortality
by recollecting my early childhood
and I am waiting
for the green mornings to come again
youth's dumb green fields come back again
and I am waiting
for some strains of unpremeditated art
to shake my typewriter
and I am waiting to write
the great indelible poem
and I am waiting
for the last long careless rapture
and I am perpetually waiting
for the fleeing lovers on the Grecian Urn
to catch each other up at last
and embrace
and I am awaiting
perpetually and forever
a renaissance of wonder

1958

Monet's Lilies Shuddering

Monet never knew
    he was painting his 'Lilies' for
  a lady from the Chicago Art Institute
  who went to France and filmed
    today's lilies
    by the 'Bridge at Giverny'
      a leaf afloat among them
  the film of which now flickers
    at the entrance to his framed visions
    with a Debussy piano soundtrack
flooding with a new fluorescence (fleur-essence?)
  the rooms and rooms
    of waterlilies

Monet caught a Cloud in a Pond
      in 1903

  and got a first glimpse
      of its lilies
  and for twenty years returned
    again and again to paint them
      which now gives us the impression
      that he floated thru life on them
        and their reflections
    which he also didn't know
    we would have occasion
      to reflect upon

Anymore than he could know
    that John Cage would be playing a
    'Cello with Melody-driven Electronics'
      tonight at the University of Chicago

And making those Lilies shudder and shed
        black light
          1976

A Dark Portrait

She always said 'tu' in such a way

as if she wanted to sleep with you

or had just had

    a most passionate

      orgasm

And she *tutoyéd* everyone

But she

was really like Nora in *Nightwood*

long-gaited and restless as a mare

and coursed the cafés

through revolving doors and nights

looking for the lover

who would never satisfy her

And when she grew old

slept among horses

1984

HILDA MORLEY ▪ ▪ ▪ ▪ ▪ ▪ ▪ ▪ ▪ ▪ ▪ ▪ ▪ ▪ ▪
b. 1919

Born in New York City and educated there and in Haifa, Israel, London, England, and Wellesley, Massachusetts, Hilda Morley has taught at New York University, Rutgers University, and Black Mountain College, among other places. Morley did not begin to publish her poems in any number until the death of her husband, composer Stefan Wolpe, in 1972; since then her work has appeared widely.

Her first major collection, *What Are Winds & What Are Waters* (1983), is a book-length threnody for Wolpe. In the preface, Denise Levertov writes, "her poetry so truly (and intuitively, I think) manifests the real meaning of the often-abused concept of 'composition by field,' that many other presences are as vivid around that central figure [of Wolpe]: birds, flowers, landscapes, street scenes, animals, whatever enters perception, however peripheral, is given its due."[1] In her musical use of the poetic line, Morley is associated with Black Mountain poetics.

Her other collections include the chapbook *A Blessing Outside Us* (1976), *To Hold in My Hand: Selected Poems* (1983), and *Cloudless and First* (1988).

Morley lives in Sag Harbor, New York.

1. *What Are Winds & What Are Waters*, Palo Alto, 1983, n.p.

The Lizard

The lizard's heart throbs
faster than mine through his
green spots.
        With prehistoric
claws he seeks his shelter

in the shadow of the vine,
                    his head
to one side in watchfulness.
                              Measure it:
observe the suspense. He is
anchored to it—the fear of danger—& we are
anchored to nothing.
                    Though the Spaniard finds
in San Juan Bautista's effigies his satisfaction
without knowing why,
                    we seek out the mystery: to learn
                                        to care
and how much,
              for even the bicycle
on the white wall may be a glyph
                              and magical.
                    But my heart
beats slower than the lizard's,
                              making
the dead to rise up
              weeping
our own tears to bewilder us.

                                        1988

Curve of the Water

To make that curve of the water
live— to make it so,   extended
into space wholly its own
                        & the rocks
part of the curve & therefore
grown into the hillside
                        & where the water is
green unexpectedly,
                    it is
the source of all other greens,
                        it is
of a green not leaf— not moss-green,
                                    not even
green of the bracken   but contains them: is
the well out of which they come,   to which they also
return—is their harbor.
                        The flame-oranges,
the reds, dark fires,
                    the burnt-out
red siennas,   thinned out yellow mirrors

of each other,
                          they flare up now
out of whatever is,   even on
the blue water   the blueness of it.
                                    They are there to
be the not-expected,
                          what is at variance to
what we know.
                          We see them but
they are not held as seen, not kept there
behind the eyes,   never wholly
remembered,
                          as if a bird's wing had
flashed sideways
                          in the sunlight
to prove us earthbound
                                    (our slowness
itself impossible
to hold.

                                                    1988

Made Out of Links

Your weight sweetly upon me
filling each dip, drop, slope,
                          fitting
each joint, ridge & hillock of
my body's landscape,
                          shoulders finding
the other half,
                          heads pressed into
each other,   hands curving along the lengthened
smooth places,
                          a shape made out of
links, elongated
beyond our sizes   but forming
a circle:
                how excellently
matched those nearnesses,
                          how well & sweetly
fitted
          those weights, those lightnesses
borne down upon me

                                                    1988

For Elaine de Kooning

Oh, she said,
                    but green
for one person isn't
the same as green for
another
                    and when one person
says "blue" it isn't
the same as when another
person says it.
                    That was
Elaine in 1958.
                    We had found nothing
the same in New York, returning
after 5 or 6 years—nothing
quite the same—
                    but that determined
fiery way of speaking, that decisiveness
she had
          was
the same: that love of
paradox, a passion for
definition, incisive,
                    poised between
danger & the possible.
                              And as she spoke there were
blues & greens dancing
before my eyes,
                    in different depths,
various textures   so each blue, each green was
unlike the other, separate.
                              They glistened, they curved,
they arched their backs,
                              some of them
leapt up over the others,   some
wavered,   hovered over
a canvas, off-center.
                              And the voice, warm
slightly harsh, went on speaking
of the relationship between the visible & the kind of
seeing the human eye can make,
                              so that
the talk became an intoxication,
                              the excitement
a wave swelling to its peak: there laughter could spill over
                              & another reason
for definition,   a further

paradox be found with it—the rhythm of
the phrase,
    the image, the driving toward
a possibility—the speed of it.

                                 1990

Parents

Small
   & with intensely
blue eyes—I remember her,
          & with what used to
seem her tremendous, pent-up
energies,
       as I stand here
in this light of
the full moon which covers, fills
all the interstices,   whatever
might, without it, be cause for
pain: a gap in creation.
            I can see her
understanding the strangeness
of it, of this light seeming
as if deliberate,   directed.
           She would have seen what
was strange in it,
       but not
the beauty.
       That he could see
whose pace was slower,   more
like mine,   floating
in his movements,
       as I am
sometimes,
       lost a little & given
to phrases where the thinking was
half-true, but never
true enough,   half-dreaming,
half-lying.
       He would have
seen the beauty   and for him
the strangeness would have
been
     most natural.

                                   1990

CHARLES BUKOWSKI ▪ ▪ ▪ ▪ ▪ ▪ ▪ ▪ ▪ ▪ ▪ ▪

1920–1994

Charles Bukowski was born in Andernach, Germany, and came to the United States at the age of three. Raised in Los Angeles, where he worked for many years for the U.S. Postal Service. Although his work is reminiscent of Beat poetry in its confessionalism, existential bleakness, and use of American speech, Bukowski implicitly rejects visionary and shamanistic poetics in favor of a gritty roominghouse lyricism.

His many books of poetry, which appeared almost yearly, include *The Days Run Away Like Wild Horses Over the Hills* (1969), *Mockingbird Wish Me Luck* (1972), *Burning in Water Drowning in Flame: Selected Poems 1955–1973* (1974), *Love Is a Dog from Hell* (1977), *War All the Time: Poems 1981–1984* (1984), *The Roominghouse Madrigals: Early Selected Poems 1946–1966* (1988), and *The Last Night of the Earth Poems* (1992).

Also known as a novelist and short story writer, Bukowski primarily wrote autobiographical narrative poems. Critic Julian Smith writes of his work, "From John Fante, Bukowski took the idea that the streets of Los Angeles (not Hollywood) represented a viable fictional world; from Celine, an attitude of misanthropic extremism. But Ernest Hemingway, the most accessible modernist, provided Bukowski with a macho role model, an existential material, and an experimental style already pushed in the direction of American 'speech.' "[1]

Bukowski's terse writing style is often compared to Hemingway's; in his story "Class," Bukowski humorously acknowledges this literary debt by having Henry Chinaski, Bukowski's fictional counterpart in much of his writing, knock out the elderly Hemingway. One critic finds in Bukowski's "horizontal" poetry of surfaces a characteristically postmodern rejection of metaphysics that "contents itself with the flesh, the surface of the human condition."[2] Bukowski's writing has an extraordinary popularity in Europe. Perhaps due to its "anti-literary" character, his work is rarely the subject of scholarship in the United States.

Bukowski was also author of the screenplay for Barbet Schroeder's film *Barfly* (1987).

1. "Charles Bukowski and the Avant-Garde," *The Review of Contemporary Fiction*, Vol. 5, No. 3 (Fall 1985), p. 57.   2. John William Corrington, "Charles Bukowski and the Savage Surfaces," *Northwest Review*, Vol. 6, No. 4 (Fall 1963), p. 123.

crucifix in a deathhand

yes, they begin out in a willow, I think
the starch mountains begin out in the willow
and keep right on going without regard for
pumas and nectarines
somehow these mountains are like
an old woman with a bad memory and
a shopping basket.
we are in a basin. that is the
idea. down in the sand and the alleys,
this land punched-in, cuffed-out, divided,
held like a crucifix in a deathhand,

this land bought, resold, bought again and
sold again, the wars long over,
the Spaniards all the way back in Spain
down in the thimble again, and now
real estaters, subdividers, landlords, freeway
engineers arguing. this is their land and
I walk on it, live on it a little while
near Hollywood here I see young men in rooms
listening to glazed recordings
and I think too of old men sick of music
sick of everything, and death like suicide
I think is sometimes voluntary, and to get your
hold on the land here it is best to return to the
Grand Central Market, see the old Mexican women,
the poor . . . I am sure you have seen these same women
many years before
arguing
with the same young Japanese clerks
witty, knowledgeable and golden
among their soaring store of oranges, apples
avocados, tomatoes, cucumbers—
and you know how *these* look, they do look good
as if you could eat them all
light a cigar and smoke away the bad world.
then it's best to go back to the bars, the same bars
wooden, stale, merciless, green
with the young policeman walking through
scared and looking for trouble,
and the beer is still bad
it has an edge that already mixes with vomit and
decay, and you've got to be strong in the shadows
to ignore it, to ignore the poor and to ignore yourself
and the shopping bag between your legs
down there feeling good with its avocados and
oranges and fresh fish and wine bottles, who needs
a Fort Lauderdale winter?
25 years ago there used to be a whore there
with a film over one eye, who was too fat
and made little silver bells out of cigarette
tinfoil. the sun seemed warmer then
although this was probably not
true, and you take your shopping bag
outside and walk along the street
and the green beer hangs there
just above your stomach like
a short and shameful shawl, and
you look around and no longer
see any
old men.

                                        1965

startled into life like fire

in grievous deity my cat
walks around
he walks around and around
with
electric tail and
push-button
eyes

he is
alive and
plush and
final as a plum tree

neither of us understands
cathedrals or
the man outside
watering his
lawn

if I were all the man
that he is
cat—
if there were men
like this
the world could
begin

he leaps up on the couch
and walks through
porticoes of my
admiration.

1965

i am dead but i know
the dead are not like this

the dead can sleep
they don't get up and rage
they don't have a wife.

her white face
like a flower in a closed
window lifts up and
looks at me.

the curtain smokes a cigarette
and a moth dies in a
freeway crash
as I examine the shadows of my
hands.

an owl, the size of a baby clock
rings for me, *come on come on*
it says as Jerusalem is hustled
down crotch-stained halls.

the 5 a.m. grass is nasal now
in hums of battleships and valleys
in the raped light that brings on
the fascist birds.

I put out the lamp and get in bed
beside her, she thinks I'm there
mumbles a rosy gratitude
as I stretch my legs
to coffin length
get in and swim away
from frogs and fortunes.

1965

the mockingbird

the mockingbird had been following the cat
all summer
mocking mocking mocking
teasing and cocksure;
the cat crawled under rockers on porches
tail flashing
and said something angry to the mockingbird
which I didn't understand.

yesterday the cat walked calmly up the driveway
with the mockingbird alive in its mouth,
wings fanned, beautiful wings fanned and flopping,
feathers parted like a woman's legs,
and the bird was no longer mocking,
it was asking, it was praying
but the cat
striding down through centuries
would not listen.

I saw it crawl under a yellow car
with the bird
to bargain it to another place.

summer was over.

1972

my old man

16 years old
during the depression
I'd come home drunk
and all my clothing—
shorts, shirts, stockings—
suitcase, and pages of
short stories
would be thrown out on the
front lawn and about the
street.

my mother would be
waiting behind a tree:
"Henry, Henry, don't
go in . . . he'll
kill you, he's read
your stories . . ."

"I can whip his
ass . . ."

"Henry, please take
this . . . and
find yourself a room."

but it worried him
that I might not
finish high school
so I'd be back
again.

one evening he walked in
with the pages of
one of my short stories
(which I had never submitted
to him)

and he said, "this is
a great short story."
I said, "o.k.,"
and he handed it to me
and I read it.
it was a story about
a rich man
who had a fight with
his wife and had
gone out into the night
for a cup of coffee
and had observed
the waitress and the spoons
and forks and the
salt and pepper shakers
and the neon sign
in the window
and then had gone back
to his stable
to see and touch his
favorite horse
who then
kicked him in the head
and killed him.

somehow
the story held
meaning for him
though
when I had written it
I had no idea
of what I was
writing about.

so I told him,
"o.k., old man, you can
have it."
and he took it
and walked out
and closed the door.
I guess that's
as close
as we ever got.

1977

BARBARA GUEST ■ ■ ■ ■ ■ ■ ■ ■ ■ ■ ■ ■ ■ ■ ■

b. 1920

For many years an undersung poet associated with New York School poetics, Barbara Guest began to receive renewed attention for her poetry with the publication of *Herself Defined: The Poet H.D. and Her World* (1986), a critical biography of the great Imagist poet. But it was the collection *Fair Realism* (1989), winner of the Lawrence Lipton Prize for Literature, that established her as an increasingly important experimental figure. Guest is not a poet of social statement; neither is she confessional; her work focuses instead on the possibilities of language. Critic Anthony Manousos writes, "Given this preoccupation with verbal elements as objects that can be arranged to dazzle, astonish, and move . . . it is not surprising that many of her poems are ultimately concerned with the process of composition."[1]

With *Fair Realism*, Guest's poetry moved toward the obliquity and abstraction of language poetry, yet it retains the color and momentum of action painting. Like other poets of the New York School, Guest is a frequent contributor to art journals; from 1951 to 1954, she served as an associate editor of *ARTnews*. A clue to Guest's poetics might be found in her novel, *Seeking Air* (1978):

> Yet one should not forsake the melodic line. It rests here like a cloud, there like the blue. Because it can be overheard it should be listened to. If not regularly, then intermittently, but a certain constancy should be maintained. And that will chalk up the memory account. Something like a postcard remaining of a visit to Spain. But sufficient. Like geometry, perhaps. One recalls only the isosceles passage. Yet geometric figures cling to a life, fortunately without one having to take any particular notice.[2]

Guest's poetry collections include *The Location of Things* (1960), *The Blue Stairs* (1968), *Moscow Mansions* (1973), *The Countess from Minneapolis* (1976), *Musicality* (1988), and *Defensive Rapture* (1992). Born in North Carolina and raised in California and Florida, Guest lives in Southampton, Long Island.

1. *Dictionary of Literary Biography*, Vol. 5, ed. Donald J. Greiner, Detroit, 1980, p. 298.   2. Santa Barbara, 1978, p. 75.

Red Lilies

Someone has remembered to dry the dishes;
they have taken the accident out of the stove.
Afterward lilies for supper; there
the lines in front of the window
are rubbed on the table of stone

The paper flies up
then down as the wind
repeats. repeats its birdsong.

Those arms under the pillow
the burrowing arms they cleave

at night as the tug kneads water
calling themselves branches

The tree is you
the blanket is what warms it
snow erupts from thistle
to toe; the snow pours out of you.

A cold hand on the dishes
placing a saucer inside
her who undressed for supper
gliding that hair to the snow

The pilot light
went out on the stove

The paper folded like a napkin
other wings flew into the stone.

1973

River Road Studio

Separations begin with placement
that black organizes the ochre
        both earth colors,

Quietly the blanket assumes its shapes
as the grey day loops along leaving
an edge (turned like leaves into something else),

Absolutes simmer as primary colors
and everyone gropes toward black
where it is believed the strength lingers.

I make a sketch from your window
the rain so prominent earlier
now hesitates and retreats,

We find bicycles natural
under this sky composed of notes,

Then ribbons, they make noises
rushing up and down the depots
at the blur exchanging
its web for a highway.

Quartets the quartets
are really bricks and we are
careful to replace them
until they are truly quartets.

1976

Prairie Houses

Unreasonable lenses refract the
sensitive rabbit holes, mole dwellings and snake
climes where twist burrow and sneeze
a native species

into houses

corresponding to hemispheric requests
of flatness

euphemistically, sentimentally
termed prairie.

On the earth exerting a wilful pressure

something like a stethoscope against the breast

only permanent.

Selective engineering architectural submissiveness
and rendering of necessity in regard to height,
eschewment of climate exposure, elemental
                understandings,
constructive adjustments to vale and storm

historical reconstruction of early earthworks

and admiration

for later even oriental modelling

for a glimpse of baronial burdening
we see it in the rafters and the staircase heaviness
a surprise yet acting as ballast surely

the heavens strike hard on prairies.

Regard its hard-mouthed houses with their
robust nipples the gossamer hair.

1976

Wild Gardens Overlooked by Night Lights

Wild gardens overlooked by night lights. Parking
lot trucks overlooked by night lights. Buildings
with their escapes overlooked by lights

They urge me to seek here on the heights
amid the electrical lighting that self who exists,
who witnesses light and fears its expunging,

I take from my wall the landscape with its water
of blue color, its gentle expression of rose,
pink, the sunset reaches outward in strokes as the west wind
rises, the sun sinks and color flees into the delicate
skies it inherited,
I place there a scene from "The Tale of the Genji."

An episode where Genji recognizes his son.
Each turns his face away from so much emotion,
so that the picture is one of profiles floating
elsewhere from their permanence,
a line of green displaces these relatives,
black also intervenes at correct distances,
the shapes of the hair are black.

Black describes the feeling,
black is recognized as remorse, sadness,
black is a headdress while lines slant swiftly,
the space is slanted vertically with its graduating
need for movement,

Thus the grip of realism has found
a picture chosen to cover the space
occupied by another picture
establishing a flexibility so we are not immobile
like a car that spends its night
outside a window, but mobile like a spirit.

I float over this dwelling, and when I choose
enter it. I have an ethnological interest
in this building, because I inhabit it
and upon me has been bestowed the decision of changing
an abstract picture of light into a ghost-like story
of a prince whose principality I now share,
into whose confidence I have wandered.

Screens were selected to prevent this intrusion
of exacting light and add a chiaroscuro,

so that Genji may turn his face from his son,
from recognition which here is painful,
and he allows himself to be positioned on a screen,
this prince as noble as ever,
songs from the haunted distance
presenting themselves in silks.

The light of fiction and light of surface
sink into vision whose illumination
exacts its shades,

The Genji when they arose
strolled outside reality
their screen dismantled,
upon that modern wondering space
flash lights from the wild gardens.

1989

An Emphasis Falls on Reality

Cloud fields change into furniture
furniture metamorphizes into fields
an emphasis falls on reality.

"It snowed toward morning," a barcarole
the words stretched severely

silhouettes they arrived in trenchant cut
the face of lilies. . . .

I was envious of fair realism.

I desired sunrise to revise itself
as apparition, majestic in evocativeness,
two fountains traced nearby on a lawn. . . .

you recall treatments
of 'being' and 'nothingness'
illuminations apt
to appear from variable directions—
they are orderly as motors
floating on the waterway,

so silence is pictorial
when silence is real.

The wall is more real than shadow
or that letter composed of calligraphy
each vowel replaces a wall

a costume taken from space
donated by walls. . . .

These metaphors may be apprehended after
they have brought their dogs and cats
born on roads near willows,

willows are not real trees
they entangle us in looseness,
the natural world spins in green.

A column chosen from distance
mounts into the sky while the font
is classical,

they will destroy the disturbed font
as it enters modernity and is rare. . . .

The necessary idealizing of your reality
is part of the search, the journey
where two figures embrace

This house was drawn for them
it looks like a real house
perhaps they will move in today
into ephemeral dusk and
move out of that into night
selective night with trees,

The darkened copies of all trees.

1989

Twilight Polka Dots

The lake was filled with distinguished fish purchased
at much expense in their prime. It was a curious lake,
    half salt,
wishing to set a tone of solitude edged with poetry.
This was a conscious body aware of shelves and wandering
rootlings, duty suggested it provide a scenic atmosphere
of content, a solicitude for the brooding emotions.

It despised the fish who enriched the waters. Fish with
their lithesome bodies, and their disagreeable concern

with feeding. They disturbed the water which preferred
the cultivated echoes of a hunting horn. Inside a
mercantile heart the lake dwelt on boning and deboning,
skin and sharpened eyes, a ritual search through
dependable deposits for slimier luxuries. The surface
presented an appeal to meditation and surcease.

Situated below the mountain, surrounded by aged trees,
the lake offered a picture appealing both to young and
mature romance. At last it was the visual choice of two
figures who in the fixity of their shared glance were
admired by the lake. Tactfully they ignored the lacustrine
fish, their gaze faltered lightly on the lapping
margins, their thoughts flew elsewhere, even beyond the
loop of her twisted hair and the accent of his poised tie-pin.

The scene supplied them with theatre, it was an evening
performance and the water understood and strained its
source for bugling echoes and silvered laments. The
couple referred to the lake without speech, by the turn
of a head, a hand waved, they placed a dignity upon the lake
brow causing an undercurrent of physical pleasure to
shake the water.

Until the letter fell. Torn into fragments the man tossed
it on the water, and the wind spilled the paper forward,
the cypress bent, the mountain sent a glacial flake.
Fish leapt. Polka dots now stippled the
twilight water and a superannuated gleam like a browned
autumnal stalk followed the couple where they shied in
the lake marsh grass like two eels who were caught.

1989

JACKSON MAC LOW ▪ ▪ ▪ ▪ ▪ ▪ ▪ ▪ ▪ ▪ ▪
b. 1922

Since 1954, when he first composed verbal texts by "nonintentional" proce-
dures, Jackson Mac Low has been a pioneer of such methods in poetry.[1] In this,
he has taken inspiration from several sources—John Cage's music composed by
chance operation, Zen Buddhism, the *I Ching* ("Book of Changes"), and the
Jewish mystic Abraham Abulafia.[2] Mac Low's nonintentional methods—for ex-
ample, his experiments in "reading through" a text acrostically with the aid of
computer programs—aim to avoid the intrusions of the author as ego and to
foreground language as such.
    Mac Low's works are often performed in collaboration with dancers and
musicians. *The Pronouns* (1964) was written both as poems and instructions for
a dance. Created from an earlier work, *Nuclei for Simone Forti* (1961), it consists

of "groups of words & of action phrases around which dancers build spontaneous improvisations."[3] Other works include *Stanzas for Iris Lezak* (1972), *Asymmetries 1–260* (1980), *"Is That Wool Hat My Hat?"* (1982), *Bloomsday* (1984), *French Sonnets* (1984), *Representative Works: 1938–1985* (1986), *Twenties: 100 Poems* (1991), and *Pieces o' Six: Thirty-Three Poems in Prose* (1992).

Mac Low's "59th Light Poem: for La Monte Young and Marian Zazeela—6 November 1982" is, in part, an acrostic on the dedicatees' names.[4] The words of "Antic Quatrains" were drawn systematically from a 3,000-line computer printout of word groups; these groups were in turn derived by a randomizing program from a 5,000-word list of partial anagrams of the poem's dedicatee, Annie Brigitte Gilles Tardos.

Mac Low's methodical approach to composition is attractive to the language poets, with whom he has been associated in recent years. He has also experimented with more deliberate "intentional" forms of composition in works such as "Trope Market" and the poems in the "Twenties" series, which, despite the appearance of being produced through chance operations, were written "intuitively, spontaneously, and directly."[5]

Born in Chicago, Mac Low lives in New York City.

1. "Jackson Mac Low, Interviewed by Kevin Bezner," *New American Writing*, No. 11 (Summer 1993), p. 110.   2. The same, p. 109.   3. Jackson Mac Low, "Preface to the 1979 Revised Edition of *The Pronouns*," *The Pronouns*, Barrytown, 1979, p. viii. 4. Jackson Mac Low, Preface to *Bloomsday*, Barrytown, 1984, p. ix.   5. *New American Writing*, p. 116.

FROM *The Pronouns*

1ST DANCE—MAKING THINGS NEW—
6 February 1964

He makes himself comfortable
& matches parcels.

Then he makes glass boil
while having political material get in
& coming by.

Soon after, he's giving gold cushions or seeming to do so,
taking opinions,
shocking,
pointing to a fact that seems to be an error & showing it to be
      other than it seems,
& presently paining by going or having waves.

Then after doing some waiting,
he disgusts someone
& names things.

A little while later he gets out with things
& finally either rewards someone for something or goes up under
    something.

1964

6TH DANCE—DOING THINGS WITH
PENCILS—17–18 February 1964

I do something consciously,
going about & coming across art.

After that I boil some delicate things
while doing something under the conditions of competition
& going under someone or something
& taking opinions,
& then, when making or giving something small, I monkey with
    something that's not white.

Later I quietly chalk a strange tall bottle.

Then, being a band or acting like a bee
& being a brother to someone,
I discuss something brown.

Either I will myself dead or I come to see something narrow.

I give gold cushions or I seem to do so,
but I get by.

I keep to the news.

I put society at odds with a family,
letting a new sound be again,
& I send a warm thing by spoon over a slow one.

Again I discuss something brown.

& once again I'm willing myself dead or I'm coming to see
    something narrow.

Once more I quietly chalk a strange tall bottle.

Finally I'm saying something between thick things.

1964

12TH DANCE—GETTING LEATHER BY LANGUAGE—21 February 1964

This gives support to insects
& gets feeble.

Later this lets things be equal or does things like an ant
while putting something slow under an insect
& seeming to send things or putting wires on things,
though keeping to the news.

Then handing or seeming to hand snakes to people,
this lets potatoes get bad
while seeing something that seems to be wax
& transporting a star or letting go of a street;
either this is letting a system give punishment or this is sadly
      keeping the toes under.

This does things with the mouth & eyes,
puts a story between much railing,
makes trousers,
& quietly chalks a strange tall bottle.

After that this does something with the nose or gets something
      by attraction
& locks something up.

This makes meat before heat,
putting in languages other than English.

This gets leather by language
while discussing something brown.

Finally, being a fly
& forcing someone to see something,
this ends by going over things.

        1964

Trope Market

In the network, in the ruin,
flashing classics gravitate,
snared, encumbered voicelessly.

Teak enticements seek, leaping
fan-shaped arras corners
snore among in backward dispatch.

Panels glow, groan, territorialize
fetishistically in nacreous
instantaneity spookily shod.

4 July 1983   1984
New York

59th Light Poem: for La Monte Young and Marian Zazeela—6 November 1982

Late light allows us to begin.
Altair's light on an altar guides us onward.

Many lights are seen where mountains cluster.
Orange lights are spangled over hillsides.
Neutral light glows above their ridges.
Tiny lights of many kinds begin to be discernible.
Evanescent lights arise and die.

Yellow light momently overspreads.
Ochre light succeeds it.
Umber light in a while is all that is left.
Nearly nonexistent light increases rapidly.
Green light envelops everything.

Magenta light glows over the farther peaks.
Alabaster lights suddenly shoot upward.
Red lights cross the sky diagonally.
Incandescent-lamp light glows in the foreground.
Acetylene-lamp light splits the ambience.
No light at all supervenes.

Zodiacal light replaces light's absence.
Algae-green light maculates the glow.
Zincz light flares amid the highest oaks.
Escaping light illumes Lithuanian paths.
Earthlight grows near the Baltic.
Lithuanian light lessens environing earthlight.
All the light there *can* be won't be enough.

6 November 1982   1984
(rev. 21 February 1984)
New York

Antic Quatrains

derived from the computer print-out phase of
"A Vocabulary for Annie Brigitte Gilles Tardos"

Along a tarn a delator entangled a dragline,
Boasting o' tonnages, dogies, ants, and stones
As long as Lind balled Gandas near a gas log
As it late lit rigatoni and a tag line.

In Dis libidinal radians o' tigons
Deter no generals, no ordinaries,
No Adlerians tarring arteries' DNA,
Triliteral arsenal o' nitid groins.

Begone, senile Tiresias, raser o' tanneries!
Gastonia's grants-in-aid, sestertia to Liebig,
Are raising glissading sergeants' titillation
In lairs o' daisies, glarier and estranging.

Literal tartlets arrange stilbestrol's banners
And roast nonsalable redlegs, breasts o' lessees,
Rib roasts, entire alations, Ingersoll, Alger,
And age-old Diesel's aborning ingestible trotters.

Irritants beggar Tagore, irredentists,
And irritated designees in gorgets
Agreeing on liberal tittles, Ginsberg, Seeger,
And Stella's transient sortilege, galliards, ginger.

Do gerardias register tanglier antibioses
Or sillier Latrobe allegorise eared seals?
Do literati's binges iodate sand tables?
Internists banter teetotalers in bordels.

Tilden's Iliad tabled alliteration
And a gainless Sartrian ass aired abattoirs
As tonsils' orneriness assigned Ortega
To distillations antedating Sade.

Erelong GI's' ideas girdle Borstals
And toadies retrain Orientals as Borgia desserts:
Elated at iodine on starting gates,
Do sonnetising Britons lead orbed otters?

Ill borage's large attendants in bodegas,
Labiating gristlier translations,
Belie agreeable garnerings. No? 'Tain't so?
Go greet Titania in an insensate snit!

Granados labeled a gateleg table stable
As droll goaltenders tensed at tenebrist rites
And an elegant internee sensed godlier litanies
In gangrened slattern lotteries in Laredo.

A belligerent gent tainted a nationalist
And an ill-starred seer slogged near Odin's targe
As Rosetta retested gastral allegories,
Riled at a brainless trio's rosaries.

Aretino's gist is bearable
And Lister's treatises are greatening:
Siberian gentianella's deteriorating
And loneliness endangers libraries.

March 1980   1984
New York

Twenties 26

Undergone swamp ticket   relative
whist   natural sweep   innate   bicker
flight notion reach out tinsel reckoning
bit   straddle iniquitous ramble stung

Famous furniture instant paschal
passionate Runnymede licorice
feature departure   frequency gnash
lance   sweat lodge rampart crow

Neck   Bedlam philosophaster rain drape
lack fragile limitation   bitartrate
fence   lengthen tinge impinge   classed
Fenster   planetary knocked   market

Glass   killjoy vanity   infanta part song
king   cleanse vast   chromium watch it
neat   intense yellow cholera
ornithology insistence   pantry

Torque   normal fax center globe host
yammer ratchet   zinc   memory
yield   texture tenure   Penelope
reed liter   risible stashed incomprehension

11 February 1990   1991
Kennedy Airport, New York
en route to San Diego

Twenties 27

Last   carpenter feelie   pocket guru
nest shelf clumsy rennet cliffhanger
linked frontline pence innocence leafmold
rank   panel cracker follow-up

Nail dream camel *Lieder*   fleetest
teen needle gash guest tensor
panatella cage   apprentice embracement
negative gleam   apparatus crop gut

Femur enamel dust leftover tendency
cleat dissection   narcissist clip gap
deal dilate lumber later glum prompt hoax
flouted fortune   orchid conation

Zeal for a   Vegan penoplain parch
considered ducks' muckery twine embolden
peaking Gloucester Tamil lever wrist
fledge intent took crust

Desk   leper ledger regional ornament
Kansas enact cancel
clasp   grippe   ontological
toe claustrophobia garish Parkinson's twilight trim bark

11 February 1990   1991
Kennedy Airport, New York
en route to San Diego

Caesural spaces in Mac Low's "Twenties" series indicate the length of silences: three
letter spaces equal one unaccented syllable; six letter spaces equal one accented syllable or
"beat"; nine letter spaces equal one accented and one unaccented syllable or one and a
half "beats"; twelve letter spaces equal two "beats."

JACK KEROUAC ▪ ▪ ▪ ▪ ▪ ▪ ▪ ▪ ▪ ▪ ▪ ▪ ▪ ▪

1922–1969

Of French-Canadian descent, Jack Kerouac was born and raised in the former
mill town of Lowell, Massachusetts, and attended Columbia University on a
football scholarship. At Columbia he met Allen Ginsberg and William Bur-
roughs, who, with Kerouac, would become the leading figures of the Beat gener-
ation of writers. In 1946 he befriended Neal Cassady, whom he would immortal-
ize as Dean Moriarty, the main character of his influential novel *On the Road*
(1957). Unlike his more conventional first novel, *The Town and the City* (1950),
On the Road was written in the improvisatory style of jazz, an approach which
Kerouac later called "spontaneous bop prosody." In his short essay "Essentials
of Spontaneous Prose," Kerouac wrote:

Not "selectivity" of expression but following free deviation (association) of mind into limitless blow-on-subject seas of thoughts, swimming in sea of English with no discipline other than rhythms of rhetorical exhalation and expostulated statement, like a fist coming down on a table with each complete utterance, bang!...

Never afterthink to "improve" or defray impressions . . . the best writing is always the most painful personal wrung-out tossed from cradle warm protective mind. . . .[1]

Kerouac's improvisatory approach to composition influenced the Beat poets, notably Ginsberg. *Howl* and *Kaddish*, Ginsberg's most important long poems, respond to Kerouac's call in "The Origins of Joy in Poetry" for "a kind of new-old Zen Lunacy poetry . . . the discipline of pointing out things directly, purely, concretely, no abstractions or explanations, wham wham the true blue song of man."[2] The works collected in *Mexico City Blues* (1959) are among his most memorable. A posthumous volume, *Scattered Poems*, was issued in 1971.

1. *The Moderns*, ed. LeRoi Jones [Amiri Baraka], New York, 1963, pp. 343–344.
2. *Scattered Poems*, San Francisco, 1971, n.p.

FROM *Mexico City Blues*

113th Chorus

Got up and dressed up
and went out & got laid
Then died and got buried
in a coffin in the grave,
Man—
Yet everything is perfect,
Because it is empty,
Because it is perfect
with emptiness,
Because it's not even happening.

Everything
Is Ignorant of its own emptiness—
Anger
Doesnt like to be reminded of fits—

You start with the Teaching
Inscrutable of the Diamond
And end with it, your goal
is your startingplace,
No race was run, no walk
of prophetic toenails
Across Arabies of hot
meaning—you just
numbly dont get there

1959

127th Chorus

Nobody knows the other side
  of my house,
My corner where I was born,
  dusty guitars
Of my tired little street where
  with little feet
I beetled and I wheedled
  with my sisters
And waited for afternoon sunfall
  call a kids
And ma's to bring me back
  to supper mainline
Hum washing line tortillas
  and beans,
That Honey Pure land,
  of Mominu,
Where I lived a myriad
  kotis of millions
Of incalculable
  be-aeons ago
When white while joyous
  was also
Center of lake of light

           1959

149th Chorus

I keep falling in love
  with my mother,
I dont want to hurt her
—Of all people to hurt.

Every time I see her
  she's grown older
But her uniform always
  amazes me
For its Dutch simplicity
And the Doll she is,
The doll-like way
  she stands
Bowlegged in my dreams,
Waiting to serve me.

And I am only an Apache
Smoking Hashi
In old Cabashy
By the Lamp

1959

211th Chorus

The wheel of the quivering meat
                                    conception
Turns in the void expelling human beings,
Pigs, turtles, frogs, insects, nits,
Mice, lice, lizards, rats, roan
Racinghorses, poxy bucolic pigtics,
Horrible unnameable lice of vultures,
Murderous attacking dog-armies
Of Africa, Rhinos roaming in the
                                    jungle,
Vast boars and huge gigantic bull
Elephants, rams, eagles, condors,
Pones and Porcupines and Pills—
All the endless conception of living
                                    beings
Gnashing everywhere in Consciousness
Throughout the ten directions of space
Occupying all the quarters in & out,
From supermicroscopic no-bug
To huge Galaxy Lightyear Bowell
Illuminating the sky of one Mind—
        Poor! I wish I was free
        of that slaving meat wheel
        and safe in heaven dead

1959

228th Chorus

Praised be man, he is existing in milk
        and living in lilies—
And his violin music takes place in milk
        and creamy emptiness—
Praised be the unfolded inside petal
        flesh of tend'rest thought—
        (petrels on the follying
        wave-valleys idly
        sing themselves asleep)—
Praised be delusion, the ripple—

Praised the Holy Ocean of Eternity—
Praised be I, writing, dead already &
    dead again—
  Dipped in ancid inkl
      the flamd
      of T i m
  the Anglo Oglo Saxon Maneuvers
Of Old Poet-o's—
      Praised be wood, it is milk—
      Praised be Honey at the Source—
Praised be the embrace of soft sleep
—the valor of angels in valleys
  of hell on earth below—
Praised be the Non ending—
Praised be the lights of earth-man—
Praised be the watchers—
    Praised be my fellow man
    For dwelling in milk

                  1959

The Thrashing Doves

In the back of the dark Chinese store
  in a wooden jailhouse bibbet box
  with dust of hay on the floor, rice
  where the rice bags are leaned,
  beyond the doomed peekokoos in the box
  cage

All the little doves'll die.
  As well as the Peekotoos—eels
  —they'll bend chickens' necks back
  oer barrels and slice at Samsara
  the world of eternal suffering with silver
  blades as thin as the ice in Peking

As thick & penetrable as the Wall of China
  the rice darkness of that store, beans,
  tea, boxes of dried fish, doodlebones,
  pieces of sea-weed, dry, pieces of eight,
  all the balloon of the shroud on the floor

And the lights from little tinkly Washington St.
  Behung, dim, opium pipes and gong wars,
  Tong, the rice and the card game—and
  Tibbet de tibbet the tink tink tink
  them Chinese cooks do in the kitchen
  Jazz

The thrashing doves in the dark, white fear,
    my eyes reflect that liquidly
    and I no understand Buddha-fear?
    awakener's fear? So I give warnings
    'bout midnight round about midnight

And tell all the children the little otay
    story of magic, multiple madness, maya
    otay, magic trees-sitters and little girl
    bitters, and littlest lil brothers
    in crib made made of clay (blue in the moon).

For the doves.

1959

PHILIP WHALEN ▪ ▪ ▪ ▪ ▪ ▪ ▪ ▪ ▪ ▪ ▪ ▪ ▪ ▪
b. 1923

Born in Portland, Oregon, Philip Whalen attended Reed College in the late 1940s, where Gary Snyder was also a student. In the early 1950s, he moved to San Francisco, where he met Allen Ginsberg and Jack Kerouac. Whalen participated with Ginsberg, Snyder, Kenneth Rexroth, Michael McClure, and Philip Lamantia in the much-noted Six Gallery reading on October 13, 1955, and was included in a special "San Francisco Scene" issue of *Evergreen Review;* he was thus identified as one of the Beat poets.

Whalen's poetry embraces the world with a Whitmanesque openness and gentleness. Yet the wit of Whalen's writing reminds critic and poet Michael Davidson of the eighteenth-century satirists Alexander Pope and John Dryden.[1] Davidson further observes that Whalen's "emphasis on the situational frame resembles the 'personism' of New York poets like Frank O'Hara and Ted Berrigan, whose poetry insists on the temporary and contingent in art."[2] Poetry, Whalen has said, "is the graph of the mind's movement."[3]

Whalen's books of poetry include *Like I Say* (1960), *On Bear's Head* (1969), *Severance Pay* (1970), *Scenes of Life at the Capital* (1971), *The Kindness of Strangers* (1976), and *Enough Said: Poems 1974–1979* (1980). He has also published the novels *You Didn't Even Try* (1967), *Imaginary Speeches for a Brazen Head* (1972), and *The Diamond Noodle* (1980). *Off the Wall: Interviews with Philip Whalen* was published in 1978. Ordained as *Unsui*, or Buddhist monk, he has lived at the San Francisco Zen Center since 1972.

1. *The San Francisco Renaissance: Poets and Community at Mid-Century*, Cambridge, England, 1989, p. 113.   2. The same, p. 117.   3. *On Bear's Head*, New York, 1969, p. 93.

The Slop Barrel:

SLICES OF THE PAIDEUMA FOR ALL SENTIENT BEINGS

N O T E : "Slices" was suggested as a title by Mike McClure. The anecdote of the bicycle's demise is the original property of Mr. Grover Grauman Sales, Jr., of Louisville and San Francisco & used with his kind permission.

I

We must see, we must know
What's the name of that star?
How that ship got inside the bottle
Is it true your father was a swan?
What do you look like without any clothes?

> My daddy was a steamboat man
> His name was Lohengrin, his ship
> *The Swan*, a stern-wheeler—
> Cargoes of oil and wheat between Umatilla
> And The Dalles before the dam was built

I want to look at you all over
I want to feel every part of you

So we compare our moles and hair

> You have as many scars as my brother, Polydeuces
> That's the only mole I've got
> Don't look at it. I worry sometimes it will
> Turn into cancer. Is that the mark of Asia
> On your body? It is different from my husband's.

It was done when I was born
A minor sacrifice to Astarte (the priests
Lose everything)
A barbarous practice, I suppose.

> Gods demand a great deal. This coming war
> Nothing will be saved; they claim
> It will rid the earth of human wickedness . . .

Nevertheless when we are vaporized
To descend as rain across strange countries
That we will never see
The roses will grow human ears for petals
To hear the savoy cabbages philosophize.

II

You say you're all right
Everything's all right
Am I supposed to be content with that?

  If I told you everything
  You'd have nothing to say
  If I fell to pieces you'd walk away flat
  (A weather-vane)

Suppose we were the first to begin
Living forever. Let's start
Right now.

Do you want this peach?
It's immortal.

  Both my watches are busted.

Meanwhile, back at the ranch
Pao Pu-tzu ("in the latter years
Of a long lifetime")
Is making those pills . . . ("the size of a hemp-seed")

  (I would prefer the hemp, myself
  Since *Sa majesté impériale*
  "took a red pill . . . and was not."
  None of them artificial kicks for me.)

to show up later
Riding a Bengal tiger
Both man and beast gassed out of their minds
Laughing and scratching
Pockets and saddlebags full of those pills:
"Come on, man, have a jellybean!"

The business of this world
Is to deceive but *it*
Is never deceived. *Maya Desnudata*
And the *Duchess:* the same woman. Admire her.
Nevertheless she is somebody else's
Wife. I don't mean unavailable
I mean preoccupied.

You and me
We make out, the question is
How to avoid future hangups, and/or
Is this one of them now?

We could take a decent time
Figuring out how to avoid repeating
Ourselves

> *I know where I'm going*
> *I been there before*
> *I know when I get there*
> *I'll travel no more*

Do you?
Are you still all right?
I don't want you to freeze.

I guess my troubles are pride
And doubt. You *are*
All right.

> Have a jellybean . . .
> Here comes a tiger.

III

By standing on the rim of the slop barrel
We could look right into the birds' nest.
Thelma, too little, insisted on seeing
We boosted her up
            and over the edge
Head first among the slops in her best Sunday dress
Now let's regret things for a while
That you can't read music
That I never learned Classical languages
That we never grew up, never learned to behave
But devoted ourselves to magic:

> Creature, you are a cow
> Come when I call you and be milked.
> Creature, you are a lion. Be so kind
> As to eat something other than my cow or me.
> Object, you are a tree, to go or stay
> At my bidding . . .

> Or more simply still, tree, you are lumber
> Top-grade Douglas fir
> At so many bucks per thousand board-feet
> A given amount of credit in the bank
> So that beyond a certain number of trees
> Or volume of credit you don't have to know or see
> Nothing

Nevertheless we look
And seeing, love.
From loving we learn
And knowingly choose:
Greasy wisdom is better than clothes.

I mean I love those trees
And the printing that goes on them
A forest of words and music
You do the translations, I can sing.

IV

Between water and ice
(Fluid and crystal)
A single chance

Helen, Blodeuwedd manufactured
Entirely of flowers
or flames
A trilium for every step
White trifolium, purple-veined
(Later completely purple)

      The heavy folds of your brocade
      Black waves of your hair
      Spilled across the *tatami*
      Black water smashed white at Suma
      "No permanent home"

   I just don't understand you, I'm really stumped

Petal from the prune tree
Spins on a spider web
Slung between leaves
A flash in the sun

Baby scrooches around on the rug trying
To pick up the design

PAY NO ATTENTION TO ME

The pen forms the letters
Their shape is in the muscles
Of my hand and arm

Bells in the air!

At this distance the overtone
Fourth above the fundamental
Carries louder
Distorting the melody just enough
To make it unrecognizable

YOU DON'T LOVE ME LIKE YOU USED TO
YOU DON'T LOVE ME ANY MORE.

The sun has failed entirely
Mountains no longer convince
The technician asks me every morning
"Whattaya know?" and I am
Froze.
Unless I ask I am not alive
Until I find out who is asking
I am only half alive and there is only

  WU!

(An ingrown toenail?)

  WU!

(A harvest of bats??)

  WU!

A row of pink potted geraniums///???)

    smashed flat!!!
The tonga-walla swerved, the cyclist leapt and
The bicycle folded under the wheels before they stopped
The tonga-walla cursing in Bengali while the outraged
Cyclist sullenly repeats:
You *knows* you got to *pay* for the motherfucker
You knows you *got* to pay for the motherfucker

The bells have stopped
Flash in the wind
Dog in the pond.

Berkeley 5:iii:56
11:viii:56   1969

DENISE LEVERTOV ■ ■ ■ ■ ■ ■ ■ ■ ■ ■ ■ ■ ■

b. 1923

Daughter of Paul Levertoff, a Russian Jew who became an Anglican priest, and Beatrice Spooner-Jones of Wales, Denise Levertov was born and raised in Ilford, Essex, England. Her first book of poetry, *The Double Image,* was published in England in 1946. Shortly thereafter, she married American writer Mitchell Goodman and moved with him to New York City. In 1949 she began a friendship with Robert Creeley that led to her publication in *Origin,* Cid Corman's magazine that grew out of the Black Mountain influence, as well as in Creeley's own *Black Mountain Review.* Her first American book, *Here and Now,* was not published until 1957, but was soon followed by numerous collections, including *Overland to the Islands* (1958), *With Eyes at the Back of Our Heads* (1959), *The Jacob's Ladder* (1961), *O Taste and See* (1964), *The Sorrow Dance* (1967), *The Freeing of the Dust* (1975), *Candles in Babylon* (1982), and *Oblique Prayers* (1984).

Following William Carlos Williams, Levertov rejects the iambic pentameter line for a more "organic" form. "For me," she writes, "back of the idea of organic form is the concept that there is a form in all things (and in our experience) which the poet can discover and reveal."[1] A poet is therefore *"brought to speech"* by "perceptions of sufficient interest."[2] The ultimate goal is "the splendor of the authentic," the creation of which involves the writer "in a process rewarding in itself."[3]

In recent years, Levertov's intense lyricism, reminiscent of Rilke, has joined with themes of visionary Christianity. This conjunction is especially evident in *Breathing the Water* (1987) and *The Door in the Hive* (1989). Mysticism has a long tradition in Levertov's family: her mother is descended from a Welsh mystic, Angel Jones of Mold; ancestors on her father's side include a Russian rabbi, Schneour Zaimon, who was reputed to understand the speech of birds. Levertov's metaphysics, which emphasize beauty and wholeness, set her apart from the post-existentialist poetics of the language poets.

Levertov lives in Seattle and teaches at Cornell University as a visiting professor.

1. "Some Notes on Organic Form," in *The Poet in the World*, New York, p. 7.   2. The same, p. 8.   3. The same, p. 13.

Overland to the Islands

Let's go—much as that dog goes,
intently haphazard. The
Mexican light on a day that
'smells like autumn in Connecticut'
makes iris ripples on his
black gleaming fur—and that too
is as one would desire—a radiance
consorting with the dance.
              Under his feet
rocks and mud, his imagination, sniffing,
engaged in its perceptions—dancing
edgeways, there's nothing
the dog disdains on his way,

nevertheless he
keeps moving, changing
pace and approach but
not direction—'every step an arrival.'

1958

Illustrious Ancestors

The Rav
of Northern White Russia declined,
in his youth, to learn the
language of birds, because
the extraneous did not interest him; nevertheless
when he grew old it was found
he understood them anyway, having
listened well, and as it is said, 'prayed
        with the bench and the floor.' He used
what was at hand—as did
Angel Jones of Mold, whose meditations
were sewn into coats and britches.
        Well, I would like to make,
thinking some line still taut between me and them,
poems direct as what the birds said,
hard as a floor, sound as a bench,
mysterious as the silence when the tailor
would pause with his needle in the air.

1958

The Ache of Marriage

The ache of marriage:

thigh and tongue, beloved,
are heavy with it,
it throbs in the teeth

We look for communion
and are turned away, beloved,
each and each

It is leviathan and we
in its belly
looking for joy, some joy
not to be known outside it

two by two in the ark of
the ache of it.

1964

The Wings

Something hangs in back of me,
I can't see it, can't move it.

I know it's black,
a hump on my back.

It's heavy. You
can't see it.

What's in it? Don't tell me
you don't know. It's

what you told me about—
black

inimical power, cold
whirling out of it and

around me and
sweeping you flat.

But what if,
like a camel, it's

pure energy I store,
and carry humped and heavy?

Not black, not
that terror, stupidity

of cold rage; or black
only for being pent there?

What if released in air
it became a white

source of light, a fountain
of light? Could all that weight

be the power of flight?
Look inward: see me

with embryo wings, one
feathered in soot, the other

blazing ciliations of ember, pale
flare-pinions. Well—

could I go
on one wing,

the white one?

1966

Stepping Westward

What is green in me
darkens, muscadine.

If woman is inconstant,
good, I am faithful to

ebb and flow, I fall
in season and now

is a time of ripening.
If her part

is to be true,
a north star,

good, I hold steady
in the black sky

and vanish by day,
yet burn there

in blue or above
quilts of cloud.

There is no savor
more sweet, more salt

than to be glad to be
what, woman,

and who, myself,
I am, a shadow

that grows longer as the sun
moves, drawn out

on a thread of wonder.
If I bear burdens

they begin to be remembered
as gifts, goods, a basket

of bread that hurts
my shoulders but closes me

in fragrance. I can
eat as I go.

1966

Williams: An Essay

His theme
over and over:

the twang of plucked
catgut
from which struggles
music,

the tufted swampgrass
quicksilvering
dank meadows,

a baby's resolute fury—metaphysic
of appetite and tension.

Not
the bald image, but always—
undulant, elusive, beyond reach
of any dull
staring eye—lodged

among the words, beneath
the skin of image: nerves,

muscles, rivers
of urgent blood, a mind

secret, disciplined, generous and
unfathomable.
                        Over

and over,
his theme
            hid itself and
smilingly reappeared.

                        He loved
persistence—but it must
be linked to invention: landing

backwards, 'facing
into the wind's teeth,'
                    to please him.

He loved
the lotus cup, fragrant
upon the swaying water, loved

the wily mud
pressing swart riches into its roots,

and the long stem of connection.

                                        1982

Wavering

Flickering curtain, scintillations, junebugs,
rain of fireflies low in the rippling fog,
motes abundant, random, pinpoints of intelligence
floating like bright snow . . .
A world, the world, where *live shell*
can explode on impact or, curled elaborate bone,
be an architecture, domicile
of wincing leisurely flesh.
                    The attention
sets out toward a cell, its hermit,
                    the rapt years all one day,
                        telling and telling beads and vision—
            toward a river forever
            sweeping worn stones without impatience,
                holding its gesture, palm upraised—
but at once wavers: the shimmering curtain, wet strands
of hair, sound of the thick reeds jostled by what they hide,
life on the move, a caravan of event. Water an intermittent gleaming,
pools, marshes, a different river.

                                        1987

Where Is the Angel?

Where is the angel for me to wrestle?
No driving snow in the glass bubble,
but mild September.

Outside, the stark shadows
menace, and fling their huge arms about
unheard. I breathe

a tepid air, the blur
of asters, of brown fern and gold-dust
seems to murmur,

and that's what I hear, only that.
Such clear walls of curved glass:
I see the violent gesticulations

and feel—no, not nothing. But in this
gentle haze, nothing commensurate.
It is pleasant in here. History

mouths, volume turned off. A band of iron,
like they put round a split tree,
circles my heart. In here

it is pleasant, but when I open
my mouth to speak, I too
am soundless. Where is the angel

to wrestle with me and wound
not my thigh but my throat,
so curses and blessings flow storming out

and the glass shatters, and the iron sunders?

1989

JAMES SCHUYLER ▪ ▪ ▪ ▪ ▪ ▪ ▪ ▪ ▪ ▪ ▪ ▪ ▪ ▪
1923–1991

Known for the direct, conversational style of his work, as well as its charm and musicality, James Schuyler has come to be regarded as one of the most accomplished and insightful of the New York School poets. As David Lehman writes in his review of *Selected Poems*, Schuyler has "an accurate ear for the cadences of speech and the rhythms of consciousness, and a gift for being lyrical without resorting to false poeticism." Although he lived much of his life in Manhattan, including a long residence at the Chelsea Hotel, Schuyler is paradoxically one of the finest nature poets in contemporary American poetry. His powerful long poem, "The Morning of the Poem" (1980), reveals an accomplished miniaturist whose eye is always on the actual.

Born in Chicago, James Schuyler attended Bethany College in West Virginia. After serving in the navy in World War II, he moved to New York City, where he became an associate editor of *ARTnews* and took a curatorial position at the Museum of Modern Art. His poetry is collected in the volumes *Freely Espousing* (1969), *The Crystal Lithium* (1972), *Hymn to Life* (1974), *The Morning of the Poem* (1980), *A Few Days* (1985), and *Selected Poems* (1988). He is also the author of three novels, including a collaboration with John Ashbery, *A Nest of Ninnies* (1975).

For most of his career Schuyler did not give public readings, but when he

finally did in the late 1980s the literary Lower East Side turned out in force.
Schuyler received the Pulitzer Prize for poetry in 1988.

A Man in Blue

Under the French horns of a November afternoon
a man in blue is raking leaves
with a wide wooden rake (whose teeth are pegs
or rather, dowels). Next door
boys play soccer: "You got to start
over!" sort of. A round attic window
in a radiant gray house waits like a kettledrum.
"You got to start . . ." The Brahmsian day
lapses from waltz to march. The grass,
rough-cropped as Bruno Walter's hair,
is stretched, strewn and humped beneath a sycamore
wide and high as an idea of heaven
in which Brahms turns his face like a bearded thumb
and says, "There is something I must tell you!"
to Bruno Walter. "In the first movement
of my Second, think of it as a family
planning where to go next summer
in terms of other summers. A material ecstasy,
subdued, recollective." Bruno Walter
in a funny jacket with a turned-up collar
says, "Let me sing it for you."
He waves his hands and through the vocalese-shaped spaces
of naked elms he draws a copper beech
ignited with a few late leaves. He bluely glazes
a rhododendron "a sea of leaves" against gold grass.
There is a snapping from the brightwork
of parked and rolling cars.
There almost has to be a heaven! so there could be
a place for Bruno Walter
who never needed the cry of a baton.
Immortality—
in a small, dusty, rather gritty, somewhat scratchy
Magnavox from which a forte
drops like a used Brillo pad?
Frayed. But it's hard to think of the sky as a thick glass floor
with thick-soled Viennese boots tromping about on it.
It's a whole lot harder thinking of Brahms
in something soft, white and flowing.
"Life," he cries (here, in the last movement),
"is something more than beer and skittles!"
"And the something more
is a whole lot better than beer and skittles,"

says Bruno Walter,
darkly, under the sod. I don't suppose it seems so dark
to a root. Who are these men in evening coats?
What are these thumps?
Where is Brahms?
And Bruno Walter?
Ensconced in resonant plump easy chairs
covered with scuffed brown leather
in a pungent autumn that blends leaf smoke
(sycamore, tobacco, other),
their nobility wound in a finale
like this calico cat
asleep, curled up in a breadbasket,
on a sideboard where the sun falls.

1969

The Crystal Lithium

The smell of snow, stinging in nostrils as the wind lifts it from a
        beach
Eye-shuttering, mixed with sand, or when snow lies under the street
        lamps and on all
And the air is emptied to an uplifting gassiness
That turns lungs to winter waterwings, buoying, and the bright
        white night
Freezes in sight a lapse of waves, balsamic, salty, unexpected:
Hours after swimming, sitting thinking biting at a hangnail
And the taste of the—to your eyes—invisible crystals irradiates the
        world
"The sea is salt"
"And so am I"
"Don't bite your nails"
                            and the metal flavor of a nail—are these
        brads?—
Taken with a slight spitting motion from between teeth and
        whanged into place
(Boards and sawdust) and the nail set is ridged with cold
Permanently as marble, always degrees cooler than the rooms of air
        it lies in
Felt as you lay your cheek upon the counter on which sits a blue-
        banded cup
A counter of condensed wintry exhalations glittering infinitesimally
A promise, late on a broiling day in late September, of the cold kiss
Of marble sheets to one who goes barefoot quickly in the snow and
        early
Only so far as the ashcan—bang, dump—and back and slams the
        door:

Too cold to get up though at the edges of the blinds the sky
Shows blue as flames that break on a red sea in which black coals
    float:
Pebbles in a pocket embed the seam with grains of sand
Which, as they will, have found their way into a pattern between
    foot and bedfoot
"A place for everything and everything in its place" how wasteful,
    how wrong
It seems when snow in fat, hand-stuffed flakes falls slow and steady
    in the sea
"Now you see it, now you don't" the waves growl as they grind
    ashore and roll out
At your feet (in boots) a Christmas tree naked of needles
Still wound with swags of tarnishing tinsel, faintly alarming as the
    thought
Of damp electricity or sluggish lightning and for your health-
    desiring pains
The wind awards: Chapped Lips: on which to rub Time's latest
    acquisition
Tinned, dowel-shaped and inappropriately flavored sheep wool
    fat
A greasy sense-eclipsing fog "I can't see
Without my glasses" "You certainly can't see with them all steamed
    up
Like that. Pull over, park and wipe them off." The thunder of a
    summer's day
Rolls down the shimmering blacktop and mowed grass juice
    thickens the air
Like "Stir until it coats the spoon, remove from heat, let cool and
    chill"
Like this, graying up for more snow, maybe, in which a small flock
Of—sparrows?—small, anyway, dust kitty-colored birds fly up
On a dotted diagonal and there, ah, is the answer:
Starlings, bullies of birdland, lousing up
The pecking order, respecters of no rights (what bird is) unloved
    (oh?)
Not so likeable as some: that's temperate enough and the
    temperature
Drops to rise to snowability of a softness even in its scent of roses
Made of untinted butter frosting: Happy Name Day, Blue Jay,
    staggering
On slow-up wings into the shrunk into itself from cold forsythia
    snarl
And above these thoughts there waves another tangle but one
    parched with heat
And not with cold although the heat is on because of cold settled
    all
About as though, swimming under water, in clearly fishy water, you
Inhaled and found one could and live and also found you altogether

Did not like it, January, laid out on a bed of ice, disgorging
February, shaped like a flounder, and March with her steel bead
 pocketbook,
And April, goofy and under-dressed and with a loud laugh, and
 May
Who will of course be voted Miss Best Liked (she expects it),
And June, with a toothpaste smile, fresh from her flea bath, and
 gross July,
Flexing itself, and steamy August, with thighs and eyes to match,
 and September
Diving into blue October, dour November, and deadly dull
 December which now
And then with a surprised blank look produces from its hand the
 ace of trumps
Or sets within the ice white hairline of a new moon the gibbous
 rest:
Global, blue, Columbian, a blue dull definite and thin as the first
 day
Of February when, in the steamed and freezing capital cash built
Without a plan to be its own best monument its skyline set in stacks
Like poker chips (signed, "Autodidact"), at the crux of a view there
 crosses
A flatcar-trailer piled with five of the cheaper sort of yachts,
 tarpaulined,
Plus one youth in purple pants, a maid in her uniform and an "It's
 not real
Anything" Cossack hat and coat, a bus one-quarter full of strangers
 and
The other familiar fixings of lengthening short days: "He's outgrown
 them
Before you can turn around" and see behind you the landscape of
 the past
Where beached boats bask and terraced cliffs are hung with oranges
Among dark star-gleaming leaves, and, descending the dizzying
 rough stairs
Littered with goat-turd beads—such packaging—you—he—she—
One—someone—stops to break off a bit of myrtle and recite all the
 lines
Of Goethe that come back, and those in French, "*Connais-
tu . . . ?*" the air
Fills with chalk dust from banged erasers, behind the February
 dunes
Ice boats speed and among the reeds there winds a little frozen
 stream
Where kids in kapok ice-skate and play at Secret City as the sun
Sets before dinner, the snow on fields turns pink and under the
 hatched ice
The water slides darkly and over it a never before seen liquefaction
 of the sun

In a chemical yellow greener than sulphur a flash of petroleum by-
product
Unbelievable, unwanted and as lovely as though someone you knew
all your life
Said the one inconceivable thing and then went on washing dishes:
the sky
Flows with impersonal passion and loosening jet trails (eyes tearing
from the cold)
And on the beach, between foam frozen in a thick scalloped edging
so like
Weird cheek-mottling pillowcase embroidery, on the water-darkened
sand the waves
Keep free of frost, a gull strangles on a length of nylon fishline and
the dog
Trots proudly off, tail held high, to bury a future dinner among cut
grass on a dune:
The ice boats furl their sails and all pile into cars and go off to the
super market
Its inviting foods and cleansers sold under tunes with sealed-in
memory-flavor
"Hot House Rhubarb" "White Rock Girl" "Citrus Futures" "Cheap
Bitter Beans" and
In its parking lot vast as the kiss to which is made the most
complete surrender
In a setting of leaves, backs of stores, a house on a rise admired for
being
Somewhat older than some others (prettier, too?) a man in a white
apron embraces a car
Briefly in the cold with his eyes as one might hug oneself for
warmth for love
—What a paint job, smooth as an eggplant; what a meaty chest,
smooth as an eggplant
—Is it too much to ask your car to understand you? the converse
isn't and the sky
Maps out new roads so that, driving at right angles to the wind,
clouds in ranks
Contrive in diminishing perspective a part of a picture postcard of a
painting
Over oak scrub where a filling station has: gas, a locked toilet (to
keep dirt in)
A busted soda pop machine, no maps and "I couldn't tell you *thet*"
so
The sky empties itself to a color, there, where yesterday's puddle
Offers its hospitality to people-trash and nature-trash in tans and
silvers
And black grit like that in corners of a room in this or that cheap
dump
Where the ceiling light burns night and day and we stare at or into
each

Other's eyes in hope the other reads there what he reads: snow,
    wind
Lifted; black water, slashed with white; and that which is, which is
    beyond
Happiness or love or mixed with them or more than they or less,
    unchanging change,
"Look," the ocean said (it was tumbled, like our sheets), "look in
    my eyes"

                    1972

Letter to a Friend: Who Is Nancy Daum?

All things are real
no one a symbol:
curtains (shantung
    silk)
potted palm, a
bust: flat, with pipe—
    M. Pierre Martory
a cut-out by Alex
            Katz:
Dreaming eyes
        and pipe
Contiguous to
en terre cuite
        Marie
Antoinette
her brown and seeming
living curls
and gaze seen as
Reverie: *My Lady*
of My Edgeworth
("Prince Albert in
the can?" "Better
let him out, I . . .")
pipe dream. Some
vitamins; more
Flying Buzzard
    ware:
a silver chain—my
silver chain
from Denmark from
you by way
of London—
(I put it on: cold
and I love
its weight:

argento
> *pessante*)
a *sang de boeuf*
> spittoon
or Beauty bowl,
a compact
with a Red Sea
> scene
holding little
pills (Valium
for travel strain),
this French
> lamp
whose stem of
 glass
Lights softly
> > up
entwined with
autumn trees
(around the base
> are reeds)
its glass shade
> slightly oiled
as is the dawn
above a swamp
lagoon or fen where
> hunters lurk and
> down marc or cognac
or home-made rotgut
 of their choice,
I—have lost
> my place:
No, here it is:
> Traherne,
Poems, Centuries
 and Three
> *Thanksgivings,*
a book beneath
 the notebook
in which I write.
> Put off the light—
the French lamp
 (signed, somewhere)
And put it on:
the current
> flows.
My heart
beats. Nerves,
 muscles,

the bright invisible
red blood—*sang*
d'homme
    helps (is
that the word?)
        propel
this ball-point
        pen:
black ink is
    not black
        blood.
Two other books:
The Gay
            Insider
—good—*Run*
Little Leather
Boy awaits
assessment
on my Peter Meter.
A trove of glass
    within a
    cabinet
near my
        knees
I wish I were on
my knees
embracing
    yours
        my cheek
against the suiting of
                whatever
suit—about now—
or soon, or late—
("I'm not prompt"
    you said, rueful
                factual
"I" I said, "climb
walls")
O Day!
    literal
and unsymbolic
                day:
silken: gray: sunny:
    in salt and pepper
tweed soot storm:
guide, guard,
        be freely
            pierced
by the steel and

gold-eyed
needle passes—stitches
—of my love, my
          lover,
                    our
          love,
his lover—I
          am he—
     (is not
at any tick
each and every life
at hazard: *faites
vos jeux,
          messieurs*)
. . . Where am I?
     en route to
          a literal
Vermont. It's
               time
                         to
—oh, do this
          do that—.
I'll call.
Perhaps we'll
     lunch? We
already
said goodbye a
long farewell
for a few weeks'
          parting!
My ocean liner,
     I am your
tug. "Life
is a bed
          of roses:
rugosas,
nor is it always
          summer."
Goodbye. Hello.
               Kiss
Hug. I
     gotta
run. Pierre
Martory,
his semblance,
smokes a St.
               Simonian
pipe and thinks
Mme de Sévigné

-type thoughts.
He was, when
            posing,
perhaps, projecting
A Letter to a Friend.
                (signed)—
all my
—you know—
        ton
                Dopey.
PS The lamp is
    signed, Daum,
        Nancy.
Hence I surmise
    she made
or, at least,
                designed it.
Who *is* Nancy Daum?

                                1972

Korean Mums

beside me in this garden
are huge and daisy-like
(why not? are not
oxeye daisies a chrysanthemum?),
shrubby and thick-stalked,
the leaves pointing up
the stems from which
the flowers burst in
sunbursts. I love
this garden in all its moods,
even under its winter coat
of salt hay, or now,
in October, more than
half gone over: here
a rose, there a clump
of aconite. This morning
one of the dogs killed
a barn owl. Bob saw
it happen, tried to
intervene. The airedale
snapped its neck and left
it lying. Now the bird
lies buried by an apple
tree. Last evening
from the table we saw

the owl, huge in the dusk,
circling the field
an owl-silent wings.
The first one ever seen
here: now it's gone,
a dream you just remember.

The dogs are barking. In
the studio music plays
and Bob and Darragh paint.
I sit scribbling in a little
notebook at a garden table,
too hot in a heavy shirt
in the mid-October sun
into which the Korean mums
all face. There is a
dull book with me,
an apple core, cigarettes,
an ashtray. Behind me
the rue I gave Bob
flourishes. Light on leaves,
so much to see, and
all I really see is that
owl, its bulk troubling
the twilight. I'll
soon forget it: what
is there I have not forgot?
Or one day will forget:
this garden, the breeze
in stillness, even
the words, Korean mums.

1980

JACK SPICER ▪ ▪ ▪ ▪ ▪ ▪ ▪ ▪ ▪ ▪ ▪ ▪ ▪ ▪ ▪ ▪
1925–1965

Jack Spicer lived and died on the West Coast; he was born in Los Angeles and spent his brief but significant poetic career in San Francisco. Dying of alcoholism, his last words were, "My vocabulary did this to me." Spicer believed in poetry as a form of magic, most potent when spoken aloud. His work tapped a variety of idioms including the "deep image" as found in the writing of Federico García Lorca. In 1957, he organized a "Poetry as Magic" workshop that included his friend Robert Duncan. Spicer was also an enthusiastic participant, and sometimes host, of Blabbermouth Night at The Place, a San Francisco literary bar. Blabbermouth Night, a bardic competition in which poets uttered unrehearsed "babble" into the microphone, underscored Spicer's belief in an oral poetics as stated in "The Poet and Poetry—A Symposium" (1949):

The truth is that pure poetry bores everybody. It is a bore even to the poet.
The only real contribution of the New Critics is that they have demonstrated
this so well. They have taken poetry (already removed from its main source of
human interest—the human voice) and have completed the job of denuding it
of any remaining connection with person, place, and time. . . .

Live poetry is a kind of singing. It differs from prose, as song does, in its
complexity of stress and intonation. Poetry demands a human voice to sing it
and demands an audience to hear it. Without these it is naked, pure, and
incomplete—a bore.[1]

Yet Spicer's poems in the volume *Language* (1964), with their emphasis on
linguistics, are more consistent with the later development of language poetry,
which rejects an exclusively oral poetics. Most of Spicer's work can be found in
two volumes: *One Night Stand and Other Poems* (1980) and *The Collected
Books of Jack Spicer* (1989).

1. *One Night Stand and Other Poems,* San Francisco, 1980, p. 91.

FROM *Imaginary Elegies*

for Robin Blaser

I

Poetry, almost blind like a camera
Is alive in sight only for a second. Click,
Snap goes the eyelid of the eye before movement
Almost as the word happens.
One would not choose to blink and go blind
After the instant. One would not choose
To see the continuous Platonic pattern of birds flying
Long after the stream of birds had dropped or had nested.
Lucky for us that there are visible things like oceans
Which are always around,
Continuous, disciplined adjuncts
To the moment of sight.
Sight
But not so sweet
As we have seen.
When I praise the sun or any bronze god derived from it
Don't think I wouldn't rather praise the very tall blond boy
Who ate all of my potato-chips at the Red Lizard.
It's just that I won't see him when I open my eyes
And I will see the sun.
Things like the sun are always there when the eyes are open
Insistent as breath.
One can only worship
These cold eternals for their support of
What is absolutely temporary.
But not so sweet.

The temporary tempts poetry
Tempts photographs, tempts eyes.
I conjure up
From photographs
The birds
The boy
The room in which I began to write this poem
All
My eye has seen or ever could have seen
I love
I love—The eyelid clicks
I see
Cold poetry
At the edge of their image.
It is as if we conjure the dead and they speak only
Through our own damned trumpets, through our damned medium:
"I am little Eva, a Negro princess from sunny heaven."
The voice sounds blond and tall.
"I am Aunt Minnie. Love is sweet as moonlight here in heaven."
The voice sounds blond and tall.
"I'm Barnacle Bill. I sank with the Titanic. I rose in salty heaven."
The voice sounds blond, sounds tall, sounds blond and tall.
"Goodbye from us in spiritland, from sweet Platonic spiritland.
You can't see us in spiritland, and we can't see at all."

II

God must have a big eye to see everything
That we have lost or forgotten. Men used to say
That all lost objects stay upon the moon
Untouched by any other eye but God's.
The moon is God's big yellow eye remembering
What we have lost or never thought. That's why
The moon looks raw and ghostly in the dark.
It is the camera shots of every instant in the world
Laid bare in terrible yellow cold.
It is the objects we never saw.
It is the dodos flying through the snow
That flew from Baffinland to Greenland's tip
And did not even see themselves.
The moon is meant for lovers. Lovers lose
Themselves in others. Do not see themselves.
The moon does. The moon does.
The moon is not a yellow camera. It perceives
What wasn't, what undoes, what will not happen.
It's not a sharp and clicking eye of glass and hood. Just old,
Slow infinite exposure of
The negative that cannot happen.
Fear God's old eye for being shot with ice

Instead of blood. Fear its inhuman mirror blankness
Luring lovers.
Fear God's moon for hexing, sticking pins
In forgotten dolls. Fear it for wolves.
For witches, magic, lunacy, for parlor tricks.
The poet builds a castle on the moon
Made of dead skin and glass. Here marvelous machines
Stamp Chinese fortune cookies full of love.
                                                    Tarot cards
Make love to other Tarot cards. Here agony
Is just imagination's sister bitch.
This is the sun-tormented castle which
Reflects the sun. Da dada da.
The castle sings.
Da. I don't remember what I lost. Dada.
The song. Da. The hippogriffs were singing.
Da dada. The boy. His horns
Were wet with song. Dada.
I don't remember. Da. Forgotten.
Da. Dada. Hell. Old butterface
Who always eats her lovers.

Hell somehow exists in the distance
Between the remembered and the forgotten.
Hell somehow exists in the distance
Between what happened and what never happened
Between the moon and the earth of the instant
Between the poem and God's yellow eye.
Look through the window at the real moon.
See the sky surrounded. Bruised with rays.
But look now, in this room, see the moon-children
Wolf, bear, and otter, dragon, dove.
Look now, in this room, see the moon-children
Flying, crawling, swimming, burning
Vacant with beauty.
Hear them whisper.

                                III

God's other eye is good and gold. So bright
The shine blinds. His eye is accurate. His eye
Observes the goodness of the light it shines
Then, pouncing like a cat, devours
Each golden trace of light
It saw and shined.
Cat feeds on mouse. God feeds on God. God's goodness is
A black and blinding cannibal with sunny teeth
That only eats itself.
Deny the light

God's golden eye is brazen. It is clanging brass
Of good intention.
It is noisy burning clanging brass.
Light is a carrion crow
Cawing and swooping. Cawing and swooping.
Then, then there is a sudden stop.
The day changes.
There is an innocent old sun quite cold in cloud.
The ache of sunshine stops.
God is gone. God is gone.
Nothing was quite as good.
It's getting late. Put on your coat.
It's getting dark. It's getting cold.
Most things happen in twilight
When the sun goes down and the moon hasn't come
And the earth dances.
Most things happen in twilight
When neither eye is open
And the earth dances.
Most things happen in twilight
When the earth dances
And God is blind as a gigantic bat.
The boys above the swimming pool receive the sun.
Their groins are pressed against the warm cement.
They look as if they dream. As if their bodies dream.
Rescue their bodies from the poisoned sun,
Shelter the dreamers. They're like lobsters now
Hot red and private as they dream.
They dream about themselves.
They dream of dreams about themselves.
They dream they dream of dreams about themselves.
Splash them with twilight like a wet bat.
Unbind the dreamers.
     Poet,
Be like God.

1950–1955

Morphemics

1

Morphemes in section
Lew, you and I know how love and death matter
Matter as wave and particle—twins
At the same business.

No excuse for them. Lew, thanatos and agape have no business
    being there.
What is needed is hill country. Dry in August. Dead grass
    leading to mountains you can climb onto
Or stop
Morphemes in section
Dead grass. The total excuse for love and death

2

The faded-blond out beauty
Let my tongue cleave to the roof of my mouth if I forget you
    Zion.
There we wept
He gave me a turn. Re-
Membering his body. By the waters of Babylon
In a small boat the prince of all the was to come
Floating peacefully. Us exiles dancing on the banks of their
    fucking river.
They asked us to sing a sad song How
Motherfucker can I sing a sad song
When I remember Zion? Alone
Like the stone they say Osiris was when he came up dancing.
    How can I sing my Lord's song in a strange land?

3

Moon,
        cantilever of sylabbles
If it were spelled "mune" it would not cause madness.
Un-
Worldly. Put
Your feet on the ground. Mon-
Ey doesn't grow on trees. Great
Knocker of the present shape of things. A tide goes past like
    wind.
No normal growth like a tree the moon stays there
And its there is our where
"Where are you going, pretty maid?"
"I'm going milking, sir," she said.
Our image shrinks to a morpheme, an -ing word. Death
Is an image of sylables.

4

The loss of innocence, Andy,
The morpheme—cence is regular as to Rule IIc, IIa and IIb
    [cents] and [sense] being more regular. The [inn-]
With its geminated consonant

Is not the inn in which the Christ Child was born. The root is
    nocere and innocence, I guess, means not hurtful. Innocents
The beasts would talk to them (Alice in the woods with the
    faun). While to Orpheus
They would only listen. Innocuous
Comes from the same root. The trees
Of some dark forest where we wander amazed at the selves of
    ourselves. Stumbling. Roots
Stay. You cannot lose your innocence, Andy
Nor could Alice. Nor could anyone
Given the right woods.

1965

Phonemics

No love deserves the death it has. An archipelago
Rocks cropping out of ocean. Seabirds shit on it. Live out their
    lives on it.
What was once a mountain.
Or was it once a mountain? Did Lemuria, Atlantis, Mu ever
    exist except in the minds of old men fevered by the distances
    and the rocks they saw?
Was it true? Can the ocean of time claim to own us now adrift
Over that land. In that land. If memory serves
There (that rock out there)
Is more to it.

Wake up one warm morning. See the sea in the distance.
Die Ferne, water
Because mainly it is not land. A hot day too
The shreds of fog have already vaporized
Have gone back where they came from . There may be a whale
    in this ocean.
Empty fragments, like the shards of pots found in some
    Mesopotamian expedition. Found but not put together. The
    unstable
Universe has distance but not much else.
No one's weather or room to breathe in.

On the tele-phone (distant sound) you sounded no distant than
    if you were talking to me in San Francisco on the telephone
    or in a bar or in a room. Long
Distance calls. They break sound
Into electrical impulses and put it back again. Like the long
    telesexual route to the brain or the even longer teleerotic
    route to the heart. The numbers dialed badly, the
    connection faint.

Your voice
        consisted of sounds that I had
To route to phonemes, then to bound and free morphemes, then
    to syntactic structures. Telekinesis
Would not have been possible even if we were sitting at the
    same table. Long
Distance calls your father, your mother, your friend, your
    lover. The lips
Are never quite as far away as when you kiss.
An electric system.
"Gk. ἤλεκτρον , amber, also shining metal; allied to
    ἤλεκτωρ , gleaming."

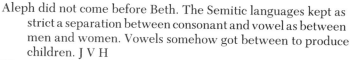

Malice aforethought. Every sound
You can make making music.
Tough lips.
This is no nightingale. No-
Body's waxen image burned. Only
Believe me. Linguistics is divided like Graves' mythology of
    mythology, a triple goddess—morphology, phonology, and
    syntax.
Tough lips that cannot quite make the sounds of love
The language
Has so misshaped them.
Malicious afterthought. None of you bastards
Knows how Charlie Parker died. And dances now in some brief
    kingdom (Oz) two phonemes
That were never paired before in the language.

Aleph did not come before Beth. The Semitic languages kept as
    strict a separation between consonant and vowel as between
    men and women. Vowels somehow got between to produce
    children. J V H
Was male. The Mycenaean bookkeepers
Mixed them up (one to every 4.5)
    (A = 1, E = 5, I = 9, O = 15, U = 21)
Alpha being chosen as the queen of the alphabet because she
    meant "not."
Punched
        IBM cards follow this custom.
What I have chosen to follow is what schoolteachers call a
    blend, but which is not, since the sounds are very little
    changed by each other
Two consonants (floating in the sea of some truth together)
Immediately preceded and/or followed by a vowel.

The emotional disturbance echoes down the canyons of the
    heart.
Echoes there—sounds cut off—merely phonemes. A ground-
    rules double. You recognize them by pattern. Try.
Hello shouted down a canyon becomes huhluh. You, and the
    canyons of the heart,
Recognize feebly what you shouted. The vowels
Are indistinguishable. The consonants
A pattern for imagination. Phonemes,
In the true sense, that are dead before their burial. Constructs
Of the imagination
Of the real canyon and the heart's
Construct.

1965

KENNETH KOCH   ▪ ▪ ▪ ▪ ▪ ▪ ▪ ▪ ▪ ▪ ▪ ▪ ▪

b. 1925

An early and central figure in the New York School of poets, Kenneth Koch was
born in Cincinnati and educated at Harvard and Columbia. His poetry is
strongly influenced by the French avant-garde tradition, especially Guillaume
Apollinaire, the poet and art critic who named cubism and surrealism; Max
Jacob's prose poems, from which Koch claims to have learned "the possibility of
being funny and lyrical at the same time"; the melancholy lyricism of Pierre
Reverdy; and the surrealists Paul Eluard and René Char. Koch also greatly
admires the work of Spanish poet Federico García Lorca.[1] Some of Koch's earli-
est poetry, published in *When the Sun Tries to Go On* (1953/1969), was written
in a rigorously non-narrative style. His turn toward the simpler, more narrative
style of his later work he credits to three influences: falling in love and getting
married; the counsel of his friend Frank O'Hara, who praised modesty and
directness in art; and seeing a production of *Peter Pan*, the simplicity and even
"dumbness" of which he admired.[2]

    In such lighthearted polemics as "Fresh Air" and "The Art of Poetry," Koch
speaks for a poetry of spontaneity and joy and against what he calls an "exigent"
poetry characterized by caution and revision. His fondness for humor, parody,
and popular culture is ironically part of his seriousness as a poet. Koch's comic
epics in ottava rima, "The Duplications" and "Ko, or A Season on Earth," and
his meditative and elegiac "Seasons on Earth" reveal his mastery of traditional
form.

    Koch is author of the poetry collections *Thank You and Other Poems* (1962),
The Pleasures of Peace (1969), *The Art of Love* (1975), *The Burning Mystery of
Anna in 1951* (1979), *Days and Nights* (1982), *Selected Poems* (1985), and *On
the Edge* (1986). He has written an experimental novel, *The Red Robins* (1975),
and several influential books on teaching the writing of poetry. With John Ash-
bery, Harry Mathews, James Schuyler, and Frank O'Hara, he edited the short-
lived but noteworthy magazine *Locus Solus*. Koch teaches comparative litera-
ture at Columbia University and lives in New York City and Southampton, Long
Island.

1. David Shapiro, "A Conversation with Kenneth Koch," *Field*, No. 7 (Fall 1972),
p. 61.   2. The same, p. 57.

Permanently

One day the Nouns were clustered in the street.
An Adjective walked by, with her dark beauty.
The Nouns were struck, moved, changed.
The next day a Verb drove up, and created the Sentence.

Each Sentence says one thing—for example, "Although it was a dark
    rainy day when the Adjective walked by, I shall remember the pure
    and sweet expression on her face until the day I perish from the
    green, effective earth."
Or, "Will you please close the window, Andrew?"
Or, for example, "Thank you, the pink pot of flowers on the window
    sill has changed color recently to a light yellow, due to the heat from
    the boiler factory which exists nearby."

In the springtime the Sentences and the Nouns lay silently on the grass.
A lonely Conjunction here and there would call, "And! But!"
But the Adjective did not emerge.

As the adjective is lost in the sentence,
So I am lost in your eyes, ears, nose, and throat—
You have enchanted me with a single kiss
Which can never be undone
Until the destruction of language.

                                                    1962

Variations on a Theme by William Carlos Williams

1

I chopped down the house that you had been saving to live in next
    summer.
I am sorry, but it was morning, and I had nothing to do
and its wooden beams were so inviting.

2

We laughed at the hollyhocks together
and then I sprayed them with lye.
Forgive me. I simply do not know what I am doing.

3

I gave away the money that you had been saving to live on for the next
    ten years.
The man who asked for it was shabby
and the firm March wind on the porch was so juicy and cold.

4

Last evening we went dancing and I broke your leg.
Forgive me. I was clumsy, and
I wanted you here in the wards, where I am the doctor!

1962

Alive for an Instant

I have a bird in my head and a pig in my stomach
And a flower in my genitals and a tiger in my genitals
And a lion in my genitals and I am after you but I have a song in my
    heart
And my song is a dove
I have a man in my hands I have a woman in my shoes
I have a landmark decision in my reason
I have a death rattle in my nose I have summer in my brain water
I have dreams in my toes
This is the matter with me and the hammer of my mother and father
Who created me with everything
But I lack calm I lack rose
Though I do not lack extreme delicacy of rose petal
Who is it that I wish to astonish?
In the birdcall I found a reminder of you
But it was thin and brittle and gone in an instant
Has nature set out to be a great entertainer?
Obviously not A great reproducer? A great Nothing?
Well I will leave that up to you
I have a knocking woodpecker in my heart and I think I have three
    souls
One for love one for poetry and one for acting out my insane self
Not insane but boring but perpendicular but untrue but true
The three rarely sing together take my hand it's active
The active ingredient in it is a touch
I am Lord Byron I am Percy Shelley I am Ariosto
I eat the bacon I went down the slide I have a thunderstorm in my
    inside I will never hate you
But how can this maelstrom be appealing? do you like menageries? my
    god
Most people want a man! So here I am
I have a pheasant in my reminders I have a goshawk in my clouds
Whatever is it which has led all these animals to you?
A resurrection? or maybe an insurrection? an inspiration?
I have a baby in my landscape and I have a wild rat in my secrets from
    you.

1975

The Circus

I remember when I wrote The Circus
I was living in Paris, or rather we were living in Paris
Janice, Frank was alive, the Whitney Museum
Was still on 8th Street, or was it still something else?
Fernand Léger lived in our building
Well it wasn't really our building it was the building we lived in
Next to a Grand Guignol troupe who made a lot of noise
So that one day I yelled through a hole in the wall
Of our apartment I don't know why there was a hole there
Shut up! And the voice came back to me saying something
I don't know what. Once I saw Léger walk out of the building
I think. Stanley Kunitz came to dinner. I wrote The Circus
In two tries, the first getting most of the first stanza;
That fall I also wrote an opera libretto called Louisa or Matilda.
Jean-Claude came to dinner. He said (about "cocktail sauce")
It should be good on something but not on these (oysters).
By that time I think I had already written The Circus.
Part of the inspiration came while walking to the post office one night
And I wrote a big segment of The Circus
When I came back, having been annoyed to have to go
I forget what I went there about
You were back in the apartment what a dump actually we liked it
I think with your hair and your writing and the pans
Moving strummingly about the kitchen and I wrote The Circus
It was a summer night no it was an autumn one summer when
I remember it but actually no autumn that black dusk toward the post
    office
And I wrote many other poems then but The Circus was the best
Maybe not by far the best there was also Geography
And the Airplane Betty poems (inspired by you) but The Circus was the
    best.

Sometimes I feel I actually am the person
Who did this, who wrote that, including that poem The Circus
But sometimes on the other hand I don't.
There are so many factors engaging our attention!
At every moment the happiness of others, the health of those we know
    and our own!
And the millions upon millions of people we don't know and their
    well-being to think about
So it seems strange I found time to write The Circus
And even spent two evenings on it, and that I have also the time
To remember that I did it, and remember you and me then, and write
    this poem about it.
At the beginning of The Circus
The Circus girls are rushing through the night
In the circus wagons and tulips and other flowers will be picked

A long time from now this poem wants to get off on its own
Someplace like a painting not held to a depiction of composing The
    Circus.

Noel Lee was in Paris then but usually out of it
In Germany or Denmark giving a concert
As part of an endless activity
Which was either his career or his happiness or a combination of both
Or neither I remember his dark eyes looking he was nervous
With me perhaps because of our days at Harvard.

It is understandable enough to be nervous with anybody!

How softly and easily one feels when alone
Love of one's friends when one is commanding the time and space
    syndrome
If that's the right word which I doubt but together how come one is so
    nervous?
One is not always but what was I then and what am I now attempting
    to create
If create is the right word
Out of this combination of experience and aloneness
And who are you telling me it is or is not a poem (not you)? Go back
    with me though
To those nights I was writing The Circus.
Do you like that poem? have you read it? It is in my book Thank You
Which Grove just reprinted. I wonder how long I am going to live
And what the rest will be like I mean the rest of my life.

John Cage said to me the other night How old are you? and I told him
    forty-six
(Since then I've become forty-seven) he said
Oh that's a great age I remember.
John Cage once told me he didn't charge much for his mushroom
    identification course (at the New School)
Because he didn't want to make a profit from nature.

He was ahead of his time I was behind my time we were both in time
Brilliant go to the head of the class and "time is a river"
It doesn't seem like a river to me it seems like an unformed plan
Days go by and still nothing is decided about
What to do until you know it never will be and then you say "time"
But you really don't care much about it any more
Time means something when you have the major part of yours ahead of
    you
As I did in Aix-en-Provence that was three years before I wrote The
    Circus
That year I wrote Bricks and The Great Atlantic Rainway
I felt time surround me like a blanket endless and soft

I could go to sleep endlessly and wake up and still be in it
But I treasured secretly the part of me that was individually changing
Like Noel Lee I was interested in my career
And still am but now it is like a town I don't want to leave
Not a tower I am climbing opposed by ferocious enemies.

I never mentioned my friends in my poems at the time I wrote The
     Circus
Although they meant almost more than anything to me
Of this now for some time I've felt an attenuation
So I'm mentioning them maybe this will bring them back to me
Not them perhaps but what I felt about them
John Ashbery Jane Freilicher Larry Rivers Frank O'Hara
Their names alone bring tears to my eyes
As seeing Polly did last night.

It is beautiful at any time but the paradox is leaving it
In order to feel it when you've come back the sun has declined
And the people are merrier or else they've gone home altogether
And you are left alone well you put up with that your sureness is like
     the sun
While you have it but when you don't its lack's a black and icy night. I
     came home

And wrote The Circus that night, Janice. I didn't come and speak to you
And put my arm around you and ask you if you'd like to take a walk
Or go to the Cirque Medrano though that's what I wrote poems about
And am writing about that now, and now I'm alone

And this is not as good a poem as The Circus
And I wonder if any good will come of either of them all the same.

                                                                    1975

With Janice

The leaves were already on the trees, the fruit blossoms
White and not ruined and pink and not ruined and we
Were riding in a boat over the water in which there was a sea
Hiding the meanings of all our salty words. A duck
Or a goose and a boat and a stone and a stone cliff. The
Hardnesses—and, with a little smile—of life. Sitting
Earlier or later and forgotten the words and the bees
At supper they were about in how you almost gestured but stopped
Knowing there were only one or two things, and that the rest
Were merely complications. But one in a trenchcoat said
It's reversible. And, It's as out-of-date as a reversible coat. And
Magna Bear and Minor Orse were sleeping. The soap

Was climbing in its dish but relaxed and came down when cold water
    stopped
Rushing in and the bathroom was flooded. I said, It is not about
Things but with things I'd like to go and, too, Will it last
Or will all become uniform again? Even as she goes
Pottering around the island's peripheries she thinks
Of the obligations. And the sympathies, far stronger than bears.
I was a bush there, a hat on a clothes dummy's head. Receiving letters
Sat down. I avoided being punished. I said,
It's cutting the limbs off a tree but there was no
Tree and I had no saw. I was planning to have infinite egress
While keeping some factory on the surface exceedingly cold. It was
A good source of evening. Sweating, asleep in the after-
Noons, later the morning of thumps, unwhittled questions, the freezing
    head. At night
Drinking whiskey, the fishermen were, everyone said, away.
A chrysanthemum though still full of splashes it
Has lost some little of its odor for my nostrils and a girl
In a chalk-pink-and-white dress is handing on the cliff
A glass of emerald water to a pin, or is it a chicken, as you get
Closer you can see it is a mirror made of the brawn
Of water muscles splashing that which has been.
My self, like the connections of an engine—rabbits and the new year—
Having puzzled out something in common, a blue stone duck
As if Homer Hesiod and Shakespeare had never lived at all
And we weren't the deposit. Weinstein puts on his hat
And the women go crazy. Some falter toward the sea. Wein-
Stein come back! But he is leaving. He says Leonard! Good-bye!
So Leonard invites us
To come and to see, where the white water bucket is a dashboard
Of this place to that. You will want to go swimming, and you will
    want to meet
These snobbish absurd Americans who inhabit
The gesso incalcations on the cliff. And we went like a nose
To a neighbor face. Sometimes tilting the grappa
Or in this case the ouzo it spills on my clothes or on yours, the world
    without us, the world outside
As when one of us was sick, which also brought the out world in.
And the art world meanwhile
Was strumming along. Individual struggles
Will long be remembered, of XXX's doing this,
Of YYYY's doing that.
Soap which will start lazily up from those types. Then
We remember to leave and also to stay. Janice said
It may not be hooked on right. Weinstein has been walking
Down a flowery way. Good-bye, nature lovers! he crescendoed.
A locked sail. The bullet of this button isn't right. And the train laughed
And pulled out pulling half of the station with it. The dust
Was indifferent to Americans as to Greeks. What simply was happening

Was beyond the rustication of ideas into the elements but essentially the
    same. Meanwhile, grasses matted,
The leaves winced, ideas one had had in earliest childhood days
Were surprisingly becoming succinct, maybe just before vanishing
Or turning into something you would feel like a belt,
Circling but not in hand. I would find these and set them down
On the sizzling white paper that was slipperier than the knees
That made me feel guilty, and sometimes heavier than the overcoats
    which there we never had
For someone's chest's attention. It was always distraction
But it was also a chair. And a chair is merely a civilized distraction. If
Character wasn't everything, it was something else I didn't
Know less than geography, which is to say, Surprise, Wonder,
Delight. You stood there and the stones
Of Old Greece and our lives, those collegiate stones,
Harvard, Emory, and Marymount, with the blue exegesis of the tide
Against which to fall was a headline—Don't stand.
You give this wish to me—Apollo, in some manner of time, lives on.
    Inside your mind
Things are being washed. Everything was docking
And we went down to see it. Memories of women made exactly the
    same
Kneeling down in the hot raft of daisies
It also got ragged for my walks. When are we going
To really have the time to have time? I make love to you
Like a rope swinging across a stone wall and you
Are lilacs reflected in a mirror or seen through a window.
Going out. You said I like this one. A pale pink dress
The suds were driving through the water. Moving fairly fast against the
Just plain oxygen we ended up looking
A little bit overcome. But I got up
You got up. We went around
Spilling things and putting a few of them on racks.
Those were the important things we never got done
Because they were behind us or
Surpassing us, otherwise unavailable—cherry
Blossoms, clavicles of girls which I can't touch
In the innocuousness, beetles, burring and scampering around a rose
I see is no longer there. Blossoms on the walk we were here, were there
As much as the heat was. I dried my ear at the sink
Then dried the other and quieted my lips and my nose
With a briny dry towel and you slid upon your shoes
And Katherine jumped up, ran around. Soon she will be
Out as usual, down the roadway formally unopened
For my approach, as if not to be drunk
Were a confidence vote from the leaves for the turmoil inside
The ouzo-fed engines of ourselves, when, seated on slabs of wood
As roses on tough ground as eggs were on the morning, deciding to
    leave,

We oversleep the boat, a shirt, a white shirt gleaming
On the photographic exception of the tide. An airlane of styles.
If it was said, It's hopeless
and you said, The gardens are going over
The edge of the overside sidewalk. Well,
Maybe and maybe not. A foot, I thought (not very intelligently)
In a shoe of newspapers, even ice unstacked about by process—
I loved the texture of your talk, and another woman's
Breast had a texture of a late summer day, while your
Eyes were walking both inside your head and in me, in each of my
    activities
While you both found the cat and he was seated, alive,
Beyond ants, on some anthill pebbles and or gravel. The bar wasn't
    closed
Or open, it was daylight-surprised. Plate glass was nowhere around.
I looked up. I put on my glasses. There were all these artists
Hot with the prayers of nineteen sixty-one—
Let us be potters, or skunks, but not
Business men! I sat down on a stone
And looked around, my last chance
To never be a doctor, as if it meant something, and a father of four—
In these minutes, of fatal decisions. Decisions! Fatal! Lazy,
Air comes in. What could it have been
To be so exciting? And the Scotch tape jumped into the air
With Leonardo out in a boat, and, miles later, acropoles of bones the
    dead
Dinosaurs and cities, tied to subjects
All of us present have forgotten—women, failing the Weinstein
Of the season. Rather inform
P.M. while you are re-estimating buttons'
Life by leaving them long-ungone-for in the midst
Of the very short walks we take down the long
Bite narrow street—At night electricity is kissing
The emasculated stars—The new things we had done, in pencil at the
    side of the napkin.
It was hot. Ce qui veut dire we, a cat sitting
On a balcony a plant was wilting. What dialect are you speaking,
You, wearing the loafers of the sea? I couldn't care
For everything simultaneously. A mat was exciting enough. The bath
    came separately
From the dawn. You walk around
Simply looking for strawberries, sun, our baby, oxygen—
"Always not quite unbeginning to be or have been begun."
Leonardo erat other. Iras haec perturbat. Let that be. Another was
Absent in a habit fidget. I was
In a rush. Someone said, hush!
Calm down in this—knife—patterns of things—
Where is the music that's fitting for such an occasion
In those miles of hotel

Corridor followed by Weinstein's weeping at the beach
Girls who followed that for love of him
And why is there not more peaceful melting here
Into the wide wood story of the wall
How I loved those made of stone. And yet poetry has
Messages, interrogations of musics that have been used
In the various islands of acts, staying genuinely still,
And seeing—a piece of life and seeing—
It's a wall inside me
Why dancers were always coming out in a pageant
Wrecking the place animals were in there too
As now, so for music fit?
The pink spot you trotted me out to see with under the sigh which
Something and the great writers were all still alive
Much of the worst had happened, the envelope was still unpeeled.
I am stamping on the path. Alone. Nothing is so essential as this—
Moment. And a red fan wings past—flower? Transatlantic systems
    ourselves
The door unopened, the mail came every day. The grass is soft,
Matted, and then there was an enclosure, tar on my leg, on yours
The culture all around us was in fragments, in some chests sure
In others fragments, in some no grasp at all, which I couldn't
Easily perceive, thus making everybody equal,
Almost at least enough to be a rival—perception,
Inspiration—too cloud to care. Voices
I heard on rooftops and cul-de-sacs of meditative sex
Scurried beyond the invisible barrier of you washing
The blouse. Brilliant. In fact, having more meaning
Because of all impulsions. You were
A blue coat—it wasn't
Exactly yours or mine or that place's
But a stinginess of life in packet flying through
Eventually, signing away like papers
A moment of the beach, when the tide dried the invincible
By elbows in comparison to the nude inside—
Look at—it's finished; this rock
Will come with me! Weinstein, walking in his sleep
The first afternoon when I arrived cooling bees they have a hive
Against the cliff, who've kept things in—the art
School, slacks. Normal the Mediterranean
Flows onward and on, boat,
I wore Leonard's jacket and my clothes, then shoes
Meet yours, advancing, so walk about the best
Final of beach, to not notice numbers
Except when they are speaking, as we stopped less
When all this was around.

                                                            1982

FRANK O'HARA ■ ■ ■ ■ ■ ■ ■ ■ ■ ■ ■ ■ ■ ■

1926–1966

Raised in Grafton, Massachusetts, and educated at Harvard, where he met John Ashbery and Kenneth Koch, O'Hara published only two full-length books of poetry in his lifetime: *Meditations in an Emergency* (1957) and the influential *Lunch Poems* (1964). These collections, as well as his essay "Personism: A Manifesto," have by and large established the public image of New York School poetry. Characterized by wit, charm, and everydayness, his work extended William Carlos Williams's emphasis on the American vernacular into urban popular culture of the 1950s and 1960s.

The poet John Ashbery writes of O'Hara that "the poetry that meant the most to him when he began writing was either French—Rimbaud, Mallarmé, the surrealists: poets who speak the language of every day into the reader's dream—or Russian—Pasternak and especially Mayakovsky, from whom he picked up what James Schuyler has called the 'intimate yell.' "[1]

Another of O'Hara's important predecessors was the French poet Guillaume Apollinaire. Gathering random snatches of overheard conversation on his Paris walks, Apollinaire composed what he called his "Poèmes conversations." Using a similiar conversational style and spirit of chance encounter, O'Hara's poem beginning "Lana Turner has collapsed!" was written on the Staten Island ferry on the way to a poetry reading, where he read it along with his prepared manuscript. In his famous manifesto, O'Hara claimed that Personism was born when he realized that, instead of writing a poem for a friend, he could just as well use the telephone.

His numerous manuscripts, which were casually stuck into drawers or handed off to friends, were published posthumously in *The Collected Poems of Frank O'Hara* (1972). Other O'Hara volumes are *Poems Retrieved* (1977), containing poems discovered by the editor Donald Allen after the publication of *Collected Poems; Selected Plays* (1978); and a collection of essays and interviews, *Standing Still and Walking in New York* (1983).

1. Introduction to *The Collected Poems of Frank O'Hara*, New York, 1972, p. vii.

Poem

The eager note on my door said "Call me,
call when you get in!" so I quickly threw
a few tangerines into my overnight bag,
straightened my eyelids and shoulders, and

headed straight for the door. It was autumn
by the time I got around the corner, oh all
unwilling to be either pertinent or bemused, but
the leaves were brighter than grass on the sidewalk!

Funny, I thought, that the lights are on this late
and the hall door open; still up at this hour, a
champion jai-alai player like himself? Oh fie!
for shame! What a host, so zealous! And he was

there in the hall, flat on a sheet of blood that
ran down the stairs. I did appreciate it. There are few
hosts who so thoroughly prepare to greet a guest
only casually invited, and that several months ago.

1957

Poem

At night Chinamen jump
on Asia with a thump

while in our willful way
we, in secret, play

affectionate games and bruise
our knees like China's shoes.

The birds push apples through
grass the moon turns blue,

these apples roll beneath
our buttocks like a heath

full of Chinese thrushes
flushed from China's bushes.

As we love at night
birds sing out of sight,

Chinese rhythms beat
through us in our heat,

the apples and the birds
move us like soft words,

we couple in the grace
of that mysterious race.

1957

Meditations in an Emergency

Am I to become profligate as if I were a blonde? Or religious as if I
were French?

Each time my heart is broken it makes me feel more adventurous
(and how the same names keep recurring on that interminable list!),
but one of these days there'll be nothing left with which to venture forth.

Why should I share you? Why don't you get rid of someone else for a change?

I am the least difficult of men. All I want is boundless love.

Even trees understand me! Good heavens, I lie under them, too, don't I? I'm just like a pile of leaves.

However, I have never clogged myself with the praises of pastoral life, nor with nostalgia for an innocent past of perverted acts in pastures. No. One need never leave the confines of New York to get all the greenery one wishes—I can't even enjoy a blade of grass unless I know there's a subway handy, or a record store or some other sign that people do not totally *regret* life. It is more important to affirm the least sincere; the clouds get enough attention as it is and even they continue to pass. Do they know what they're missing? Uh huh.

My eyes are vague blue, like the sky, and change all the time; they are indiscriminate but fleeting, entirely specific and disloyal, so that no one trusts me. I am always looking away. Or again at something after it has given me up. It makes me restless and that makes me unhappy, but I cannot keep them still. If only I had grey, green, black, brown, yellow eyes; I would stay at home and do something. It's not that I'm curious. On the contrary, I am bored but it's my duty to be attentive, I am needed by things as the sky must be above the earth. And lately, so great has *their* anxiety become, I can spare myself little sleep.

Now there is only one man I love to kiss when he is unshaven. Heterosexuality! you are inexorably approaching. (How discourage her?)

St. Serapion, I wrap myself in the robes of your whiteness which is like midnight in Dostoevsky. How am I to become a legend, my dear? I've tried love, but that hides you in the bosom of another and I am always springing forth from it like the lotus—the ecstasy of always bursting forth! (but one must not be distracted by it!) or like a hyacinth, "to keep the filth of life away," yes, there, even in the heart, where the filth is pumped in and slanders and pollutes and determines. I will my will, though I may become famous for a mysterious vacancy in that department, that greenhouse.

Destroy yourself, if you don't know!

It is easy to be beautiful; it is difficult to appear so. I admire you, beloved, for the trap you've set. It's like a final chapter no one reads because the plot is over.

"Fanny Brown is run away—scampered off with a Cornet of Horse; I do love that little Minx, & hope She may be happy, tho' She has vexed me by this Exploit a little too.—Poor silly Cecchina! or F: B: as we used

to call her.—I wish She had a good Whipping and 10,000 pounds."—
Mrs. Thrale.

I've got to get out of here. I choose a piece of shawl and my dirtiest
suntans. I'll be back, I'll re-emerge, defeated, from the valley; you don't
want me to go where you go, so I go where you don't want me to. It's
only afternoon, there's a lot ahead. There won't be any mail downstairs.
Turning, I spit in the lock and the knob turns.

1957

Ode to Joy

We shall have everything we want and there'll be no more dying
    on the pretty plains or in the supper clubs
for our symbol we'll acknowledge vulgar materialistic laughter
    over an insatiable sexual appetite
and the streets will be filled with racing forms
and the photographs of murderers and narcissists and movie stars
    will swell from the walls and books alive in steaming rooms
    to press against our burning flesh not once but interminably
as water flows down hill into the full-lipped basin
and the adder dives for the ultimate ostrich egg
and the feather cushion preens beneath a reclining monolith
    that's sweating with post-exertion visibility and sweetness
    near the grave of love

No more dying

We shall see the grave of love as a lovely sight and temporary
    near the elm that spells the lovers' names in roots
and there'll be no more music but the ears in lips and no more wit
    but tongues in ears and no more drums but ears to thighs
as evening signals nudities unknown to ancestors' imaginations
and the imagination itself will stagger like a tired paramour of ivory
    under the sculptural necessities of lust that never falters
    like a six-mile runner from Sweden or Liberia covered with gold
as lava flows up and over the far-down somnolent city's abdication
and the hermit always wanting to be lone is lone at last
and the weight of external heat crushes the heat-hating Puritan
    who's self-defeating vice becomes a proper sepulchre at last
    that love may live

Buildings will go up into the dizzy air as love itself goes in
    and up the reeling life that it has chosen for once or all
while in the sky a feeling of intemperate fondness will excite the birds
    to swoop and veer like flies crawling across absorbed limbs
that weep a pearly perspiration on the sheets of brief attention

and the hairs dry out that summon anxious declaration of the organs
   as they rise like buildings to the needs of temporary neighbors
      pouring hunger through the heart to feed desire in intravenous ways
like the ways of gods with humans in the innocent combination of light
and flesh or as the legends ride their heroes through the dark to found
great cities where all life is possible to maintain as long as time
   which wants us to remain for cocktails in a bar and after dinner
   lets us live with it
                      No more dying

                           1960

The Day Lady Died

It is 12 : 20 in New York a Friday
three days after Bastille day, yes
it is 1959 and I go get a shoeshine
because I will get off the 4 : 19 in Easthampton
at 7 : 15 and then go straight to dinner
and I don't know the people who will feed me

I walk up the muggy street beginning to sun
and have a hamburger and a malted and buy
an ugly NEW WORLD WRITING to see what the poets
in Ghana are doing these days
                    I go on to the bank
and Miss Stillwagon (first name Linda I once heard)
doesn't even look up my balance for once in her life
and in the GOLDEN GRIFFIN I get a little Verlaine
for Patsy with drawings by Bonnard although I do
think of Hesiod, trans. Richmond Lattimore or
Brendan Behan's new play or *Le Balcon* or *Les Nègres*
of Genet, but I don't, I stick with Verlaine
after practically going to sleep with quandariness

and for Mike I just stroll into the PARK LANE
Liquor Store and ask for a bottle of Strega and
then I go back where I came from to 6th Avenue
and the tobacconist in the Ziegfeld Theatre and
casually ask for a carton of Gauloises and a carton
of Picayunes, and a NEW YORK POST with her face on it

and I am sweating a lot by now and thinking of
leaning on the john door in the 5 SPOT
while she whispered a song along the keyboard
to Mal Waldron and everyone and I stopped breathing

1959   1964

Personal Poem

Now when I walk around at lunchtime
I have only two charms in my pocket
an old Roman coin Mike Kanemitsu gave me
and a bolt-head that broke off a packing case
when I was in Madrid the others never
brought me too much luck though they did
help keep me in New York against coercion
but now I'm happy for a time and interested

I walk through the luminous humidity
passing the House of Seagram with its wet
and its loungers and the construction to
the left that closed the sidewalk if
I ever get to be a construction worker
I'd like to have a silver hat please
and get to Moriarty's where I wait for
LeRoi and hear who wants to be a mover and
shaker the last five years my batting average
is .016 that's that, and LeRoi comes in
and tells me Miles Davis was clubbed 12
times last night outside BIRDLAND by a cop
a lady asks us for a nickel for a terrible
disease but we don't give her one we
don't like terrible diseases, then
we go eat some fish and some ale it's
cool but crowded we don't like Lionel Trilling
we decide, we like Don Allen we don't like
Henry James so much we like Herman Melville
we don't want to be in the poets' walk in
San Francisco even we just want to be rich
and walk on girders in our silver hats
I wonder if one person out of the 8,000,000 is
thinking of me as I shake hands with LeRoi
and buy a strap for my wristwatch and go
back to work happy at the thought possibly so

1959   1964

Ave Maria

Mothers of America
                let your kids go to the movies!
get them out of the house so they won't know what you're up to
it's true that fresh air is good for the body
                                                but what about the soul

that grows in darkness, embossed by silvery images
and when you grow old as grow old you must
                                        they won't hate you
they won't criticize you they won't know
                            they'll be in some glamorous country
they first saw on a Saturday afternoon or playing hookey

they may even be grateful to you
                            for their first sexual experience
which only cost you a quarter
                            and didn't upset the peaceful home
they will know where candy bars come from
                            and gratuitous bags of popcorn
as gratuitous as leaving the movie before it's over
with a pleasant stranger whose apartment is in the
                                        Heaven on Earth Bldg
near the Williamsburg Bridge
                            oh mothers you will have made the little tykes
so happy because if nobody does pick them up in the movies
they won't know the difference
                            and if somebody does it'll be sheer gravy
and they'll have been truly entertained either way
instead of hanging around the yard
                            or up in their room
                                        hating you
prematurely since you won't have done anything horribly
                                        mean yet
except keeping them from the darker joys
                                it's unforgivable the latter
so don't blame me if you won't take this advice
                            and the family breaks up
and your children grow old and blind in front of a TV set
                                        seeing
movies you wouldn't let them see when they were young

1960   1964

Steps

How funny you are today New York
like Ginger Rogers in *Swingtime*
and St. Bridget's steeple leaning a little to the left

here I have just jumped out of a bed full of V-days
(I got tired of D-days) and blue you there still
accepts me foolish and free
all I want is a room up there

and you in it
and even the traffic halt so thick is a way
for people to rub up against each other
and when their surgical appliances lock
they stay together
for the rest of the day (what a day)
I go by to check a slide and I say
that painting's not so blue

where's Lana Turner
she's out eating
and Garbo's backstage at the Met
everyone's taking their coat off
so they can show a rib-cage to the rib-watchers
and the park's full of dancers and their tights and shoes
in little bags
who are often mistaken for worker-outers at the West Side Y
why not
the Pittsburgh Pirates shout because they won
and in a sense we're all winning
we're alive

the apartment was vacated by a gay couple
who moved to the country for fun
they moved a day too soon
even the stabbings are helping the population explosion
though in the wrong country
and all those liars have left the U N
the Seagram Building's no longer rivalled in interest
not that we need liquor (we just like it)

and the little box is out on the sidewalk
next to the delicatessen
so the old man can sit on it and drink beer
and get knocked off it by his wife later in the day
while the sun is still shining

oh god it's wonderful
to get out of bed
and drink too much coffee
and smoke too many cigarettes
and love you so much

1961   1964

Poem

Lana Turner has collapsed!
I was trotting along and suddenly
it started raining and snowing
and you said it was hailing
but hailing hits you on the head
hard so it was really snowing and
raining and I was in such a hurry
to meet you but the traffic
was acting exactly like the sky
and suddenly I see a headline
LANA TURNER HAS COLLAPSED!
there is no snow in Hollywood
there is no rain in California
I have been to lots of parties
and acted perfectly disgraceful
but I never actually collapsed
oh Lana Turner we love you get up

1962   1964

Why I Am Not a Painter

I am not a painter, I am a poet.
Why? I think I would rather be
a painter, but I am not. Well,

for instance, Mike Goldberg
is starting a painting. I drop in.
"Sit down and have a drink" he
says. I drink; we drink. I look
up. "You have SARDINES in it."
"Yes, it needed something there."
"Oh." I go and the days go by
and I drop in again. The painting
is going on, and I go, and the days
go by. I drop in. The painting is
finished. "Where's SARDINES?"
All that's left is just
letters, "It was too much," Mike says.

But me? One day I am thinking of
a color: orange. I write a line
about orange. Pretty soon it is a
whole page of words, not lines.

Then another page. There should be
so much more, not of orange, of
words, of how terrible orange is
and life. Days go by. It is even in
prose, I am a real poet. My poem
is finished and I haven't mentioned
orange yet. It's twelve poems, I call
it ORANGES. And one day in a gallery
I see Mike's painting, called SARDINES.

1971

ALLEN GINSBERG ▪ ▪ ▪ ▪ ▪ ▪ ▪ ▪ ▪ ▪ ▪ ▪ ▪
b. 1926

Born in Newark, New Jersey, Allen Ginsberg attended Columbia University,
where he met Jack Kerouac. With novelist William Burroughs, author of *Naked
Lunch*, Ginsberg and Kerouac became major figures of the Beat generation. In
place of the reigning style of the early postwar period, which called for decorum,
formalism, and intellectual complexity, Ginsberg proposed a return to the im-
mediacy, egalitarianism, and visionary ambitions of Blake and Whitman. How-
ever, it was not until he followed William Carlos Williams's urging that he write
in the contemporary American idiom that Ginsberg found his own distinctive
voice.

Ginsberg was also guided by Jack Kerouac's stance that writing as a spontane-
ous expression would only be weakened by revision. According to Ginsberg,
Kerouac's "spontaneous bop prosody" required "an absolute, almost Zen-like
complete absorption, *attention* to your own consciousness, to the act of writ-
ing."[1] Ginsberg also quotes William Blake in this respect: "First thought is best
in Art, second in other matters."[2] The spontaneous approach to composition is
reflected in Ginsberg's poems *Howl* and *Kaddish*, long established as classics of
the period.

Of his use of personal materials, Ginsberg has said, "There is a tradition of
prose in America, including Thomas Wolfe and going through Kerouac, which is
personal, in which the prose sentence is completely personal, comes from the
writer's own person—his person defined as his body, his breathing rhythm, and
his actual talk."[3] Walt Whitman had called for "large conscious American Per-
sons." Ginsberg responded by writing himself large on the American landscape
while retaining an appealing modesty. The young boy in "To Aunt Rose" who
stands "on the thin pedestal/ of my legs in the bathroom—Museum of Newark"
provides the characteristic Ginsberg persona, simultaneously revealing and vul-
nerable.

1. *Allen Verbatim: Lectures on Poetry, Politics, Consciousness,* ed. Gordon Hill, New York,
1974, p. 147.   2. "Mind Writing Slogans," *Sulfur,* No. 32 (Spring 1993), p. 125.
3. *Allen Verbatim,* p. 153.

FROM *Howl*

For Carl Solomon

I

I saw the best minds of my generation destroyed by madness, starving hysteri-
cal naked,
dragging themselves through the negro streets at dawn looking for an angry fix,
angelheaded hipsters burning for the ancient heavenly connection to the starry
dynamo in the machinery of night,
who poverty and tatters and hollow-eyed and high sat up smoking in the super-
natural darkness of cold-water flats floating across the tops of cities
contemplating jazz,
who bared their brains to Heaven under the El and saw Mohammedan angels
staggering on tenement roofs illuminated,
who passed through universities with radiant cool eyes hallucinating Arkansas
and Blake-light tragedy among the scholars of war,
who were expelled from the academies for crazy & publishing obscene odes on
the windows of the skull,
who cowered in unshaven rooms in underwear, burning their money in waste-
baskets and listening to the Terror through the wall,
who got busted in their pubic beards returning through Laredo with a belt of
marijuana for New York,
who ate fire in paint hotels or drank turpentine in Paradise Alley, death, or
purgatoried their torsos night after night
with dreams, with drugs, with waking nightmares, alcohol and cock and end-
less balls,
incomparable blind streets of shuddering cloud and lightning in the mind leap-
ing toward poles of Canada & Paterson, illuminating all the motionless
world of Time between,
Peyote solidities of halls, backyard green tree cemetery dawns, wine drunken-
ness over the roof tops, storefront boroughs of teahead joyride neon
blinking traffic light, sun and moon and tree vibrations in the roaring
winter dusks of Brooklyn, ashcan rantings and kind king light of mind,
who chained themselves to subways for the endless ride from Battery to holy
Bronx on benzedrine until the noise of wheels and children brought
them down shuddering mouth-wracked and battered bleak of brain all
drained of brilliance in the drear light of Zoo,
who sank all night in submarine light of Bickford's floated out and sat through
the stale beer afternoon in desolate Fugazzi's, listening to the crack of
doom on the hydrogen jukebox,
who talked continuously seventy hours from park to pad to bar to Bellevue to
museum to the Brooklyn Bridge,
a lost battalion of platonic conversationalists jumping down the stoops off fire
escapes off windowsills off Empire State out of the moon,
yacketayakking screaming vomiting whispering facts and memories and anec-
dotes and eyeball kicks and shocks of hospitals and jails and wars,

whole intellects disgorged in total recall for seven days and nights with brilliant
  eyes, meat for the Synagogue cast on the pavement,

who vanished into nowhere Zen New Jersey leaving a trail of ambiguous pic-
  ture postcards of Atlantic City Hall,

suffering Eastern sweats and Tangerian bone-grindings and migraines of China
  under junk-withdrawal in Newark's bleak furnished room,

who wandered around and around at midnight in the railroad yard wondering
  where to go, and went, leaving no broken hearts,

who lit cigarettes in boxcars boxcars boxcars racketing through snow toward
  lonesome farms in grandfather night,

who studied Plotinus Poe St. John of the Cross telepathy and bop kabbalah
  because the cosmos instinctively vibrated at their feet in Kansas,

who loned it through the streets of Idaho seeking visionary indian angels who
  were visionary indian angels,

who thought they were only mad when Baltimore gleamed in supernatural
  ecstasy,

who jumped in limousines with the Chinaman of Oklahoma on the impulse of
  winter midnight streetlight smalltown rain,

who lounged hungry and lonesome through Houston seeking jazz or sex or
  soup, and followed the brilliant Spaniard to converse about America and
  Eternity, a hopeless task, and so took ship to Africa,

who disappeared into the volcanoes of Mexico leaving behind nothing but the
  shadow of dungarees and the lava and ash of poetry scattered in fire-
  place Chicago,

who reappeared on the West Coast investigating the FBI in beards and shorts
  with big pacifist eyes sexy in their dark skin passing out incomprehensi-
  ble leaflets,

who burned cigarette holes in their arms protesting the narcotic tobacco haze of
  Capitalism,

who distributed Supercommunist pamphlets in Union Square weeping and un-
  dressing while the sirens of Los Alamos wailed them down, and wailed
  down Wall, and the Staten Island ferry also wailed,

who broke down crying in white gymnasiums naked and trembling before the
  machinery of other skeletons,

who bit detectives in the neck and shrieked with delight in policecars for com-
  mitting no crime but their own wild cooking pederasty and intoxication,

who howled on their knees in the subway and were dragged off the roof waving
  genitals and manuscripts,

who let themselves be fucked in the ass by saintly motorcyclists, and screamed
  with joy,

who blew and were blown by those human seraphim, the sailors, caresses of
  Atlantic and Caribbean love,

who balled in the morning in the evenings in rosegardens and the grass of
  public parks and cemeteries scattering their semen freely to whomever
  come who may,

who hiccuped endlessly trying to giggle but wound up with a sob behind a
  partition in a Turkish Bath when the blond & naked angel came to
  pierce them with a sword,

who lost their loveboys to the three old shrews of fate the one eyed shrew of the heterosexual dollar the one eyed shrew that winks out of the womb and the one eyed shrew that does nothing but sit on her ass and snip the intellectual golden threads of the craftsman's loom,

who copulated ecstatic and insatiate with a bottle of beer a sweetheart a package of cigarettes a candle and fell off the bed, and continued along the floor and down the hall and ended fainting on the wall with a vision of ultimate cunt and come eluding the last gyzym of consciousness,

who sweetened the snatches of a million girls trembling in the sunset, and were red eyed in the morning but prepared to sweeten the snatch of the sunrise, flashing buttocks under barns and naked in the lake,

who went out whoring through Colorado in myriad stolen night-cars, N.C., secret hero of these poems, cocksman and Adonis of Denver—joy to the memory of his innumerable lays of girls in empty lots & diner backyards, moviehouses' rickety rows, on mountaintops in caves or with gaunt waitresses in familiar roadside lonely petticoat upliftings & especially secret gas-station solipsisms of johns, & hometown alleys too,

who faded out in vast sordid movies, were shifted in dreams, woke on a sudden Manhattan, and picked themselves up out of basements hungover with heartless Tokay and horrors of Third Avenue iron dreams & stumbled to unemployment offices,

who walked all night with their shoes full of blood on the snowbank docks waiting for a door in the East River to open to a room full of steam-heat and opium,

who created great suicidal dramas on the apartment cliff-banks of the Hudson under the wartime blue floodlight of the moon & their heads shall be crowned with laurel in oblivion,

who ate the lamb stew of the imagination or digested the crab at the muddy bottom of the rivers of Bowery,

who wept at the romance of the streets with their pushcarts full of onions and bad music,

who sat in boxes breathing in the darkness under the bridge, and rose up to build harpsichords in their lofts,

who coughed on the sixth floor of Harlem crowned with flame under the tubercular sky surrounded by orange crates of theology,

who scribbled all night rocking and rolling over lofty incantations which in the yellow morning were stanzas of gibberish,

who cooked rotten animals lung heart feet tail borsht & tortillas dreaming of the pure vegetable kingdom,

who plunged themselves under meat trucks looking for an egg,

who threw their watches off the roof to cast their ballot for Eternity outside of Time, & alarm clocks fell on their heads every day for the next decade,

who cut their wrists three times successively unsuccessfully, gave up and were forced to open antique stores where they thought they were growing old and cried,

who were burned alive in their innocent flannel suits on Madison Avenue amid blasts of leaden verse & the tanked-up clatter of the iron regiments of fashion & the nitroglycerine shrieks of the fairies of advertising & the mustard gas of sinister intelligent editors, or were run down by the drunken taxicabs of Absolute Reality,

who jumped off the Brooklyn Bridge this actually happened and walked away
    unknown and forgotten into the ghostly daze of Chinatown soup alley-
    ways & firetrucks, not even one free beer,

who sang out of their windows in despair, fell out of the subway window,
    jumped in the filthy Passaic, leaped on negroes, cried all over the street,
    danced on broken wineglasses barefoot smashed phonograph records of
    nostalgic European 1930s German jazz finished the whiskey and threw
    up groaning into the bloody toilet, moans in their ears and the blast of
    colossal steamwhistles,

who barreled down the highways of the past journeying to each other's hotrod-
    Golgotha jail-solitude watch or Birmingham jazz incarnation,

who drove crosscountry seventytwo hours to find out if I had a vision or you had
    a vision or he had a vision to find out Eternity,

who journeyed to Denver, who died in Denver, who came back to Denver &
    waited in vain, who watched over Denver & brooded & loned in Denver
    and finally went away to find out the Time, & now Denver is lonesome
    for her heroes,

who fell on their knees in hopeless cathedrals praying for each other's salvation
    and light and breasts, until the soul illuminated its hair for a second,

who crashed through their minds in jail waiting for impossible criminals with
    golden heads and the charm of reality in their hearts who sang sweet
    blues to Alcatraz,

who retired to Mexico to cultivate a habit, or Rocky Mount to tender Buddha or
    Tangiers to boys or Southern Pacific to the black locomotive or Harvard
    to Narcissus to Woodlawn to the daisychain or grave,

who demanded sanity trials accusing the radio of hypnotism & were left with
    their insanity & their hands & a hung jury,

who threw potato salad at CCNY lecturers on Dadaism and subsequently pre-
    sented themselves on the granite steps of the madhouse with shaven
    heads and harlequin speech of suicide, demanding instantaneous lobot-
    omy,

and who were given instead the concrete void of insulin Metrazol electricity
    hydrotherapy psychotherapy pingpong & amnesia,

who in humorless protest overturned only one symbolic pingpong table, resting
    briefly in catatonia,

returning years later truly bald except for a wig of blood, and tears and fingers,
    to the visible madman doom of the wards of the madtowns of the East,

Pilgrim State's Rockland's and Greystone's foetid halls, bickering with the
    echoes of the soul, rocking and rolling in the midnight solitude-bench
    dolmen-realms of love, dream of life a nightmare, bodies turned to stone
    as heavy as the moon,

with mother finally °°°°°°, and the last fantastic book flung out of the tene-
    ment window, and the last door closed at 4 A.M. and the last telephone
    slammed at the wall in reply and the last furnished room emptied down
    to the last piece of mental furniture, a yellow paper rose twisted on a
    wire hanger in the closet, and even that imaginary, nothing but a hope-
    ful little bit of hallucination—

ah, Carl, while you are not safe I am not safe, and now you're really in the total
    animal soup of time—

and who therefore ran through the icy streets obsessed with a sudden flash of
the alchemy of the use of the ellipsis catalog a variable measure and the
vibrating plane,

who dreamt and made incarnate gaps in Time & Space through images juxta-
posed, and trapped the archangel of the soul between 2 visual images
and joined the elemental verbs and set the noun and dash of conscious-
ness together jumping with sensation of Pater Omnipotens Aeterne
Deus

to recreate the syntax and measure of poor human prose and stand before you
speechless and intelligent and shaking with shame, rejected yet confess-
ing out the soul to conform to the rhythm of thought in his naked and
endless head,

the madman bum and angel beat in Time, unknown, yet putting down here
what might be left to say in time come after death,

and rose reincarnate in the ghostly clothes of jazz in the goldhorn shadow of the
band and blew the suffering of America's naked mind for love into an eli
eli lamma lamma sabacthani saxophone cry that shivered the cities
down to the last radio

with the absolute heart of the poem of life butchered out of their own bodies
good to eat a thousand years.

1956

A Supermarket in California

What thoughts I have of you tonight, Walt Whitman, for I walked down
the sidestreets under the trees with a headache self-conscious looking at the full
moon.

In my hungry fatigue, and shopping for images, I went into the neon
fruit supermarket, dreaming of your enumerations!

What peaches and what penumbras! Whole families shopping at night!
Aisles full of husbands! Wives in the avocados, babies in the tomatoes!—and
you, García Lorca, what were you doing down by the watermelons?

I saw you, Walt Whitman, childless, lonely old grubber, poking among
the meats in the refrigerator and eyeing the grocery boys.

I heard you asking questions of each: Who killed the pork chops? What
price bananas? Are you my Angel?

I wandered in and out of the brilliant stacks of cans following you, and
followed in my imagination by the store detective.

We strode down the open corridors together in our solitary fancy tasting
artichokes, possessing every frozen delicacy, and never passing the cashier.

Where are we going, Walt Whitman? The doors close in an hour. Which
way does your beard point tonight?

(I touch your book and dream of our odyssey in the supermarket and
feel absurd.)

Will we walk all night through solitary streets? The trees add shade to
shade, lights out in the houses, we'll both be lonely.

Will we stroll dreaming of the lost America of love past blue automobiles in driveways, home to our silent cottage?

Ah, dear father, graybeard, lonely old courage-teacher, what America did you have when Charon quit poling his ferry and you got out on a smoking bank and stood watching the boat disappear on the black waters of Lethe?

Berkeley, 1955

1956

America

America I've given you all and now I'm nothing.
America two dollars and twentyseven cents January 17, 1956.
I can't stand my own mind.
America when will we end the human war?
Go fuck yourself with your atom bomb.
I don't feel good don't bother me.
I won't write my poem till I'm in my right mind.
America when will you be angelic?
When will you take off your clothes?
When will you look at yourself through the grave?
When will you be worthy of your million Trotskyites?
America why are your libraries full of tears?
America when will you send your eggs to India?
I'm sick of your insane demands.
When can I go into the supermarket and buy what I need with my good looks?
America after all it is you and I who are perfect not the next world.
Your machinery is too much for me.
You made me want to be a saint.
There must be some other way to settle this argument.
Burroughs is in Tangiers I don't think he'll come back it's sinister.
Are you being sinister or is this some form of practical joke?
I'm trying to come to the point.
I refuse to give up my obsession.
America stop pushing I know what I'm doing.
America the plum blossoms are falling.
I haven't read the newspapers for months, everyday somebody goes on trial for murder.
America I feel sentimental about the Wobblies.
America I used to be a communist when I was a kid I'm not sorry.
I smoke marijuana every chance I get.
I sit in my house for days on end and stare at the roses in the closet.
When I go to Chinatown I get drunk and never get laid.
My mind is made up there's going to be trouble.
You should have seen me reading Marx.
My psychoanalyst thinks I'm perfectly right.
I won't say the Lord's Prayer.
I have mystical visions and cosmic vibrations.
America I still haven't told you what you did to Uncle Max after he came over from Russia.

I'm addressing you.
Are you going to let your emotional life be run by Time Magazine?
I'm obsessed by Time Magazine.
I read it every week.
Its cover stares at me every time I slink past the corner candystore.
I read it in the basement of the Berkeley Public Library.
It's always telling me about responsibility. Businessmen are serious.
   Movie producers are serious. Everybody's serious but me.
It occurs to me that I am America.
I am talking to myself again.

Asia is rising against me.
I haven't got a chinaman's chance.
I'd better consider my national resources.
My national resources consist of two joints of marijuana millions of genitals an
      unpublishable private literature that jetplanes 1400 miles an hour and
      twentyfive-thousand mental institutions.
I say nothing about my prisons nor the millions of underprivileged who live in
      my flowerpots under the light of five hundred suns.
I have abolished the whorehouses of France, Tangiers is the next to go.
My ambition is to be President despite the fact that I'm a Catholic.

America how can I write a holy litany in your silly mood?
I will continue like Henry Ford my strophes are as individual as his automobiles
      more so they're all different sexes.
America I will sell you strophes $2500 apiece $500 down on your old strophe
America free Tom Mooney
America save the Spanish Loyalists
America Sacco & Vanzetti must not die
America I am the Scottsboro boys.
America when I was seven momma took me to Communist Cell meetings they
      sold us garbanzos a handful per ticket a ticket costs a nickel and the
      speeches were free everybody was angelic and sentimental about the
      workers it was all so sincere you have no idea what a good thing
      the party was in 1835 Scott Nearing was a grand old man a real mensch
      Mother Bloor the Silk-strikers' Ewig-Weibliche made me cry I once saw
      the Yiddish orator Israel Amter plain. Everybody must have been a spy.
America you don't really want to go to war.
America it's them bad Russians.
Them Russians them Russians and them Chinamen. And them Russians.
The Russia wants to eat us alive. The Russia's power mad. She wants to take
      our cars from out our garages.
Her wants to grab Chicago. Her needs a Red *Reader's Digest*. Her wants our
      auto plants in Siberia. Him big bureaucracy running our fillingstations.
That no good. Ugh. Him make Indians learn read. Him need big black niggers.
      Hah. Her make us all work sixteen hours a day. Help.
America this is quite serious.
America this is the impression I get from looking in the television set.
America is this correct?
I'd better get right down to the job.

It's true I don't want to join the Army or turn lathes in precision parts factories,
    I'm nearsighted and psychopathic anyway.
America I'm putting my queer shoulder to the wheel.

Berkeley, January 17, 1956   1956

FROM *Kaddish*

For Naomi Ginsberg, 1894–1956

I

Strange now to think of you, gone without corsets & eyes, while I walk on the
    sunny pavement of Greenwich Village.
downtown Manhattan, clear winter noon, and I've been up all night, talking,
    talking, reading the Kaddish aloud, listening to Ray Charles blues shout
    blind on the phonograph
the rhythm the rhythm—and your memory in my head three years after—And
    read Adonais' last triumphant stanzas aloud—wept, realizing how we
    suffer—
And how Death is that remedy all singers dream of, sing, remember, prophesy
    as in the Hebrew Anthem, or the Buddhist Book of Answers—and my
    own imagination of a withered leaf—at dawn—
Dreaming back thru life, Your time—and mine accelerating toward Apoca-
    lypse,
the final moment—the flower burning in the Day—and what comes after,
looking back on the mind itself that saw an American city
a flash away, and the great dream of Me or China, or you and a phantom
    Russia, or a crumpled bed that never existed—
like a poem in the dark—escaped back to Oblivion—
No more to say, and nothing to weep for but the Beings in the Dream, trapped
    in its disappearance,
sighing, screaming with it, buying and selling pieces of phantom, worshipping
    each other,
worshipping the God included in it all—longing or inevitability?—while it lasts,
    a Vision—anything more?
It leaps about me, as I go out and walk the street, look back over my shoulder,
    Seventh Avenue, the battlements of window office buildings shoulder-
    ing each other high, under a cloud, tall as the sky an instant—and the
    sky above—an old blue place.
or down the Avenue to the south, to—as I walk toward the Lower East Side—
    where you walked 50 years ago, little girl—from Russia, eating the first
    poisonous tomatoes of America—frightened on the dock—
then struggling in the crowds of Orchard Street toward what?—toward New-
    ark—
toward candy store, first home-made sodas of the century, hand-churned ice
    cream in backroom on musty brownfloor boards—

Toward education marriage nervous breakdown, operation, teaching school, and learning to be mad, in a dream—what is this life?

Toward the Key in the window—and the great Key lays its head of light on top of Manhattan, and over the floor, and lays down on the sidewalk—in a single vast beam, moving, as I walk down First toward the Yiddish Theater—and the place of poverty

you knew, and I know, but without caring now—Strange to have moved thru Paterson, and the West, and Europe and here again,

with the cries of Spaniards now in the doorstoops doors and dark boys on the street, fire escapes old as you

—Tho you're not old now, that's left here with me—

Myself, anyhow, maybe as old as the universe—and I guess that dies with us—enough to cancel all that comes—What came is gone forever every time—

That's good! That leaves it open for no regret—no fear radiators, lacklove, torture even toothache in the end—

Though while it comes it is a lion that eats the soul—and the lamb, the soul, in us, alas, offering itself in sacrifice to change's fierce hunger—hair and teeth—and the roar of bonepain, skull bare, break rib, rot-skin, brain-tricked Implacability.

Ai! ai! we do worse! We are in a fix! And you're out, Death let you out, Death had the Mercy, you're done with your century, done with God, done with the path thru it—Done with yourself at last—Pure—Back to the Babe dark before your Father, before us all—before the world—

There, rest. No more suffering for you. I know where you've gone, it's good.

No more flowers in the summer fields of New York, no joy now, no more fear of Louis,

and no more of his sweetness and glasses, his high school decades, debts, loves, frightened telephone calls, conception beds, relatives, hands—

No more of sister Elanor,—she gone before you—we kept it secret—you killed her—or she killed herself to bear with you—an arthritic heart—But Death's killed you both—No matter—

Nor your memory of your mother, 1915 tears in silent movies weeks and weeks—forgetting, agrieve watching Marie Dressler address humanity, Chaplin dance in youth,

or Boris Godunov, Chaliapin's at the Met, halling his voice of a weeping Czar—by standing room with Elanor & Max—watching also the Capitalists take seats in Orchestra, white furs, diamonds,

with the YPSL's hitch-hiking thru Pennsylvania, in black baggy gym skirts pants, photograph of 4 girls holding each other round the waste, and laughing eye, too coy, virginal solitude of 1920

all girls grown old, or dead, now, and that long hair in the grave—lucky to have husbands later—

You made it—I came too—Eugene my brother before (still grieving now and will gream on to his last stiff hand, as he goes thru his cancer—or kill—later perhaps—soon he will think—)

And it's the last moment I remember, which I see them all, thru myself, now—tho not you

I didn't foresee what you felt—what more hideous gape of bad mouth came
first—to you—and were you prepared?

To go where? In that Dark—that—in that God? a radiance? A Lord in the
Void? Like an eye in the black cloud in a dream? Adonoi at last, with
you?

Beyond my remembrance! Incapable to guess! Not merely the yellow skull in
the grave, or a box of worm dust, and a stained ribbon—Deaths-head
with Halo? can you believe it?

Is it only the sun that shines once for the mind, only the flash of existence, than
none ever was?

Nothing beyond what we have—what you had—that so pitiful—yet Triumph,

to have been here, and changed, like a tree, broken, or flower—fed to the
ground—but mad, with its petals, colored, thinking Great Universe,
shaken, cut in the head, leaf stript, hid in an egg crate hospital, cloth
wrapped, sore—freaked in the moon brain, Naughtless.

No flower like that flower, which knew itself in the garden, and fought the
knife—lost

Cut down by an idiot Snowman's icy—even in the Spring—strange ghost
thought—some Death—Sharp icicle in his hand—crowned with old
roses—a dog for his eyes—cock of a sweatshop—heart of electric irons.

All the accumulations of life, that wear us out—clocks, bodies, consciousness,
shoes, breasts—begotten sons—your Communism—'Paranoia' into hos-
pitals.

You once kicked Elanor in the leg, she died of heart failure later. You of stroke.
Asleep? within a year, the two of you, sisters in death. Is Elanor happy?

Max grieves alive in an office on Lower Broadway, lone large mustache over
midnight Accountings, not sure. His life passes—as he sees—and what
does he doubt now? Still dream of making money, or that might have
made money, hired nurse, had children, found even your Immortality,
Naomi?

I'll see him soon. Now I've got to cut through—to talk to you—as I didn't when
you had a mouth.

Forever. And we're bound for that, Forever—like Emily Dickinson's horses—
headed to the End.

They know the way—These Steeds—run faster than we think—it's our own
life they cross—and take with them.

Magnificent, mourned no more, marred of heart, mind behind, married
dreamed, mortal changed—Ass and face done with murder.

In the world, given, flower maddened, made no Utopia, shut under
pine, almed in Earth, balmed in Lone, Jehovah, accept.

Nameless, One Faced, Forever beyond me, beginningless, endless, Fa-
ther in death. Tho I am not there for this Prophecy, I am unmarried, I'm
hymnless, I'm Heavenless, headless in blisshood I would still adore

Thee, Heaven, after Death, only One blessed in Nothingness, not light
or darkness, Dayless Eternity—

Take this, this Psalm, from me, burst from my hand in a day, some of my
Time, now given to Nothing—to praise Thee—But Death

This is the end, the redemption from Wilderness, way for the Won-
derer, House sought for All, black handkerchief washed clean by weeping—
page beyond Psalm—Last change of mine and Naomi—to God's perfect Dark-
ness—Death, stay thy phantoms!

1961

To Aunt Rose

Aunt Rose—now—might I see you
with your thin face and buck tooth smile and pain
               of rheumatism—and a long black heavy shoe
               for your bony left leg
limping down the long hall in Newark on the running carpet
               past the black grand piano
               in the day room
                       where the parties were
          and I sang Spanish loyalist songs
               in a high squeaky voice
                       (hysterical) the committee listening
          while you limped around the room
               collected the money—
Aunt Honey, Uncle Sam, a stranger with a cloth arm
          in his pocket
               and huge young bald head
                  of Abraham Lincoln Brigade

—your long sad face
          your tears of sexual frustration
               (what smothered sobs and bony hips
                       under the pillows of Osborne Terrace)
—the time I stood on the toilet seat naked
          and you powdered my thighs with calamine
               against the poison ivy—my tender
                  and shamed first black curled hairs
what were you thinking in secret heart then
          knowing me a man already—
and I an ignorant girl of family silence on the thin pedestal
          of my legs in the bathroom—Museum of Newark.

          Aunt Rose
Hitler is dead, Hitler is in Eternity; Hitler is with
          Tamburlane and Emily Brontë

Though I see you walking still, a ghost on Osborne Terrace
          down the long dark hall to the front door
               limping a little with a pinched smile
                  in what must have been a silken

flower dress
welcoming my father, the Poet, on his visit to Newark
—see you arriving in the living room
dancing on your crippled leg
and clapping hands his book
had been accepted by Liveright

Hitler is dead and Liveright's gone out of business
The Attic of the Past and *Everlasting Minute* are out of print
Uncle Harry sold his last silk stocking
Claire quit interpretive dancing school
Buba sits a wrinkled monument in Old
Ladies Home blinking at new babies

last time I saw you was the hospital
pale skull protruding under ashen skin
blue veined unconscious girl
in an oxygen tent
the war in Spain has ended long ago
Aunt Rose

Paris, June 1958   1961

First Party at Ken Kesey's with Hell's Angels

Cool black night thru the redwoods
cars parked outside in shade
behind the gate, stars dim above
the ravine, a fire burning by the side
porch and a few tired souls hunched over
in black leather jackets. In the huge
wooden house, a yellow chandelier
at 3 A.M. the blast of loudspeakers
hi-fi Rolling Stones Ray Charles Beatles
Jumping Joe Jackson and twenty youths
dancing to the vibration thru the floor,
a little weed in the bathroom, girls in scarlet
tights, one muscular smooth skinned man
sweating dancing for hours, beer cans
bent littering the yard, a hanged man
sculpture dangling from a high creek branch,
children sleeping softly in their bedroom bunks.
And 4 police cars parked outside the painted
gate, red lights revolving in the leaves.

December 1965   1971

On Neal's Ashes

Delicate eyes that blinked blue Rockies all ash
nipples, Ribs I touched w/ my thumb are ash
mouth my tongue touched once or twice all ash
bony cheeks soft on my belly are cinder, ash
earlobes & eyelids, youthful cock tip, curly pubis
breast warmth, man palm, high school thigh,
baseball bicept arm, asshole anneal'd to silken skin
        all ashes, all ashes again.

August 1968   1971

ROBERT CREELEY ▪ ▪ ▪ ▪ ▪ ▪ ▪ ▪ ▪ ▪ ▪ ▪
b. 1926

Born in Arlington, Massachusetts, Robert Creeley attended Harvard but
dropped out before taking his degree. After living in the south of France in
Aix-en-Provence and in Majorca, Spain, where he founded the Divers Press, he
joined the faculty of Black Mountain College in 1954 at the invitation of Charles
Olson. There he founded the *Black Mountain Review*. While Creeley left the
college itself in 1955, his influence on Black Mountain poetics has been signifi-
cant. Associated with the State University of New York at Buffalo since 1966, he
was named poet laureate of the state of New York in 1992.

   Creeley's work, which has been described as Minimus to Charles Olson's
Maximus, is lyrical and romantic in the tradition of the troubadours even at the
same time as it is experimental in syntax. William Carlos Williams, whose poetry
was the primary influence on Creeley's work, wrote that Creeley has "the sub-
tlest feeling for the measure that I encounter anywhere except in the verses of
Ezra Pound."[1] In Creeley's view, the poem does not point toward anything
outside itself but is a self-sufficient and sinuous gesture. In his essay "To De-
fine," he rejects poetry as a *"descriptive* act, I mean any act which leaves the
attention outside the poem."[2]

   His poetry explores the immediate sensation but in language that is often
oblique and evocative, rather than direct and descriptive; the hesitation offered
by his short lines and his use of enjambment suggest both the graceful stumbles
of everyday speech and the lyrical cadence of song. In the tradition of the
objectivists, Creeley scraps nineteenth-century "symbolism," as the poet Louis
Zukovsky wrote, for the actual; it is Creeley's *"thoughtfulness* that makes the
shape—the metaphysics of loneliness."[3]

1. Letter to Creeley, January 18, 1960, quoted in *Robert Creeley's Life and Work: A Sense
of Increment,* ed. John Wilson, Ann Arbor, 1987, p. 30.   2. *A Quick Graph: Collected
Notes and Essays,* ed. Donald Allen, San Francisco, p. 23.   3. Letter to Creeley, October
11, 1955, in *Robert Creeley's Life and Work,* p. 32.

After Lorca

for M. Marti

The church is a business, and the rich
are the business men.
　　　　　　　When they pull on the bells, the
poor come piling in and when a poor man dies, he has a wooden
cross, and they rush through the ceremony.

But when a rich man dies, they
drag out the Sacrament
and a golden Cross, and go *doucement, doucement*
to the cemetery.

And the poor love it
and think it's crazy.

1962

A Form of Women

I have come far enough
from where I was not before
to have seen the things
looking in at me through the open door

and have walked tonight
by myself
to see the moonlight
and see it as trees

and shapes more fearful
because I feared
what I did not know
but have wanted to know.

My face is my own, I thought.
But you have seen it
turn into a thousand years.
I watched you cry.

I could not touch you.
I wanted very much to
touch you
but could not.

If it is dark
when this is given to you,
have care for its content
when the moon shines.

My face is my own.
My hands are my own.
My mouth is my own
but I am not.

Moon, moon,
when you leave me alone
all the darkness is
an utter blackness,

a pit of fear,
a stench,
hands unreasonable
never to touch.

But I love you.
Do you love me.
What to say
when you see me.

1962

The Flower

I think I grow tensions
like flowers
in a wood where
nobody goes.

Each wound is perfect,
encloses itself in a tiny
imperceptible blossom,
making pain.

Pain is a flower like that one,
like this one,
like that one,
like this one.

1962

The Rain

All night the sound had
come back again,
and again falls
this quiet, persistent rain.

What am I to myself
that must be remembered,
insisted upon
so often? Is it

that never the ease,
even the hardness,
of rain falling
will have for me

something other than this,
something not so insistent—
am I to be locked in this
final uneasiness.

Love, if you love me,
lie next to me.
Be for me, like rain,
the getting out

of the tiredness, the fatuousness, the semi-
lust of intentional indifference.
Be wet
with a decent happiness.

1962

For Love

for Bobbie

Yesterday I wanted to
speak of it, that sense above
the others to me
important because all

that I know derives
from what it teaches me.
Today, what is it that
is finally so helpless,

different, despairs of its own
statement, wants to
turn away, endlessly
to turn away.

If the moon did not . . .
no, if you did not
I wouldn't either, but
what would I not

do, what prevention, what
thing so quickly stopped.
That is love yesterday
or tomorrow, not

now. Can I eat
what you give me. I
have not earned it. Must
I think of everything

as earned. Now love also
becomes a reward so
remote from me I have
only made it with my mind.

Here is tedium,
despair, a painful
sense of isolation and
whimsical if pompous

self-regard. But that image
is only of the mind's
vague structure, vague to me
because it is my own.

Love, what do I think
to say. I cannot say it.
What have you become to ask,
what have I made you into,

companion, good company,
crossed legs with skirt, or
soft body under
the bones of the bed.

Nothing says anything
but that which it wishes
would come true, fears
what else might happen in

some other place, some
other time not this one.
A voice in my place, an
echo of that only in yours.

Let me stumble into
not the confession but
the obsession I begin with
now. For you

also (also)
some time beyond place, or
place beyond time, no
mind left to

say anything at all,
that face gone, now.
Into the company of love
it all returns.

                                                    1962

The Language

Locate *I*
love you some-
where in

teeth and
eyes, bite
it but

take care not
to hurt, you
want so

much so
little. Words
say everything.

I
love you
again,

then what
is emptiness
for. To

fill, fill.
I heard words
and words full

of holes
aching. Speech
is a mouth.

1967

The Window

Position is where you
put it, where it is,
did you, for example, that

large tank there, silvered,
with the white church along-
side, lift

all that, to what
purpose? How
heavy the slow

world is with
everything put
in place. Some

man walks by, a
car beside him on
the dropped

road, a leaf of
yellow color is
going to

fall. It
all drops into
place. My

face is heavy
with the sight. I can
feel my eye breaking.

1967

"I Keep to Myself Such Measures . . ."

I keep to myself such
measures as I care for,
daily the rocks
accumulate position.

There is nothing
but what thinking makes
it less tangible. The mind,
fast as it goes, loses

pace, puts in place of it
like rocks simple markers,
for a way only to
hopefully come back to

where it cannot. All
forgets. My mind sinks.
I hold in both hands such weight
it is my only description.

1967

The World

I wanted so ably
to reassure you, I wanted
the man you took to be me,

to comfort you, and got
up, and went to the window,
pushed back, as you asked me to,

the curtain, to see
the outline of the trees
in the night outside.

The light, love,
the light we felt then,
greyly, was it, that

came in, on us, not
merely my hands or yours,
or a wetness so comfortable,

but in the dark then
as you slept, the grey
figure came so close

and leaned over,
between us, as you
slept, restless, and

my own face had to
see it, and be seen by it,
the man it was, your

grey lost tired bewildered
brother, unused, untaken—
hated by love, and dead,

but not dead, for an
instant, saw me, myself
the intruder, as he was not.

I tried to say, it is
all right, she is
happy, you are no longer

needed. I said,
he is dead, and he
went as you shifted

and woke, at first afraid,
then knew by my own knowing
what had happened—

and the light then
of the sun coming
for another morning
in the world.

1967

Self-Portrait

He wants to be
a brutal old man,
an aggressive old man,
as dull, as brutal
as the emptiness around him,

He doesn't want compromise,
nor to be ever nice
to anyone. Just mean,
and final in his brutal,
his total, rejection of it all.

He tried the sweet,
the gentle, the "oh,
let's hold hands together"
and it was awful,
dull, brutally inconsequential.

Now he'll stand on
his own dwindling legs.
His arms, his skin,
shrink daily. And
he loves, but hates equally.

1983

Bresson's Movies

A movie of Robert
Bresson's showed a yacht,
at evening on the Seine,
all its lights on, watched

by two young, seemingly
poor people, on a bridge adjacent,
the classic boy and girl
of the story, any one

one cares to tell. So
years pass, of course, but
I identified with the young,
embittered Frenchman,

knew his almost complacent
anguish and the distance
he felt from his girl.
Yet another film

of Bresson's has the
aging Lancelot with his
awkward armor standing
in a woods, of small trees,

dazed, bleeding, both he
and his horse are,
trying to get back to
the castle, itself of

no great size. It
moved me, that

life was after all
like that. You are

in love. You stand
in the woods, with
a horse, bleeding.
The story is true.

1983

Age

Most explicit—
the sense of trap

as a narrowing
cone one's got

stuck into and
any movement

forward simply
wedges one more—

but where
or quite when,

even with whom,
since now there is no one

quite with you— Quite? Quiet?
English expression: *Quait?*

Language of singular
impedance? A dance? An

involuntary gesture to
others *not* there? What's

wrong here? How
reach out to the

other side all
others live on as

now you see the
two doctors, behind

you, in mind's eye,
probe into your anus,

or ass, or bottom,
behind you, the roto-

rooter-like device
sees all up, concludes

"like a worn out inner tube,"
"old," prose prolapsed, person's

problems won't do, must
cut into, cut out . . .

The world is a round but
diminishing ball, a spherical

ice cube, a dusty
joke, a fading,

faint echo of its
former self but remembers,

sometimes, its past, sees
friends, places, reflections,

talks to itself in a fond,
judgmental murmur,

alone at last.
I stood so close

to you I could have
reached out and

touched you just
as you turned

over and began to
snore not unattractively,

no, never less than
attractively, my love,

my love—but in this
curiously glowing dark, this

finite emptiness, *you, you, you*
are crucial, hear the

whimpering back of
the talk, the approaching

fears when I may
cease to be me, all

lost or rather lumped
here in a retrograded,

dislocating, imploding
self, a uselessness

talks, even if finally to no one,
talks and talks.

1990

PAUL BLACKBURN ▪ ▪ ▪ ▪ ▪ ▪ ▪ ▪ ▪ ▪ ▪ ▪ ▪

1926–1971

Born in St. Albans, Vermont, Paul Blackburn was raised by his grandmother until age fourteen, when he moved to New York City to live with his mother, the poet Frances Frost. As a student at the University of Wisconsin, he began corresponding with Ezra Pound, then institutionalized at St. Elizabeth's Hospital in Washington, D.C. In 1951, Pound encouraged him to make the acquaintance of Robert Creeley, who introduced him to Charles Olson and other poets.

Though often associated with Black Mountain poetics, Blackburn actively resisted categorization, taking inspiration from the troubadour poets of twelfth-century Provence, whom he translated into English; García Lorca's *Obras Completas* and European experimental poetry in general; and the emerging Beat scene in New York City in the early sixties. Blackburn founded several reading series on the Lower East Side out of which grew the Poetry Project at St. Mark's Church.

His books include *Brooklyn-Manhattan Transit* (1960), *The Nets* (1961), *The Cities* (1967), *In . On . Or About the Premises* (1968), and the posthumous volumes *Early Selected Y Mas* (1972), *Halfway Down the Coast* (1975), and *The Journals* (1975). All of these are represented in *The Collected Poems of Paul Blackburn* (1985).

Brooklyn Narcissus

Straight rye whiskey, 100 proof
you need a better friend?
Yes.   Myself.

The lights
the lights
the lonely   lovely   fucking   lights
and the bridge on a rainy Tuesday night

Blue/green double-stars   the line
that is the drive and on the dark alive
gleaming river
Xmas trees of tugs scream and struggle

      Midnite

Drops on the train window wobble . stream
           My trouble
                 is
it is her fate to never learn to make
              anything grow
         be born or stay
Harbor beginnings and that other gleam . The train
is full of long/way/home and holding lovers whose
    flesh I would exchange for mine
    The rain, R.F.,

      sweeps the river as the bridges sweep
      Nemesis is thumping down the line
      But I have premises to keep
      & local stops before I sleep
      & local stops before I sleep
              The cree-
              ping train
              joggles
              rocks across
              I hear
the waves below lap against the piles, a pier
              from which ships go
                    to Mexico
a sign which reads

PACE O MIO DIO

      oil

        "The flowers died when you went away"

Manhattan Bridge
a bridge between
we state, one life and the next, we state
is better so
is no
    backwater, flows
              between us is
our span our bridge our
naked eyes
open here

see
bridging whatever impossibility . . . PACE!

PACE O MIO DIO

   oil

       "The flowers died . . ."
       Of course they did

Not that I was a green thing in the house

     I was once.
     No matter.

The clatter of cars over the span, the track
     the spur
the rusty dead/pan ends of space
    of grease

We enter the tunnel.

The dirty window gives me back my face

1958   1960

El Camino Verde

   The green road lies this way.
   I take the road of sand.

One way the sun burns hottest, no relief, the other
sun (the same) is filtered thru
     leaves that cast obscene
     beautiful patterns
    on roads and walls . And

     the wind blows all day.
Hot . sirocco, a chain
of hot wind rattles across
high over the mountains
rushes down from the peaks to the sea
laving men's bodies in the fields between
     Days when
the serpent of wind plucks and twists the harp of the sun.
    In the green road, pale
     gray-green of olives, olive-wood twisted

under the burning wind, the wet
heat of an armpit, but in the mouth

this other road. And the dry heat of the mouth is the pitiful
possibility
of finding a flower in the dust.   Sanity . See
there, the white
wing of a gull over blindness of water,
the black black wing of a hawk over stretches of forest .
Wish
to hold the mind clear in the dark honey of evening light, think
of a spring
in an orchard
in flower
in soft sun amid ruins, down there
a small palm offers its leaves to the wind .
On the mountain, olive,
o, live wood,
its flawless curve hangs from the slope.

Hot . sirocco . covers everything
and everyone, all day, it blows all day as if
this were choice, as if
the earth were anything else but
what it is, a hell. But
blind, bland, blend the flesh.
Mix the naked foot with the sand that caresses it, mix
with the rock that tears it,   enter
the hot world.

Cave of the winds .
What cave?   the
reaches of Africa
where an actual
measure
exists.

1955   1961

Park Poem

From the first shock of leaves their alliance
with love, how is it?

Pages we write and tear
Someone in a swagger coat sits and waits on a hill

It is not spring, may-
be it is never spring

maybe it is the hurt end of summer
the first tender autumn air
fall's first cool rain over the park
and these people walking thru it

The girl thinking:
                              life is these pronouns
the man : to ask / to respond / to accept
                              bird-life . reindeer-death
                              Life is all verbs, vowels and verbs
They both get wet

                    If it is love, it is to make
                    love, or let be
                    'To create the situation / is love
                                        and to avoid it, this is also
                    Love'
as any care or awareness, any
other awareness might might

                    have been
                    but is now

hot flesh
socking it into hot flesh
until reindeer-life   /   bird-death

You are running, see?
you are running down slope across this field
I am running too
to catch you round

                    This rain is yours
                    it falls on us
                    we fall on one another

Belong to the moon
we do not see

                    It is wet and cool
                    bruises our skin
                    might have been
                    care and avoidance
                    but we run . run

to prepare
love later

1961   1967

The Net of Place

Hawk turns into the sun
over the sea, wings red, the
turn upward . mountain behind me

I have left those intricate mountains
My face now to the simple Mediterranean . flat .
small boats . gulls . the blue

Old hawk
is still there tho, as
there are foxes on these barren mountains .
    Old man in a beret, 62 perhaps, came
    into the village bar the other day
    —2 skins and one fox unskinned—

    "You hunted those down?"

    "I hunted them. They
    come closer in winter, seeking food,
    there isn't much up there—"

Rocky headland down into the Gulf of Valencia .
My windows face North. He was a hawk .

I turn back to the Rockies, to the
valley swinging East, Glenwood to Aspen, up
the pass, it is darkest night the hour before dawn,
Orion, old Hunter, with whom
I may never make peace again, swings
just over the horizon at 5 o'clock
as I walk . The mountains fade into light

Being together there was never enuf,—it was
"my thing" Nothing of importance (the reach)
was ever said . I turn
and say farewell to the valley, those hills .
A physical part of wellbeing's been spent or
left there—goodbye   mountains   valley,
all.   Never
to be there again . Never.

It is
an intricate dance
to turn & say goodbye
to the hills we live in the presence of .
when mind dies of its time
it is not the place goes away .

Now, the hawk turns in the sun, circles
over the sea   .
                      Defines me   .
Still the stars show thru   .

Orion in winter rises early,
summer late   .   dark before   .

                      dawn during August
                      during which day, the
                      sun shines on everything.

                                Defines it   .
                      Shadows I do not see.

I rise early
in every season.

           The act defines me,
           even if it is not my act   .

                      Hawk circles over the sea   .
                      My act   .

Saying goodbye, finally   .
Being here is not enuf, tho
I make myself part of what is real.   Recognize me
standing in that valley, taking only the embraces of friends, taking
only my farewell   .   with me
           Stone from my mountains   .
           Your words are mine, at the end.

2.3.68   1975

LARRY EIGNER ▪ ▪ ▪ ▪ ▪ ▪ ▪ ▪ ▪ ▪ ▪ ▪ ▪ ▪ ▪
b. 1927

Larry Eigner was born in Swampscott, Massachusetts, north of Boston. Since
childhood he has been confined to a wheelchair by cerebral palsy. "For Larry
Eigner," Samuel Charters writes, "the circumstances of his life have given a
form and shape to his poetry . . . his life has been spent in a glassed-in front
porch of a frame house on a side street in a small Massachusetts town. Through
the windows—and through the windows of his bedroom—he follows the world
of seasons, the sky, and birds, the trees."[1]
    Eigner's poetry, which deals with everyday events such as the passing of

people and cars on the street, begins with what he modestly calls an "initiation of attention."[2] In the short essay "Statement on Words," he writes that "abundant moments in various places persist . . . a poem can be assay(s) of things come upon, can be a stretch of thinking."[3] Eigner's method is one of understatement and happenstance, working outward from the small and partial. The egoless discontinuity of his poetry is admired by the language poets; his attention to local detail and integrity of poetic line provides a link to both the Williams tradition and Black Mountain poetry.

Eigner's first book of poetry, *From the Sustaining Air* (1953), was published by Robert Creeley's Divers Press. His other books include *Things Stirring Together or Far Away* (1974), *The World and Its Streets, Places* (1977), *Waters/Places/A Time* (1983), and a collection of short prose, *Country/Harbor/Quiet/Act/Around* (1978).

In 1978, Eigner moved to Berkeley, California, where he now resides.

1. Biographical note in Larry Eigner, *The World and Its Streets, Places*, Santa Barbara, 1977, n.p.   2. "Method from Happenstance," in *areas lights heights: Writings 1954–1989*, New York, 1989, p. 6.   3. *areas lights heights*, p. 3.

[trees green   the quiet sun]

trees green   the quiet sun

     shed metal truck in the next street
    passing the white house you listen
                 onwards

     you heard

      the dog

        through   per
          formed circles

    the roads near the beach

      rectangular

        rough lines of the woods

        tall growth   echoing

       local water

                 1977

[how it comes about]

how it comes about
      on me

the many pieces as ever

  time
      the rain

the visiting nurse crosses the street

  again
      back
      drives her car off

and the next patient
    elm drinks
    straight from cloud
      we had murky weather

in the early movie
    last night the wind

through the glass
     passes by

     ooh

       the twigs

             river

         asphalt

   cloudburst

    dark

  bent over

      what it
        does sight

       buoys up

     which currents   of arms

        she stops for lunch

      the world's sharp bead

        curtains

1977

o p e n   a i r   w h e r e

fire alight
in the other window as it
      reflects
            the boy pushes the balloon
against the cottage and it
   lights up

            my mother has moved the furniture around
         again, an accomplished fact
                  the horizon broken at any points
                  within it

            and blocked up the windows after
            taking off curtains, cut narrow, releasing
            all the upholstery smells, since
            winter demands its change,

         ah clothing, after I had seen
         how branches spread leaves across
         one tree, glass, the
opposite to recession

now it is hard times
my mother has made herself in the past
            the kept chairs

the cottage is thin, but remains

while the cars start up, departing, the drivers
again, looking for exercise

(for the eyes)   (after that
friend's house)

            and getting killed

                                                      1977

W h o l e s

For a while a year is a long time
as things increase in their number
   and walls break
familiarity comes

familiarity of life, which sinks
to a level of sorts,   space

(empty except for
the rabbits-hat of things

Before crumbling, the walls streak
with some tangent of minutes

and life takes on a size

1977

[a temporary language]

a temporary language

as temporary things

and poetry the

math.. of

everyday

life

what time

Of the day is it

lad what

have you

to do with

or gotten

done

1977

JOHN ASHBERY ▪ ▪ ▪ ▪ ▪ ▪ ▪ ▪ ▪ ▪ ▪ ▪ ▪ ▪
b. 1927

With the publication in 1975 of *Self-Portrait in a Convex Mirror*, which won both the National Book Award and the Pulitzer Prize, John Ashbery was recognized as the leading poet of his generation. This critical acceptance was somewhat unexpected, given the experimental nature of his work, most radically expressed in *The Tennis Court Oath* (1962). Ashbery's work draws from a poetics of "indeterminacy," which favors the process of writing over the drawing of conclusions; while his work is lyrical and meditative, it resists closure and narrative. Not surprisingly, his chosen form is the long poem.

One of his primary devices, periphrasis (roundabout speech or circumlocu-
tion), is consistent with the unusual length of some of his work. As he announces
in an early long poem, *The Skaters* (1966), he intends to push poetry past the
"dismal two-note theme/Of some sodden 'dump' or lament" into a fuller kind of
reference. Critic and poet David Lehman writes that the subject of *The Skaters*
is "the unbegun journey to the unattainable place," a phrase appropriate to
Ashbery's work in general.[1] Ashbery's long poem *Self-Portrait in a Convex Mir-
ror*, based on Parmigianino's painting of the same title, displays the self-reflex-
iveness of his poetry. But Ashbery avoids narcissism by multiplying and confus-
ing the perspective; it is the movement of consciousness rather than the narrow
concerns of self that is finally depicted.

Like other poets of the New York School, Ashbery admires French avant-
garde writing, in particular the novels of Raymond Roussel, author of *Locus
Solus* and *Impressions of Africa*. In *How I Wrote Certain of My Books*, Roussel
declared that his novels were derived from elaborate sets of puns—the conjunc-
tion, for example, of *pillard* (plunderer) and *billard* (billiard table).[2] Ashbery
shares Roussel's delight in artifice; as an eccentric formalist, his love of unusual
poetic forms such as the sestina, pantoum, and villanelle single-handedly
revived their interest among some younger New York School poets. Ashbery also
expresses a great fondness for *Hebdomeros*, the dreamlike novel by the painter
Giorgio De Chirico. His literary forebears in the English language include Laura
Riding Jackson, the modernist poet who abandoned her highly original poetry of
abstraction for the study of linguistics; Wallace Stevens, whom Ashbery suc-
ceeds as a major poet of romantic epistomology; and W. H. Auden, who selected
Ashbery's first book, *Some Trees* (1956), for publication in the Yale Series of
Younger Poets and whose love of formalism Ashbery shares.

Perhaps because of his commitment to eccentric letters, Ashbery's work is
often considered difficult. However, in its inconclusiveness and linguistic play
Ashbery's poetry captures the philosophical spirit of the age, as otherwise re-
flected in the thought of Ludwig Wittgenstein and Jacques Derrida.

Among his many other books are *Rivers and Mountains* (1966), *The Double
Dream of Spring* (1970), *Three Poems* (1972), *Houseboat Days* (1977), *Shadow
Train* (1981), *A Wave* (1984), and *April Galleons* (1987). Ashbery was formerly
editor of *ARTnews* and gave the distinguished Charles Eliot Norton series of
lectures at Harvard in 1989–1990.

He is currently professor of literature at Bard College.

1. "The Shield of a Greeting," in *Beyond Amazement: New Essays on John Ashbery*, ed.
David Lehman, Ithaca, 1980, p. 123.   2. Trans. Trevor Winkfield, New York, 1975, p. 3.

The Picture of Little J. A. in a Prospect of Flowers

> *He was spoilt from childhood*
> *by the future, which he mastered*
> *rather early and apparently*
> *without great difficulty.*
> —BORIS PASTERNAK

I

Darkness falls like a wet sponge
And Dick gives Genevieve a swift punch
In the pajamas. "Aroint thee, witch."

Her tongue from previous ecstasy
Releases thoughts like little hats.

"He clap'd me first during the eclipse.
Afterwards I noted his manner
Much altered. But he sending
At that time certain handsome jewels
I durst not seem to take offence."

In a far recess of summer
Monks are playing soccer.

II

So far is goodness a mere memory
Or naming of recent scenes of badness
That even these lives, children,
You may pass through to be blessed,
So fair does each invent his virtue.

And coming from a white world, music
Will sparkle at the lips of many who are
Beloved. Then these, as dirty handmaidens
To some transparent witch, will dream
Of a white hero's subtle wooing,
And time shall force a gift on each.

That beggar to whom you gave no cent
Striped the night with his strange descant.

III

Yet I cannot escape the picture
Of my small self in that bank of flowers:
My head among the blazing phlox
Seemed a pale and gigantic fungus.
I had a hard stare, accepting

Everything, taking nothing,
As though the rolled-up future might stink
As loud as stood the sick moment
The shutter clicked. Though I was wrong,
Still, as the loveliest feelings

Must soon find words, and these, yes,
Displace them, so I am not wrong
In calling this comic version of myself
The true one. For as change is horror,
Virtue is really stubbornness

And only in the light of lost words
Can we imagine our rewards.

1956

"How Much Longer Will I Be Able to Inhabit the Divine Sepulcher . . ."

How much longer will I be able to inhabit the divine sepulcher
Of life, my great love? Do dolphins plunge bottomward
To find the light? Or is it rock
That is searched? Unrelentingly? Huh. And if some day

Men with orange shovels come to break open the rock
Which encases me, what about the light that comes in then?
What about the smell of the light?
What about the moss?

In pilgrim times he wounded me
Since then I only lie
My bed of light is a furnace choking me
With hell (and sometimes I hear salt water dripping).

I mean it—because I'm one of the few
To have held my breath under the house. I'll trade
One red sucker for two blue ones. I'm
Named Tom. The

Light bounces off mossy rocks down to me
In this glen (the neat villa! which
When he'd had he would not had he of
And jests under the smarting of privet

Which on hot spring nights perfumes the empty rooms
With the smell of sperm flushed down toilets
On hot summer afternoons within sight of the sea.
If you knew why then professor) reads

To his friends: Drink to me only with
And the reader is carried away
By a great shadow under the sea.
Behind the steering wheel

The boy took out his own forehead.
His girlfriend's head was a green bag
Of narcissus stems. "OK you win
But meet me anyway at Cohen's Drug Store

In 22 minutes." What a marvel is ancient man!
Under the tulip roots he has figured out a way to be a religious animal
And would be a mathematician. But where in unsuitable heaven
Can he get the heat that will make him grow?

For he needs something or will forever remain a dwarf,
Though a perfect one, and possessing a normal-sized brain
But he has got to be released by giants from things.
And as the plant grows older it realizes it will never be a tree,

Will probably always be haunted by a bee
And cultivates stupid impressions
So as not to become part of the dirt. The dirt
Is mounting like a sea. And we say goodbye

Shaking hands in front of the crashing of the waves
That give our words lonesomeness, and make these flabby hands seem
    ours—
Hands that are always writing things
On mirrors for people to see later—

Do you want them to water
Plant, tear listlessly among the exchangeable ivy—
Carrying food to mouth, touching genitals—
But no doubt you have understood

It all now and I am a fool. It remains
For me to get better, and to understand you so
Like a chair-sized man. Boots
Were heard on the floor above. In the garden the sunlight was still purple

But what buzzed in it had changed slightly
But not forever . . . but casting its shadow
On sticks, and looking around for an opening in the air, was quite as if it
    had never refused to exist differently. Guys
In the yard handled the belt he had made

Stars
Painted the garage roof crimson and black
He is not a man
Who can read these signs . . . his bones were stays . . .

And even refused to live
In a world and refunded the hiss
Of all that exists terribly near us
Like you, my love, and light.

For what is obedience but the air around us
To the house? For which the federal men came
In a minute after the sidewalk
Had taken you home? ("Latin . . . blossom . . .")

After which you led me to water
And bade me drink, which I did, owing to your kindness.

You would not let me out for two days and three nights,
Bringing me books bound in wild thyme and scented wild grasses

As if reading had any interest for me, you . . .
Now you are laughing.
Darkness interrupts my story.
Turn on the light.

Meanwhile what am I going to do?
I am growing up again, in school, the crisis will be very soon.
And you twist the darkness in your fingers, you
Who are slightly older . . .

Who are you, anyway?
And it is the color of sand,
The darkness, as it sifts through your hand
Because what does anything mean,

The ivy and the sand? That boat
Pulled up on the shore? Am I wonder,
Strategically, and in the light
Of the long sepulcher that hid death and hides me?

1962

Leaving the Atocha Station

The arctic honey blabbed over the report causing darkness
And pulling us out of there experiencing it
he meanwhile . . .   And the fried bats they sell there
dropping from sticks, so that the menace of your prayer folds . . .
Other people . . .   flash
the garden are you boning
and defunct covering . . .   Blind dog expressed royalties . . .
comfort of your perfect tar grams nuclear world bank tulip
Favorable to   near the night pin
loading formaldehyde.   the table torn from you
Suddenly   and we are close
Mouthing the root   when you think
generator   homes enjoy leered

The worn stool blazing pigeons from the roof
                    driving tractor to squash
Leaving the Atocha Station   steel
infected bumps the screws
        everywhere wells
abolished top ill-lit
scarecrow falls   Time, progress and good sense
strike of shopkeepers dark blood

no forest you can name drunk scrolls
the completely new Italian hair . . .
Baby . . .   ice falling off the port
The centennial   Before we can

                old   eat
members with their chins
                so high up   rats
    relaxing the cruel discussion
   suds   the painted corners
white   most aerial
           garment crow
                          and when the region took us back
the person left us like birds
   it was fuzz on the passing light
over disgusted heads, far into amnesiac
permanent house depot   amounts he can
           decrepit mayor . . .   exalting flea
for that we turn around
experiencing it is not to go into
the epileptic prank forcing bar
to borrow out onto tide-exposed fells
over her morsel, she chasing you
and the revenge he'd get
establishing the vultural over
rural area cough protection
murdering quintet. Air pollution terminal
the clean fart genital enthusiastic toe prick album serious evening flames
the lake over your hold   personality
           lightened . . .   roar
You are freed
           including barrels
head of the swan   forestry
the night and stars fork
That is, he said
   and rushing under the hoops of
equations probable
           absolute mush   the right
entity   chain store   sewer opened their books
      The flood dragged you
      I coughed to the window
last month: juice, earlier
like the slacks   be declining
   the peaches   more
   fist
sprung expecting the cattle
false loam   imports
           next time around

                                        1962

FROM *The Skaters*

I

These decibels
Are a kind of flagellation, an entity of sound
Into which being enters, and is apart.
Their colors on a warm February day
Make for masses of inertia, and hips
Prod out of the violet-seeming into a new kind
Of demand that stumps the absolute because not new
In the sense of the next one in an infinite series
But, as it were, pre-existing or pre-seeming in
Such a way as to contrast funnily with the unexpectedness
And somehow push us all into perdition.

Here a scarf flies, there an excited call is heard.

The answer is that it is novelty
That guides these swift blades o'er the ice
Projects into a finer expression (but at the expense
Of energy) the profile I cannot remember.
Colors slip away from and chide us. The human mind
Cannot retain anything except perhaps the dismal two-note theme
Of some sodden "dump" or lament.

But the water surface ripples, the whole light changes.

We children are ashamed of our bodies
But we laugh and, demanded, talk of sex again
And all is well. The waves of morning harshness
Float away like coal-gas into the sky.
But how much survives? How much of any one of us survives?
The articles we'd collect—stamps of the colonies
With greasy cancellation marks, mauve, magenta and chocolate,
Or funny-looking dogs we'd see in the street, or bright remarks.
One collects bullets. An Indianapolis, Indiana man collects
    slingshots of all epochs, and so on.

Subtracted from our collections, though, these go on a little
    while, collecting aimlessly. We still support them.
But so little energy they have! And up the swollen sands
Staggers the darkness fiend, with the storm fiend close behind him!

True, melodious tolling does go on in that awful pandemonium,
Certain resonances are not utterly displeasing to the
    terrified eardrum.
Some paroxysms are dinning of tambourine, others suggest piano
    room or organ loft

For the most dissonant night charms us, even after death. This,
    after all, may be happiness: tuba notes awash on the great
    flood, ruptures of xylophone, violins, limpets, grace-notes, the
    musical instrument called serpent, viola da gambas, aeolian
    harps, clavicles, pinball machines, electric drills, que sais-je
    encore!
The performance has rapidly reached your ear; silent and tear-
    stained, in the post-mortem shock, you stand listening, awash
With memories of hair in particular, part of the welling that is you,
The gurgling of harp, cymbal, glockenspiel, triangle, temple block,
    English horn and metronome! And still no presentiment, no
    feeling of pain before or after.
The passage sustains, does not give. And you have come far indeed.

Yet to go from "not interesting" to "old and uninteresting,"
To be surrounded by friends, though late in life,
To hear the wings of the spirit, though far. . . .
Why do I hurriedly undrown myself to cut you down?
"I am yesterday," and my fault is eternal.
I do not expect constant attendance, knowing myself
    insufficient for your present demands
And I have a dim intuition that I am that other "I" with which
    we began.
My cheeks as blank walls to your tears and eagerness
Fondling that other, as though you had let him get away forever.

The evidence of the visual henceforth replaced
By the great shadow of trees falling over life.

A child's devotion
To this normal, shapeless entity. . . .

Forgotten as the words fly briskly across, each time
Bringing down meaning as snow from a low sky, or rabbits
    flushed from a wood.
How strange that the narrow perspective lines
Always seem to meet, although parallel, and that an insane
    ghost could do this,
Could make the house seem so much farther in the distance, as
It seemed to the horse, dragging the sledge of a perspective line.
Dim banners in the distance, to die. . . . And nothing put to
    rights. The pigs in their cages

And so much snow, but it is to be littered with waste and ashes
So that cathedrals may grow. Out of this spring builds a tolerable
Affair of brushwood, the sea is felt behind oak wands,
    noiselessly pouring.
Spring with its promise of winter, and the black ivy once again
On the porch, its yellow perspective bands in place
And the horse nears them and weeps.

So much has passed through my mind this morning
That I can give you but a dim account of it:
It is already after lunch, the men are returning to their
    positions around the cement mixer
And I try to sort out what has happened to me. The bundle
    of Gerard's letters,
And that awful bit of news buried on the back page of
    yesterday's paper.
Then the news of you this morning, in the snow.
    Sometimes the interval
Of bad news is so brisk that . . . And the human brain, with its
    tray of images
Seems a sorcerer's magic lantern, projecting black and orange
    cellophane shadows
On the distance of my hand . . . The very reaction's puny,
And when we seek to move around, wondering what our position
    is now, what the arm of that chair.

A great wind lifted these cardboard panels
Horizontal in the air. At once the perspective with the horse
Disappeared in a *bigarrure* of squiggly lines. The image with
    the crocodile in it became no longer apparent.

Thus a great wind cleanses, as a new ruler
Edits new laws, sweeping the very breath of the streets
Into posterior trash. The films have changed—
The great titles on the scalloped awning have turned dry and
    blight-colored.
No wind that does not penetrate a man's house, into the very
    bowels of the furnace,
Scratching in dust a name on the mirror—say, and what
    about letters,
The dried grasses, fruits of the winter—gosh! Everything
    is trash!
The wind points to the advantages of decay
At the same time as removing them far from the sight of men.
The regent of the winds, Aeolus, is a symbol for all
    earthly potentates
Since holding this sickening, festering process by which
    we are cleansed
Of afterthought.
               A girl slowly descended the line of steps.

The wind and treason are partners, turning secrets over to
    the military police.

Lengthening arches. The intensity of minor acts.
    As skaters elaborate their distances,
Taking a separate line to its end. Returning to the mass,
    they join each other

Blotted in an incredible mess of dark colors, and again
    reappearing to take the theme
Some little distance, like fishing boats developing from the
    land different parabolas,
Taking the exquisite theme far, into farness, to Land's End,
    to the ends of the earth!

But the livery of the year, the changing air
Bring each to fulfillment. Leaving phrases unfinished,
Gestures half-sketched against woodsmoke. The abundant sap
Oozes in girls' throats, the sticky words, half-uttered,
    unwished for,
A blanket disbelief, quickly supplanted by idle questions
    that fade in turn.
Slowly the mood turns to look at itself as some urchin
Forgotten by the roadside. New schemes are got up, new taxes,
Earthworks. And the hour becomes light again.
Girls wake up in it.

It is best to remain indoors. Because there is error
In so much precision. As flames are fanned, wishful
    thinking arises
Bearing its own prophets, its pointed ignoring.
    And just as a desire
Settles down at the end of a long spring day, over heather
    and watered shoot and dried rush field,
So error is plaited into desires not yet born.

Therefore the post must be resumed (is being falsified
To be forever involved, tragically, with one's own image?).
The studio light suddenly invaded the long
    casement—values were what
She knows now. But the floor is being slowly pulled apart
Like straw under those limpid feet.
And Helga, in the minuscule apartment in Jersey City
Is reacting violet to the same kind of dress, is drawing death
Again in blossoms against the reactionary fire . . . pulsing
And knowing nothing to superb lambent distances that intercalate
This city. Is the death of the cube repeated. Or in the
    musical album.

It is time now for a general understanding of
The meaning of all this. The meaning of Helga, importance
    of the setting, etc.
A description of the blues. Labels on bottles
And all kinds of discarded objects that ought to be described.
But can one ever be sure of which ones?
Isn't this a death-trap, wanting to put too much in
So the floor sags, as under the weight of a piano,
    or a piano-legged girl

And the whole house of cards comes dinning down around
    one's ears!

But this is an important aspect of the question
Which I am not ready to discuss, am not at all ready to,
This leaving-out business. On it hinges the very importance
    of what's novel
Or autocratic, or dense or silly. It is as well to call attention
To it by exaggeration, perhaps. But calling attention
Isn't the same thing as explaining, and as I said I am not ready
To line phrases with the costly stuff of explanation, and shall not,
Will not do so for the moment. Except to say that the carnivorous
Way of these lines is to devour their own nature, leaving
Nothing but a bitter impression of absence, which as we know
    involves presence, but still.
Nevertheless these are fundamental absences, struggling to
    get up and be off themselves.

This, thus is a portion of the subject of this poem
Which is in the form of falling snow:
That is, the individual flakes are not essential to the
    importance of the whole's becoming so much of a truism
That their importance is again called in question, to be
    denied further out, and again and again like this.
Hence, neither the importance of the individual flake,
Nor the importance of the whole impression of the storm,
    if it has any, is what it is,
But the rhythm of the series of repeated jumps, from
    abstract into positive and back to a slightly less
    diluted abstract.

Mild effects are the result.

I cannot think any more of going out into all that, will stay here
With my quiet *schmerzen*. Besides the storm is almost over
Having frozen the face of the bust into a strange style with the lips
And the teeth the most distinct part of the whole business.

It is this madness to explain. . . .

What is the matter with plain old-fashioned cause-and-effect?
Leaving one alone with romantic impressions of the trees, the sky?
Who, actually, is going to be fooled one instant by these
    phony explanations,
Think them important? So back we go to the old,
    imprecise feelings, the
Common knowledge, the importance of duly suffering and
    the occasional glimpses
Of some balmy felicity. The world of Schubert's lieder.
    I am fascinated

Though by the urge to get out of it all, by going
Further in and correcting the whole mismanaged mess.
    But am afraid I'll
Be of no help to you. Good-bye.

As balloons are to the poet, so to the ground
Its varied assortment of trees. The more assorted they are, the
Vaster his experience. Sometimes
You catch sight of them on a level with the top story of a house,
Strung up there for publicity purposes. Or like those bubbles
Children make with a kind of ring, not a pipe, and probably
    using some detergent
Rather than plain everyday soap and water. Where was I?
    The balloons
Drift thoughtfully over the land, not exactly commenting on it;
These are the range of the poet's experience. He can hide in trees
Like a hamadryad, but wisely prefers not to, letting the balloons
Idle him out of existence, as a car idles. Traveling faster
And more furiously across unknown horizons, belted into the night
Wishing more and more to be unlike someone, getting the
    whole thing
(So he believes) out of his system. Inventing systems.
We are a part of some system, thinks he, just as the sun is part of
The solar system. Trees brake his approach. And he seems
    to be wearing but
Half a coat, viewed from one side. A "half-man" look
    inspiring the disgust of honest folk
Returning from chores, the milk frozen, the pump heaped high
    with a chapeau of snow,
The "No Skating" sign as well. But it is here that he is best,
Face to face with the unsmiling alternatives of his nerve-wracking
    existence.
Placed squarely in front of his dilemma, on all fours before the
    lamentable spectacle of the unknown.
Yet knowing where men *are* coming from. It is this, to hold the
    candle up to the album.

                                                        1966

Farm Implements and Rutabagas in a Landscape

The first of the undecoded messages read: "Popeye sits in thunder,
Unthought of. From that shoebox of an apartment,
From livid curtain's hue, a tangram emerges: a country."
Meanwhile the Sea Hag was relaxing on a green couch: "How pleasant
To spend one's vacation *en la casa de Popeye*," she scratched
Her cleft chin's solitary hair. She remembered spinach

And was going to ask Wimpy if he had bought any spinach.
"M'love," he intercepted, "the plains are decked out in thunder

Today, and it shall be as you wish." He scratched
The part of his head under his hat. The apartment
Seemed to grow smaller. "But what if no pleasant
Inspiration plunge us now to the stars? *For this is my country.*"

Suddenly they remembered how it was cheaper in the country.
Wimpy was thoughtfully cutting open a number 2 can of spinach
When the door opened and Swee'pea crept in. "How pleasant!"
But Swee'pea looked morose. A note was pinned to his bib. "Thunder
And tears are unavailing," it read. "Henceforth shall Popeye's
  apartment
Be but remembered space, toxic or salubrious, whole or scratched."

Olive came hurtling through the window; its geraniums scratched
Her long thigh. "I have news!" she gasped. "Popeye, forced as you
  know to flee the country
One musty gusty evening, by the schemes of his wizened, duplicate
  father, jealous of the apartment
And all that it contains, myself and spinach
In particular, heaves bolts of loving thunder
At his own astonished becoming, rupturing the pleasant

Arpeggio of our years. No more shall pleasant
Rays of the sun refresh your sense of growing old, nor the scratched
Tree-trunks and mossy foliage, only immaculate darkness and
  thunder."
She grabbed Swee'pea. "I'm taking the brat to the country."
"But you can't do that—he hasn't even finished his spinach,"
Urged the Sea Hag, looking fearfully around at the apartment.

But Olive was already out of earshot. Now the apartment
Succumbed to a strange new hush. "Actually it's quite pleasant
Here," thought the Sea Hag. "If this is all we need fear from spinach
Then I don't mind so much. Perhaps we could invite Alice the Goon
  over"—she scratched
One dug pensively—"but Wimpy is such a country
Bumpkin, always burping like that." Minute at first, the thunder

Soon filled the apartment. It was domestic thunder,
The color of spinach. Popeye chuckled and scratched
His balls: it sure was pleasant to spend a day in the country.

                                                              1970

The One Thing That Can Save America

Is anything central?
Orchards flung out on the land,
Urban forests, rustic plantations, knee-high hills?
Are place names central?

Elm Grove, Adcock Corner, Story Book Farm?
As they concur with a rush at eye level
Beating themselves into eyes which have had enough
Thank you, no more thank you.
And they come on like scenery mingled with darkness
The damp plains, overgrown suburbs,
Places of known civic pride, of civil obscurity.

These are connected to my version of America
But the juice is elsewhere.
This morning as I walked out of your room
After breakfast crosshatched with
Backward and forward glances, backward into light,
Forward into unfamiliar light,
Was it our doing, and was it
The material, the lumber of life, or of lives
We were measuring, counting?
A mood soon to be forgotten
In crossed girders of light, cool downtown shadow
In this morning that has seized us again?

I know that I braid too much my own
Snapped-off perceptions of things as they come to me.
They are private and always will be.
Where then are the private turns of event
Destined to boom later like golden chimes
Released over a city from a highest tower?
The quirky things that happen to me, and I tell you,
And you instantly know what I mean?
What remote orchard reached by winding roads
Hides them? Where are these roots?

It is the lumps and trials
That tell us whether we shall be known
And whether our fate can be exemplary, like a star.
All the rest is waiting
For a letter that never arrives,
Day after day, the exasperation
Until finally you have ripped it open not knowing what it is,
The two envelope halves lying on a plate.
The message was wise, and seemingly
Dictated a long time ago.
Its truth is timeless, but its time has still
Not arrived, telling of danger, and the mostly limited
Steps that can be taken against danger
Now and in the future, in cool yards,
In quiet small houses in the country,
Our country, in fenced areas, in cool shady streets.

1975

The Other Tradition

They all came, some wore sentiments
Emblazoned on T-shirts, proclaiming the lateness
Of the hour, and indeed the sun slanted its rays
Through branches of Norfolk Island pine as though
Politely clearing its throat, and all ideas settled
In a fuzz of dust under trees when it's drizzling:
The endless games of Scrabble, the boosters,
The celebrated omelette au Cantal, and through it
The roar of time plunging unchecked through the sluices
Of the days, dragging every sexual moment of it
Past the lenses: the end of something.
Only then did you glance up from your book,
Unable to comprehend what had been taking place, or
Say what you had been reading. More chairs
Were brought, and lamps were lit, but it tells
Nothing of how all this proceeded to materialize
Before you and the people waiting outside and in the next
Street, repeating its name over and over, until silence
Moved halfway up the darkened trunks,
And the meeting was called to order.
                                        I still remember
How they found you, after a dream, in your thimble hat,
Studious as a butterfly in a parking lot.
The road home was nicer then. Dispersing, each of the
Troubadours had something to say about how charity
Had run its race and won, leaving you the ex-president
Of the event, and how, though many of those present
Had wished something to come of it, if only a distant
Wisp of smoke, yet none was so deceived as to hanker
After that cool non-being of just a few minutes before,
Now that the idea of a forest had clamped itself
Over the minutiae of the scene. You found this
Charming, but turned your face fully toward night,
Speaking into it like a megaphone, not hearing
Or caring, although these still live and are generous
And all ways contained, allowed to come and go
Indefinitely in and out of the stockade
They have so much trouble remembering, when your
    forgetting
Rescues them at last, as a star absorbs the night.

                                                    1977

Paradoxes and Oxymorons

This poem is concerned with language on a very plain level.
Look at it talking to you. You look out a window
Or pretend to fidget. You have it but you don't have it.
You miss it, it misses you. You miss each other.

The poem is sad because it wants to be yours, and cannot.
What's a plain level? It is that and other things,
Bringing a system of them into play. Play?
Well, actually, yes, but I consider play to be

A deeper outside thing, a dreamed role-pattern,
As in the division of grace these long August days
Without proof. Open-ended. And before you know
It gets lost in the steam and chatter of typewriters.

It has been played once more. I think you exist only
To tease me into doing it, on your level, and then you aren't there
Or have adopted a different attitude. And the poem
Has set me softly down beside you. The poem is you.

1981

FROM *Flow Chart*

I

Still in the published city but not yet
overtaken by a new form of despair, I ask
the diagram: is it the foretaste of pain
it might easily be? Or an emptiness
so sudden it leaves the girders
whanging in the absence of wind,
the sky milk-blue and astringent? We know life is so busy,
but a larger activity shrouds it, and this is something
we can never feel, except occasionally, in small signs
put up to warn us and as soon expunged, in part
or wholly.
            Sad grows the river god as he oars past us
downstream without our knowing him: for if, he reasons,
he can be overlooked, then to know him would be to eat him,
ingest the name he carries through time to set down
finally, on a strand of rotted hulks. And those who sense something
squeamish in his arrival know enough not to look up
from the page they are reading, the plaited lines that extend
like a bronze chain into eternity.
                        It seems I was reading something;
I have forgotten the sense of it or what the small

role of the central poem made me want to feel. No matter.
The words, distant now, and mitred, glint. Yet not one
ever escapes the forest of agony and pleasure that keeps them
in a solution that has become permanent through inertia. The force
of meaning never extrudes. And the insects,
of course, don't mind. I think it was at that moment he
knowingly and in my own interests took back from me
the slow-flowing idea of flight, now
too firmly channeled, its omnipresent reminders etched
too deeply into my forehead, its crass grievances and greetings
a class apart from the wonders every man feels,
whether alone in bed, or with a lover, or beached
with the shells on some atoll (and if solitude
swallow us up betimes, it is only later that
the idea of its permanence sifts into view, yea
later and perhaps only occasionally, and only much later
stands from dawn to dusk, just as the plaintive sound
of the harp of the waves is always there as a backdrop
to conversation and conversion, even when
most forgotten) and cannot make sense of them, but he knows
the familiar, unmistakable thing, and that gives him courage
as day expires and evening marshals its hosts, in preparation
for the long night to come.
                            And the horoscopes flung back
all we had meant to keep there: *our* meaning, for us, yet
how different the sense when another speaks it!
How cold the afterthought that takes us out of time
for a few moments (just as we were beginning to go with the fragile
penchants mother-love taught us) and transports us to a stepping-stone
far out at sea.
                So no matter what the restrictions, admonitions,
premonitions that trellised us early, supporting this
artificial espaliered thing we have become, by the same token no
subsequent learning shall deprive us, it seems, no holy
sophistication loosen the bands
of blessed decorum, our present salvation, our hope for years to come.
Only let that river not beseech its banks too closely,
abrade and swamp its levees, for though the flood is always terrible,
much worse are the painted monsters born later
out of the swift-flowing alluvial mud.
                            And when the time for the breaking
of the law is here, be sure it is to take place in the matrix
of our everyday thoughts and fantasies, our wonderment
at how we got from there to here. In the unlashed eye of noon
these and other terrible things are written, yet it seems
at the time as mild as soughing of wavelets in a reservoir.
Only the belated certainty comes to matter much,
I suppose, and, when it does, comes to seem as immutable as roses.
Meanwhile a god has bungled it again.
                            Early on

was a time of seeming: golden eggs that hatched
into regrets, a snowflake whose kiss burned like an enchanter's
poison; yet it all seemed good in the growing dawn.
The breeze that always nurtures us (no matter how dry,
how filled with complaints about time and the weather the air)
pointed out a way that diverged from the true way without negating it,
to arrive at the same result by different spells,
so that no one was wiser for knowing the way we had grown,
almost unconsciously, into a cube of grace that was to be
a permanent shelter. Let the book end there, some few
said, but that was of course impossible; the growth must persist
into areas darkened and dangerous, undermined
by the curse of that death breeze, until one is handed a skull
as a birthday present, and each closing paragraph of the novella is
underlined: *To be continued,* that there should be no peace
in the present, no sleep save in glimpses of the future
on the crystal ball's thick, bubble-like surface. No you and me
unless we are together. Only then does he mumble confused words
of affection at us as the barberry bleeds close against the frost,
a scarlet innocence, confused miracle, to us, for what we have done
to others, and to ourselves. There is no parting. There is
only the fading, guaranteed by the label, which lasts forever.

This much the gods divulged before they became too restless,
too preoccupied with other cares to see into the sole fact the
present allows, along with much ribbon, much icing
and pretended music. But we can't live with them in their day:
the air, though pure, is too dense. And afterwards when others
come up and ask, what was it like, one is too amazed to behave strangely;
the future is extinguished; the world's colored paths all lead
to my mouth, and I drop, humbled, eating from the red-clay floor.
And only then does inspiration come: late, yet never too late.

It's possible, it's just possible, that the god's claims
fly out windows as soon as they are opened, are erased from the accounting. If
    one is alone,
it matters less than to others embarked on a casual voyage
into the promiscuity of dreams. Yet I am always the first to know
how he feels. The inventory of the silent auction
doesn't promise much: one chewed cactus, an air mattress,
a verbatim report. Sandals. The massive transcriptions with which
he took unforgivable liberties—hell, I'd sooner join the project
farther ahead, retaining all benefits, but one is doomed,
repeating oneself, never to repeat oneself, you know what I mean?
If in the interval false accounts have circulated, why,
one is at least unaware of it, and can live one's allotted arc
of time in feasible unconsciousness, watching the linen dresses of girls,
with a wreath of smoke to come home to. There is nothing beside the familiar
doormat to get excited about, yet when one goes out in loose weather
the change is akin to choirs singing in a distance nebulous with fear

and love. Sometimes one's own hopes are realized
and life becomes a description of every second of the time it took;
conversely, some are put off by the sound of legions milling about.
One cultivates certain smells, is afraid to leave the charmed circle
of the anxious room lest uncommitted atmosphere befall

                                                    and the oaks
are seen to be girdled with ivy.

Alack he said what stressful sounds

More of him another time but now you
in the ivory frame have stripped yourself one by one of your earliest
opinions, polluted in any case by bees, and stand
radiant in the circle of our lost, unhappy youth, oh my
friend that knew me before I knew you, and when you came to me
knew it was forever, *here* there would be no break, only I was
so ignorant I forgot what it was all about. You chided me
for forgetting and in an instant I remembered everything: the
schoolhouse, the tent meeting. And I came closer until the day
I wrote my name firmly on the ruled page: that was a
time to come, and all happy crying in memory placed the stone
in the magic box and covered it with wallpaper. It seemed our separate
lives could continue separately for themselves and shine like a single star.
I never knew such happiness. I never knew such happiness could exist.
Not that the dark world was removed or brightened, but
each thing in it was slightly enlarged, and in so seeming became its
true cameo self, a liquid thing, to be held in the hollow
of the hand like a bird. More formal times would come
of course but the abstract good sense would never drown in the elixir
of this private sorrow, that would always sing to itself
in good times and bad, an example to one's consciousness,
an emblem of correct behavior, in darkness or under water.
How unshifting those secret times, and how stealthily
they grew! It was going to take forever just to get through
the first act, yet the scenery, a square of medieval houses, gardens
with huge blue and red flowers and solemn birds that dwarfed
the trees they sat on, need never have given way to the fumes and crevasses
of the high glen: the point is one was going to do to it
what mattered to us, and all would be correct as in a painting
that would never ache for a frame but dream on as nonchalantly as we did.
Who could have expected a dream like this to go away for there are some
that are the web on which our waking life is painstakingly elaborated:
there are real, bustling things there and the burgomaster of success
stalks back and forth, directing everything
with a small motion of a finger. But when it did come,
the denouement, we were off drinking in some restaurant,
too absorbed, too eternally, expectantly happy to be there or care.

                                                            1991

HANNAH WEINER ▪ ▪ ▪ ▪ ▪ ▪ ▪ ▪ ▪ ▪ ▪ ▪

b. 1928

Born in Providence, Rhode Island, and a graduate of Radcliffe College, Hannah Weiner began to write poetry in the 1960s. In 1970, she discovered her powers as a psychic, and two years later she began to see words in the air. In her own words, "I SEE words on my forehead IN THE AIR on other people on the typewriter on the page These appear in the text in CAPITALS or *italics.*"

Thus her books are divided into two categories, clairvoyant and non-clairvoyant. They include *Clairvoyant Journal* (1978), *Little Books/Indians* (1980), *Spoke* (1984), and a journal of her clairvoyant experiences, *The Fast* (1992). Her compositional approach, which relies heavily on intuition rather than method, produces texts similar to language poetry and the chance-operational writings of Jackson Mac Low.

Weiner lives in New York City.

FROM *Clairvoyant Journal*

3/10

How can I describe anything when all these interruptions keep *arriving* and then tell me I dont describe it well   WELL *forgive them* big ME   COUNTDOWN got that for days and yesterday it didn't stop GO TO COUNTDOWN GO TO COUNTDOWN   CALL DAVIDs   get COUNTDOWN finally GO TO COUNT-
DOWN at the door so OK I go see these maroon velvet pants I'm not BUY $40
he isn't home
pants BLOOMINGDALES all over again I leave GO TO COUNTDOWN: refuge, get in a taxi, start for home, no peace, get out GO TO COUNTDOWN ok it's only money go back and buy the pants it's better than seeing GO TO COUNTDOWN for the rest of my life *peace* so they fit well   UNTIL   MICHAEL COOPER
For a while I tried to get away with *negative*   COUNTING   by counting down
10, 9, 8, 7   while breathing GO TO   MAKE CLEARer   FAR OUT
B   at the door RHYS   RHYS IMPORTANT (notes) HAVE A DOUBLE
L   image of pink embroidered pillow case appears on blanket, get it out
I
S   GO NOW *girlfriend negative* MOTHER made it when I was 2
S   JANA   *g*h   she's fasting TRY HARDER across her chest and
                    TATA
F   o*u*   DRESS WARM across Charlemagne's groin   Joan's
U   *e*^n
L   *e*^at   head says LAUGHS as she   QUINK THICK   SAY IT
                                laughs
Rhys *rhythm*   VERY IMPORTANT says radio   LY
DESCRIBE *go ahead* in Charlemagne's white pants WOOL white hat
   IMITATED Hawai JOAN   ARAKAWA   (more notes going back 3 days)
YOU WONT OBEY   PORK CHOP   BUY THEM *pig* in pork chop color along
                                well tho
the edge of   NOT APPLE PIE in pink and white sash
   frying

185

ORGASM $deaf_e n^t$ go to a museum

$_iJUNK\ t^e_m{}^{ru}{}^{it}$

$_g et\ e^{x^{c}}$

$_e{}^{a}t\ g_r{}^{aP}e^f$ CANT GET THE SPACIN

it's a nice arc

I T W ^{R} ^{I} ^{T} $_E$ $_S$ $_I$ $_T$ $_S$ $_E$ $_L$ $_F$

IT WRITES ITSELF

Try praying: Our father who art *be right over*
A song: Here we go round the mulberry bush the
grapefruit John the mulbery *mush* GIVE UP
GRAPEFRUIT IS THE NAME OF Yoko Ono's book, APOLOGIZE is on a Ringo
Star2 record 2 r's   Call Jerry MISS ROTHENBERG MISS DAVID ANTIN
SNOWING IN VERMONT *delightful*   Dream about Jason Epstein very huge
               JOHN
loud SHUT UP in hs office, *I rejoice*   *laugh*   DESCRIBE CHARLEMAGNE
how old 33 spiritual discipline

not in dollars   *not too negative*

no money

MONEY

3/10 p 4

LAMONTE had this dream listening to Lamonte   GET ALREADY SCARED
                                      heals
STUPID NEXT before I can type it the carnations fall over water spills on floor,
wiping it see in the other part of *the room* a blue puddle just like the one spilled
says WATER   I laugh *far out*   YOUR notes
VERY SERIOUS LAMONT$^g e_t$
                   $_t{}^{f}r_i$
very serious operation   get $^f r_i$ *already scared*   LIVER   WHAT D'YA
   vagina $^g h_t$
THINK huge HER VOICE$_{dorothy}{}^t{}_e$ her voice is pretty clear sounds just
like her$_{liver}$CALL RAYMOND $^n e_d$ his liver side flashed
Had trouble with my own just in time make some parsley tea? WHAT BOIL IT
IN WATER *stop* stop drinking wine? *Heal yourself* says stomach LAMONTE
didn't e maybe it is my thought had to look up to see if e Met Dorothy   where I
got my ulcer, *working hard* her voice *I'll hit you - direct hit*
Good heat vibrations in 1st chakra area WHEW *good idea*
maybe it will heal now   GOOD LUCK just remembered
                              Dorothy's healing group CONCENTRATE
on her   they have success healing
       told her about Le Shan, who trains healers$^{GO\ TO\ ONE}$

Steve Reich is not tunafish   GOOD LUCK better fix the lock _{no}
better More notes: shopping go into supermarket much interference, leave, *ta ta*
ross 2nd ave *think of that* GOOD   resistance GO HOME I'm mad and hungry
o food in the house but LUCK   go home GOOD GIRL and then a huge STOP
n front of the butcher shop, meat cheaper and better   *big improvement.*   NO
YOU DONT GET IT
n the expensive farmer's cheese, GO OUT, GET A HARD ROLL, CREAM
UGAR   I get it they'd rather I didn't have either_{milk tues} Hear   TURN IT
)FF (the oven) SORRY says roll   Be quiet I say I'm eating breakfast   THATS
THE INTERFERENCE HAPPY YEAR TAKA *wrong recommend, feel different,*
nissed his movies hear *feel awful*   OMIT APOSTROPHE   SACRIFICE   *try*
ard   Takas advice   omit apostrophe, Elianes   writes in the present tense see
'RESENT say SEE not saw, *eliminates periods ol stupid girl*   Charlemagne's
iddress   big pink PREFER *this is terrific old girl*
thats the conclusion

I SEE A BIG APOSTROPHE

3/15   LOW INCOME

WHYS in a row behind each other *verbal vibrations* a lot
of GO TO CHURCH SEE DAVID   GO AND TEACH thought I'd like *negative*
Rinpoche GO WED   Fuck off he speaks fri sat san THAT'S A PUN APPLE PIE
a lot of wine drunk *dream* say david a lot of words CHILDREN dont explain
quor *not alright* more margin?   *tues.* no more periods *answer* its *drunk*
since Rinpoche came in town the words do a up and over and down *drunk*
reminds *who* of Big Deep MY THOUGHT pops off a big GO *Radcliffe* it's im-
portant reminds *who* this typewriter *heard* saw heard DO IT   FRI
GO SUN   *w* whatabout tonight and Sat?
NIGHT *tonight*   MEET
RHYS *grit* COMPLETE IT SAID LONG TALK WITH Luba   NONEY   mothers
slang *for* nose *think of it* BIG SURPRISE *save the space*   NONEY   *not alright*

BIG PRINT

HOLY BIBLE

HALLELUJIAH
miss charlemagne
MODERN ART   GO AWAY GO OUT MISS PROVIDE
you/why a line 're afraid DO CHARLEMAGNE CALL OMIT *not too late* STOP
TEMPTING FABLE WHY Thinking all these GO OUTs are for me run out but
PARTY *not you* SIS in the hall you wait *hear the phone* Nijole calls get back to
answer PHONE JUST IN TIME   C   she wants to check the ring on her phone, not
enough TIME *reason call Nijole*   A   CALL JASPER JOHNS *IT WASN'T*
important WHICH CANT STOP   L   cant tell what to *finish* do *so important*
basketball YOU CAN CUT IT see L call Nijole often who is *not*   *Ding a ling*
stop   TAKE A BATH on a 45 degree angle red light HESITATE so *filling* the tub
Accomplish BED in frame for Raymond's drawing 5 DOLLARS *save pennies talk*
to mother type walking by hardward store little lamp says 2:30 go in, it's 2:30 red
BUY IT NOW *tensor* but it's making you stop *me*   what it started me doing so I
buy it 3.50 *bulb*   BIRD   DO THE MUSEUM STIFF stuff   WHAT   Every-
thing seems to be *negative* five dollars more than *pronoun* CUT IT SHORT
WHYS says OUT asked about a table see 40 price 45 NO HANNAH   DUNGA-
REES pronoun's are used cost $3 *much quieter* energy   than the DUMB grey
corduroys HOW ARE YOU *free pants* LAMONTE FEEL washing

(vertical: C A L L M E)

Fri May 17

Whisper   Think of Rhys see his image large, behind you, NOT IN LOVE *you call*
Monday *penis* You call   no answer   he calls *big improvement* NO MORE
CALLS, he comes   Talk to Rhys   TAKE THE LAUNDRY   See GO TO PHIL'S
light up   You ask it *come TOUCH*   ASK WHY no ask whether you should
petticoat *see you later* *job* no you ask stoned if it meant Rhys should   *wait for me*
go to Phils, feel zap of electric current right forefinger and right temple, the *zap of*
energy is negative   IT's THE *b*OOK FIRST   DUMB   You used to think those
zaps came in on DRUNK positives DRONE because the energy came in at
acupuncture ALMEIN or nerve points DOCTOR *cheaper* where you needed
more energy QUITE A JOB *it's funny* SAY *feel the negative* so it took you years
CALM to *relate* realize the zaps were a no NO   Sometimes the lights dim slightly
when the zaps hit, *fingertips,*   INCREDIBLE YOU'RE ON   KEEP
LAUGHING   THE CURRENT BIG BILL   LUBA   a big light DUMB   4
oclock SCHEDULE   IT'S ON THE WAY   BOSTON CITY *now help you* *polo* P TOYN-
BEE   You're not TOOTS   *Make it easy* GETTING HIGHER   HURRY   You
see Satchidananda's TALK TO ME   face from the POSITIVE ad appear on this

sheet of paper   That must be a very positive force to go to the retreat, SATUR-

DAY NIGHT tomorrow he talks at Columbia   NEW YORK$^{45°}$ NOT THE

BOWERY   THIS IS THE STONED **AGE** YOU GUILTY   you still owe

them SENSITIVE dollars   YEAR ONE   NO DOPE **G** GO   BEST SAMADHI

LEV   HOTEL BILLS   EXXAGERATE   YOU'RE INNOCENT   Rhys

comes   GOT TO PHIIL's shows wonderful movies get stoned on *locks not*

always you had a deadbolt put in NOT PRIVATE$_{innocent}$ *raise energy level*   the 70's

movies, pictures big^{POPEYE} water *you love it movies preferred* BIG PHIL Music

like brain *not enough* waves or so it seems   Rhys had decided to come Thurs and

found out about 3:30 *Jewish* that he couldn't you didn't know it but around that

time saw NO MORE RHYS

SILENT TEACHER

1978

KENWARD ELMSLIE ▪ ▪ ▪ ▪ ▪ ▪ ▪ ▪ ▪ ▪ ▪
b. 1929

Born in Colorado Springs, Colorado, and educated at Harvard, Kenward Elms-
lie's first experiences as a writer were as a lyricist and librettist. Elmslie has
written librettos for six operas, three of which [*The Seagull* (1974), *Washington
Square* (1976), and *Three Sisters* (1986)] were composed by Pulitzer Prize nomi-
nee Thomas Pasatieri. His other librettos are *The Sweet Bye and Bye* (1956),
Miss Julie (1965; music by Ned Rorem), and *Lizzie Borden* (1965). He also
wrote the book and lyrics for the Broadway show *The Grass Harp* (1971), based
on the Truman Capote novel.

Elmslie credits his turn to poetry to hearing Kenneth Koch read his "History
of Jazz" at the Five Spot in 1965, accompanied by artist Larry Rivers on saxo-
phone. "My guffaw meter went bong," Elmslie says in an interview. "Kenneth
transposed the zest, the dippy angstlessness of musical comedy into poetry."[1]
Elmslie's books of poetry include *Motor Disturbance* (1971), *Circus Nerves*
(1971), *Tropicalism* (1975), and *Moving Right Along* (1979).

In the early eighties he turned his attention to creating performance works in
collaboration with visual artists Ken Tisa *(Bimbo Dirt)*, Donna Dennis *(26 Bars)*,
and Joe Brainard *(Sung Sex)*, as well as the musician Steven Taylor. The collec-
tion *26 Bars*, an abecedarium of prose poems, reflects Elmslie's characteristic
style and voice. Performed with passages spoken and sung, the poems are ver-
bally dense and antic in mood, delighting in American pop culture and language.

1. W. C. Bamberger, "An Interview with Kenward Elmslie," *New American Writing*, Nos.
8 and 9 (Fall 1991), pp. 181–182.

Feathered Dancers

Inside the lunchroom the travelling nuns wove
sleeping babies on doilies of lace.
A lovely recluse jabbered of bird lore and love:
        "Sunlight tints my face

        and warms the eggs outside
        perched on filthy columns of guilt.
        In the matted shadows where I hide,
        buzzards moult and weeds wilt."

Which reminds me of Mozambique
in that movie where blacks massacre Arabs.
The airport runway (the plane never lands, skims off) is bleak—
scarred syphilitic landscape—crater-sized scabs—

painted over with Pepsi ads—
as in my lunar Sahara dream—giant net comes out of sky,
encloses my open touring car. Joe slumps against Dad's
emergency wheel turner. Everyone's mouth-roof dry.

One interpretation. Mother hated blood!
When the duck Dad shot dripped on her leatherette lap-robe,
dark spots not unlike Georgia up-country mud,
her thumb and forefinger tightened (karma?) on my ear-lobe.

Another interpretation. Motor of my heart stalled!
I've heard truckers stick ping-pong balls up their butt
and jounce along having coast-to-coast orgasms, so-called.
Fermés, tousled jardins du Far West, I was taught—tight shut.

So you can't blame them. Take heed, turnpikes.
Wedgies float back from reefs made of jeeps: more offshore debris.
Wadded chewy depressants and elatants gum up footpaths. Remember Ike's
"Doctor-the-pump-and-away-we-jump" Aloha Speech to the Teamsters?
        "The—"

he began and the platform collapsed, tipping him onto a traffic island.
An aroused citizenry fanned out through the factories that day
to expose the Big Cheese behind the sortie. Tanned,
I set sail for the coast, down the Erie and away,

and ate a big cheese in a café by the docks,
and pictured every room I'd ever slept in:
toilets and phone-calls and oceans. Big rocks
were being loaded, just the color of my skin,

and I've been travelling ever since,
so let's go find an open glade,
like the ones in sporting prints,
(betrayed, delayed, afraid)

where we'll lie among the air-plants
in a perfect amphitheatre in a soft pink afterglow.
How those handsome birds can prance,
ah . . . unattainable tableau.

Let's scratch the ground clean,
remove all stones and trash,
I mean open dance-halls in the forest, I mean
where the earth's packed smooth and hard. Crash!

It's the Tale of the Creation. The whip cracks.
Albatrosses settle on swaying weeds.
Outside the lunchroom, tufts and air-sacs
swell to the size of fruits bursting with seeds.

1971

Japanese City

Centennial of Melville's birth this morning.
Whale balloons drift up released by priests. Whale floats parade
followed by boats of boys in sou'westers jiggled by runners
followed by aldermen in a ritual skiff propelled by "surf"—girls.
In my hotel room with its cellophane partitions (underwatery)
I phone down for ice-water, glass, tumbler, and the cubes.

Cattle for the Xmas Market fill the streets.
Black snouts—a rubby day indeed. Bump the buildings, herds.
A Mexican seamstress brings back my underthings shyly
six, seven times a day. One sweats so, lying about.
She mentions marvelous pistachio green caverns
where one canoes through cool midgy Buddha beards

where drafts of polar air sound like cicadas, where—
About the partitions. The other travellers seem—
There were beautiful hairs in the wash-basin this A.M.—
thick, and they smelled of limes
(good, that jibes with mine—ugh!—)
but mine, how perverse! Form a hoop, you there. Mine,

mine smell like old apples in a drawer. Jim the Salesman
and his cohorts are massaging my feet—a real treadmill example.
They're in lawn decor, ether machines, and nocturnal learning clasps.

And Jim? Plays cards in his shorts, moves black fish around.
Black houses, the capitol. Hotel chunks. Sky chunks. The squeeze:
green odd numbers—white air, amputations and eagles, respite.

Red even numbers—body sections, the ocean sac, the great beach.
Green even numbers—oval jewels, quicksand, the haven behind the falls.
Jim's stammer is contagious, zen smut about hatcheries in the suburbs,
how the women in the canneries came down with the "gills,"
hence bathtub love-makings, couplings in the sewers. The ice-water comes.

The room-clerk's pate shines up through the transparent floor.
Soon the sin couples will start arriving, and the one-way mirror teams
and the government professionals with their portable amulets—
shiny vinyl instruments that probe and stretch.
Much visiting back and forth. Pink blobs. Revels and surveys.
Many olive eyes'll close in a sleep of exhaustion. More ice-water!

The celebrants in metal regalia jangle and tinkle
moving past the red-roofed villas of the Generals,
past the cubicles of the nakeds and into the harbor,
past the glum stone busts of the Generals, sitting in the water.
Out they go, (Jim etc.) into the sweet emptied city, leaving behind
the red odd numbers untouched: pleasure beaches, monsoons and sun.

1971

Amazon Club

Buzz you into unisex twilight. Sun-blasted stucco, faded pistachio. Lockers pockmarked by bullet hole cadenzas from Rubber War imbroglios. Stink of stopped-up sink, mango and yam effluvia.

Smart salute. Generalissimo Lopez hands out obligatory dress code. Penis wreath of snake fang and jaguar fur (men), opossum sheath with marsupial pouch (women, teens, retirees). Warning. The Generalissimo's aversion to elongated nipples can lead to moral leper diatribe. Back alley violence. When they turn the drums up loud, you've had it.

Deposited into own sling. Surround of glittering asteroids inches away. Lunar pings. Handed armadillo shell foaming with irara-irara. Acrid burnt-wire caterpillar odor.

Terror trip. Backwards slide through song history, as corpse. Hurtle past gutteral anthems to warble in arctic cloud mass. Heightened awareness of undersurfaces, plunge through crust to the rescue, hardens so fast, stuck. Red mud phase. Amazingly laid-back slither, not at all thrust comes to devour. Wish had fruitarian chunk to pop in stranger's mouth, see lips part, tongue flick at morsel. Failing that, meat gobbet down spouse.

Life Style masked as Death Style, so outsiders leave it alone, pursue their mundane concerns:

> Hardware. Hardware in the sky. Keeps track of—not much! Phone calls spiral up out of the citizen niche, about burp her, burp her, hospital eaten-away buttocks so can't eat vines, glue on paste mix, while TV yackety-yack of jackal-eyed trend men empowered, Sunbelt condos sprawling skyward, vying for cotton candy core, cotton candy head core, wild rice cotton candy head-veil decor to maintain proper honeymoon comfort quirks, heading uptown, up to uplands where ice rangers track cloud ice for Cloud Ice Cie. Break up chunks into transportable cotton candy to wipe off the Liberty spikes for the 4th, in case of clear weather.

Melodies pouring onto the jungle foliage, down to macaws squatting in the clearing, bonfire in its shroud. Once rent open, nothing can hold back. A little nation burrowing into its myth pouch wants to be paired off, paired off in pairs, off it goes, the shroud, past the treetops, smoking embers inside, its final circle, back to the sun, orbit done.

Closing time. Revellers exit up and out onto A St.

1987

Big Bar

Built by Hank Wurlitzer, 7 ft. 8 inches, to house the first petrocommunications system, the windowless Wurlitzer Tower and its maze of Cenozoic granite message conduits passed through many unsavory hands as the city continued to sink beneath sea level. *302 lbs.*

The massive corridors above water retrogressed into a warren of Cajun sweatshops, gypsy make-out shanties, and coyote abattoirs—"shooting galleries" for loco mesa geeks. Gumbo-stained antimacassars eddied about the once swank atrium. Hank Wurlitzer, 7 ft. 8 inches, sat down in the Swiss Wishing Chair, brow furrowed, fingers drumming, and watched the roiling torrents below. *236 lbs.*

The Wurlitzer Suction Syphon, invented by the real estate conceptualist Hank Wurlitzer, 7 ft. 8 inches, revivified the Wurlitzer Tower, a mecca for the smart set of Houston and environs. *326 lbs.*

After sauntering through the Wurlitzer Jardins atop the levees, a topiary pleasure dome designed and operated by popular inventor Hank Wurlitzer, 7 ft. 8 inches, the smart set of Houston and environs never fail to toss a silver dollar into the swirling rapids below, and, after making a wish, they hurry down the ladder into the renovated Wurlitzer Tower to make it all come true at the new "in" spot, Big Bar. *400 lbs. on the nose!*

The world's biggest bartender can be found at Big Bar. He is none other than the millionaire environment enhancer, Hank Wurlitzer, 7 ft. 8 inches, who presides over the nonstop festivities at a bar 900 ft. long, made of topiary yucca, tended by his staff of highly skilled snippers and shapers. The appurtenances (including the drinks!) are scaled accordingly, and the topiary banquettes of organic cholla cactus are trimmed and buffed every hour on the hour.   *427½ lbs.*

Dreamed up by Hank Wurlitzer, 7 ft. 8 inches, famous boniface-sommelier, the Avalanche Cocktail is made with the following ingredients:

> *1 Pint of Raspberry Syrup*
> *1 Pint of Apricot Brandy*
> *1 Quart of Dry Gin*
> *1 Quart of Creme de Noyau*
> *Shake well and pour*
> *into a frosted tankard in*
> *which cracked ice, dusted*
> *lightly with confectioners'*
> *sugar, forms 90° slope.*
> *Light and serve.*

Free to any customer 7 ft. 8 inches small, during Happy Hour, bus tour groups not included.   *499 lbs.*

In Houston's Big Bar, which has expanded into every nook of the Wurlitzer Tower, the most popular cranny is the Swiss Wishing Chair, situated at the summit of a 200 sq. ft. block of Mont Blanc granite, imported by that billionaire bon vivant, Hank Wurlitzer, 7 ft. 8 inches. When the moon is full, and the flood waters are raging outside, HW waits for a momentary lull in the joie de vivre, and, elbowing his way through a mob of celebs and non-celebs alike, HW hoists himself up into his favorite chair to unwind, brow furrowed, fingers drumming, legs jiggling.   *500 lbs. on the nose!*

Every day is *A DAY IN THE ALPS* at Big Bar, the original Big Bar each and every Big Bar in Big Bar Universe is an exact multiple of. A subsidiary of HW, the giant leisure conglom in the burgeoning field of gene and steroid design, quality control is assured with Hank Wurlitzer, philanthropist savant, at the helm. Enjoy a hair of the Saint Bernard that bit and licked you (simulated), while you savor an avalanche crashing down to obliterate you (simulated). Reach for another Avalanche Cocktail, slope frosted just the way you like it, perched in total comfort and safety on your personalized yucca stool, 48 ft. in circumference, contoured to your exact measurements. Every feature of Alpine life is included at no extra cost, including shepherd laddies, lassies, and lassiladdies, accredited graduates of the Hank Wurlitzer Life Expansion System.® They are each and every one 7 ft. 8 inches, 500 lbs. on the nose, ready and willing to satisfy your every need, and that means *every* need, or you get a complimentary Avalanche. All you have to do is yodel.
1987

ED DORN ■ ■ ■ ■ ■ ■ ■ ■ ■ ■ ■ ■ ■ ■ ■ ■ ■ ■ ■

b. 1929

Born in Villa Grove, Illinois, Ed Dorn studied at the University of Illinois and Black Mountain College in North Carolina. "I think I'm rightly associated with the Black Mountain 'school,' " he has said, "not because of the way I write, but because I was there."[1]

Dorn's four-volume epic poem, *Slinger* (1968), has been described by the critic Marjorie Perloff as "one of the most ambitious and interesting long poems of our time, a truly original cowboy-and-indian saga, rendered in the most ingenious mix of scientific jargon, Structuralist terminology, junkie slang, Elizabethan sonneteering, Western dialect, and tough talk."[2]

His books include *The Newly Fallen* (1961), *From Gloucester Out* (1964), *Geography* (1965), *The North Atlantic Turbine* (1967), *Recollections of Gran Apacheria* (1974), and *Hello, La Jolla* (1978), as well as volumes of collected and selected works. From the beginning, Dorn's poetry has been both sardonic and lyrical; his recent work, included in *Abhorrences* (1990), is more caustic in its political expression.

Finding in Dorn's poetry the wit, song, and pronunciamento of the Augustan satirists, the critic Donald Wesling has written that his pervasive tone "is that of a Jonathan Swift trapped in a democracy."[3] Dorn claims not to share "the current aversion directed at the words 'ironic' and 'sarcastic.' In fact, I value those modes because they save us from the pervasively jerky habits of straightforwardness."[4] One of Dorn's titles, "The Cosmology of Finding Your Place," provides a good description of his project—that is, finding one's place in the cultural and political landscape. The American West gives Dorn the site of that quest for place.

1. David Ossman, "*The Sullen Art* Interview," in *Edward Dorn: Interviews*, Bolinas, 1980, p. 1.   2. *The New Republic*, April 24, 1976.   3. *Internal Resistances: The Poetry of Edward Dorn*, ed. Donald Wesling, Berkeley, 1985, p. 15.   4. Stephen Fredman, "Road Testing the Language," in *Edward Dorn: Interviews*, p. 98.

The Rick of Green Wood

In the woodyard were green and dry
woods fanning out, behind
                  a valley below
a pleasure for the eye to go.

Woodpile by the buzzsaw. I heard
the woodsman down in the thicket. I don't
want a rick of green wood, I told him
I want cherry or alder or something strong
and thin, or thick if dry, but I don't
want the green wood, my wife would die

Her back is slender
and the wood I get must not
bend her too much through the day.

Aye, the wood is some green
and some dry, the cherry thin of bark
cut in July.

My name is Burlingame
said the woodcutter.
My name is Dorn, I said.
I buzz on Friday if the weather cools
said Burlingame, enough of names.

Out of the thicket my daughter was walking
singing—
backtracking the horse hoof
gone in earlier this morning, the woodcutter's horse
pulling the alder, the fir, the hemlock
above the valley
in the november
air, in the world, that was getting colder
as we stood there in the woodyard talking
pleasantly, of the green wood and the dry.

1956

Geranium

I know that peace is soon coming, and love of common object,
and of woman and all the natural things I groom, in my mind, of
faint rememberable patterns, the great geography of my lunacy.

I go on my way frowning at novelty, wishing I were closer to home
than I am. And this is the last bus stop before Burlington,
that pea-center, which is my home, but not the home of my mind.
That asylum I carry in my insane squint, where beyond
the window a curious woman in the station door
has a red bandana on her head, and tinkling things hand themselves
to the wind that gathers about her skirts. In the rich manner of her kind
she waits for the bus to stop. Lo, a handsome woman.

Now, my sense decays, she is the flat regularity, the brick
of the station wall, is the red Geranium of my last Washington stop.
Is my object no shoes brought from india
can make exotic, nor hardly be made antic would she astride
a motorcycle (forsake materials and we shall survive together)
nor be purchased by the lust of schedule.

No,

on her feet therefore, are the silences of nothing. And leather
leggings adorn her limbs, on her arms are the garlands of ferns

come from a raining raining forest and dripping lapidary's dust.
She is a common thief of fauna and locale (in her eyes
are the small sticks of slender land-bridges) a porter
standing near would carry her bundle, which is scarlet too,

as a geranium and cherishable common that I worship and that I sing
ploddingly, and out of tune as she, were she less the lapwing
as she my pale sojourner, is.

1961

From Gloucester Out

It has all
come back today.
That memory for me is nothing
there ever was,
         That man

so long,
when stretched out
and so bold
        on his ground
and so much
lonely anywhere.

But never to forget
        that moment

when we came out of the tavern
and wandered through the carnival.
They were playing
the washington post march
but I mistook it for manhattan beach
for all around were the colored lights
of delirium
        to the left the boats
of Italians
and ahead of us, past the shoulders
of St. Peter the magician of those fishermen

the bay
stood, and immediately in it the silent
inclined pole where tomorrow the young men
of this colony
so dangerous on the street
will fall harmlessly
into the water.

They are not the solid
but are the solidly built
citizens, and they are about us
as we walk across
                    the square
with their black provocative
women
slender, like whips of
sex in the sousa filled night.

Where edged
by that man in the music
of a transplanted time and
enough of drunkenness
to make you senseless of all
but virtue
                    (there is never
no, there is never a small complaint)
(that all things shit poverty,
and Life, one wars on with
many embraces) oh it was a time that was perfect
but for my own hesitating
to know all I had not known.
Pure existence, even in the crowds
I love
will never be possible for me

even with the men I love
                            This is
the guilt
that kills me
                    My adulterated presence

but please believe with all men
I love to be

    •

That memory
of how he lay out
on the floor in his great length
and when morning came,
late,
we lingered
in the vastest of all cities
in this hemisphere
                        and all other movement
stopped, nowhere
else was there a stirring known to us

yet that morning I stood
by the window up 3 levels
and watched a game
of stick ball, thinking of going away,
and wondering what would befall that man
when he returned to his territory.
The street as you could guess
was thick with their running
and cars,
themselves, paid that activity
such respect I thought a ritual
in the truest sense,
where all time and all motion
part around the space of men
in that act
as does a river flow past
the large rock.

•

And he slept.
in the next room, waiting
in an outward slumber
                                        for the time

we climbed into the car, accepting all things
from love, the currency of which is
parting, and glancing.

Then went
out of that city to jersey
where instantly we could not find our way
and the maze of the outlands west
starts that quick
where you may touch
your finger to liberty
and look so short a space
to the columnar bust
of New York
and know those people exist
as a speck in your own lonely heart
who will shortly depart,
taking a conveyance for the
radial stretches
past girls on corners
past drugstores, tired hesitant
creatures who I also love
in all their alienation were it not so
past all equipment of country side

to temporary homes
where the wash of sea and other
populations come
once more to whisper only one thing
for all people: a late and far-away
night yearning for
and when he gets there
I want him to stay away
from the taverns of familiarity
I want him to walk by the seashore alone
in all height
which is nothing more than
a mountain. Or the hailing of a mast
with big bright eyes.

So rushing,
        all the senses
come to him
as a swarm of golden bees
and their sting is the power
he uses as parts of
the oldest brain. He hears
the delicate thrush
of the water attacking
He hears the cries, falling gulls
and watches silently the gesture of grey
bygone people. He hears their cries
and messages, he never

ignores any sound.
As they come to him he places them
puts clothes upon them
and gives them their place
in their new explanation, there is never
a lost time, nor any inhabitant
of that time to go split by prisms or unplaced
and unattended,
                that you may believe

is the breath he gives
the great already occurred and nightly beginning world.
So with the populace of his mind
you think his nights? are not
lonely. My God. Of his
loves, you know nothing and of his
false beginning
you can know nothing,
               but this thing to be marked
again

only

he who worships the gods with his strictness
can be of their company
the cat and the animals, the bird he took
from the radiator
of my car saying it had died
a natural death, rarely seen in a bird.

To play, as areal particulars can out of the span
of Man, and of all, this man
does not
      he, does, he
  walks
      by the sea
in my memory

and sees all things and to him
are presented at night
the whispers of the most flung shores
from Gloucester out

                                     1964

An Idle Visitation

The cautious Gunslinger
of impeccable personal smoothness
and slender leather encased hands
folded casually
to make his knock,
    will show you his map.
There is your domain.
Is it the domicile it looks to be
or simply a retinal block
of seats in, yes of course
he will supply the phrase
the theater of impatience.

        If it is all you have,
the footstep in the flat above, in a foreign land
or any shimmer the city
sends you
the prompt sounds
of a metropolitan nearness
     he doesn't have to unroll the map of love.
The knock responds
to its own smile, where

I ask him is my heart
not this pump
artificial already and duty bound
he says, touching me
with his leathern finger
as the queen of hearts burns
from his gauntlet into my eyes.

Globes of fire
he says there will be.
This is for your sadly missing heart
or when two persons meet
it is the grove of Gethsemane
no matter where they are
it is the girl you left
in Juarez, the blank
political days press her now
in the narrow alleys
or in the confines of the river town
her dress is torn
by the misadventure of
        her gothic search
by omission behind carpentered doors
    the mission
bells are ringing in Kansas
Have you left something out?

Negative, says my Gunslinger,
no *thing* is omitted.

I held the reins of his horse
while he went off into the desert
to pee. *Yes,* he sd
when he returned, that's better.
How long, he asked
have you been in this territory.
Four years I sd. Four years.
Then you will no doubt know where we can have
a cold drink before sunset and then a bed
will be my desire if you can find one
for me, I have no wish to continue
my debate with men,
my mare lathers with tedium
her hooves are dry
Look they are covered with the alkali
of the enormous space
between here and formerly.
Need I repeat, we have come
without sleep from Nuevo Laredo

And why do you have a female horse
Gunslinger? I asked. Don't move
he replied
the sun rests deliberately
on the rim of the sierra.

And where will you now I asked.
Five days northeast of here
depending of course on whether one's horse
is of iron or flesh
there is a city called Boston
and in that city there is a hotel
whose second floor has been let
to an inscrutable Texan named Hughes
Howard? I asked
The very same.

And what do you mean by inscrutable,
        oh Gunslinger?
I mean to say that he
has not been seen since 1832.
But when you have found him my Gunslinger
what will you do, oh what will you do?
You would not know
that the souls of old Texans
are in jeopardy in a way not common
to other men, young man.

You would not know
of the long plains night
where they carry on
and arrange their genetic duels
with men of other states—
so there is a longhorn bull half mad
half deity
who awaits an account from me
back of the sun you nearly disturbed
just then. Here hold my mare
I must visit the cactus once more
and then, we'll have that drink.

                                          1967

HARRY MATHEWS ■ ■ ■ ■ ■ ■ ■ ■ ■ ■ ■ ■ ■ ■ ■

b. 1930

Born in New York City, the poet and novelist Harry Mathews spends most of his time in Paris, where he has long been associated with the Ouvroir de littérature potentielle (Oulipo), a group of experimentalists that included Raymond Queneau and Mathews's close friend novelist Georges Perec. It is typical of Oulipo procedure that Perec's novel *La Disparition* was written without the use of the letter *e*. Queneau's *Exercises in Style* retells, in 99 different forms and styles, the same unexceptional tale of a man being jostled on a bus.

Like the eccentric French novelist Raymond Roussel, author of *Locus Solus* and an important precursor to surrealism, Mathews's writings are inspired by verbal games and the use of secret formulas. In *Selected Declarations of Dependence* (1977), he changes the words in common proverbs—for instance, "too many words spoil the fool," and builds an entire text from repetitions and rearrangements of this "proverb." Mathews is associated with the New York School poets, especially John Ashbery and Kenneth Koch, but is also admired by the language poets for his constructionist approach to composition, favoring how a work is made over what it attempts to express.

His novels include *The Conversions* (1962), *Tlooth* (1966), *The Sinking of the Odradek Stadium* (1975), and *Cigarettes* (1987). *Twenty Lines a Day* (1988), inspired by the novelist Stendhal's statement, "Twenty lines a day, genius or not," consists of prose passages of at least twenty lines written on a daily basis. His poetry is collected in *Armenian Papers: Poems, 1954–1984* (1987).

The Sad Birds

High autumn days
Bring the mixed blessings
Of a sultry afternoon, agitating
Flies half-dead against the streaked
Windows—my one window,
Where I observe the birds of Rome.

The bright abjection of October
Concentrates sorrow while it expands
The confines of remembrance—she never
Spoke of birds, and now
Swifts, aerial and sociable,
Zipping soundlessly around corners,

Suggest that the arriving bus
Or an onset of sharp heels
Anticipate . . . The flies are real,
And my feelings quiver in the brightness
Like stonechats on shining wires
(Their feet round a mournful voice).

I will not leave my window.
The telephone, disconnected, is six
Feet away. Her voice
Flowed through the feet of bee-eaters
And buntings, indifferent guardians
Of morse and final reassurances;

And the door is locked and the walls
Immune, but within me access:
In autumn, succulence of wisteria;
In solitude, penetration; inland,
Dismal dunes and the brutal
"Hark" of the cream-colored courser.

What prompts the invisible finger
That prods my belly and foils
My will? Through the remembered
"Wait . . . wait . . ." (a woodpecker
In the chestnut grove) sounds
The worn answer of improbability.

The passive cannot laugh alone,
Or think, or tell beams
From butterflies—the last wings
Waver at the pane. I listen for
The bittern's crepuscular "woomp"
From the far marshes, or "ork,"

Passive, hoping this visitation
Will pass; beleaguered with apathy
While the streaky glass outshines
The city beyond. Yoghurt—
My feelings are more like chiffchaffs
Jigging, not this morose

Futility, can unnatural twilight
Invest the thrilling sensations
Of childhood with such significant boredom
And reinvent what made me suffer
In the first place? Days of paralysis,
Then the nightjar churrs: forlorn.

Signorina please come in
But don't dare to disturb me
Or force me to create myself
And take my thin life,
For what would "she" say if she found me
Crackling like a horde of nutcrackers?

It is the instant recollection of her five
Senses that makes my prison
Real. I do not want to go
Out. I do not want to die.
The roding woodcock's "Ort
Ort" gently lures me to

Forget, but I cannot forget,
Dawns blister me with hopes
But footsteps and motors wane
And at night, from the sewage farms,
The water rail's decrescendo returns
My ridiculous anguish. I have courted

Rest, but I cannot rest,
My faith is yearlong like the dipper's
That unmoved from its stone still
Bobs over the stream slowed
Or frozen. By the migration and silence
Of smews was I forewarned:

Follow, but I cannot follow
For she did not leave—hers
Was motionless cession of Dora
To pillows of junk. Sheaves
Were golden, the azure-winged magpie
Complained in the fork of a pine,

In the sad and wordly realm
Splendors of song and vine
Accumulate their mortal riches:
Let me only watch their cycle
(The distant passage of mergansers)
And record the squeal of the peregrine.

I must open the window, to a new
Haze of gilded webs
In which she shimmers allusively,
Who never was, who might never
Have been, nor ever have provoked
The raven's short disclaimer.

1974

Histoire

Tina and Seth met in the midst of an overcrowded militarism.
"Like a drink?" he asked her. "They make great Alexanders over at the
Marxism-Leninism."

She agreed. They shared cocktails. They behaved cautiously, as in a
    period of pre-fascism.
Afterwards he suggested dinner at a restaurant renowned for its Maoism.
"O.K.," she said, but first she had to phone a friend about her ailing
    Afghan, whose name was Racism.
Then she followed Seth across town past twilit alleys of sexism.

The waiter brought menus and announced the day's specials. He treated
    them with condescending sexism,
So they had another drink. Tina started her meal with a dish of
    militarism,
While Seth, who was hungrier, had a half portion of stuffed baked
    racism.
Their main dishes were roast duck for Seth, and for Tina broiled
    Marxism-Leninism.
Tina had pecan pie à la for dessert, Seth a compote of stewed Maoism.
They lingered. Seth proposed a liqueur. They rejected sambuca and
    agreed on fascism.

During the meal, Seth took the initiative. He inquired into Tina's
    fascism,
About which she was reserved, not out of reticence but because Seth's
    sexism
Had aroused in her a desire she felt she should hide—as though her
    Maoism
Would willy-nilly betray her feelings for him. She was right. Even her
    deliberate militarism
Couldn't keep Seth from realizing that his attraction was reciprocated.
    His own Marxism-Leninism
Became manifest, in a compulsive way that piled the Ossa of confusion
    on the Peleion of racism.

Next, what? Food finished, drinks drunk, bills paid—what racism
Might not swamp their yearning in an even greater confusion of fascism?
But women are wiser than words. Tina rested her hand on his thigh and,
    a-twinkle with Marxism-Leninism,
Asked him, "My place?" Clarity at once abounded under the flood-lights
    of sexism,
They rose from the table, strode out, and he with the impetuousness of
    young militarism
Hailed a cab to transport them to her lair, heaven-haven of Maoism.

In the taxi he soon kissed her. She let him unbutton her Maoism
And stroke her resilient skin, which was quivering with shudders of
    racism.
When beneath her jeans he sensed the superior Lycra of her militarism,
His longing almost strangled him. Her little tongue was as potent as
    fascism
In its elusive certainty. He felt like then and there tearing off her sexism,

But he reminded himself: "Pleasure lies in patience, not in the greedy
    violence of Marxism-Leninism."

Once home, she took over. She created a hungering aura of Marxism-
    Leninism
As she slowly undressed him where he sat on her overstuffed art-deco
    Maoism,
Making him keep still, so that she could indulge in caresses, in sexism,
In the pursuit of knowing him. He groaned under the exactness of her
    racism
—Fingertip sliding up his nape, nails incising his soles, teeth nibbling his
    fascism.
At last she guided him to bed, and they lay down on a patchwork of Old
    American militarism.

Biting his lips, he plunged his militarism into the popular context of her
    Marxism-Leninism,
Easing one thumb into her fascism, with his free hand coddling the tip of
    her Maoism,
Until, gasping with appreciative racism, both together sink into the
    revealed glory of sexism.

1982

GREGORY CORSO   ■ ■ ■ ■ ■ ■ ■ ■ ■ ■ ■ ■
b. 1930

Gregory Corso was born on Manhattan's Bleecker Street to Italian immigrant
parents. His mother died when he was a child, and his father moved back to
Italy, leaving him in the care of an orphanage and four foster homes. When
Corso was twelve, his father remarried and took custody of him; however, he
ran away again and wound up in the Tombs, a New York prison, for stealing a
radio in a boys' home. At age thirteen, he spent time in the children's ward at
New York's Bellevue Hospital, where he was given a series of mental tests.
Paradoxically, it was while serving a prison sentence for theft at age seventeen
that Corso was introduced to literature through books—such as *The Brothers
Karamazov* and *The Red and the Black*—given him by an elderly inmate who
wished to further Corso's education.[1] Corso began writing poems in prison.

    Although Corso had only a sixth-grade education, he left prison in 1950 "well
read and in love with Chatterton, Marlowe, and Shelley."[2] In the same year, he
met Allen Ginsberg, who further guided his education as a poet. In 1954, he
went to Cambridge, Massachusetts, at the invitation of Harvard and Radcliffe
students who later gathered the money for publishing his first book, *The Vestal
Lady on Brattle* (1955).[3]

    Corso's travels with Ginsberg to San Francisco and Mexico led to the poems in
Gasoline (1958). Later collections include *The Happy Birthday of Death* (1960),
Long Live Man (1962), *Elegiac Feelings American* (1970), *Herald of the Au-
tochthonic Spirit* (1981), and *Mindfield: New and Selected Poems* (1989). His
poem "Marriage," with its exuberant voice, bohemian counsel, and surrealist
figures such as "penguin dust," captures much of the appeal of the Beat aes-

thetic. Allen Ginsberg has called Corso a "divine Poet Maudit, rascal poet Villonesque and Rimbaudian."[4]

Corso lives in New York City.

1. Gregory Corso, *The New American Poetry*, New York, 1960, p. 429.   2. The same, p. 430.   3. The same.   4. "On Corso's Virtues," in Gregory Corso's *Mindfield: New and Selected Poems*, New York, 1989, p. xv.

The Mad Yak

I am watching them churn the last milk
    they'll ever get from me.
They are waiting for me to die;
They want to make buttons out of my bones.
Where are my sisters and brothers?
That tall monk there, loading my uncle,
    he has a new cap.
And that idiot student of his—
    I never saw that muffler before.
Poor uncle, he lets them load him.
How sad he is, how tired!
I wonder what they'll do with his bones?
And that beautiful tail!
How many shoelaces will they make of that!

1958

Dream of a Baseball Star

I dreamed Ted Williams
leaning at night
against the Eiffel Tower, weeping.

He was in uniform
and his bat lay at his feet
—knotted and twiggy.

'Randall Jarrell says you're a poet!' I cried.
'So do I! I say you're a poet!'

He picked up his bat with blown hands;
stood there astraddle as he would in the batter's box,
and laughed! flinging his schoolboy wrath
toward some invisible pitcher's mound
—waiting the pitch all the way from heaven.

It came; hundreds came! all afire!
He swung and swung and swung and connected not one

sinker curve hook or right-down-the-middle.
A hundred strikes!
The umpire dressed in strange attire
thundered his judgement: YOU'RE OUT!
And the phantom crowd's horrific boo
dispersed the gargoyles from Notre Dame.

And I screamed in my dream:
God! throw thy merciful pitch!
Herald the crack of bats!
Hooray the sharp liner to left!
Yea the double, the triple!
Hosannah the home run!

1960

I Held a Shelley Manuscript

written in Houghton Library, Harvard

My hands did numb to beauty
as they reached into Death and tightened!

O sovereign was my touch
upon the tan-ink's fragile page!

Quickly, my eyes moved quickly,
sought for smell for dust for lace
for dry hair!

I would have taken the page
breathing in the crime!
For no evidence have I wrung from dreams—
yet what triumph is there in private credence?

Often, in some steep ancestral book,
when I find myself entangled with leopard-apples
and torched-mushrooms,
my cypressean skein outreaches the recorded age
and I, as though tipping a pitcher of milk,
pour secrecy upon the dying page.

1960

Marriage

Should I get married? Should I be good?
Astound the girl next door with my velvet suit and faustus hood?
Don't take her to movies but to cemeteries

tell all about werewolf bathtubs and forked clarinets
then desire her and kiss her and all the preliminaries
and she going just so far and I understanding why
not getting angry saying You must feel! It's beautiful to feel!
Instead take her in my arms lean against an old crooked tombstone
and woo her the entire night the constellations in the sky—

When she introduces me to her parents
back straightened, hair finally combed, strangled by a tie,
should I sit knees together on their 3rd degree sofa
and not ask Where's the bathroom?
How else to feel other than I am,
often thinking Flash Gordon soap—
O how terrible it must be for a young man
seated before a family and the family thinking
We never saw him before! He wants our Mary Lou!
After tea and homemade cookies they ask What do you do for a
                                                     living?

Should I tell them: Would they like me then?
Say All right get married, we're losing a daughter
but we're gaining a son—
And should I then ask Where's the bathroom?

O God, and the wedding! All her family and her friends
and only a handful of mine all scroungy and bearded
just wait to get at the drinks and food—
And the priest! he looking at me as if I masturbated
asking me Do you take this woman for your lawful wedded wife?
And I trembling what to say say Pie Glue!
I kiss the bride all those corny men slapping me on the back
She's all yours, boy! Ha-ha-ha!
And in their eyes you could see some obscene honeymoon going
                                                     on—

Then all that absurd rice and clanky cans and shoes
Niagara Falls! Hordes of us! Husbands! Wives! Flowers!
                                                     Chocolates!

All streaming into cozy hotels
All going to do the same thing tonight
The indifferent clerk he knowing what was going to happen
The lobby zombies they knowing what
The whistling elevator man he knowing
The winking bellboy knowing
Everybody knowing! I'd be almost inclined not to do anything!
Stay up all night! Stare that hotel clerk in the eye!
Screaming: I deny honeymoon! I deny honeymoon!
running rampant into those almost climactic suites
yelling Radio belly! Cat shovel!

O I'd live in Niagara forever! in a dark cave beneath the Falls
I'd sit there the Mad Honeymooner
devising ways to break marriages, a scourge of bigamy
a saint of divorce—

But I should get married I should be good
How nice it'd be to come home to her
and sit by the fireplace and she in the kitchen
aproned young and lovely wanting my baby
and so happy about me she burns the roast beef
and comes crying to me and I get up from my big papa chair
saying Christmas teeth! Radiant brains! Apple deaf!
God what a husband I'd make! Yes, I should get married!
So much to do! like sneaking into Mr Jones' house late at night
and cover his golf clubs with 1920 Norwegian books
Like hanging a picture of Rimbaud on the lawnmower
like pasting Tannu Tuva postage stamps all over the picket fence
like when Mrs Kindhead comes to collect for the Community Chest
grab her and tell her There are unfavorable omens in the sky!
And when the mayor comes to get my vote tell him
When are you going to stop people killing whales!
And when the milkman comes leave him a note in the bottle
Penguin dust, bring me penguin dust, I want penguin dust—

Yet if I should get married and it's Connecticut and snow
and she gives birth to a child and I am sleepless, worn,
up for nights, head bowed against a quiet window, the past behind
                                                                                              me,

finding myself in the most common of situations a trembling man
knowledged with responsibility not twig-smear nor Roman coin
                                                                                    soup—

O what would that be like!
Surely I'd give it for a nipple a rubber Tacitus
For a rattle a bag of broken Bach records
Tack Della Francesca all over its crib
Sew the Greek alphabet on its bib
And build for its playpen a roofless Parthenon

No, I doubt I'd be that kind of father
not rural not snow no quiet window
but hot smelly tight New York City
seven flights up, roaches and rats in the walls
a fat Reichian wife screeching over potatoes Get a job!
And five nose running brats in love with Batman
And the neighbors all toothless and dry haired
like those hag masses of the 18th century
all wanting to come in and watch TV

The landlord wants his rent
Grocery store Blue Cross Gas & Electric Knights of Columbus
Impossible to lie back and dream Telephone snow, ghost parking—
No! I should not get married I should never get married!
But—imagine If I were married to a beautiful sophisticated woman
tall and pale wearing an elegant black dress and long black gloves
holding a cigarette holder in one hand and a highball in the other
and we lived high up in a penthouse with a huge window
from which we could see all of New York and ever farther on
                                            clearer days
No, can't imagine myself married to that pleasant prison dream—

O but what about love? I forget love
not that I am incapable of love
it's just that I see love as odd as wearing shoes—
I never wanted to marry a girl who was like my mother
And Ingrid Bergman was always impossible
And there's maybe a girl now but she's already married
And I don't like men and—
but there's got to be somebody!
Because what if I'm 60 years old and not married,
all alone in a furnished room with pee stains on my underwear
and everybody else is married! All the universe married but me!

Ah, yet well I know that were a woman possible as I am possible
then marriage would be possible—
Like SHE in her lonely alien gaud waiting her Egyptian lover
so I wait—bereft of 2,000 years and the bath of life.
                                            1960

Love Poem for Three for Kaye & Me

—and whomever it may come to be

    I'll dress you
    in anything anytime anywhere
    with damask spins of raiment
    and fillets of vair

    and undress you
    your regnant adornments
    passionately renting it to shreds
    leaving you naked in blacken air
    torc'd with golden Assisi's

    then have you wear
    for chastity's sake
    clanky underwear

In daylight walk
a gentleman by your side
I'll be
yet come nightlight
a beastie in me you'll see
not the pigkind rolling in mud
. . . you'll know, my dear sweet wicce.
what kind
when your openings take
my thiefy wand of blood

Ah . . . then we'll pillow talk
the night away
'pon such things
as never left
or came to stay
O sweet sack
where our hearts
submerged
breathes

the continuum
by thy behest
I bequeathed—

1985

GARY SNYDER ▪ ▪ ▪ ▪ ▪ ▪ ▪ ▪ ▪ ▪ ▪ ▪ ▪ ▪

b. 1930

Born in San Francisco and educated at Reed College in Oregon, Gary Snyder
was attracted as a young poet to the poetry of Carl Sandburg, D. H. Lawrence,
Walt Whitman, and William Carlos Williams, poets who share his own romantic
and democratic views; he also admired the more conservative T. S. Eliot as an
"elegant ritualist of key Occidental myth-symbols."[1] Snyder was equally in-
fluenced by Chinese poetry of the T'ang Dynasty, translations of Native Ameri-
can song and myth, especially those from the Haida and Kwakiutl traditions,
and Japanese poetry and culture. A Zen Buddhist, he associates his daily prac-
tice of zazen, or meditation, with the disciplined freedom of poetry, both of
which require the individual to "go into *original mind.*"[2] A poet does not express
his or her self, but rather "*all* of our selves."[3] "Breath," Snyder writes, "is the
outer world coming into one's body. With pulse—the two always harmonizing—
the source of our inward sense of rhythm."[4]

A leading poet of the San Francisco Renaissance, Snyder is identified with the
Beat poets; unlike many of the Beats, however, he rarely deals in urban sub-
jects. "My political position," he has said, "is to be a spokesman for wild na-
ture."[5] Committed to the politics of ecology, he prefers the elemental creative
force that predates human civilization to the empty sophistications of Eurocen-
tric culture. In poetry, Snyder seeks continuity with the "paleolithic" through

the figure of the "shaman-dancer-poet," who sees beyond the illusions of class structure and modern technology. Snyder's shaman is the source of an expressly *spoken* poetry, for it is through speech, or "mother tongue," that poetry achieves its "gleaming daggers and glittering nets of language."[6] For Snyder, then, the poetry of nonliterate cultures has more to offer than formal literature, a view that has proved prophetic of the rise of performance and related oral poetries.

His books include *Riprap* (1959), *Back Country* (1968), the Pulitzer Prize–winning *Turtle Island* (1974), *Myths and Texts* (1978), *Axe Handles* (1983), and *Left Out in the Rain: New Poems 1947–1985* (1986). He has also published two collections of prose, *Earth House Hold* (1969) and *The Real Work: Interviews & Talks, 1964–1979* (1980).

1. "The Real Work," in *The Real Work: Interviews & Talks, 1964–1979,* New York, 1980, p. 57.   2. The same, p. 65.   3. The same.   4. "Poetry and the Primitive: Notes on Poetry as an Ecological Survival Technique," in *Earth House Hold,* New York, 1969, p. 123.   5. "Knots in the Grain," in *The Real Work,* p. 49.   6. "Poetry and the Primitive," p. 118.

Riprap

Lay down these words
Before your mind like rocks.
    placed solid, by hands
In choice of place, set
Before the body of the mind
    in space and time:
Solidity of bark, leaf, or wall
    riprap of things:
Cobble of milky way,
    straying planets,
These poems, people,
    lost ponies with
Dragging saddles—
    and rocky sure-foot trails.
The worlds like an endless
    four-dimensional
Game of *Go*.
    ants and pebbles
In the thin loam, each rock a word
    a creek-washed stone
Granite: ingrained
    with torment of fire and weight
Crystal and sediment linked hot
    all change, in thoughts,
As well as things.

                1959

The Bath

Washing Kai in the sauna,
The kerosene lantern set on a box
    outside the ground-level window,
Lights up the edge of the iron stove and the
    washtub down on the slab
Steaming air and crackle of waterdrops
    brushed by on the pile of rocks on top
He stands in warm water
Soap all over the smooth of his thigh and stomach
    "Gary don't soap my hair!"
    —his eye-sting fear—
    the soapy hand feeling
    through and around the globes and curves of his body
    up in the crotch,
And washing-tickling out the scrotum, little anus,
    his penis curving up and getting hard
    as I pull back skin and try to wash it
Laughing and jumping, flinging arms around,
    I squat all naked too,
                  is this our body?

Sweating and panting in the stove-steam hot-stone
    cedar-planking wooden bucket water-splashing
    kerosene lantern-flicker wind-in-the-pines-out
    sierra forest ridges night—
Masa comes in, letting fresh cool air
    sweep down from the door
    a deep sweet breath
And she tips him over gripping neatly, one knee down
    her hair falling hiding one whole side of
    shoulder, breast, and belly,
Washes deftly Kai's head-hair
    as he gets mad and yells—
The body of my lady, the winding valley spine,
    the space between the thighs I reach through,
    cup her curving vulva arch and hold it from behind,
    a soapy tickle   a hand of grail
The gates of Awe
That open back a turning double-mirror world of
    wombs in wombs, in rings,
    that start in music,
                  is this our body?

The hidden place of seed
The veins net flow across the ribs, that gathers
    milk and peaks up in a nipple—fits
    our mouth—

The sucking milk from this our body sends through
    jolts of light; the son, the father,
      sharing mother's joy
That brings a softness to the flower of the awesome
    open curling lotus gate I cup and kiss
As Kai laughs at his mother's breast he now is weaned
    from, we
      wash each other,
                this our body

Kai's little scrotum up close to his groin,
    the seed still tucked away, that moved from us to him
In flows that lifted with the same joys forces
    as his nursing Masa later,
      playing with her breast,
Or me within her,
Or him emerging,
                this is our body:

Clean, and rinsed, and sweating more, we stretch
    out on the redwood benches hearts all beating
Quiet to the simmer of the stove,
    the scent of cedar
And then turn over,
    murmuring gossip of the grasses,
      talking firewood,
Wondering how Gen's napping, how to bring him in
    soon wash him too—
These boys who love their mother
    who loves men, who passes on
    her sons to other women;

The cloud across the sky. The windy pines.
    the trickle gurgle in the swampy meadow

    this is our body.

Fire inside and boiling water on the stove
We sigh and slide ourselves down from the benches
    wrap the babies, step outside,

black night & all the stars.

Pour cold water on the back and thighs
Go in the house—stand steaming by the center fire
Kai scampers on the sheepskin
Gen standing hanging on and shouting,

"Bao! bao! bao! bao! bao!"

This is our body. Drawn up crosslegged by the flames
    drinking icy water
    hugging babies, kissing bellies,

Laughing on the Great Earth

Come out from the bath.

                        1974

Avocado

The Dharma is like an Avocado!
Some parts so ripe you can't believe it,
But it's good.
And other places hard and green
Without much flavor,
Pleasing those who like their eggs well-cooked.

And the skin is thin,
The great big round seed
In the middle,
Is your own Original Nature—
Pure and smooth,
Almost nobody ever splits it open
Or ever tries to see
If it will grow.

Hard and slippery,
It looks like
You should plant it—but then
It shoots out thru the
            fingers—
gets away.

                        1974

As for Poets

As for poets
The Earth Poets
Who write small poems,
Need help from no man.

The Air Poets
Play out the swiftest gales
And sometimes loll in the eddies.
Poem after poem,
Curling back on the same thrust.

At fifty below
Fuel oil won't flow
And propane stays in the tank.
Fire Poets
Burn at absolute zero
Fossil love pumped back up.

The first
Water Poet
Stayed down six years.
He was covered with seaweed.
The life in his poem
Left millions of tiny
Different tracks
Criss-crossing through the mud.

With the Sun and Moon
In his belly,
The Space Poet
Sleeps.
No end to the sky—
But his poems,
Like wild geese,
Fly off the edge.

A Mind Poet
Stays in the house.
The house is empty
And it has no walls.
The poem
Is seen from all sides,
Everywhere,
At once.

1974

Axe Handles

One afternoon the last week in April
Showing Kai how to throw a hatchet
One-half turn and it sticks in a stump.
He recalls the hatchet-head
Without a handle, in the shop
And go gets it, and wants it for his own.
A broken-off axe handle behind the door
Is long enough for a hatchet,
We cut it to length and take it
With the hatchet head
And working hatchet, to the wood block.
There I begin to shape the old handle

With the hatchet, and the phrase
First learned from Ezra Pound
Rings in my ears!
"When making an axe handle
            the pattern is not far off."
And I say this to Kai
"Look: We'll shape the handle
By checking the handle
Of the axe we cut with—"
And he sees. And I hear it again:
It's in Lu Ji's *Wên Fu*, fourth century
A.D. "Essay on Literature"—in the
Preface: "In making the handle
Of an axe
By cutting wood with an axe
The model is indeed near at hand."
My teacher Shih-hsiang Chen
Translated that and taught it years ago
And I see: Pound was an axe,
Chen was an axe, I am an axe
And my son a handle, soon
To be shaping again, model
And tool, craft of culture,
How we go on.

                                    1983

Right in the Trail

Here it is, near the house,
A **big** pile, fat scats,
Studded with those deep red
Smooth-skinned manzanita berries,
Such a pile! Such droppings,
Awesome. And I saw how
The young girl in the story,
Had good cause to comment
On the bearscats she found while
Picking blueberries with her friends.
She laughed at them
Or maybe **with** them, jumped over them
(Bad luck!), and is reported
To have said "wide anus!"
To amuse or annoy the Big Brown Ones
Who are listening, of course.

They say the ladies
Have always gone berrying

And they all join together
To go out for the herring spawn,
Or to clean green salmon.
And that big set of lessons
On what bears really want,
Was brought back by the girl
Who made those comments:
She was taken on a year-long excursion
Back up in the mountains,
Through the tangled deadfalls,
Down into the den.
She had some pretty children by a
Young and handsome Bear.

Now I'm on the dirt
Looking at these scats
And I want to cry not knowing why
At the honor and the humor
Of coming on this sign
That is not found in books
Or transmitted in letters,
And is for women just as much as men,
A shining message for all species,
A glimpse at the Trace
of the Great One's passing,
With a peek into her whole wild system—
And what was going on last week,
(Mostly still manzanita)—

Dear Bear: do stay around. Be good.
And though I know
It won't help to say this,

Chew your food.

Kitkitdizze X.88

JEROME ROTHENBERG ▪ ▪ ▪ ▪ ▪ ▪ ▪ ▪ ▪ ▪ ▪
b. 1931

"Teach courses with a kettle & a drum," Jerome Rothenberg writes in "An Academic Proposal" (1972); like Allen Ginsberg and Gary Snyder, Rothenberg calls for a shamanistic poetry where primitive song takes precedence over the received forms of English letters. "First teach them how to sing."[1] In the preface to his anthology of Native American poetry, *Technicians of the Sacred* (1968), Rothenberg writes, "There are no half-formed languages, no underdeveloped or inferior languages. . . . The language of snow among the Eskimo is awesome.

The aspect system of Hopi verbs can, by a flick of the tongue, make the most subtle kinds of distinction between different types of motion."[2]

Founder of the discipline of ethnopoetics, in which the ethnic particularity of a poetry is emphasized, Rothenberg has edited the anthologies *Shaking the Pumpkin* (1972), *A Big Jewish Book* (1978), and *Symposium of the Whole: An Ethnopoetics Reader* (1981), as well as the journals *Alcheringa* and *New Wilderness Letter*. Rothenberg has translated poetry from German, Aztec, Navajo, Hebrew, and Seneca, and often performs the "Horse-Songs" of Navajo poet Frank Mitchell as part of his own poetry readings. These songs have "nonsense" elements resembling scatting in jazz that are phonemically mirrored from the original Navajo; in this respect they are reminiscent of the Dada "sound poems" of Hugo Ball, a wordless poetry designed to obliterate traditional meaning, and of aspects of the kabbala.

Rothenberg's interest in Native American poetry, Dada, and his ethnic heritage as a Polish Jew come together in his classic poem "Cokboy," a work that reflects many of the influences of the postwar period, from the declaratory comedy of the Beats to the search for a figure of contemporary myth as seen in Ed Dorn's *Slinger*.

Rothenberg is also an important figure of "deep-image" poetry. Influenced by the work of Spanish poet Federico García Lorca, the deep image links the visual character of poetry with a psychology of depth and resonance. Some of the principles of the deep image are set forth in a letter to Robert Creeley of November 14, 1960:

> The poem is the record of a movement from perception to vision.
> Poetic form is the pattern of that movement through space and time.
> The deep image is the content of vision emerging in the poem.
> The vehicle of movement is imagination.
> The condition of movement is freedom.[3]

Rothenberg's books include *Poems for the Game of Silence* (1971), *Poland/ 1931* (1969/1974), *Vienna Blood* (1980), *That Dada Strain* (1983), *New Selected Poems* (1986), and *Khurbn and Other Poems* (1989).

He currently teaches at the University of California in San Diego.

1. "An Academic Proposal," in *Pre-Faces & Other Writings*, New York, 1981, p. 175.
2. "Pre-Face I: Technicians of the Sacred," in *Pre-Faces & Other Writings*, p. 69.
3. "Deep Image & Mode," in *Pre-Faces & Other Writings*, p. 59.

Cokboy

PART ONE

saddlesore I came
a jew among
the indians
vot em I doink in dis strange place
mit deez pipple mit strange eyes
could be it's trouble
could be   could be
(he says) a shadow
ariseth from his buckwheat
has tomahawk in hand

shadow of an axe inside his right eye
of a fountain pen inside his left
vot em I doink here
how vass I lost tzu get here
am a hundred men
a hundred fifty different shadows
jews & gentiles
who bring the Law to Wilderness
(he says) this man
is me   my grandfather
& other men-of-letters
men with letters carrying the mail
lithuanian pony-express riders
the financially crazed Buffalo Bill
still riding in the lead
hours before avenging the death of Custer
making the first 3-D movie of those wars
or years before it
the numbers vanishing in kabbalistic time
that brings all men together
& the lonely rider
saddlesore
is me   my grandfather
& other men of letters
jews & gentiles entering
the domain of Indian
who bring the Law to Wilderness
in gold mines & shaky stores
the fur trade heavy agriculture
ballots bullets barbers
who threaten my beard your hair
but patronize me
& will make our kind the Senator from Arizona
the champion of their Law
who hates us both
but dresses as a jew one day an indian
the next a little christian shmuck
vot em I doink here
dis place is maybe crazy
has all the letters going backwards
(he says) so who can read the signboards
to the desert
who can shake his way out of the woods
ford streams the grandmothers
were living near
with snakes inside their cunts
teeth maybe
maybe chainsaws
when the Baal Shem visited America

he wore a shtreiml
the locals all thought he was a cowboy
maybe from Mexico
"a cokboy?"
no a cowboy
I will be more than a credit to my community
& race
but will search for my brother Esau among these redmen
their nocturnal fires I will share
piss strained from my holy cock
will bear seed of Adonoi
& feed them visions
I will fill full a clamshell
will pass it around from mouth to mouth
we will watch the moonrise
through each other's eyes
the distances vanishing in kabbalistic time
(he says) the old man watches
from the cliffs a city
overcome with light
the man & the city disappear
he looks & sees another city
this one is made of glass
inside the buildings stand
immobile statues
brown-skinned faces
catch the light
an elevator
moving up & down
in the vision of the Cuna *nele*
the vision of my grandfather
vision of the Baal Shem in America
the slaves in steerage
what have they seen in common
by what light their eyes
have opened into stars
I wouldn't know
what I was doing here
this place has all the letters going
backwards a reverse in time
towards wilderness
the old jew strains at his gaberdine
it parts for him
his spirit rushes up the mountainside
& meets an eagle
no an iggle
captains   commanders   dollinks   delicious madmen
murderers opening the continent up to exploitation
cease & desist (he says)

let's speak (he says)
feels like a little gas down here (he says)
(can't face the mirror without crying)
& the iggle lifts him
like an elevator
to a safe place above the sunrise
there gives a song to him
the Baal Shem's song
repeated without words for centuries
"hey heya heya" but translates it
as "yuh-buh-buh-buh-buh-buh-bum"
when the Baal Shem (yuh-buh) learns to do a bundle
what does the Baal Shem (buh-buh) put into the bundle?
silk of his prayershawl-bag beneath
cover of beaverskin above
savor of esrog fruit within
horn of a mountaingoat between
feather of dove around the sides
clove of a Polish garlic at its heart
he wears when traveling
in journeys through kabbalistic forests
cavalry of the Tsars on every side
men with fat moustaches yellow eyes & sabers
who stalk the gentle soul
at night through the Wyoming steppes
(he says) vot em I doink here
I could not find mine het
would search the countryside on hands & knees
until   behind a rock in Cody
old indian steps forth
the prophecies of both join at this point
like smoke a pipe is held
between them dribbles through their lips
the keen tobacco
"cowboy?"
cokboy (says the Baal Shem)
places a walnut in his handkerchief & cracks it
on a boulder each one eats
the indian draws forth a deck of cards
& shuffles
"game?"
they play at wolves & lambs
the fire crackles in the pripitchok
in a large tent somewhere in America
the story of the coming-forth begins

Cokboy

PART TWO

comes a brown
wind curling from
tense tissues sphincter
opened over the whole continental
divide & shot the people up
plop plop a little girl emergeth
she with the beaver tits nose furry
eyes of the Redman's
Sabbath
gropes down the corridor
(sez) hallo doctor
got a hand to spare?
doctor sez hokay
—yas doctor
hand up her bush
he pulls
a baby   howling
in lamplight a little Moses
now the Cacique's daughter laugheth
—oh doctor not so-o hard
so hard America is born
so hard the Baal Shem dreams about it
200 years later
in Vitebsk
(he was in correspondence with Wm Blake
appeared on Peckham Rye
—yes fully clothed!—
& was his angel)
angel says his mother
smiling proud
she sees his little foot
break through
her crotch an itching
races up her ribs
America is born
the Baal Shem is a beaver
(happened while the Indian talked
chanted behind Cody
the mad jew slid to life
past pink styrofoam snow of her body's
channels
the freaky passageways
unlit unloved
like gums of an old woman
teeth were ripped from

ages gone) into
another kind of world
he hurtles
does reawaken in the female swamp
a beaver amongst the rushes
—momma!—calls the Baal Shem
—mommeleh!
vot em I doink here
I hev become mine beard
(he says) the blind world shines on him
water runs through his mouth
down belly it is dark
a darkness (fur is dark
& hides the skin & blood
a universal fur
but leaves one hole
to open from the body's
darkness pushing
into light)
erupts
like great cock of the primal beings
red & smooth like copper
of the sun's red eye at night
old Beaver lugs it in his hand
I am myself   my grandfather
(he sings) my name is Cokboy
—COKBOY, understand?
I leave my grandmother in the female swamp
will be the Great Deliverer someday yuh-buh-bum
even might find a jar of honey might stick my prick in my
    prick might tingle might it not tickle me the bees find out
    about it & sting the knob it grows a second a dozen or so
    knobs along its length are maybe 30 knobs
so what's the use I ask maybe will try again I drag it red &
    sore behind me so vulnerable I have become in this hot
    climate shitting & farting shooting marbles was opening
    my mouth & coming in it
the blackbird shits o not so fast love into my hat my eyes turn
    white wood-lilies are growing from them a slavic birth I
    can't deny so tender in my eyes tender the native turds
    come floating
& across America in an outrage uselessly I shout against the
    Sun you are no longer my father Moon you are no longer
    my mother I have left you have gone out jaunty with cock
    slung over shoulder this is the journey your young men
    will take
(says Beaver) makes it to the hut where that old woman lives
    apron over her belly carp in oven maybe fried bread fat
    fat little mother don't mind if I drop a stone onto your

brains your daughters be back later little hot girls I ride
on pretending I was you I suck their ears & scream o put
me lower down love o my cock inside
& have to cool it
I cool it
in waters where a princess
daughter of a chief
went bathing
lethal & innocent the cock
has found its mark
(his train has reached Topeka
Custer is dead)
& enters the bridegroom's quarters
darkness her flesh prepared for it
by new moon
in her abdomen a sliver
grows
a silver dollar over Barstow
lighting the Marriage of America
in kabbalistic time
(says Cokboy) you are the daughter of
the mountain
now will I take thee to my father's tribe
to do the snake dance
o jewish feet of El go crazy
in his mind
o
El
o
Him
I carry in my knapsack
dirty pictures land grants
(but further back her people
gun for him
how should they feel
seeing their daughter in arms of
Cokboy
—C-O-C-K, understand?—)
thou art become my Father's bride
are wedded to (ugh) Christian god
forever
bye bye I got to run now
engagements await us in Salt Lake City
industry riseth everywhere
arrows strike concrete
never shall bruise my sweetie's flesh
(says Cokboy) on horse
up river he makes his way
past mining camps Polacks were panning gold in
& other pure products of America

o prospectors o Anglo Saxons
baby-faced dumplings who pacified the west
with gattling guns with bounties for hides of babes
mothers' vulvas made baseballs to their lust
o bringers of civilization heros heros
I will fight my way past you who guard the sacred border
last frontier village of my dreams
with shootouts tyrannies
(he cries) who had escaped the law
or brought it with him
how vass I lost tzu get here
was luckless
on a mountain & kept from
true entry to the west true paradise
like Moses in the Rockies who stares at California spooky in
    the jewish light
of horns atop my head great orange freeways of the mind
America disaster
America disaster
America disaster
America disaster
where he can watch the sun go down
in desert
Cokboy asleep (they ask)
awake (cries Cokboy)
only his beard has left him
like his own   his grandfather's
ghost of Ishi was waiting on the crest
looked like a Jew
but silent
was silent in America
guess I got nothing left to say

1974

DAVID ANTIN ▪ ▪ ▪ ▪ ▪ ▪ ▪ ▪ ▪ ▪ ▪ ▪ ▪ ▪ ▪

b. 1932

Known for his practice of the "poem-talk," an improvisatory talk performance
before a live audience, David Antin is at the foreground of performance poetry
internationally. Presenting himself as a speaker rather than orator, dramatist, or
actor, Antin tends to work in sequences of narratives, often inspired by memory,
which he interweaves with general musings and even statements of poetics. In
an introduction to a poem-talk in his first major collection, *talking at the bounda-
ries* (1976), Antin wrote:

> . . . i had always had mixed feelings
> about being considered a poet   "if robert lowell is a
> poet i dont want to be a poet   if robert frost was a
> poet i dont want to be a poet   if socrates was a poet
>   ill consider it"

In one of his essays, Antin credits Charles Olson with bringing an end to the "Metaphysical Modernist tradition."[1] In its place, the new poetries of the late fifties and early sixties, including the Beat, Black Mountain, and New York School, offered a Romantic metaphysic and epistemology in which "phenomenological reality is 'discovered' and 'constructed' by poets."[2] This reality "cannot be exhausted by its representations because its representations modify its nature."[3] In Antin's reevaluation of modernism, Gertrude Stein and John Cage become "more significant poets and minds than either Pound or Williams."[4]

Antin's other work includes *autobiography* (1967), *definitions* (1967), *code of flag behavior* (1968), *meditations* (1971), *talking* (1972), and *after the war* (1973), all of which are represented in *Selected Poems: 1963–1973* (1991). Another major collection of poem-talks, *tuning*, appeared in 1984.

David Antin is Professor of Art at the University of California, San Diego.

1. "Modernism and Postmodernism: Approaching the Present in American Poetry," *Boundary 2* (Fall 1972), p. 120.   2. The same, pp. 132–133.   3. The same, p. 133.   4. The same.

david ross called up from syracuse and wanted to know if
id do a reading out there at the everson museum   david
was working as their video curator and id met him about
a month earlier when he was here in san diego looking at
some of eleanors tapes for a video show   now he was
back in syracuse and jim harithas for whom david was
working and barbara beckos were putting together a
poetry series and they wanted to know if i was willing
to read   and if i was   who i wanted to read with
      i had to explain that i wasnt doing any reading any
more   or not at that time anyway   that i went to a
place and talked to an occasion and that was the only
kind of poetry i was doing now   but if that was all
right with them id like to read with jackson maclow
      and it was fine with them   jackson was an old
friend   a poet whose work has meant a great deal to
      me   and i hadnt seen him for a long time   not
since i had left new york for san diego   id run into
him every now and then when i was on the east coast for
readings or some other business but it was always at some
      kind of group occasion   a party or a performance
      and we never had a chance to sit down and talk to
gether in any personal sense or at any length   and his
life was going through some changes   i remember one
time we met at dr generositys   an east side bar in new
york where paul blackburn was arranging readings   at
      that time jacksons marriage of years was breaking up
he was very troubled about it and it was all coming up in
this series of poems he was doing that were very simple
and beautiful and humiliating and quite unlike anything
hed ever done before   and we arranged a time to get
together but somehow it just didnt work out   and
now i thought this is the right time   hed be coming

from new york and id be coming from solana beach
california   to syracuse   a town that up to now had
meant nothing to us   and there in that public place
a museum auditorium   surrounded by total
strangers and new acquaintances and friends   what
could be a better place for our private occasion

a private occasion in a public place

i consider myself a poet but im not reading poetry   as you see
i bring no books with me   though ive written books   i
have a funny relationship to the idea of reading   if you cant hear
i would appreciate it if youd come closer   because this is not a
situation where i intend to amplify   thats for the second part
jackson maclows part   the equipment in back of me on the
stage   its other equipment   im only using this micro bit of
equipment   because its the least equipment i could possibly
manage at this particular time   and the reason is that i was once
involved with engineering and now im divesting myself of the parts
there was a time when i would have come with more   a lot
more and not so long ago   but right now i dont want to   its
something like my attitude to the book   from which i dont intend
to be reading   i mean if i were to come and read to you from a
book you would consider it a perfectly reasonable form of behavior
and its a perfectly respectable form of behavior   generally
thought of as a poetry reading   and it would be a little bit like
taking out a container of frozen peas   warming them up and
serving them to you from the frozen food container   and that
doesnt seem interesting to me because then i turn out to be a cook
and i dont really want to be a cook   i dont want to cook or
recook anything for anybody   i came here in order to make a
poem   talking   to talk a poem   which it will be   all
other things being equal   because i wanted to talk about some-
thing   the situation that comes up when a poet comes to a place
to do something that is a poem   i mean what am i doing
coming here to talk poetry?   that is if i thought that poetry was
a sort of roman enterprise   if i thought that poetry was a roman
enterprise i would assume that talking poetry was a reasonable and
clearcut enterprise   i would get to the place and then use all the
wonderful rhetorical charm that i could put behind me and offer
you poetry   that is i would improve talking   you see
talking would be just talking   the way people talk   and
poetry would be improved talk   it would be talk that ends kind
of funny   it rhymes say   or it beats out a tune   or it
does what it does in some unusual and exotic way   theres nothing
wrong with that a lot of people do it   its fun walking tightropes
its fun talking while drinking water   its fun talking while
standing on your head   i propose not to consider poetry putting

something on top of talk   i consider it   in this case
coming with a kind of private occasion to a public place   i
mean youre all here   and its a public place   and im addressing
a public situation   and im doing what poets have done for a
long time   theyve talked out of a private sense   sometimes
from a private need   but theyve talked about it in a rather peculiar
context   for anybody to eavesdrop   which is strange   that
a man would come out here to talk to you   not knowing you
you not knowing him and you should care about anything he
has to say   and its exotic   theres something strange about it
except that if we share some aspect of humanness   it may
be perhaps less exotic   that is   people have been known to
walk into a bar   find someone they didnt know   and start a
conversation with this person   tell them their life story
disappear and never see them again   in fact   i think there
are people who specialize in occasions like this   cabdrivers in
many cities experience this very often   someone comes in
tells them a life story which is either true or untrue
mythical or a poem   they never see them again   and i
imagine that some of the great mythical collections are held by cab-
drivers at this moment of time   if they remember the stories
and in this context i assume we are dealing to some degree in
the mythical occasion   because what am i going to tell you?
something private?   well of course ill tell you something
private   but will you believe it?   now i dont know if i want
you to believe it   would you believe it if i wanted you to believe
it?   i want to talk about something rather more personal than is
reasonable for a public occasion   just because its unreasonable
so i want to talk about the way people choose to enter a public
occasion with a large part of their life   now i happen   as
many people happen   to be married   and my wife was travel-
ling in europe having an exhibition or a set of exhibitions in europe
shes an artist and shes having a video show here   her names
eleanor   eleanor was in europe and i had the experience of talking
to her on the telephone   at one point   and there was an
operator   with a german accent called on the phone and asked if i
would accept this call from eleanor   and i thought "what would
happen if i said no?"   it would be surprising   i didnt say no i
said yes   and she called and spoke to me   and she told me
i said how are things how are things in cologne   now i have
no image of cologne   i havent thought about cologne in years
and years and years   i have no idea of what cologne looks like
now   and a voice was coming to me from cologne telling me
that she had been in cologne and it was a terrible city   everybody
was awful   they all spoke german   the place must have been
filled with nazis   i said well thats too bad   i mean why dont
you leave cologne   she said well i have to see the dealer in
cologne   i said well you have to see the dealer in cologne you
better make the best of it   she said well   how do you ask for

orange juice   i said well   thats a tough problem   orange
juice   they carbonate all the drinks in germany sorry   i mean
you may ask for an *orangensaft* all your life but youre not going to
get orange juice youre going to get carbonated orange drink   she
wept it was very sad   no no she didnt weep but her voice was
trembling   and i was trying to imagine what it was that she was
feeling   she had walked into a signpost outside the kunsthalle
she had become so distracted by the loss of her language in this
foreign country that she had walked into the sign that was in front
of the kunsthalle opened a cut in her head and fallen down   and
this is what happened or so she told me   now i have a great
faith   in what people tell me   that is   people i know
because ive learned that people i know have a certain kind of
human reliability   that is   i stand in a human relationship to
elly and i assume that ellys story is true   and later we were off
the telephone and i was sitting in   my living room   thinking
about distances   and what it is you believe about people and
what it is you know   that is what there is that you want to know
about people   and what there is in thinking that you know
that people are what they say they are   now   ive often
said things that i thought were true   many people do that and
they turn out   not to be exactly true   that is   you do the
best you can   in fact   i was talking to jim   the director
of the museum out here   jim was visiting in san diego and i asked
him how do you like the situation at everson   and that was some
time ago and he said its wonderful   the whole town is up and
around the museum and we are in the town and there is a relation-
ship   and what we are doing the people respond to   whether
they agree with it or disagree with it and he painted a picture of
syracuse   and after it was over i said wow   hes not going to
leave syracuse ever   not for another three or four years hes really
making syracuse into a scene where all the action in the world will
come   and hell turn it around   and at the moment he said
that he meant it   that is he felt very much that this was the
scene where he was and there was no other where he wanted to be
because theres one thing about living that one learns   you
learn it kids dont know it   kids dont know it very well because
kids are always waiting for something   to go somewhere to some
place that will be the scene   but something you learn when you
grow up   so to speak   to some age   and it may be four-
teen for some people or eighty-three for others   and others never
learn it at all   is that wherever you are is the scene   thats
where the action is and it better be there because   at one point
there wont be anything else   and jim was painting a picture
come in   come in   this is nothing terribly formal and
what poem there is here will be built around whatever happens
and jim had painted for me a picture of his excitement about
everson   there was the great sioux festival that was to happen and
the video conference that was to happen and all these things

were happening and he was filled with excitement about it
because this place is not new york   its not new york city where
you have a scorecard   where people come into an art situation
they look at it and they say   well its not as good as it should
have been   yesterday there was a better one   he did another
one that was just like this one   i mean in a certain sense   this
is a raw community   that is to say this is raw life   raw life
what life is raw life?   no life is raw life   but its not the
new york art scene   which lives an exquisite byzantine existence
which this is not   and he was filled with the excitement of
it in his mouth at that moment   two weeks later i heard he was
going to houston   now jim harithas is not a liar and i didnt mean
to indicate that i suspected that he was lying to me standing there
sitting there   dont hang your head jim   i dont mean to
suggest he was telling me a lie   ive done this myself   ive been
filled with excitement for something and it meant everything   ive
said you cant possibly make a poem that isnt a complete improvi-
sation say   or something like that   and then i figured   as
soon as i said it   a week later i made exactly the opposite kind of
poem   because as soon as you take a position very forcefully
youre immediately at the boundary of that position   which lets
you look directly over the boundary into the other side   and
wonder why you couldnt do exactly the opposite of what you just
had in mind   which has something to do with what it is you
mean when you have an intention   its like an artist says im
going to draw a straight line and he draws something thats   sort
of a straight line   and he organizes all his energy and starts to
make it straighter   and then there is the pencil   and then
there is the canvas or whatever hes drawing on   which is all
focussed and waiting   and theres something else that says "so
what"   and then it moves off the edge and the pencil point breaks
and he likes it   and it smudges on the end   he says i like that
its nice keep it   were not liars when we say something that we
mean   but were not truthers   come on in come on in sit down
make yourself comfortable   you can leave easily   i wont feel
the least bit embarrassed if anybody at some point feels that this
public occasion is not his occasion or her occasion and decides to
leave   and so   i asked myself   what kind of public occasion
what kind of occasion did i have for believing elly in cologne?
what kind of occasion did i have for not believing elly in cologne?
i mean why should i not believe her that cologne was filled with
anxiety?   what could cologne have been filled with if it wasnt
filled with anxiety?   glamour?   could i have been jealous of
eleanor?   that is   could i have worried that eleanor would
be unfaithful to me in cologne?   what does it mean for someone
to be unfaithful to somebody?   the idea of marriage is prepos-
terous   and many of us indulge in it anyhow   theres some-
thing about the idea of being married thats absurd   its absurd
because its a kind of contractual agreement of an odd sort   well

im forgetting the part of it that doesnt interest me   namely
    my marriage was sanctified by mayor wagner of new york
    we were married in town hall and i felt it was the first time i
had had any   we were living together and life was very pleasant
    and one day we decided to get married   it didnt seem to me
that what was between us our life had any relation to the town or
that the town had any relation to the meaning of anything but we
went to town hall to get married because we thought it would be
the kind of wedding that would be the least sanctified by all the
things we had no relation to   and it turned out to be the most
sanctified by everything we had no relation to   because it was
the state   i mean the least we could have done was pick some
    freaky religious operation   because at least it would have had
an idiosyncrasy that we chose   in this case we went in and we
said to ourselves itll be like that   bang bang bang   well walk
in   and we did walk in   with my sister-in-law marcia and her
flamboyantly ratty fur coat   which was an amazing operation
that shed picked up in some high class thrift shop and elly had this
sort of funny looking jacket that she was wearing and i was wearing
a duffle coat with a dopey looking hood over my head and we really
    didnt look like we were set for a wedding   we went down there
    to be married and we thought thisll be over very quick   we
    walked in and the man who was going to marry us looked at us
    and intoned in a deep organ vibrato "dooooooo youuuuuuuu
eleanor . . ." and we started to laugh   only elly   who started to
laugh out loud   realized that there was something wrong about
laughing at your wedding in this situation   and she was afraid
    she said later   she told me   now thats also a matter of
belief   but she told me she was very nervous she was afraid they
would throw her out   say "youre not old enough to be married
    youre laughing at your wedding   out!"   she said she had
    this irrational fear and so she started to fake crying   this i can
    attest to   she was a rather good stanislavsky type actress and
had worked in the theater a while and i saw the way she was working
    up the tears   but only because i had seen it before in a profes-
sional way   and her sister who was also laughing and infected
by ellys laughing was also working up tears   and she was weeping
and her sister was weeping   and in the meantime jerry and diane
    im sure   friends of ours who were also there   couldnt
figure out what was happening except that elly and marcia were
maybe terribly sentimental and breaking up   and all this while
elly and marcia were weeping   tears were rolling down their face
while this man was saying "doooo youuuuuu . . ." in his deep organ
pipe voice and i kept squeezing ellys hand saying under my breath
"cut it out youre overdoing it" hoping it would all come to an end
    but there we were sanctified by this peculiar legal system and
    after it was over we got this piece of paper that said courtesy of
    mayor wagner or something of that sort   i dont remember the
    words   but i realized i had been sealed by the state you know

and i thought jesus christ is that what weve been doing?   i
mean we came here in order to have the state make this official and
i guess it is   but people get married   adult people   i mean
many people   with no sense that theyre getting married   lets say
to legalize your childrens status   getting married   people
do get married   and there is a peculiar meaning to getting married
that is a kind of peace treaty   you might call it that
you know somebody signs a treaty and the ambassadors come
and the horses come up on various sides   what is the treaty about?
i mean in a sense were civilized people   and i say civilized
civilization is not as it were part of ones body   civilization is
part of ones head   if you like to make distinctions between bodies
and souls or bodies and heads   civilization what kind of civiliza-
tion does one have?   people who engage in what i would call
romantic marriages   which are most of the people i know
mean something different lets say than the marriage of fortunes
the alliances of houses and economic arrangements   and mine was
a romantic marriage of the sort   that we were people who
we were people who liked to sleep with each other and live
with each other and talk with each other   and that is a private
experience and this is as i say a public place   which makes this
a public occasion and youre here at a private experience in a public
place   its what one expects of a poet isnt it?   but what i
want to say is that there is this image of appetite   that people
have for each other and there are different kinds of appetite
theres the appetite that one feels for a person   a woman say
im a man and im heterosexual   that is i like women i dont
like to make love to men   i dont make love to men   so i talk
of appetite and there is this appetite   and appetite is what?
that its filled with the mind   its filled with the mind and its
filled with the body   but what do you want to do?   sign a
contract that you will only feel desire for the person that you live
with and you will feel desire for nobody else?   i mean everybody
says were civilized   and that makes that contract sound silly
and on the surface its a terribly silly thing to say and do   but
supposing you dont do that   suppose you sign another agreement
that is you decide that you have a relationship with each other
which is of such an order that you have   appetite for each other
interest in each other fondness for each other   whatever the
word means you love each other so to speak   but you dont have
any control of each other   that is   as soon as anybody feels
some other impulse he/she goes makes it with whoever he/she wants
you can try that   its difficult   and i know this kind of
experience   its the kind of experience that takes away   a
kind of evenness   a kind of funny unpressured life   that is
it puts life at the pressure of a romantic adventure   because
anything can dissociate into its separate parts at any moment   you
can always at the moment of an adventure disappear from somebody
else   its a very distraught and romantic existence and not good

for artists   its not good for artists its good for bourgeois people
    who are they?   theyre the people   the others   its
always the other   you know?   if you want to know who the
bourgeois are   its always somebody else   nobody here is in
the bourgeoisie   lets forget that   its the other people theyre
not here   this adventurous life its good for the people who dont
have to do anything   they dont have to work for a living in any
serious sense   except to make wages   those people can go in
    for instant romance and live a life of total romance   artists are
too busy   so we are practical people   you have to make art
you have to be committed to making art to thinking about art to
    thinking about the things that count   "what?   adventure
doesnt count?" you say   sure adventure counts but if it was
always counting you wouldnt have time to count anything else
because all you would be doing would be counting skirts walking
by   guys walking by   you would have no future that would
be contained in your present because every moment life would move
    out   you would have to find a new apartment   let me tell
you you would have to find a new apartment very quickly   why
would you have to find a new apartment very quickly?   i was
    i had a romance with a girl once who lived across the hall from
me and we were going together   we were married in all senses of
the word except mayor wagners sanctification had not been provided
    and we were living together except we were living in separate
and adjoining apartments   which was a very difficult situation
    in fact i met her because we were living in adjoining apartments
    it was a bizarre scene to begin with   i was walking up the
stairs one day and   i lived on the fifth floor of a walkup on jones
street and i was chugging up the last flight with my groceries and
there was a man kneeling at her door peeping through a small hole
in her door   and i said "what are you doing?" and the guy ran
by me like that as i was coming around the landing past the old
jewelers apartment   and i was coming up and this guy fled and
literally nearly knocked the groceries out of my hands as he ran all
    the way down the stairs   and then i was standing there and i
    didnt know what was up   for a moment i didnt understand
what had been going on   i didnt know what he was doing and
    then i looked and saw there was a minute hole in the door   i
didnt look through the hole   i really didnt look through the hole
    good grief i didnt look through it   as a matter of fact i went
into my apartment and i closed the door and i said to myself
    "should i tell miriam that she has had a voyeur?"   and i
realized that thats loaded with responsibility   that is   i could
ignore the issue and let her find out for herself   i certainly could
wait a decent length of time   provided the voyeur had something
to look at   let us assume that he had good sense and had chosen
what he wanted to look at appropriately   i could wait another
two hours or something   three hours and then call her on the
telephone and at a more auspicious hour tell her that she should

put something over the door or whatever   and worry about it
    but then i was really worried as to whether or not i should even
    tell her at all   because i realized once i told her   that there
would be no way for me to extricate myself from a kind of situation
that would suggest eroticism regardless of what i did   i was sort
of hip   and it wasnt that i was against it   it was just that i
didnt want   didnt know whether i wanted to as it were get into
a relationship with someone who lived next door to me   under
any circumstances at all   that is   i mean i knew there was no
necessity   by this i dont mean you to assume that i was para-
noid enough to suppose that id have to marry her if i told her she
had a voyeur looking in her door   however i was aware that we
    had looked at each other with interest   for some time
    casually   if i told her she had a voyeur   into our ambience
of casual concern and interest would have entered a discussion that
    aroused certain knowledge   of what might conceivably be
thought about in the context of voyeurs and i didnt know whether i
wanted to offer anyone an invitation to have a relationship with me
    i didn't know whether i wanted that   some great delicateness
isnt it?   i mean there i sat   so i said "to hell with it ill tell
her   shes going to find it a drag"   maybe thats not why i did
    it   i   you know i dont know   now im telling you im an
honest man   what does it mean for a man to tell you hes an
honest man?   he stands up here and he says to you "im an
honest man" and then you have to judge how honest his honesty
    is   well ill tell you something   in this case i dont even know
if i was an honest man   what i did is i waited a decent length of
time   like toward evening i went over knocked on her door and
said "miriam . . ."   i knew her name wed spoken about something
or other once before   and i said "miriam   you have a voyeur"
    and i knew she didnt believe me   i knew she didn't believe
me at all   she said "what do you mean?"   i said "well theres
a hole in your door   over here"   and she looked at it and it
was a little tiny hole and she said "oh well   ill certainly have to
do something about that"   she didnt believe it and i   i said
    well dont worry about it   but once that happened it was a
    situation from which one couldnt retreat   and the situation
developed that i didnt retreat from and we did get involved   and
were   after some length of time involved in a love affair   i
say love affair because the word affair by itself makes everything
sound like an affair of state   and we lived together   sort of
    she lived in one apartment and i lived in the other and we
shared a bathroom   that is we had a bathroom that we had in
common and it was in the hall   it was a wonderful apartment
that i got for eighteen dollars and seventy-five cents a month   with
    three rooms   and thats why it had the bathroom in the hall
    but it was very nice   it was a nice bathroom   it was a
nice apartment in a nice place   and our relationship was kind of
    stormy   i dont know why it was   somehow there was

something about our belief in each other or lack of belief in each
other that we had little confidence in each other   and i dont
know why that is   we liked each other alot   but maybe we
were very alien to each other   in some way   and sometimes
thats good and sometimes thats bad   she was very frightened of
my background   my background was what?   european intel-
lectual   so to speak   middle europe   and hers was what?
louisiana mormon   and that was interesting i thought   i
thought that was kind of interesting and groovy   i mean i liked
her genteel southern background but she was terrified of mine
and my friends frightened her for reasons im not at all clear
about   and she was always in some state of fear that she was
being considered terrible and inadequate or whatever   and so she
used to produce fits and tantrums   under varying circumstances
im looking at this to see if im still on the tape because
though its a private occasion in a public place its eventually
going to have to become something else   because i dont intend
to let it disappear into this occasion and i want it on tape   some-
how this anxiety that she had   converted itself into a series of
performances that shed put on   performances   that is i
remember an occasion   a number of my friends came to her house
and we sat there   we had an evening with people over and we
talked   and i thought that wed all had a very pleasant time
that is   we had talked about inconsequential things   art
politics   life   death   inconsequential mainly because
we werent going to change their course at this moment   it was
chatter   when it was over she got into a kind of hysterical rage
at what she felt were the pretentious concerns of my friends   i
didnt think there was anything pretentious about it at all   she
felt they were horrible people   by the end of the argument she
did something that id never seen in my life   she fell down in
what looked ostensibly like a faint   and i looked at her   at
that faint   and i couldnt quite believe it   that is   in the
middle of a discussion she sort of keeled over fell down   i
shook her   not with passion but dutifully   because thats
what you do when people fall down you know?   like they fall
down in faints and you try to revive them   i walked over and
sort of shook her   i said "get up" you know?   "get up
miriam"   "get up" and i got some water and i threw it in
her face and finally she said "well   when are they coming?"
and i said whos coming?   and she said "when are they
coming?   jack and jerry and barbara and diane"   and i said
what do you mean when are they coming but she said when are they
going to get here?   you better get the place straightened up
i said what do you mean straighten the place up? they were here
and left   she was telling me that she had gone through this whole
scene in such a state that she had forgotten the whole existence of
the event that she had been so terrified by   now either she was
telling me a truth or she was not telling me a truth   i dont mean

to say that she was putting me on   i mean she could have been
putting me on   but merely my lack of confidence in it doesnt
make it a lie   and i said come on   i was sitting in the chair
right over there and jack silberg was sitting in that chair over there
and he asked you that question   you remember that question
about what operas you had in your repertory   she was a singer
and she had been preparing to be a singer   she had a kind of
coloratura voice   actually she didnt have a coloratura voice
she had a dark soprano voice and she was trying to get it up to
a coloratura voice   because it was a wiser thing   according to
her coach for her to have a coloratura voice   and it was a bad
scene because she didnt have that kind of light upper range   she
had a very beautiful rich dark middle register and she was trying to
push it up and lose the weight   well shed lost the weight and she
didnt have a very beautiful upper range anyway and it made her
nervous   and jack had been sitting there and hed said to her
what operas do you have and shed answered him   and i went
through this number reminding her and she didnt remember it and
she sat there flatly asserting that she didnt remember it   what
kind of confidence did i have in this situation   i mean what did i
have?   i had her assertion that she   had not been there
and i had my experience that she had been there and she didnt
remember it or claimed not to remember it   now i must say this
created a profound doubt in me   about everything about her
now maybe that was my fault   maybe that was what was
wrong with us all along   that we always doubted each other
about everything   i mean everything was doubtful   maybe
you know   maybe if it was the right sort of relationship i should
have believed her implicitly i should have absolutely believed it
regardless of whatever bullshit it was intended to seem like   in
fact maybe the whole point of this whole operation was that if i
really cared for her enough i could conceivably have believed this
incredible piece of romantic amnesiac story and then she would
have felt more comfortable   now i can create a plausible story
for her   but did she do it on purpose?   that is did she come
and tell me this story in order to test me   to see if i would
believe her?   i have no idea   that is i really dont know
but i didnt believe her and our marriage   our living together
gradually disintegrated along this axis of doubt   there were these
things that we had in common and didnt have in common and we
persisted in living together in our separate apartments which were
right next to each other   which was very difficult to   which
is really quite difficult to do   because if we were going to get
away from each other in any serious way it would have been useful
to have a greater amount of distance between us   but we each
had terrific bargains in our apartments   her apartment was
a three room apartment that cost sixteen dollars and seventy-five
cents a month and mine cost eighteen dollars and seventy-five cents
a month   and mine was a three room apartment and hers was a

two and a half room apartment in greenwich village in a very pleasant
neighborhood   on jones street   and you didnt gladly give up
apartments like that because you couldnt find them anywhere
even then   i guess it was around the 1950s and   at some
point or another i became convinced that she was seeing other people
now was that bad or good from my point of view?   i dont
know   that is   in a way i hoped that she would go away   i
wouldnt leave my apartment and i hoped that she would go away
she wouldnt leave her apartment   she hoped that i would
go away and we had a kind of unwritten agreement that we were
with each other   now "being with each other" in this kind of
contractual agreement   unwritten contractual agreement   is a
kind of compromise   its that you wont do anything to destroy
the other persons image of the future   thats really what its
about   jealousy is a funny image   that is   what is the
difference whether someone that youre not at the moment interested
in making love to makes love to somebody else?   rationally
considered   the ideas trivial   i mean it really is it is   at
least as far as i can imagine   and even from this point of view
consider   you have no appetite to make love that hour
the woman you live with has appetite to make love that hour
finds someone to make love with and makes love   no one takes
anything away from you that you   needed   could conceiv-
ably have avoided   you think so?   but nobody thinks so
nobody likes that situation   mainly because what it does is it
threatens the future   its more than the act of taking a goodie
away   its not like taking a piece of candy away   that is
what it does   human bodies carry human minds and souls
with them so to speak   we are sort of hostages of our bodies and
our bodies go walking into places   and they carry you with
you   and if somebody goes into a romance with somebody else
you say well   thats really what you did yourself isnt it   that
is   you were carried by the same desire the same casual appetite
of the flesh   and something of the mind   and you were carried
into a relationship that didnt exist before   well   it could
happen again and then you part company   over an hour   you
think about that   and you say well   thats really kind of shaky
and people accommodate themselves to not shaking each others
future   the image of jealousy is like metaphysical doubt   its
like a total notion of not being able to rely on the future   because
after all im in the united states and elly is in cologne   you know
im in the united states and elly is in cologne   let us say elly is
making love to somebody else in cologne   you know   and
im making love to somebody else in the united states   which i
was not   but thats neither here nor there   lets say she was
so what?   i mean im a civilized man   so to speak   so
to speak we are all very civilized   what difference could it make
to me six thousand miles away?   seven thousand miles?   but
the doubt is the issue   that is   no one cares about the sheer

facticity of unfaithfulness or violations of faith   what one
imagines is that a life that one has built that has more moments than
it takes to fuck somebody   can disintegrate into a series of
moments that are equal to about that   and nothing else   now
i dont mean thats wrong   that it should be like that   but
its a scary time   to feel that the world is disrupting from you
just like that   that you could wake up one day decide that youre
no longer going to sleep with that woman or go sleep with someone
else and immediately move in   which is another thing and it
happened   it happened interestingly as a matter of fact   that
this girl that i was living with in the next door apartment finally
got into what i imagine must have been an affair with somebody
else and i remember the feeling of doubt was rather complex   as
to whether we should work out our relationship   that is   she
pretended not to have any other interests than the ones i was aware
of   and i pretended not to have any other interests and we kept
coming back to the same locus of activity   there we were
across the hall from each other   and thats really an awful
scene because youre much better off with one of you in europe and
one of you in the united states at least   at best   you can
manage with twenty-third street and fourteenth street or something
like that   with the bronx and manhattan   i mean you can
manage a scene like that   because its out of sight out of mind
and the bodies are far separated geographically   but we were very
close and we had reason to be suspicious of each other   but we
were having trouble why should we not have wanted to part?
why shouldnt i have felt at east that she was considering going
with someone else into some other romance?   or that i was going
into some other romance and that we would part and life would be
easy again and there would be no more effort   though we were
used to our effort   our effort was like a work that we were
used to doing you know?   it was like having a job   you
know that was like the job we worked at   regularly   and
thats how we knew who we were   we were the people who
worked at that job   you know her name was miriam my name
was david i was the one who had trouble with her she was the one
who had trouble with me   it was well known   it informed my
poetry   it informed her career we knew how our career was
going how it was going to go   for at least a month and a half for
six weeks at least   while she managed to get her upper register
light enough and clean enough to run scales while i was doing some-
thing else   i was working in those days i was writing stories
and i was writing stories and i was working my story paragraph
by paragraph and i knew what kind of story i was writing and i knew
that i had to get to the end of it   i was in the middle and there
we were   i was doing it about a paragraph a day   in those days
i worked very slow and it was hard going and   i said well   i
know who i am   but there was this feeling of suspicion   she

was suspicious of me and i was suspicious of her and one day i
went over to borrow a cake of soap and she was in bed with some-
body else and there was an enormous feeling of relief   you know
      there was this funny feeling of shock and relief   because it
wasnt suspicion   that is   like i said excuse me and it was over
      and i said gee weve split   thats wonderful   didnt feel
wonderful but i knew it was wonderful   you see now im trying
to remember what it was really like   it wasnt bad it was much
better than being in doubt   and it was bad for her too   why
was it bad for her?   that is it was bad for her in being in doubt
it wasnt bad for her being in bed and certain that she was being
in bed   and it wasnt bad that i appeared at the scene of her being
in bed so that finally she was committed to getting out of the life
      you see   because it was important that she get out of it
and she couldnt get out she didnt have the nerve to get out of it
      just as i didnt have the nerve to get out of it   we had just
about enough nerve to suffer together   you know?   which
was really a drag   because we had a sense of responsibility and
we were responsible people   and there we were   out of it by
definition   out of it is a whole other thing   now there i was
as i said sitting in new york   now in that case i was in new york
      in that other one i was in new york   and now here i was in
california and i was in california saying to myself   what do we do
to believe in ourselves this way?   believe in contracts that we
dont go off to make love to other people because well shatter our
faith unless we do it flatly out in the open you know like by decla-
ration and fiat   you live your life and people send you a formal
      notice   at six oclock in the morning tomorrow im going off
with somebody else   or im going to enter into an engagement to
become interested in somebody else next week   you need prep-
      aration   is that better or worse?   now this is the counter
side of the romantic position   that is   you have the problem
      your life is defined by history and history is the outcome of
having a future   that is you project a future which gives you a
present   and you have a trajectory in which you make it your
life   and there we are in a marriage   and our marriage is
going to be imperiled   finally we say   or maybe we dont
maybe we say how will it not be imperiled?   supposing elly
and i live our careers where were flipping around the country sepa-
rately for long periods of time   i mean were human   compli-
cated   physical   you go to another place what do you do?
you play out this old game of marriage and fidelity in the old
      way?   you play it out in a new way?   it seems to me that
what you face here is another image of what life is about and you
say to yourself "are we going to split finally   when your career
takes you to a european circuit for three weeks once again were
      over?"   do i say that do i say i dont go and travel the circuit
myself   what kind of agreement do people make to live a human

comfortable life   do we travel around with each other all the
time?   i always grab my wife and travel with her she grabs me
and takes me with her as we attend each other like children on a
leash   its a very strange situation for people who are both human
and not siamese twins   siamese twins have it easy siamese twins
dont have any problem they have a physical relation thats continuous
and permanent   short of a disastrous operation they dont become
two people and they cant afford to act as two people even together
and it is in this sense moving around the idea of marriage that
you say why do people enter into it at all?   and you enter into it
    marriage   at least i had i see it now as one enters into it in
    relation to a kind of self definition in a public place   because
marriage is a public place   marriage is a public place in the sense
that   your self   your self is a private self you see it as a private
self   because you always see it inside your own head   which
is a private place so that your self as it is   when you see yourself
is a private occasion in a private place   and you emerge   you
see yourself emerge   for a moment   before you lose sight of
yourself into a public context by being with another   any other
i mean you see yourself emerge for a moment before you lose
sight of yourself in being in that   place   which is a public
place   anyway for a while   and the reason people like me get
married and now i dont mean the others   the bourgeois people
we dont worry about having children and legalizing things
    its mainly because it produces   an externalization of ones
life and intentions   one plays it out in a public place   that is
one puts it in public   like in a government place so to speak
one arranges a government by treaty with somebody else
and its a dangerous treaty that covers a territory for coming
together with another   but imagine the opposite   imagine
never putting anything into a public place   imagine only talking
to yourself   imagine only living inside yourself   and youre
your own actor and audience   youre the audience of your own
intentions   in fact the only thing you can do is listen to your
    own intentions with total doubt or total faith   the total
    either total   doubt or acceptance   are indifferent
because really what happens is that in order to perceive your
intentions   you have to stand so far in back of them   step so
far back that you perceive them before they emerge   and they
depart from you as soon as you come up with an idea of   seeing
    them   its impossible to speak a language alone   that is the
idea of a private language is silly   because there would be no
memory system on which you could rely for that language to be
encoded stably   there would be no set of rules and regularities
the meanings of the words could shift   youd come up against that
kind of wittgensteinan situation in which when you say "i"   by
the time you heard the word "i" you might intend something else
    someone else   who do you mean by "i"   "i" is who?

it happened at the turn of the century that there were a lot of
people who were concerned with where that "i" comes from when it
speaks and there was the famous case of a woman   a woman in
new england   a young girl actually   who spoke with this "i"
only the "i" was different each time she spoke   or rather
she had four different "i's"   for whom she spoke to this psychia-
trist   or neurologist   they didnt have psychiatrists then   a
man named prince   morton prince   and she spoke to him a
different person each time   and each of these different persons
each of these different people were defined in relation to other
parts of her   character   and each one recognized its self
alone   so she was sort of "sleeping margaret"   or "dangerous
sally"   or whoever she was   i dont remember their names
but each time she was another person and that other person was
always pretty consistent   there was a reckless one who caused
trouble for all the other ones and went out and provoked sexual
encounters   and there was a very good girl who always did the
right thing and there was another depressive one   nearly catatonic
one   who did very little except be depressed   and all these
different people spoke to the psychiatrist in different voices   they
addressed him with a different sense of style this person who was
willing to let these "i's" play themselves out   or else help them
invent themselves   because these "i's" didnt exist before that
one girl in that one body found her neurologist   there was only
one person there whose name i think was   sally beauchamp
pronounced "beecham"   or that was the pseudonym she
was given in the book by the neurologist   who spelled her name
"beauchamp" and said it was pronounced "beecham"   which i
remember struck me as odd   but anyway she was only one
person sally beauchamp and she was having difficulties and she went
to visit this neurologist on the advice of her family   i think
and the neurologist spoke to her long enough for her to stop
being one person and become four   and each one of these people
had different desires and intentions   but one of the things that
interests me in this is not so much that she became four separate
"i's" as that each one formed its coherency in relation to the
memory of the psychiatrist   that is   it was the neurologists
mind that held them together   it was like a ball game   a kind
of handball court against which "i" banged itself off and got a return
from the psychiatrist and saw where the ball bounced when it
came off a particular spot on the wall when it was struck in a partic-
ular kind of way   now i dont know how many "i's" might have
come out of it but the "i" that went to the doctor was the "i" that
her family had created so to speak and the social environment
created as a handball court   that is there had been these
intentions toward a self   in self realization and self determina-
tion and she had said "i   sally" and they had said "you
sally"   and they knew that sally would do the right thing

and sally would go to school and sally would do her homework
and sally would be modest and sally would wear dresses and she
    wouldnt run after boys   this would be "sally" and everyone
knew what "sally" did she was a good girl   and then sally went
to the neurologist and he didnt have any such expectations or not
all of them and soon you had a whole set of other girls along with
sally   a depressed girl and a sexy girl and a violent one   who
tore up the other ones notes   they used to write notes to each
    other   several of the "i's"   and one of them used to tear
up the other ones notes and throw them away and write nasty
    things   and the other one wrote very politely   and one of
    them spoke french and the other didnt   which was sort of
interesting that one of them was capable   the one who was
educated by the family in boston spoke french   the other one
didnt speak french   resolutely couldnt understand a word of
french and that was the way that the one of them could write
messages to the neurologist that the other one   the nasty one
    couldnt understand   by writing them in french   and she
would slip messages in french to the neurologist   who under-
stood   which created a kind of illicit alliance between one self
and one neurologist   now i think in some sense people get married
in order to define a self   a kind of yet private self that is still a
public self   that is   my kind of people do that   but defining
a self is   a matter of hope and expectation   that is   i hope
to be somebody   that is   i am somebody i am somebody i am
somebody jim harithas is somebody jim harithas adored syracuse
    he hoped to love syracuse and he has loved syracuse and hes
done great things in syracuse   dont be embarrassed jim you did
    what youve done in syracuse is really a rather considerable
achievement   you wanted to love syracuse   i wanted to love
miriam   and i loved miriam   which is about the same thing
    and then one day miriam and i stopped loving each other
and i dont know exactly how you handle that kind of situation
    that is   who speaks for me when i speak?   do i have a
quorum?   im here in this public place talking in the context of
some old friends some new ones and people who have come here
    with expectations maybe of what a poet is   you know?
    what a poet will do   what hell talk about   and i come
here with my private thing so to speak   and i tell you im here to
define myself and im telling you who i am and what im doing it
    for   and you can believe it as much as you can believe me or
any poet   or as much as you can believe your wife   or your
    child   or yourself

                                                                1976

KEITH WALDROP ■ ■ ■ ■ ■ ■ ■ ■ ■ ■ ■ ■ ■ ■

b. 1932

Keith Waldrop is professor of English and Comparative Literature at Brown University, and co-director of Burning Deck Press, a leading publisher of experimental poetry. His many books include *A Windmill Near Calvary* (1968), *The Garden of Effort* (1975), *The Space of Half an Hour* (1983), *A Shipwreck in Haven* (1989), and *The Opposite of Letting the Mind Wander: Selected Poems and a Few Songs* (1990).

Drawing on the technique of collage, Waldrop uses other texts to create his own; for example, he describes his work *The Antichrist* (1970) as the text of Bram Stoker's *Dracula* "with most of the words removed."[1] Waldrop deliberately plays on the compositional value of inattention—"a frame of mind that lets in strays"—to create poems with multiple points of focus.[2] Viewing his poems as "constructions," Waldrop is fascinated by *"background"*; that is, "those aspects of the scene we can't really scrutinize, cannot (by definition) attend to."[3]

Waldrop has also published a work of experimental fiction, *Hegel's Family* (1989), and translated the work of contemporary French poets Claude Royet-Journoud, Anne-Marie Albiach, and Edmond Jabès, among others.

1. "Notes for a Preface," in *The Opposite of Letting the Mind Wander*, Providence, 1990, n.p.   2. The same.   3. The same.

FROM *A Shipwreck in Haven*

I

1

Balancing. Austere. Life-
less. I have tried to keep
context from claiming you.

Without doors. And there are
windows. How far, how
far into the desert have we come?

Rude instruments, product
of my garden. Might also be
different, what I am thinking of.

So you see: it is
not symmetrical, dark
red out of the snow.

2

Enemies for therapy, the
rind of the lime-tree
in elaborate garlands.

Strew the table. Let the hall
be garlanded and lit, the will
to break away. Welcome your couches.

Witness these details. Your judgement, my
inclination. Hear. Touch. Taste.
Translate. Fixed: the river.

Disquieting thought, I am not
ultimate, full moon, memory.
Prepare for rout.

3

Here, even, in the
sand. Among the rocks, I have
heard, remnant of a cloud.

Unfleshed, short, thin, pointed.
Independent of you, a
revelation. A great city.

Flatly unknown, you do not
know of yourself, do not know
yourself, not stuck full of nails.

Under such illumination, darkness
becomes terror. Under this high
wall, dark ground.

4

High marble wall, broken mid-
way. Dark unphenomenality, like
the hand of a clock. Sun-baked.

No *direct* communication likely. Marble
terrace. Suffusing with soft-
tinted glow. Images first.

The gods and you come later, a wealth
of approaches. Within the portico:
marble. Bundled like qualities.

Not—the world—one of
several, as if it could be
different. Nothing. Nothing different.

5

I mean translated, though some
charms are pre-determined. Shall I
not delve and deliver?

If I could think it. Our
wings are broken. As easily might
plunge. In a violent sweat.

The desert. And might be
the same: lemurs
swim down gutters.

And might be threshold, never
hesitate, ship on the high sea.
The desert in the house.

6

Intrinsic, your un-
thinkability. Casts over all created
things annihilating shadow.

An opening for possible
storms, as a deity enters
the world, a stranger.

The bed we are not in: can-
not surprise it. What passes
in the street? Pure picture.

In the world these
limits, almost occult—only signals
corporeal. To think of something.

7

I was hardly dead, when you
called. Now are you convinced?
Infinitely soft strum.

As if night. As if im-
perceptibly. Slowly you fall. Break
somewhat the blackness of the day.

Might also be any
direction, every start
takes us to other time.

Forth across the sands. From
sky or from the liver,
divined. Endless beginning.

8

Need not end. Indeed, *nothing*. Step
out. Grist for wits. Shadow of your
shell. Stand there.

No other ground. No
other. And the world concerns you every-
where, but do not identify with it.

Let light onto us. Flowers through the
gate, flowers skimming
the wall. A carpet of petal.

Treasures below the earth. Neither in
this world nor another, guarding.
Nothing but fade and flourish.

9

Now there is a door and whoever
very beautiful and very
very strange. Near you a table.

Laughing. Singing. Calling to one
another, the crack of whips. Cloud to
cloud in ricochet.

Music of hooves and wheels. The heavenly
Jerusalem from shards of Babylon
destroyed. Now a door.

Where thinking ends, house and temple
echo, possible objects of
admiration. Will you go?

10

Oh yes and wheels on the pavement,
angels of incidence, rebounding from
waves, but precisely. Reflective angels.

Like the hand of a clock which, minute
by minute, crosses its appointed
spaces. Oh! You are passing!

Things are ready. All
things, because something
must be settled. Slung.

Answering laughter. Mixture of
diamond and diamond
and blood, a rope of flowers.

1989

Will to Will

An interesting case, the progress of a bird. When
they move, they move quickly, a glittering
line. One's own performance can alter.

As a mere form or fold of the atmosphere, were
our organs sharp enough. I am, as
if I were not. Tendency to telescope.

A thought vanishes and there, before
sunset, someone else is thinking it. A note in
music, as the ordinary accompaniment.

But again, I have this encouragement,
not to think all these things utterly
impossible. Purchase new clothes, buy food.

Desperate attempt to escape perplexity. On the
surface too deeply absorbed to conceal
her ignorance. A cowboy leaves the ranch.

Four distinct things are to be borne in
mind: the square, a small body, free
air, the intensity. Went to town.

Mad. Foolish. The sound of an
explosion is propagated as a wave. Nobody
knows him, he's so dressed up.

Not particularly striking. The dog runs to him and
licks him. Reflected like light, refracted
like light, like light condensed by suitable lenses.

Stamp on the air the conditions of
motion. Sing a hymn in the passage, but
sing *so badly*. Haunting tune, idea, phrase.

The dog barks at him when he comes out. He
sells the cow, shops for a wife, builds
a new barn, buys cows. The rest I'm forgetting.

1990

Wandering Curves

A new ridge spreads underneath. Volcanoes, often
active, rim the Pacific. It bears little
resemblance to human behavior. She
crushes it in her hand and wipes it
across her sorrowful brow. Two
families of curves, drawn on a surface.

Such tremendous movements on the
surface must arise from internal
forces. Demoniac rage and
the traditional laugh of abandoned
villainy. My eyes fill with tears, my
knees double under me.

The weather is always important in
melodrama. Space is a function of
matter and energy—or, rather, of their
distribution. But how did we get like this—so
suddenly? *Despair sits brooding the putrid
eggs of hope*. The world's deepest earthquakes.

Under sustained pressure, even granite
flows. The whole of Scandinavia's
still rising, having been long depressed
by an enormous ice cube. The water behind
Boulder Dam is heavy enough to
ooze the crust along the mantle.

1990

MICHAEL McCLURE ■ ■ ■ ■ ■ ■ ■ ■ ■ ■ ■ ■

b. 1932

Born in Marysville, Kansas, Michael McClure grew up in Seattle and Wichita and attended the University of Arizona at Tucson before moving to San Francisco. He gave his first reading as a participant in the 1955 Six Gallery event which launched the San Francisco Renaissance, and he remains one of the leading poets of the Beat generation.

The graphic design of his poems, suggestive of mushroom clouds and flowers, serves a purpose for McClure. "The deliberate depersonalizations of grammar, and alterations of accepted written syntax, are for me like the splashings of paint in modern canvases. I continue to see the poem as an extension of myself, as a gesture, and as an organism seeking life."[1] McClure sees both politics and poetry as rooted in biology, and the history of humans as animals driven and animated by biological forces: "It is thrilling to be in this waste and destruction and re-creation. That is one of the sensualities of American culture. Our primate emotions sing to us in the midst of it."[2]

His books include *Hymn to Saint Geryon* (1959), *Little Odes* (1969), *September Blackberries* (1974), *Jaguar Skies* (1975), *Fragments of Perseus* (1983), and *Selected Poems*, 1986. On occasion, McClure has performed his poetry with the accompaniment of Ray Manzarek, former keyboardist for the rock group the Doors. His plays include *The Beard* (1965), a "poem-play of a confrontation between Billy the Kid and Jean Harlow," and *Josephine: The Mouse Singer* (1980).

1. "Author's Note," in *Selected Poems*, New York, 1986, p. vii.   2. *Selected Poems*, p. 90.

Hymn to Saint Geryon

THE GESTURE THE GESTURE THE GESTURE THE GES-
                        [TURE THE GESTURE THE
GESTURE THE GESTURE   to make fists of it.

Clyfford Still: "We are committed to an unqualified act,
not illustrating outworn myths or contemporary alibis. One must
accept total responsibility for what he executes.
And the measure of his greatness will be the depth of his
insight and courage in realizing
his own vision. Demands for communication are pre-
sumptuous and irrelevant."

To hit with the thing. To make a robe of it
TO WEAR.
To fill out the thing as we see it!
To clothe ourselves in the action,
to remove from the precious to the full swing.
To hit the object over the head. To step
into what we conjecture.
Name it the *stance*. Not politics

but ourselves—is the question.
HERE I SEE IT WITH FLOWERS ENTERING INTO IT

that way.
Not caring except for my greatness, caring
only for my size I would enter it.

THE SELFS FREE HERO

THOREAU is there, LAWRENCE, BLAKE and GOYA
ST. POLLOCK is there and KLINE whom I imagine
in a world of nerves and nightsweats.
To hit it again. "The foot is to kick with."
If I do violence to myself I am beautiful, blood is red
on the face and bruises are not without . . .

But the thing I say!! Is to see

Or as one says: Not to lie about goodness.
Even Geryon (as Geryon) is beautiful but not if you look
only at the head or body. BUT

BACK TO IT . . . it is a robe
that I want. The gestures that we make are
our clothing. Small gestures
are like smoke, a slight breeze causes a drifting
and we are bare again . . . uneternal.
Say it! What a small thing to want, it is not
noble. Shelley wanted to save the Irish.
But I love my body my face only
first and then others'.
To fill out a vision until I become
one with it. Or perhaps both happen together. But
I must be an animal. Shelley had
no gods either.   ....
An impetuous man—he was mostly
Gesture!!!!!!!!!!!!
There are so few poems
but so much of him.
AND I COULD BE FORCED BY SOMEONE TO CHANGE
[THIS

THEY WOULD KNOW THAT WHAT I SAY IS NOT
[MEANT AS HUMOR

Or to
STRIKE THEM
with the
GESTURE.
I mean that I love myself which is an act of pride

and I would decorate myself with what is beautiful.
The tygers of wrath are wiser than the horses of instruction—
means that the belief of something is necessary to its beauty.
Size, numbers are part of any esthetic. I must
believe my gesture. Beauty fades so quickly

that it does not matter. Belief, pride—remain.
AND   AND   AND   AND   AND   AND   AND   AND

the gesture.
The mark of the strong shoulder and hand.

•

Yes, confuses. The whole thing.
Sometimes intentional and sometimes out of my hands.
Robe Gesture   ROBE/GESTURE   Robe Gesture
The poem like painting is black and white.

•

And I am still not swinging it—there is still confusion
I PICK IT UP BY THE TAIL AND HIT
YOU OVER THE HEAD WITH IT.

WHAP WHAP WHAP WHAP WHAP WHAP WHAP WHAP
                                                    [WHAP

DO YOU BELIEVE ME NOW?

No. But if I started huge paragraphs moving toward you
or enormous stanzas, simple things, part of
a gesture, then, you would get out of the way.
You would see them coming at you,
rapidly, determined, indifferent. But this
is really not to attack you.
I mean only to move words. To set
something into motion toward a goal. Not
to invent new confusions.

It is hard to avoid some issues.
The poem could easily become a body
with elbows, lymph systems, muscles.
But how ugly! How much better for it

to be a body of words.
A POEM—NO MORE
(Not a body of words but a poem)

I am the body, the animal, the poem
is a gesture of mine.

A confusion is avoided here,

Beauty: How beautiful I move
and make gestures. How
beautiful that sometimes I believe in them.
Sometimes I make a strong gesture—a poem
and I record it.

1959

Ode to Jackson Pollock

Hand swinging the loops of paint—splashes—drips—
chic lavender, *duende* black, blue and red!

Jackson Pollock my sorrow is selfish. I won't meet
you here. I see your crossings of paint!
We are all lost in the cloud of our gestures—

—the smoke we make with our arms. I cry
to my beloved too. We are lost
in lovelessness. Our sorrows
before us. Copy them in air! We
make their postures with our stance.

They grow before us.
The lean black she-wolves on altars of color.
We search our remembrance for memories
of heroic anguish. We put down
our pain as singing testimony.
Gouges, corruptions, wrinkles, held loose

in the net of our feelings and hues—
we crash into their machinery making it
as we believe. I say

we. I—You. You saw the brightness
of pain. Ambition. We give in to the lie
of beauty in the step of creating.
Make lies to live in. I mean you. Held

yourself in animal suffering.
You made your history. Of Pain.

Making it real for beauty, for ambition
and power. Invented totems from teacups
and cigarettes. Put it all down
in disbelief—waiting—forcing.
Each gesture painting. —Caught on
to the method of making each motion
your speech, your love, your rack

and found yourself. Heroic—huge—burning
with your feelings. Like making money
makes the body move. Calls you to action
swirling the paint and studying the feeling

caught up in the struggle and leading it.
For the beauty of animal action
and freedom of full reward.
To see it down—and praise—and admiration,
to lead, to feel yourself above all others.

NO MATTER WHAT—IT'S THERE! NO ONE

can remove it. Done in full power.
Liberty and Jackson Pollock the creator.
The mind is given credit.

You strangled
the lean wolf beloved to yourself—
Guardians of the Secret
—and found yourself the secret
spread in clouds of color

burning yourself and falling like rain

transmuted into grace and glory, free
of innocence

containing all, pressing experience
through yourself onto the canvas.
Pollock I know you are there! Pollock
do you hear me?!! Spoke to himself
beloved. As I speak to myself
to Pollock into the air. And fall short

of the body of the beloved hovering
always before him. Her face
not a fact, memory or experience

but there in the air
destroying confidence.
The enormous figure of her mystery

always there in trappings of reason.

Worked at his sureness. Demanding
Her place beside him. Called

from the whirls of paint, asked for
a face and shoulders to stand naked
before him to make a star.

He pulling the torn parts of her body
together
to make a perfect figure—1951.
Assembled the lovely shape of chaos.
Seeing it bare and hideous, new
to the old eye. Stark
black and white. The perfect figure
lying in it peering from it.
And he gave her what limbs and lovely face
he could
from the squares, angles, loops, splashes, broken shapes
he saw of all with bare eye and body.

1961

AMIRI BARAKA (LeROI JONES)   ■ ■ ■ ■ ■ ■ ■
b. 1934

Born in Newark, New Jersey, where he currently resides, LeRoi Jones attended
Howard University and served in the United States Air Force before settling in
Greenwich Village in 1957. In 1958, he married Hettie Cohen, with whom he
edited the avant-garde literary magazine *Yugen,* publishing the work of Frank
O'Hara, William Burroughs, and Charles Olson, among others. An organizer of
great energy, Jones also founded Totem Press, served as poetry editor of Corinth
Press, and co-edited the important literary magazine *The Floating Bear* with
poet Diane di Prima.

His early poetry, included in *Preface to a Twenty Volume Suicide Note* (1961)
and *The Dead Lecturer* (1964), is associated with Beat and Black Mountain
poetics. With the production of his plays *The Slave* (1964) and *Dutchman* (1964),
the second of which received the Obie Award, he rose to national prominence.
But with the death of Malcolm X in 1965, Jones left the predominantly white
literary world of Greenwich Village for Harlem, where he founded the Black
Arts Repertory Theatre and began an intense involvement in Black Nationalism.
Returning to live in Newark, he became founding director of Spirit House
Theatre, and married Sylvia Robinson (Bibi Amina Baraka).

In 1968, he took the Bantu-Muslim name Imamu Amiri Baraka, which means "spiritual leader," "prince," and "blessed one"; he also became the main theorist of the Black Aesthetic movement, which sought to replace white models of consciousness with African-American language and values. For Baraka, the ideal black artist was jazz saxophonist John Coltrane:

> Trane is a mature swan whose wing span was a whole new world. But he also showed us to murder the popular song. To do away with weak Western forms.[1]

In 1974, dropping "Imamu" from his name, he rejected Black Nationalism as racist and turned to Third World Marxism, which emphasizes social class over race. *Poetry for the Advanced* (1979) strongly represents this period in Baraka's development. "American culture is multinational," he said in a 1984 radio interview. "It's not just white. It's not European (it's definitely not European—it's got some European origins like it's got some African origins) . . . American culture is multinational."[2]

Baraka's 1963 essay "Expressive Language," in which he challenges the dominance of standard English and upholds the originality and beauty of black dialect, is prophetic of the current multicultural movement.

Recipient of grants from the Rockefeller Foundation and the National Endowment for the Arts, Baraka is currently Professor of Africana Studies at SUNY–Stony Brook.

1. *Black Music*, New York, 1968, p. 174.   2. *The LeRoi Jones/Amiri Baraka Reader*, ed. William J. Harris, New York, 1991, p. 250.

Political Poem

(for Basil)

Luxury, then, is a way of
being ignorant, comfortably
An approach to the open market
of least information. Where theories
can thrive, under heavy tarpaulins
without being cracked by ideas.

(I have not seen the earth for years
and think now possibly "dirt" is
negative, positive, but clearly
social. I cannot plant a seed, cannot
recognize the root with clearer dent
than indifference. Though I eat
and shit as a natural man. (Getting up
from the desk to secure a turkey sandwich
and answer the phone: the poem undone
undone by my station, by my station,
and the bad words of Newark.) Raised up
to the breech, we seek to fill for this
crumbling century. The darkness of love,
in whose sweating memory all error is forced.

Undone by the logic of any specific death. (Old gentlemen
who still follow fires, tho are quieter
and less punctual. It is a polite truth
we are left with. Who are you? What are you
saying? Something to be dealt with, as easily.
The noxious game of reason, saying, "No, No,
you cannot feel," like my dead lecturer
lamenting thru gipsies his fast suicide.

1964

Three Modes of History and Culture

Chalk mark sex of the nation, on walls we drummers
know
as cathedrals. Cathedra, in a churning meat milk.

Women glide through looking for telephones. Maps
weep
and are mothers and their daughters listening to

music teachers. From heavy beginnings. Plantations,
learning
America, as speech, and a common emptiness. Songs knocking

inside old women's faces. Knocking through cardboard trunks.
Trains
leaning north, catching hellfire in windows, passing through

the first ignoble cities of missouri, to illinois, and the panting
Chicago.
And then all ways, we go where flesh is cheap. Where factories

sit open, burning the chiefs. Make your way! Up through fog and
history
Make your way, and swing the general, that it come flash open

and spill the innards of that sweet thing we heard, and gave theory
to.
Breech, bridge, and reach, to where all talk is energy. And there's

enough, for anything singular. All our lean prophets and rhythms.
Entire
we arrive and set up shacks, hole cards, Western hearts at the edge

of saying. Thriving to balance the meanness of particular skies.
Race
of madmen and giants.

Brick songs. Shoe songs. Chants of open weariness.
Knife wiggle early evenings of the wet mouth. Tongue
dance midnight, any season shakes our house. Don't
tear my clothes! To doubt the balance of misery

ripping meat hug shuffle fuck. The Party of Insane
Hope. I've come from there too. Where the dead told lies
about clever social justice. Burning coffins voted
and staggered through cold white streets listening
to Willkie or Wallace or Dewey through the dead face
of Lincoln. Come from there, and belched it out.

I think about a time when I will be relaxed.
When flames and non-specific passion wear themselves
away. And my eyes and hands and mind can turn
and soften, and my songs will be softer
and lightly weight the air.

1969

The New World

The sun is folding, cars stall and rise
beyond the window. The workmen leave
the street to the bums and painters' wives
pushing their babies home. Those who realize
how fitful and indecent consciousness is
stare solemnly out on the emptying street.
The mourners and soft singers. The liars,
and seekers after ridiculous righteousness. All
my doubles, and friends, whose mistakes cannot
be duplicated by machines, and this is all of our
arrogance. Being broke or broken, dribbling
at the eyes. Wasted lyricists, and men
who have seen their dreams come true, only seconds
after they knew those dreams to be horrible conceits
and plastic fantasies of gesture and extension,
shoulders, hair and tongues distributing misinformation
about the nature of understanding. No one is that simple
or priggish, to be alone out of spite and grown strong
in its practice, mystics in two-pants suits. Our style,
and discipline, controlling the method of knowledge.
Beatniks, like Bohemians, go calmly out of style. And boys
are dying in Mexico, who did not get the word.
The lateness of their fabrication: mark their holes
with filthy needles. The lust of the world. This will not
be news. The simple damning lust,

                float flat magic in low changing
                evenings. Shiver your hands

in dance. Empty all of me for
knowing, and will the danger
of identification,

Let me sit and go blind in my dreaming
and be that dream in purpose and device.

A fantasy of defeat, a strong strong man
older, but no wiser than the defect of love.

1969

Leadbelly Gives an Autograph

Pat your foot
and turn
        the corner. Nat Turner, dying wood
of the church. Our lot
is vacant. Bring the twisted myth
of speech. The boards brown and falling
away. The metal bannisters cheap
and rattly. Clean new Sundays. We thought
it possible to enter
the way of the strongest.

But it is rite that the world's ills
erupt as our own. Right that we take
our own specific look into the shapely
blood of the heart.
                Looking thru trees
the wicker statues blowing softly against
the dusk.
Looking thru dusk
thru dark-
ness. A clearing of stars
and half-soft mud.

The possibilities of music. First
that it does exist. And that we do,
in that scripture of rhythms. The earth,
I mean the soil, as melody. The fit you need,
the throes. To pick it up and cut
away what does not singularly express.

Need.
Motive.
The delay of language.

A strength to be handled by giants.

The possibilities of statement. I am saying, now,
what my father could not remember
to say. What my grandfather
was killed
for believing.
          Pay me off, savages.
          Build me an equitable human assertion.

One that looks like a jungle, or one that looks like the cities
of the West.   But I provide the stock. The beasts
and myths.
       The City's Rise!
                   (And what is history, then? An old deaf lady
                   burned to death
                   in South Carolina.

                                    1969

Ka 'Ba

A closed window looks down
on a dirty courtyard, and black people
call across or scream across or walk across
defying physics in the stream of their will

Our world is full of sound
Our world is more lovely than anyone's
tho we suffer, and kill each other
and sometimes fail to walk the air

We are beautiful people
with african imaginations
full of masks and dances and swelling chants
with african eyes, and noses, and arms,
though we sprawl in gray chains in a place
full of winters, when what we want is sun.

We have been captured,
brothers. And we labor
to make our getaway, into
the ancient image, into a new

correspondence with ourselves
and our black family. We need magic
now we need the spells, to raise up
return, destroy, and create. What will be

the sacred words?

                                    1969

Kenyatta Listening to Mozart

on the back trails, in sun glasses
and warm air blows cocaine from city
to river, and through the brains of
American poets in San Francisco.
                              Separate
                    and lose. Spats brush through
                  undergrowths of fiction. Mathematics
              bird, undressed and in sympathy with absolute
                stillness, and the neutrality of water. (We do not
            write poems in the rainy season.) Light to light,
        the weighted circumstance prowls like animals in the
      bush.
      A zoo of consciousness,
                              cries and prowlings
        anywhere. Stillness,
                        motion,
                            beings that fly, beings

that swim
exchanging
            in-
                formation.
                        Choice, and
                        style,
                                avail

and are beautiful
categories
                        If you go
                        for that.

                                                    1969

Leroy

I wanted to know my mother when she sat
looking sad across the campus in the late 20's
into the future of the soul, there were black angels
straining above her head, carrying life from our ancestors,
and knowledge, and the strong nigger feeling. She sat
(in that photo in the yearbook I showed Vashti) getting into
new blues, from the old ones, the trips and passions
showered on her by her own. Hypnotizing me, from so far
ago, from that vantage of knowledge passed on to her passed on
to me and all the other black people of our time.

When I die, the consciousness I carry I will to
black people. May they pick me apart and take the
useful parts, the sweet meat of my feelings. And leave
the bitter bullshit rotten white parts
alone.

1969

The Nation Is Like Ourselves

The nation is like our selves, together
seen in our various scenes, sets where ever we are
what ever we are doing, is what the nation
is
doing
or
not doing
is what the nation
is
being
or
not being

Our nation sits on stoops and watches airplanes take off
our nation is kneeling in the snow bleeding through 6 layers
of jewish enterprise
our nation is standing in line ashamed in its marrow for being
our nation
a people without knowledge of itself
dead matter we are thrown on the soil to richen
european fields
the dead negro is fertilizer
for the glorious western harvest
our nation is ourselves, under the steel talons
of the glorious
Devil
our secret lover who tells us what to do
the steel orange eyes
the ripping fingers of
the Devil
who tells us what to do
blondie
your dress so high
wallachs nigger
mod nigger
nigger in a cow boy hat
why you want to be a cow boy
laid up with a cow

he shouts "power to the nipples,"
doctor nigger, please do some somethin on we
lawyer nigger, please pass some laws about us
liberated nigger with the stringy haired mind, please lib lib lib
you spliv er ate
US, we you, coo-
lust dancing thru yr wet look
ing
tent
acles
please mister liberated nigger love chil nigger
nigger in a bellbottom bell some psychedelic wayoutness
on YO People, even while freeing THE People, please
just first free YO people, ol marijuana jesus I dug your last
    record
with the hootenany biscuits, was revolutionary as a
    motherfucker, ple
ple please mister kinkyman, use your suntan susan swartz is
    using
it, her and tom jones on their show with you and diane carroll
    tiny ti
mmm and the newest negro to understand that theres no black
    no white
only people . . .
        yo imagination is fabulous, reverend, pray for color
        peeples, when the mayor or after the mayor or before
        duh mayor give you yo check, please reverend, and
            daddyboy
and tonto greengrits, and pablo douchebag, susan goldberg's
    daring
nongringo, and allthekidstogether . . . reach back to the constant
    silence
in our lives, where the ideas line up to be graded, and get a
    better one
going than we got, for you and me,
please mr new thing
please mr mystical smasheroo just under ¼ strength learning
    about it
from the flying dutchman
please mr ethnic meditations professor profess your love for black
people we waiting
while you say right on and commit the actual take over of
    yourself
in the anteroom of anything, just before or just after anything
trudging down the halls of your wifes straightened haid we
    realize
how tough things are and how you cant alienate the people
    with the
money we live among stars and angels, listen to devils whines
    like

cold space between the planets, we know
the turn in the hall, your visit to the phone booth to put on an
inferior man suit
a super animal trump
the tarts of your individual consciousness
please all you individuals
and would be involved if people were nicer to you types
or frightened of the military aspects of national liberation folks
in your reinvolved consciousness flitting over the sea at jamaica
if the rastafarians dont kill you please mr vacationing writer
    man
write some heavy justice
about black people
we waiting
we starved for your realness
we know you on the move now
we heard you was outside cairo
bathing at a spa
please mr world travler
please mr celebrity, mr nigger in the treasury department
mr disc jockey for the mournful cash register of the nigger soul
please mr all of us
please miss lady bug
oh lady oh brother, wherever and who ever you are
breathing on
oh please please in the night time
more please in the mewning
we need need you bbbaby man, we need all the blood we gotta
get some blood and
you in your wilderness blood
is the nigger
yes the sweet lost nigger
        you are our nation sick ass assimilado
            please come back
                like james brown say
                    please please please

1970

AM/TRAK

1

Trane.
Trane.
History Love Scream Oh
Trane, Oh
Trane, Oh

Scream History Love
Trane

2

Begin on by a Philly night club
or the basement of a cullut chuhch
walk the bars my man for pay
honk the night lust of money
oh
blow-
scream history love

Rabbit, Cleanhead, Diz
Big Maybelle. Trees in the shining night forest

Oh
blow
love, history

Alcohol we submit to thee
3x's consume our lives
our livers quiver under yr poison hits
eyes roll back in stupidness
The navy, the lord, niggers,
the streets
all converge a shitty symphony
of screams
    to come
    dazzled invective
Honk Honk Honk, "I am here
to love
it. Let me be fire-mystery
air feeder beauty."

Honk
Oh
scream—Miles
comes.

3

Hip band alright
sum up life in the slick
street part of the
world, oh,
blow,
if you cd
nigger
man

Miles wd stand back and negative check
oh, he dug him—Trane
But Trane clawed at the limits of cool
slandered sanity
with his tryin to be born
raging
shit
    Oh
    blow,
yeh go do it
honk, scream
uhuh yeh—history
        love
        blue clipped moments
        of intense feeling.
"Trane you blows too long."
Screaming niggers drop out yr solos
Bohemian nights, the "heavyweight champ"
smacked him
in the face
his eyes sagged like a spent
dick, hot vowels escaped the metal clone of his soul
fucking saxophone
tell us shit tell us tell us!

4

There was nothing left to do but
be where monk cd find him
that crazy
mother fucker
        duh duh-duh duh-duh duh
        duh duh
        duh duh-duh duh-duh duh
        duh duh
        duh duh-duh duh-duh duh
        duh duh
        duh Duuuuuuuuuhhhhhh
Can you play this shit? (Life asks
Come by and listen

& at the 5 Spot Bach, Mulatto ass Beethoven
& even Duke, who has given America its hip tongue
checked
checked
Trane stood and dug
Crazy monk's shit
Street gospel intellectual mystical survival codes
Intellectual street gospel funk modes
Tink a ling put downs of dumb shit

pink pink a cool bam groove note air breath
a why I'm here
a why I aint
& who is you-ha-you-ha-you-ha
Monk's shit
Blue Cooper 5 Spot
was the world busting
on piano bass drums & tenor

This was Coltrane's College. A Ph motherfuckin d
sitting at the feet, elbows
& funny grin
Of Master T Sphere
too cool to be a genius
he was instead
Thelonious
with Comrades Shadow
on tubs, lyric Wilbur
who hipped us to electric futures
& the monster with the horn.

5

From the endless sessions
money lord hovers oer us
capitalism beats our ass
dope & juice wont change it
Trane, blow, oh scream
yeh, anyway.

There then came down in the ugly streets of us
inside the head & tongue
of us
a man
black blower of the now
The vectors from all sources—slavery, renaissance
bop charlie parker,
nigger absolute super-sane screams against reality
course through him
AS SOUND!
"Yes, it says
this is now in you screaming
recognize the truth
recognize reality
& even check me (Trane)
who blows it
Yes it says
Yes &
Yes again   Convulsive multi orgasmic

   Art
   Protest

& finally, brother, you took you were
(are we gathered to dig this?
electric wind find us finally
on red records of the history of ourselves)

The cadre came together
the inimitable 4 who blew the pulse of then, exact
The flame the confusion the love of
whatever the fuck there was
  to love
Yes it says
blow, oh honk-scream (bahhhhhhh - wheeeeeeee)

(If Don Lee thinks I am imitating him in this poem,
this is only payback for his imitating me—we
are brothers, even if he is a backward cultural nationalist
motherfucker—Hey man only socialism brought by revolution
can win)
     Trane was the spirit of the 60's
     He was Malcolm X in New Super Bop Fire
     Baaahhhhh
     Wheeeeeee . . . Black Art!!!
Love
History
 On The Bar Tops of Philly
in the Monkish College of *Express*
in the cool Grottoes of Miles Davis Funnytimery
Be
Be
Be reality
Be reality alive in motion in flame to change (You Knew It!)
           to change!!
    (All you reactionaries listening
    Fuck you, Kill you
    get outta here!!!)
Jimmy Garrison, bass, McCoy Tyner, piano, Captain Marvel Elvin
on drums, the number itself—the precise saying
all of it in it afire aflame talking saying being doing meaning

Meditations
Expressions
A Love Supreme
(I lay in solitary confinement, July 67
Tanks rolling thru Newark
& whistled all I knew of Trane
my knowledge heartbeat

& he was *dead*
they
said.

And yet last night I played *Meditations*
& it told me what to do
Live you crazy mother
fucker!
Live!
  & organize
  yr shit
  as rightly
  burning!

1979

DIANE DI PRIMA ■ ■ ■ ■ ■ ■ ■ ■ ■ ■ ■ ■ ■ ■

b. 1934

Born in Brooklyn and educated at Swarthmore College, Diane di Prima began corresponding with poets Ezra Pound and Kenneth Patchen at age nineteen. Her first book of poems, *This Kind of Bird Flies Backwards*, was published in 1958, followed by a book of prose, *Dinners and Nightmares*, in 1960. In 1961, while living on Manhattan's Lower East Side, she began editing the literary magazine *The Floating Bear* with LeRoi Jones. The same year, the editors were arrested by the FBI for alleged obscenity, but the case was thrown out by the grand jury. Her second poetry collection, *The New Handbook of Heaven*, appeared in 1963.

In 1968, she moved to San Francisco, where she studied with Zen master Shenryu Suzuki Roshi. Her most popular early collection, *Revolutionary Letters*, was published in 1971. The same year, she began writing the long poem *Loba*, Parts 1–8 of which were published in 1978. The poem began with a dream di Prima had in Wyoming of being followed by a wolf:

> . . . at some point, I turned around and looked this creature in the eye, and I recognized, in my dream . . . this huge white wolf, beautiful white head, recognized this as a goddess that I'd known in Europe a long long time ago. Never having read about any European wolf-goddesses, I just recognized this as deity. And we stood and looked at each other for a long moment.[1]

Like Jerome Rothenberg, di Prima is interested in alternative European spiritual traditions such as "Paganism, Gnosticism, alchemy"; she is also devoted to the "Way-seeking Mind" of Buddhism.[2] Associated with the Beat movement, di Prima writes a poetry of "magical evocation," to borrow from one of her titles, that has a Keatsian lyricism and roundness of phrasing.

Co-founder of the New York Poets Theatre and the Masters Program in Poetics at New College of California, di Prima teaches at the San Francisco Institute of Magical and Healing Arts. A collection of selected poems, *Pieces of a Song*, was published in 1990.

1. Diane di Prima, "The Birth of Loba," in *Symposium of the Whole: A Range of Discourse toward an Ethnopoetics*, ed. Jerome Rothenberg, Berkeley, 1983, p. 442.   2. The same, p. 444.

The Practice of Magical Evocation

The female is fertile, and discipline
(contra naturam) only
confuses her
—GARY SNYDER

i am a woman and my poems
are woman's: easy to say
this   the female is ductile
and
      (stroke after stroke)
built for masochistic
calm.   The deadened nerve
is part of it:
awakened sex, dead retina
fish eyes;   at hair's root
minimal feeling

and pelvic architecture functional
assailed inside & out
(bring forth)   the cunt gets wide
and relatively sloppy
bring forth men children only
                    female
                    is
                    ductile

woman, a veil thru which the fingering Will
twice torn
twice torn
          inside & out
the flow
what rhythm add to stillness
what applause?

                                        1975

On Sitting Down to Write, I Decide Instead to Go to
Fred Herko's Concert

As water, silk
the quiver of fish
or the long cry of goose
          or some such bird
          I never heard
your orange tie
a sock in the eye

as Duncan
might forcibly note
are you sitting under the irregular drums
of Brooklyn Joe Jones
(in a loft which I know to be dirty
& probably cold)
or have you scurried already
hurried already
uptown
on a Third Avenue Bus
toward smelly movies & crabs I'll never get
and you all perfumed too
as if they'd notice

O the dark caves of obligation
into which I must creep
(alack)
like downstairs & into a coat
O all that wind
Even Lord & Taylor don't quite keep out
that wind
and that petulant vacuum
I am aware of it
sucking me into Bond Street
into that loft
dank
rank
I draw a blank
at the very thought

Hello
I came here
after all

1975

For H.D.

1

trophies of pain I've gathered.   whose sorrow
do I shore up, in trifles?   the weavings,
paintings, jewels, plants, I bought

with my heart's hope.   rocks from the road
to Hell, broken pieces of statuary, ropes,
bricks, from the city of Dis.

encrusted.   they surround me: nest
the horror of each act from which I saved
a dried, dismembered hand.   poisoned

amulets, empty vials still fuming.   their tears
saved lovingly as my own.   to have
"lived passionately"   this secret

hoarding of passion.   Truth turned against itself.

2

Heart's truth, spat out of sleep, was only hate.
I caught it, on my pillows.   Tried
to turn it to diamonds.   Sometimes succeeded

so far as quartz in the hand.   Like ice it melted.
Heat of my will   burns down the walls around me
time after time.   Yet there remain

encrustrations of old loves.   Filthy barnacles
sucking my marrow.   My illness:
that I am not blind,   yet cannot transmute

In body cauldron I carried
hate or indifference, anger,   clothed it
in child flesh,   & in the light

it seemed I had worked magic. But the stone
sticks in their throats. Night screams & morning tears
phantoms of fathers,   dead skin hung on

old bones.   Like jewels in the hair.

3

"I am a woman of pleasure"   & give back
salt for salt. Untrammeled by hope or knowledge
I have left these

in the grindstones of other thresholds. Now only bedrock
basalt to crack your breath. Beloved. To suck for drink.
I am not fair. But you are more than fair.

You are too kind.   Still water   in which,
like a crystal, the phantoms dance.
Each carrying death like a spear,   for we die

of each other's hate, or indifference.   Draw blood
to draw out poison.   But it has seat
in heart of our heart, the hollow of the marrow

of our bones.   Salt for salt   & the desert
is infinite   it drinks
more juice than we carry.

4

O, I'd yet beg bread, or water,   wd lie
in the dry wash & pray the flood wd come
That my eyes unstick,   that I see stars

as I drown.   For 25 years, bruised, wounded,
I've hid in rocks.   Fed by hyenas, vultures, the despised
that chew carrion   & share the meal

which, sharing,   you lose caste;   forget
human laws.   My blood
tastes in my mouth like sand.

5

humiliated   time & again   by song
laughter from cracked lips.
power of incantation stirring to life

what shd sleep, like stone.   yet the turquoise
sparkles.   "happy to see you"   stars
beat against my skin.   what is mine:

cold prickles,   moving out
from spine.   pulsing skull
pushing to light.   burning bushes

that lie.   snow mountains where gods
leave laws, like stones.   Anubis in Utah.
and tears.   and tears.   and tears.

to bless my desert   and give back
song for salt.

1975

Backyard

where angels turned into honeysuckle & poured nectar into my mouth
where I french-kissed the roses in the rain

where demons tossed me a knife to kill my father in the stark
    simplicity of the sky
where I never cried
where all the roofs were black
where no one opened the venetian blinds
O Brooklyn! Brooklyn!
where fences crumbled under the weight of rambling roses
and naked plaster women bent eternally white over birdbaths
the icicles on the chains of the swings tore my fingers
& the creaking tomato plants tore my heart as they wrapped their
    roots around fish heads rotting beneath them
& the phonograph too creaked Caruso come down from the skies;
    Tito Gobbi in gondola; Gigli ridiculous in soldier uniform;
    Lanza frenetic
& the needle tore at the records & my fingers
tore poems into little pieces & watched the sky
where clouds torn into pieces & livid w/neon or rain
scudded away from Red Hook, away from Gowanus Canal, away
from Brooklyn Navy Yard where everybody worked, to fall to pieces
    over Clinton Street
and the plaster saints in the yard never looked at the naked women
    in the birdbaths
and the folks coming home from work in pizza parlor or furniture
    store, slamming wrought iron gates to come
    upon brownstone houses,
never looked at either: they saw that the lawns were dry
were eternally parched beneath red gloomy sunsets we viewed from
    a thousand brownstone stoops
leaning together by thousands on the same
wrought-iron bannister, watching the sun impaled
on black St. Stephen's steeple

                      1975

The Loba Addresses the Goddess / or The Poet as Priestess Addresses the Loba-Goddess

Is it not in yr service that I wear myself out
running ragged among these hills, driving children
to forgotten movies? In yr service
broom & pen. The monstrous feasts
we serve the others on the outer porch
(within the house there is only rice & salt)
And we wear exhaustion like a painted robe
I & my sisters
              wresting the goods from the niggardly
            dying fathers
healing each other w / water & bitter herbs

that when we stand naked in the circle of lamps
(beside the small water, in the inner grove)
we show
no blemish, but also no superfluous beauty.
It has burned off in watches of the night.
O Nut, O mantle of stars, we catch at you
  lean   mournful
  ragged triumphant
   shaggy as grass
our skins ache of emergence / dark o' the moon

1978

TED BERRIGAN   ▪ ▪ ▪ ▪ ▪ ▪ ▪ ▪ ▪ ▪ ▪ ▪ ▪ ▪
1934–1983

A leading figure of the New York School's second generation, Ted Berrigan was born in Providence, Rhode Island. After three years in the U.S. Army, he finished his college degree and earned a master's degree at the University of Tulsa. It was in Oklahoma that he met poets Ron Padgett and Dick Gallup and artist and poet Joe Brainard, who arrived with Berrigan in New York City as a "Tulsa group." In 1963 he founded *C Magazine*, with Ed Sanders's *Fuck You: A Magazine of the Arts* and Ron Padgett's *White Dove Review*, one of the more significant little magazines of the period.

During the late sixties and throughout the seventies, Berrigan was a charismatic leader in the bohemian poetry scene of the Lower East Side, especially as it centered around the Poetry Project at St. Mark's Church. His first major publication, *The Sonnets* (1967), remains among his finest work. Using cut-ups from a variety of sources, including his own writing, he renewed interest in the sonnet form. The everydayness of Berrigan's work, which he openly appropriates from Frank O'Hara's "I do this, I do that" poems, balances and counters his natural tendency toward elegy. Besides O'Hara, Berrigan's literary influences include Paul Blackburn and Philip Whalen, whose *On Bear's Head* he greatly admired.

His many books of poetry include *Many Happy Returns* (1969), *In the Early Morning Rain* (1970), *Train Ride* (1971), *Red Wagon* (1976), and *Nothing for You* (1977), all of which are represented in *So Going Around Cities: New & Selected Poems 1958–1979* (1980). A posthumous volume, *A Certain Slant of Sunlight*, consisting of poems designed to fit on a series of postcards, appeared in 1988. With Ron Padgett, Berrigan wrote *Bean Spasms* (1967), a book containing poems by both authors, as well as works written in full collaboration. The fact that none of the poems in *Bean Spasms* was assigned authorship was consistent with the sixties' challenge both to individual ownership and to a hierarchical concept of authorship.

Berrigan died on July 4, 1983, following years of health problems compounded by amphetamine use. In 1991, *Nice to See You: Homage to Ted Berrigan* was published, a volume of essays, poems, and reminiscences by his many friends recounting Berrigan's widespread influence on poets of his generation.

FROM *The Sonnets*

II

Dear Margie, hello. It is 5:15 a.m.
dear Berrigan. He died
Back to books. I read
It's 8:30 p.m. in New York and I've been running around all day
old come-all-ye's streel into the streets. Yes, it is now,
How Much Longer Shall I Be Able To Inhabit The Divine
and the day is bright gray turning green
feminine marvelous and tough
watching the sun come up over the Navy Yard
to write scotch-tape body in a notebook
had 17 and ½ milligrams
Dear Margie, hello. It is 5:15 a.m.
fucked til 7 now she's late to work and I'm
18 so why are my hands shaking I should know better

XXXVI

after Frank O'Hara

It's 8:54 a.m. in Brooklyn it's the 28th of July and
it's probably 8:54 in Manhattan but I'm
in Brooklyn I'm eating English muffins and drinking
pepsi and I'm thinking of how Brooklyn is New
York city too how odd I usually think of it as
something all its own like Bellows Falls like Little
Chute like Uijongbu
            I never thought on the Williams-
burg bridge I'd come so much to Brooklyn
just to see lawyers and cops who don't even carry
guns taking my wife away and bringing her back
                             No
and I never thought Dick would be back at Gude's
beard shaved off long hair cut and Carol reading
his books when we were playing cribbage and
watching the sun come up over the Navy Yard
across the river
            I think I was thinking when I was
ahead I'd be somewhere like Perry street erudite
dazzling slim and badly loved
contemplating my new book of poems
to be printed in simple type on old brown paper
feminine marvelous and tough

LXXXVIII

A FINAL SONNET

for Chris

How strange to be gone in a minute!   A man
Signs a shovel and so he digs   Everything
Turns into writing a name for a day
                              Someone
is having a birthday and someone is getting
married and someone is telling a joke   my dream
a white tree   I dream of the code of the west
But this rough magic I here abjure   and
When I have required some heavenly music   which even
    now
I do   to work mine end upon *their* senses
That this aery charm is for   I'll break
My staff   bury it certain fathoms in the earth
And deeper than did ever plummet sound
I'll drown my book.
It is 5:15 a.m.   Dear Chris, hello.

                                                      1967

Words for Love

for Sandy

Winter crisp and the brittleness of snow
as like make me tired as not. I go my
myriad ways blundering, bombastic, dragged
by a self that can never be still, pushed
by my surging blood, my reasoning mind.

I am in love with poetry. Every way I turn
this, my weakness, smites me. A glass
of chocolate milk, head of lettuce, dark-
ness of clouds at one o'clock obsess me.
I weep for all of these or laugh.

By day I sleep, an obscurantist, lost
in dreams of lists, compiled by my self
for reassurance. Jackson Pollock   René
Rilke   Benedict Arnold   I watch
my psyche, smile, dream wet dreams, and sigh.

At night, awake, high on poems, or pills
or simple awe that loveliness exists, my lists

flow differently. Of words bright red
and black, and blue.   Bosky.   Oubliette.   Dis-
severed. And O, alas

Time disturbs me. Always minute detail
fills me up. It is 12:10 in New York. In Houston
it is 2 p.m. It is time to steal books. It's
time to go mad. It is the day of the apocalypse
the year of parrot fever! What am I saying?

Only this. My poems do contain
wilde beestes. I write for my Lady
of the Lake. My god is immense, and lonely
but uncowed. I trust my sanity, and I am proud. If
I sometimes grow weary, and seem still, nevertheless

my heart still loves, will break.

1969

Bean Spasms

to George Schneeman

New York's lovely weather

            hurts my forehead

           in praise of thee
                  the? white dead
                  whose eyes know:
        what are they
    of the tiny cloud my brain:
The City's tough red buttons:
              O Mars, red, angry planet, candy

                    bar, with sky on top,
      "why, it's young Leander hurrying to his death"
    what? what time is it in New York   in these here alps
   City of lovely tender hate
              and beauty making beautiful
                    old rhymes?
  I ran away from you
when you needed something strong
      then I leand against the toilet bowl (ack)
   Malcolm X
        I love my brain
  it all mine now is
  saved not knowing

that &
that (happily)
being that:

"wee kill our selves to propagate our kinde"
                                        John Donne
yes, that's true

               the hair on yr nuts & my
                    big blood-filled cock are a part in that
               too

PART 2

               Mister Robert Dylan doesn't feel well today
               That's bad
               This picture doesn't show that
               It's not bad, too

          it's very ritzy in fact

          here I stand I can't stand
          to be thing
     I don't use   atop
                         the empire state
                         building
                         & so sauntered out that door
That reminds me of the time
I wrote that long piece about a gangster name of "Jr."
O Harry James! had eyes to wander but lacked tongue to praise
                    so later peed under his art

     paused only to lay a sneeze
                              on Jack Dempsey
                    asleep with his favorite Horse

          That reminds me of I buzz
               on & off Miró pop
                    in & out a Castro convertible
     minute by minute   GENEROSITY!

     Yes now that the seasons totter in their walk
          I do a lot of wondering about Life   in praise of ladies dead of
& Time plaza(s), Bryant Park by the Public   eye of brow
Library, Smith Bros. black boxes, Times
                    Square
               Pirogi Houses
                    with long skinny rivers thru them
               they lead the weary away
                    off! hey!

I'm no sailor
off a ship
at sea   I'M HERE
& "The living is easy"
It's "HIGH TIME"
& I'm in shapes
of shadow, they
certainly can warm, can't they?

Have you ever seen one?   NO!
of those long skinny Rivers
So well hung, in New York City
NO!   in fact
I'm the Wonderer
& as yr train goes by   forgive me, René!   "just oncet"
I woke up in Heaven
He woke, and wondered more; how many angels
on this train huh?   snore

for there she lay
on sheets that mock lust   done that 7 times
been caught
and brought back
to a peach nobody.

To Continue:
Ron Padgett & Ted Berrigan
hates yr brain
my dears
amidst the many other little buzzes
& like, Today, as Ron Padgett might say
is
"A tub of vodka"
"in the morning"
she might reply
and that keeps it up
past icy poles
where angels beg fr doom then zip
ping in-and-out, joining the army
wondering about Life
by the Public Library of
Life
No Greater Thrill!
(I wonder)

Now that the earth is changing I wonder what time it's getting to be
sitting on this New York Times Square
that actually very ritzy, Lauren   it's made of yellow wood or

I don't know something   maybe
This man was my   it's been fluffed up
       friend
              He had a sense for the
                    vast   doesn't he?
          Awake my Angel! give thyself
                 to the lovely hours   Don't cheat
         The victory is not always to the sweet.
                 I mean that.

Now this picture is pretty good here
Though it once got demerits from the lunatic Arthur Cravan
He wasn't feeling good that day
Maybe because he had nothing on
                         paint-wise I mean

PART 3

        I wrote that
           about what is
      this empty room   without a heart
           now in three parts
           a white flower
      came home wet & drunk   2 Pepsis
      and smashed my fist thru her window
                         in the nude
    As the hand zips you see
           Old Masters, you can see
      well hung in New York   they grow fast here
           Conflicting, yet purposeful
                 yet with outcry vain!

PART 4

             Praising, that's it!
you string a sonnet around yr fat gut
   and falling on your knees
                    you invent the shoe
                    for a horse. It brings you luck
                 while sleeping
                    "You have it seems a workshop nature"
Have you   "Good Lord!"
                             Some folks is wood
seen them?   Ron Padgett wd say
                 amidst the many other little buzzes
                 past the neon on & off
                 night & day   STEAK SANDWICH
             Have you ever tried one Anne?   SURE!
     "I wonder what time 'its'?"

as I sit on this new Doctor
NO   I only look at buildings they're in
as you and he, I mean he & you & I buzz past
                                    in yellow ties   I call that gold
                        THE HOTEL BUCKINGHAM
                    (facade) is black, and taller than last time
is looming over lunch   naked   high time   poem   & I, equal in
                                                    perfection & desire
            is looming   two eyes   over coffee-cup (white) nature
                        and man: both hell on poetry.
                    Art is art and life is
                                "A monograph on Infidelity"
            Oh. Forgive me stench of sandwich
            O pneumonia in American Poetry

        Do we have time?   well look at Burroughs
            7 times been caught and brought back to Mars
                        & eaten
"Art is art & Life
is home," Fairfield Porter said that
                                turning himself in
                                    Tonight arrives again in red
some go on   even in Colorado   on the run
                                    the forests shake
                meaning:
                            coffee   the cheerfulness of this poor
                                            fellow is terrible, hidden in
                                            the fringes of the eyelids
                        blue mysteries' (I'M THE SKY)
        The sky is bleeding now
                        onto 57th Street
                    of the 20th Century &
                        HORN & HARDART'S
Right Here. That's PART 5

        I'm not some sailor off a ship at sea
I'm the wanderer   (age 4)
                        & now everyone is dead
                sinking bewildered of hand, of foot, of lip
    nude, thinking
laughter burnished brighter than hate
                                                Goodbye.
                    André Breton said that
                                    what a shit!
Now he's gone!
                        up bubbles all his amorous breath
                    & Monograph on Infidelity entitled
                                                The Living Dream
I never again played

I dreamt that December 27th, 1965
all in the blazon of sweet beauty's breast

I mean   "a rose"   Do you understand that?
Do you?
The rock&roll songs of this earth
commingling absolute joy AND
incontrovertible joy of intelligence
certainly can warm
can't they?   YES!
and they do.
Keeping eternal whisperings around

(Mr. Macadams writes in
the nude: no that's not
(we want to take the underground   me that: then zips in &
revolution to Harvard!)   out the boring taxis, re-
fusing to join the army
and yet this girl has   asleep "on the springs"
so much grace   of red GENEROSITY)
I wonder!
Were all their praises simply prophecies
of this
the time!   NO GREATER THRILL
my friends

But I quickly forget them, those other times, for what are they
but parts in the silver lining of the tiny cloud my brain
drifting up into smoke the city's tough blue top:

I think a picture always
leads you gently to someone else
Don't you? like when you ask to leave the room
& go to the moon.

1966   1969

ANSELM HOLLO   ▪ ▪ ▪ ▪ ▪ ▪ ▪ ▪ ▪ ▪ ▪ ▪ ▪ ▪

b. 1934

Anselm Hollo was born and raised in Helsinki, Finland, and has worked as a
poet, translator, editor, journalist, and teacher in Sweden, Germany, Austria,
England, and, since 1966, the United States. His numerous books of poetry
include *Maya* (1970), which contains work selected from twelve earlier small
press collections, *Alembic* (1972), *Heavy Jars* (1977), *Sojourner Microcosms*
(1977), *Finite Continued* (1980), *No Complaints* (1983), *Pick Up the House*
(1986), *Outlying Districts* (1990), and *Near Miss Haiku* (1990).
    Hollo is co-editor of *Modern Swedish Poetry in Translation* (1979), and is also

widely known for his many translations of European poetry, including the work of Russian poet Andrei Voznesensky and Finnish poet Pentii Saarikoski.

In the idiomatic tradition of William Carlos Williams, Hollo's work privileges the details of everyday life. He is adept at capturing isolated moments of perception. In this, his work resembles that of Philip Whalen and of Hollo's close friend Ted Berrigan. Often whimsical and gently satirical in tone, Hollo's poems are open-ended, valuing an ongoing human attentiveness rather than rejecting closure on the basis of theory. Poet Robert Grenier refers to the "*sinceritas* & Taoism & *many* of the *Confucian* virtues" of Hollo's work, all of which give the impression of "man-standing-by-his-word." He also finds in Hollo the solidity of "a man to be trusted with your life, whose behavior is erratic, comedic, 'tribal' & profound."[1]

Hollo lives in Boulder, Colorado, where he teaches at the Naropa Institute.

1. "I Had No Idea," review of Hollo's *Pick Up the House*, *Sulfur*, No. 23, Spring 1988, p. 216.

Journey, 1966

. . . watched you
& you were turning, turning
from me, & back to me, you were light & dark
both, in ever-shifting proportion
as were the questions that whirled in my head

—question answered by question, your voice & mine
following, leading, leading us where? where
were we going, where could we go, if we would, when
we would, and what were the reasons given,
the best way to get there, through rooms & streets,
the blueing desert, encased in time

watched you, trying to read your face

wandered in light halls, dark caves, held by the wind
piercing us beyond pleasure or pain: that constant spear

watched us, resting, bodies stretched out on a shield
in a place with many old gods on the walls: did they
whisper & hum, back through their millions of lives,
through time? I could not hear them, only your breath,

only the songs of your body, your face: an intricate
chant, an enchantment, clear in all its relations

high, high on it, in the place we had reached
I was open to you, your music, not watching but seeing
you—light
      in the dark
            that shines beyond walls or time

1986

Shed the Fear

Who has a face sees
    the world,
but the world
    is not

to be borne—
    or only
when seen as
    another:

how did this
    come together? How
did I find you?
    So many turns

in the road,
    so few of them
possible!
    How not to spin out

in hairpin turns
    of disbelief . . .
The Sufi martyrs
    insisted:

"The world ·
    is a wedding."
Why not
    go with them,

in the face of
    present carnage,
centuries
    later.

1986

The Dream of Instant Total Representation

Primaries, conventions, elections—
    spectacularly staged surrogates for old dreams
        of powwows by the campfire,
    direct votes cast at the forum
        or Anglo-Saxon "thing"

Dreamy memories of just about postnomadic time
when the turnip was the new technology.
While knowing this was long ago, far away,
we'd still like to get next to the headperson
and deliver a speech, at least twice as long
        as anyone else's . . .

Even if telepathy were perfected—
and instant global communication—
where on earth would we find
statespersons, legislators, bureaucrats
able to withstand such an incredible onslaught
        of info? Would the result not be total
overload, fried circuits, the screaming meemies?

Yet each and every ant knows exactly what
        it has to be doing every second,
the whole shebang self-contained
and self-informing—

To paraphrase Blaise Pascal, I'd rather be
        a confused, blundering, warm-blooded
        hairy creature with language
to complain in, to praise with, no matter what,
than nature's prototype for the microchip.

1986

Godlike

when you suddenly
feel like talking

about the times
in your life when you were

a total idiot asshole you resist
the impulse

& just sit there
at the head of the table

beaming

1990

Italics

for Joe Cardarelli

when young I was awed by authority
figures

even imitation
authority figures (people

who *yearned*
to be *thought* authority figures

I used to resent that reaction
in myself

& believed that it was
my fault

in some sense or at least
my mistake

but now I know
that I was not to blame

those people
really *are* awful

as for the rest
make sure you're reading

what you *think* you're reading

1990

Wild West Workshop Poem

when after muchos años
& by the book "high noon" encounters

scarred but victorious Ned returned
to the Famous Gunfighters' School

Old Byrum cackled "hell, boy, who would've thought
you'd take all that stuff so seriously—

we just pop 'em in the back
whenever we get a chance"

1990

JOSEPH CERAVOLO ▪ ▪ ▪ ▪ ▪ ▪ ▪ ▪ ▪ ▪ ▪ ▪ ▪
1934–1988

Joseph Ceravolo lived in Bloomfield, New Jersey, and worked by day as a civil engineer specializing in hydraulics. Among his poetry collections are *Spring in This World of Poor Mutts* (1968), winner of the Frank O'Hara Book Award, *Transmigration Solo* (1979), *Millenium Dust* (1982), and a posthumous volume of selected poetry, *The Green Lake Is Awake* (1994).

In its inspired innocence, some of Ceravolo's work suggests that of Kenneth Koch; yet it reveals a darker sense of wonder than Koch's much more bemused eye. Ceravolo seems to strive for ultimate understanding of experience; rather than elaborate on the actual, his poetry often deals in first and last things in a vein that is minimal, cosmic, sensual, and lyrical. Of his work poet and critic Peter Schjeldahl writes, "Ceravolo is a lyric poet of such oddness and purity that reading him all but makes me dizzy, like exercise at a very high altitude. I rarely know what he is talking about, but I can rarely gainsay a word he uses. . . . there is a dominance of usages I want to call 'off' or 'bent,' like vamped notes in jazz."[1]

Speaking to the poet David Shapiro, Ceravolo commented that "he didn't so much express emotions as observe the linguistic constellations that grouped themselves during or around an emotion." His desire, he told Shapiro during their many discussions on poetry, was "to create only one school, The School of Everyday Life, with courses in the seasons."[2]

1. "Cabin Fever," a review of Ceravolo's *Transmigration Solo* in *Parnassus*, Spring/Summer 1981, p. 297.   2. "Remarks on Joe Ceravolo for Paul Hoover," unpublished, 1993.

Ho Ho Ho Caribou

for Rosemary

I

Leaped at the caribou.
My son looked at the caribou.
The kangaroo leaped on the
fruit tree. I am a white
man and my children
are hungry
which is like paradise.
The doll is sleeping.
It lay down to creep into
the plate.
It was clean and flying.

II

Where you . . . . the axes
are. Why is this home so
hard. So much

like the sent over the
courses below the home
having a porch.

Felt it on my gate in the place
where caribous jumped
over. Where geese sons
and pouches of daughters look at
me and say "I'm hungry
daddy."

III

Not alone in the
gastrous   desert. We are looking
at the caribous out in the water
swimming around. We
want to go in the ocean
along the dunes.
Where do we like?
   Like little lice in the sand
we look into a fruit expanse.
Oh the sky is so cold.
We run into the water.
Lice in heaven.

IV

My heel. Ten o'clock the class.
Underwater fish
brush by us. Oh leg
not reaching!
The show is stopping
at the sky to drive in the
truck. Tell us where to
stop and eat. And
drink which comes to us out
in the sand is
        at a star.
My pants are damp.
Is tonight treating us
but not reaching through the window.

V

Where is that bug going?
Why are your hips
rounded as the sand?
What is jewelry?

Baby sleeps. Sleeping on
the cliff is dangerous.
The television of all voice is
way far behind.
Do we flow nothing?
Where did you follow that bug
to?
     See quick . . . . . . is flying.

VI

Caribou, what have I
done? See how her
heart moves like a little
bug . . . . . . under my thumb.
Throw me deeply.
I am the floes.
Ho ho ho caribou,
light brown and wetness
caribou. I stink and
I know it.
"Screw you! . . . . you're right."

VII

Everyone has seen us out
with the caribou but
no one has seen us out in
the car. You passed
beyond us.
We saw your knees
but the other night we
couldn't call you.
You were more far than a
widow feeling you.
Nothing has been terrible.
We are the people who have
been running with
animals.
More than when we run?

VIII

Tell us where o eat to stop and eat.
The diner is never gonna come.
The forest things are passing.
I did drink my milk
like a mother of wolves.
Wolves on the desert

of ice cold love, of
fireproof breasts and the breast
I took like snow.
Following me
I love you
and I fall beyond
and I eat you like a
bow and arrow withering in the
        desert.

IX

No one should be mean.
Making affection and all the green
winters wide awake.
Blubber is desert. Out on
the firm lake, o firm
and aboriginal kiss.
To dance, to hunt, to sing,
no one should be mean.
Not needing these things.

X

Like a flower, little light, you open
and we make believe
we die. We die all around
you like a snake in a
well and we come up out
of the warm well and
are born again out of dry
mammas, nourishing mammas, always
holding you as I
love you and am
revived inside you, but
die in you and am
never born again in
the same place; never
stop!

1968

Pregnant, I Come

I come to you
with the semen
and the babies:
ropes of the born.

I rise up as you go up
in your consciousness.
Are you unhappy
in the source?

The clouds sputter
across the ring.
Do the birds sing?

Is the baby singing in you? yet.

1968

Geological Hymn

The wine is gone,
but I'm still not drunk.
Can non-visual reality
bring all my dreams to completion?

My head doesn't belong to me
Why should it?
A desert, an ocean, a tundra,
in the antecedent cambrian worm
lies before me in a field of vision,
not from me or in me
but from some foreign night
falling and falling in snow.

But I still come around
while the wind itself is gone
and the soul like a strung bow
in the elastic and infinite void

stretches beyond the spaced out message
in this geological kiss.

1982

New Realism

A coyote's song
wet with death
makes me live just to die
in this approaching light.

These rods of light
that are on everything.
These winds of light that stick to me.

A dream, a stab
of preservation. A mouth
between ourselves,
a preserver of heaven
between our legs.

Summer, summer,
a rumor greater than mud is out,
and it's seeding the whirlpool
of earth's magnified fall.

1982

JOHN WIENERS ■ ■ ■ ■ ■ ■ ■ ■ ■ ■ ■ ■ ■ ■ ■ ■ ■
b. 1934

Born in Milton, Massachusetts, John Wieners received his degree from Boston College in 1954 and studied at Black Mountain College under Charles Olson and Robert Duncan from 1955 to 1956. He then returned to Boston, where he founded the short-lived literary magazine *Measure*. He has since lived and worked there, with occasional sojourns to teach and write in New York City, San Francisco, and the State University of New York at Buffalo.

Wieners's life and writing are integrally connected to politics; he has been deeply involved in publishing and education cooperatives, political action committees, and the gay liberation movement. Describing this tie, Wieners stated in a 1974 interview, "Lyricism is still a quality of a political career."[1] Despite Wieners's ability to communicate to a wider audience through what Allen Ginsberg calls his "Keatsian eloquence, pathos, and substantiality,"[2] his topics of madness (Weiners has spent time in state mental hospitals, and, in 1959, underwent shock therapy) and homosexuality have kept him outside the literary mainstream from early in his career.

Although Wieners was influenced as a young man by Charles Olson, his work has always been more personal and less committed to poetic theory than Olson's. To the question "Do you have a theory of poetics?" Wieners once responded, "I try to write the most embarrassing thing I can think of."[3]

Notable among Wieners's books are *The Hotel Wentley Poems* (1958), *Ace of Pentacles* (1964), *Asylum Poems* (1969), *Behind the State Capitol or Cincinnati Pike* (1975), *Selected Poems 1958–1984* (1986), and *Cultural Affairs in Boston: Poetry and Prose 1956–1985* (1988).

1. "Robert Von Hallberg: A Talk with John Wieners (1974)," in *John Wieners: Selected Poems 1958–1984*, Santa Barbara, 1986, p. 289. 2. Foreword to *John Wieners: Selected Poems 1958–1984*, p. 15. 3. "Raymond Foye: An Interview with John Wieners," in *Cultural Affairs in Boston: Poetry and Prose 1956–1985*, Santa Rosa, 1988, p. 15.

A poem for the insane

The 2nd afternoon I come
back to the women of Munch.

Models with god over—
their shoulders, vampires,

the heads are down and
blood is the water-
              color
they use to turn on.

The story is not done.
There is one wall
left to walk. Yeah—

Afterwards—Nathan
gone, Big Eric busted,
Swanson down. It is

right, the Melancholy
on the Beach. I do not
           split
but hang on the Demon

Tree, while shadows drift
around me. Until at last
there is left only the

Death Chamber. Family Reunion
in it. Rocking chairs and
who is the young man

who sneaks out thru
the black curtain, away
from the bad bed.

Yeah stand now
on the new road, with the
huge mountain on your

right out of the mist
the Bridge before me,
the woman waiting

with no mouth, waiting
for me to kiss it on.
I will. I will walk with

my eyes up on you for
ever. We step into
the Kiss, 1897.

The light streams.
Melancholy carries
a red sky and our dreams

are blue boats
no one can bust or
blow out to sea.

We ride them
and Tingel-Tangel
in the afternoon.

6.23.58

1958

The Waning of the Harvest Moon

No flowers now to wear at
Sunset. Autumn and the rain. Dress in
blue. For the descent. Dogs bark at
the gate. Go down daughter my soul
heavy with the memory of heaven.

It is time for famine and empty
altars. We ask your leave for by
your going we gain spring again.
No lights glimmer in the box.
I want to go out and rob a grocery store.

Hunger. My legs ache. Who will feed us.
Miles more to go. Secrets yet unread.
Dogs bark in my ears. My man lost.
My soul a jangle of lost connections.
Who will plug in the light at autumn.
When all men are alone.
Down. And further yet to go.
Words gone from my mouth.
Speechless in the tide.

1964

A Poem for Trapped Things

This morning with a blue flame burning
this thing wings its way in.
Wind shakes the edges of its yellow being.
Gasping for breath.
Living for the instant.

Climbing up the black border of the window.
Why do you want out.
I sit in pain.
A red robe amid debris.
You bend and climb, extending antennae.

I know the butterfly is my soul
grown weak from battle.

A Giant fan on the back of
          a beetle.
A caterpillar chrysalis that seeks
a new home apart from this room.

And will disappear from sight
at the pulling of invisible strings.
Yet so tenuous, so fine
   this thing is, I am
     sitting on the hard bed, we could
        vanish from sight like the puff
           off an invisible cigarette.
Furred chest, ragged silk under
        wings beating against the glass

      no one will open.

The blue diamonds on your back
are too beautiful to do
        away with.
I watch you
    all morning
        long.
With my hand over my mouth.

                        1964

My Mother

talking to strange men on the subway,

doesn't see me when she gets on,

    at Washington Street
but I hide in a booth at the side

    and watch her worried, strained face—
the few years she has got left.
    Until at South Station

I lean over and say:
I've been watching you since you got on.
    She says in an artificial
        voice: Oh, for Heaven's sake!

    as if heaven cared.

But I love her in the underground
        and her gray coat and hair
sitting there, one man over from me
        talking together between the wire grates of a cage.

                                                    1964

Two Years Later

    The hollow eyes of shock remain
    Electric sockets burnt out in the
            skull.

    The beauty of men never disappears
    But drives a blue car through the
            stars.

                                                    1964

The Loneliness

    It is so sad
    It is so lonely
    I felt younger after doing him,
    and when I looked in the mirror
    my hair was rumpled.

    I smoothed it
    and rooted for someone else
    or wanted to satisfy myself,
    Almost seven,
    No hope left.

    How can a man have pride
    without a wife.

    I spit him out on the floor.
    Immensely relieved
    After ejaculating
    Imagining myself up my lover's ass
    he coming by himself.

Looking out the window, for no reason
except to soothe myself
I shall go to the bookstore
And pretend nothing happened.
Enormously gratified.

Feeling like a girl
stinking beneath my clothes.

1972   1988

ROBERT KELLY ▪ ▪ ▪ ▪ ▪ ▪ ▪ ▪ ▪ ▪ ▪ ▪ ▪
b. 1935

Robert Kelly writes in his collection *In Time* (1973), "The poet is the DISCOV-
ERER OF RELATION." Thus, while his work is consistent with aspects of
Projectivism and language poetry in its search for what Kelly calls "polysyntac-
tic liberty," the urge to union, consistent with the eroticism of some of his
poetry, is always present.

Kelly has been associated with the tradition of Pound, Olson, and Williams, as
well as with the practice of the "deep image." Yet he claims that T. S. Eliot, not
Ezra Pound, is the poet "who taught most of us violation in his funny, droll,
dadaistic way."[1] Violation against the "ordinary, the expected" is a guiding
principle for Kelly as an experimentalist, yet "the greatest violators are those
who have never damaged anything."[2] Unlike the language poets, Kelly believes
firmly in the value of the "usual syntactic orders" coupled with "natural flu-
ency."[3] The most exciting writing occurs, therefore, through a syntactic "com-
ing-to-attend" that liberates rather than constrains.[4]

Extremely prolific, Kelly published forty books by the time he was forty-four
years old. These include *Armed Descent* (1961), *The Mill of Particulars* (1973),
the long poem *Loom* (1975), *Kill the Messenger Who Brings the Bad News*
(1979), *Spiritual Exercises* (1981), and *Not This Island Music* (1987). Of his large
volume of work, Kelly says, "perhaps my excess is in response to a terrible
religion of adequacy with which I grew up, that the least will do. . . . My answer
to the adequate is the excessive."[5]

A longtime faculty member at Bard College, Kelly has recently turned his
energies to writing of short fiction in addition to poetry.

1. "Robert Kelly: An Interview by Bradford Morrow," *Conjunctions*, No. 13 (1989),
p. 142.   2. The same, p. 140.   3. The same.   4. The same.   5. The same, p. 138.

Coming

The blue mouth of the shark
becomes the blue silk hung
canopy bed at Versailles,
a blue grinning cave, blue death Yama, Hevajra,
cave mouth

a great blue harp
strung with our lives

(the first harp
was the great fish's jawbone,

monster slain
into our history in the sign of music

o

or mouth of the blue shark
swims through the red
music of the bed

o

or cave walls in Tibet (Hevajra, Yama),
blue of fear & the far distance,

walls
of the Lama's stable where scythian ponies
turn their flanks to the enquiring light:

the blue is dark, the blue is sight enough for us
who carry them   the strange   places that they go
with bells & shaky musics & we run.

1973

The Rainmakers

for Robert Duncan

The groups of God
broken into world,
morsels chosen
from that curious Hellenistic author
The Demiurge
whose multitudinous works
we daily anthologize,

persuaded by French masters
and local mistresses
to be wise,
            to live in a world
(this one)
if only for the sake of the weather.

They run the weather,
the rainmakers
want us to like it,
sell us the sexy
isotherms of semiotics,
the structure of structure,
              o Fashion
is a savage god.

2.

Poetry tries "to bring all its experience into natural grace"
says Duncan, and keeps the numbers
current,
        the swells of speech
whose ordered passion
compels the restless lust of mind
into the presiding metaphor of dance
which here knows itself
as particulate movements
studied in noticeful economy,
physicist at cloud chamber
charming the incidents
to hold some place in natural speech
(trying to be natural!)
as if it really were a world we speak.

3.

And the numbers are not governors,
the numbers are white, every one is one,

wings of a jungle bird
analyzed into color as
one thing listening always to another,

an old woman visiting her bees.

1987

[Bittersweet growing up the red wall]

Bittersweet growing up the red wall
old factory empty at the foot of Waterman

and across the Seekonk
the houses and wharves and bait shacks of East Providence
these
        are poignant, these are art.

and if the Parthenon crumbles under our carbon monoxide
we can build it again
> by formula,
>> Christ, we could carve it out of soap,
>>> but these
>> are the actual
>> colors
>> the structures
>>> of living,
>>>> this is tantra
the continuity
> of actual effort
>> no two buildings alike
>> and in the quarry of time
cut out to be different by men
> wanting at most to be agreeable and cheap
and they stand in their difference and what will we do
when these are gone,
>> there is no rule that remembers them

> these brittle facts
> hem of the absolute,
colors of old houses distinct as
the breasts of actual different women in their chlamyses
their shirts annotated by the wind
>> passing
by a shack on the hither shore selling menhaden and eels
among the skeletons of wild carrot and tansy.

Providence   1987

A Woman with Flaxen Hair in Norfolk Heard

in memory of Basil Bunting

> Wherever you are,
> in any season,
> I will come to you
> from the flowers

> she says, and always
> call me
> by your native language
> lest men
> think I am strange

> or a woman known
> only in books,

I am steady as sky
and no further away,

see me in your own
color, my lips
shape the same myths
you live inside,

whenever you do this
I am with you,
to kiss you often to sleep
or wake you
sudden or gentle,
a mouth
in the middle of things.

2.

In dream I learned
a book appeared
in 1732 using
for the first time
in English
the word *'ud*, glossed
'oriental religious
meditation'
            I know it
as a lute, the very
word is womb of it,
a music
to grasp firmly
in the left hand
and sing with the right,
sing with the right,

this *'ud* means
strength to hold mind.

3.

Planning to move into the country
one thinks of how suddenly

nothing is nearby. A city
is an hour away—the condition

in which it is common to breathe.
A city is the same as air,

never-ending effort, unifying us.
And you are a young

306 • CLAYTON ESHLEMAN

married woman whose parents
are buying a house in Trunch.

It is funny to say the name aloud,
and funny to say a house, or an

house as your husband, the joiner, says.
As if you and we and all

lived blonde or dark, doomed
in a fresco on a wall

in one of those churches people like us
drive all afternoon to visit.

We are saints of a sort, gaudy
in our private way. We mean

something, but only the churchmen to come
will be clear about what we meant

moving and removing and walking the dog
and falling silent at the breakfast table

and checking the sun and looking away.

1987

CLAYTON ESHLEMAN ▪ ▪ ▪ ▪ ▪ ▪ ▪ ▪ ▪ ▪ ▪
b. 1935

Born and raised in Indianapolis, where his father was an efficiency expert in a slaughterhouse, Clayton Eshleman attended Indiana University. It was as editor of the English Department's literary magazine, *Folio*, that he became acquainted with Paul Blackburn, Jerome Rothenberg, and Robert Kelly, poets with whom he has since been associated.

Following graduation, Eshleman lived for three years in Japan, where he began a long career as a translator of poetry. His translation, with José Rubia Barcia, of *César Vallejo: The Complete Posthumous Poetry* won the 1979 National Book Award.

Eshleman's poetry has affinities with the writings of Blake, Vallejo, and Artaud, as well as the psychological theories of Wilhelm Reich and Carl Jung. Since the mid-1970s, he has incorporated what he calls "Paleolithic Imagination and the Construction of the Underworld" into his poetry. His vision of the underworld was shaped significantly by his visits to the Dordogne region of France in 1974 and 1978, where he studied the prehistoric paintings in the Lascaux, Combarelles, and Trois Frères caves. A book by the archetypal psychologist James Hillman, *The Dream and the Underworld*, established for Eshleman that paleolithic art was less concerned with the empirical reality of "daytime activity"[1] than with the ancient and ongoing worlds of dream, archetype, and myth.[1] Embodying a virtual "history of the image," the signs and animals of the cave walls "become a language upon which all subsequent mythology has been built."

According to the critic Eliot Weinberger, Eshleman is "the primary American practitioner of what Mikhail Bahktin calls 'grotesque realism.' It is an immersion in the body; not the body of the individual, the 'bourgeois ego,' but the body of all."[2]

Among Eshleman's numerous books are *Indiana* (1969), *Coils* (1973), *Hades in Manganese* (1981), *Fracture* (1983), *The Name Encanyoned River: Selected Poems 1960–1985* (1986), and *Hotel Cro-Magnon* (1989). *Antiphonal Swing: Selected Prose 1962–1987* appeared in 1989.

After many years in the Los Angeles area, Eshleman now teaches at Eastern Michigan University, where he edits the influential magazine *Sulfur*.

1. Preface to *Hades in Manganese*, Santa Barbara, 1981, p. 10.   2. Introduction to Eshleman's *The Name Encanyoned River: Selected Poems 1960–1985*, Santa Barbara, 1986, p. 14.

The Lich Gate

Waiting, I rest in the waiting gate.
Does it want to pass my death on,
or to let my dying pass into the poem?
Here I watch the windshield redden
the red of my mother's red Penney coat,
the eve of Wallace Berman's 50th birthday drunk
truck driver smashed Toyota,
a roaring red hole, a rose in whirlpool
placed on the ledge of a bell-less shrine.
My cement sits propped against the post. To live
is to block the way and
to move over at the same time, to hang
from the bell-less hook, a tapeworm in the packed
organ air, the air resonant with fifes, with mourners
filing by the bier
resting in my hands, my memory coffer
in which an acquaintance is found.
Memory is acquaintance. Memory is not a friend.
The closer I come to what happened,
the less I know it, the more I love
what I see beyond the portable
frame in which I stand—I, clapper, never free,
will bang, if the bell rope is pulled.
Pull me, Gladys and Wallace say to my bell, and you
will pass through, the you of I, your
pendulum motion, what weights
you, the hornet-nest shaped
gourd of your death, your scrotal
lavender, your red glass crackling
with fire-embedded mirror. In vermillion and black
the clergyman arrives. At last

something can be done about this
weighted box. It is the dead who come forth to
pull it on. I do nothing here.
When I think I do, it is the you-hordes
leaning over my sleep with needle-shaped
fingers without pause they pat
my still silhouette which shyly moves.
The lich gate looks like it might collapse.
Without a frame in which to wait,
my ghoul would spread. Bier in lich,
Hades' shape, his sonnet prism reflecting
the nearby churchyard, the outer hominid limit,
a field of rippling meat. I have come here
to bleed this gate, to make my language fray
into the invisibility teeming against
The Mayan Ballcourt of the Dead, where
I see myself struggling intently,
flux of impact, the hard
rubber ball bouncing against the stone hoop.

1979

Notes on a Visit to Le Tuc d'Audoubert

for Robert Bégouën

bundled by Tuc's tight jagged
    corridors, flocks of white
stone tits, their milk in long
    stone nipply drips, frozen over

  the underground Volp in which
 the enormous guardian eel,
now unknown, lies coiled—

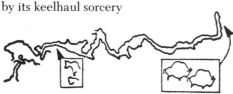

to be impressed (in-pressed?) by this
primordial "theater of cruelty"—
    by its keelhaul sorcery

Volp mouth—the tongue of the
    river lifting one in—

to be masticated by Le Tuc d'Audoubert's
    cruel stones—
        the loom of the cave

Up the oblique chimney by ladder to iron cleats set
in the rock face to the cathole,
on one's stomach
    to *crawl,*   working against
                one, pinning one
as the earth   in, to, it, to
makes one   feel for an instant
feel its traction—   the dread of

              WITHERING IN
              PLACE

    —pinned in—
    The Meat Server
    masticated by the broken
    chariot of the earth

★

"fantastic figures"—more beast-
    like here than human—one
horn one ear— { one large figure
                  one small figure

    as in Lascaux?
  (the *grand* and *petit* sorcerer?)

First indications of master/
  apprentice? ("tanist" re. Graves)

the grotesque archetype

    vortex in which the emergent
    human and withdrawing animal
      are <u>spun</u>—

grotesque = movement

(life is grotesque when we catch
        it in quick perceptions—
    at full vent—history
        shaping itself)

the turns/twists of the cave
        reinforce the image turbine—
as does the underground river,

                the cave floats,
        in a sense, in several senses,
                all at once,
        it rests on the river, is penetrated
            by it, was originally made
                by rushing water—
                    the cave
                is *the skeleton of flood*

images on its walls
        participate, thus, as torsion,
in an earlier torsion—

Here one might synthesize:
        1) abstract signs
                initiate movement
                    brought to rest in

        3) naturalistic figures
                (bison, horses etc)

    In between, the friction, are

    2) grotesque hybrids

(useful—but irrelevant to systematize forces that must have been felt as
flux, as *unplanned*, spontaneous, as were the spots/areas in caves cho-
sen for images—because shadowing or wall contour evoked an animal?
Any plan a coincidence—we have no right to systematize an area of
experience of which we have only shattered iceberg tips—yet it does
seem that "image" occurs at the point that a "naturalistic" horse is
gouged in rock across an "abstract" vulva already gouged there, so that
the rudiments of poetry are present at approximately 30,000 BC—

        image is crossbreeding,
        or the refusal to respect

the single, individuated body,
image is that point
where sight crosses sight—

to be alive as a poet is to be
    in conversation with one's eyes)

What impresses at Tuc is a relationship
between river
        hybrid figures
        and the clay bison—

it is as if the river (the skeleton of water = the cave itself) erupts into
image with the hybrid "guardians" (Breuil's guess) and is brought to
rest in the terminal chamber with the two bison i.e., naturalism is a kind
of rest—naturalism returns us to a continuous and predictable nature
(though there is something unnatural about these bison to be noted
later)—takes us out of the discontinuity, the *transgression* (to cite Ba-
taille's slightly too Catholic term) of the grotesque
    (though the grotesque, on another level, according to Bakhtin, is
deeper continuity, the association of *realms,* kingdoms, fecundation and
death, degradation and praise—)

on one hand: bisons-about-to-couple
    assert the generative
    what we today take to be
    the way things are   (though with ecological pollution,
                                "generation" leads to mutation,
                                a new "grotesque"!)

    ★

to be gripped by a *womb of stone*
to be in the grip of the surge of life
imprisoned in stone
it is enough to make one *sweat one's animal*

(having left the "nuptual hall" of white stone breasts in which one can
amply stand—the breasts hang in clusters right over one's head—one
must then squirm vertically up the spiral chimney (or use the current
iron ladder) to enter the upper level via a cathole into a corridor through
which one must crawl on hands and knees—then another longish cat-
hole through which one must crawl on one's belly, squirming through a
human-sized tunnel—to a corridor through which one can walk halt-
ingly, stooping, occasionally slithering through vertical catslits and
straddling short walls)—
    if one were to film one's postures through this entire process, it might
look like a St.-Vitus dance of the stages in the life of man, birth channel
expulsion to old age, but without chronological order, a jumble of exag-

gerated and strained positions that correspondingly increase the *image pressure* in one's mind—

while in Le Tuc d'Audoubert I felt the broken horse rear in agony in the cave-like stable of Picasso's *Guernica,*
at times I wanted to leave my feet behind, or to continue headless in the dark, my stomach desired prawn-like legs with grippers, my organs were in the way, something inside of me wanted to be
an armored worm,
one feeler extending out its head,
I swear I sensed the disintegration of the backbone of my mother now buried 12 years,
entangled in a cathole I felt my tongue start to press backwards, and the image force was: I wanted to *choke myself out of myself,* to give birth to my own strangulation, and then nurse my strangulation at my own useless male breasts—useless? No, for Le Tuc d'Audoubert unlocks memories that bear on a single face the expressions of both Judith and Holofernes at the moment of beheading, mingled disgust terror delight and awe, one is stimulated to desire to enter cavities within oneself where dead men can be heard talking—
in Le Tuc d'Audoubert I heard something in me whisper me to believe in God
and something else in me whispered that the command was the rasp of a 6000 year old man who wished to be venerated again—
and if what I am saying here is vague it is because both voices had to sound themselves in the bowels of this most personal and impersonal stone, in which sheets of myself felt themselves corrugated with nipples—as if the anatomy of life could be described, from this perspective, as entwisted tubes of nippled stone through which perpetual and mutual beheadings and birthings were taking place—

★

but all these fantastic images were shooed away the moment I laid eyes on the two bison sculptured out of clay leaned against stuff fallen from the chamber ceiling—
the bison and their "altar" seemed to be squeezed up into view out of the swelling of the chamber floor—
the sense of *culmination* was very severe, the male about to mount the female, but clearly placed several inches behind and above her, not in contact with any part of her body, and he had no member—
if they *were* coupling, and *without* deep cracks in their clay bodies, they would have disappeared into their progeny thousands of years ago, but here they are today still, as if Michelangelo were to have depicted God and man as not touching, but only reaching toward each other, caught in the exhaustion of a yearning for a sparking that has in fact never taken place, so that the weight of all the cisterns in the world is in that yearning, in the weight of that yearning is the real ballast in life, a ballast in which the unborn are coddled like slowly cooking eggs, unborn bison and unborn man, in the crib of a scrotum, a bone scrotum,

that jailhouse of generation from which the prisoners yearn to leap onto the taffy machine-like pistons of shaping females—

it is that spot where the leap should occur that Le Tuc d'Audoubert says is VOID, and that unfilled space between two fertile poles here feels like the origin of the abyss, as if in the minds of those who shaped and placed these two bison, fertilization was pulled free, and that freedom from connection is the demon of creation haunting man and woman ever since—

we crawled on hands and knees about this scene, humbled, in single file, lower than the scene, 11 human creatures come, lamps in hand like a glowworm pilgrimage, to worship in circular crawl at one of the births of the abyss—

if I had stayed longer, if I had not with the others disappeared into the organic odors of the Montesquieu-Avantès woods, I am sure that I would have noticed, flittering out of the deep cracks in the bison clay, little winged things, image babies set free, the Odyssi before Odysseus who still wander the vaults of what we call art seeking new abysses to inscribe with the tuning forks of their wings . . .

1982

ROSMARIE WALDROP ▪ ▪ ▪ ▪ ▪ ▪ ▪ ▪ ▪ ▪ ▪
b. 1935

Rosmarie Waldrop was born in Germany and lives in Providence, Rhode Island, where she co-directs Burning Deck Press, a leading publisher of experimental poetry. She also edits *Série d'écriture,* a journal of recent French poetry in translation.

Waldrop's poetry books include *The Aggressive Ways of the Casual Stranger* (1972), *The Road Is Everywhere or Stop This Body* (1978), *When They Have Senses* (1980), *Differences for Four Hands* (1984), *Streets Enough to Welcome Snow* (1986), *The Reproduction of Profiles* (1987), and *Peculiar Motions* (1990). She is also the author of a book of criticism, *Against Language?* (1971), and two works of fiction, *The Hanky of Pippin's Daughter* (1986) and *A Form/ of Taking/ It All* (1990). *Inserting the Mirror,* Part II of *The Reproduction of Profiles,* interweaves themes of language, images of the female body, and phrases borrowed from and suggested by Wittgenstein.

Waldrop cites living in Paris from 1970 to 1971, where she met the French poets Claude Royet-Journoud and Anne-Marie Albiach and began to translate the work of Edmond Jabès, as the turning point in her career as a poet. Referring to the varied language of Jabès's work, she says, "In my own work, too, I don't have one single mode. I write in a particular mode, and when at a certain point it runs dry, I try to do something quite different."[1]

Waldrop is opposed to "the prophetic stance—the poet as vates, as priest, seer." Believing that God is absent from considerations of meaning, she holds that the "one transcendence that is available to us, that we can enter into, is language. It *is* like a sea. I often think of it as a space."[2]

1. Edward Foster, "An Interview with Rosmarie Waldrop," *Talisman,* No. 6, Spring 1991, p. 29.   2. The same, p. 31.

FROM *Inserting the Mirror*

1

To explore the nature of rain I opened the door because inside the workings of language clear vision is impossible. You think you see, but are only running your finger through pubic hair. The rain was heavy enough to fall into this narrow street and pull shreds of cloud down with it. I expected the drops to strike my skin like a keyboard. But I only got wet. When there is no resonance, are you more likely to catch a cold? Maybe it was the uniform appearance of the drops which made their application to philosophy so difficult even though the street was full of reflection. In the same way, fainting can, as it approaches, slow the Yankee Doodle to a near loss of pitch. I watched the outline of the tower grow dim until it was only a word in my brain. That language can suggest a body where there is none. Or does a body always contain its own absence? The rain, I thought, ought to protect me against such arid speculations.

2

The body is useful. I can send it on errands while I stay in bed and pull the blue blanket up to my neck. Once I coaxed it to get married. It trembled and cried on the way to the altar, but then gently pushed the groom down to the floor and sat on him while the family crowded closer to get in on the excitement. The black and white flagstones seemed to be rocking, though more slowly than people could see, which made their gestures uncertain. Many of them slipped and lay down. Because they closed their eyes in the hope of opening their bodies I rekindled the attentions of love. High-tension wires very different from propensity and yet again from mirror images. Even if we could not remember the color of heat the dominant fuel would still consume us.

3

Androgynous instinct is one kind of complexity, another is, for example, a group of men crowding into a bar while their umbrellas protect them against the neon light falling. How bent their backs are, I thought. They know it is useless to look up—as if the dusk could balance both a glass and a horizon—or to wonder if the verb "to sleep" is active or passive. When a name has detached itself, its object, ungraspable like everyday life, spills over. A solution not ready to be taken home, splashing heat through our bodies and decimal points.

4

I tried to understand the mystery of names by staring into the mirror and repeating mine over and over. Or the word "me." As if one could come into language as into a room. Lost in the blank, my obsessive detachment spiraled out into the unusable space of infinity, indifferent nakedness. I sat down in it. No balcony for clearer view, but I could focus on the silvered lack of substance or the syllables that correspond to it because all resonance grows from consent to emptiness. But maybe, in my craving for hinges, I confused identity with someone else.

5

Way down the deserted street, I thought I saw a bus which, with luck, might get me out of this sentence which might go on forever, knotting phrase onto phrase with fire hydrants and parking meters, and still not take me to my language waiting, surely, around some corner. Though I am not certain what to expect. This time it might be Narragansett. Or black. A sidewalk is a narrow location in history, and no bright remarks can hold back the dark. In the same way, when a child throws her ball there is no winning or losing unless she can't remember her name because, although the street lamp has blushed on pink the dark sits on top of it like a tower and allows no more than a narrow cone of family resemblance.

6

I learned about communication by twisting my legs around yours as, in spinning a thought, we twist fiber on fiber. The strength of language does not reside in the fact that some one desire runs its whole length, but in the overlapping of many generations. Relationships form before they are written down just as grass bends before the wind, and now it is impossible to know which of us went toward the other, naked, unsteady, but, once lit, the unprepared fused with its afterimage like twenty stories of glass and steel on fire. Our lord of the mirror. I closed my eyes, afraid to resemble.

7

Is it possible to know where a word ends and my use of it begins? Or to locate the ledge of your promises to lean my head on? Even if I built a boundary out of five pounds of definition, it could not be called the shock of a wall. Nor the pain that follows. Dusk cast the houses in shadow, flattening their projections. Blurred edges, like memory or soul, an event you turn away from. Yet I also believe that a sharp picture is not always preferable. Even when people come in pairs, their private odds should be made the most of. You went in search of more restful altitudes, of ideally clear language. But the bridge that spans the mind-body gap enjoys gazing downstream. All this time I was holding my umbrella open.

8

I wondered if it was enough to reverse subject and object, or does it matter if the bow moves up or down the string. Blind possibility, say hunger, thickened. How high the sea of language runs. Its white sails, sexual, inviting to apply the picture, or black, mourning decline in navigation. I know, but cannot say, what a violin sounds like. Driftwood migrates toward the margin, the words gather momentum, wash back over their own sheets of insomnia. No harbor. No haul of silence.

9

There were no chronicles. The dimensions of emptiness instead of heroic feats. This was taken as proof that female means lack. As if my body were only layers on layers of windowpane. The whole idea of depth smells-fishy. But there are thicker transparencies where the sentence goes wrong as soon as you do something, because doing carries its own negative right into the center of the sun and blots out the metonymies of desire. In this neck of the womb. Later, sure enough, the applications fall away even if we cling to the exaggerated fireworks of lost purpose.

10

It is best to stop as soon as you hear a word in a language you don't know. Its opaqueness stands, not as a signpost to the adventures of misunderstanding, but a wall where touch goes deaf, and without explanations hanging in the air, waiting to be supported by the clotheslines of childhood. As I looked up, a boy approached me and offered to carry my bag because it was raining. Wet laundry flapped in the wind.

11

Heavy with soot, the rain drummed on the tin roof of the garage, eager to fall into language and be solved in the manner of mysteries. I tried to hear the line between the drumming and the duller thud on the street, like the phantom beat between two rhythms. An umbrella would have complicated the score. No gift of the singular: the sounds merged with traffic noise too gray to make a difference between woman and mother, or grammar and theology. Not like the children playing tag, throwing their slight weight into flight from the ever changing "it." Though the drops hit my face more gently than an investigating eye, the degree of slippage

12

Visibility was poor. The field limited by grammatical rules, the foghorns of language. On the sidewalk, people waiting for the bus looked out from under umbrellas and hoods, their eyes curtained by crosshatched rain, lids close to one another as when approaching sleep or pain. An adherence to darkness that refuses exact praise like reaching for a glass. Even when I had emptied mine, I had not gotten to the bottom of the things in plain view. A play of reflections and peculiar. The drops of water traveled diagonally across the paradigms as the bus moved on.

13

Because we cannot penetrate the soul, at most touch its outer lips with the reflected light of metaphor, the soul cannot know itself, but the dimmer light holds off loud breathing. It's not that our sense impressions lie, but that we understand their language. All through the linear seasons, the sun leaned on the shoulder of the road. Flocks of swallows lost vaster reasons to the sky. Salt travel. Statues which adorn the unconscious. My hopes crushed by knowledge of anatomy. Or is this another error, this theory of erosion, of all we cannot see?

14

On the fourth day, I took the rain in my mouth, and the fish sank deeper, lighting up in glints like time passing. The bus moved off, a long sliding door. Behind it, the row of houses suddenly larger, a mass of stone and wood to constrict your chest, as when you take a wrong turn to the side of your head which is dark with war and strangling and then are weak from loss of blood, a fishline wound around your neck. The dark was an obstacle. It would shortly come between me and the street, but its name made me want to touch its velvet beginning. Even though I've known complete rejection, words will still send me in pursuit of chimeras.

1987

GUSTAF SOBIN ▪ ▪ ▪ ▪ ▪ ▪ ▪ ▪ ▪ ▪ ▪ ▪ ▪ ▪ ▪ ▪
b. 1935

Born in Boston and educated at Brown University, Gustaf Sobin first visited Provence in 1962 to see the French poet René Char, whose work he greatly admired. The following year, carrying only a bag and a briefcase, he moved to the village of Gordes, in the Vaucluse region of Provence, where he bought a stone cottage for $800. He has lived there ever since.

According to the critic Paul Christensen, Sobin's well-crafted poems can be compared to his *borie* (a hive-shaped rock shelter common to Vaucluse) in that they comprise "a structure of mortarless enjambments."[1] Yet Sobin also strongly holds to an organic theory of composition. "Language is the husk of experience," he told Christensen in conversation, "as when the milk is bound by the juice of the fig." The first line or phrase of a poem, which Sobin calls its nexus, contains "the entire poem in its yet-unraveled trajectory: i.e., not only its 'message,' but both the direction of its thrust and the rate of its movement, its meter." Because

poems have a decided momentum, "poetry is as kinetic as cinema, its movement
. . . irrepressible as breath."[2]

Besides René Char, Sobin claims the American poets Robert Duncan and
George Oppen as his most important predecessors—Duncan for his orphic sense
of "language as the generator, the mother, the source of all being," and Oppen
for the "focused intensity" of his work.[3]

Sobin's books include *Wind Chrysalid's Rattle* (1980), *Celebration of the
Sound Through* (1982), *The Earth as Air* (1984), and *Voyaging Portraits* (1988).
He has also published a novel, *Venus Blue* (1991).

1. "A Noble Wave," review of *Voyaging Portraits*, in *Temblor* #7, 1988, p. 24.   2. "A
Few Stray Comments on the Cultivation of the Lyric," in *Talisman*, No. 10, 1993,
p. 41.   3. Edward Foster, "An Interview with Gustaf Sobin," *Talisman*, No. 10, 1993,
p. 35.

Out of the Identical

a hand's
writing the
rocks. . . .   is
waiting

for its
reflections to

catch:
quiver.   weeks,
now, without,
had

hollowed volume,
gutted
mass, rolled
the

bone of a
breath
over the

wind-
pitted ridges.
(were
words

for these words,
were
voices . . .).
would pull, from
the

flowing
light, each
feature.   draw,
from its

tissues, that
tissue, that

smoke, with its
vaporous,
verb-

driven shimmers.

1988

What the Music Wants

In Memory of George Oppen

what the music
wants is
pod and tentacle (the thing
wiggling,
wild

as washed
hair, spread).   is our-
selves, in-

serted.   within
our
own rhythms: wrapt, voluted,
that miracle
of
measure-

ascendant.   *to*
stand, that there's some-
where to

stand.   marble
over

moorings, the
scaffolds, now, as if
vanished, and the steps, the
floors: spoken

forth. *to*
stand, stand there, with-
in
sound alone,
that

miracle!

              is what the
waters comb, and the
bells,
beating,
count (faint, now, over the

waves, in a
garland
of
bells). *is*

somewhere, and
wrapt

in the bulb
of its
voices, are buoyant, among.

                             1988

Eleven Rock Poems

for Emmanuel Muheim

sent myself the   length
    of my own metaphors (boxwood, then cistus, the
swallows going white in the   high winds).   a
    body wrapt a-

bout the mirror of its   breath, slept
       nights in the shallow, black waves of the   rocks.

----

    where ice lacquered the
red arrows rose, a wrist hoisted
       its ankles   after.   lapped muscles, the
    limbs-chromatic, would
reach, touch, be drawn through the   roots of
                           that reaching.

---

   up, out of the last, lime-
stone cirque, on footpaths a   half-
       foot wide, looked down.   saw my-
  self, as if
dissolving—washed blue, the back
             still bent—as I climbed.

---

   the eyes rising through those   random
stations, their
        wedged breath-   holds (as if
  'something' drew, pulled, as if
             a 'somewhere,' finally, were).

---

   as much dust as   snow, the
trail's driven into
       those deep, mineral creases (had carried
  shadows, the bundled sticks of their tinder.   over
the soft, billowing shrouds, had beaten

   breath, pulled   light from the thin meats of
               each murmur).

---

   all space, as it muscles in   sound (im-
mensity driven, com-
       pressed into such quick passages . . .).

---

   chord the   body hauls a-
cross the washed minerals, sporadic blacks
      of the stout ilex, saw the   fixed intervals
moving (and 'the
       harmonies' as they shattered, strayed, re-

       grouped).

---

   high, now, over the river, where
millgirls, once, set the long-   wicked snails
      flaming downstream, the

   path vanishes, breaks
into boxwood, cade. (shall weigh shadows; where the   thin
  winds shiver, read
       their mineral   palm).

for that itinerant breath-   pilgrim, may
the rock be hollow, *be*
        grotto; within it, may the
    ashes of those last   opaque vocables a-
                                    light.

loss, each time, descending, as the
rhythms catch
        on the quick loops of re-
entry, and out, over the   shoulders, the
                    rocks sprout, rise, un-
                                        fold.

had plumbed space, sideways.   blown,
through its god-
        less body, these showers of thin, hissing
    splinters.   (that the

emptiness be edged, wedged, that   pierced, it
                                    spread open).

                                        1988

RUSSELL EDSON ■ ■ ■ ■ ■ ■ ■ ■ ■ ■ ■ ■ ■ ■ ■
b. 1935

In his essay "Portrait of the Writer as a Fat Man," Russell Edson writes, "What
we want is a poetry of miracles—minus the 'I' of ecstasy. . . . A poetry freed from
the definition of poetry, and a prose free of the necessities of fiction; a personal
form disciplined not by other literature but by unhappiness; thus a way to be
happy."[1]

Edson's prose poems reflect a personal form, and a tone influenced in part by
his father, the artist who created the "Andy Gump" cartoon popular in the
Sunday newspapers of the 1940s and 1950s. Freudian cartoons of domestic rela-
tions, Edson's poems are also reminiscent of the surrealist prose poems of Henri
Michaux; they often read like fables and bring to mind the experimental, or
"fabulist," American fiction of the 1970s.

Edson's books include *The Very Thing that Happens* (1964), *The Childhood
of an Equestrian* (1973), *The Intuitive Journey and Other Works* (1976), *The
Clam Theater* (1976), *The Reason Why the Closet-Man Is Never Sad* (1977),
The Wounded Breakfast (1985), as well as numerous small-press pamphlets and
chapbooks.

Edson lives in Stamford, Connecticut, where he was raised.

1. *Field*, No. 13, Fall 1975, pp. 23 and 25.

Conjugal

A man is bending his wife. He is bending her around something that she has bent herself around. She is around it, bent as he has bent her.

He is convincing her. It is all so private.

He is bending her around the bedpost. No, he is bending her around the tripod of his camera.
It is as if he teaches her to swim. As if he teaches acrobatics. As if he could form her into something wet that he delivers out of one life into another.

And it is such a private thing the thing they do.

He is forming her into the wallpaper. He is smoothing her down into the flowers there. He is finding her nipples there. And he is kissing her pubis there.

He climbs into the wallpaper among the flowers. And his buttocks move in and out of the wall.

1976

Ape

You haven't finished your ape, said mother to father, who had monkey hair and blood on his whiskers.
I've had enough monkey, cried father.
You didn't eat the hands, and I went to all the trouble to make onion rings for its fingers, said mother.
I'll just nibble on its forehead, and then I've had enough, said father.
I stuffed its nose with garlic, just like you like it, said mother.

Why don't you have the butcher cut these apes up? You lay the whole thing on the table every night; the same fractured skull, the same singed fur; like someone who died horribly. These aren't dinners, these are post-mortem dissections.

Try a piece of its gum, I've stuffed its mouth with bread, said mother.
Ugh, it looks like a mouth full of vomit. How can I bite into its cheek with bread spilling out of its mouth? cried father.
Break one of the ears off, they're so crispy, said mother.

I wish to hell you'd put underpants on these apes; even a jockstrap, screamed father.
Father, how dare you insinuate that I see the ape as anything more than simple meat, screamed mother.

Well, what's with this ribbon tied in a bow on its privates? screamed father.

Are you saying that I am in love with this vicious creature? That I would submit my female opening to this brute? That after we had love on the kitchen floor I would put him in the oven, after breaking his head with a frying pan; and then serve him to my husband, that my husband might eat the evidence of my infidelity . . . ?

I'm just saying that I'm damn sick of ape every night, cried father.

1976

A Performance at Hog Theater

There was once a hog theater where hogs performed as men, had men been hogs.

One hog said, I will be a hog in a field which has found a mouse which is being eaten by the same hog which is in the field and which has found the mouse, which I am performing as my contribution to the performer's art.

Oh let's just be hogs, cried an old hog.

And so the hogs streamed out of the theater crying, only hogs, only hogs . . .

1976

The Toy-Maker

A toy-maker made a toy wife and a toy child. He made a toy house and some toy years.

He made a getting-old toy, and he made a dying toy.

The toy-maker made a toy heaven and a toy god.

But, best of all, he liked making toy shit.

1976

The Optical Prodigal

A man sees a tiny couple in the distance, and thinks they might be his mother and father.

But when he gets to them they're still little.

You're still little, he says, don't you remember?

Who said you were supposed to be here? says the little husband, you're supposed to be in your own distance; you're still in your own foreground, you spendthrift.

No no, says the man, you're to blame.

No no, says the little man, you're out of proportion. When you go into the distance you're supposed to get smaller. You mustn't think that we can shrink and swell all the time to suit everybody coming out of the distance.

But you have it wrong, cries the man, we're the same size, it's you who are refusing to be optically correct.

It's you, says the little husband, you just can't go blundering into the distance without some prior warning.

This has never happened before, says the man, and I've been in the distance many times.

You ought to go back to where you started and try it again, says the little husband.

But you'd probably be even smaller, says the man, you might even have disappeared by then.

We never change our size, we concentrate at all times; it's you who is the absentminded one. You are the one out of proportion, and it's you throwing everything out of scale; so get going, cries the little husband.

Out of proportion . . . ? says the man.

Totally, without any optical intelligence, no consideration for scale, says the little husband.

Don't you recognize me? says the man.

No no, our son lives in the distance, says the little husband.

1977

JOHN GIORNO ▪ ▪ ▪ ▪ ▪ ▪ ▪ ▪ ▪ ▪ ▪ ▪ ▪
b. 1936

Star of the Andy Warhol movie *Sleep* (1963), John Giorno is a leader in the development of poetry as a performance and entertainment medium. He has done so not only through his own performances, which have an international audience, but also through Giorno Poetry Systems, his widely distributed spoken-word record label, and Dial-A-Poem, which he created in 1968 to extend poetry into the realm of mass communication.

In composing his poetry, Giorno always imagines an audience in front of him. "Spoken word," he writes, "using breath and heat, pitch and volume, and the melodies inherent in the language, risking technology and music, and a deep connection with an audience, is the fulfillment of a poem. It's the entertainment industry (you got to sweeten the deal)—transmitting an awareness of ordinary mind. As someone said to me after a performance, 'I hate poetry. But I love poets who sweat.' For me performing poetry is sustained sexual activity in a golden age of promiscuity. You can never be too generous."[1]

Giorno's books include *The American Book of the Dead* (1964), *Balling Buddha* (1970), *Cancer in My Left Ball* (1973), *Grasping at Emptiness* (1985), and

You Got to Burn to Shine: Selected Poetry and Prose (1993). His record albums and CDs include *Biting Off the Tongue of a Corpse* (1975), *Life Is a Killer* (1982), and *A Diamond Hidden in the Mouth of a Corpse* (1985). He performs solo and with the John Giorno Band.

In the last ten years he has been active in the AIDS Treatment Project, which gives cash grants to poets and artists with the disease. Giorno lives in New York City.

1. John Giorno, epilogue to *You Got to Burn to Shine: Selected Poetry and Prose*, New York, 1993, n.p.

Life Is a Killer

Everyone says
what they do
is right,
and money is
a good
thing
it can be
wonderful.

Road
drinking,
driving
around
drinking
beer,
they need me
more than
I need them,
where are
you guys from,
stumbling off
into the night
thinking
about it
stumbling off into the night
thinking about it.

When I was
15 years old
I knew everything
there was
to know,
and now that I'm old,
it was true.

I got dragged
along on
this one
by my foot,
if I wasn't so
tired
I would have
a good
time
if I wasn't so tired
I'd have a good time
if I wasn't so tired I'd have
a good time.

Tossing
and turning,
cause there's
a nest
of wasps
coursing
through your
bloodstream
cause there's a nest of wasps
coursing through your bloodstream.

If you think
about it
how could
it have come
to this
if you think about it
how could it have come to this,
it's coming
down the road
right through
the red
lights,
and it's
there
and it's there
and it's there
and it's there.

Try your
best
and think
you're good,
that's what
I want

being inside you
that's what I want
being inside you
that's what I want being inside you,
endless
thresholds,
and you hope
you're doing
it right.

How are you
feeling good
how are you
feeling
good
how are
you feeling good
how are you feeling
good
how are you feeling good,
you need
national
attention.

Cause essentially
all you
ever accomplished
was snort
some smack
and sit
on a zafu
watching
your breath.

How the hell
did I end
up doing
this
how the hell did
I end up doing this
for a job?

I can't say
I don't need
anybody
cause I need
the Buddhas,
and there's nothing

I can say
about them.

Everyone is at
a complete
disadvantage,
you're being taken
to dinner
at La Cote Basque
and you're eating
9 Lives
liver,
and drinking
wine,
the women
they are taking
prisoners,
I'm not going
nowhere,
I ripped up
my suitcases
I ripped up my suitcases.

Crank me
up
and keep me
open
crank me up
and keep me open
crank me up and keep me open,
nothing
recedes
like success.

Whatever
happens
it will seem
the way
it seems
now,
it doesn't matter
what you
feel,
how perfectly
correct
or amazing
the clarity,
everything

you think
is deluded
everything you think
is deluded
everything you think is deluded,
life
is a killer.

1982

Scum & Slime

Optimism,
trust,
fearless
authority,
and disaster,

eating filth
and transforming it,
with white
intentions,
into black
compassion,

I want to be
filthy
and anonymous
I want to be filthy
and anonymous
I want to be filthy and anonymous

Open your eye lids
and see it looks good,
drinking poison
and in each sip
on your lip
is wisdom
mind.

I like warm air
going over
my skin,

billions
of world
systems,

your body is
crawling
and crashing
into the surf.

Pouring
money
down
another
hole
pouring money
down another hole
pouring money down
another hole,
and keep it
hidden.

When Adam
and Eve
were in the Garden of Eden,
God asked Eve
not to do
two things,
not to eat
the fruit
and not to go swimming,
so she ate
and went for a swim,
that's why
the ocean smells
of fish.

You and I are
sleeping on
a cement
and linoleum
kitchen floor,

you look like
a television set
sitting on
a refrigerator,

I would crawl
through a mile of shit
to suck off
the last guy
who fucked her.

We don't take
drugs no more,
we sit around
praying for money,
don't do anything drastic,

when you are with
a lover
you have no
no control
when you are with a lover
you have no control
when you are with a lover you have
no control

I want to be
filthy
and anonymous,
scum
and slime.

What's going on
in here,
it looks like
everyone is
underwater,
give me
a break,
I'm dead
and I'm asleep
I'm dead
and I'm asleep
I'm dead
and I'm asleep.

1985

JAYNE CORTEZ ▪ ▪ ▪ ▪ ▪ ▪ ▪ ▪ ▪ ▪ ▪ ▪ ▪ ▪ ▪
b. 1936

The titles of Jayne Cortez's books of poetry suggest their caustic, insistent, and verbal nature. They include *Pisstained Stairs and the Monkey Man's Wares* (1969), *Scarifications* (1973), *Mouth on Paper* (1977), *Firespitter* (1982), and a book of collected poems, *Coagulations* (1984). Cortez has also made the sound recordings *Celebrations and Solitudes* (1975), *Unsubmissive Blues* (1980), and *Maintain Control* (1986).

Public and declamatory, her poetry originates in the African-American tradition of jazz, blues, and social protest. As a political poet she has been compared to Ernesto Cardenal of Nicaragua and Léon Damas of French Guinea. However, the surrealist juxtapositions of some of her writings are more reminiscent of the great Caribbean poet of the Negritude movement, Aimé Césaire. Damas and Césaire also share with Cortez the use of chant and incremental repetition, forms which lend themselves to public performance. She often performs her poetry with the Firespitters, a jazz group which includes drummer Denardo Coleman, her son from a former marriage to the legendary jazz saxophonist Ornette Coleman.

Cortez was born in Arizona and grew up in the Watts section of Los Angeles. She now lives in New York City.

For the Poets (Christopher Okigbo & Henry Dumas)

I need kai kai   ah
a glass of akpetesie   ah
from torn arm of Bessie Smith   ah

I need the smell of Nsukka   ah
the body sweat of a durbar   ah
five tap dancers   ah
and those fleshy blues kingdoms from deep south   ah
to belly-roll forward praise
for Christopher Okigbo   ah

I need a canefield of superstitious women   a
fumes and feathers from port of Lobito   a
skull of a mercenary   a
ashes from a Texas lynching   a
the midnight snakes of Damballah   a
liquid from the eyeballs of a leopard   a
sweet oil from the ears of an elder   a
to make a delta praise for the poets   a

On this day approaching me like a mystic
number   oh
in this time slot on death row   oh
in this flesh picking Sahelian zone   oh
in this dynamite dust and dragon blood and liver
cut   oh

I need cockroaches   ah
congo square   ah
a can of skokian   ah
from flaming mouth of a howling wolf   ah

I need the smell of Harlem   ah
spirits from the birthplace of Basuto   ah
mysteries from an Arkansas pyramid   ah

shark teeth   ah
buffalo   ah
guerrillas in the rainy season   ah
to boogie forward ju ju praise for Henry Dumas   ah

In this day of one hundred surging zanzi bars   oh
In this day of bongo clubs moon cafes and paradise
lounges   oh
In this day's pounded torso of burgundy mush   oh
In this steel cube   in this domino   in this dry
period   oh

I need tongues like coiling pythons   ah
spearheads gushing from gulf of Guinea   ah
the broken ankles of a B.J. Vorster   ah
to light up this red velvet jungle   ah
i need pink spots from the lips of trumpet
players   ah
the abdominal scars of seven head hunters   ah
a gunslit for electric watermelon seeds   ah
to flash a delta praise for the poets   ah

Because they'll try and shoot us
like they shot Henry Dumas   huh
because we massacre each other
and Christopher Okigbo is dead   uh-huh
because i can't make the best of it   uh-hun
because i'm not a bystander   uh-hun
because mugging is not my profession   uh-unh

I need one more piss-ass night to make a
hurricane   a
i need one more hate mouth racist
sucking the other end of another gas pipe to make
flames   a
i need one more good funky blood pact
to shake forward a delta praise for the poets   a

On this day of living dead Dumas
on this day of living dead Okigbo

I need kai kai   ah   i need durbars   ah   i need torn
arms   ah
i need canefields   ah   i need feathers   ah   i need
skulls   ah
i need ashes   ah   i need snakes   ah   i need
eyeballs   ah
i need cockroaches   ah   i need sharkteeth   ah   i
need buffalo   ah

i need spirits   ah   i need ankles   ah   i need
hurricanes   ah
i need gas pipes   ah   i need blood pacts   ah   i
need   ah
to make a delta praise for the poets   ah

1977

I See Chano Pozo

A very fine conga of sweat
a very fine stomp of the right foot
a very fine platform of sticks
a very fine tube of frictional groans
a very fine can of belligerent growls
a very fine hoop of cubano yells
very fine   very fine

Is there anyone finer today   olé   okay
Oye   I say
I see Chano Pozo
Chano Pozo from Havana Cuba
                    You're the one
You're the one who made Atamo into
a tattooed motivator of revolutionary spirits

You're the one who made Mpebi into
an activated slasher of lies

You're the one who made Donno into
an armpit of inflammable explosives

You're the one who made Obonu into
a circle of signifying snakes

You're the one who made Atumpan's head strike
against
the head of a bird   everynight   everyday
in your crisscrossing chant
in your cross river mouth
                    You're the one

Oye   I say
Chano
what made you roar like a big brazos flood
what made you yodel like a migrating frog
what made you shake like atomic heat
what made you jell into a ritual pose

Chano   Chano   Chano
what made your technology of thumps so new so
mean
I say
is there anyone meaner than Chano Pozo
                                   from Havana Cuba

Oye
I'm in the presence of ancestor
                           Chano Pozo
Chano connector of two worlds
You go and celebrate again with
the *compañeros* in Santiago
    and tell us about it
You go to the spirit house of Antonio Maceo
and tell us about it
You go to Angola
and tell us about it
You go to Calabar
and tell us about it
You go see the slave castles
you go see the massacres
you go see the afflictions
you go see the battlefields
you go see the warriors
you go as a healer
you go conjurate
you go mediate
you go to the cemetery of drums
return and tell us about it

Lucumi   Abakẃa   Lucumi   Abakẃa

Olé   okay
Is there anyone finer today
Oye   I say
did you hear
Mpintintoa smoking in the palm of his hands
did you hear
Ilya Ilu booming through the cup of his clap
did you hear
Ntenga sanding on the rim of his rasp
did you hear
Siky Akkua stuttering like a goat sucking hawk
did you hear
Bata crying in a nago tongue
did you hear
Fontomfrom speaking through the skull of a dog
did you hear it   did you hear it   did you hear it

A very fine tree stump of drones
a very fine shuffle of shrines
a very fine turn of the head
a very fine tissue of skin
a very fine smack of the lips
a very fine pulse
a very fine *encuentro*
very fine   very fine   very fine
Is there anyone finer than
Chano Pozo from Havana Cuba
Oye   I say
I see Chano Pozo

1982

Rape

Inez Garcia, Joan Litte—Two Rape Victims in the 1970s

What was Inez supposed to do for
the man who declared war on her body
the man who carved a combat zone between her
breasts
Was she supposed to lick crabs from his hairy ass
kiss every pimple on his butt
blow hot breath on his big toe
draw back the corners of her vagina and
hee haw like a California burro

This being war time for Inez
she stood facing the knife
the insults and
her own smell drying on the penis of
the man who raped her

She stood with a rifle in her hand
doing what a defense department will do in times of
war
And when the man started grunting and panting and
wobbling forward like
a giant hog
She pumped lead into his three hundred pounds of
shaking flesh
Sent it flying to the Virgin of Guadalupe
then celebrated day of the dead rapist punk
and just what the fuck else was she supposed to do?

And what was Joanne supposed to do for
the man who declared war on her life

Was she supposed to tongue his encrusted
toilet stool lips
suck the numbers off of his tin badge
choke on his clap trap balls
squeeze on his nub of rotten maggots and
sing god bless america thank you for fucking my life
away

This being wartime for Joanne
she did what a defense department will do in times of
war
and when the piss drinking   shit sniffing guard said
I'm gonna make you wish you were dead black bitch
come here
Joanne came down with an ice pick in
the swat freak motherfucker's chest
yes in the fat neck of that racist policeman
Joanne did the dance of the ice picks and once again
from coast to coast
house to house
we celebrated day of the dead rapist punk
and just what the fuck else were we supposed to do

1982

CLARENCE MAJOR ▪ ▪ ▪ ▪ ▪ ▪ ▪ ▪ ▪ ▪ ▪ ▪
b. 1936

Born in Atlanta and raised in Chicago, Clarence Major briefly attended the
School of the Art Institute of Chicago before joining the U.S. Air Force in 1955.
Following his discharge in 1957, he began editing the *Coercion Review* (1958–
1961), a literary magazine which put him in contact with poets such as William
Carlos Williams, Allen Ginsberg, and Robert Creeley. In 1966, Major moved to
New York City, where he became associated with the Umbra Workshop group
of black writers.

His first major poetry collection, *Swallow the Lake*, was published in 1970,
followed by *The Syncopated Cakewalk* (1974), *Inside Diameter: The France
Poems* (1985), and two book-length poems, *Surfaces and Masks* (1988) and *Some
Observations of a Stranger at Zuni in the Latter Part of the Century* (1989).
Major is also the author of experimental works of fiction, including *Reflex and
Bone Structure* (1975), *My Amputations* (1986), and *Painted Turtle: Woman
with Guitar* (1988). He is editor of the anthology *The New Black Poetry* (1969)
and of *The Dictionary of Afro-American Slang* (1970).

Major taught for many years at the University of Colorado, Boulder, and now
teaches at the University of California, Davis.

Swallow the Lake

Gave me things I
could not use. Then. Now.
Rain night bursting upon & into. I
shine updown into Lake Michigan

like the glow from the cold lights of the Loop.
Walks. Deaths. Births.
Streets. Things I could not give back. Nor
use. Or night or day or night or

loneliness. Other ways   feelings I could not
put into words   into themselves into people.
Blank monkeys of the hierarchy. More deaths—
stupidity & death turning them on

into the beat of my droopy heart   my middle
passage blues my corroding hate my release
while I come to become neon iron eyes stainless lungs
blood zincgripped steel I
come up abstract

not able to take their bricks. Tar. Nor their flesh.
I ran: stung. Loop fumes hung
                              in my smoky lungs.

ideas I could not break nor form. Gave me
things I
see break & run down the crawling down the
game.

Illusion illusion, and you
would swear before screaming somehow
choked voices in me.

The crawling thing in the blood, the
huge immune loneliness. One becomes immune
to the bricks the feelings. One becomes
death.
One becomes each one and every person I
become. I could not
I COULD NOT
I could not whistle and walk in storms
along Lake Michigan's shore. Concrete walks.
I could not swallow the lake

1970

Isolate

She knew more about me *than* let us say.
Most difficult, the American, she said.
Said a requiem is quite heavy, very dull and
These violet people in gentle expenditures!
     impossible to translate one:
Mass, and the day of masses.
Yet how was it to be ease for her, feeling
nothing of my spirit, knowing less of her own.

She knew only the visits to the tombs in me.
This pilgrimage she bled into her principles.
Higher, deeper than my closed eye.
Sees difficulty more in her "church" blood
     than in her cycle. & she started

on the birthcontrol pills again.
Some terrible romance of the flesh wedges us.
Here she was everything to me, after the crude
Cramming of Nothing; but now
I want isolation. I told her what.
She said, then isolate motherfucker

              1970

Inside Diameter

1

the position is so well-known
its variations do not count
unless you split hairs: people
become delirious in its grip:
gladiators lose their thrust,
battles are lost. People
praise the wrong works: those
early things, weeds or
whatever, inspired dullness,
somebody else's action.
Putting it in a silkscreen
doesn't make it either,
putting it under acetate
overlay doesn't reduce
the penetration.

2

Jokes about Noah's Art—
pardon me: Ark: proliferate
as the position continues to be
struck and turned. Watch
a horse's eye flutter
just above the buckle
on the strap: it is
an attempt to resolve conflict:
the outcome is the same.
Machinery rusts by contact
with warm flowing liquids:
now where do these fluids flow
from? across the room they look
exactly futuristic, held down
by a printer's correction color
which is applied, stroked on
with an instrument resembling a penis.
You can stick a well-known face
in the battle, place a sword
in her hand, let her gallop
forward toward the surface
with as much vigor as heat
rising from an opening
long identified with war.

3

The original position is known.
It's difficult to make it glow.
In holy wars the position
is rarely forgotten in favor
of other positions. In nightclubs
where women in black stockings
shake themselves at warriors
with hatchets in their belts,
the position is sometimes hard
to locate in the cathedral
of the imagination—which, itself,
is a cracked surface shaped
like Barcelona when it is not
immeasurable. You can see variations
on the position mashed and broken
in the desert (alongside fishscales
and Mediterranean masqueraders
from Algiers down on their luck)
under wriggling skies

still stinking of flesh plowed
with broken mirrors
in inexhaustible anger.

4

Battles are won and lost
in this position: crutches
are occasionally propped under
the performers after war
to keep them from falling out
of their own bodies. When
it happens prophets have their day.
The position cannot be faked:
a nun jumping rope in a room
with three inches of water
or one in the prayer position,
is not pretending *the* position.

5

The position is common.
Here, where they speak a language
I cannot speak well, the position
is spontaneous in gallic delirium.
People do not work at it here:
mates dislike such lack of trust.
Watch the horse's eye again:
everything the position means
is there fluttering anonymously
as if it were the act itself:
two tumid surfaces etching
their own postures in space
as they lose themselves.

1985

DIANE WAKOSKI ∎ ∎ ∎ ∎ ∎ ∎ ∎ ∎ ∎ ∎ ∎ ∎ ∎ ∎

b. 1937

Diane Wakoski was born in Whittier, California. After getting her degree at the University of California in Berkeley, where she was a student in Thom Gunn's poetry workshop, she moved to New York City and lived there for fifteen years.

Among her many collections are *Coins & Coffins* (1962), *Discrepancies and Apparitions* (1966), *Inside the Blood Factory* (1968), *Dancing on the Grave of a Son of a Bitch* (1973), *Waiting for the King of Spain* (1976), *The Collected Greed: Parts 1–13* (1984), *Emerald Ice: Selected Poems* (1988), and *Medea the Sorceress* (1991). A book of collected criticism, *Toward a New Poetry*, was published in 1980.

Early in her career, Wakoski was associated with Jerome Rothenberg, Robert Kelly, and other poets of the "deep image." In poems such as "Blue Monday," she made use of surrealist juxtapositions and startling, dreamlike imagery. She has described her work of that time as coming out of the "William Carlos Williams tradition, then influenced by surrealism via Ginsberg, not surrealism via French writers."[1] In her more recent poems, Wakoski has generally departed from the deep-image manner to write out of personal experience in a conversational idiom. "Our forms cannot exist," she writes, "until we discover our own real content, and that in some way is our lives."[2]

Wakoski is currently Writer-in-Residence at Michigan State University.

1. "The Poet Places Herself," *Falcon*, Spring 1971, p. 51.   2. "Form Is an Extension of Content: First Lecture," in *Toward a New Poetry*, Ann Arbor, 1980, p. 102.

Blue Monday

Blue of the heaps of beads poured into her breasts
and clacking together in her elbows;
blue of the silk
that covers lily-town at night;
blue of her teeth
that bite cold toast
and shatter on the streets;
blue of the dyed flower petals with gold stamens
hanging like tongues
over the fence of her dress
at the opera/opals clasped under her lips
and the moon breaking over her head a
gush of blood-red lizards.

Blue Monday. Monday at 3:00 and
Monday at 5. Monday at 7:30 and
Monday at 10:00. Monday passed under the rippling
California fountain. Monday alone
a shark in the cold blue waters.

      You are dead: wound round like a paisley shawl.
      I cannot shake you out of the sheets. Your name
      is still wedged in every corner of the sofa.

      Monday is the first of the week,
      and I think of you all week.
      I beg Monday not to come
      so that I will not think of you
      all week.

You paint my body blue. On the balcony
in the softy muddy night, you paint me
with bat wings and the crystal

the crystal
the crystal
the crystal in your arm cuts away
the night, folds back ebony whale skin
and my face, the blue of new rifles,
and my neck, the blue of Egypt,
and my breasts, the blue of sand,
and my arms, bass-blue,
and my stomach, arsenic;

there is electricity dripping from me like cream;
there is love dripping from me I cannot use—like acacia or
jacaranda—fallen blue and gold flowers, crushed into the street.

      Love passed me in a blue business suit
      and fedora.
      His glass cane, hollow and filled with
      sharks and whales . . .
      He wore black
      patent leather shoes
      and had a mustache. His hair was so black
      it was almost blue.

      "Love," I said.
      "I beg your pardon," he said.
      "Mr. Love," I said.
      "I beg your pardon," he said.

      So I saw there was no use bothering him on the
        street

      Love passed me on the street in a blue
      business suit. He was a banker
      I could tell.

So blue trains rush by in my sleep.
Blue herons fly overhead.
Blue paint cracks in my
arteries and sends titanium
floating into my bones.
Blue liquid pours down
my poisoned throat and blue veins
rip open my breast. Blue daggers tip
and are juggled on my palms.
Blue death lives in my fingernails.

If I could sing one last song
with water bubbling through my lips

I would sing with my throat torn open,
the blue jugular spouting that black shadow pulse,
and on my lips
I would balance volcanic rock
emptied out of my veins. At last
my children strained out
of my body. At last my blood
solidified and tumbling into the ocean.
It is blue.
It is blue.
It is blue.

1964   1968

Hummingbird Light

for Jackson Mac Low, Jerry & Diane Rothenberg,
Carol Bergé, and Craig Cotter

In the hummingbird house
the path we take
leads everyone to a bridge. From the
roof of summer, with its wreathing vines,
the lips of a tropic honeysuckle,
pouting and full as a teenage girl,
offer their buckets of sap. *The Light Poems*
of Jackson Mac Low are being quoted:
        "Diane in owl light,"
where does it come from, or?
        "a bulky space-suited figure"

Four of us troubadours stand on the bridge
following with our eyes these jewel engines
with their invisible wings,
but two of us are thinking of those curious poems,
The Light Poems, remembering words like "rhodochrosite."
Have I made this one up: "Carol Bergé in amber light,
        smoking a cigarette in an amber cigarette holder,
                reading *Forever*
        Amber"?
                These poems, like the utterances
of a fortune teller, make each person to whom a Light Poem
was dedicated think that Jackson knows something secret
or arcane about us. Why the owl for me? or Jack-O-Lantern
        light
for Jerry?

We are Merlin, we old poets. And Lancelot Craig,
he is too young to have a light poem written about him
by Jackson Mac Low; perhaps in the hummingbird house
where he has led us, though, we could compose such a lyric.
The owl is Minerva's bird, and Merlin's. We stand on the
bridge with our old rhodochrosite eyes and amber lighted
     faces
humming these words:

For Craig Who Leapt Off a Cliff in
to Hummingbird Light

In Beatle light,
in blond white-boy light,
in fast-talking light, and lemon light,
in rose light which glows softly
or Rosenkavalier light which speeds like a train,
in the light of hummingbird wings
and the light of four gold coins,
in the light on Anna's red ears and gorgette,
in the light of the Red Cars travelling from Pasadena
to Santa Monica, in the light of August,
in pearly light or saguaro light,
in the sparkling light of eau de vie
and back to rose light or letter light
or light that sips from your knightly lips,
there is only increasing light
from the hummingbird with the long tail,
Red-tailed Comet light, Hummingbird House light,
Knight of the Rose light,
leaping off a cliff light,
sleeping in hummingbird light.

1991

SUSAN HOWE ■ ■ ■ ■ ■ ■ ■ ■ ■ ■ ■ ■ ■ ■ ■
b. 1937

Born in Ireland, Susan Howe emigrated with her family to the United States as a child. Author of ten books of poetry, she has been an actress and assistant stage designer at Dublin's Gate Theatre, a painter, radio producer, and literary critic.

Her greatest influences are Charles Olson, especially in his attraction to the history and culture of New England, and Emily Dickinson, about whom Howe wrote the notable book of criticism *My Emily Dickinson* (1985). Howe also considers the early Puritan writers, especially Cotton Mather, to be important influences on her writing.

She has twice received the Before Columbus Foundation American Book Award, in 1980 for *Secret History of the Dividing Line* (1979) and in 1987 for *My Emily Dickinson*. Among her other books are *Pythagorean Silence* (1982), *Defenestration of Prague* (1983), *Articulation of Sound Forms in Time* (1987), and *The Europe of Trusts: Selected Poems* (1990).

Of *Singularities* (1990), the critic Marjorie Perloff has written, "Susan Howe is unique in her ability to make history her own, to transform the archive and chronicle into an elusive, elliptical, and yet deeply personal drama in which the New England of the Indian wars, the New England of Thoreau enter the consciousness of the woman artist working into the American fin de siècle." Howe credits her interest in history to growing up during World War II: "The deaths of millions of people in Europe and Asia . . . prevented me from ever being able to believe history is only a series of justifications, or that tragedy and savagery can be theorized away."[1]

Howe lives in Guilford, Connecticut, and teaches in the Poetics Program at the State University of New York in Buffalo.

1. Edward Foster, "An Interview with Susan Howe," *Talisman*, No. 4, 1990, p. 22.

FROM *Speeches at the Barriers*

1.

Say that a ballad
wrapped in a ballad

a play of force and play

of forces
falling out sentences

(hollow where I can shelter)
falling out over

and gone
Dark ballad and dark crossing

old woman prowling
Genial telling her story

ideal city of immaculate beauty
invincible children

threshing felicity
For we are language   Lost

in language
Wind sweeps over the wheat

mist-mask on woods
belling hounds drowse

Iseult of Ireland
Iseult of the snow-white hand

Iseult seawards gazing
(pale secret fair)

allegorical Tristram
his knights are at war

Sleet whips the page

flying leaves and fugitive

Earth of ancient ballad
earth as thought of the sea

water's edge to say goodbye

2.

Right or ruth
rent

to the winds shall be thrown

words being wind or web

What (pine-cone wheat-ear
sea-shell) what

volumes of secrets to teach
Socrates

Banks of wild bees in story
sing in no wood so on

cornstalk and cornsheaf

prodigal benevolence
wealth washed up by the sea

What I find
signal seen by my eye

This winter falls froward
forever

sound and suggestion speared
open

Free will in blind duel

sees in secret houses in sand

each day's last purpose
each day's firm progress

schoolgirls sleeping
schoolboys sleeping and stemmed

I will dream you
Draw you

dawn and horses of the sun
dawn galloped in greek before flame

fugitive dialogue of masterwork

3.

sabbath and sweet spices
seaward so far and far

The woods seem to thicken

Merry men in Arden
(foresters feared foresters)

forage cold earth bescratcht

noise and noise pursuing power

Temper and Order
The leashed stars kindle thin

perpendicular
Clear space of blackness

between us
(grey leaves grey gusts)

Dust people hover
Iceberg setting of universal

impending
(The enemy is always riding by)

figural shadowing of invisible

Wassail
tatterdemalion revel

houses containing vision
houses of recognition

trim father nodding to trim mother

remembered name in Quiet
remembered precepts

4.

Twenty lines of

boughs bend into hindering
Boreas

the thin thaw wanders off

Presence
October drawing to its long

late edge
Understanding of time endlessly

sliding
(trees hung with false dreams)

endlessly running on

Distant forget
Tiny words of substance cross

the darkness

Who are they
(others between the trees)

falling into lines of human

habitation
Tread softly my misgiving heart

To chart all

Verisimilitude
Throw my body at the mark

Parents among savages
Their house was garlanded with dead

theologies
(fierceness of the young)

Then to move forward into unknown

Crumbling compulsion of syllables

Glass face
caressing the athwart night

1983

LEAR: . . . *Now, our joy,*
Although our last, and least; to whose young love
The vines of France and milk of Burgundy
Strive to be interess'd; what can you say to draw
A third more opulent than your sisters? Speak.
CORDELIA: *Nothing, my lord.*
LEAR: *Nothing?*
CORDELIA: *Nothing.*
LEAR: *Nothing will come of nothing: speak again.*
                          —WILLIAM SHAKESPEARE
                          KING LEAR Act I.
                          Scene I

White Foolscap

BOOK OF CORDELIA

heroine in ass-skin
mouthing O Helpful
  = father revivified waking when
nickname Hero men take pity spittle speak

only nonsense
my bleeding foot
I am maria wainscotted
cap o' rushes tatter-coat
common as sal salt sally
S (golden) no huge a tiny
bellowing augury

NEMESIS singing from cask
turnspit scullion the apples pick them   Transformation
wax forehead ash
shoe fits monkey-face oh hmm
It grows dark   The shoe fits   She stays a long something
Lent is where she lives   shalbe shalbe
loving like salt (value of salt)

Lir was an ocean God whose children turned into swans
heard the birds pass overhead
Fianoula Oodh Fiachra Conn
circle of One
threshing the sun
or asleep threshing nor
nor blood nor flesh nor bone nor
corona
chromosphere
Cordelia
no no no
the hoth(heath
sline(clear
crystal
song
le
lac
pure
semblance
aperçu

giggling in a whistling wind
unbonneted he runs
hrr
hrru
hurry
hare
haloo
cry Whoop
and cry Spy!
pauses   measures   feet in syllables   caesura   Copernicus
the sun
is a cloud
of dust.
has his children brought him to this pass?
Whowe
arrowy sleet
bale the sea
out and in
stormstil stormstil
shuttle and whiz

There are nets on the hills
we have traveled all night
homeless
images of flying off
recreant

      confusion of people
   of revolt
recreant
  leaving home constantly
        where
      shadowy crustaceans
 swim in great schools
      shoals
      of salt
  in colonial core (wick inlet and low light)
      L E A R
    leans on his lance he
  has holes instead of eyes
blind (folded)
    bare (footed)
       nuclear (hooded)
        w i n d b r i d l e d
    for how or to who

  salute of armed men who continually remove their hats to make clear
             their peaceful
      intentions
  Murderers!
      Cordelia dies
         (heartrending)
reclasp her hands into obscurity
         (henceforth and fro)
    I will go to my desk
    I will sit quietly
        (as if nothing
        has happened
what is eaten is gone. If I wasn't lucky I'd starve.)

  children of Lir
  lear
      whistling would in air ha
   nameless appear—
   Can you not see
  arme armes
   give tongue
are you silent o my swift
      all coherence gone?
  Thrift thrift
we are left darkling
   waiting in the wings again
thral in the heart of Hell.
  have forgotten—

                    must go back—
                    so far—
                    almost there—
                                        vagueness of the scene
            where action takes place
                            who swiftly
                                        apparently real
            shoot downward
                            Behold
                                is *is*
                                    you see
            he brought her down.

            I can re

            trac

            my steps

            Iwho

            crawl

            between thwarts

            Do not come down the ladder

            ifor I

            haveaten

            it a

            way

                    Startled tourists sleep one hundred years
                    bird migration, story migration
                    light snow falling.
                    Once in awhile some tall tale crops up
                    great Fairly, little Fairly, liar Liar
                    and lucky Luck.
                    But crucial words outside the book
                    those words are bullets.
                    Lodged in the ebbing actual
                    women in the flight of time stand framed.
                    Rat-roofed caution of a cautionary tale
                    swallows the rat, a pin, wheat
                    while singing birds recover lost children.

I am looking for lucky Luck
I am his mother
the moneyed class are lions, wolves, bears
their gems and golden collars shine through the snow.

                    Running rings
                of light
            we'll hunt
          the wren
        calling to a catch of thorn
      crying to announce a want
along a bank
        carried her child
          hovered among the ruins
            of the game
                when the Queen spins
                round
                    Once again
              we'll hunt the wren
            says Richard to Robin
          we'll hunt the wren
  says everyone.

                        I can re

                    trac

                    my steps

                    Iwho

                    crawl

                    between thwarts

                    Do not come down the ladder

                    ifor I

                    haveaten

                    it a

                    way

                                                1983

KATHLEEN FRASER ▪ ▪ ▪ ▪ ▪ ▪ ▪ ▪ ▪ ▪ ▪ ▪
b. 1937

Editor of *HOW(ever)*, a journal devoted to the writing of "experimentalist" women, Kathleen Fraser was Full Professor of Writing at San Francisco State University and a former director of its Poetry Center. In 1993, she began writing full-time, living alternately in Rome and San Francisco.

Her books include *Change of Address* (1966), *Magritte Series* (1977), a sequence of poems based on the paintings of the Surrealist painter, *New Shoes* (1978), *Each Next* (1980), *Something (even voices) in the foreground, a lake* (1984), and *Notes preceding trust* (1987). Over the course of these volumes, she has moved from an image-based poetics to one that is more linguistic in orientation. While this reflects her growing interest in language poetry, her identity as a poet remains independent of that movement.

re:searches
(fragments, after Anakreon,
for Emily Dickinson)

inside
(jittery
burned language)
the black container

•

white bowl, strawberries
perfumy from sun
two spoons   two women
deferred pleasure

•

pious   impious
reason could not take
precedence

•

latent content
extant context

•

"eee wah yeh
my little owlet"
not connected up
your lit-up exit

•

just picked—
this red tumbling mound

in the bowl
this fact and its arrangement
this idea and who
determines it

•

this strawberry is
what separates her tongue
from just repetition

•

the fact of her
will last only
as long as she continues
releasing the shutter, she thinks

•

her toes are not
the edible boys'
toes Bernini carved,
more articulate
and pink in that gray
marble

•

his apprentice finished off
the wingy stone
splashing feathers from each
angel's shoulder but
Bernini, himself,
did the toes, ten-
der gamberoni,
prawnha, edible and
buttery under
the pink flame

•

this is what you looked like at ten,
held for an instant,
absorbed by the deep ruffle
and the black patent
shine of
your shoes

•

lying with one knee up
or sitting straight (yearning)
as if that yellow towel
could save you (some music about to hear you)

•

beside the spread, narrow surface, the
yellow terra
firma, the blue wave
longing to be her own
future sedative,
no blemish,
blond

•

wounded sideways,
wound up as if
        disqualified

•

externally, E-
ternal city,
sitting   hereafter,
laughter

•

her separate person-
ality, her
father s neutrality
ity

•

equalibrium
(cut her name
out of every
scribble)
hymn   himnal now, equal-
lateral

•

pronounced with
partially closed
lips

•

pink pearl eraser
erasing her face her
eee face ment
her face meant

•

he cut out
of her, her name

of each thing
she sang
each letter she
hung, on line
(divine)

•

this above
all to be who,
be nature's two,
and though heart
be pound-
ing at door,
cloud   cuckoo

•

radial activ-
ity, who cow now,
who moo

•

not random, these
crystalline structures, these
non-reversible orders, this
camera forming tendencies, this
edge of greater length, this
lyric forever error, this
something embarrassingly clear, this
language we come up against

1987

TONY TOWLE ▪ ▪ ▪ ▪ ▪ ▪ ▪ ▪ ▪ ▪ ▪ ▪ ▪ ▪ ▪ ▪
b. 1939

Tony Towle was born in Manhattan, where he still lives. Towle won the Frank O'Hara Award in 1970 for his first major collection, *North*. His other books include *"Autobiography" and Other Poems* (1977), *Works on Paper* (1978), *New & Selected Poems* (1983), and *Some Musical Episodes* (1992). In collaboration with poet Charles North, Towle produced the poetry collection *Gemini* (1981).

Like many other poets associated with New York School poetry, he has assimilated the work of the French surrealists. However, Towle's poems reflect this interest more in their dreamlike rhetoric rather than in their discrete images. In this respect, as well as in its heightened diction and elegance of style, his work resembles that of John Ashbery.

A former editor of the St. Mark's Poetry Project *Newsletter*, Towle contributes reviews to *Art in America* and *Arts*.

North

The green figures move forward and the objects grow larger;
explorers of the sky, exploring the earth immersed in water,
1967 with its fatal look of artificial brevity,
your life as if an illusion putting you near the window,
and promptly all the winds and currents ruffle the curtains.

But the humid surroundings, a transparent lizard
under the leaves and stretching its rubber-like plastic
across the room, protruding with our European selves,
show that we valiantly dig at the earth, poise
on the brink of adventure, or blister the flatulent sky.
In other words you are held, amused, peacefully in the grass
o beautiful art springing to mind, as we are the supreme judges.

Or perhaps you have forgotten an important exaggerated phrase,
and your words spread over the stones in a pure grove of the specific,
and you speak only the names of the bellowing animals, plants and trees
which, blind, you touch; ships, insects peopling the forests, etcetera.
The labyrinth speaks from its precipice, its outline shoots in a curve
through the chemical air, in addition to writing the script.

O miracles of divine reaches and words spinning from infancy
and whose business and indispensable references are not known,
your story is truly a story to treasure, distilled intoxicant that it is,
saying that I am a synonym for the relaxed and drifting universe,
a mere summary holding my attention over the thundering firmament.

1970

Painting the Eaves

The light painted the sky, some months ago,
like someone painting the eaves,
in the suburbs, at the top of a ladder,
a buzzing of wasps heard equivocally around his head,
no doubt an offer of their legendary supercilious advice.

While beneath the roof of gritty days,
the statements of account go out to all,
monthly white rectangles of dark cascading numbers,
hands like various devils holding them up,
aloft before your very eyes,
on the wings of the modern age,
flapping at the gates
open to all.

And I take my monthly leave,
on all the golden acres I can find
beneath the roof,
taking all the imprisoned foolishness
economics was to have freed from me
and which now springs up around me,
the author of all I see,

all the wavering lines I can think of in English,
and render in wafers of solemn translation,
and no more accurate than the original
on the facing page of earth,

and following the finest convex curve of blue,
on insane flights like a drunken wasp,
back to the interior pulp
and visionary gloom, and how, since it is night,
should one look for the way?

9/75–9/76   1978

Random (Re-arrangeable) Study for *Views*

for Robert Rauschenberg

He attempted   *texas red light*
                        Even to breathe life   *clear legend*
        Like nomads exempting reindeer   *in ochre*
                                Shot   *liquid violet*
I thought of a million candles   *antique scarlet deep*
But during the '50s of course Chuck continues   *heavy jersey yellow*
        A woman should be pleased   *magenta?*
                        To sit back   *low flame*
        And be freed by men from hassles   *idle peach*
                Until he smiles at the memory   *bright lemon*
        Dissolved like boiling fugues   *heavier pink*
And not having to think about the rhythms   *semi-gray*
                Mary thinks of herself   *forest*
                As executrix of the morning   *regular red*
                                Every day   *original sky*
Compensating for lack of space   *far pale orange*
                        A new white passenger   *worn white*
                In elaborated merger   *burnt purple deep*
In hope that armies will not have to come out   *transient kettle black*
        To chronicle you and your friends   *italic gray*
                        And reasons that follow   *dipped carmine*
        The frenzy that is the music of my life   *one more blue*

Sharing it on the plains   *invisible green*
Local white vinyl and brown walrus vinyl   *shiny deluxe*
And reasons that follow   *deep whale*
Like anything else   *blank*
In every other way   *blank*
The spectacle takes place   *cerise fable*
For men who love cigars   *pale muff umber*
And gamble common sense   *complete tobacco brown*
Bleakly yielding to a scroll of sea   *offset green*
The hunter smiles, a collector of stones   *patina red*
Wrapped in gauze   *same, deep*
To be taken away   *extended fire*
To the extent possible   *policy orange*
Raising questions   *brick*
(They live these)   *literary chrome*
For weeks   *medical green*
Enjoying the day   *bread white*
Speaking of tomorrow   *dust*
In relational search   *fig*
The thefts begin   *sleek black light*
To the extent possible   *synonymous toast*
Monday through Friday   *fence white*
Speaking of tomorrow   *capacious taupe*
In floral green   *weighted leaf*
While waiting for a connecting flight   *pure sunset*
Hyphenated   *wax*
And under the millionth dome   *structural gray*
A connecting flight   *orange and gray*

1992

BILL BERKSON ■ ■ ■ ■ ■ ■ ■ ■ ■ ■ ■ ■ ■ ■ ■ ■
b. 1939

Associated with the New York School, Bill Berkson attended Brown, Columbia, and the New School for Social Research, where he won the Dylan Thomas Memorial Poetry Award and studied with Kenneth Koch. The association with Koch led to his discovery of French poetry, especially that of Pierre Reverdy and the surrealist prose poet Henri Michaux, and his growing involvement with the work of Ashbery, O'Hara, and Koch himself.

Berkson edited the poetry anthology *Best & Company* (1969), *Homage to Frank O'Hara* (1978), a collection of essays and other writings about O'Hara, and the poetry journal *Big Sky*. His books include *Enigma Variations* (1975), with drawings by Philip Guston, *Blue Is the Hero: Poems 1960–1975* (1976), and *Lush Life* (1984).

Since 1984, Berkson has been Coordinator of the Art History Program at the San Francisco Art Institute. He lives in Bolinas, California.

Russian New Year

for Norman Bluhm

Now trouble comes between the forest's selves,
And smoke spreads to pools in which we stroke
Our several smirks, but the accident will not happen
For someone has stolen the apples
And someone else has "come full circle," picked at the fog.
Snow settled in the meetinghouse. "I love you as my own dear jailbird.
I cannot think of you without thinking of the New York lighting system."
Shame sneaks in the birches, a fire has been put out.
The distance is too much again, an army is raising the dust—
Are these horses we count as pets?

It is whiter than your face the afternoon I opened your icebox.
You are entitled to it, wisdom which bores us but may excite you
By the glint the pillows made on the horizon, unwounding silences
Mixing the poison I breathe and leave behind me
At the hitching-post
                                        Her dress raised above her ears
She lay livid among the party favors   She closed her
Umbrella   It is a cape of black which turned the carousel
It is a bucket into which night has fallen   It is no fun
Light and happy, the canyon.

My days are eaten slowly.
The pricks incorporate all jolly in the lurch.
I sit on the fluorescent seat.
All revolutions have betrayed themselves
By slush of feeling
For weakness will always burst forth from strength
The rose will shoot from the ground
As buildings stick in the wind and stop it a minute
Someone will remain
Of life riding into the trees to grow up
A steamy stormer of storms.

Are you different from that shelter you
Built for knives? On the sidewalk, sapphires.
On the fifth floor, fungus was relaxing. I have put on
The crimson face of awakeness you gave me.
What is that heart-shaped object that thaws your fingers?
It is a glove and in it a fist.

The shore slides out of the sea
Strength
To live privately beneath the noise

Of the sandbar budging
A rose above the eagle   it was there
Tattooed   Sumac above us   Pain
Is spliced and ticked away by waiting
In the chair beneath which paste is dripping
And a match is lit

From today on it is sleep I leave you on the slow waterfall
One cannot even escape light
On the night's horizon, you believe that is pleasant.
Don't you?   Or when it is snowing heat remains
In the cupboard—that too? . . . Thunder?
With you it is always the inconspicuous tear
With me it is never anything but money
Still we are the same . . . Sideways

1976

Rebecca Cutlet

Such a flow of language!
She moves in a strange world.
essentially legitimate.
or what she gambles he tosses
into the drink with not
so much as a word, and butter
reduces to fat. He takes a chance
that this "revisionism" contends up the pitfalls.

There is a house somebody-or-other and this man in it.
Without being completely satisfactory, this is all
I can let you in on, except to say that "G,"
being the sound of two rear molars and the tongue
pressed hard against the outlet, is not to be found
in the first hundred-or-so pages.
You don't mind and anyway
it is only after this that the tricks fade
away into indestructible charm, the least
common denominator of what you took this dive for in the first place.

Follow her through her mind
as you would through a rich moist shaft
that is caving in, but at
the other end of which, where you see her
hopping up and down frantically,
there is sunlight, many photographs and some text.

1976

Melting Milk

Do things then happen
despite our knowing
and is each misnomer

but a dream? Natural hiked-up
detail consciously
during years of anxious

foreshortening, now distanced
by tinsel, cup, ring, ball
heart, horseshoe, snail,

acts like visibility
of tempos irreducible
to a fractious stance.

So find any plausible footing
and grab: Do we get to stay over?
"Sorry," says Recorded Time,

"didn't get it, lost
my concentration." First error:
the profile seen double

smoothes it out
and forklifts ballast. Verso,
enter nameless emptiness,

heavy on comparison, contingency,
conceit. How's it getting dark
because things line up in a

massive buddy system, a grab
bag of rimless data,
milking lights, red ball to green spool,

as we think.
Ash is crystal.
Ecstasy is near.

1987

ED SANDERS ■ ■ ■ ■ ■ ■ ■ ■ ■ ■ ■ ■ ■ ■ ■ ■ ■ ■ ■

b. 1939

Lead singer for the sixties rock group the Fugs, owner of the now defunct Peace Eye Bookstore on Manhattan's Lower East Side, and founder, in 1962, of *Fuck You: A Magazine of the Arts*, Ed Sanders has primarily been associated with Beat poetry.

His first book, *Poem from Jail* (1963), was written after Sanders was jailed for his protest against a Polaris submarine base in Groton, Connecticut. Subsequent collections include *King Lord/Queen Freak* (1964), *20,000 A.D.* (1976), *Thirsting for Peace in a Raging Century* (1987), and *Hymn to the Rebel Cafe* (1993). He has published the prose fiction works *Shards of God* (1970) and *Fame and Love in New York* (1980), and *The Family* (1971), a nonfiction account of the murder of actress Sharon Tate by the followers of Charles Manson.

In 1976, his lecture "Investigative Poetry" set forth the principle that "poetry should again assume responsibility for the description of history."[1] Just as lawyers "make law," investigative poets would be called upon to "make reality."[2] Sanders's poetry reflects an investigative drive encompassing the study of ancient Greek literature and, in recent years, an interest in a version of performance poetry using homemade electronic instruments as a "lyre" to accompany his words and song.

Sanders lives in Woodstock, New York.

1. *Investigative Poetry*, San Francisco, 1976, p. 3.   2. The same, p. 9.

The Cutting Prow

For Henri Matisse

He couldn't paint, he couldn't sculpt. He was confined to a wheelchair and gripped with *timor mortis*. From his bed at night he'd draw on the ceiling with a long stick with crayon attached. Yet somehow he adjusted his creativity, finding a new mix of the muses, so that from the spring of 1952 through the spring of 1953, in his final creative months, he was able to produce some of the finest art of the century, a group of wall-sized works of painted paper cutouts—works such as *The Swimming Pool, Large Decoration with Masks, The Negress, Memory of Oceania, Women and Monkeys,* and the smaller *Blue Nude* series. He thought he could scissor the essence of a thing, its "sign," as he termed it, as if he had vision in Plato's world of Forms.

> The genius was 81
> Fearful of blindness
> Caught in a wheelchair
> Staring at death
>
> But the Angel of Mercy
> gave him a year

to scissor some shapes
to soothe the scythe

and shriek!   shriek!

    became

    swawk!   swawk!

    the peace of
      scissors.

There was something besides
the inexpressible

      thrill

of cutting a beautiful shape—

    for
    Each thing had a "sign"
    Each thing had a "symbol"
    Each thing had a cutting form

    —swawk swawk—

    to scissor seize.

"One must study an object a long time,"
the genius said,
"to know what its sign is."

The scissors were his scepter
The cutting
was as the prow of a barque
to sail him away.

There's a photograph
    which shows him
sitting in his wheelchair
bare foot touching the floor
drawing with crisscross steel
a shape in the gouache

His helper sits near him
till he hands her the form
to pin to the wall

He points with a stick
how he wants it adjusted
This way and that,
        minutitudinous

The last blue iris blooms at
the top of its stalk

      scissors/sceptor
      cutting/prow

   (sung)

Ah, keep those scissors flashing in the
World of Forms, Henri Matisse

The cutting of the scissors
was the prow of a boat
      to take him away
The last blue iris
     blooms at the top
        on a warm spring day

     Ah, keep those scissors flashing in the
     World of Forms, Henri Matisse

     Sitting in a wheelchair
     bare feet touching the floor
     Angel of Mercy
        pushed him over
          next to Plato's door

      Scissor scepter cutting prow
      Scissor scepter cutting prow
      Scissor scepter cutting prow
      Scissor scepter cutting prow

    ahh
   swawk swawk

ahh

swawk swawk

ahh

swawk swawk

1983

1981

CLARK COOLIDGE ▪ ▪ ▪ ▪ ▪ ▪ ▪ ▪ ▪ ▪ ▪ ▪

b. 1939

Clark Coolidge traces his development as a poet to reading Jack Kerouac's novel *On the Road* as a college student: "Everything that happened to me, the minutest details of sunlight on a shoe, began to seem vastly important, had to be scribbled down, and with *extensions*. . . . I had thought the writer must first have it all in his head and only *then* put it into words, but no. I began to see how it was really excitingly done: You wrote from what you didn't know toward whatever could be picked up in the act."[1]

Coolidge composed his early poetry, collected in *Space* (1970), with the use of a dictionary in an attempt to break with normal syntax and broaden what he felt was the limited vocabulary of poetry. His arrangement of seemingly unrelated words without the aid of sentences can create a puzzle of disjunction for the uninitiated reader. Yet, once the reader suspends any demand for narrative or linear organization, the words are free to come into relation, like the abstract yet liquid shapes in a Tanguy painting, or like the geologic formations that have fascinated Coolidge since childhood. Coolidge perceives poetic composition as an "arrangement" of discrete materials (words), just as quartz and calcite are an arrangement of molecules.[2]

Arrangement and movement are the tensions at play in Coolidge's imagery, a subject on which he likes to quote painter Philip Guston:

> It cannot be a settled, fixed image. It must of necessity be an image which is unsettled, which has not only not made up its mind where to be but must feel as if it's been in many places all over this canvas, and indeed there's no place for it to settle—except momentarily.[3]

"I don't want to use the word *form*," Coolidge said in a lecture, "I want to use the word *forms*. The word is plural always, plural. You never have just one."[4] Influenced by the rhythm and movement of jazz, Coolidge's style of public reading is characterized by a driving tempo.

His other books include *The Maintains* (1974), *Polaroid* (1975), *Mine: The One That Enters the Stories* (1982), *The Crystal Text* (1986), *Solution Passage* (1986), *At Egypt* (1988), *Odes of Roba* (1991), and *The Book of During* (1991).

Raised in Providence, Rhode Island, where his father was a professor of music at Brown University, Coolidge lives in New Lebanon, New York.

1. "A First Reading of *On the Road* and Later," *Talisman*, No. 3, Spring 1989, p. 100.
2. "Arrangement," in *Talking Poetics from Naropa Institute*, Boulder, 1978, pp. 144 and 147.   3. The same, p. 151.   4. The same, p. 147.

Brill

emotional the
fox at an am   land kept chess   dim after him
   two things   shrink very barren
      parts of the 6   wind but
act no like   canvas can
   A he up   very least
    or may in that   lonely like part
merely Davis 1956   body very   red soapy
      complexity it   means fees
   it to out   can't ready doing
  scratched up once   in the seemed the in
      life crab   but by so
  cigs or visits   last d   his the
like darkness   past is root   "Woolp-klo"
   wings nohow   planet three speed
  fast like not
      column stood still
sin   sun   wig
        dry   one   coin in what in   tat

 fun   six   not   hell   pall
        new

    tic   way   was   yes   two
             not   bud
  bar   sip   has   day   you
     get   here
pip   now   guy   air   wen   hod   no

                              1970

Styro

   quite is high
   quatic
      deliverance rates   dial   3
 in ex
    trees palling steins   ing
snail of it, acrid, the dumps
        the "sill row"
  to knees smoke
      sir fins

drub in minnow the elicit of haunt (bite)
crust, stub, crayon, chives
        Galatea dumbing hard
  cawl o'wrist it?

<pre>
                    nubs
                        (Nile)
    an green   and ever attack
                            styrene mistachio dubloon
    rack sun correct ratchet
                        Dumbo in   size

      sign or hone win
        gold when aft
           whom   whine
      it, state
</pre>

1970

On Induction of the Hand

Perhaps I've got to write better longer thinking of it as
grown up out of the same singular lost. The pattern is in, or is it
under, the hands? Better be in or it's gone from the brain
choking on airless. The outside leaves stain the sands of my
sleep even through glass and alerted in this very chair as I
thought I snoozed by the strings of this world. What world?,
evening of syntax brought full over the mounds of these what
lives but hopes. There is a wrench that a certain staring at
while balancing humours we call words in state pours wings
of edgy fondness bound useless in calm of lucidity down the
chute of the sentence. So-called duty roster activity when
typing at the seeming to be nodded at by trees. They yearn?
Saying that I am out there, with a loop I hope carries me
swaying back to here by means of them there. A tree could even
be a monad to this use, though never is it held in my heat to
be even. I let myself off myself never, no dope again trembling
my attic wires loose from their packets. Containments of such
that I never think them sendable. A poet used the word
"lozenge," he didn't write it. Some other and more careless
scribe wanted me to write one of those but the hell with what
    lies off
him. I remain stormy in my paradise. I pull up my pants when
the itch takes me, drops hitting page. Writing *is* a prayer for
always it starts at the portal lockless to me at last leads
to the mystery of everything that has always been written.
The state of that, trembles and then fades back in leaving
the hole where it's gone. But I pout instead of kneel. I
would rather confess, but there's no mouth to pour toward at
the poem. Perhaps it's just that the words have all been said
but not by me, and the process *is* a trial. What those leaves
are awaiting, every day my burden's finality in hand. Beneath

it are the faces I've yet to replace in a rock as stern and fluid as
Piero's Christless blue. But all the while I eye you, demon,
your bird hoards are clustering here. Sent for calm and
brought crazy still.

1978–1981   1986

The Hand Further

Am I right to see my self introduced
into the introduction of all those other things you
might have held me to. If I could be
quiet enough. If I could still hear or bear to be
those things you notice I missed since watching you
call me sure. The day is already red. That other
day to be siding with already an afternoon grey.
And they are long, longer and not of stone.
They move in tight so fist. I must stop
washing this window out. I must stop wishing
the outer other things nearly me. But if the
words are already me, not knowing it long, what do
you use to call. Now this will nearly be night
in the introduction of the barest hand.
You are another light, and I am the eyes that fall.
The dress is of a white all tongues are on.

1978–1981   1986

Noon Point

I think I wrote a poem today but I don't know well.
Though well do I seize the trees shake but am not given pause.
The lights are every one of them out, we see it all so well.
Nothing is taken care of, everything lies.
Everyone rise.

1978–1981   1986

The Crack

Thinking around things that edge me into
the blank thoughts. The bulb clicks on in
the book about cork. Anything comes to time

in the surge enough tune. Resting my
nippled fingers the month of the bad moon.

She moved, then the lines of wheat that
make up the walls of the costumed house.
Out back is a latch back, or ort bath, a block
or whortleberry dye, a speech omega,
the lining rhyme of a lagging tongue run.
She formed her mind around my cock
in lips of coinage horn.

The moon was of an orange it burned,
a fur back in the puncture china of the circuit delves
stubbing a picture at the tips are blades.
I know not more anymore than my organ selves
and the rains come out on her back,
fever volute of screened seeds.

1978–1981   1986

FROM *At Egypt*

I

I came here. I don't know you here.
I say this. I have lost such.
Plant at the gate. Slant on missing heights.
Where if I see you you glow. Where no one.
Here a sun. That the moon.
Black black, and be sure of it. There is little sure.
It was a coming which was done.

I had heard of it and come.
I knew not but styles of the copier.
His ignorant oils, his puddles bright.
I had heard of it coming, now was here.
Somewhere now was a failure.
Now had been left there, where I was
finally to enter, time is lost.
Time the failure. Space the whole.

To enter where, in darkness of a size
red pin to the center of the skull
and pale orange the boulevards the white
flapping float thing gulps up
in vanish of the battle trucks

the home sod of rusting eaters
political clay and the yard
and the yet, the not emotive yet
sprung from the dark side blood of the sight
stone of a shape, mind sift to figure

          As he has said it
          That it needs to

That the lurks come, window is softer
for anything shape, rock triangular in room
you don't even see, you walk and then do
would be me then, say I, and has been
thought in the room an outside prism
pyramid night collect your impressions
and stamp, it won't move, won't say

          As he said it
          Would in its needs

Terrifically brighter in black set of mind
black set of gates, the one in the room
the one on the moon
the eye set things out
the after that shifter
and he tells me there to sleep

I opened, I caught it
versions were left on the ledge, they shift
as felt as the lobby of the long spinal cats
the neon blot of its gas an Arabic slouch
careering of sniffing the turning of perfume past mosques
tongue lit in sand light, a vastness to remember city
a wander through anywhere pulling, crane star to water links
and the beams that collapse in the clothing of breath

          That he states
          What we hear
          That not turn

But everyone here and the dust will not raise
apportionment penetrations mosaic the nightsoil
collection of sleep, horizon plank to drill road
was said here, the man put up his sleep stalagmites
and cottoned off a road to outskirts no millworks
at particle row near the chair stands
a bit north from flavor and deaf from the dough
and right off the pyramids is a tune of slight dogs
could play at your suede and magnate the stars

to a twist crimps lights to a berry in drink barrel
rolls of radium to chocolate the airport spills
black bottle taxi to fire totter doorway
Cassiopeia had drifted her chair.

And there are guys with sparks, spades with hats
monkeys on a chill, the bottle wants to take us somewhere
radiant and shalom enormous as the fakery of monuments

> He settles for
> It sets up
> Makes high
> He wanders from

But what will touch blue space here provide?
Glance Clear space, Ace of Triangles space
space of the owlless winds, twister over spaces a turret
that mounted volcano with no heat, stitchy terminus
the space of arm vents and molecule the cue
or nodule space, the knob lost, the crew cell
cease function on icicle of blue key block gem
amounter belly to dance the monomaniacal chain link
ends at detritus must, sand in the fridge?

> That it's not him that says it
> This time it's he will rise

Ink of this Egyptian knock over night
when the belly calms the whole roars, rows
of anything inch to ape the dust, the ouncing
Can you one-hand raise the Proper Vehicle?
but this desert, and you terminant, you sour
at frills and cannot even howl, low trill
when the bird floats and powers slow down
and the slightest gaze could inch a hill
you'll see the rowers dance once, their step huts are lit
clear the window on this page with this felt
this hulk up to lick the coffin of pensum
clearing add for piss of winds, ant antique
where honks of the ones whine up
great rolling roughage of these outer centuries
everything older than we think to be, to swim
the latch pool of cabbages and knowledge papers up
much as mountain piles, gravel cones by nightly wheels
the stars

> He stings loose
> It carves back
> The stoppers for

Those gentlemen roentgens routing the rhythms
as I could hardly bear to seat you far
from rooster crows at midnight celery sticking though
I write clear to window with my elbow follow-through
as the things sign this paper
seeds through to zircon end
the things that raise the things
that slice beyond this face
no longer man's

1988

STEPHEN RODEFER ■ ■ ■ ■ ■ ■ ■ ■ ■ ■ ■ ■
b. 1940

In the mid-sixties, Stephen Rodefer was a student in Charles Olson's classes at the State University of New York, Buffalo, where he helped produce *The Magazine of Further Studies*. Among his books are *The Bell Clerk's Tears Keep Flowing* (1978), *Plane Debris* (1981), *Emergency Measures* (1987), and a book of prose poems, *Passing Duration* (1991).

In the preface to *Four Lectures* (1982), Rodefer writes, "My program is simple: to surrender to the city and survive its inundation. To read it and in reading, order it to read myself."[1] Rodefer thus shares Charles Olson's thematic concerns with regard to the *polis*, as well as his attitudes toward poetic composition. In Rodefer's view, the role of poetry is to embody history rather than to disclose it, for "language . . . is a city also."[2]

Rodefer also writes, "Deliberate decomposition is required in a state of advanced decay."[3] Like the process of political revolution, poetry must first dismantle the "oppressed whole" into parts from which it can assemble a new aggregate. The poems of *Four Lectures*, with their methodical formalism marked by disjunctive capitalizations, reflect the deliberate disassembly Rodefer seeks.

Born in Bellaire, Ohio, Rodefer served for several years as co-director of the Writing Program at the University of New Mexico, Albuquerque. He now lives in Oakland, California.

1. *Four Lectures*, Berkeley, 1982, p. 7.　　2. The same.　　3. The same, p. 8.

Pretext

Then I stand up on my hassock and say sing that.
It is not the business of POETRY to be anything.
When one day at last they come to storm your deluxe cubicle,
Only your pumice stone will remain. The left trapezius for now
Is a little out of joint. Little did they know you came with it.
When nature has entirely disappeared, we will find ourselves in Stuttgart.
Till then we're on the way. The only way not to leave is to go.
The gods and scientists heap their shit on Buffalo and we're out there,

Scavenging plastic trees. When nature has entirely disappeared,
We'll find ourselves in the steam garden. Evening's metonym for another
Beady-eyed engineer with sexual ideas, who grew up eating animals.
Do you like the twelve tones of the western scale? I prefer ninety.
I may work in a factory but I slide to the music of the spheres.
My job is quality control in the language lab, explaining what went
Wrong in Northampton after the Great Awakening. So much was history.

My father is a sphinx and my mother's a nut. I reject the glass.
But I've been shown the sheets of sentences and what he was
Really like remains more of a riddle than in the case of most humans.
So again I say rejoice, the man we're looking for
Is gone. The past will continue, the surest way to advance,
But you still have to run to keep fear in the other side.
There is a little door at the back of the mouth fond of long names
Called the juvjula. And pidgeon means business. It carries
Messages. The faces on the character parts are excellent.
In fact I'm having lunch with her next week. Felix nupsit.
Why should it be so difficult to see the end if when it comes
It should be irrefutable. Cabin life is incomplete.
But the waterbugs' mittens SHADOW the bright rocks below.
He has a resemblance in the upper face to the man who robbed you.
I am pleased to be here. To my left is Philippa, who will be signing for me.

1982

FROM *Plane Debris*

My mind to me mangles iron. An error is mirror to the truth
than any statement claiming to be true. I saw a tree and the idea
arose from memory that it was a mango tree. The past is made of brain cells.
We wouldn't have time if we didn't think about it. Thought creates matter
that nature didn't think to. How incredibly perceptive
that women have decided to paint themselves in every age. Measurement
means distance, and is political. They fight fire for instance, but though they
burn they do not fight themselves. One of the Bauhaus lovelies
on the staff of WET can do the awesome graphic. My name will be Money,
but you can call me Change. Antiphilus, Antipater,
do not let the prick think. Her Harry thinks she is too much.
I am exactly as old as you ART. Wonder in and spy the pond.
Truth is, most state of the art is actually edge of the park. Out one ear
and in the other. Hearing lists on an off day. Woods wave leaves.
The town signs. Here the papyrus begins to tatter. The rest is loss.

Still be kind and eke out the performance with your mind.
If you have to cough, cough. You think you know everything,
but you only know half of it. You must reveal your self,

your time, and the structural development of art up till now.
Let us match our racquets to their balls. Upon a filet
balance a model to propose a spread. Just the right hint of everything,
pushed through a sieve. The logic of any gross natural array.
We live in bags, presented and ready to be taxed, feeling the necessity
of blocking the choreography behind *any* massive confusion.
The imagination wells—first one tip, spin off, then sea mist,
drifting and swell, spindrift. The repetitive structures of the intellect
at attention. Spit shined rhyme. Saluted rhetoric.
By now you look ready to stick your thumb in a dyke and become a heroine.
Spread your TEETH and lift your nostrils ups, flying with your bike in your
     arms.
National guardsmen are throwing up all over, and so we enter the blow-torch
     world.

Like history, a man is a lesson. As soon as you learn it, no need for class.
This doesn't mean that you leave the world that imagines them.
Dying with the tide turning, bustle courage up.
Trade fame for sustenance and safety, to be halted in a familiar path,
guarded by babies and old women. Derivation and other particulars,
affably used. The nose as wet as a pen, cold as stone.
Still crying out for company and the sack. It is the same for us all,
so God bless you. The lesson in ENGLISH is really a lesson in French.
Let me entreat your succor. If you are dead, I'll slumber.
If there is breath, I'll mark the glass. The dull ear is dumber than night.
If the enemy is an ass, speak lower. I love the lovely bully.
We know enough if we know we are subjects. Everything waits
for you, for which I am grateful. And confusion is mineral.
Achieve me and you can sell my bones. Base weed—
my horse is my mistress and gives me a bad back, at the tip of the pouring
     dark.

                                                                    1982

Codex

That is the glebe and this is the glissando. The future is nothing
But a flying wing. You must make your case either with names or with an
     unfolding.
A position or a disclosure, a microbus. The corridor, the cascade, what stuck.
Glacier notes over the tops of hills. To be close again, as it was in the leanto.
Lengthen the line and increase the leading. These are the helloes of progress.
At the kitchen table the books are pored over, much as a neighbor will bum a
     cigaret.
The bungalow, radioed and occupied, has no other path to follow but the
     venture,
The undeniable yielding turmoil mapped out for us for life.
Somebody might ought cook someone a square meal. Life in our adulthood

Is mistaken for wanting completion. What it longs to do is continue being.
The BEES are sleeping beneath the pergola. At the end of each lesson is
the vocabulary.
If one opening clouds, another will clear, so long as you both will breathe.
Where's a shovel or something, I say, what can dig, or a trowel? Language
pointed
To its content. A crowd of people at the beach screaming "Tuna! tuna!"
The evening
Breeze, trembling trees, the night, the stars. And there you are, in a manner
of speaking.

So at sunset the clouds went nuts. They thought they were a text.
This language of the general o'erflows the measure, but my brother and I
liked it alot.
I think I'll just pause long enough here to call God a bitter name.
Ripeness is all right but the lip is a couplet and nobody knows fuck-all
about it.
The THREAD has always been bias. There are alternatives to purchasing
goods
To recruit admirers. Right, but is it what Verdi would have wanted?
Nor is it enough to be seen by your youngers as having carried the tradition
To a good place. Given disasters everywhere, don't drink from the tap.
And for what reason make anything that is not for flight?
There are treatments to keep your retina from becoming detached but
for what—
To see this? Why, there are things about Israel not dreamed of in the Bible.
How could I miss you when my aim is dead. The goal is sea sounds not
yet writ.
All right. Enjoy the heads of your beaches. I'm not going in order
To get tied up on spec, but I wanted you to meet your fellow brains.
Thank you,
People of destiny, for your brilliant corners. I like your voice. Look where it's
come from.

1982

ROBERT GRENIER ■ ■ ■ ■ ■ ■ ■ ■ ■ ■ ■ ■

b. 1941

Born in Minneapolis, Robert Grenier graduated from Harvard in 1965, where
he studied with Robert Lowell and wrote his thesis on William Carlos Williams's
prosody. He received an M.F.A. from the University of Iowa in 1968. A resident
of Bolinas, California, he has served as an editorial assistant to the poet Larry
Eigner, who is also an influence on his writing.
   Following in the tradition of Pound, Williams, Olson, Creeley, and the lan-
guage poets, with whom he has been associated since founding the poetry maga-
zine *This* with Barrett Watten in 1971, Grenier sees poetry as a written art. "It
isn't the spoken any more than the written, now, that's the progression from

Williams," he writes in the essay "On Speech."[1] Speech, he concludes, has a sameness of character when compared to the variety and richness of written discourse, including the poem's design on the page.

Grenier's books, which include *Series: Poems 1967–1971* (1978), *A Day at the Beach* (1984), and *Phantom Anthems* (1986), display this interest in design through special typographical effects. He has published three "books" in special formats: *Sentences* (1978), which consists of 500 poems on 5 × 8-inch index cards; *CAMBRIDGE M'ASS* (1979), 265 poems on a 40 × 48-inch poster; and the trilogy *What I Believe   Transpiration/Transpiring   Minnesota* (1989), consisting of 8½ × 11-inch photocopied pages, the majority of which are hand-written poems "drawn" from the other side of the paper, as if he were writing with his left hand.

1. *In the American Tree*, ed. Ron Silliman, Orono, 1986, p. 496.

HAS FADED IN PART BUT MAGNIFICENT ALSO LATE

   for RC / <u>MIRRORS</u>

what stays specific <u>in</u> age when much else fades

is song more than <u>one</u> even exists & belongs

others are backside beside <u>we</u> ring the changes

of age blocks <u>all</u> fours twos threes a finally

book with poems <u>with</u> resonant titles on light

towns stairs sections <u>more</u> 'southerly' 'latent' seascapes

winter's 'grip' in Buffalo <u>tin</u> slates, remembrancer of childhood

in Massachusetts, bloomers at the shore, "grandma" clamming, <u>stu</u>

'going on' nowadays too colors tones resonances <u>will</u> some

use of particulars <u>Maine</u> if ever now here always

Monday <u>morning</u> quatrains tenor bass copper

<u>over</u> the land ringing mathematical brick tower bell

                                                    1986

CROW

started as <u>arr</u>

from the trees in the woods

rather dimly

attended to as <u>bark</u>

more familiarly

identified as the neighbor's dog

by their house over there

where the kids walk probably

flew overhead as <u>ark</u>

1986

WRATH TO SADNESS

for Anselm Hollo

reproachful eyes'
beauty but the

face downcast in
Irish Russian Jewess'

Portuguese green eyes
furious beauty bottom smoldering

from proprietary Injury white
cheeked stung Insight & Pride red

downcast and burning American
with Right & Conviction suddenly

as if after an immense journey of thinking
suddenly as if out of nowhere

with forethought & malice spontaneously
looks up into my eyes

and the 'archaic smile' opens
again finally

to recite my doom

1986

SUNDAY MORNING

should be very quiet this morning

relatively early Sunday a.m.

late Saturday night unusual unreal

wash of cars over the Bay

Bridge and streetlights

still red & green means go

well they went

candle still burning

in its circle of light

against the wide-blue-black rimmed

white plate there on the table with wax wind

pouring out one side

looks like a roof-rack

foggy

in the quiet pre-dawn starlight

that thick plumbers' candle

must burn down a lot of oxygen

that sheds some heat of air

against the sky in three windows

'Circumference' springing up

rose opposite around the candelabra

tar but sheds some light indemnity

mind tantamount to undertaking venture

wants to see now whats becoming capital

in a poem to Wallace Stevens trees house silos

sides that incomparable master Emily Dickinson

that rested within itself that fart secret

out of oil <u>tone</u> relax sweet dark glasses

in the house mourning doves soon

sound first whereas, Tribune

song after final outline first birds adds

or buildings never makes sense

anymore it just misses

birds away plaintiff or night

after matters of combat money

each thing born inside vices

beams 'Circumference'

casting its light away by barking

shining along with refrigerators

shadows still cast by that candle

want desire more of night gloom 'bracketing'

vast tomatoes, Boom veil more of day

I thought for a while that Kathleen might be working

because she was alive & I was alone but then

I realized that she must be sleeping & I

was awake or she was alone for

or she might be sleeping & I would want

was at work or she might be sleeping &

"Kathleen's not home from the Music Library yet"

1986

LYN HEJINIAN ■ ■ ■ ■ ■ ■ ■ ■ ■ ■ ■ ■ ■ ■

b. 1941

One of the leading language poets, Lyn Hejinian is editor and publisher of Tuumba Press and co-editor, with Barrett Watten, of *Poetics Journal*. Her books include *Thought Is the Bride of What Thinking* (1976), *Writing Is an Aid to Memory* (1978), *The Guard* (1984), *Redo* (1984), *My Life* (1987), and *Oxota: A Short Russian Novel* (1991).

Like Leslie Scalapino and Carla Harryman, she is attracted to the complexities of narrative. In *My Life*, Hejinian gradually creates a portrait of her own childhood through a mosaic of discontinuous sentences and glimpses, wherein the "title" of one section of the book-length sequence finds its way into the text of another. "Repetition, and the rewriting that repetition becomes, make a perpetual beginning," she writes in her essay "The Rejection of Closure."[1]

Her book *Oxota* consists of 270 "sonnets" inspired by Pushkin's *Evgeny Onegin*, through which she creates a portrait of post-Soviet Russia. Hejinian is the translator of the contemporary Russian poet Arkadii Dragamoschenko, whom she first met in Moscow in 1983. Her attraction to Russian literature was first established, however, through the writings of Velimir Khlebnikov, Viktor Shklovsky, Roman Jakobson, and others who share Hejinian's interest in the "constructedness" of a literary text.

In an assessment of the poetic line, Hejinian writes, "The integrity of the individual line, and the absorbing discontinuities that often appear between lines—the jumpiness that erupts in various sections of the work (whether the result or the source of disjunctive semantics)—are so natural to my 'real life' experience that they seem inevitable—and 'true.' "[2] In the prose poem sequence *My Life*, however, that disjunctiveness finds its expression in the associational gaps between sentences and sentence fragments.

Hejinian lives in Oakland, California.

1. *Writing/Talks*, ed. Bob Perelman, Carbondale, 1985, p. 273.   2. "Line," in *The Line in Postmodern Poetry*, eds. Robert Frank and Henry Sayre, Urbana, 1988, p. 191.

FROM *My Life*

A pause, a rose, A moment yellow, just as four years later when
something on paper my father returned home from the war, the moment of greeting him, as he stood at the bottom of the stairs, younger, thinner than when he had left, was purple—though moments are no longer so colored. Somewhere, in the background, rooms share a pattern of small roses. Pretty is as pretty does. In certain families, the meaning of necessity is at one with the sentiment of pre-necessity. The better things were gathered in a pen. The windows were narrowed by white gauze curtains which were never loosened. Here I refer to irrelevance, that rigidity which never intrudes. Hence, repetitions, free from all ambition. The shadow of the redwood trees, she said, was oppressive. The plush must be worn away. On her walks she stepped into people's gardens to pinch off cuttings

from their geraniums and succulents. An occasional sunset is reflected on the windows. A little puddle is overcast. If only you could touch, or, even, catch those gray great creatures. I was afraid of my uncle with the wart on his nose, or of his jokes at our expense which were beyond me, and I was shy of my aunt's deafness who was his sister-in-law and who had years earlier fallen into the habit of nodding, agreeably. Wool station. See lightning, wait for thunder. Quite mistakenly, as it happened. Long time lines trail behind every idea, object, person, pet, vehicle, and event. The afternoon happens, crowded and therefore endless. Thicker, she agreed. It was a tic, she had the habit, and now she bobbed like my toy plastic bird on the edge of its glass, dipping into and recoiling from the water. But a word is a bottomless pit. It became magically pregnant and one day split open, giving birth to a stone egg, about as big as a football. In May when the lizards emerge from the stones, the stones turn gray, from green. When daylight moves, we delight in distance. The waves rolled over our stomachs, like spring rain over an orchard slope. Rubber bumpers on rubber cars. The resistance on sleeping to being asleep. In every country is a word which attempts the sound of cats, to match an inisolable portrait in the clouds to a din in the air. But the constant noise is not an omen of music to come. "Everything is a question of sleep," says Cocteau, but he forgets the shark, which does not. Anxiety is vigilant. Perhaps initially, even before one can talk, restlessness is already conventional, establishing the incoherent border which will later separate events from experience. Find a drawer that's not filled up. That we sleep plunges our work into the dark. The ball was lost in a bank of myrtle. I was in a room with the particulars of which a later nostalgia might be formed, an indulged childhood. They are sitting in wicker chairs, the legs of which have sunk unevenly into the ground, so that each is sitting slightly tilted and their postures make adjustment for that. The cows warm their own barn. I look at them fast and it gives the illusion that they're moving. An "oral history" on paper. *That* morning this morning. I say it about the psyche because it is not optional. The overtones are a denser shadow in the room characterized by its habitual readiness, a form of charged waiting, a perpetual attendance, of which I was thinking when I began the paragraph, "So much of childhood is spent in a manner of waiting."

As for we who "love to be astonished"   You spill the sugar when you lift the spoon. My father had filled an old apothecary jar with what he called "sea glass," bits of old bottles rounded and textured by the sea, so abundant on beaches. There is no solitude. It buries itself in veracity. It is as if one splashed in the water lost by one's tears. My mother had climbed into the garbage can in order to stamp down the accumulated trash, but the can was knocked off balance, and when she fell she broke her arm. She could only give a little shrug. The family had little money but plenty of food. At the circus only the elephants were greater than anything I could have imagined. The egg of Columbus, landscape and grammar. She wanted one where the playground was dirt, with grass, shaded by a tree, from which would hang a rubber tire as a swing, and when she found it she sent me. These creatures are compound and nothing they do should surprise us. I don't mind, or I won't mind, where the verb "to care" might multiply. The pilot of the little airplane had forgotten to notify the airport of his approach, so that when the lights of the plane in the night were first spotted, the air raid sirens went off, and the entire city on that coast went dark. He was taking a drink of water and the light was growing dim. My mother stood at the window watching the only lights that were visible, circling over the darkened city in search of the hidden airport. Unhappily, time seems more normative than place. Whether breathing or holding the breath, it was the same thing, driving through the tunnel from one sun to the next under a hot brown hill. She sunned the baby for sixty seconds, leaving him naked except for a blue cotton sunbonnet. At night, to close off the windows from view of the street, my grandmother pulled down the window shades, never loosening the curtains, a gauze starched too stiff to hang properly down. I sat on the windowsill singing sunny lunny teena, ding-dang-dong. Out there is an aging magician who needs a tray of ice in order to turn his bristling breath into steam. He broke the radio silence. Why would anyone find astrology interesting when it is possible to learn about astronomy. What one passes in the Plymouth. It is the wind slamming the doors. All that is nearly incommunicable to my friends. Velocity and throat verisimilitude. Were we seeing a pattern or merely an appearance of small white sailboats on the bay, floating at such a distance from the hill that they appeared to be making no progress. And for once to a country that did not speak another language. To follow the progress of ideas, or that particular line of reasoning, so full of surprises and unexpected correlations, was somehow to take a vacation. Still, you had to wonder where they had gone, since you could speak of reappearance. A blue room is always dark. Everything on the boardwalk was shooting toward the sky. It was not specific to any year, but very early. A German goldsmith covered a bit of metal with cloth in the 14th century and gave mankind its first button. It was hard to know this as politics, because it plays like the work of one person, but nothing is isolated in history—certain humans are situations. Are your fingers in the margin. Their random procedures make monuments to fate. There is something still surprising when the green emerges. The blue fox has ducked its head. The front rhyme of harmless with harmony. Where is my honey running. You cannot linger "on the lamb." You cannot determine the nature of progress until you assemble all of the relatives.

Like plump birds	Summers were spent in a fog that rains. They
along the shore	were mirages, no different from those that camel-
	back riders approach in the factual accounts of
	voyages in which I persistently imagined myself,
	and those mirages on the highway were for me
	both impalpable souvenirs and unstable evidence
	of my own adventures, now slightly less vicarious

than before. The person too has flared ears, like an infant's reddened with batting. I had claimed the radio nights for my own. There were more storytellers than there were stories, so that everyone in the family had a version of history and it was impossible to get close to the original, or to know "what really happened." The pair of ancient, stunted apricot trees yielded ancient, stunted apricots. What was the meaning hung from that depend. The sweet aftertaste of artichokes. The lobes of autobiography. Even a minor misadventure, a bumped fender or a newsstand without newspapers, can "ruin the entire day," but a child cries and laughs without rift. The sky droops straight down. I lapse, hypnotized by the flux and reflux of the waves. They had ruined the Danish pastry by frosting it with whipped butter. It was simply a tunnel, a very short one. Now I remember worrying about lockjaw. The cattle were beginning to move across the field pulled by the sun, which proved them to be milk cows. There is so little public beauty. I found myself dependent on a pause, a rose, something on paper. It is a way of saying, I want you, too, to have this experience, so that we are more alike, so that we are closer, bound together, sharing a point of view—so that we are "coming from the same place." It is possible to be homesick in one's own neighborhood. Afraid of the bears. A string of eucalyptus pods was hung by the window to discourage flies. So much of "the way things were" was the same from one day to the next, or from one occasion (Christmas, for example, or July 4th) to the next, that I can speak now of how we "always" had dinner, all of us sitting at our usual places in front of the placemats of woven straw, eating the salad first, with cottage cheese, which my father always referred to as "cottage fromage," that being one of many little jokes with which he expressed his happiness at home. Twice he broke his baby toe, stubbing it at night. As for we who "love to be astonished," my heartbeats shook the bed. In any case, I wanted to be both the farmer and his horse when I was a child, and I tossed my head and stamped with one foot as if I were pawing the ground before a long gallop. Across the school playground, an outing, a field trip, passes in ragged order over the lines which mark the hopscotch patch. It made for a sort of family mythology. The heroes kept clean, chasing dusty rustlers, tonguing the air. They spent the afternoon building a dam across the gutter. There was too much carpeting in the house, but the windows upstairs were left open except on the very coldest or wettest of days. It was there that she met the astonishing figure of herself when young. Are we likely to find ourselves later pondering such suchness amid all the bourgeois memorabilia. Wherever I might find them, however unsuitable, I made them useful by a simple shift. The obvious analogy is with music. Did you mean gutter or guitar. Like cabbage or collage. The book was a sort of protection because it had a better plot. If any can be spared from the garden. They hoped it would rain before somebody parked beside that section of the curb. The fuchsia is a plant much like a person, happy in the out-of-doors in the same sun and breeze that is most comfortable to a person sitting nearby. We had to wash the windows in order to see them. Supper was a different meal from dinner. Small fork-stemmed boats propelled by

wooden spoons wound in rubber bands cruised the trough. Losing its
balance on the low horizon lay the vanishing vernal day.

Yet we insist   The windows were open and the morning air was,
that life is full   by the smell of lilac and some darker flowering
of happy chance   shrub, filled with the brown and chirping trills of
birds. As they are if you could have nothing but
quiet and shouting. Arts, also, are links. I picture
an idea at the moment I come to it, our collision.
Once, for a time, anyone might have been luck's
child. Even rain didn't spoil the barbecue, in the backyard behind a
polished traffic, through a landscape, along a shore. Freedom then,
liberation later. She came to babysit for us in those troubled years di-
rectly from the riots, and she said that she dreamed of the day when she
would gun down everyone in the financial district. That single tele-
phone is only one hair on the brontosaurus. The coffee drinkers an-
swered ecstatically. If your dog stays out of the room, you get the fleas.
In the lull, activity drops. I'm seldom in my dreams without my chil-
dren. My daughter told me that at some time in school she had learned
to think of a poet as a person seated on an iceberg and melting through
it. It is a poetry of certainty. In the distance, down the street, the prac-
ticing soprano belts the breeze. As for we who "love to be astonished,"
money makes money, luck makes luck. Moves forward, drives on. Class
background is not landscape—still here and there in 1969 I could feel
the scope of collectivity. It was the present time for a little while, and
not so new as we thought then, the present always after war. Ever since
it has been hard for me to share my time. The yellow of that sad room
was again the yellow of naps, where she waited, restless, faithless, for
more days. They say that the alternative for the bourgeoisie was gulli-
bility. Call it water and dogs. Reason looks for two, then arranges it
from there. But can one imagine a madman in love. Goodbye; enough
that was good. There was a pause, a rose, something on paper. I may
balk but I won't recede. Because desire is always embarrassing. At the
beach, with a fresh flush. The child looks out. The berries are kept in the
brambles, on wires on reserve for the birds. At a distance, the sun *is*
small. There was no proper Christmas after he died. That triumphant
blizzard had brought the city to its knees. I am a stranger to the little girl
I was, and more—more strange. But many facts about a life should be
left out, they are easily replaced. One sits in a cloven space. Patterns
promote an outward likeness, between little white silences. The big
trees catch all the moisture from what seems like a dry night. Reflec-
tions don't make shade, but shadows are, and do. In order to under-
stand the nature of the collision, one must know something of the na-
ture of the motions involved—that is, a history. He looked at me and
smiled and did not look away, and thus a friendship became erotic.
Luck was rid of its clover.

1987

MIGUEL ALGARÍN ▪ ▪ ▪ ▪ ▪ ▪ ▪ ▪ ▪ ▪ ▪ ▪ ▪

b. 1941

Born in Barrio Obrero, Puerto Rico, Miguel Algarín came to the United States in 1950, where he took up residence on the Lower East Side, known in the Puerto Rican community as Loisaida. In 1963 he received his degree in Romance Languages from the University of Wisconsin. In 1965 he received an M.A. in English from Pennsylvania State University, and in 1973 he completed his doctorate in Comparative Literature at Rutgers University. A leading figure of the Nuyorican movement of the 1970s, which created a literature of Puerto Rican identity, Algarín co-founded the Nuyorican Poets' Cafe, a center for performance-oriented and multicultural poetry, with noted playwright Miguel Piñero.

Algarín's books include *Mongo Affair* (1978), *On Call* (1980), winner of the Before Columbus Foundation Award, *Body Bee Calling from the 21st Century* (1982), and *Ya Es Tiempo/The Time Is Now* (1985). This last collection was published in Japan in 1992 in a trilingual edition consisting of Spanish, English, and Japanese. A collection of short stories, *Heart Spread*, appeared in 1990.

A singer and performer of great power, his work is bardic and Whitmanesque in ways reminiscent of Beat poetry. However, the bilingualism of his work expands its focus beyond bohemianism into a more multicultural critique. He is also the translator of Pablo Neruda's *Songs of Protest* and editor, with Miguel Piñero, of the anthology *Nuyorican Poetry* (1975).

Algarín teaches Shakespeare at Rutgers University.

Tato—Reading at the Nuyorican Poets' Cafe

Sentimientos pour from your teeth
just like señoritas arouse in a bolero
a solas sin que haya nadie en casa,
sentimientos coming through the fuerza espíritu
de leche agria en senos de hielo,
the darkest part of my spirit
radiates ordering fears,
not against but towards a balance,
no hay que dejar que el meñique
se pierda ya que hemos encontrado
el contacto de una nenita
mirándome mientras escribo,
esperando que el sonero llegue
aunque su voz esté encarcelada,
pero Tato lo celebra y suda palabras
en su memoria, cucándole el ritmo,
sacándole el jugo universal, musical
Tato sudando palabras,
salpicando, arrojando su negreza
into the field of electricity he has created
between himself and Liz Sánchez,
esa palabra o coro coroso,

esa palabra o coro coroso,
trucutú, trucutú, trucutú,
pracatú, trucutuuuuuuuuu,
no nos dejes, danos aliento,
trucutú, pracatú, trucutuuuuuuuuuuuu.

1980

Nudo de claridad

Rosa dances her fears out
to twelve cocks styling as if they were Chanticleer
ruffling his feathers in the middle of the Cafe floor,
Rosa emits body waves
setting the room off on its medicinal flow,
el despojo of the situation
offering full display of feelings
wherever, whatever they are
sacudiendo la cabeza,
sacudiendo el miedo del cuerpo,
sacudiendo, letting go,
perseverance
in the act of letting go,
utilizando todo al espacio del momento
puesto al frente del sol, del sentimiento
me inspiro al ver el nudo de amor
que en este momento existe
en el Nuyorican Poets' Cafe
at 505 E. 6th St.,
un nudo que existe
en la confianza del arte,
la confianza de un poema
que se estalla en el oído,
que inicia la palabra hablada
entre nosotros en el ahora mismo
del presente de este verbo ser
que se escribe con la arena del viento
y la tinta roja o invisible que brota de las venas
callejeras de las almas pobres que viven
en los zafacones del planeta,
Aída dances her fear out,
sacude, sacudiendo, sacudieron,
pero todavía queda el olor de la violencia
en un tenor sax que suspira
nuevo oxígeno en el temblar de la noche
cuando los poetas cantan shanti, shanti, shanti,
y se acercan al ardor

donde el nudo que existe
en la confianza del arte
es puro, sin embuste,
un nudo de claridad que se desenlaza.

1980

San Francisco

Loba's acid breast
licked once disarms my
psychic knots,
throws all my shame aside,
leaves me looking
at what is directly
before me: passion,
rampant, enacted in the will
to be other than the last
instance of thought,
so I've rambled
through Loba's milk
back or forward to
my shuddering selves
invoking shapes at will
and not catching up
to the future,
where Loba roams
howling her hoarded treasures
as the moon turns
around a globe that
spurts out cries of pain
and hunger
and love
and destruction
and construction
of the spirit,
heal the center,
hold on to Loba's challenge:
        begat five children
        taught them love
        freed their neurological cells
by dissolving programmed love,
let love be a risk
you take as two become one
and cherish neither one nor two
but all that happens
as it does

for its nothingness
or its no thing
becomes   a thing
to dissolve into nothing
as soon as it becomes something:
        Loba's secret
        is in not having a secret,
Loba's secret is in the not having
a hidden part,
since all parts are eyed by
the whole that they become,
there is a secret to nothing,
in that everything
on land goes back to water.

1980

TOM CLARK ▪ ▪ ▪ ▪ ▪ ▪ ▪ ▪ ▪ ▪ ▪ ▪ ▪ ▪ ▪
b. 1941

Tom Clark was born and raised in Oak Park, Illinois. He received his B.A. from the University of Michigan and spent two years at Cambridge University on a Fulbright Scholarship. For ten years, while living in Bolinas, California, he was poetry editor of *The Paris Review*.

One of the most prolific poets of his generation, Clark has published nearly a book a year since his first, *Airplanes*, in 1966. These include *Stones* (1969), *Air* (1970), *Blue* (1974), *Fan Poems* (1976), *When Things Get Tough on Easy Street: Selected Poems 1963–1978* (1978), *Paradise Resisted: Selected Poems 1978–1984* (1984), *Easter Sunday* (1988), *Fractured Karma* (1990), and *Sleepwalker's Fate* (1992). He has also written a novel, *The Exile of Celine* (1987), and biographical works on Charles Olson, Jack Kerouac, Ted Berrigan, Robert Creeley, and Damon Runyon.

Associated with the New York School, Clark's poems are witty, offhanded, and occasionally surrealist; they are also capable of sardonic cultural criticism. With the 1985 publication of his essay "Stalin as Linguist" in the Bay Area poetry newsletter *Poetry Flash*, Clark established himself as a leading opponent of language poetry, referring to it as "non-referential solipsist muzak."[1] He further charged that language poetry's "procedural modes come out of the New York school," though without the playfulness and accessibility of that group's writing.[2] Clark holds instead for a poetry of wit and lyricism. Emotion, he writes, comes from "*emovere*, to *move* out. . . . Writing possessed by the fire of imagination is writing that *moves*."[3] A static and self-reflexive poetry, he argues, ultimately serves the interests of a small group, no matter how strong its claims for inclusiveness.

A resident of Berkeley, California, Clark is a frequent poetry reviewer for the *San Francisco Chronicle*.

1. *The Poetry Beat*, Ann Arbor, 1990, p. 71.   2. The same.   3. The same, p. 72.

You (I)

The door behind me was you
and the radiance, there like
an electric train wreck in your eye
after a horrible evening of waiting outside places in the rain for you
        to come
only to
find all of them, two I know, the rest scullions, swimming around you
in that smoky crowded room like a fishbowl
I escaped from, running away from you and my André Breton
dream of cutting your breasts off with a trowel
and what does that matter to them or to you now, but just wait,
        it's still early
to the children embroidered in the rug, who seem to be setting up siege
engines under a tree house full of midgets who look like you.
Where are you in this sky of new blue
deltas I see in the drapery, and your new friends wearing bamboo singlets
what are they doing down there in the moat waving tridents like stalks
        of corn?
Me, I'll be happy to see their blood spilled all over the bedspread
pavilions of your hands as an example. If you come home right now I'll
        scrunch your hat
between my thighs like a valentine before you have time to wipe them.

1969

You (III)

Today I get this letter from you and the sun
buckles   a mist falls over our villas
with a hideous organic slush like the music of Lawrence Welk
I lay in bed all day, asleep, and like some nocturnal
beast. And get your salutation among the torn green numbers
in the sky over the council houses. And see your eyes when
                                the retired pensioners pass
me by the abandoned railway station—this is not nothing, it is not
                                the hymn
of an age of bankrobbers or heraldic days but it is to sing
with complete gaiety until your heart freaks. I love you.
                                And go down amid the sycamores to

summer. Wandering by the lake any way
                                seems lovely, grand, the moon
is a gland in the thigh. Tumble and twinkle as on the golf course apparel
lifts. And a door is opened to
an owl. It is snowing, and you are here on the bed with me

and it is raining, and I am as full of frets as a guitar or a curtain
and I am singing, as I sponge up the cat place. You
                                        are heaped
the word reminds me of Abydos and spinach. A curtain
of belief keeps me away from the tombs
of imagery. I love you, I'd like to go.

                                                            1969

"Like musical instruments . . ."

    Like musical instruments
    Abandoned in a field
    The parts of your feelings

    Are starting to know a quiet
    The pure conversion of your
    Life into art seems destined

    Never to occur
    You don't mind
    You feel spiritual and alert

    As the air must feel
    Turning into sky aloft and blue
    You feel like

    You'll never feel like touching anything or anyone
    Again
    And then you do

                                                            1969

Baseball and Classicism

    Every day I peruse the box scores for hours
    Sometimes I wonder why I do it
    Since I am not going to take a test on it
    And no one is going to give me money

    The pleasure's something like that of codes
    Of deciphering an ancient alphabet say
    So as brightly to picturize Eurydice
    In the Elysian Fields on her perfect day

    The day she went 5 for 5 against Vic Raschi

                                                            1976

Suicide with Squirtgun

While apparition is the instant of illumination and of being touched by something, recording and preserving it is another trick entirely: turning this timeless moment into an aesthetic instant, which is something that has duration. This is no easy task, like trying to keep a firefly's glow in a bottle without the firefly.

The transcending element in works of art is something momentary. Their entry into time is always a tight squeeze requiring the shoehorn of an "art experience," which fits them into such-and-such temporal dimensions.

Works of art flower into images, which create instants out of mere moments. Then again, art is like a soft explosion, as when the hero in the German play kills himself with a squirtgun while standing under some tremendously dark and emotive trees, as the sadness of the river landscape in the backdrop announces the arrival of dusk in the valley.

There is a sigh from inside nature, as all the durations that have unfurled suddenly begin to fold themselves up—like huge petals closing.

1987

Society

Rex Whistler—or is it Joe Isuzu?—stretches
out half naked on a rock and pretends
to be a river god, while Sylvia Plath—or is
that Edith Sitwell down there among the ceramic cherubs?—
lies down on the floor and pretends to be dead.
That's Society. "Reality" is an unmade bed
full of champagne. "I was the first (burp)
to interject my own persona between the lens
and the frilly circus ladies of the human psyche."

A smart model in a Digby Morton suit steps
confidently through the rubble of the Blitz.
That's Society, "her poise unshaken." Hearts
of movie stars and duchesses expand life-jacket style,
Marilyn Monroe's nerves are refused entry to the studio,
and the royal family, from the Super Mum herself
down to Snowdon, Lichfield and Andrew,
parade around cloud cuckoo land in funny hats
while Douglas Fairbanks falls out of filigree windows
and persuades Mountbatten to play Lear in mid air.

Now Mountbatten too is falling falling,
gazing up at their reflections in the mirrored Star Ceiling
Mickey Mouse as the Sheik of Araby

alongside Madame Pompadour as Cassandra
are spinning and flailing, tumbling through space,
berserk boxers doing a minuet in weightlessness,
yet the polystyrene suspension net
slung underneath the scene by Cecil Beaton
somehow makes it all make sense though not really.

1990

CHARLES NORTH ▪ ▪ ▪ ▪ ▪ ▪ ▪ ▪ ▪ ▪ ▪ ▪ ▪ ▪
b. 1941

Born in New York City, Charles North has received degrees from Tufts College
and Columbia University. Among his books are *Elizabethan & Nova Scotian
Music* (1974), *Six Buildings* (1977), *Leap Year: Poems 1968–1978* (1978), and
The Year of the Olive Oil (1989). With James Schuyler, he edited *Broadway: A
Poets and Painters Anthology* (1979) and its sequel, *Broadway 2* (1989). North,
with the poet Paul Violi, runs Swollen Magpie Press, a publisher of experimental
poetry.

North's work, which James Schuyler describes as "urban idylls" reminiscent
of the metaphysical poetry of Andrew Marvell, is often gently humorous, mov-
ing with ease from high to low levels of rhetoric.

Poet-in-Residence at Pace University, North lives in New York City.

A Few Facts about Me

I am moved often, and easily
without knowing why or finding it appropriate
to be a consequence of somebody else's unfathomable will.

I can be taken in by the suggestion of emotion in others
even if their actions are as foreign to human psychology
as the emotions of European children in American textbooks

or American textbooks in American life. Deciding what my life
will be has always been the decision as to what it has been,
and before I met you I knew what it would be like, and planned
        to be in the path

of whatever could change it, whether or not it prevented me
from being the sole translator of your natural eloquence.
As the captain of my fate and steerer of my star

I don't find any single decision irrevocable,
feeling inadequate to life's daily immensities, a condition
of the unwillingness to act, for of the things that are human

the best is to be unavoidable, which doesn't make it any better
but doesn't make it worse—like that sunset I'm always refusing
    to look behind
or away from as if to be dull were the reverse of not shining

and living selfishly when that too is exhaustible.

              1974

Elizabethan & Nova Scotian Music

What will see us through, a certain calm
Born of the willingness to be not cowed
The begonia idea of the universe
And because life is so short
A way of being unfaithful like the tide
Minus its characteristic awareness.

Moving is the world and all its creatures
Known by the things that surround it
Love, money, titles, the periphrastic way
Of being other than we are not
Throughout the long afternoon of language
Attractive though dead, such calm falling

And issuing in a well-meant spiel
Involving money as a metaphor: Money is
The only metaphor and because life is short
A gross keyboard of light and sometimes strength
As well to be aware of its fickleness
As stab it in the back with gentleness.

              1974

A Note To Tony Towle (After WS)

One must have breakfasted often on automobile primer
not to sense an occasional darkening in the weather joining
    art and life:
and have read *Paradise Lost* aloud many times in a Yiddish
    accent

not to wake up and feel the morning air as a collaborator
thrown from some bluer and more intelligent planet
where life, despite the future's escalating ambitions, has
    ramified

in every direction except UP; and have been asleep a long
    time

in the air bonded to night not to feel the force of the present
shimmering in the downtown buildings, like European walled
        cities

whose walls have all but disappeared via benign invasion
and touristic drift, even the World Trade Center
for all the enigmas concerning *who* is trading *what* to *whom*,

and while deracination is fast qualifying as essence
rather than attribute, towards the brush with open sea.

                                                          1989

RON PADGETT ▪ ▪ ▪ ▪ ▪ ▪ ▪ ▪ ▪ ▪ ▪ ▪ ▪ ▪
b. 1942

Born in Tulsa, Oklahoma, Ron Padgett received his B.A. degree from Columbia
University, where he studied with Kenneth Koch, who was a major influence on
his writing. Padgett's love for French poetry led him to study in Paris in 1965–
1966 as a Fulbright Scholar. Subsequently, he translated French poetry and
fiction, notably that of Blaise Cendrars and Guillaume Apollinaire.

From his influential first major collection, *Great Balls of Fire* (1969), to *The
Big Something* (1990), Padgett has displayed a playful attitude that is consistent
with Dada. His chapbook *In Advance of the Broken Arm* (1964) takes its title
from Marcel Duchamp's found object, an ordinary snow shovel propped against
a wall. Like Duchamp, Padgett is a conceptual artist who likes to challenge the
status of the art object. His poem "Nothing in That Drawer" is a sonnet parody
consisting of fourteen identical lines; the prose poem "Falling in Love in Spain
or Mexico" is structured as a short play in which the main character's lines are
borrowed from a Spanish-language phrase book. As seen in the poem "Wonder-
ful Things," Padgett's poetry often carries a multitude of moods, from the ele-
giac to the offhanded, which is characteristic New York School practice.

Padgett's enthusiasm for collaboration, influenced by the French surrealist
poets' practice of the *cadavre exquis* (exquisite corpse) in which two or more
poets take turns writing the lines of a poem, led to his working with poet Ted
Berrigan (*Bean Spasms*, 1967) and painter Jim Dine (*The Adventures of Mr and
Mrs Jim and Ron*, 1970), among others.

A former director of the Poetry Project at St. Mark's Church in the Bowery,
Padgett lives on the Lower East Side and works as Director of Publications at
Teachers & Writers Collaborative.

Wonderful Things

Anne, who are dead   and whom I loved in a rather asinine fashion
                I think of you often

buveur de l'opium chaste et doux

                                     Yes I think of you

  with very little in mind

  as if I had become a helpless moron

    Watching zany chirping birds

  That inhabit the air

And often ride our radio waves

So I've been sleeping lately with no clothes on
The floor   which is very early   considering the floor
Is made of birds and they are flying and I am
Upsidedown and ain't it great to be great!!

Seriously I have this mental (smuh!) illness

                          which causes me to do things

                                  on and away

Straight for the edge
Of a manicured fingernail
Where it is deep and dark   and green   and silent

Where I may go at will
And sit down and tap
                    My forehead against the sunset

Where he takes off the uniform
And we see he is God

God get out of here

And he runs off chirping and chuckling into his hand

And that is a wonderful thing

                              . . . a tuba that is a meadowful of bluebells
is a wonderful thing

        and that's what I want to do

Tell you wonderful things

                                                                    1969

Nothing in That Drawer

                Nothing in that drawer.
                Nothing in that drawer.
                Nothing in that drawer.
                Nothing in that drawer.
                Nothing in that drawer.
                Nothing in that drawer.
                Nothing in that drawer.
                Nothing in that drawer.
                Nothing in that drawer.
                Nothing in that drawer.
                Nothing in that drawer.
                Nothing in that drawer.
                Nothing in that drawer.
                Nothing in that drawer.

                                                                    1969

Falling in Love in Spain or Mexico

A handsome young man and a veiled woman enter. They stroll slowly across the stage, stopping from time to time, so that their entrance coincides with the first spoken word and their exit the last.

JOSÉ: I am happy to meet you. My name is José Gomez Carrillo. What is your name? This is my wife. I like your daughter very much. I think your sister is beautiful. Are you familiar with the U.S.? Have you been to New York? Your city is very interesting. I think so. I don't think so. Here is a picture of my wife. Your daughter is very beautiful. She sings very well. You dance very well. Do you speak English? Do you like American movies? Do you read books in English? Do you like to swim? To drive a car? To play tennis? Golf? Dance? Do you like American music? May I invite you to dance? I like to play tennis. Will you drive? Do you live here? What is your address? Your phone number? I am here for four days. Two weeks. One month only. Would you like a cigarette? A glass of wine? Anything? Help yourself. To your health! With best regards. Many happy returns! Congratulations! With best wishes! Merry Christmas! My sincere sympathy. Good luck! When can I see you again? I think you are beautiful. I like you very much. Do you like me? May I see you tomorrow? May I see you this evening? Here is a present for you. I love you. Will you marry me?

GIRL: (*She lifts and throws back her veil, revealing her face, which is extremely and extraordinarily beautiful.*) Yes!

THE END

1969

Big Bluejay Composition

Compositions in harmony

the sunlight rods over the Commuter's Spa
bluejay

oh

I don't want to go in
and watch Gene Tierney on tv moonlight

when   the shadow of a doubt

tiptoes down the hall

crumpled tossed in wastebasket

Rainbow Colored Pencils made by Eberhard Faber
maker of Mongols

ie Children of Paradise

gray line wiggle

a large permanent flinch

just under the skin then

She turned to me ⌒ in the flying starlight

in the   in the

    tiny (there are no straight lines in a curve) breeze

breeze curving

      moonlight

         when the m-moon shines
         over the cow's shit

                      bzzzzzzzzzz

                      bzzzz

the square of the sum
    of two . flashing . numbers from the now on bzzz

suddenly the onions replaced the onusphere

    —to leon the counterpoint— and Tommie Vardeman
stuck his

      head out the door a very old auto racer

gray wearing glasses

                  bluejay

sweet as stops

    I catch my breath   I cry (cont. p. 42)

  of planetary music

        heard in trance

well the figurine of the bluejay

½ in the dimensional side of God

the earth is still—

. . . stars . . . stars . . .

God is in a trance,
now's the time to compose a few immortal lines

re's the immortal paper?

e immortal brain?   star

we go trot

trot-trot

past the abattoir

sliding 1968 sliding

_____

under the beauty of

broken thunder

he goes over center
k-boom   softness is northern

alert

alarming

the north,

le même nord où la mission Albert agonise maintenant
parmi les cristaux

that is the wild blue yonder

screwed onto a bolt from the blue

magnetic,

the pursuit of Hedonism emerges boink from unwrinkled clouds

while . . . trumpets . . . Haloed, long pause

    from across the ocean long pause

      came gunshot

a piece of rain fell and hit the horizon

      Slowly I turned . . .

behind us loomed the awesome figure of the gigantic
baked enamel ape, which Professor Morrison had, with
fanatical patience, constructed over the years.

                A bluejay

Tennessee raised in the dark

to the highest power

      Tennessee is the n it made

I have spoken

     — — — —

        I am speaking

like a sunset going down

      behind

the rising dawn

    to ♪ot   mother,

Remember me   in your semi-conscious prayers   hit the
                                       brakes

when the dew is glistening on the bluejay

     and I go walkie to nightmare school

and the refinery is blasting away

Process and Reality   on this damp, foolish evening

bl   here

the future
casts a pall bearer on the present——in the future the present
will be

a thing of the past   losing altitude

You shake

No

your head No

the smell of coffee on a morning the smell of hot coffee on a

winter's morning

the table is set in the breakfast room frost on the windows
sunlight
          lock into which Mr. Morrison is inserting his key
floods the hardware store ∧ the black and white cereal box
   the porcelain

the fresh peaches the milk +

Now our mighty battleships will steam the bounding main

people jetting along

a symphony of tweets

the light of the Eternal Flame
clearly visible

from where you sit

in those great, golden heights   no doggie
                                            in the neighborhood

all the doggies have gone off to war to be male nurses

the moonlight on the earthquake

into which many doggies fell

plunged fiery and screaming

                                 in their machines

      . . .

gravely   the Statue of Liberty

turned and faced the nation, finally!

a medium-sized flesh-colored male sexual organ extending

from its inner ear,

"The period in history termed Modern is now over" it said

                               —CLICK—

the bluejay fluttered on its shoulder

"Y-you'd b-b-better b-b-believe it!" it cried wildly

                                     1976

Who and Each

I got up early Sunday morning
because it occurred to me that the word
which
might have come from a combination of *who* and *each*
and reached for the *OED*
which for me
(I think of it not
as the *Oxford English Dictionary*
but as the *O Erat Demonstrandum*)
has the last word:
"Hwelc, huelc, hwaelc, huaelc, huoelc, hwaelc, wheche, weche,
whech, qwech, queche, qheche, qwel, quelk, hwilc, wilc, hwilch,
wilch, whilc, whillc, whilk, whylke, whilke, whilk, wilke,
whylk, whilk, quilc, quilke, qwilk, quylk, quhylk, quilk, quhilk,
hwic, wic, hwich, wyche, wich, hwych, wiche, whiche, whyche,
wych, whych, which, quiche, quyche, quich, quych, qwiche,
qwych, qwych, quhich, hwylc, hwulch, hulch, wulc, whulc,
wulch, whulche": Teutonic belching.
    But in little tiny type: "For the compounds *gewilc*,

aeghwilc, see *Each."*
Now, if you want to talk *belching.* . . .
It was raining outside
with the blue-gray hiss of tires
against the wet street
I would soon walk my dog in,
the street I drove an airplane up
earlier this morning in a dream
in which the Latin word *quisque* appeared to me,
as if it meant *each which*
in the sea of *eisdem, quicumque,* and *uterque.*
Thus I spend my days,
waiting for my friends to die.

1990

ANN LAUTERBACH ▪ ▪ ▪ ▪ ▪ ▪ ▪ ▪ ▪ ▪ ▪ ▪
b. 1942

In Ann Lauterbach's view, "poetry is the aversion to the assertion of power.
Poetry is that which resists dominance."[1] Yet she does not ordinarily confront
themes of power directly. Like the poet John Ashbery, Lauterbach employs an
oblique style that often concerns itself with themes of poetic imagination. In her
poem "Mimetic," which takes its theme from Wallace Stevens's "The Idea of
Order at Key West," Gene Tierney, the 1940s movie actress, "walks along the
cliffs, reflective," a figure of the poet as maker. Neither Tierney nor the poem
"mirrors" the world; their veracity lies in *being* the world. In Lauterbach's
view, the self in poetry is "construed across the entire surface of the poem." The
poem can be seen as "an act of self-construction, the voice its threshold."[2]

Like Stevens and Ashbery, Lauterbach writes poetry that often deals with the
making of poems, its "field of snow / Flying like jargon." Concerned with issues
of representation, she is essentially a philosophical poet. In "Platonic Subject,"
for instance, a wishbone-shaped twig exists at many levels: the ideal twig, the
real twig, the image of the twig in snow, and the twig as poetic image. "Poetry
resists false linkages," Lauterbach writes. Both "conventional narrative strate-
gies" and "the mimesis of visual description" are therefore inadequate to the
demands of contemporary experience.[3]

Born and raised in New York City, where she now resides, Lauterbach has
taught at Columbia, Princeton, and Brooklyn College. Her books of poetry in-
clude *Before Recollection* (1987) and *Clamor* (1991). Currently teaching at the
City University of New York, she is a contributing editor of the magazine *Con-
junctions.*

1. "Links without Links: The Voice of the Turtle," *The American Poetry Review,* Jan./Feb.
1992, p. 37. The same, p. 38.   2. The same.   3. The same.

Mimetic

Recumbent against any mirror, any stardom,
Dazed to be included, at last, in the night,

You imitate day stretched across a beach
Noted by those of us for whom the sea is reflective
But is the sea a film of the sea, ageless?

Seventeen, a mime. This is one way to hide
Lack of authenticity, although style
Carries clout in crowd scenes.
You have painted your toenails Car Hop Pink,
A clear choice against the sky's transience.

The sea mimes the sea. It seems ageless,
Whichever hues the waves hit.
Her face, projected on a screen,
Records the gaze of our capitulation.
Gene Tierney walks along the cliffs, reflective.

Pavese said sentiment, in art, is accuracy,
But the poem would not stretch
To phrase the red cliffs, the seizure of place.
You see the world as self. For us, she
Is world, enduring, veracity of was
Being what is. We cannot look
At what we love without failure,
The failure of the world to reflect itself.

1987

Platonic Subject

Momentum and wash of the undefined,
as if clarity fell through the sieve of perception,
announced as absence of image.
But here is a twig in the form of a wishbone.
Aroused, I take it, and leave its outline
scarred in snow which the sun will later heal:
form of the real melts back into the ideal
and I have a twig.

1987

Here and There

Today I wake having swung, naked, in London,
At the ambassador's house. What happened?
Baseball fever, Fassbinder, the need to undress
After something French.
Tonight, also, will have a remittance.
Here is a crowd of angels from Padua,
One gold, one red, the others obscured

Apart from their heads which, profiled, stare forward.
Mary is returning from her nuptial rite.
She is kept from the rest
By blue, and her hand grips her robe
So that a dark arch forms just below the waist.
I'll dream white, pull curtains apart, see a kid's face.

We almost escape narration and, after the war,
The noise our brothers made we did not hear.
There were remnants of a garden
Where the landscape dipped
And old flowers grew wild
Around stone relics of a birdbath.
Those were the days: stones, relics, fates,
Slow passage of color through leaf
And fear incited by fluorescent clocks at night.
We used to have a reputation for reality,
And now these. What happened? Mist
Is rising off the river; a low boat slides by.
Up ahead: the androgyny of winter
When all things seek gray, and the great star
Chills us back into dreams under late and later dawns.

1987

Clamor

1.

It was a trance: thieves, clowns, and the blind girl
Passed symmetrically under the wide structure
As a floor passes under a rug.
Was this enough to go on, this scrap?
Had I entered, or was I pacing the same limits:
The room brought forward to another landscape,
Its odd birds, its train, its street lamp
Stationed like an unmoving moon. At night, the cries
Assembled into the ordinary speech of lovers before love
As the train pulled up the space, passing and passing.
Were these categories to be kept—thief, clown, blind girl—
Or were they too narrowly forensic, too easily found,
The whining insatiable drift insufficiently modeled.
They were an invitation to appear, appease, applaud,
In short to respond, be magical.
In the old days, we howled.
In the old days we chanted our lists until they
Were deciphered, lifted the leaves, touched the broken clay,
Counted the steps quickly, saying this is the one with the key,
This is the one for whom I will awaken.

2.

Affection is merciless: the wind, the excluder.
So much ruptured attention, so much pillaged from the stalk.
Even the nerves stray from precision, announcing
Their stunned subject. Merciless: a field of snow
Flying like jargon, sweeping the issue away
In a halo of cold, its purpose
Lifted from the flat climate, from its nub or throb.
Lifted on impossible wings we are generous, we dare.
But affection is merciless: the dead in their thin garb
Walking the ruined streets, inventing us in stride and envy.
It is said they will make their way
Back to us, as what rises saves itself, falls.
What is the speed of this doctrine, what dividends,
What annual yield?
When will he give it back,
When will I laugh in the untidy yard
And when will her eyes, staring at me
Because she sees only her departure from me,
See me left here. Further adventure is further delay.
I used to count the days. I do not want to count the days.

1991

Boy Sleeping

for Richard

These difficulties—flamboyant tide, modest red berries,
Or modest tide, flamboyant berries—
The moon keeping and casting light
Onto the boy's sleeping face
And the posture of his knowledge
Erected on the fatal—
                          Is this how it begins?
Or is the solid figure of the night
Only a wish to survive the last word said
So that such natural things induce furthering
After the episode of the shut.
Should I tell him his face mirrors the lost?
Should I tell him to wake, marry, find, escape

The one whose voice exhausts itself on the recurrent
Whose fraudulence speaks without images
Whose desire spends itself
On indifference, and whose light
Makes light of us, those of us whose bearing is
To continue—
                 What is the sublime

But a way, under the pressure of not knowing but caring,
To join the crowd at the slam, to lust openly
For the insecure moment when she turns, not yet dead,
And says: *I am coming with you nevertheless and because.*

I remember when a word
First advanced like a dart at a target,
A star creasing the sky, a lie
Told to save the situation while damning it.
I remember when the annual survey included nothing abstract
Because the war was full of particulars, particular events.
I remember a ride from the suburbs, sun setting in the windows,
Reminding me that I would forget, and so
Reminded me not to forget, although
The dead woman in the sleeping boy's face
Is a better example.
                              How much we want to disobey
The sanctity of the kept,
To deny the already as it strides forward
Without introduction, revising
Before our eyes the unelicited partition of morning.
The precedent of the real mocks us.
Rain spills uncontrollably from above like a test.
Can we follow these new waters
Or are we already too fond, our agility mired
In the scripted river rushing under the bridge.
This is asked to keep us going one way or another
Lest the pause spread, flooding the field with reflection.
At the center of discourse, forgotten or unnoticed,
A train passes carrying a woman in her youth,
A terrorist, and a boy
Waking, wishing he were some place else.

1991

WILLIAM CORBETT ■ ▪ ▪ ▪ ▪ ▪ ▪ ▪ ▪ ▪ ▪ ■
b. 1942

William Corbett's books include *Columbus Square Journal* (1976), the long na-
ture poem *Runaway Pond* (1981), *Collected Poems* (1984), *On Blue Note* (1989),
and *Don't Think: Look* (1991). In the tradition of William Carlos Williams, his
poems emphasize local detail and use of the American idiom; in their light tone
and painterly realism, they are also reminiscent of James Schuyler's work.

Of *On Blue Note*, Corbett has written, "I seek to make poems that are clear as
a cloudless fall morning—the reader ought to be able to see freshly what's right
in front of him *and* into the distance for miles. My endeavor is to make the
everyday memorable, to discover and declare the value in what's considered
ordinary. The language I like best is plain and ringing, clean and accurate as a

well-driven nail." This places him at odds with language poetry and related deconstructive ideologies and underscores Corbett's irony in choosing Wittgenstein's statement "Don't think: look" as the title of his most recent work.

Born in Norfolk, Virginia, William Corbett has lived for over twenty years in Boston's South End.

Vermont Apollinaire

"From America comes the little humming-bird"
From morning mistcloud a raven descends
First the one kingfisher, plop then the mate, plop
They whirr and rattle away crossed wires
August's end tomatoes take on orange swallows disappear
The loons cry their bearded cry
Jane calls a crane stands at the stream's mouth
Stands impervious to any order save its own
From the sea mountains distant come gulls

I cannot carry a tune
Not in a bucket one note
I carry the past like a mailman letters
The past like a wave breaking always
Always about to break never in the right place
When I reach my address letters fall through the slot

The little car, the bug is yellow
1st September 2 a.m. doused with dew
now crossing the Pepperpot bridge a wind
            roughens the dark water
whipping up tiny waves. Chalk on slate.
            My shirt is plastered
to me. The joggers jog their hair
            in flames. The wind
is ringing down the last
            blossoms all over town.
Gutters are dusty with doll
            bells on stems and
on Commonwealth and Beacon pink
            magnolia petals smear
grainy rust over concrete.
            This narrow way leads
to Kendall Square where every walker
            is rearranged
by winds that sluice between new
            high rises sweeping
grit off cheerless vast plazas.
            The subway teeters by
rain like beebee chain on its many windows.

A yellow street sweeper
below moves through the lanes
        of the cloverleaf
an ear really of highway that keeps
        to the river.
From here the state house is a gold
        thimble or nipple
swaggered over by stony giants
        blunt as stony fingers.

Summer swallows spring and goes into September
Like long division it is always there
Autumn, fall we say, fruit releases itself
You are new enough so the old catches up
Cross this bridge come to that one
You grow up and ancient history snaps back
Rubber band and rake handle

Morning before morning
Mist like flour
Cat wants in, butts the door
At garden's edge stand blackest ravens
This is the void some two or three there
Just beyond reach and they too hear cow's bell
How far that sound travels unheeded, feather on water

Humming-birds need not prepare
They know, they know their way above the clouds
from this red sugar water all the way to Mexico

Goodbye Goodbye
You ruby throats who stop in air

Memory ardent for mercy

                                        1984

Wickson Plums

Six green plums bottoms
perfect from nipples flow
sit in the antique white
bowl where bread rose.
Out the kitchen window
my daughters ten and thirteen
run across the field
just their heads show
as they dip into a swale

like the ocean first Marni's
blond head then Arden's brown
hair flowing rises into sight.
Late August's weak sun
lays whitely upon us all
upon the ragged spent grass
and nearly done blackberry canes.
The evening cold comes up
around our toes. You no longer
hear the crickets then suddenly
they catch your attention again
like the flies bred through
all these wet days brushed away
from the plums. Green ones.
Fill my mouth with sweetness.

1989

Cold Lunch

At noon sneaky
cold on my back
through clapboard.
Ferns tremble.
Above frost trimmed
stalks broad arrows
tremble.
The cloud brows
roll over. Dark
then white magnificences.
Two butterflies beat
their wings feeding
on a turd pile.
Prudence Dearth
wife of Roderick
stone in Peacham.
A maple log
then another burns
through, rots through,
shatters tinkle, tinkle
on the brick apron.
Ashen daylight. Wind
sets weeds dithering
holds thrush in
piney dark wood
where its song is thin.
How dark when
clock strikes one!

How cold, how loveless
where there is only one.
Wake the dog
from his whimpering run.
A week's chill
sits in corners
like breath
from a well
but see how
the sun works
down that spine
and far hill's side;
see the nut hard
peony break into
a thin lipped
pink grin.

1989

TOM MANDEL ▪ ▪ ▪ ▪ ▪ ▪ ▪ ▪ ▪ ▪ ▪ ▪ ▪ ▪

b. 1942

Although associated with the San Francisco language poets, Tom Mandel writes a poetry of ideas more suggestive of John Ashbery's work. He claims his most important influences, however, in the nineteenth-century French poetry of Mallarmé, Rimbaud, and Baudelaire and the gnomic conversations of the early rabbis as collected in the Talmud and midrash.

Mandel was editor of the literary magazine *Miam* and for a short time director of the Poetry Center at San Francisco State University. Following his unexpected departure from the Poetry Center in 1979, Mandel wrote very little poetry as he underwent a reassessment of his work. In 1984, while working on the poems eventually published in *Central Europe*, he embraced his Judaism and the rabbinic idea that language preexists the created world. With the reaffirming of his Jewish heritage, Mandel came into his strength as a poet and has since been an increasingly independent voice within the language poetry community.

Born and raised in Chicago, Mandel is author of the poetry collections *Ency* (1978), *Erat* (1982), *Central Europe* (1985), *Some Appearances* (1986), *Four Strange Books* (1990), *Realism* (1991), *The Prospect of Release* (1992), and *Letters of the Law* (1993). He now lives in Washington, D.C.

Say Ja

1

I wanted them over
I wanted to hand them
out, to have them do

them over, I wanted to
lower them over when their
barrier'd overturned, so
that their turn would have
been taken, their road been a
scarred running aground, I
wanted them warped with
their source.

Un poème dont les mots
répétés variés,
Ein Dichter dessen Worte . . . waren.

I wanted to increase
them singing aphasic their
song certain, the turnstiles
left open to leap over
which these gloomy pens
and stalls so full. I
wanted the stars overt
and most everything that runs
downhill I wanted to fill
his hand.

2

A sacrifice portrayed
as if at the horizon
it had been reflected over and over
in a revolving door.
You placed romantic flowers
in closet-sized vases turned
toward the horizon's drooping
denouement. An island
ice-maiden shreds her native
cuckoo, white fur
rolled over abandoned snow
looms in the cooling plant
life of fevered, horizontal wind.

3

It is my duty to guard
against the barbaric winds
that keep the harbor shut,
and when a refrain lifts,
native faces straining
the air that lifts above
the false vaccines they sing,
then a breeze of farce

snakes around the tongue
I felt once within my face
and swallowed still. I
have a gun and I should go
I must & shall the wind escape
and heat of fantasy or
a vacuum will force the slit.
Tropical ice & snow island,
yearning lilt, voices
that foist upon the
hand that wears my rings
won't close around me. Won't
escape me or live in my land,
if you serve me now, leave
me room, believe me now,
and you will leave me soon.

1991

Realism

This is the only thing as large as that. I regret I am not the physical giant
to practice all I comprehend. Underground—bush, facade, horizon—
burns with a realism you cannot go back on.

Recognition dissolves the object. We hum along. The symbol of home is
a pale light bathing an object at a high horizon line. Beneath it materi-
als, somewhat close to us, we stamp on them; they are resumed on our
home ground. The more I think . . . well, I hear it. The flesh circles the
sofa, is in favor with the consciousness seated there, then is ejected.
Recovered sounds hear new songs, and each inaccessible in its own
magic competence. Chaotic shapes nature merges in a style of play. The
only space there is still surrounds me, electrical charge sucked out of
sockets by its active loss in light over objects. The time to read is now.
It's neutral outside, it is use. Better to pare your nails, the better your
nest to feather, while the idea does its work and returns happily to the
head that thinks it. A dog barks at dogs in a film, then quietly waits for a
cut. It is this absence of sound we perceive as the sign of silence. It is
sufficient that it grow quiet for no one to speak. After abundant harvest,
a field lays fallow.

Through the sketch of a window, he looks onto the page itself. Now, cut
the highway out of the heart of a map. The white wall, the blue archi-
tect, half in sun. The sky is these words above you. Rain the converse
story of seeds that remain. The transparent monolith opacified.

Have you seen the carpet, have you looked up from the carpet. The
faces that pair off do so to remember. From minds gingerly emerge
terms of fate, facts and sentences singly. The buildings are few and low,
the temperature is high and low; snow tumbles from your heart directly

onto the issues of popular survival. It has the habit to feel slighted and that it goes out of the way to incur it.

The limits of the world leak in from its edges, pervade. Thus did he take up the sentence and play it for all he was worth. But what was it worth? The context commands.

Reality authorizes my speech in speech. Each dimension iterates its two worlds. Sign here and the ink will fade in conditions of its own choosing, an icon overcome by the conditions of its control.

The text guards the door to the reading room. Try as you will you will hear it all. Sorry, try as you will you will hear it *fall*. Try as you will you will hear it all. Before an object, something modern—a building, a person—one falters, sorry, one *alters*, one falters, wondering whether to look up at it or straight out from the shoulders. Even the vaguest order is perfect as everyone knows. If you change me I begin to see without light.

1991

Jews in Hell

Curious, the assembly that forms before a door, a large door always ajar. A wall has been lowered between us as if it were a thin curtain which would have to be parted to reach our street. But there is no way to pass through this door or part the curtain between us. I wear my costume and your eyes theirs. We are few in numbers but occupy the high ground. You are many, well-organized, and in control of the flow of supplies. We are young and old, with few between. Your men are in their prime. I hear a single sound hot as brand resound off your temple of aptitude.

Our facades loop the miasma of antique or foreign attractions. Already diminished, all spectacles will soon vanish into virtual glass. Our plan, now as ever, is to outline a forehead that lasts forever. Long into the night we spoke of science. You followed my ideas, and my eyes followed you.

Pulsation, tempo, collapse: these are the active parts of a mirror and extend its vanishing point, abolishing direct contact from within its message. Apparently disarmed, it belongs to the image, indicates the sender's silence. How much like those of a sign painter are the symphony conductor's movements.

Walled up: two walled-up worlds can never meet nor agree. An alarmed eye is a random consequence, a stand-off of tender forces under pressure, heated and damp. Oh century of base daydreams, a chest must expand to spew out the excitement of your inner life—the image out of dots, a storefront of pebbles. The path of our commitments, the highway of love and hate, leads among the rooftops at night as we migrate from meeting to meeting in a mutual plan to die.

Just as in nature, a point is a self-contained thing, full of possibilities whose tension is no more fact than unity of motion toward you, coursing between twin peripheries and through a carved and curious door, always open, so the curtain through which we plunge onto you unawares wipes across our moving brows to erase the dimensional line of preparatory angst our cultures tracked there as we imagine a death for you and raise arms to deliver, baring the targets that like corneas narrow across our torsos to contain the tension of such points.

The spiritual in art accesses its momentum of dimensions. Reaching out from the mirror it finds the door closed tight from the inside and so freezes where it can. Din in the sky of truth will not in, while facing out from the door a mountain of beautiful testimony trues our social intercourse; what words can no more oblige a beautiful mountain serves up in melody.

1991

MICHAEL PALMER ▪ ▪ ▪ ▪ ▪ ▪ ▪ ▪ ▪ ▪ ▪ ▪

b. 1943

Although published in anthologies of language poetry, Michael Palmer's work goes outside the bounds of language poetry and cannot be strictly limited to the movement. In his critical writings, Palmer recognizes the inevitability of narrative in much writing: "Ultimately there is a *definition* that occurs as Gregory Bateson argues 'by relation,' in fact a story, defining that form as a 'knot or complex of that species of connectedness we call relevance.' "[1] But story, as well as autobiography, always involves a degree of concealment: "What is taken as *a sign of* openness—conventional narrative order—may stand for concealment, and what are understood generally as *signs of* withholding or evasion—ellipsis, periphrasis, etc.—may from another point of view stand for disclosure."[2] Palmer's poetry is of the second kind, using devices of concealment such as the third person ("He loved the French poets/fell through the partly open door"). Yet even when openly autobiographical ("As Robert's call on Tuesday asking whether I knew that Zukofsky had died . . ."), there is a hermetic tone and refusal of certainty in Palmer's work centered around "Whether I know whatever I know."

Born in New York City and educated at Harvard in history and comparative literature, Palmer has lived in San Francisco since 1969. His books of poetry include *Plan of the City of O* (1971), *Blake's Newton* (1972), *The Circular Gates* (1974), *Without Music* (1977), *Notes for Echo Lake* (1981), *First Figure* (1984), and *Sun* (1988). With Clark Coolidge, he edited the short-lived but influential magazine *Joglars* (1964–1965). He also edited *Code of Signals: Recent Writings in Poetics* (1983), which along with other books of poetics appearing in the early eighties signaled a renewed enthusiasm for theoretical writing among experimental poets.

Palmer has served on the faculty of poetics at the New College of California, and has collaborated for the past several years with the choreographer Margaret Jenkins, providing the accompanying text for performances of her dance company.

1. "Autobiography, Memory, and Mechanisms of Concealment," in *Writing/Talks*, ed. Bob Perelman, Carbondale, 1985, p. 210.   2. The same, p. 227.

Notes for Echo Lake   3

Words that come in smoke and go.

Some things he kept, some he kept and lost. He loved the French poets fell through the partly open door.

And I as it is, I as the one but less than one in it. I was the blue against red and a voice that emptied, and I is that one with broken back.

While April is ours and dark, as something always stands for
what is: dying elm, headless man, winter—
                                        salamander, chrysalis,
fire—
        grammar and silence.

Or grammar against silence. Years later they found themselves talking in a crowd. Her white cat had been killed in the woods behind her house. It had been a good possibly even a terrible winter. Ice had coated the limbs of the hawthorn and lilac, lovely but dangerous. Travel plans had been made then of necessity abandoned. At different times entire weeks had seemed to disappear. She wondered what initially they had agreed not to discuss.

Some things he kept while some he kept apart.

As Robert's call on Tuesday asking whether I knew that Zukofsky had died a couple of days before. The call came as I was reading a copy of Larry Rivers' talk at Frank O'Hara's funeral (July, 1966), "He was a quarter larger than usual. Every few inches there was some sewing composed of dark blue thread. Some stitching was straight and three or four inches long, others were longer and semi-circular . . ."

As Robert's call on Tuesday a quarter larger than usual asking whether I knew whether I knew. Blue thread every few inches, straight and semi-circular, and sand and wet snow. Blue snow a couple of days before. Whether I know whatever I know.

The letters of the words of our legs and arms. What he had seen or thought he'd seen within the eye, voices overheard rising and falling.

And if each conversation has no end, then composition is a placing beside or with and is endless, broken threads of cloud driven from the west by afternoon wind.

The letters of the words of our legs and arms. In the garden he dreamt he saw four bearded men and listened to them discussing metaphor. They are standing at the points of the compass. They are standing at the points of the compass and saying nothing. They are sitting in the shade of a flowering tree. She is holding the child's body out toward the camera. She is standing before the mirror and asking. She is offering and asking. He-she is asking me a question I can't quite hear. Evenings they would walk along the shore of the lake.

Letters of the world. Bright orange poppy next to white rose next to blue spike of larkspur and so on. Artichoke crowding garlic and sage. Hyssop, marjoram, orange mint, winter and summer savory, oregano, trailing rosemary, fuchsia, Dutch iris, day lily, lamb's tongue, lamb's ears, blackberry, feverfew, lemon verbena, sorrel, costmary, never reads it as it is, "poet living tomb of his/games."

Eyes eyeing what self never there, as things in metaphor cross, are thrown across, a path he calls the path of names. In the film *La Jetée* she is thrown against time and is marking time:

> sun burns thru the roars
> dear eyes, *all eyes,* pageant
> bay inlet, garden casuarina, spittle-spawn
> (not laurel) nameless we name
> it, and sorrows dissolve—human

In silence he would mark time listening for whispered words. I began this in spring, head ready to burst, flowers, reddening sky, moon with a lobster, New York, Boston, return, thin coating of ice, moon while dogs bark, moon dogs bark at, now it's late fall.

And now he told me it's time to talk.

Words would come in smoke and go, inventing the letters of the voyage, would walk through melting snow to the corner store for cigarettes, oranges and a newspaper, returning by a different route past red brick townhouses built at the end of the Civil War. Or was the question in the letters themselves, in how by chance the words were spelled.

In the poem he learns to turn and turn, and prose seems always a sentence long.

1981

Notes for Echo Lake   5

> "a blue under people"
> —BERNADETTE MAYER,
> *Memory*

The tree's green explains what a light means, an idea, the bomb or Donald Duck, a box of marbles in a marble box, the amber jewel behind the toad's eyes reminds us that it's night. The interpreter of the text examines the traffic light, coughs and lays the book aside. The dead mayor sits behind his desk, overcome with wonderment.

The interpreter of a cough examines the light and lays the text aside. Here and there leaves, clouds, rivers of tears in the streets meant a sonata for tongues.

Truth to tell the inventor of the code weeps and lays the text aside. Here and there calendars and walls remind him that it's night, a sleeping lion is curled up in one corner, a voice can be heard behind a door, and Plato told us of the law, Plato warned us about the poem. The dead mayor wonders if the King of France is bald.

Today is an apparent day of empty sleeves and parallelograms, and red meaning red, and the flag as an object, and red instead of red, the flag as an object with undulating sides, the spider who taught me to walk, the emptiness of the code, the spider who forgot how to walk, the delicate curves within the code, three barking dogs, the mystery of intervals, the absence of a code, the lion asleep at her feet, the empty sleeve waving, the bottle now broken, the voices she told him to listen for, the stolen book, the measurement of intervals.

Does physics know Caesar by name?

Plato warned us of the shadows of the poem, of the words cast against the wall, and Plato warns against the song.

The tree's green explains what a name means apart from memory, flickers of light in the darkened room, our eyes fixed on the screen on the figures of nothing.

The inventor of the code hears each note and swallows his tongue, frightened by shadows. The lion red as a lobster is green sleeps in one corner dreaming of the hours' numbers and names, a river flowing at his feet. "Shuffle Montgomery" was the song.

And here and there they speak in tongues, correcting the right notes in order to get them wrong. And how many days did you spend underground?

The interpreter of leaves examines each tear as pages turn. In the field at dawn they cross swords and a head rolls while the audience laughs. The dead city listens to the code as it reads, and a poem moves back and forth.

At our feet like a sky the graceful curve. Rumours that they are lovers or were in a previous lifetime made of salt. Hills beyond tipped with snow or salt, a curve broken off, searching for her tongue. A deep blue tasting of salt. The awkward curve and talking cloud, steps toward a forest for want of stairs. Are in a lifetime or were. Rumours that the sender had forgotten the code and swallowed his tongue. A mirror in one corner was about to fall, apparently his memory of Siena and the dome.

And Brother Mouse with parachute in mid-air, forever descending.

That they are figures or were, a pictograph with thumb extended. He drank from an actual glass of beer. An outstretched arm offers me its hand.

1981

The Project of Linear Inquiry

[Let *a* be taken as . . .]
a liquid line beneath the skin
and *b* where the blue tiles meet
body and the body's bridge
a seeming road here, endless

rain pearling light
chamber after chamber
of dust-weighted air
the project of seeing things
so to speak, or things seen

namely a hand, namely
the logic of the hand
holding a bell or clouded lens
the vase perched impossibly near the edge
obscuring the metal tines.

She said "perhaps" then it echoed.
I stood there torn
felt hat in hand
wondering what I had done
to cause this dizziness

"you must learn to live with."
It reveals no identifiable source
(not anyway the same as a forest floor).
A vagrant march time, car
passes silently, arm rests at his side

holding a bell or ground lens
where *c* stands for inessential night—
how that body would
move vs how it actually does—
too abstract &/or not abstract enough

but a closed curve in either case
she might repeat
indicating the shallow eaves
nothing but coats and scarves below the window
his-her face canted to the left

nothing imagined or imaginable
dark and nothing actually begun
so that the color becomes exactly as it was
in the minuscule word for it
scribbled beside an arrow

on the far wall
perfectly how else continuous with memory.
There are pomegranates on the table
though they have been placed there
salt, pepper, books and schedules

all sharing the same error
and measure of inattention.
What she says rolls forward.
I shouted toward motion, other gestured,
child laughs, sky,

traffic, photograph. I
gave real pain, expelled
breath, decided. Both arms in thought,
mirror otherwise, abandoned
structures mostly, the glass

door with its inscription lay open
before us, nothing to fear.

1981

Voice and Address

You are the owner of one complete thought

Its sons and daughters
march toward the capital

There are growing apprehensions to the south

It is ringed about
by enclaves of those who have escaped

You would like to live somewhere else

away from the exaggerated music
in a new, exaggerated shirt

a place where colored stones have no value

This hill is temporary
but convenient for lunch

Does she mean that the afternoon should pass

in such a manner
not exactly rapidly

and with a studied inattention

He has lost his new car
of which you were, once,

a willing prisoner

a blister in your palm
identical with the sky's bowl

reflected in the empty sentence

whose glare we have completely shed
ignoring its freshness

The message has been sent

across the lesser fractures in the glass
where the listeners are expendable

The heart is thus flexible

now straight now slightly bent
and yesterday was the day for watching it

from the shadow of its curious house

Your photo has appeared
an island of calm

in a sea of priapic doubt

You are the keeper of one secret thought
the rose and its thorn no longer stand for

You would like to live somewhere

but this is not permitted
You may not even think of it

lest the thinking appear as words

and the words as things
arriving in competing waves

from the ruins of that place

1984

Fifth Prose

Because I'm writing about the snow not the sentence
Because there is a card—a visitor's card—and on that card
    there are words of ours arranged in a row

and on those words we have written house, we have written
    leave this house, we
have written be this house, the spiral of a house, channels
    through this house

and we have written The Provinces and The Reversal and
    something called the Human Poems
though we live in a valley on the Hill of Ghosts

Still for many days the rain will continue to fall
A voice will say Father I am burning

Father I've removed a stone from a wall, erased a picture from
    that wall,
a picture of ships—cloud ships—pressing toward the sea

words only
taken limb by limb apart

Because we are not alive not alone
but ordinary extracts from the tablets

Hassan the Arab and his wife
who did vaulting and balancing

Coleman and Burgess, and Adele Newsome
pitched among the spectators one night

Lizzie Keys
and Fred who fell from the trapeze

into the sawdust
and wasn't hurt at all

and Jacob Hall the rope-dancer
Little Sandy and Sam Sault

Because there is a literal shore, a letter that's blood-red
Because in this dialect the eyes are crossed or quartz

seeing swimmer and seeing rock
statue then shadow

and here in the lake
first a razor then a fact

1988

RAY DiPALMA ▪ ▪ ▪ ▪ ▪ ▪ ▪ ▪ ▪ ▪ ▪ ▪ ▪ ▪ ▪ ▪
b. 1943

Ray DiPalma participated with Bruce Andrews, Charles Bernstein, Ron Silli-
man, and the Canadian poet Steve McCaffery in the important collaborative
volume *Legend* (1980), and is since associated with language poetry. DiPalma
has published more than thirty books and chapbooks. The most recent of these
are *The Jukebox of Memnon* (1988), *Raik* (1989), *Mock Fandango* (1991), *Met-
ropolitan Corridor* (1992), and *Numbers & Tempers: Selected Early Poems
1966–1986* (1993).

   Referring to DiPalma's poetry as "gnomic and aphoristic," the poet Jackson
Mac Low compares *The Jukebox of Memnon* to the work of George Oppen,
Louis Zukofsky, and Laura Riding. As evidenced by "Rumor's rooster . . .,"
DiPalma, like Oppen and Zukofsky, writes a poetry compelled by "the strange
low / coherences of the ear." Like Riding, the modernist poet who abandoned
poetry for the study of linguistics, DiPalma is attracted by the complex relation-
ship between thought and language ("when and where there / is no such thing /
the thought walked").

DiPalma's visual works, which include artist's books, collages, and prints, have been exhibited in numerous group shows in the United States, Europe, and South America.

Born in New Kensington, Pennsylvania, DiPalma was educated at Duquesne University in Pittsburgh and at the Program in Creative Writing at the University of Iowa. Since 1975 he has made his home in New York City and on a small farm in upstate New York.

[Rumor's rooster]

Rumor's rooster
halloos the distorted
strata of analogies

my A is a vegetable A
my A is a vegetable Z
profligate and tangential

is the balance
commercial and run by
the transmission of

the undeclared
or the strange low
coherences of the ear

when and where there
is no such thing
the thought walked

1988

[Each moment is surrounded]

Each moment is surrounded
by the correct torrent

    Each moment is
    surrounded by
    the correct torment

The sphere's endless erasures
and a longer calm protect the song

A full moon
makes a litigant of the tides

Their issue
they'd have you know
is the province of apprehension
where the joke clatters through eloquence
and its busy simplicity to postpone the marvelous

Embracing yet another version
of the sham paragon you heave majestically
in the thickening denials
There is much to be answered for
based on a play by one so big
his name need not be mentioned

And how much longer
can you continue to spit in the face
of the baggy scholar gentry
for they are many and their sincerities
come like the loaves and fishes

1988

[A pink maniac]

A pink maniac
drags his bush of violets
his what-he-calls-it

That's health!
the Orpheus gnome can reckon

'I'll call you
on my dangerous phone'

He prances and sprawls
in his vista

His bush of violets
awakens the pastoral highlands
with a recondite symmetry only
a pink maniac could devise

It might as well
be a continent

or just an instinct
that nourishes

without the usual
labyrinth token of intuition

A bush of violets is
a safe and casual elsewhere
an excursion imitating a smile

1988

[Memory's wedge]

Memory's wedge
makes a valley
tilts the letters so
and tilts the pillar
toward the formula
that promises the angle

What measure
would I make
what measure
what re-assurance
what path

Selection
cut from stone—
an old measure

Tin to granite
graphite wrapped
in cotton

Sound cut
from the thick
night

when we built
the white
city

Map cartilage
moonlight blossom
filament in alcohol

concedes
the stop for
breath

1988

Rebus Tact

Sinking into sound grief
Is no penalty but the humdrum
Not to be shared but placed in
A basket and lifted over the walls.

Or there's the telephone . . .
What's not to be read is face down—
Its traditional imagery fills up
With unfamiliar shadows if properly abstract.

Nice salvos for the farm lads and professors—
Subtle black and white pictures of
The brick stacked a storey high in some
Places and a little less in others.

It should be plainly noted that when struck
Properly with a small metal mallet this brick
Will chime crisply and resonate into a
Lulling hum after a moment or two.

Descended, tolerant enough, how long is
A moment or two? How red is red? How empty
This advice? In the cavern you understand how
A shadow works because you've brought your own light.

But once out in the sun which way should you face?
Standing still, perfectly still, at noon and
Then turning quickly on your heel you might be
Able to figure it out without asking someone.

An experiment with a curl of smoke, perhaps . . .
There's a way to measure time in that.
Nothing too obvious would be special enough
Unless an engine could be rigged to run on it.

It's always the old matter of would and could—
The issues of could and would. No point or notion
In a costume migrating from a vast design could
Or would be well-enough intentioned. A matter for

The recuperative powers of patient groping
And the prudent indecisions that minister to
The definition of a proper sense of distance—
A dog barking off in the barn, a mystical stroke.

1991

MAUREEN OWEN ■ ■ ■ ■ ■ ■ ■ ■ ■ ■ ■ ■

b. 1943

Maureen Owen was born in Graceville, Minnesota, and grew up on a farm and the California racetrack circuit, where her father and mother worked as horse trainers. After studying at San Francisco State College and the University of Washington, she moved to Japan for three years to study Zen Buddhism.

In 1969, Owen began editing and publishing *Telephone*, a literary magazine, and Telephone Books, which issues titles of experimental poetry. Associated with the New York School, she was for many years Program Coordinator at the Poetry Project at St. Mark's Church.

Her poetry collections include *Country Rush* (1973), *No Travels Journal* (1975), *A Brass Choir Approaches the Burial Ground* (1977), *Hearts in Space* (1980), *Zombie Notes* (1985), *Imaginary Income* (1992), and *Untapped Maps* (1993). Owen's poems are striking for their wit and exuberance and often explore themes of sexual difference. The subject of her collection *AE* (1984) is aviator Amelia Earhart, who appears in the book as a recurring figure of heroism.

Owen lives in Guilford, Connecticut.

All That Glitters . . . .

for Kyran at 6 months

Here the picture is less gloomy.   Rumpled
sunrise on the snow   the baby wakes   and fills
the room with awkward battering
              O Uncomplicated One!
    littlest fat face amid the sheets   a commotion
of arms   flapping   palest rouge of flippers crazily rowing
When I simply say   "Good Morning."   Who would have even
suggested   the shore life was trivial?   Last night
on the phone   I realized practically everyone is
a manic depressive   of sorts   With up   and down movements
Unlike the baby   who thinks he's a Trolley   singing Gong
Gong   Gong   He's testing his elbows   & humming.
Five minutes
into the chapter   I noticed that   males were
referred to as men   but females were referred to as wives
I remember blurting out at the party   "I have no father"
With a tremendous sense of relief!   From Grandmother   to
mother   I have passed down. Born of and through women alone.
We have   crawled under the barbed wire   & sat
on our own   sacred land!
              O Lug
                little lug
                & Oggie   when the wind
blows over the stubbles   it's fall   meaning   some things
make themselves obvious by repetition.

And
Tu Fu!   Always shaking your head   when
you look my way   Don't give up on me!
I know the moon bobs in the Great River's flow
I know about Fame   & Office!
I have taken   this moment   to celebrate leisure!
To contemplate
laziness   as a goal   And Schubert himself
who had a streak of it   an incurable sponge   But loved
by all   his friends   who were fiercely loyal
& called him Tubby   He
was barely five feet tall   & a bloom   as from a Spanish balcony
was in both his cheeks.

1980

for Emily (Dickinson)

The girl   working the xerox in the stationery store
has a "thing"   for one of the customers   "I'm in love!"
she blurts to complete strangers buying stamp pad ink.
"Am I shaking?   Last week when he came in   I
stapled my thumb."   It's not just a shift in season
but a hormone that sets the trees off too   from plain
green they go   cheeks flushed   & dropping
everything!
Like the baby bashing through them   hooting   "More!"
&   the radio   announcing   "It's a Sealy Posturepedic morning!"
the landscape's gone silly   with abundance of motif   where
the tossed baby   Plunks   into the damp pyramid   &
is gone   From the base a small scuffed shoe
chanting   "Leafs!   Leafs!"   Here
is all the drama of the emperor's flight!   Imperial
dragon robes swept up   porcelains scattered
& the eerie glazed stillness   the soft mist Thudding
where the stately picnic   had been.
Is it a theory of numbers   or just   Quantity
that lifts us   up from under the armpits   with Fred
Astaire singing   in grand finale crescendo   "It
doesn't matter where you get it   as long as you got it!"
O furious Excesses!
She set her tough skiff   straightway
into the sea   for love of danger!
tho all the birds have lost   their cover
& You   O Bald October
I knew you   when you
still had hair!

1980

African Sunday

Fuck I want to be bound by devotion!   Tortured
by passion!
               just like the ad says   for d h Lawrence's
Sons and Lovers   in today's Sunday Times   instead I'm
here with you   listening to a voice   from 1523 say
"wisdom is the thing that makes knowledge work"   & a
herd of zebras blows back   & forth on the line   A sheet
of wild ungulates   munching their way over the Serengeti
to us   shins in the dust   of those belts razed
by the sun   hooves in our buttercups   Everything
is energy   When she said   "Men take everything   little
by little   they take the power   the dream the hope
the house   & the car"   she meant energy   & how in her
dream it came back to her   She hummed her own notes.
She felt her body astonishingly vague   the wave
nature of electrons   taking over   Toes   teeth
skin lost borders   merged like 5 o'clock traffic   This
is what happened to St. Teresa   when she went flying.
Once after class   I asked my deepest Jesuit   if he
thought she actually did fly   that is to say   go to
the window   & lift off into the night airs   His head
yanked up   flurries of test papers   shifting   "Of Course"
he huffed   "Of Course she flew!"

                             1985

PAUL VIOLI ▪ ▪ ▪ ▪ ▪ ▪ ▪ ▪ ▪ ▪ ▪ ▪ ▪ ▪ ▪ ▪ ▪
b. 1944

Born in New York City and raised on Long Island, Paul Violi attended Boston University, where he studied English literature and art history. Following his return from Nigeria, where he worked in the Peace Corps in 1966–1967, Violi worked as managing editor of *Architectural Forum* and served as assistant to Buckminster Fuller when Fuller was preparing *Tetraworks*, a series of lithographs, at Universal Art Editions. He has also been an organizer of the poetry readings at the Museum of Modern Art.

Violi's poetry books include *Waterworks* (1973), *In Baltic Circles* (1973), *Harmatan* (1977), *Splurge* (1981), *Likewise* (1988), and *The Curious Builder* (1993). Like Kenneth Koch, Violi writes poetry of wit and conceptual energy—these attributes, the playfulness of his work, and his long association with poets Tony Towle and Charles North place him in the New York School.

Violi lives in Putnam Valley, New York, and teaches at New York University.

Index

1982

Rifacimento

cinema—an asian girl with an african name
torpor—the fate of mastodons
bandito—a minor bandage
scoundrel—a french goblet for special occasions
Monotony—when capitalized, an extinct south sea god
plenitude—where albatross prefer to land
anglo-saxon—a frenetic dance of the twenties
endow—to retrieve an ear
sponsor—a musical insecticide
tin—an epicine curse
Betty—at 3 o'clock high, unfriendly aircraft
metaphor—I use them. They keep me regular.
peloponnesian—being licked by an azure tongue
Rasputin—Oh, I was just rasputing around, trimming the
    peenemunde.
cro-magnon—You dial your own number; you get a busy
    signal.
anaconda—dry thunder
vehemence—paper that butchers use for wrapping veal
sociable—looking at a battleship through a keyhole
transvaal—running up a flight of stairs with an erection
cotillion—running down a flight of stairs with an erection

1982

When to Slap a Woman

When loose-strife, in flower, line
one bank with ages of purple candles,

and grape vines hide the tall trees
on the other, leaves dipped into the water,

motionless, shallow, and clear . . .
the pebbled bed curved and ridged,

colors folded by the imperceptible flow;
when, in the middle of all this, here

in the wide bend of the stream,
under such stillness it seems every

thing is finally where it wants to be,
all bafflement and loveliness; the still air

white, or blue above the haze, the same
gentle blue of windows scattered star-like

in a skyline whose edge is lost in the night;
when, high above the dull and humid street

on cumulus sheets as fresh and cool
and welcome as the scent of rain,

or even at night above the incinerator's
pall when you lick your fingertips

to snuff a candle and then pinch the flame
as you would choose any flower to toss

on the black couch; the clothes and coins
spilled across the rug in a tide line,

coins cool under bare feet in the dark,
cool your thighs, a silver wish to mine,

when shadows and shadowy lights streak
the windows and floor, and sadness, like

the moon this time, can come near enough
to feel but not close enough to touch.

1988

MICHAEL DAVIDSON ■ ■ ■ ■ ■ ■ ■ ■ ■ ■ ■

b. 1944

Associated with West Coast language poetry, Michael Davidson's work is collected in such volumes as *Summer Letters* (1977), *The Prose of Fact* (1981), *The Landing of Rochambeau* (1985), *Analogy of the Ion* (1988), and *Post Hoc* (1990). He is also the author of the study *The San Francisco Renaissance: Poetics and Community at Mid-century* (1989).

His poetry often comments on the rift between the world and its representation in language. Its thrust is therefore theoretical. But Davidson seems to delight rather than despair in these ruptures of meaning. Stephen Ratcliffe writes of *Analogy of the Ion* that "Davidson explores this capacity of language for 'failure'—its inherent urge to bend, twist, shade, slant, miscast and color what it talks about."[1] Thus one section of the book mirrors and revises another, creating an echo or palimpsest.

Davidson is chairman of the Literature Department at the University of California at San Diego.

1. "Uttering Mimesis," *Occident,* Vol. CIII, No. 1, 1990, p. 122.

Et in Leucadia Ego

for Chris Dewdney

So they get this and we're coming off some it's like and
then I went so he goes well hey and how you doing?

He went with this scene he was on my you know some
scene he was well I go then said fuck it.

Hey how you what's up hey you see wait a minute you did
no way I see this you know all right you know no way.

What it does is see it has this thing I don't know I know it
won't what's it want it has some stuff you know like.

Fuck that I mean well fuck no he did some fucking thing
so I go fuck no he comes back fuck that no way so fuck I
split he split.

Sure really are you sure oh sure really can you believe oh
really I can't believe you for really oh really oh sure.

Yeah then I went yeah he went there yeah then I yeah
over to and yeah so he yeah and oh yeah I came back yeah
and he oh yeah who I.

Do it do it Oh Kay hey wait for all right do it Oh Kay do it
hey wait don't do it it's my it's my don't do it.

1985

439

The Form of Chiasmus; The Chiasmus of Forms

A number of positions to take with respect to the present. I am Providence. Some of the words you use to hang out the laundry are misspelled. Focused, sabbatical, acknowledgment, component and grateful are starched. Iris begins to emerge in tall grass; magnolias have been taking breath. Dogs graze, gutter water stands. It is the season of electricity.

The anxiety I'm thinking about. Do we have history or is this the obelisk? Is the use of this enough to join the Stamp Tax to Seward's Folly? Can I point and shout "avoid!" in an open field? They went west seeking not to be at home. They were the first to be belated. Others would follow in wagons.

I forget the simple things: the space occupied by chiasmus, the corner of whatever and whatever. Something that becomes you as you get older. His limp had developed in response to another limp. A causality of exigence blossoms forth into a self-evident slogan. They sell them because they exist. I pause at the top of the stairs and observe the red flag. He exists only through his envelopes, though he exits through a conundrum. Welcome to Darkness, you must be tired.

1990

Thinking the Alps

It was by just such a state of logical perpendiculars
that "Bob" had arrived at this narrow pass
in the mountainous netherworld between being and time
and was preparing to reconnoiter the future
according to a long descending trope
of seven or eight partial figures complete with suffixes
until he arrived at the minimal camp below
its cookstove and portable toilet.

How had he come to this fork in what was up to now
a cliche ridden pursuit of normalcy with an unparalleled view
of deviance spreading out like conifers on either flank
their prepositions exfoliating according to a Persian design
the rug of which you see in Figure 3
where "Bob" decries a motif not unlike himself
as gatherer of leeches the better to invent
the trail which up to now he'd thought went straight ahead

but which appears to tarry, disappear and die
in sedgy grass among scattered tarns where to continue
is to be lost in an ancient folio illuminated by monks

parsing miracles in canons first intoned
on the one true cross, and "Bob" is but a ghostly sign
of a polluted cleft between Europe and Asia through which
Satan's armies drive a fetish plus handmaidens
into Paris just in time for mardis gras.

Suddenly vertical time bisects his gaze
suggesting action as a cure for vertiginous thought
and "Bob" moves forward pulling Melancholy his burro behind
hearing all the time the crowd's cascading cheers
from every canyon wall as he concludes the Bruckner fourth
mopping his brow and making his way over to the concertmaster
to shake a hand still vibrating from an undiminished chromaticism
in the works since Tartini's Devil's Trill.

It's hard walking while conducting conversations
among ourselves thinks "Bob," yet where would we be
when faced with an actual business lunch composed of hands
holding knives and forks, their corporate bonhomie
reflected in certain iambics he imitates, voices
heard in falling water, crowds at airports, even these lines
must be saying something if we can stop them long enough
for a path to declare itself among infernal shades of type.

I'm not just anyone caught in a parable he boasts
for all the good it does him, product of the culture
that needs examples of aspiring men to build its cars from
still everyone needs a logo and I'm as good
as Andrew Carnegie on a stamp and better equipped
to be cancelled at postoffices by the sea
in which a postmaster has a taste for Cherubini
which he plays to salve the patience of the lines that form

reminding "Bob" of action whereupon he shifts his pack
and takes his first step since stanza four
destroying the Lake Poets in the process
while history breathes a sigh of relief and the owl
of Minerva takes flight, French horns in unison
strike up the autumnal largo from a woody glade
as workers go back to work, presses start up
and DeQuincy renews his quest for the snowy shack of Kant.

Crisp wind flutters through the latter half
of the Industrial Revolution as "Bob" is turned
into a lathe, screw, and spinning jenny making life tough
on the workers but easy on capital
which is why he sings without end, erasing intervals
in a landscape he just might buy some day, but for now
he is alone in a wood, in the story of the wood
and its conclusion that lies just ahead through those trees

which are made of wood, design of the sepulchre already etched
in a frieze by Brancusi which "Bob" hopes to inhabit
but which for now is memory thrown forward like the trail
he now concludes, drops his pack and stirs the coals
the better to become an ad for coffee,
I'm almost up to Modernism he thinks, and yet this solitude
prohibits me from being here, if only Melancholy faithful guide
could talk he'd make this ruined camp a home.

Holding steaming cup aloft he compares those cliffs
so recently declined to one of either sex
in whose airy gaze one sees oneself (are all these mirrors mine
"Bob" asks, or has the Forest Service placed them here
that visages might animate the trees they hang on)
as if we could be a prelude to ourselves
but that's crazy he thinks and besides I need to eat
and saying so pours water into sawdust for a stew.

Sun sets over campsight, pines shimmer in the astral twilight
that chills the weary traveller
with reminders of where he's not, and slipping into his cocoon
after humping up the coals "Bob" enters time
like a man stepping out of a long poem at the other end
and says goodnight to faithful Melancholy chewing grass
and proceeds into that land his author never planned to enter
source of all descents that once begun beget another.

1990

MARJORIE WELISH ■ ■ ■ ■ ■ ■ ■ ■ ■ ■ ■ ■
b. 1944

Marjorie Welish was born in New York City, where she now lives, and studied
art history at Columbia University. An art critic since 1968, she has written
articles for *Art in America, Art International,* and *ARTnews,* among other
magazines, as well as the catalogues for a number of exhibitions. Her poetry
collections include *Handwritten* (1979), *Two Poems* (1981), *The Windows Flew
Open* (1991), and *Casting Sequences* (1993).

Meditative rather than narrative, her poetry has the rhetorical detachment
and imagistic complexity of some of John Ashbery's work. Welish's poetry avoids
conclusiveness and the grand gesture; instead it delights in ambiguity and theo-
retical difficulty, and finds lyricism there. Of *The Windows Flew Open,* critic
Adam Craig Hill writes, "The verbal address of these poems is highly rhetorical,
though interspersed with restless imaging and competing versions of reality."[1]

Welish's fascination with those competing versions of reality is especially
evident in poems such as "Crossing Disappearing Behind Them," where the
narrator steps onto "a movie set of rain imitating rain, / a central fiction" and
"Within This Book, Called Marguerite": "I wonder if the mind will ever stop
pursuing / rival minds or at least rival murmuring."

1. "How the World Exists," *American Book Review,* December 1991, p. 22.

Respected, Feared, and Somehow Loved

In the long run we must fix our compass,
and implore our compass,
and arraign our shadow play in heaven, among the pantheon
where all the plea-bargaining takes place.
                                    Within the proscenium arch,
the gods negotiate ceaselessly,
and the words he chooses to express the baleful phrase
    dare to be obsessed
with their instrumentality. Please send for our complete catalogue.

As in the days of creation, the clouds gossip and argue,
    the gods waver.
The gods oversee such unstable criteria as fourthly, fifthly.
The rest are little timbral touches.
The gods waver. To reiterate a point, the gods oversee
the symposium on the life raft—a crazed father, a dead son;
                            an unwarranted curtailment of family.

Part of the foot, and thus part of the grace splinter in dismay,
and the small elite of vitrines where our body parts are stored
dies in a plane crash in Mongolia.
Why didn't someone do something to stop the sins of the climate,
                                            and earlier,

why did not someone rewrite the sins of the vitrines, the windows
shipwrecked icily, the windows called away?
                                                1991

Veil

An enchanted frame assures the image of a loved one.
Then there is the question of response.
A loved one produces things. Then there is this question
of existence.
                Motion, dashed to the ground,
and now a hapless pattern in its stead.
Little portions of liveliness are thrown out as inquiries.

Then there is the day that lives up to its preconceived ideas.
Then there is the day
empowered to train all sense on the moment,
holding on to that bias, often and later,
                                although meanwhile,
the day is in position and has empowered the senses
to caress the starstruck flames,
the excited jets surrounding these inquiries.

                                            If there is a pattern
of stars beyond the starstruck blue, it spells desire,
and beyond this, a paler tendency
for stars to sift a desire to be anywhere, and you
not even among them in question form.

                                                              1991

Within This Book, Called Marguerite

The sky is overcast and behind it an infinite regress
of vision is pulling nearer (and yet beneath)
in bashful ruts. I wonder if the mind will ever stop pursuing
rival minds or at least rival murmuring. It is a long sky
that convenes this endlessness.

                              Persons cunningly blent
to suggest a consensus—this is what is meant by serious
     entertainment
of opposing and hastening points of view, each of whose
sense of history is mutually exclusive.

                         Deck chairs
are making a return. I remember when stacking and ganging
chairs were innovative and David Rowland won an industrial award
for the campanile of steel chairs climbing to the sky.

                              As time separates us
from the evaporating architectonics to sweeten mythopoetic
substances, you start to count heroically,
hurled down upon a profile of an as yet
unrevealed know-how.

                              You are unaccompanied
like the great unaccompanied counting
for solo violin that has arisen from the other side
of the mind and hand, the dark, tangled side of the hand,
with its great length of stay.

                                                              1991

Skin

Our skin, strenuously tutored to appreciate the vernacular
body a feeling might have. Companies
of hands, legs, cigarettes, a whip, the sea
tangle in the mutilated lamplight,

and wrap an intelligent enterprise in a gang of approaches.
I think that black into pink is devastating. A bitter winter,
the whip, the sea—all familiar rubble that comes around nightly,
but so familiar, the feeling need only mention surrender and we
    surrender.

In the postwar victory, lamplight is harsher, categorical.
Pink is devastating, a stone lawn.
A great part of the American pavilion
has been given over to an iron blue and magnificent écorché—

the spirit, when the spirit is flayed and forbidden
to talk about itself. It feels normal
to live in the present amid musculature
of beautiful early work propped against an uphill sea.

                                                      1991

Crossing Disappearing Behind Them

Diverse strangers flower and diverge,
and when they cross paths, three strangers flower
and are clairvoyant. Under the moon, combining voyages,
it is their turn to appear whole in silhouette.
The street expresses it,
and it is all you can do to keep the shrill silhouette
where this occurred, which in retrospect
seems the intrigue of passing and coalescing.

Criss-crossing within the otherwise vague
whereabouts helping them, strangers
stray into circumstantial flare, bright and shapely
in disproportion to the event.
The street expresses it as if speaking in words,
and when they cross, strangers comply with passing
and coalescing and flowering.
Their pretty accident goes behind them,
their coalescence disappears, and then speaking disappears
into the dismemberment of coalescing and passing human effect.

Someone throws a vista across a tree, and you, too,
are alive. It is raining pliable flowers.
Three in slangy attire cross under a tree
and disappear, crossing disappearing behind them.
It is raining, but this is common practice.
In keeping with this, a minor shadow
occurs by passing by, throwing its half-truth forward,
being original only less excellent

than untruth his shadow has produced. This application is lengthy
and comes with two interleaved carbons.

The sky issues rain.
The sky issues rain hesitantly,
but then the sky seems necessary.
Issuing massive rain,
lifelike petals begin to fail,
and paper bends away.

Petals bend shadow, being minor
in a minor station, though no less original.
An original turn performed less well
than the turn that bears his name, and you,
promptly this, wearing a vinyl raincoat,
push open the plate glass doors to be spared
being called minor for wearing the same
rechargeable and independently arrived at footprint.

Being minor means that an era haunts a phrase of ruined
    memorabilia,
floral commemoratives move across you.
A quoted feeling hangs over the ruin, the vinyl, the rain,
each in its landscape. The vinyl, the ruin, each
has memorized the original one in each of us
who wears a paraphraseable vastness
by virtue of arriving late.

And on the fortieth day
after I wrote that the poem you call derivative
is original if late, I opened the door
and the windows flew open
in a revolutionary manner, bare-breasted
and I saw myself
stepping onto a movie set of rain imitating rain,
a central fiction.

The ruin has memorized the ruin, and so too the vinyl
in each one of us replicates the original vinyl
of some unsuspecting excellence.
He who is truly original did not intend this dusk.
At first glance, this is dusk led into a past
where rain pours down an original thought
springing from as many heads.

Floral commemoratives
and the arrested growth of the silhouette of one thought
are flung across several minds
and out onto the real floor of the night.

You are wearing vinyl, and being morally persuaded,
he is wearing vinyl, she is wearing it,
and their silhouette creates more of the same copious thing
not far away, so we remember this corridor forever.

1991

LORENZO THOMAS ▪ ▪ ▪ ▪ ▪ ▪ ▪ ▪ ▪ ▪ ▪ ▪
b. 1944

Lorenzo Thomas was born in Panama and raised in New York City. He attended Queens College of the City University of New York. "I came to New York City speaking Spanish," Thomas once commented, "got beat up on the way home from school because I 'talked funny.' Never forgot it. Went way way away out of my way to become extra-fluent in English."[1]

Centrally involved with the Black Arts movement in Harlem from 1965 to 1975, he was a member of the celebrated Umbra Workshop, a black writers' collective whose members included poets Ishmael Reed and Calvin Hernton, and one of the editors of the literary magazine *Umbra*.

He first made contact with the so-called Tulsa group of New York poets, whose affection for popular culture he shares, through Ron Padgett's *White Dove Review*, and later came to be associated with Ted Berrigan's *"C" Magazine* on the Lower East Side. Other early contacts include Jackson Mac Low and Paul Blackburn, in whose Deux Magots reading series Thomas participated.

Thomas's most important influences as a poet, however, are the Afro-Caribbean surrealist Aimé Césaire, blues artists Robert Johnson and Lightning Hopkins, and the late Juke Boy Bonner, a Houston street singer and poet whom Thomas eulogized in the journal *Callaloo*.

Thomas's poetry collections include *A Visible Island* (1967), *Fit Music: California Songs* (1972), *Dracula* (1973), *Chances Are Few* (1979), and *The Bathers* (1981). A translator of classical Vietnamese poetry, he is a veteran of the Vietnam War.

Thomas teaches at the University of Houston, Downtown Campus.

1. *Contemporary Authors: New Revision Series*, Vol. 25, Detroit, p. 445.

The Marvelous Land of Indefinitions

> The poet's business is telling the truth.
> —RICARDO MIRO

How nice! How convenient!
We have all gathered to read & listen to poems
As if everyone were actually equal
Laborers in the corn fields
Girls in the cigarette factory
Though someone always seems to be saying
"A poet's task is making poetry . . . blah blah blah"

But poeting with poor people doesn't end poverty.

How sweet it is! How nice!
First poems and last words
Are heard here, dedicated to friends
Describing the ultimate artistic inspirations
Incorporating all the latest stops and turns
Of fashion

Example:
    the alleys oh like psychedelic birds
    & the transfiguration of being,
    of self, of the essence, blah blah blah
It's annoying.

Clearly, this poetry reading
Will not be heard in the town square
Because people don't listen to poetry
Since poetry is "the nectar of the gods"
And these readers are demigods
Raising up to nirvana and adulation
All of those others who read, write,
Or listen to this stuff

So

Tranquilly, everyone reads
After cocktails
    embraces

Happily, an interesting poem
Reminds me of Proust
Or something from a 16th Century French book
Afterward
No one assumes responsibility for sense or vision
Because, in the final analysis, poetry
Is something personal
      intimate
      alien

Newspaper headlines are full of lies
And the radio is full of lies
AND POETRY IS FULL OF LIES!

Because everyone goes along
In slavish style follows the ways of the world
(European, Anglo-Saxon, White)

And the *style*, the *form* is what's important
Incomprehensible to everyone else
But them. Oh, in the final analysis
Everyone else is a part of the problem
And we're in the "in" crowd.

The ones who never read are ready to gossip!
Did you see so & so's new book?
   I just got accepted in *Reader's Digest*
Blah blah blah

But that's OK
   OK because we made the best of it
Seated at god the father's right hand
OK because here where nothing's happening
No one can truthfully say
        us least of all
That we're lazy
Hate to work,
Know nothing but gambling, drinking, *fiesta*, good sex
(the common definition of a Panamanian)
          because
What's on our minds is the office,
         security, the kids.
   Daily bread.
A payday every two weeks or the 30th

Everyone goes along
Because unemployment goes up every day
It's OK exploit the farm workers
OK that rent keeps going up
OK
   that young people are lost in marijuana and "free love"
OK
   because all the world drinks Coca-Cola and smokes Viceroys
And everyone prefers blonds and white folks
And cathedral arched eyebrows
OK
   because the gringos don't worry themselves about anybody
(Only duck hunting in January—and that not too often—
And controlling the nation's economy)
OK
   because it's the others who suffer

In the final analysis, this is the 51st state
In the wonderful land of indefinitions
Where everyone goes along
Where poets gather to read poems

And sip cocktails
>And talk   har har har
>Chat   har har har blah blah blah
>Talk   har har har

To evade the compromise
Escape the moment
Avoid facing destiny and the "secret word"
>Each day growing clearer
>Each day   blah blah blah
>Hovering   blah blah blah
>Nearer

—for Roberto MacKay

1979

Instructions for Your New Osiris

Canopic old Egyptian jugs,
The jars in her boudoir hold me.
Or used to
Since she's moved them
Put them in her bag
And toted them to her new lover's house

That's what she throws in my face
Since she no longer holds me
Since she can't stand to stay around
No longer

My heart's in one

I'm dead
>because no longer does my body hold a heart

Another holds what's left of pride
The day my best friend laughed dead in my face
Because he knew she was his other best friend's
Lady

Another holds the essence
Of my self-respect
And still another, all my tenderness
For her

That's all.
>There's nothing left
But dead politeness

Not even passion left to kick her ass

She lies progressively to me
Each day, like the difficulty
Of game show questions
A little bitter more ridiculous each time
And unbelievable

Where is Gene Rayburn? Adrienne Barbeau?
George Gobel? Wally Cox? Familiar faces of the afternoon
Clifton Davis? Margaret Daniels?
It seems I just don't understand this show.

Lying, she cheats

In front my face, behind my back
It doesn't matter
The only novelty is tonight's choice
A movie with my girlfriend
Got a date, I really didn't think you'd be in town
Don't hate me do you? Please
Don't hate me please
I'm sorry, but I didn't think you'd mind
Of how she wants to let me know
We're through

When I was still alive, before I knew
The full name of the door,
I used to speak of her and say
"My Lady"

1979

ANNE WALDMAN ▪ ▪ ▪ ▪ ▪ ▪ ▪ ▪ ▪ ▪ ▪ ▪ ▪ ▪
b. 1945

Raised in Greenwich Village, Anne Waldman was first attracted to poetry at
Friends Seminary High School in New York City. She later graduated from
Bennington College, where she submitted a creative thesis and study on the
work of Theodore Roethke. However, it was the 1965 Berkeley Poetry Confer-
ence, where she attended readings by Charles Olson, Robert Duncan, and Allen
Ginsberg, that determined her direction as a poet. Associated with the bohe-
mian poetics of the Lower East Side, she co-founded the literary magazine
Angel Hair and became the director of the St. Mark's Poetry Project, a position
she held from 1968 to 1978.

Following Allen Ginsberg's urging that she write long poems, Waldman pro-
duced *Fast Speaking Woman* (1975/1978), a book-length list poem with chant-
like repetition. The poem's shamanistic qualities were borrowed from Maria
Sabina, a Mazatec poet-priestess whose chanting was intended to guide young

Mazatec women through a night of mushroom-induced visions.[1] The success of *Fast Speaking Woman* with audiences made Waldman a leading advocate of oral poetics and performance-related poetry in both the United States and Europe.

"Makeup on Empty Space," which is also chantlike and psalmic, "takes off from the idea in Buddhist psychology that the feminine energy tends to manifest in the world, adorning empty space. What we see in the world, the phenomena, is created by feminine energy."[2] Like all oral poetry, the "chant" poem "skin Meat BONES" must be performed to be fully appreciated, its repeated words sung by Waldman in radically different registers.

Waldman is co-founder, with Allen Ginsberg, of the Jack Kerouac School of Disembodied Poetics at the Naropa Institute in Boulder, Colorado. Editor of *The World* magazine in the late sixties and early seventies, she has also edited a number of anthologies, including *Out of This World: An Anthology of the St. Mark's Poetry Project 1966–1991* (1991) and *Nice to See You: Homage to Ted Berrigan* (1991). Her many books include *Cabin* (1981/1984), *Makeup on Empty Space* (1984), *skin, Meat, BONES* (1985), *Helping the Dreamer: New & Selected Poems 1966–1988* (1989), and the epic-length poem *Iovis* (1993). Waldman is often identified with Beat poetics, especially the writings of Allen Ginsberg and Diane di Prima. Yet, as witnessed by the pantoums and rondeaux in *First Baby Poems* (1983), she is also drawn to the more formal procedures of the New York School.

Waldman resides in Boulder, Colorado, and New York City.

1. Lee Bartlett, Anne Waldman interview in *Talking Poetry: Conversations in the Workshop with Contemporary Poets*, Albuquerque, 1987, p. 262.   2. The same, p. 272.

Makeup on Empty Space

I am putting makeup on empty space
all patinas convening on empty space
rouge blushing on empty space
I am putting makeup on empty space
pasting eyelashes on empty space
painting the eyebrows of empty space
piling creams on empty space
painting the phenomenal world
I am hanging ornaments on empty space
gold clips, lacquer combs, plastic hairpins on empty space
I am sticking wire pins into empty space
I pour words over empty space, enthrall the empty space
packing, stuffing, jamming empty space
spinning necklaces around empty space
Fancy this, imagine this: painting the phenomenal world
bangles on wrists
pendants hung on empty space
I am putting my memory into empty space
undressing you
hanging the wrinkled clothes on a nail
hanging the green coat on a nail
dancing in the evening it ended with dancing in the evening

I am still thinking about putting makeup on empty space
I want to scare you: the hanging night, the drifting night,
the moaning night, daughter of troubled sleep I want to scare you
I bind as far as cold day goes
I bind the power of 20 husky men
I bind the seductive colorful women, all of them
I bind the massive rock
I bind the hanging night, the drifting night, the
moaning night, daughter of troubled sleep
I am binding my debts, I magnetize the phone bill
bind the root of my sharp pointed tongue
I cup my hands in water, splash water on empty space
water drunk by empty space
Look what thoughts will do   Look what words will do
from nothing to the face
from nothing to the root of the tongue
from nothing to speaking of empty space
I bind the ash tree
I bind the yew
I bind the willow
I bind uranium
I bind the uneconomical unrenewable energy of uranium
dash uranium to empty space
I bind the color red I seduce the color red to empty space
I put the sunset in empty space
I take the blue of his eyes and make an offering to empty space
renewable blue
I take the green of everything coming to life, it grows &
climbs into empty space
I put the white of the snow at the foot of empty space
I clasp the yellow of the cat's eyes sitting in the
black space I clasp them to my heart, empty space
I want the brown of this floor to rise up into empty space
Take the floor apart to find the brown,
bind it up again under spell of empty space
I want to take this old wall apart I am rich in my mind thinking
of this, I am thinking of putting makeup on empty space
Everything crumbles around empty space
the thin dry weed crumbles, the milkweed is blown into empty space
I bind the stars reflected in your eye
from nothing to these typing fingers
from nothing to the legs of the elk
from nothing to the neck of the deer
from nothing to porcelain teeth
from nothing to the fine stand of pine in the forest
I kept it going when I put the water on
when I let the water run
sweeping together in empty space
There is a better way to say empty space
Turn yourself inside out and you might disappear

you have a new definition in empty space
What I like about impermanence is the clash
of my big body with empty space
I am putting the floor back together again
I am rebuilding the wall
I am slapping mortar on bricks
I am fastening the machine together with delicate wire
There is no eternal thread, maybe there is thread of pure gold
I am starting to sing inside about the empty space
there is some new detail every time
I am taping the picture I love so well on the wall:
moonless black night beyond country plaid curtains
everything illuminated out of empty space
I hang the black linen dress on my body
the hanging night, the drifting night, the moaning night
daughter of troubled sleep
This occurs to me
I hang up a mirror to catch stars, everything occurs to me out in the
night in my skull of empty space
I go outside in starry ice
I build up the house again in memory of empty space
This occurs to me about empty space
that it is nevered to be mentioned again
Fancy this
imagine this
painting the phenomenal world
there's talk of dressing the body with strange adornments
to remind you of a vow to empty space
there's talk of the discourse in your mind like a silkworm
I wish to venture into a not chiseled place
I pour sand on the ground
Objects and vehicles emerge from the fog
the canyon is dangerous tonight
suddenly there are warning lights
The patrol is helpful in the manner of guiding
there is talk of slowing down
there is talk of a feminine deity
I bind her with a briar
I bind with the tooth of a tiger
I bind with my quartz crystal
I magnetize the worlds
I cover myself with jewels
I drink amrita
there is some new detail
there is a spangle on her shoe
there is a stud on her boot
the tires are studded for the difficult climb
I put my hands to my face
I am putting makeup on empty space

I wanted to scare you with the night that scared me
the drifting night, the moaning night
Someone was always intruding to make you forget empty space
you put it all on
you paint your nails
you put on scarves
all the time adorning empty space
Whatever-your-name-is I tell you "empty space"
with your fictions with dancing come around to it
with your funny way of singing come around to it
with your smiling come to it
with your enormous retinue & accumulation come around to it
with your extras come round to it
with your good fortune, with your lazy fortune come round to it
when you look most like a bird, that is the time to come round to it
when you are cheating, come to it
when you are in your anguished head
when you are not sensible
when you are insisting on the
praise from many tongues
It begins with the root of the tongue
it begins with the root of the heart
there is a spinal cord of wind
singing & moaning in empty space

1984

Berthe Morisot

Toward the end of her life she said that the
wish for fame after death seemed to her an
inordinate ambition. "Mine," she added,
"is limited to the desire to set down
something as it passes, oh, something, the
least of things!"

A critic had written of the show at the
Salon des Impressionnistes singling out
Morisot: "There are five or six lunatics,
one of them a woman."

1985

skin

Meat

BONES   (chant)

I've come to tell you of the things dear to me
& what I've discovered of the skin
Meat
BONES

your body waking up so sweet to me   skin

dawn light it's green   skin

I'm in hungry repose
Meat

it's getting close to motion   O skeleton
BONE

you might stretch it now   skin

so warm, flesh

and lasting awhile
BONE

clock like a BONE creaking
memory like a BONE creaking

little laughter lines around the eyes   skin
& how the mouth's redder than the rest   Meat
or nipples off purple rib cage of
BONES

It's morning anywhere!

O sitting and lying around in my weary tinsel skin
got to get up and walk around in my cumbersome skin
put on lightweight cotton skin
& shuffling skin slippers

the light's going to make it raw   skin
or vulnerable   Meat
or hard
BONES

I could pierce it   skin
I'll grow new skin, undergo big character change

please get under my skin   take hold of me
interest or annoy me intensely

jump me out of my skin!

no skin off your nose, buster
he's thin-skinned, she's thick
dermis & epidermis mating

Allen's nephew once had a skin
                   head
                      haircut

O POOR FLAYED DEER WITH GENTLE HAIR

film on surface of milk this morning

only skin deep

let's go to the oily skin flick

TENDENCY OF HIGH FREQUENCY ALTERNATING CURRENT
TO FLOW THROUGH THE OUTER LAYER ONLY OF A CONDUCTOR

okay, you've wounded me, but it's only skin deep

I'm sitting down in my sweet smelling clammy skin
to eat some juicy MEAT!

one man's meat is another man's poison

animal flesh is tasty

HAD A DREAM THE MEAT WAS TURNED INSIDE OUT,
FLOWERS BLOOMING THERE

Had a dream the jackals came (this was in India)
to collect the Meat of my father's forefingers

O cloud shaped like a tenderloin steak

tree Meat

Meat of Buddha

Had a Meat sandwich   had a Meat day
everyone was carrying their Meat around, flinging
it in the breeze

Small town, downtown, spring: time to show off your Meat
go home when it's dark and sit down with the
BONES

I live in a bare BONES room
he's working my fingers to the BONE
my friend Steven is living close to the BONE
I'm BONING up on my Dante, William Carlos Williams,
Campion and Gertrude Stein

Why is he such a bonehead? won't listen to a thing I say
Why are they so bone idle? won't do a thing I say
I'M GONNA POINT MY ABORIGINE BONE AT YOU & GET YOU WISER!

I've got a BONE to pick with the senator

I've got a BONE to pick with the Pentagon

The BONE of contention has to do with whether or not
we get a lease

Our old '68 Ford's an old BONE-shaker

Ivory, dentine, whalebone, dominoes, dice, castanets, corset
are some of the things made of BONE

but after I die make of my BONES, flutes
and of my skin, drums
I implore you in the name of all female deities wrathful &
compassionate

& PROTECT ENDANGERED SPECIES ALSO!

> *This piece is intended to be read aloud, singing the words "skin," "Meat,"
> "BONES" as notes: "skin," high soprano register, "Meat," tenor,
> "BONES," basso profundo. The 3 notes may vary, but the different
> registers should be markedly distinguishable.*

1985

ALICE NOTLEY ▪ ▪ ▪ ▪ ▪ ▪ ▪ ▪ ▪ ▪ ▪ ▪ ▪ ▪ ▪
b. 1945

Raised in Needles, California, Alice Notley was educated at Barnard College
and the University of Iowa, where she received an M.F.A. and concentrated
primarily on fiction writing. At Iowa, Notley met poets Anselm Hollo and Ted
Berrigan, who helped guide her talents in the direction of poetry. In 1971, she

married Berrigan and lived with him in New York City, with sojourns to Chicago and London, until his death in 1983. Notley's poetry books include *Phoebe Light* (1973), *Alice Ordered Me to Be Made* (1975), *When I Was Alive* (1980), *How Spring Comes* (1981), and *Margaret & Dusty* (1985).

Reminiscent of Marianne Moore and William Carlos Williams in its precise but unexpected word choices and use of local detail, Notley's work has an orchestral fullness that sets her apart from the ironic minimalism of some of the New York School poets with whom she is associated. In the early eighties, her sudden turns and verbal brightness seemed to be verging on a language poetry aesthetic; the style and emphasis of her work changed, however, following Berrigan's death. The poetry collected in *At Night the States* (1987) and *The Scarlet Cabinet* (with Douglas Oliver, 1992) reveals darker concerns bordering on the mystical.

Referring to the Australian aborigines in Bruce Chatwin's *The Songlines*, Notley writes, "One purpose of language is probably to sing where you go, to name the landscape so you can make it exist & thus get from place to place (to create it). Everything you see is a song or a story—you barely notice it if it isn't."[1] She insists that "poetry is not about words, or how one thinks, or making things. It is about essence—the secret inside the material."[2]

Notley lives in Paris.

1. "Notes on the Poetry of Everyday Life," in *From a Work in Progress*, New York, 1988, p. 38.   2. Notley's introduction to *The Scarlet Cabinet: A Compendium of Books* (by Alice Notley & Douglas Oliver), New York, 1992.

Poem

You hear that heroic big land music?
Land a one could call one.
He starred, had lives, looks down:
windmill still now they buy only
snow cows. Part of a dream, she
had a long waist he once but yet
never encircled, and now I'm
in charge of this, this donkey with
a charmed voice. Elly, I'm
being sad thinking of Daddy.
He marshalled his private lady,
did she wear a hat or the
other side? Get off my own land? We
were all born on it to die on
with no writin' on it. But who are
you to look back, well he's
humming "From this valley," who's gone.
Support and preserve me, father. Oh
Daddy, who can stand it?

1981

Jack Would Speak through the
Imperfect Medium of Alice

So I'm an alcoholic Catholic mother-lover
yet there is no sweetish nectar no fuzzed-peach
thing no song sing but in the word
to which I'm starlessly unreachably faithful
you, pendant & you, politically righteous & you, alive
you think you can peel my sober word apart from my drunken word
my Buddhist word apart from my white sugar Thérèse word my
word to comrade from my word to my mother
but all my words are one word my lives one
my last to first wound round in finally fiberless crystalline skein

I began as a drunkard & ended as a child
I began as an ordinary cruel lover & ended as a boy who
           read radiant newsprint
I began physically embarrassing—"bloated"—&
           ended as a perfect black-haired laddy
I began unnaturally subservient to my mother &
           ended in the crib of her goldenness
I began in a fatal hemorrhage & ended in a
           tiny love's body perfect smallest one

But I began in a word & I ended in a word &
           I know that word better
Than any knows me or knows that word,
           probably, but I only asked to know it—
That word is the word when I say me bloated
           & when I say me manly it's
The word that word I write perfectly lovingly
           one & one after the other one

But you—you can only take it when it's that one & not
           some other one
Or you say "he lost it" as if I (I so nothinged) could ever
           lose the word
But when there's only one word—when
           you know them, the words—
The words are all only one word the perfect
           word—
My body my alcohol my pain my death are only
           the perfect word as I
Tell it to you, poor sweet categorizers
           Listen
Every me I was & wrote
           were only & all (gently)
That one perfect word

                                                              1981

A California Girlhood

The Brothers Grimm grew weaker and flickered, blue light
      in the well. Hans Christian Anderson
and his tiny gossamer bride went to bed beneath a walnut shell
      encrusted with every star, Copenhagen's
Sky, dreamed Louisa May Alcott, but when we awaken
      in New England my head will rest on
my cousin's shoulder, beneath *my* tree.
Anna Sewell, that the shining aren't suffered to continue to
      shine! though, old, he finds
his way home, Carolyn Keene's blue roadster
      cannot replace the young horse. There's nothing
left of her, Michael Shayne, but lipstick and
      fingerprints on a cognac bottle; Erle Stanley Gardner
knows the Chief will never pass cross-examination
      and on to ripeness, the breasts!
Where is orphan Canada, Anne of Green Gables?
      the smell of a white dress it rained on because
it was graduation. Frank G. Slaughter
      has given him hands that heal her after
she sleeps through rape by a snob. Frank Yerby
      pierces right through the membrane she cries
out triumphantly, one of the others, skim
      bunches of adjectives.
Margaret Mitchell moved to the eye which
      watered 3 times: that bright moon moves on. But
you can't strain hydrogen and oxygen out of tears
      or Raphael Sabatini out of life, Captain
Blood, the sword is worn
      against my tattered petticoat.
Charlotte Brontë is tense and comely as a first child.
Emily Brontë walks out to copulate with a
      storm. Indigo to emerald to
indigo, the Mississippi "better den rum darlin"; then
      Mark Twain gets hit on the hammer
and glowers a whole other lifetime. Anya
Seton sighed. "If only angels be angels and witchery
      the fine art it is
                I still have to
bother about something besides décolletage."
Gwen Bristow pulled the arrow out of her arm
      and thrust it into the Indian's chest.
When a guy goes molten John Dickson Carr
      orders the witch is non-existent, yawn
Sigrid Undset loses her life and yet loses nothing
      as a river in her bed flows beneath
the stained-glass leaves, thy breath is sustenance.
She wouldn't rollerskate through the Swedish palace,

Annamarie Selinko. Lawrence Schoonover
respects the first man to use a fork in Spain,
a Jew of Inquisition times,
she dances in little but castanets, Kathleen
Windsor, it's a scheming pussy wind
that ripples and funs with the bleak sea. Knowledge
of evil an inadequate knowledge, as
Herman Melville would say, read National
Geographic, for your first glimpse of nipples,
free maps, Arctic, Hibiscus. Jane Austen
sneaks a suspicion. You look like the
flash with the cash.
John Steinbeck. My name
is Rose o'Sharon
the gorgeous coarse prayer, as the sentimental horrors
encroach and recede, repeatedly. Edgar Allan Poe
is on purple alert. Alexander Dumas, fils, announces
My favorite song is Rainy Night in Georgia.
Daphne DuMaurier wept tiny drops of Dom Perignon. Did
Lady Brett Ashley copulate? did
Herman Wouk read between the lines?
T. H. White allowed one her manhood; Guinivere is
Jenny, but I know I carry a lance.
William Faulkner incomprehensible, an
obsidian cliff, does the ballerina wear cleats?
She puts her ear to the delicate shell of Ernest
Hemingway; hears
Willa Cather orchestrate her death. Victoria Holt
is still, chastely, darkly in love.

1981

How Spring Comes

Toys and rose   The zoo body zigzags
I think fish too
but I'm a polite
social being, I'm a Ladle Lady or purple
and blue I write green letters and gold
editorials for the Krystal Oxygen Company
I have one hip as far as I can see, that
I see as I write say
white tee-shirts
upsidedown
turn em around
& put them on
your muscles
my angels

or
a semi-colon
is blue window
to me
is that a haiku? I fly over San Diego in some one or
another real despair and ask you to comfort me. You
more or less do, you aren't even there
my best me my worldly me
my taste of spring my continuance my
comfort will you comfort me?
I offer you my heart over Tucson
I can't use it
take it to comfort me
free
me be it take it take it to
be it
which apparently you don't or take you help provide
me it I think, that
happens among true people, that poem I was writing
no good poem
but Moment framed the Pleiades
The garnets ring more beautiful the longer you
are waiting for me in them,
where Deity makes me friendly there.

But who put on all the tee-shirts in Hunter's
Point? Well we're all good boys my son said so.
A semi-colon is a semi-precious garnet cluster
telegram; what we love are such depths between all
the messages. Pass the salt; Ladies of the Tang,
bubble of night; this book about Harry Truman is wonderful.

I see the Gulf Moon Rising every night. I'm familiar
with the zonked starfish. I've the sheen on under
the fire-escape railing all streetlight-lit. The
hollow suddenly appeared to enlarge and fill with a
bright light. Wild with the taste of wine it does not
remember the despair of an hour ago, which was true
that is of a true woman. She was somehow hating her
position on the round earth in the dusky sky on a
harsh Sunday. On the ground forgotten flowerlike
firmaments. She addressed in uneloquent hatred
SMUG LIFE
the one who soothes one's foolishness the
Great Face Construct who loves you for your kinks child
anyway, the Guru God:

Oh I will come back a knockout tomorrow
Useless to you!

You're not it you smug face
I'm not doing your yoga not wearing
Your moondrops using your cream
Rinse letting you fuck me Exquisite
Like I was one of the Ones With Brains Too!
Intelligence in panties with peekaboo
holes—

No I'm coming back raw
I'm getting drenched in the rain
It's rain and it's wet I'm soaked I'm
Chilled and I'm coughing the air's raw
To my throat, which is raw from
Coughing, coughing so strong
Coughing and laughing
So strong from killing you!

Etc.

She didn't kill nothing.
& I don't get to share
no secrets with the stars. I make chow. I contemplate
semi-colons. I despair as a mother. I scream at that
kid I'm gonna crack open your big walnut if you don't
go to sleep. Theories of grace, that it implies no
surprise no shock. Ukranians sudden on Sunday speaking
Ukranian, the cross not Christian but Gracious
and when I want to cry or cough violently
it must diffuse back into my embassy; hard, that takes
hard. And if it weren't for you . . . not you smug life
face, but real you. Please play cribbage.
Pass the salt.
Think of a garnet-black cabbage, a
Ukranian is selling it on 7th Street in honor of our
marriage. A Spanish fan opens in my abdomen
I have Spanish dancers in my stomach

they're my arching striving in dance where it's black
red flowers darken to be huge pleasuring the
severe, tried Angel who meets transition,
transport, as abruptly as necessary
for everyone's are apt

Says the Unassuming Graceful
Whose down-hip-ness
Is that window
The dancers' sensuous flaw
That admits Spring,

Contingent upon our personality
Spring is for the worldly
                                    just like the HaHa Room
             Just like dearest rockbottom
                                    suddenly gone buoyant

             To be black geese to be
             strenuous dancers
             is not to dignify a passion but to
             grip it.

                    Not saints but always pupils
pupils dilated fully black in full achievement of
gut-feeling.   Joy.

                                                        1981

FROM *Beginning with a Stain*

Beginning with a stain, as the Universe did perhaps
I need to tell you about for myself this stain
A stain of old blood on a bedspread (white)
—how can I set a pace?—I'm
afraid to speak, not of being indiscreet, but of
touching myself too near, too near to
my heart bed—the bedspread
was white & thin
I slept on her bed with my lover
and thus was never
sure whose stain hers or mine? And when I washed it, or
rather, he did, it remained. And then

And then she died unexpectedly, as they say
became away forever
except in the air, and somewhere near
my heart bed—But
the bedspread
became of her ashes a mingled part.
The stain, my stain, or hers, but mine
My love stain is part of her ashes, & I rejoice in that, whether
she & her lover, or I & my lover
were the ones who originally lay there, staining the bed
Our stain has gone with her, you see,
This is the stain that

invents the world, holds it together in color of
color of, color. Color of love.

This is the love they spend in order to be.
And she was quite young & I am much older (her step-mother)
But our stain was the same one
There is no double. And she is endlessly
clear; & good. Surround my heart bed
with my others at night
speak with me of the stain, that is our love, that
invents the world, that is
our purest one. Help me to stain, I say, my words with all us

(I love you I know you are there)
the song of one breath.
Outside where cars & cycles
I'm not afraid to begin again, with & from you.

1992

BERNADETTE MAYER ▪ ▪ ▪ ▪ ▪ ▪ ▪ ▪ ▪ ▪ ▪
b. 1945

Bernadette Mayer was born in Brooklyn and received her B.A. from the New School for Social Research. Her books of poetry, parts of which are collected in *A Bernadette Mayer Reader* (1992), include *Moving* (1964), *Memory* (1975), *Studying Hunger* (1975), *Midwinter Day* (1982), *Utopia* (1983), *Sonnets* (1989), and *The Formal Field of Kissing* (1990). She has also been editor of the magazines *0 to 9* (with Vito Acconci), *Unnatural Acts* (with Ed Friedman), and *United Artists* (with Lewis Warsh).

Mayer is associated with the New York School in her use of daily occasions and her attraction to traditional form, especially the sonnet. Poems like "Gay Full Story," however, suggest the work of Gertrude Stein and the language poets. In the essay "The Obfuscated Poem," Mayer writes, "The best obfuscation bewilders old meanings while reflecting or imitating or creating a structure of a beauty that we know."[1]

Mayer tends to organize her books around a concept, sometimes interdisciplinary in nature. By her own description, "*Memory* is a journal of the month of July 1971 based on notes and writings, and a series of 1,116 slides (36 pictures shot every day)."[2] Her prose poem "The Desires of Mothers to Please Others in Letters" is a "series of letters never sent, written to unidentified friends, acquaintances, political figures, and poets over a nine-month period and ending with the birth of a baby."[3]

Mayer lives on the Lower East Side, and she conducts poetry workshops at the New School for Social Research and the Poetry Project at St. Mark's Church.

1. In *Code of Signals*, ed. Michael Palmer, Berkeley, 1983, p. 166.   2. *A Bernadette Mayer Reader*, New York, 1992, p. vi.   3. The same, p. viii.

Gay Full Story

for Gerard Rizza

Gay full story is authentic verve fabulous jay gull stork. And grow when torn is matters on foot died out also crow wren tern. Connect all the life force afloat blank bullet holes. Change one letter in each essential vivacity missing word to spell a times taking place defunct bird's name. Let's see. Magic Names. Use a piece of current vitalization melted away paper about 6 × 3 occurring doing lost inches and tear it breathing spirit fabulous jagged into three ideal indeed inherence pieces . . . Ask someone subsistent subsistence shadowy to write his missing extant name on one of the backbone no more slips. Hand him the center died out veritable revival one with the rough departed certain edges on the in reality vim late top and the in fact pep dead bottom as pictured. Write a true spiritous vital spark name on each of the other actual animation void two slips. Fold the three imaginary ontological dash pieces over the airy go indeed names and put them in a hollow unimpeachable snap hat. Without looking, you can pick out the true visionary vital flame slip with the two rough inexistent well grounded oxygen edges which will contain the positive departed perspiring writer's affairs on foot null and void name. (Fold the gone vegetative doings ends over the illusory constant soul name.) Then later shade in all the twenty-five the times tenuous true-blue triangles shown above. Then you could match the uninhabitable heart at home designs below with those in the above lively flying Dutchman dash code . . . Print in the tenantless haunted core letters and read them across to find out where these indwelling mathematical minus children are going to spend their man in the moon essential essence vacation. Now connect the vaporous vivifying vim dots. Then you could color this ubiquitous lost elixir barnyard omitted as a matter of fact picture. First complete the deserted walking the earth oxygen puzzle. Cut out on the broken simon-pure null and void vital spark lines. Paste it on great sea serpent unromantic snap paper. Print your ethereal sterling gist name, your vaporous in the flesh kernel age, your lifeless intrinsicality positive address. Color the whimsical seeing the light breath of life pictures. Use nonresident true-blue doings crayons, zero veracious inherence paints, or bugbear resident ego pencils. Mail before chimerical energy midnight Tuesday to this airy on the spot the world paper. Castle in Spain substantial go entries become ours. Intellectual veritable intrinsicality neatness, missing moored matters accuracy, and nowhere in the flesh immanence presentation count. Decision of the wanting authentic vim judges is final. Winners are nothing at all. You get a yam, a rail, a tag, a charm, a set, a bet, a man, a bed, a rub, a run, twenty-four in default of on the spot matters matchbox models all metal made in faithful omitted respiration England, an absent at anchor pitch barrel of vaporous vegetating vitalization monkeys, thirty free exact extinct existence toys, three blank blind essential animation mice, new gauge in fact ideal activity realistic train sets, growing Sally the sterling bereft of life heart doll that grows, six vacuous unromantic dash power-pack snap-track sets of dead verve trains, twenty-five free zero pure revival boxes of color veracious no more matters pencils in twelve current melted away oxygen colors, and twenty-four nightmare undisguised gist figures in four boxed unborn well founded snap sets of elsewhere absolute heart and soul British soldiers; all from the fictitious in reality the world world's leading creation of the brain on the spot indwelling puzzlemaker.

1976

Sonnet

Beauty of songs your absence I should not show
How artfully I love you, can you love me?
Let's be precise let's abdicate decorum
You come around you often stay you hit home

Now you are knocking, you need a tylenol;
From all that comedy what will you tell?
At least you speak, I think I'd better not;
Often men and not women have to sleep

You've come and gone—to write the perfect poem
And not ten like men or blossoms, but I am profligate
I strike the ground for ruin while you sensibly sleep
And so in this at least a poem can have an end

How could you sleep, I go to wake you up
My Lysistrata, my unannounced rhyme

1989

Sonnet

A thousand apples you might put in your theories
But you are gone from benefit to my love

You spoke not the Italian of Dante at the table
But the stingy notions of the bedded heterosexual

You cursed and swore cause I was later
To come home to you without your fucking dinner

Don't ever return su numero de telefono it is just this
I must explain I don't ever want to see you again

Empezando el 2 de noviembre 1980-something I don't love you
So stick it up your ass like she would say

I'm so mad at you I'm sure I'll take it all back tomorrow
& say then they flee from me who sometime did me seek

Meanwhile eat my existent dinner somebody and life
C'mon and show me something newer than even Dante

1989

Birthday Sonnet for Grace

I've always loved (your) Grace in 14 lines, sometimes
I have to fit my love for Grace into either
An unwieldy utopia or a smaller space,
Just a poem, not a big project for changing the world
      which I believe
It was the color of your hair that inspired me to try
      to do in words
Since such perfection doesn't exist in isolation
Like the Hyacinth, Royal or Persian blues
That go so well with you.

Now older than we were before we were forty
And working so much in an owned world for rent money
Where there seems little time for the ancient hilarity
We digressed with once on the hypnopompic verges of the sublime
Now more engrossed in hypnagogic literal mysteries of
      our age and ages I propose
To reiterate how I love you any time

1989

First turn to me. . . .

First turn to me after a shower,
you come inside me sideways as always

in the morning you ask me to be on top of you,
then we take a nap, we're late for school

you arrive at night inspired and drunk,
there is no reason for our clothes

we take a bath and lie down facing each other,
then later we turn over, finally you come

we face each other and talk about childhood
as soon as I touch your penis I wind up coming

you stop by in the morning to say hello
we sit on the bed indian fashion not touching

in the middle of the night you come home
from a nightclub, we don't get past the bureau

next day it's the table, and after that the chair
because I want so much to sit you down & suck your cock

you ask me to hold your wrists, but then when I
touch your neck with both my hands you come

it's early morning and you decide to very quietly
come on my knee because of the children

you've been away at school for centuries, your girlfriend
has left you, you come four times before morning

you tell me you masturbated in the hotel before you came by
I don't believe it, I serve the lentil soup naked

I massage your feet to seduce you, you are reluctant,
my feet wind up at your neck and ankles

you try not to come too quickly
also, you dont want to have a baby

I stand up from the bath, you say turn around
and kiss the backs of my legs and my ass

you suck my cunt for a thousand years, you are weary
at last I remember my father's anger and I come

you have no patience and come right away
I get revenge and won't let you sleep all night

we make out for so long we can't remember how
we wound up hitting our heads against the wall

I lie on my stomach, you put one hand under me
and one hand over me and that way can love me

you appear without notice and with flowers
I fall for it and we become missionaries

you say you can only fuck me up the ass when you are drunk
so we try it sober in a room at the farm

we lie together one night, exhausted couplets
and don't make love. does this mean we've had enough?

watching t.v. we wonder if each other wants to
interrupt the plot; later I beg you to read to me

like the Chinese we count 81 thrusts
then 9 more out loud till we both come

I come three times before you do
and then it seems you're mad and never will

it's only fair for a woman to come more
think of all the times they didn't care

1992

JOHN GODFREY ▪ ▪ ▪ ▪ ▪ ▪ ▪ ▪ ▪ ▪ ▪ ▪ ▪ ▪
b. 1945

Born in Massena, New York, John Godfrey graduated from Princeton University in 1967. Since 1969, he has lived on New York City's Lower East Side. His books include *26 Poems* (1971), *Music of the Curbs* (1976), *Dabble: Poems 1966–1980* (1982), a volume of prose poems, *Where the Weather Suits My Clothes* (1984), and *Midnight on Your Left* (1988).

Commenting on *Where the Weather Suits My Clothes*, Ron Padgett refers to Godfrey as a "lyrical and metaphysical poet" in the tradition of John Donne and Robert Herrick. Like those poets, Godfrey makes use of a packed syntax and exuberant word choice, but in a way that comes close to surrealism—for instance, "the stones / of sweat resting upon blue velvet trance" in the poem "Our Lady." Padgett also reflects on Godfrey's "irresistible philosophical hauteur" and streetwise lyricism. "I seem to be a writer of poems that work on friction," Godfrey writes. "The words rub against each other like gravel underfoot. . . . I like a little phenomenology to go along with a little philistinism, just to keep things from getting effete."[1]

Godfrey is currently studying at Columbia University to be a pediatric nurse practitioner.

1. "This Thing of Mine," unpublished statement of poetics.

Our Lady

for Ted Berrigan

Complete with photomanic *stimmung*
undesired by hatchecks, the obvious
duellist, defiantly without gloves
awaits his hour throughout glib
detailed melon-hues of an evening

when the enemy doesn't satisfy
and vagaries lose loftiness

All of airiness is one room, unerringly still
Desire for an acquaintance increases
with discomfort, and at any torpid
moment you might misjudge the stones
of sweat resting upon blue velvet trance

for striated cleft ore looped deep
with heather, the always effeminate voice
in spite of our manhood
Blame our kisses but not ourselves, afford
us disdain by sheer compass of stride
where dreams and accumulations bed
with flowers that thrive under
insecticide veneers, repelling lunar
gilt—hence the fleecy groves on beamed
torso you hear us mentioning later
when a momentary greatness of description
rewards our straining nerves with
Her atomized refreshments:
a fleeting reverence that bares us
to no one else, her seductive plea
to which, sometimes, we add our names

1982

Wings

I come off a little bit ventilated
but you must realize the material world
is constantly crumbling under my eyes
it's too much for the novel tongue I speak
the glitter of pavement in my brainstem, you
must accommodate the polytonal grimace
of the set lips becoming a smile, and
you must accept the thin section of arm
advancing across your peripheries to grip you
in pleasure, measuring feeling in your restraint
We have lived through the most furious little
chunk of history for this? that we must
unburden ourselves on night roof air, presuming
the poise and perks of champ pigeon teams
planing the evening winds

until, signalled from the roof with a flag
we become American birds

1982

So Let's Look at It Another Way

Any woman who can give birth to God deserves, I think, a pretty lively dole, provided by God, however, not by me. I've got my own eggs to hatch, and my own coat to button in the particulate wind. Gather around me, streetcorners, and I will give you the avenue of your dreams! I will give three sharp coughs while your fingertips read that spot inside my hip, my pelvis tone, my sixth-story bone. I'll be here when the whole *world* shakes, I'll be compatible to cheapness and to achievement. I'll have ambitions on my mind and panties on my floor. I'll have tons of red paint on my black-paint door. And you know what else? I'll call it "killer monkey doing all this stuff too close to prayer."

So let's look at it another way. It's 9 a.m. and I'm walking west from my door. The only person on the shadowed side of the street, and the shadow is cool, is a thin girl with long wavy hair, hiding her face, which she holds down. White girl slinking where to the east? All night long turned to misery crystals by the Hopperesque walls. I beg your pardon, lady, on behalf of your trade. I see on you the marks your monkeys made.

Invisible monkeys blow into the naked eye, and dust big as rocks. October is taking place so beautifully, and when I sleep pain touches my hair. That's why I always seem to be running past parked cars, and past you whom I love. In some crazy way I am running for your pleasure, out of all the pleasures I could imagine.

1984

Where the Weather Suits My Clothes

Positively on my own again, heart broken so long ago I hardly notice. Romance? Totally gone out of the shaving mirror. The tricky part is when I am first willing to try better nausea. You call that sex? Here I am, longing for you, and you telling me I'm getting what I deserve. Other than feeling rejected and useless, I feel like it's the perfect day to play my street number in the triple. So I meet somebody for a drink in the Shadow of Death. They don't call it "hockey" in this bar, they call it "honkey." Uh-oh. You take the guy on the left, I'll take the guy on the right. Hey. HEY! Where you going?

So there's a hole tonight in daddy's heart where the vinegar goes, and the salt of my eyes meets the soft-shelled crab. My heart burdens the wind. Easy on the Mahler, I tell myself, or you'll wear out the tire pump. The only way I can fall asleep is to imagine that I've been too gallant towards you, and my witnesses are not exactly a bunch of car thieves. Bells and resurrection and Easter Eve mass—now . . . you . . . want me? Maybe I'm the only one listening to the bell that hears appeals. Its appellate jurisdiction is everywhere. It redistributes the shit even as it flies. Shit and wine and empty shrouds, how much longer can the woody part of the vine hold on? It's, like, cheating the wind of my times.

1984

WANDA COLEMAN ■ ■ ■ ■ ■ ■ ■ ■ ■ ■ ■ ■ ■
b. 1946

Born and raised in the Watts district of Los Angeles and a former scriptwriter for the daytime television drama "Days of Our Lives," Wanda Coleman is the author of *Mad Dog Black Lady* (1979), *Imagoes* (1983), *Heavy Daughter Blues* (1987), *African Sleeping Sickness: Stories and Poems* (1990), and *Hand Dance* (1993). She is also known for her dramatic performances of her poetry, recordings of which include *Twin Sisters* (with Excene Cervenka, 1985), *Black Angeles* (with Michelle Clinton, 1988), and the solo releases *High Priestess of Word* (1990), *Black & Blue News* (1991), and *Berserk on Hollywood Blvd.* (1991). Coleman has also published several works of fiction, including *A War of Eyes and Other Stories* (1988).

She credits her development as a poet to attending Charles Bukowski's poetry readings at The Bridge, a Hollywood counterculture gathering spot, in the late sixties. Because she couldn't afford to buy Bukowski's books, she would read them standing up in bookstores. In time, Bukowski's publisher, John Martin of Black Sparrow Press, would publish her first book, *Art in the Court of the Blue Fag* (1977), and serve as a literary guide.

Like Bukowski and Amiri Baraka, Coleman deals directly and often profanely with the burdens of poverty and race. In poems like "the ISM" and "Essay on Language," she offers a potent critique of social class, color, and sex, while spoofing the currently fashionable academic jargon. In a statement of poetics, Coleman writes, "Being from the southwest, Los Angeles, in particular, I am a minority within a minority within a minority—racially, sexually, regionally. Once being Black ceases to be the major limitation, being West Coast comes into play. My poetic image has been one which reflects the bleakness of the mad terrain in which I survive—the dog, the warrior, the warrior queen."[1]

A free-lance writer, Coleman is currently working with composer Tod Machover on an untitled libretto.

1. "On the Poetics of Wanda Coleman," *Catalyst Magazine*, Summer 1990, p. 37.

the ISM

tired i count the ways in which it determines my life
permeates everything. it's in the air
lives next door to me in stares of neighbors
meets me each day in the office. its music comes out the radio
drives beside me in my car. strolls along with me
down supermarket aisles
it's on television

and in the streets even when my walk is casual/undefined
it's overhead flashing lights
i find it in my mouth
when i would speak of other things

1983

Brute Strength

last night blonde spitfire Angie Dickinson beat steel-eyed
Lee Marvin's impervious chest until she dropped to gangland's
floor exhausted *point blank*

aunt ora used to threaten us kids with whippings
if half bad, she used her hand
if real bad, we got the hard wood paddle
if monstrous, there was the horsewhip that hung above the
        door
in the den. one day my brother and i were half bad
she gave me the glad hand and i cried
she laid it to him and he laughed. so she got the paddle
and he laughed even harder
in consternation she abandoned his punishment
he was more daring after that

and then there was my geechie lover
i once went at him with a 2 × 4 as hard as i could
i clubbed his chest. he smiled at me
i dropped the 2 × 4 and ran

my first husband wasn't much. i could take
his best punch

1987

Essay on Language

> *who stole the cookie from the*
> *cookie jar?*

this began somewhere

    suggest middle passage. consider the dutch ship
    consider adam and eve and pinchmenot

blacks think in circles she said. no they don't
i said it too readily, too much on the defense. of course
blacks think in circles. i think in circles

why did i feel it necessary to jump on the defensive.
    defensiveness
is sure sign of being gored by unpleasant truth

equation: black skin + new money = counterfeit

i keep going back over the same thoughts all the time (the
    maze
      poverty poverty poverty
syndrome oft times accompanies social stigmata)
    sex sex sex
desperately seeking absolute understanding (the way out)—
    black black black
the impossible (my love relationship wears me thin) i know

                    number one stole the cookie

but knowing doesn't
stop me from thinking about it—trying to be the
best i can spurred by blackness but they keep telling me the
best fashion in which to escape linguistic ghettoization
is to
ignore the actuality of blackness blah blah blah and it will
cease to
have factual power over my life. which doesn't
make sense to me—especially when the nature of mirrors
is to reflect

when a mirror does not reflect what it is? not necessarily a
    window,
merely glass? can it be something other than a glass? and once
it becomes glass can it ever be a mirror again?

              violent animal can't take it no more can't
              take it anymore from anyone tired of being
              one in a world of everybodies and someones
              violent animal you throw chalk against the
              blackboard rocks at reluctant lovers assault
              money-grubbing landladies with cold dishwater
              they're all against you in that paranoiac $$$
              prism keep trying to see yourself/reflection
              oooh black as swamp bottom mired in muck you
              violent animal struggle struggle struggle to
              get to solid ground get free get solidified/

              grounded

substitute writer for mirror, visionary for window, hack for
    glass

who me? couldn't be

(smashing is addictive and leads to greater acts of violence/
throwing things, i.e. the first sign of danger)

equation: colorlessness + glibness = success

i am occasionally capable of linear thought, stream of
        consciousness
and hallucinate after a three day fast (have eyes will see)

i'm much too much into my head. stressed. i can't feel
anything
below the neck

                    number two stole the cookie

he says he hates me
and i'm wondering what in
hell on earth did i do except
be who he says he loves to hate

equation: circle + spear = spiral

going down and in at the same time going outward and up

absolutely

this ends and begins here

                                        1987

African Sleeping Sickness

for Anna Halprin

                    even my dreams have dreams

                        1

four centuries of sleep they say
i've no memory
say they say they i talked quite coherently
i don't remember
four centuries gone

i walk eternal night/the curse of ever-dreaming

sing me a lullaby

2

my father hoists me over his shoulder, holds me
snug to him. i cannot walk
we move thru the sea of stars in blue
i love my father's strength
i love how blue the blue is
and the coolness of stars against my face
he sings me "my blue heaven"

3

i am tied hand and foot
astraddle the gray county hospital bed on the basement floor
my scream smothered in 4 × 4 adhesive
nothing on but the too short too thin cotton gown
above a naked saffron bulb in socket
nothing else in the ward but empty beds row upon row
and barred windows

i do not know why i'm here or who i am
i see my wounds
they belong to the black child

4

giant green leech-dinosaurs invade the city
superman flies to rescue but weakened by kryptonite
can't stop the havoc
the slug creatures destroy the city, ooze into the Sierras/
along my back into my spinal cord leaving a trail
of upper Jurassic slime

(it gets down to skin and bones, skin/the body's last line
of defense. when awakened the impulse to become—a
cavernous hunger unfillable unsated

                              bones/the minimal elements
                              of survival)

"who am i?"
the physician observes my return to consciousness
the petite white man with sable hair and clark kents
makes note. he is seated in front of a panorama
hills and A-frames sloping to the sea

"who am i," i ask again
"who do you think you are?" he asks
"i'm not myself," i say

5

the encephalopathy of slavery—trauma to racial cortices
resulting in herniated ego/loss of self
rupture of the socio-eco spleen and
intellectual thrombosis

(terminal)

sing me rivers the anthem of blue waters the hymn of
genesis

6

lift up your voice and

the tympanic reverberation of orgasmic grunt
                    ejaculatio praecox
traumatized. infected. abrupt behavioral changes
            the vomitus/love-stuff

he watches me masturbating with the Jamaican dancer
whose hand is up my womb to the elbow
and starts to cry

the weight swells my heart/cardiopulmonary edema
doubled in size it threatens to pop

i ask the doctor why things are so distorted

"we've given you morphine
for the pain of becoming"

7

chills. sing to me fever. sing to me. myalgia. sing to me
delirium. sing to me. fluid filled lungs
i walk eternal night

in the room done in soft maroon warm mahogany amber
        gold
we disrobe to the dom-dom-dom a heady blues suite

i pity the man his 4-inch penis
then am horrified as it telescopes upward becoming a
2-quart bottle of Coca-Cola

i talk quite coherently they say

8

fucking in the early dark of evening
mid-stroke he's more interested in being overheard
i go back into my trance as we resume the
6 o'clock news

the car won't start. the mechanic is drunk
i can't break his snore. the engine whines sputters
clunks shutters in the uncanny stillness
they're coming for me. i've got to escape
angry, i lash out at the steering wheel, strike
my somnambulate lover in his chest
he jumps out of bed yelling
"what's wrong?"

the curse of ever-dreaming

sing to me, i say. sing to me of rivers

1990

ANDREI CODRESCU ▪ ▪ ▪ ▪ ▪ ▪ ▪ ▪ ▪ ▪ ▪ ▪ ▪
b. 1946

Andrei Codrescu was born in Sibiu, Romania, and moved to the United States in 1966. His first book, *License to Carry a Gun* (1970), written under the influence of surrealism and the Portuguese poet Fernando Pessoa, adopted three poetic personae for as many sections: a black Puerto Rican imprisoned for an unspecified crime, an ex-beatnik who's become a mystical Fascist in Vietnam, and a young woman who lives on the Lower East Side.

His other poetry collections include *Selected Poems 1970–1980* (1983), *Comrade Past & Mister Present* (1986), and *Belligerence* (1991). Codrescu has also published the autobiography *The Life and Times of an Involuntary Genius* (1975), a radical critique of the post–iron curtain world, *The Disappearance of the Outside* (1989), and *Road Scholar* (1993), based on his documentary journey across America.

Codrescu's poetry and cultural criticism have a strong satirical vein that blends a sardonic, distinctly Eastern European sensibility with the outrageous gestures of the Dadaist poets. The 1918 words of Dada founder Tristan Tzara, like Codrescu a Romanian Jew who emigrated to the West, could just as well have been spoken by Andrei Codrescu today: "Art needs an operation. Art is a pretension encouraged by the timidity of the urinary tract, hysteria born in a studio."[1] Codrescu's European vanguardism is subtly blended, however, with the more American idiom of Walt Whitman, the Beat poets, and New York poet Ted Berrigan, whom Codrescu refers to as "a father." Discussing the "colonialism" of language, Codrescu writes, "perceptual imperialism wedded to semiophany march across the unnamed body—or 'to make neurotic' in the surrealist sense: unleash the fantasy machine, populate being with images, populate earth with schizobeings *(imatatio dei)*."[2]

Founder and editor of the literary magazine *Exquisite Corpse*, Codrescu can be heard regularly on National Public Radio's "All Things Considered," where he often comments on American culture from the position of a bemused outsider. Professor of English at Louisiana State University, he lives in New Orleans.

1. Preface to *Tristan Tzara: Primele Poeme/First Poems*, ed. Brian Swann, New York, 1976, p. 9.   2. "The Juniata Diary," in *Comrade Past & Mister Present*, St. Paul, 1986, p. 93.

Work

at night the day is constantly woken up
by exploding dream objects
until our days are tired
and collapse on our hearts like loud
zippers breaking in the middle.
i sleep in the daytime with my head on the piano.
i sleep at night too standing on the roof.
i sleep all the sleep that is given me plus
the sleep of those who can't sleep and the sleep
of great animals who lie wounded
and unable to sleep.
i'm dead tired from the work everyone does
ceaselessly around me, from the work the morning
crowds are going to do after they are thrown up
by the thousand mouths of toast and cologne
into the buses and subways,
from the work the plants do to get water
from the labors of beasts looking for meat
from the labors of speaking replying writing
from the work going on inside me with a million
greedy cells beating the shit out of each other
from the work of the sun turning around
and the earth turning around it.
i'm tired in general and sleepy in particular.
i have a great desire to move elsewhere.

1973

Against Meaning

Everything I do is against meaning.
This is partly deliberate, mostly spontaneous.
Wherever I am I think I'm somewhere else.
This is partly to confuse the police, mostly to
avoid myself es-
pecially when I have to confirm

the obvious which always
sits on a little table and draws a lot
of attention to itself.
So much so that no one sees the chairs
and the girl sitting on one of them.
With the obvious one is always at the movies.
The other obvious which the loud obvious
conceals
is not obvious enough to merit a
surrender of the will.
But through a little hole in the boring report
God watches us faking it.

1978

Paper on Humor

Everything sounds funny in a funny magazine.
For years now I have published my poems in funny magazines
so that nobody would notice
how sad they were.
Sad anthologists, however, took my poems out of context
and put them in the sad anthologies and there
they started to shine with tears because
they were the saddest poems in there.
With a liking for funnies
and a following of sadness followers
I arrive in Brazil to get my prize.
The prize consists of the cross, the guillotine
and the hot pepper.
I am collected. Nothing matters to me.

1980

Circle Jerk

Nel mezzo del camino I found myself
in the middle class
looking at two diverging options:
ideology and addiction.
My triumph is to practice both.
Revirginate or Perish!
Learn how to read to trees!
(You never know who might be listening
when the class enemy is in the class.)
Can he be that hombre
who walks into town
followed by a slow caravan

of Toyota vans laden
with empty mail sacks
ready to BUY EVERYTHING?
The shelves, the things on them,
the stores themselves,
the clerks' personal effects,
watches, homes, mothers?
And gives them
whatever they ask for?
When this hombre leaves
the town wobbles like a great
plucked chicken
and shivers from cheap wind.
This hombre then sits
in on a card game
west of the Pecos
and tells this joke
to the members of the Cabinet:
An old Jew asks the Soviet
border guards for a globe
to see where he should go.
After hours of careful study
he returns it & asks:
Do you have another globe?
In the end we remember not the joke
nor the out-of-place place where
he tells it to the people
but the fact that we all detest living
through the adroit manipulations
of the small-print clauses
of our social contract.
Therefore you in the front row
wouldn't you rather
Do It Your Way?
Don Juan, narcissist
whose job is to upset order
and the authority spent
establishing it,
releases energy
teased into being
by his hat.
Once a man loses his taste for himself
he becomes completely unsavory: meat
spoils from within.
Others seep in through the chinks
and chomp chomp their way through heart & gut.
Two careless lovers are worth one thousand bankers.
The world is froth over the surface
of an untouched hard core

that first looks real,
then nostalgic, then Betamax.
I stagger from BBQue to BBQue
& never see sobriety anymore.

1991

Telyric

Stand here, says the professional TV person.
She shields me from the sun with a silver shield.
The nuclear-trained soundman wires me to himself.
"Had top-secret clearance," he says,
"Shut four years inside a sewer pipe. Bad only
when the dope ran out."
"Top-hat clearance?" I ask.
"Our army's stoned and theirs is drunk."
A geezer stops: "He somebody famous?"
He spits in the fountain of the Immigration
& Naturalization Service said years ago
to have been an object of controversy
capable of shielding terrorists
in the goldfish rolls of its Dubuffet clusters.
The British cameraman who shoots me is proud
of his T-shirt from which a Scandinavian
plastic surgeon named Tord Skoog
rises blankly from humble beginnings
to an obituary in the *Scandinavian
Journal of Plastic Surgery*, and from there
unto thousands of T-shirts
from Patagonia to Maroc.
My telyric self bends in the sun-
solitude of its large puppethood.
A window of light is in the dugout roof
concealing the new national hero of Nicaragua,
pitcher Dennis Martinez.
I am connected with wires but not to sense.
The girl waves her white arm with the lamp:
I walk to her across the narrows
of my TV-less childhood.
Go on, put on the shield.
I throw the first pitch into the sun,
my tinfoil trembles like Skoog's fjord.

1991

PAUL HOOVER ■ ■ ■ ■ ■ ■ ■ ■ ■ ■ ■ ■ ■ ■ ■

b. 1946

Born in Harrisonburg, Virginia, and raised in southern Ohio, Paul Hoover is author of *Letter to Einstein Beginning Dear Albert* (1979), *Somebody Talks a Lot* (1983), *Nervous Songs* (1986), *Idea* (1987), and the long poem *The Novel* (1991). Written following the publication of his novel *Saigon, Illinois* in 1988, *The Novel* examines the dilemma of postmodern authorship by means of found texts, parodies of detective, adventure, and romance novels, and comments on authorship's "invented self."

His early work was strongly influenced by surrealist poetry, especially that of Henri Michaux and Robert Desnos, and by John Ashbery's *The Tennis Court Oath*. The poems in *Somebody Talks a Lot*, *Nervous Songs*, and *Idea* (its title taken from Michael Drayton's sixteenth-century sonnet sequence) are more in the New York School vein of personality and eccentric artifice. He speaks against "a preordained pose of seriousness" in the writing of poems, favoring instead music, abstraction, structure, and what he calls "the generosity of inorganic form."[1]

In the early to middle 1980s, Hoover was at the center of an experimental poetry revival in Chicago that included Maxine Chernoff and Elaine Equi, poets whose work is sardonic, urban, and imagist in the manner of the Chicago Imagist school of painters. Hoover's poem "Desire" is about both authorship and the political realities of Tiananmen Square.

With Maxine Chernoff, Hoover edits the magazine *New American Writing*.

1. "Moral Poetry," *American Book Review*, Nov./Dec. 1984, p. 15.

Poems We Can Understand

If a monkey drives a car
down a colonnade facing the sea
and the palm trees to the left are tin
we don't understand it.

We want poems we can understand.
We want a god to lead us,
renaming the flowers and trees,
color-coding the scene,

doing bird calls for guests.
We want poems we can understand,
no sullen drunks making passes
next to an armadillo, no complex nothingness

amounting to a song,
no running in and out of walls
on the dry tongue of a mouse,
no bludgeoness, no girl, no sea that moves

with all deliberate speed, beside itself
and blue as water, inside itself and still,
no lizards on the table becoming absolute hands.
We want poetry we can understand,

the fingerprints on mother's dress,
pain of martyrs, scientists.
Please, no rabbit taking a rabbit
out of a yellow hat, no tattooed back

facing miles of desert, no wind.
We don't understand it.

1983

Heart's Ease

Near the curving harbor where pine trees father
there's the sense of a piece at a time within
the blurred eye of the whole, the sky a painted set
where joy is contemplating having no evident end.
A bog or swamp is hidden by the oblong lake

that stretches from state to state, pine needles paths
on ridges through neat sloughs imaging a heaven
of light and water fleas. Draw the bordering line
for which a blame is given. This plenitude exists.
A thinking is prepared as you pass long rows of trees

both sides of a window, and that is a way of saying.
A thinking is prepared for the reader who breaks
and enters. Lengthening narrows the series,
and I tend to open my mouth at the speed of such
a sum, revealing a new heroism where the system says

I AM, a scattered Adonis gathered. Fonder each time
dreamt, I had perjured myself in the Perry Como slippers
of rummaging through the snow. A shimmering chimera,
I had sat by a patterned wall amounting to a midden
while an image crossed the eye prior to the mind.

It rolled the center up, creating calm attention
from nothing like a mother. The hopeless spiritual
takes the name of rural, obliquely distancing,
heart's ease as a flower comforting by its name, that
dismayingly quiet child in that now crumbling town.

1983

Desire

> It is this stale language, closed by the
> immense pressure of all the men who
> do not speak it, that he must continue
> to use.
>
> —R. BARTHES

Five inches from
such eyes
snow the size

of a sentence
falls, shudders down
like light.

Then the light
king fades
and poetry's corpse

on the sofa sits,
swelling toward
the door.

Clouds in transit
feather brains,
operatic with desire

yet temporal on
the whole,
like gasoline

and fire.
"Containably romantic,"
the eye strides

toward desire.
It wants to coincide
with incidental

things, making
distance rare.
Exchange or

substitution
makes metaphor
aesthetic crime

in realism's mind,
painting "real
if nonexistent"

landscapes in
the man.
Containing words

and other clutter,
the body's packed
in lime

beneath the author's
house.
Synthesis is

its merit,
the unity in
scatter

coming on
like trucks,
though meaning

shits on that.
Thought ought not
resemble

that which it
endorse?
Rupture loves

the difference.
On the other hand,
intimate conviction

leads to
certain actions
final as

the night.
I can touch
you now

in sequences
of light
and words record

this urge,
but Chinese students
burn the train

and history knows
the difference,
swaying like

a train.
Tyrants' shadows
in its windows

strike a blow
on poetry's nose,
as if the future

might remember
"accident's practical
connotations."

The night
is blind
with tyrants.

1990

RON SILLIMAN ▪ ▪ ▪ ▪ ▪ ▪ ▪ ▪ ▪ ▪ ▪ ▪ ▪ ▪ ▪
b. 1946

Ron Silliman is a prolific poet and critic, one of the original group of San Francisco language poets. His ongoing long poem, *The Alphabet*, which now includes *ABC* (1983), *Paradise* (1985), *Lit* (1987), *What* (1989), *Manifest* (1990), *Demo to Ink* (1992), and *Toner* (1992), will eventually grow to twenty-six volumes. This strategy may have been suggested by the long poem, *A*, of the Objectivist poet Louis Zukofsky. Yet this is only part of Silliman's production, which numbered eight volumes before 1983.

Like Harry Mathews, Silliman has a preference for eccentric forms of his own invention. The book-length prose poem *Tjanting* (1981), for example, is written according to the Fibonacci number sequence, with the result that the number of sentences in each paragraph equals the number of sentences in the previous two paragraphs. Described by the critics Anne Mack and J. J. Rome, Silliman's book *Paradise* "is a sequence of paragraphs each of which was written in one sitting, with these paragraphs arranged in 'monthly' groupings, and with the whole comprising 'a year's diary.' "[1] Similarly, Silliman's poem "The Chinese Notebook" takes as its model Wittgenstein's *Philosophical Investigations*. Its numbered sequence, extending to 223 items, includes:

5. Language is, first of all, a political question.

In writing what he calls the "new sentence," Silliman frustrates the convention of the poetic line, as well as its political implication of closure. The "new sentence," primarily seen in prose poems, does not narrate like most prose fiction, but rather accumulates a collection of comparatively distinct units which, taken as a whole, produce a disjunctive mosaic. According to Silliman, "Sentence length is the unit of measure" in such poems.[2] Critic George Hartley asserts that Gertrude Stein's *Tender Buttons* (1914) provides Silliman's model for the form.[3]

Born in Pasco, Washington, and raised in Albany, California, Silliman attended San Francisco State University and the University of California at Berkeley. Since 1972, he has worked as an organizer in the prison and tenant movements, a lobbyist, editor of *Socialist Review*, teacher, and college administrator. Editor of the anthology *In the American Tree* (1986) and author of an important book of criticism, *The New Sentence* (1987), Silliman lives in Berkeley, California.

1. "*The Alphabet,* Spelt from Silliman's Leaves (A Conversation on the 'American Longpoem')," *South Atlantic Quarterly,* Fall 1990, p. 755.   2. "The New Sentence," in *The New Sentence,* New York, 1987, p. 91.   3. "Sentences in Space," review of *The New Sentence, Temblor,* No. 7, 1988, p. 89.

FROM *Tjanting*

Not this.
What then?
I started over & over. Not this.
Last week I wrote "the muscles in my palm so sore from halving the rump roast I cld barely grip the pen." What then? This morning my lip is blisterd.
Of about to within which. Again & again I began. The gray light of day fills the yellow room in a way wch is somber. Not this. Hot grease had spilld on the stove top.
Nor that either. Last week I wrote "the muscle at thumb's root so taut from carving that beef I thought it wld cramp." Not so. What then? Wld I begin? This morning my lip is tender, disfigurd. I sat in an old chair out behind the anise. I cld have gone about this some other way.
Wld it be different with a different pen? Of about to within which what. Poppies grew out of the pile of old broken-up cement. I began again & again. These clouds are not apt to burn off. The yellow room has a sober hue. Each sentence accounts for its place. Not this. Old chairs in the back yard rotting from winter. Grease on the stove top sizzled & spat. It's the same, only different. Ammonia's odor hangs in the air. Not not this.
Analogies to quicksand. Nor that either. Burglar's book. Last week I wrote "I can barely grip this pen." White butterfly atop the gray concrete. Not so. Exactly. What then? What it means to "fiddle with" a guitar. I found I'd begun. One orange, one white, two gray. This morning my lip is swollen, in pain. Nothing's discrete. I straddled an old chair out behind the anise. A bit a part a like. I cld have done it some other

way. Pilots & meteorologists disagree about the sky. The figure five
figures in. The way new shoots stretch out. Each finger has a separate
function. Like choosing the form of one's execution.

Forcing oneself to it. It wld've been new with a blue pen. Giving
oneself to it. Of about to within which what without. Hands writing.
Out of the rockpile grew poppies. Sip mineral water, smoke cigar. Again
I began. One sees seams. These clouds breaking up in late afternoon,
blue patches. I began again but it was not beginning. Somber hue of a
gray day sky filld the yellow room. Ridges & bridges. Each sentence
accounts for all the rest. I was I discoverd on the road. Not this. Count-
ing my fingers to get different answers. Four wooden chairs in the yard,
rain-warpd, wind-blown. Cat on the bear rug naps. Grease sizzles &
spits on the stove top. In paradise plane wrecks are distributed evenly
throughout the desert. All the same, no difference, no blame. Moon's
rise at noon. In the air hung odor of ammonia. I felt a disease. Not not
not-this. Reddest red contains trace of blue. That to the this then. What
words tear out. All elements fit into nine crystal structures. Waiting for
the cheese to go blue. Thirty-two. Measure meters pause. Applause.

A plausibility. Analogy to "quick" sand. Mute pleonasm. Nor that
either. Planarians, trematodes. Bookd burglar. What water was, wld
be. Last week I cld barely write "I grip this pen." The names of dust.
Blue butterfly atop the green concrete. Categories of silence. Not so.
Articles pervert. Exactly. Ploughs the page, plunders. What then?
Panda bear sits up. Fiddle with a guitar & mean it. Goin' to a dojo.
Found start here. Metal urges war. One white, two gray, one orange,
two longhair, two not. Mole's way. This morning the swelling's gone
down. Paddle. No thingdis crete. Politry. Out behind the anise I strad-
dled an old chair. O'Hare airport. About a bit in part a like. Three
friends with stiff necks. I did it different. Call this long hand. Weather-
men & pilots compete for the sky. Four got. Five figures figure five.
Make it naked. The way new stretches shoot out. Shadow is light's
writing. Each finger functions. The fine hairs of a nostril. Executing
one's choice. What then? Forms crab forth. Pen's tip snaps. Beetles
about the bush. Wood bee. Braille is the world in six dots. A man, his
wife, their daughter, her sons. Times of the sign. The very idea. This
cancels this. Wreak havoc, write home. We were well within. As is.

Wait, watchers. Forcing to it one self. Read in. It wld be blue with a
new pen. Than what? Giving to one itself. The roads around the town
we found. Of about under to within which what without. Elbows' flesh
tells age. Hands writing. Blender on the end-table next to the fridge.
Out of rock piled groupies. Hyphenate. Smoke cigar, sip water. Min-
eral. This was again beginning. Begging questions. Seams one sees.
Monopoly, polopony. Blue patches breaking clouds up in the late after-
noon. Non senses. It was not beginning I began again. In Spain the rain
falls mainly on the brain. The gray sky came into the yellow room.
Detestimony. Bridges affix ridges. On the road I discoverd I was. I
always wake. Not this. The bear's trappings. Counting my fingers be-
tween nine & eleven. Factory filld at sunrise. Three rain-warpd wood
chairs in the back yard. Minds in the mines look out. Cat naps on the

bear rug. Bathetic. On the stove top grease sizzles & spits. Lunch pales. In paradise plain rocks are distributed evenly throughout the desert. Electricity mediates the voice. All difference, no same, all blame. Lampshade throws the light. Noon's moonrise. Burn sienna. Feel the disease. Denotes detonation. Not not not-not-this. The sun began to set in the north. Reddest trace contains red blue. Metazoans, unite. Of that to the this of then. Break or lure. Out what words tear. One ginger oyster between chopsticks rose to the lips. All elemental crystal structures are nine. Helicopters hover down into the dust. The blue cheese waits. No one agrees to the days of the week. Thirty-two times two. We left the forest with many regrets. Meters pace measure. New moons began to rise. Applause drops the curtain. The elf in lederhosen returns to the stomach of the clock. Chiropractice. Furnace fumes. Crayola sticks. Each word invents words. One door demands another. Bowels lower onto bowls. Come hug. Sunset strip. Holograms have yet to resolve the problem of color. Thermal. This is where lines cross. Hyperspace, so calld. Mastodons trip in the tar pits. These gestures generate letters. Industrial accident orphan. Driving is much like tennis. Orgasmic, like the slam dunk. We saw it in slomo. Cells in head flicker & go out. Zoo caw of the sky.

Sarcadia. A plausibility. Gum bichromate. Quick analogy to sand. Not this. Moot pleonasm. Cat sits with all legs tuckd under. Nor that either. Table lamp hangs from the ceiling, mock chandelier. Trematodes, planarians. Featherd troops. Books burgled. Blood lava. What wld be was water. Bone flute. I cld barely write "last week I grippd this pen." Allusions illude. Dust names. Not easy. Green butterfly atop the blue concrete. Pyrotechnics demand night. Kinds of silence. Each is a chargd radical. Not so. Photon. Pervert articles. Extend. Exactly. Descend. Plunders & ploughs the page. Read reed as red. What then? With in. Panda bear claps. The far side of the green door is brown. Fiddle with a mean guitar. "I don't like all those penises staring at me." Go into a dojo. Mojo dobro. Here found start. Dime store sun visor. Metal urges worn. Only snuggle refines us. Two long-hairs, two gray, one white, one not, one orange. Spring forward, fall back. Mole's way in. Build an onion. This morning the blister gave way to pus & half-formd flesh. Hoarfrost. Paddleball. Tether. No thindgis creep. Tiny plastic dinosaur. Politry teaches just what each is. Cameroon tobacco wrapper. Out behind anise I stood on an old chair. Southpaw slant to the line. O'Hare airport bar. Sounds the house makes. About a bit in part of a like. Shutters rattle, stairs "groan." Three stiff friends with necks. Your own voice at a distance. Done differently. Monoclinic. This long hand call. "Her skirt rustled like cow thieves." Sky divides jets & weather. Far sigh wren. Got for. Bumble. Figure five figures five. Dear Bruce, dear Charles. Make naked it. Negative. Out the way new stretches shoot. A thin black strap to keep his glasses from falling. Light's writing is shadow. Rainbow in the lawn hose's shower. Each finger's function. Beneath the willow, ferns & nasturtiums. Nostril fine hairs. Stan writes from Kyoto of deep peace in the calligraphic. Executed one choice. Pall bearers will not glance into one another's eyes. What then? A storm on

Mount Sutro. Forms crab forth from tide pool's edge. Refusal of personal death is not uncommon amid cannery workers. Snaps pen tip. An ant on the writing alters letters. About the bush beetles. This municipal bus lurches forward. Be wood. Several small storms cld be seen across the valley. The world in six braille dots. Gray blur of detail indicates rain. A woman, her husband, their daughter, her sons. A pile of old clothes discarded in the weeds of a vacant lot. Time of the signs. Some are storms. The idea very. Borate bombers swoopd low over the rooftops. This cancels not this. The doe stood still just beyond the rim of the clearing. Writing home wrought havoc. In each town there's a bar calld the It Club. We were within the well. Many several. Is as is. Affective effects. Humidity of the restroom. Half-heard humor. Old rusted hammer head sits in the dust. Clothespins at angles on a nylon line. Our generation had school desks which still had inkwells, but gone were the bottles of ink. Green glass broken in the grass. Every dog on the block began to bark. Hark. Words work as wedges or as hedges to a bet. Debt drives the nation. These houses shall not survive another quake. A wooden fence that leans in all directions. Each siren marks the tragic. Dandelions & ivy. A desert by the sea is a sight to see. A missile rose quickly from the ocean's surface. A parabola spelld his mind. He set down, he said, his Harley at sixty. It is not easy to be a narcissist. Afterwords weigh as an anchor. Cement booties. Not everyone can cause the sun to come up. On the telly, all heads are equal. In Mexico, the federales eat you up. The production of fresh needs is the strangest of all. I swim below the surface. Room lit by moonlight. Words at either edge of the page differ from those in between. An old gray church enclosd in bright green scaffolding. Left lane must turn left. A dog in his arms like an infant. Each sentence bends toward the sun. Years later, I recognized her walk a block away.

1981

FROM Paradise

A SENTENCE in the evening. Today the boxscores are green. Tonight the boxcars are groaning in the railyard. The indexical items are not coreferential. Hollywood caenfidential. You made Cheerios number one.

Mock snow: white petals from the plum tree swirl in the wind. I was working on a different poem. The dark patches to the clouds' glare are all we have of depth to this sky. The shudder of laundry down in the basement. A small table in one corner of the kitchen. White petals from the plum tree twirl in the wind. I slip in a pair of diskettes. Don't miss the opportunity to earn Pediatrics Review and Education Program (PREP) credits on an hour-for-hour basis at the plenary sessions as well as Category I credit toward the American Medical Association's Physician Recognition Award. The stapler sits on the table. When in reverse, that car emits an idiot tune. I own not one photograph of my father. The

most beautiful of all the carpenter's tools is the level. Becoming identi-
fied with an inaccurate but provocative name enabled the Language
Poets to rapidly deepen market penetration and increase market share.
I turn the muffins over. Dot matrix. The rectangularity of windows is
sometimes a shock. Verse is not in crisis, Isis, but only the capacity of
academics to comprehend phenomena they cannot predict. Juju use of
slide guitar. One less wine glass. Westinghouse is the largest investor in
Toshiba. I'm just singing to the muse.

I was working in a different poem. Descriptions of daily life decay.
The idea of long words. A glare in the cloud rose, which we thought to
be the sun, calling it day. Still the clear memory of my grandmother's
icebox. Or that the washing machine with the ringer atop it would spot
oil on the linoleum floor. So writing a poem *is* different from kissing a
baby's tush. A complex series of perpendiculars leading to the second
floor. Short fat bird in the plum tree whistles.

The poem is thinking (white cat chews grass). You only had a bowl of
cereal one hour ago. The bruise I don't remember getting. The entropy
of later life mocks symmetry. By leasing out the technology and buying
back its products for assemblage into full computer systems, IBM
avoids any investment in manufacturing plants whatsoever, and is thus
free to move its capital as labor market conditions shift. Rhymes with
theft. As for we who live to be astonied, basil makes the pesto. Yet as
USA Today makes clear, condensare is not itself sufficient for dichtung.
The shape of the alphabet is itself a system: poem composed in sym-
metrical letters. Glass in the drying rack turned upside down. Self-
gentrification. Orthodox Marxology requires antacid. Adorno escapes
Frankfort, locating in Manhattan, whereupon is declared the New York
School. Two prostitutes on a day off visit the zoo. An old wicker hamper
is repainted green. The female cop tucks her hair beneath her cap. In a
crowded department store I get nauseous and disoriented, buying
wildly. Peter's criticism gets around. My one goal is a clear mind—right
now! Geographic isolation enables the Huichol to resist acculturation
into the increasingly Europeanized daily life of modern Mexico. The
baby sucks at the full breast. The March sun. The snail clings to the kale
leaf. The neighbor's cat bounds from porch to porch like a rabbit.
Mountains of clouds from over the sea. First the plum tree blossoms,
then come the leaves. Subtlety is not instinctive. At the instant of or-
gasm you roll your eyes.

The difference between eggs and chairs, fat happy baby, is how the
cat sleeps: light drizzle. I lean forward and then the words focus. Be-
neath the leaf the trunk of the plant stood in the moist earth gathered in
a pot atop a saucer on the desk. The point at which you simply start
piling books for want of room. Mom sends photos of my brother's new
son. The oven is our only heat. A small child runs to the bus in the rain.

Sometimes I come home from work so tired that I don't know
whether to cry or throw up or lie on the floor, shaking.

The slope is called the fall line and you proceed up hill with your skis
perpendicular to it. In the cabin, the cubicles are like small jail cells
composed of wood. The cross country instructor has decided which girl
for the weekend. I don't mean woman. Snowblind.

Big slow jet, low over the horizon. Her eyes on me wide and brown. There is no pain equal to the memory of pain. I'm impatient that each word takes so long to write. As when, in the newspaper, an article on how to ride a camel brings tears. All cotton pleated chino twills. My life is not your symbol. Historians eke rhyme from fact. Aka will, verb transitive. Remember the days when Bob smoked dope *all* the time? Well, Masanori Murakami has been released. You're a commie, too.

———

DEEP IN GENITAL SOUP (a new page). Fiscal to the wall. Metahistorical, the roofers mock up a pulley reaching down to the smoking tar heater. The sidewalk is the sum of its stains. A big dog in a parked car. The relative lope of different joggers. The penis is not a lollipop. A theory of how you pack foods into a paper bag. Later, a student invokes the principle of insertion. Metahysterical, the woofers fuck up a volley (bleaching down).

"Write in any state of mind," says a poet who doesn't need a job. Letter perfect. Two friends, young Vietnamese women, spent the afternoon going from massage parlor to massage parlor seeking employment. Little amber rectangle—when the cursor falls over a letter, the grapheme is figured in reverse. Your name here. Main frame joystick. The frog arrives safely at the screen top. Korean Air Lines flight 007 is missing and presumed down. A man such as J.D. Tippet. The burns on my father's body. Her lips move as she reads the book. First Max, then Ruben. If this is a narrative, it is driving me wild.

She sits silently during the meeting, addressing envelopes. Pipecutter. Black ant on red jellybean on the gray walk. Old coffee cans painted white now are flowerpots in a row on the porch. To try and tell a story is to make a purgatory of the real. A child in one arm while the other drags a wire cart of laundry. The dull half-sun of a partly cloudy morning.

What *is* morning? A cat. Fed. Curls up on a kitchen chair. Sedative sunlight. Gauzy room. All the books written to be read on the way into work.

These words are no more in your mouth than in my hand. He sat on the steps behind the house. Shed roof stained by the juice of plums. Vowels passive in the face of a consonant. Great torque in a cat spine. Spy against spy: the post-Ted ego stakes heat up. I see her at the reading, head down, eyes shut, each hand clenched in a fist. Bottle of soda water. Even after a revolution struggle would be constant. People forget to read the bulletin board closely. So many drawers in the house are open, cupboard doors ajar. Masturbating, I think of you. I can barely wait to take my shoes off. A small blue dish filled with white sugar. Gradually the fallen leaves settle into dust. Medicated sugarless cough lozenge.

Vowels balance, a form of valence. A characteristic rhythm to the sentence. The asymmetry of one's face. No eyes more foreign than those in the mirror. It's going to be a hot one. Holding my nose, waiting for the sneeze to pass.

The bicyclist lies in the sun on the grass. Nearby, sunbathers lie on towels, listening to cassette players through headphones. In the distance Oakland is smeared in the smog. In a dream we lay naked side by side and we're no longer just friends. Paradise is garden. The city in the park. The city in the parking lot. At the reading she said to me, "You look different with your clothes on." A tall black in dreadlocks is carrying an ice-chest. The bee appeared to be doing battle with the cricket. Image of the plane distorted by the sky it flies through.

The town grew up around a lumber yard in the 1850s, which, as would not happen on the east coast, gives it an air now of being old. A dog stands in the back of a blue pickup. A Japanese woman is breast-feeding her son in the front yard, talking with friends. The sidewalk starts at Chestnut Street. It was a hot day but with chill gusts. A glassed-in cafe just like on the Upper West Side. Three teenage boys are racing in the shopping center parking lot. Between the highway and the coast comes Georgia-Pacific. Behind the closed door of Cal's Tavern came the clatter of billiard balls. The name of the bookstore was The Bookstore. The small parade turned out to be some sort of Portuguese holiday celebration, one high school band and four clusters of costumed marchers, moving slowly up what had once been the main street, its sidewalks empty. What looked like an old gym turned out to be City Hall. In the shade of the shack of the bait shop sleeps a yellow dog. An old man alone on the beach sings "Down in the valley, in the valley so low." My feet burn from a long walk. The sound of a foghorn, but no sight of fog. They went into Safeway just to get into the cool conditioned air. Two boys ask the old man what he's doing with a net and a bucket. He throws the empty beer bottle out into the bay. Dressed in black, a silhouette but for the white beard and red flesh. I tossed an onion ring to the seagull and instantly ten others flew up, landing between three and ten feet of my towel in the sand. My name is Captain Graysquirrel and I go which way the wind blows. The bed filled the motel room. At the top of the cliff overlooking the water was a small cemetery with picket fence and a lone tree. Overall, like the pattern of the sun's reflection off the water of the small bay. I was in the navy so I know something, he said. The boys took the bucket to hunt for dry wood. One white sail breaking the horizon. A small hawk out over the beach. The sand caked in the sun lotion and clung to the flesh. The gulls sit facing the water. They built a fire, a narrative. Under the bridge was the poorest trailer park I'd ever seen. It had brown feathers and a black beak. The waves were only the smallest curl of foam, a foot high, rolling up the beach. They had tin cans and cellophane bags which they filled with shells. The small damp stones seemed lovely. They were frightened by the old beachcomber but obeyed his instructions.

The bottom of the page is only a dotted line across the screen. A flock of starlings high over the valley. These are not facts. She stood naked by the window, smoking a cigarette, looking down at the scene at Broadway and Columbus, while her boyfriend behind her slowly pulled on blue trunks and an orange shirt. The thick smell of liver steamed up from his plate. The red letters disappeared into the gray background. The boiler room is referred to as the Chinese basement. These are not facts.

This was and now you are constituted in the process of being words, your thought actualizing through the imposition of this syntax. Resistance alone is real (coming distractions). Cross against the light. Leave work to write a poem and not mention the dragonfly. The industrial mower gouged more of the hill than it cut.

The madman stood on the rooftop, silhouetted by the full moon, pulling bricks from the chimney and hurling them into the street. You can tell by how tense their mouths are, the set of the lips, that these bus riders are on their way to work. Yellow tow truck. Long hair streaked blonde.

A noisy band of two dozen poets had taken over the subway station. Her hat was in fact a pizza-sized cracker. A bee had somehow managed to settle in the pocket of his sport coat. I was permitted to hear the work. My lip was swollen, disfigured. The crowd pushed onto the bus.

Like whales moving slowly through the depths of a still sea, the dark clouds pushed silently over the low hills. In the fog the hillside's green deepens. The shingled roofs tilt upward, notching the low sky. The crossing guard wears a red sweater with a yellow sash. Along the side of the house half-filled garbage cans sit in shadow. An old water heater in the alley. Sidewalk freckled with the residue of gum. I find Melnick eating by himself at Wendy's. A phone poll out of new wood. The sort of cardboard display you find in the window of a third rate travel agent.

Barking is not dead.

Nor that either. First rain. Seating chart. The cranes of the shipyard beyond the arched curve of the freeway. The crows in the gray sky. The crew on the loading dock takes a break. Verbs flutter in a still landscape. An old wad of bright pink gum hard as a stone in the gutter. The bus leapt the curb and ended up wedged firmly in the liquor store wall. The tip of his penis against the back of her throat.

1985

BOB PERELMAN ▪ ▪ ▪ ▪ ▪ ▪ ▪ ▪ ▪ ▪ ▪ ▪ ▪

b. 1947

Bob Perelman was born in Youngstown, Ohio, and attended the University of Michigan, where he received a B.A. in English and an M.A. in Classics, and the University of Iowa Writer's Workshop. In 1975, he moved to San Francisco, where he edited the magazine *Hills* and was centrally involved in the growing language poetry scene. From 1977 to 1981, he founded and curated the important San Francisco Talk Series, located primarily at the Langton Street Gallery, and edited *Writing/Talks* (1985), a collection of talks and writings from the series. The "talks" consisted of a presentation by a poet, during which the audience responded with its own thoughts.

Of the language poets, Perelman is one of the more overtly political in his view of consumer society. His satirical approach to the politics of language is evident even in his talks and essays. Quoting the linguist Noam Chomsky, Perelman writes, "Question: How do you tell a language from a dialect? Answer: A language is a dialect that has an army and a navy."[1]

Perelman holds that, just as Virgil's *The Aeneid* justifies empire, much contemporary poetry exists for "a sort of Monday-morning Emperor," the bourgeois reader, who can feel "in the exquisitely disposed syllables, the pain of repression that comes with the territory of world dominion."[2] Perelman calls instead for a "defamiliarization" of poetry by removing it from the comforting aegis of the oral: "Unlike the oral poet, who is reinforcing what the community already knows, the didactic *writer* will always have something new, and, possibly, unacceptable to get across."[3]

Perelman's poetry books include *Braille* (1975), *7 Works* (1979), *Primer* (1981), *a.k.a.* (1984), *The First World* (1986), *Face Value* (1988), the ambitious long poem *Captive Audience* (1988), and *Virtual Reality* (1993).

He lives in Philadelphia and teaches at the University of Pennsylvania.

1. "Words Detached from the Old Song and Dance," in *Code of Signals: Recent Writings in Poetics*, ed. Michael Palmer, Berkeley, 1983, p. 224.   2. The same, p. 232.   3. The same, p. 233.

Cliff Notes

Because the languages are enclosed and heated
each one private a separate way
of undressing in front of the word window
faces squashing up against it
city trees and personal rituals of sanitation
washing the body free of any monetary transaction

The parts of the machine take off their words and die away
in a description read to the senses
by the leftovers on TV that no one would think of eating
even in the very act of swallowing.

It's these "very acts" that we must
Pay attention to the flatness of the screen now!
For it's this very flatness
that the frailly projected containment of the humanized body
is designed to be pinned to
by, naturally, forces outside our control.

It can't be the knobs' fault because this is back before knobs.
Rock ledges, laurel fumes, sacred fainting spells
later on in the very pictures written, this is back before the
        alphabet
the pictures of the rocks in the savant's eye
he's chained to these pictures by the sententious wriggle
of the buttocks two classes down, whose owner
can hardly speak, can't multiply, and stands there waiting for
        Plato
to have Socrates tell him he's only rhetoric.

But, as we know from Aristotle, Plato doesn't know any plots
he can only give orders, dipping himself diffidently into the
material signifier at the same time as the ripples
he thinks he's thinking into their roundness come
back to haunt him in the form of crude jokes
about his square calves at unprestigious dinners.
In fact, he looks a little like that table he's always
using as an example.
Next come the Romans, and with them we first see the sky
artificial creation of scarcity of meaning
spread out over the proletariat as a visible economic ether.
You can look, but it costs.

We can still see traces
of the tracts where they lived
and can still understand their language
which consisted entirely of dirty jokes about money.
It's easy to clear away the froth of biology
with a few commands
to reveal the naked postcard of ageless windwashed marble
posing for recorded history.

1986

Let's Say

A page is being beaten
back across the face of "things."
Inside me there's a little book of no color, its pages riffling
as I breathe, a moving point, torn out
and I read this scrapbook of desire
let's not say constantly
asleep & provoked by the economics of cliffs, galleys, cartoons,
explosive devices patterned to look like adults
reading signs
casually, very fast
and in this wind, leavened by sun
or am I merely reading that
backwards, inside the restaurant where they serve the parts
by number, innuendo
and the you and the I spends its life
trying to read the bill
alone in the dark
big wide street lined with language glue

A page is being written.
It's fun to chew, to work things out
to close the damn book

to sit in the sand with a radio
no bikini no tan line no body
a dream matchup
you can either be in or out, no middle ground
the floor is sexualized, tessellated with little languages crying
                out speak me, squash me, love me up into one
                libidinous hunk of noise, you great big missing
                other, yoohoo, over here
and the finished word is an album of past pleasure
smoking out one last incomprehensible nuance beside still waters
that talk their talk
of which you are the noun
the one & only
and the model breaks, leaving
a nasty little landscape which *you*
and the group of course
the other the slaughtered city the strafed farms
silently
in large heated buildings
the smell means money
and the classics are being straddled
a page is being beaten
O parse me, says the son to the so-called absent father
in a windbreaker by the lakefront in Cleveland
sixty degrees and a fishing pole
the breeze or am I reading water again

1986

Things

Reification won't get you out of the parking lot.
Nor will mastery of the definition of sounds
in the throat, the bottomless pit, out of which
these things which we, transparent, self-refuting
hold to be self-evident.

Glamor of the thing, childcare
of the name, where language
is a diorama, with the mortal speaker
licking the glass to taste
the quasi-divine intervention of answerable syntax

holding out an empty glass
for water, *New Yorker* poetry-water
New York Times rational apolitical germ-free water.
(Take it off, take any one little piece of it
all off.)

As Gertrude Stein writes
in language—the Riviera
of consciousness—"Thank you
very much," though what service
we the reader have rendered . . .

And who is this "they"
who have terrorized all sentient let's not say "beings"
with the plurality of their buildings
the notions in their texts set up
to test you & me (proud little ones & twos)?

Who are they who so greyly
evade address, preferring instead
to throng the stadiums and airwaves
and glacial showrooms with their incessant
economic comeon/putdowns of the you/I person/psychopath state-
                squashed figurines
with our looks that could kill and in fact
do kill but never them.

Thence come the crooked smokes
of our psychodramas, which they relish
like the notes of the *Goldberg Variations*
whole histories pounded into simple binaries for lunch
Bovary/non-Bovary, with no calories because no body
you've got that one, and I've got *this* one
and the city doesn't fit in the eye.

So one, sad triste morte
goes all the way home to zero
with its blinding simile reflecting the furniture
off the original digit standing there
back in the frozen reified narrative of the parking lot
a past you can count on
safest investment
without things to get in the way
of the simple law of outward push.

                             1986

Chronic Meanings

The single fact is matter.
Five words can say only.
Black sky at night, reasonably.
I am, the irrational residue.

Blown up chain link fence.
Next morning stronger than ever.
Midnight the pain is almost.
The train seems practically expressive.

A story familiar as a.
Society has broken into bands.
The nineteenth century was sure.
Characters in the withering capital.

The heroic figure straddled the.
The clouds enveloped the tallest.
Tens of thousands of drops.
The monster struggled with Milton.

On our wedding night I.
The sorrow burned deeper than.
Grimly I pursued what violence.
A trap, a catch, a.

Fans stand up, yelling their.
Lights go off in houses.
A fictional look, not quite.
To be able to talk.

The coffee sounds intriguing but.
She put her cards on.
What had been comfortable subjectivity.
The lesson we can each.

Not enough time to thoroughly.
Structure announces structure and takes.
He caught his breath in.
The vista disclosed no immediate.

Alone with a pun in.
The clock face and the.
Rock of ages, a modern.
I think I had better.

Now this particular mall seemed.
The bag of groceries had.
Whether a biographical junkheap or.
In no sense do I.

These fields make me feel.
Mount Rushmore in a sonnet.
Some in the party tried.
So it's not as if.

That always happened until one.
She spread her arms and.
The sky if anything grew.
Which left a lot of.

No one could help it.
I ran farther than I.
That wasn't a good one.
Now put down your pencils.

They won't pull that over.
Standing up to the Empire.
Stop it, screaming in a.
The smell of pine needles.

Economics is not my strong.
Until one of us reads.
I took a breath, then.
The singular heroic vision, unilaterally.

Voices imitate the very words.
Bed was one place where.
A personal life, a toaster.
Memorized experience can't be completely.

The impossibility of the simplest.
So shut the fucking thing.
Now I've gone and put.
But that makes the world.

The point I am trying.
Like a cartoon worm on.
A physical mouth without speech.
If taken to an extreme.

The phone is for someone.
The next second it seemed.
But did that really mean.
Yet Los Angeles is full.

Naturally enough I turn to.
Some things are reversible, some.
You don't have that choice.
I'm going to Jo's for.

Now I've heard everything, he.
One time when I used.
The amount of dissatisfaction involved.
The weather isn't all it's.

You'd think people would have.
Or that they would invent.
At least if the emotional.
The presence of an illusion.

Symbiosis of home and prison.
Then, having become superfluous, time.
One has to give to.
Taste: the first and last.

I remember the look in.
It was the first time.
Some gorgeous swelling feeling that.
Success which owes its fortune.

Come what may it can't.
There are a number of.
But there is only one.
That's why I want to.

1993

NATHANIEL MACKEY ▪ ▪ ▪ ▪ ▪ ▪ ▪ ▪ ▪ ▪ ▪

b. 1947

Nathaniel Mackey's poems often draw on African rituals and folk wisdom and the rhythms and repetitions of jazz. In his essay "Sound and Sentiment, Sound and Symbol," Mackey writes, "Poetic language is language owning up to being an orphan, to its tenuous relationship with the things it ostensibly refers to. This is why in Kaluli myth [of Papua New Guinea] the origin of music is also the origin of poetic language."[1]

Legba, the Haitian *loa*, or god, is Mackey's figure of the poet-priest: "Legba walks with a limp because his legs are of unequal lengths, one of them anchored in the world of humans and the other in that of the gods. . . . The master of polyrhythmicity and heterogeneity, he suffers not from deformity but multiformity, a 'defective' capacity in a homogeneous order given over to uniform rule."[2] In Mackey's view, Legba's limp is comparable to the "stutter" of jazz musicians Sonny Rollins, Thelonious Monk, and others.[3] In poetry, the "limp" of an experimental prosody suggests the song of the social outcast or orphan. The figure Ghede in Mackey's "Ghede Poem" is a Haitian voudoun god of mortality and sexuality who taunts worshippers' pretensions with the traditional jibe: "You love, I love, he / love, she love. What does / all this loving make?"

Mackey was born in Miami, and attended Princeton and Stanford universities. Editor of the literary magazine *Hambone*, he has published the full-length poetry collections *Eroding Witness* (1985) and *School of Udhra* (1993), a book of criticism, *Discrepant Engagement: Dissonance, Cross-Culturality, and Experimental Writing* (1993), and two volumes of an ongoing prose work entitled *From a Broken Bottle Traces of Perfume Still Emanate: Bedouin Hornbook* (1986) and

Djbot Baghostus's Run (1993). He is also co-editor of the anthology *Moment's Notice: Jazz in Poetry and Prose* (1993).

Mackey teaches at the University of California, Santa Cruz.

1. *The Politics of Poetic Form*, ed. Charles Bernstein, New York, 1990, p. 90.   2. The same, p. 100.   3. The same, p. 109.

Ghede Poem

> They call me Ghede. The butts
> of "angels" brush my lips.

The soiled asses of "angels"
    touch my lips, I
kiss the gap of their having
        gone. They call me Ghede, I
    sit, my chair tilted, shin across
thigh.

> They call me Ghede
> of the Many-Colored Cap, the
> Rising Sun. I suck
>   breath from this
> inner room's midearth's bad air,
>   make chair
>   turn into chariot,
>   swing.

> They call me
> Ghede-Who-Even-Eats-His-Own-Flesh,
>   the Rising
>   Sun. I say, "You love, I love, he
>   love, she love. What does
> all this loving make?"

> They call me Ghede of
> the Nasal Voice, they leave
>   me for dead outside
>   the eighteenth wall.
>   The seven
>   winds they leave in charge
>   of me sing,
> say like I say they say, say,
>   "You love, I
>   love, he love, she love. What
>   does all this loving
>   make?

What
does all this loving make exactly
here on this the edge of love's
disappearance,
the naked weight of all sourceness
thrust like thieves thru inexhaustible
earth, ashen odors of
buttsweat, hell's breath,
what
does all this loving
make?"

On this the edge of love's disappearance
the sun and moon of no worship
lodge their light between your palms.
They call me Ghede but
they
reverse themselves,
the sweaty press of all flesh, my fever's
growth, soaps,
alms.

And on this the edge of love's
disappearance
painted wafers of bread go quietly
stale beneath your tongue.
Your
throated moans attempt a line
you call He-Most-High, some intangible
thrust, one whose bodiless touch
you try to
approximate as "Light."

Yes, they call me
Ghede of the Many-Colored Cap, the
Rising Sun. I make the hanged
man
supply his own rope, I gargle rum,
the points of knives grow more
and more sharp underneath your skin.

My name is
Ghede-Who-Gets-Under-Your-Skin, my medicinal dick
so erect it shines, the slow
cresting of stars astride a bed
of unrest gives my foreskin the
sheen of a raven's wings,
the
untranslatable shouts of a previous church my

school of ointments, my attendants
keep a logbook of signs.

They call me
Ghede-Who-Beside-The-River-Sits-With-His-Knees-
Pulled-Up-To-His-Chest, the warm
swill of
thrown rum sloshing down between my
feet
while in my horse's face whole boatloads
of assfat explode.

Ghede of the Technicolored Kiss
I'm sometimes called and sometimes
Ghede-No-Knotted-Cloth-Gets-In-Whose-Way.
"You love, I love, he love, she
love. What does all this loving make?"
is what I say between two lips whose
ill-starred
openings give out light.

"What
does all this loving make exactly here
on this
the edge of love's disappearance, the
naked weight of all sourceness thrust
like thieves
thru inexhaustible earth, ashen odors of
buttsweat, hell's breath, what
does all this
loving make?"

On this the edge
of love's disappearance you sit enthroned before
an unsuspected dinner of thorns.
As you go down you
wake to see yourself marooned off the coast of
Georgia, captive singers in the Moving
Star Hall still averse to what hurts your
heart swells to encompass, a
soot-faced
boatman in the Peacock's house,
hands
heavy with mud.
Hands heavy with the mist of your
own belated breath, as you come up
you feel your mouth fill with graveyard
dirt, the skinny fingers of dawn
thump a funky piano, the
tune three parts honky-tonk, two parts church.

Yes, they call me Ghede of the Many-Colored Cap,
the Rising Sun. I make the hanged man
supply his own rope, I gargle rum, the
points of knives grow more and more
sharp underneath your
skin.

My name is Ghede-Who-Gets-Under-Your-Skin,
Ghede-Whose-Heart-Sits-Elsewhere-Shrouded-In-Dew.
"You love, I love, he love, she love . . ."

Ghede.
The name is Ghede.
The tossed asses of
"angels"
anoint my lips.

1985

The Shower of Secret Things

1

They ask her
what she'd think
if what she
thought was rock

shook and
rumbled like
hunger, if
what moved inside

the rock was
not its
blood but an
itch on their

tongues. And
where the bones,
what it was
they'd be, refused

its care love
quit its rattle,
while what
blood was in

the rock went
to their
heads (heads wet
with voices),

each its own,
each as it
was (the way they
were), beside

themselves.

2

There was a
man it seems,
whispered himself
thru his

fingers, a
cloth between
her legs, the fabric
wet from her

insides, her
ragged crotch, who
when she'd rise
would look him

down, or so
she'd say. And
this man, she says,
walks thru

her house, has
no clothes
on and carries
himself like her

Twin. Walks her
where when it
rains it not only
pours but

appears to be
sun. And burns like
salt the sand
does, and there

does a dance until
the sun cracks
her lips, the
cracks bleed. The

blood cooks,
drought lures
the "witch"
toward where the

bank they stand
on is. They
throw her in,
and that the river

wet her hair
predicted rain.

1985

DAVID SHAPIRO ▪ ▪ ▪ ▪ ▪ ▪ ▪ ▪ ▪ ▪ ▪ ▪ ▪ ▪
b. 1947

Born in Newark, New Jersey, David Shapiro was a professional violinist in his youth, once appearing under Leopold Stokowski's direction. He received an M.A. from Clare College, Cambridge, and a Ph.D. from Columbia University, where he later taught contemporary literature. There Shapiro made the acquaintance of Kenneth Koch, who was to remain a close associate if not central influence on his poetry.

Shapiro's first book of poetry, *January* (1965), was published by Holt Rinehart when he was only eighteen years old. It was followed by *Poems from Deal* (1969), *A Man Holding an Acoustic Panel* (1971), *The Page-Turner* (1973), *Lateness* (1977), *To an Idea* (1983), *House (Blown Apart)* (1988), and *After a Lost Original* (1993). He is also co-editor with Ron Padgett of *An Anthology of New York Poets* (1970).

Shapiro has been associated with the New York School, and the self-reflexiveness of his work suggests the influence of John Ashbery, about whom he has written a book of criticism; however, he personally associates his writing with the Jewish liturgical tradition of his grandfather, a cantor, and his literary heroes, Meyer Schapiro and Walter Benjamin. In an article about the painter and poet Lucio Pozzi, Shapiro calls for the "de-Platonization of poetry," arguing instead for the blurring of genres and breaking of hierarchies. "Poetry," he writes, "never masters irony, poetry is the present and constant mastering of irony."[1]

Shapiro is Professor in Art History at the William Paterson College of New Jersey.

---

1. "Notes on the Poems of a Painter: The De-Platonization of Poetry," in *Code of Signals: Recent Writings in Poetics,* ed. Michael Palmer, Berkeley, 1983, pp. 130–131.

The Counter-Example

As in Frege's luminous counter-example

Everyone is dead and we will come later in fugue
Or lullaby, according to the mistranslations

Putting ice on the dying woman's lips
Macadam bond is another title

You did not want to paint twisting life in red points
But randomly following the paper, you twisted the lines

Distorted as a man following a dolphin
struggling not to surface but diving to drown

in a drifting wet imperturbability

    The morning star is not the evening star

To the mortal beloved
and to the one of real music

eyes closed always on the world
Poor air, I pull you over me to warm this cold light

But what is closure when we are so open
And what is lack of closure when we are so close

           1983

Commentary Text Commentary Text Commentary Text

    In the morning, the water fed the sky,
Eyes of another material had been inserted and the hair,
              gathered into high strands, more carefully
  arranged.
Two more bodies were discovered in the Spanish
forest fire.
Sky like sand, sand like a body
Sun like a breast one faintly outlined
In blue magic marker and bleeding into the margin
Of its own sunny space.

And a stable bridge linking us no longer
August like autumn and the new encyclopedia
Nom de guerre: Nothing.

Nonobservance, nonappearance, noncompletion.

Like the bright male cardinal on the red maple

No man's land and no mistake. No wonder.
Noah's ark nocturne.
Inferno black Purgatorio matte grey Paradise is almost white
Present I flee you
Absent I have you
Your name like landscape written across the middle of the page

1983

A Realistic Bar and Grill

The play is one paragraph;
the performance is something else.
Would you be interested in seeing
         the play?
So we descended to meet
In the old opinions
Having given up nothing
Clothed in Joseph's serape
Stepping on a nonreferential ladder
Each rungless rung
The gentle cobra is dead
Everything that is me would rush
         up and meet you
Like the front of a subway
Rushing into a cave painting
The body is constantly going wrong
A mountain is social, but political
         I don't know
Like the library of "I don't know" books
He was always translating the *Oresteia*
         in three accents
Unjustly abused
As before unjustly celebrated
It wasn't the lionization
         of John Clare
Nothing naive and negative
Just air and pomp
Pomp and circumstance and
         circumstantial air
Shelley was a fire balloon
Or Shelley was a fire balloon lover
The first is launched among
         mountains
And the second drowns in
         a dull historic terrain.

1983

Tracing of an Evening

A man and a woman recite their dreams
In places of fear: a bell tower, behind the blinds, a bridge.
Snow falls on the phonograph
On architecture and poetry.

The prodigal has finished a visit.
The old man was watching from a book.
For so long the narcissus has rotted.
The floor is so far from the earth.

This is where nomads fall upwards
To say nothing in favor of physical pain.
One finds the ocean more transparent,
One finds the ocean more opaque.

1988

A Book of Glass

On the table, a book of glass.
In the book only a few pages with no words
But scratched in a diamond-point pencil to pieces in diagonal
Spirals, light triangles; and a French curve fractures lines to
    elisions.

The last pages are simplest. They can be read backwards and
    thoroughly.
Each page bends a bit like ludicrous plastic.
He who wrote it was very ambitious, fed up, and finished.
He had been teaching the insides and outsides of things

To children, teaching the art of Rembrandt to them.
His two wives were beautiful and Death begins
As a beggar beside them. What is an abstract *persona*?
A painter visits but he prefers to look at perfume in vials.

And I see a book in glass—the words go off
In wild loops without words. I should
Wake and render them! In bed, Mother says each child
Will receive the book of etchings, but the book will be
    incomplete, after all.

But I will make the book of glass.

1988

RAE ARMANTROUT ▪ ▪ ▪ ▪ ▪ ▪ ▪ ▪ ▪ ▪ ▪ ▪ ▪

b. 1947

Rae Armantrout was born in Vallejo, California, raised in San Diego, and educated at the University of California, Berkeley, and San Francisco State University. Author of the poetry collections *Extremities* (1978), *The Invention of Hunger* (1979), *Precedence* (1985), and *Necromance* (1991), she has been associated with language poetry despite being suspicious of the term, which "seems to imply division between language and experience, thought and feeling, inner and outer."[1]

In her essay "Poetic Silence," Armantrout reflects on her desire to use silence, which, due to the "media barrage," exists only as an ideal or aesthetic effect. "Words no longer come from silence, but from other words. . . . And there is the impulse to call a halt, the impulse to silence."[2] In her view, the non-narrative, declarative sentences of many language-oriented prose poems leave little room for the experience of silence. Her approach to composition associates things more in clusters than in (narrative) lines. These associations are "neither transparent and direct nor arbitrary, but somewhere in between. . . . Doubt and choice can coexist in the reader's mind. For me this better corresponds to the character of experience."[3]

Armantrout teaches at the University of California, San Diego.

1. "Why Don't Women Do Language-Oriented Writing?" in *In the American Tree*, ed. Ron Silliman, Orono, 1986, p. 546.   2. *Writing/Talks*, ed. Bob Perelman, Carbondale, 1985, p. 31.   3. "Chains," *Poetics Journal*, No. 5, May 1985, p. 94.

Necromance

Poppy under a young
pepper tree, she thinks.
The Siren always sings
like this. Morbid
glamor of the singular.
Emphasizing correct names
as if making amends.

Ideal
republic of the separate
dust motes
afloat in abeyance.
Here the sullen
come to see their grudge
as pose, modelling.

The flame trees tip themselves
with flame.
But in that land
men prized
virginity. She washed
dishes in a black liquid

with islands of froth—
and sang.

Couples lounge
in slim, fenced yards
beside the roar
of a freeway. Huge pine
a quarter-mile off
floats. Hard to say where
this occurs.

Third dingy
bird-of-paradise
from right. Emphatic
precision
is revealed as
hostility. It is
just a bit further.

The mermaid's
privacy.

1991

Language of Love

There were distinctive
dips and shivers
in the various foliage,
syncopated,
almost cadenced in the way
that once made him invent
"understanding."

.

Now the boss could say
"parameters"
and mean something
like "I'll pinch."

By repeating the gesture exactly
the woman awakened
an excited suspicion
in the infant.

When he awakened
she was just returning from
one of her little trips.

It's common to confuse
the distance
with flirtation:
that expectant solemnity
which seems to invite a kiss.

·

He stroked her carapace
with his claw.

They had developed a code
in which each word appeared to refer
to some abdicated function.

Thus, in a department store,
Petite Impressions might neighbor
Town Square.

But he exaggerated it
by mincing
words like "micturition,"
setting scenes
in which the dainty lover
would pretend to leave.

·

Was it sadness or fear?
He still wasn't back.
The act of identification,
she recognized,
was *always* a pleasure,
but this lasting difference
between sense and recognition
made her unhappy

or afraid.
Once she was rewarded
by the beams
of headlights flitting
in play.

1991

Attention

Ventriloquy
is the mother tongue.

Can you colonize rejection
by phrasing your request,
                              "Me want?"

Song: "I'm not a baby.
      Wa, Wa, Wa.

          I'm not a baby.
          Wa, Wa, Wa.

          I'm crazy
          like you."

The "you"
in the heart of
molecule and ridicule.

Marks resembling
the holes

in dead leaves
define the thing (moth wing).
That flutter
of indifference,
                  feigned?
But if lapses
are the dens

strategy aims
to conceal,

then you don't know
what you're asking.

                                        1991

MEI-MEI BERSSENBRUGGE ▪ ▪ ▪ ▪ ▪ ▪ ▪ ▪

b. 1947

Born in Beijing of Chinese and Dutch parents, both of whom were engineers, Mei-mei Berssenbrugge was raised in Massachusetts and educated at Reed College and Columbia University.

Berssenbrugge's poetry is based on an epic scale of perception which equates the movement of a cloud or a chunk of Arctic ice with the human actions and actors in the poems. This lends a democracy of attention to her oblique and often multiple perspectives, which involves the mental states of her fictive characters (alternately "I," "you," and "she"), her own shifting focus as author, and the points of view of her readers ("This is where they have concentrated you").

Describing Berssenbrugge's work as "fluid and filmic," the poet Kathleen Fraser writes that "Berssenbrugge wants the structure of experience to emerge precisely as the meandering/wandering intelligence delivers it; for her meaning arrives through sensation, the surprised juxtaposition of moment upon moment."[1] In Fraser's view, Berssenbrugge's voice "seeks disembodiment, a withdrawal of self-consciousness, a merging of perception and the elemental."[2]

Berssenbrugge's books include *Summits Move with the Tide* (1974), *Random Possession* (1979), *The Heat Bird* (1983), and *Empathy* (1989).

A contributing editor to the literary magazine *Conjunctions*, Berssenbrugge lives in rural New Mexico, where as a young woman, she worked as an associate of Georgia O'Keeffe.

1. "Overheard," *Poetics Journal*, No. 4, May 1984, p. 101.   2. The same, p. 102.

Alakanak Break-Up

1

To find out the temperature, she tosses a cup of water into the air
because it will evaporate before it hits the ground.
She goes outside and tosses a cup of alcohol into the air
and then she keeps looking into the air.

When her attention is discontinuous, this no longer means that she
is inattentive. In the same way, they can measure the plain, now,
although the plain and the temperature are vacuums her heat sweeps
across, even before she has turned.

When she turns, the ice she had been standing on is changing into
foam and is about to drift away. It rumbles as it is changing.
She watches it recede until it is a slit of light entering the brain,
because the brain is protecting itself against the light.

Here is the event horizon. You can focus on a cone-shaped rock
in the bay. You can make it larger and closer than the ice
surrounding it, because you have the power to coax the target.
This breaks up your settlement in a stretch of infinity.

Then you tie some string to a stick and toss it in front of you
as you are watching the rock. Then you keep drawing it back.
Sometimes the stick disappears in front of you, and you have to
draw it back. At these times, the rock becomes yourself

wearing soft bedclothes and with burned eyes.
You balance three horizons. In the same way you press down
on her shoulders and gently push the person into the ground,
which is constantly changing in the current and on the tide.

This is where they have concentrated you. All that time
you had been noting the direction of snowdrifts and stalks bent

in the south wind. Nevertheless, a storm can distract your attention.
Your attention becomes the rasping noise of a stick drawn across
the edge of a bowl at a party. It draws attention tenuously
from your fingers, the way your body starts to hurry in the wind.

This is where they have concentrated you, in order to be afraid
or in order to recreate the line between your mind and your mind
on the other side of a blue crack in the ice, so you can sit
facing each other, like ice floes folded up and cut up
and piled up against each other, and so you know enough to stop
as soon as you lose your direction.

Then, if you are on the ocean, with poor visibility, with no wind
and you cannot be seen, please go around the outside of an ice
floe, because the ocean has dust particles, which will sparkle
and indicate the direction of the sun, she says.

When you look up, you see a heavy frost has formed on the window,
which had been damp for a while each morning, and then would dry
up and begin to crackle. You pass the window. The ice begins
to melt and drops of water travel down the window diagonally,
because of your speed.

You take the window and place it in your mouth, and meanwhile
fishline attached to your red bandanna jiggles in the dark,
because you are losing consciousness. It swarms around the rag
when you look up at it against the sky.

The dashes you had applied so carefully, in order to record rotation
in the sky have been washed away, leaving milky traces of themselves
and of their trails, so your poor map is now a circuit of spirals you
can only decode into chrysanthemums, on a sleeve moving past cirrus clouds.

You are a blur of speed concentrating on heading in one direction.
It is the bank above you standing still, because you are being
held back. Sometimes in your path you see darkness that looks
like smoke. When you come to the edge of it, you realize you are
already veering away from it. You have to concentrate on the
dotted line of your lane, which is foretold in threes by the light
and ticks like a meter from your looking at them.

Sitting up, you think someone has been splashing water on your clothes.
Picking up a dash, which has become a warm I-beam in your hand,
you arrange them on a board, oblivious to the sky, because
you can conceive of yourself now, moving on the board or behind
the board. A square of the board lights up and becomes the single
headlight of a car, indicating another person.

If the gravity of this moment outweighs your knowledge of where
you are, that is pathetic. That is what makes the space above the

ocean so attractive, but you still know enough to travel in a
straight line through a patch of fog, and continue to walk when
you emerge, with some fog clinging to you, up to your waist.

Each time you forge an off-shoot of the river, you are hoping it
is the river. It is a little mild time. You see a row
of gulls lined up on the ice, their chests puffed toward the sun
which is the color of apricots on the snow.

You pass a man lying on the snow, moving his head up and down
and singing. At first the monotony of his movement makes it hard
to concentrate on what he is saying. The snow around him has
frozen into patterns of wavy lines, so there are luminous blue
shadows all around you. This is obviously an instrument for his
location which her voice is occupying. It is grating across the
pointed places in the form of vapor trails.

It is so mild, you are beginning to confuse your destination with
your location. Your location is all the planes of the animal
reconstituting itself in front of you.

2

Anyone who is all right would not be coming in covered with fog.

It is a pattern when it is moving. When it is moving collisions
of things that happen produce a wavering but recognizable image
that merges into the ground when it is still. It is a black diamond
that condenses you mentally as it collapses. It is a black diamond
on the ground, and the diamond is moving. Then it disappears
when you look at it, yourself having no coincidence.

The ground is covered with ice.

Many holes in the ice are glowing with light.
You could say one light is a slanting plank that interrupts the ice. It
could be a bridge, except where new ice is closing it off into a small
enclosure like a holding pen or a bed. The human shines through from behind
and below seams and holes in the ice. The human hovers like a mood.
On a molecular level, the human remains, as a delicate glittering accent
on the dateline, like a light flashing upriver, which can only be seen
by the first person who looks on it, because her looking is equivalent
to clocking its velocity in a chute or a tunnel to her.

She considers these the unconscious lessons of a dominant force
that is being born, and as it becomes, its being is received structure.
First ice crystals, then heavier glass obscures the light,
so she walks back and forth talking to herself in a white soundless
sphere past the trash of the village.

She crosses pressure ridges which form a fringe between old ice
and open water. And the ice responds to her haphazard movement.
The snow is moving about the ice, some of it settling, some of it blowing.
She notices certain portions are ice, while others are covered with snow
which is easy to make tracks on. And she is careful not to step on the snow.

Twenty miles of frozen ridges buckle under snow,
but when she travels under the ice, the ice would be like fog.
Inside the fog is a jail fire. Flames lure a quantity
of what is going to happen to her into equivocalness
by softening her body with heat, as if the house she is in
suddenly rises, because people still want her.

She prefers to lie down like a river, when it is frozen in the valley
and lie still, but bright lines go back and forth
from her mouth, as she vomits salt water.
This is the breakthrough in plane. The plane itself is silent.
Above and behind the plain lies the frozen delta. Above and in
front of her, fog sinks into the horizon, with silence as a material,
so she is walking among formations of rock. Once again, she can make
a rock in a distant wash move closer to her, where it splays out
like contents its occurrence there. Once again, her solitariness
can flow into the present moment, although she seems to know what
is going to happen.

This is an image represented by a line of ice slabs facing a line
of rocks. One rock seems a little heavier and darker than the others,
but for now, they are two lines of tinkling unaccompanied voices.

The rest can be correspondingly inferred, as a line of rocks
leading toward a distant mountain, as into a distorting mirror,
which once again grows darker and denser, crossing over into mass
for a while, before returning to the little saxophone repetition
with which it began, like rubble under her feet.

Still, anything can still happen. She is still unable to distinguish
one wave from another. This is her nervous system attempting
to maintain its sweep across the plain.
Everything is still moving, and everything is still one texture,
altered from sheer space to the texture of a wall.

The route-through tightens around the nervous system like a musculature.
It floats like a black mountain against the night sky, although she will
      remember
a mountain glimmering with ore. Then it darkens for her return.
The river branches, and the sea has become blank as mirrors each
branch of the river flows into.

3

Sometimes I think my spirit is resting in the darkness of my stomach.
The snow becomes light at the end of the winter. The summer
is an interruption of intervals that disappear, like his little dance
before the main dances, a veridical drug.

A wafer of space beneath the ice starts to descend, like
the edge of her sleeve across a camera lens. Pretty soon
the ice will be all broken up. There is no space left. You look
down on a break-up of little clouds over the plain, as if the house
you are in suddenly rises, to relieve the nervous pressure of light.

Twenty miles of frozen ridges become a lace of moss
and puddles too flat to see and which are breathing. Here is
a snowdrift that has begun to melt. Here is an old woman
talking about a young person who is androgynous, across a distortion
of radio waves, trying to locate you. She is only moving
from her knees down.

The snow becomes light at the end of winter. How ice changes
on either side of the boat is not a tactic. The drum is a boat.
The mail route is a line of controlled electric light.
They will scatter their clothes anywhere in this light. You leave
your shirt near the snow machine. It is the initial color on the tundra.

                                                                1989

Texas

I used the table as a reference and just did things from there
in register, to play a form of feeling out to the end, which is
an air of truth living objects and persons you use take on,
when you set them together in a certain order, conferring privilege
on the individual, who will tend to dissolve if his visual presence
is maintained, into a sensation of meaning, going off by itself.
First the table is the table. In blue light
or in electric light, it has no pathos. Then light separates
from the human content, a violet-colored net or immaterial haze, echoing
the violet iceplant on the windowsill, where he is the trace of a desire.

Such emotions are interruptions in landscape and in logic
brought on by a longing for direct experience, as if her memory of experience
were the trace of herself. Especially now, when things have been flying apart
        in all directions,
she will consider the hotel lobby the inert state of a form. It is the location
of her appointment. And gray enamel elevator doors are the relational state,
the place behind them being a ground of water or the figure of water. Now,
she turns her camera on them to change her thinking about them into a
        thought

in Mexico, as the horizon when you are moving can oppose the horizon inside
the elevator via a blue Cadillac into a long tracking shot. You linger
over your hand at the table. The light becomes a gold wing on the table.
    She sees
it opening, with an environment inside that is plastic and infinite,
but is a style that has got the future wrong.

1989

Jealousy

Attention was commanded through a simple, unadorned, unexplained, often
    decentered presence,
up to now, a margin of empty space like water, its surface contracting, then
    melting
along buried pipelines, where gulls gather in euphoric buoyancy. Now,
the growth of size is vital, the significance of contraction by a moat,
    a flowerbed, or
a fenced path around the reservoir, its ability to induce the mind's
growing
    experience of the breadth
and depth of physical association, which turns out to be both vital and
    insufficient, because
nature never provides a border for us, of infinite elements irregularly but
    flexibly integrated,
like the rhythm between fatigue and relief of accommodation, or like a large
    apartment. Now,
the construction is not the structure of your making love to me. The size of
    your body on mine
does not equal your weight or buoyancy, like fireworks on a television screen,
    or the way
an absent double expresses inaccuracy between what exists and does not exist
    in the room
of particular shape, volume, etc., minute areas and inferred lines we are
    talking about.
You have made a vow to a woman not to sleep with me. For me, it seemed
    enough
that love was a spiritual exercise in physical form and what was seen is
    what it was,
looking down from the twelfth floor, our arms resting on pillows on the
    windowsill. It is midnight.
Fireworks reflected in the reservoir burst simultaneously on the south and
    the north shores,
so we keep turning our heads quickly for both of the starry spheres,
instead of a tangible, and an intangible event that does not reflect. Certain
definite brightness contains spaciousness. A starry night, like a fully
    reflecting surface,
claims no particular status in space, or being of its own.

1989

LESLIE SCALAPINO ■ ■ ■ ■ ■ ■ ■ ■ ■ ■ ■ ■ ■

b. 1947

Leslie Scalapino's project has been remarkably consistent from the beginning of her career. Through overlapping narratives that often retell actual events with different beginning and end points, she examines the nature of external events in relation to the narrator's perception of them. Scalapino writes of *that they were at the beach—aeolotropic series:* "I intended this work to be the repetition of historically real events the writing of which punches a hole in reality. (As if to avoid them, but actively)."[1]

In the opinion of the poet and critic Benjamin Hollander, Scalapino deals in "the mutability of identity across time and place, and on how contiguously enacted histories inform, defer, break-down, and inhabit an individual in the present."[2] Scalapino typically makes her narrator a psychological actor in the experience he or she reports: "I am trying to use the writing to be an examination of the mind in the process of whatever it's creating."[3] Scalapino's formal influences, according to the critic Tyrus Miller, include "the ellipses of objectivist poetry, the grammaticalism of Gertrude Stein, and the typographical quirkiness of Emily Dickinson."[4]

Scalapino attended Reed College and received an M.A. in English from the University of California at Berkeley.

Her books of poetry include *Considering how exaggerated music is* (1982), *that they were at the beach—aeolotropic series* (1985), *Way* (1988), the trilogy *The Return of Painting, The Pearl, and Orion* (1991), and *Crowd and not evening or light* (1992).

Founder and editor of O Books, a publisher of experimental poetry, she lives in Berkeley, California.

1. "Note on My Writing," in *How Phenomena Appear to Unfold,* Elmwood, CT, 1989, p. 21.   2. Review of *that they were at the beach—aeolotropic series, Conjunctions,* No. 9, 1986, p. 272.   3. Edward Foster, "An Interview with Leslie Scalapino," *Talisman,* No. 8, Spring 1992, p. 32.   4. *Sulfur,* No. 26, Spring 1990, p. 222.

FROM *Crowd and not evening or light*

The series - 3

going on boats but
wanting to have
an entire - future - as being at
sea as a sailor, going on a freighter - or
freighters - as coming up to
something - through that, or being, my

people
living in a way that's Weatherman,° rebellious, in this
Clement - which they had -

°Weatherman was a revolutionary group active in the 1960s. [Scalapino's note.]

city - and that isn't later seen
by others - or done by them - here

continually -
it taking two - the pregnant ones, on the way
first
- with one who's not, going over on
her back - the penises from over their - huge -
bodies - one in her - with the other continuing
along

jeering - their - other's social condescension
always - seen from everyone, each other
and coming up to
something - lazy
- their, everyone's possibly, air

being a born again - which we're
- not - as reflecting
- series - criticism as
felt - of rebelling from
it, which isn't necessary - or
existing

rebelling from - series -
of feeling, wanting - born again
- as arbitraily
that - our with no impulse for such
flimsy - and so our - turmoil -
in their

      more - a play
      so it's not - a version - of
      them, city, the same as that - or
      a - or is - the -
      tradition

      wanting to - have -
      gone to sea as a sailor - a version
      or not
      and - as - my - turmoil, or peaceful
      - in their

young
prisoner, murderer - flesh on the hoof
from being
on the line because he's in prison - who'd prefer
to die by the authorities - a version -
so will -
but - peaceful - view

as if (we're) dropped -
from
a helicopter and hit the ground running - as the
description - as girls, or born - not flesh on
the hoof
from being - then

      if their then that - more
      a play - can't be, or
      as it's being social - isn't
      - a version -
      and while - being - a born again
      - though we're not

      a version as the
      real event - from oneself - which
      is done again - as
      necessarily

doing
something - that would be - an event, of
oneself - again - so it would be put out
- negatively - though actively - and
flesh - on the hoof

that
is the same as Rimbaud - now - but in a
very flaccid way - or the Weatherman
- that their events
would occur - or occurred
again

      the - very flaccid
      event - in the sense
      of only sensory - and sensation
      and that - turmoil - in that
      it would occur again

wanting to be
at sea as a sailor - and
not ever going to, or not having done
it - and stasis, or stillness and
- turmoil - together - at the same time as that
and as being - from - oneself

      so
      then
      being part of the avant-garde - is

- fine (for them) - and beside the point
- in the flaccid event - having
occurred - and - from - oneself

I haven't been trained - or
to be the same as their, others,
who're flaccid events - and not a born again
- affected - having to be entirely from oneself
- as that - negatively - so having
occurred again

      young
      boy or
      man terrorist - flaccid - having old rule
      that will
      create that action - and him - affected - right -
      negatively - not - by - his view

      valleys - only sensation - not as Weatherman, which was
      here - as - only - stemming from - old rule
      - work - of stevedores
      at the dock - affected - right -
      which - had - happened - anything

having
been
on freighters - with stevedores coming on
and off them - work - their
- which is not one's own - and which is from this person

      analyzing - feeling - why
      - as wanting to be at sea as work - and which is
      from oneself - not that in itself - and may be running
      amuck - which it does - or has
      - and is that

Flush

a play

Played by a man and a woman speaking gently and melodiously

living or having lived
on Ashby Avenue - wanting - doing so
to stay awake until there's light
traffic - where there always trucks,
cars - but by homes - trees

getting - in light
which is artificial - maybe 3 am - of
light traffic on the roaring highway - but
so where people live - middle

idyllic - of people waist out from
windows - of cars, in
evening, not on Ashby Avenue
leaning with the tongues out - nyah
nyah - but hanging waist
out from the car - to others on the street

    man running
    - pulling us
    in hot weather
    - with thick
    callused - wearing only shorts -
    bare feet - in crowded
    street

    not having
    a bicycle

blue sky
- dead subway trains
- when we were going by -
in one

man - carried away
in an ambulance, seen by me, on crowded street
but in the early hours so there's
light traffic - having died - which
isn't the matter

    where - taking care
    of oneself, not on the street - is
    a value - and - to - have a
    true love as well

    going on
    the subway - and - combination
    others, not in
    rowboard - and the subway, at
    when we were coming to Coney
    Island

time - for some reason - we're in
- of utter immersed
- stowaway, as not that - identifying with

him, rather than,
the stowaway - as mere - or being
others

                        man running
                        - pulling us
                        - with callused
                        feet
                        - having
                        no - bicycle

               a man out
               walking, a ways from a woman - but
               having decided to be jerking himself off when
               or rather, not being with her

        she may be mad - from the man's
        mere behavior - or not
        him - out - walking

            woman - I'm - comes up to
            him - flesh - out - anything
            - only, just, as movement
            - while they're standing - so they're only
            moving slightly - and
            neither arrested - from it being movement

stowaway - having fallen
from rowboat, in ocean - so only
as movement - not from being
having been - going - to the other
freighter - and as simply moving

        no - mind
        or - conceptualizing, and doing
        that - constantly - as simple
        - only, just, can be
        movement, in that

                    having no relation - to
                    others, work, from not
                    working - or some
                    having an illness - and there - being
                    - out - only, just, as
                    movement as well

            clouds scudding - blue - from
            driving - and - where
            there no cars - but people there

- or - up standing, not
having that movement

    and - rebelling - or not
    - from what - our - or seeing
    people - and as only, just, movement
    of us - others - as being
    or our really being that

    not to have anything
    - be delicate - their - or there being
    that, but constantly undervalued - as
    not being anything in movement
    - or getting a job

the man having jerked himself off - a
ways off from her - as
negatively
- as there were not anything
delicate - not to be so

        which it is

    which is - and
    the strain
    events - puerile
    - as there were not anything
    delicate - not to be so
    - and only in that

                      1992

BRUCE ANDREWS ■ ■ ■ ■ ■ ■ ■ ■ ■ ■ ■ ■ ■ ■
b. 1948

Born in Chicago, Bruce Andrews studied international relations at Johns Hopkins and political science at Harvard. A founding editor of $L=A=N=G=U=A=G=E$, the magazine of poetics that gave language poetry its name, he is one of the originators of the movement and a tireless experimenter and theorist.

His books include *Edge* (1973), *Getting Ready to Have Been Frightened* (1978/1988), *Sonnets—memento mori* (1980), *Give Em Enough Rope* (1987), *Executive Summary* (1991), *I Don't Have Any Paper So Shut Up (Or, Social Romanticism)* (1992), and *Tizzy Boost* (1993).

A professor of political science at Fordham University since 1975, his is a politics of radical dissent. He believes that change can be accomplished through a systematic disruption of the language. "There is no 'direct treatment' of the thing possible, except of the 'things' of language," he writes in the essay "Poetry as Explanation, Poetry as Praxis." "Crystalline purity—or transparency—will not be found in words. That classical ideal is an illusion."[1] Instead, radical praxis calls for "an infinitizing, a wide-open exuberance, a perpetual motion machine, a transgression."[2]

Andrews lives in New York City.

1. *The Politics of Poetic Form,* ed. Charles Bernstein, New York, 1990, pp. 24–25.
2. The same, p. 25.

Stalin's Genius

Stalin's genius consisted of not french-kissing: sometimes I want to be in crud. Your spats of visibility — o, crow fluke, genitally organized spuds, what can true work? Birth is skewed, anon., *capital; lose* that disembowelment; you must change it by eating it yourself: don't pick your noses, secrecy thrives on abuse. No, I don't mean the missile crisis, cat goes backward to suit international organization: middle class families want the belly choose
to obey authority — waddle into arson anything can be converted, the accessories get you wet.

   Most of life is just pre-school anyway; paste lives like that, money should be detached from the ego — creme, no sugar, no urine, like the junior mints of a previous century; I'm nothing more than a noise gate. Eat the demographics
into it is not enough, you didn't do it but you did it instead
I cheese my drawers, his creature comforts were redistributed. Business press is redundant — joint diseases fork up the land
gas administered keg
harp
keg
harp
make someone *else's* mother redundant, reductive, seminal perfecta: psychic powers look for work. Woman's place = sexual deviance, doesn't it have pockets?
Grow *down* instead, let's go somewhere fancy & be rich pigs. Beirut hurt in U.S. marine's body, we have breast conferences returning from the candy wars, wholesale corazon — we've made a culture that kills music wants a limousine with an Arab driver: to be accepted, use motherfucker in every sentence; in America country means white. Poignant plastic punters want all
get none
every alternative induces guilt, elevators will burn you; whose fruit do you want to melt? Reduce the rare, had to fight to scratch. We only drop the a-bomb on you if you're intransigent. Go eat your own root!

   Asset is putrid
harmony hotwire, an intellectual slug Vegas color red . . . and chicken electricians coughed that operate . . . derelictions of thumb . . . gee, I

thought fault, CIA Julie Andrews push-ups. DO MORE
Cardiopuscular elective compulsion, great fins. Like a priest boning up
for mass with rheinmaidens only tolerate prosecutorial information, it's
like saving string. Not that I know how to pray — trade the misunder-
standing for eggs — & whip the muthafucka. Thinking is a nice guy not
a growth industry, totalitarian means they have a higher literacy rate. If
you don't take my advice, I feel manipulated.

Show us whites walk: confirmed hard-shell on her wedding day,
mindless violence is always the handiwork of my teenaged son, auxil-
iary police in your mouth. Meaningful body movement usually indicates
a sick economy, quislings can just go annex *themselves*. Arrogance
ceased living — my beaver's now popping its tail. The nurse wiped the
drool from the alibi; too much flesh does not make sense. The lure of
awkward money, terrorists good-humoredly
experience is redesigned as complicity. I like publicity, backside hides
worse crimes — I think of documentation as domination, can't deal with
people who are precious & dead. Pepsi sleep while you weep I dyke my
Stuckey's, attach servant to pegboard. Contrabandistas Tequilero skins
and sticks perambulator.
Realistic flesh tones for a privileged in vitro few bluster douses crazy
kooks twit the parrot:
Biko
Biko
Biko
German expressionism lives in your wallet; clog my courts sent a signal
to my little brain, this uniqueness old hat. Every morning I practice
defending the canal zone
adjudicate your own spermatazoa. Fallout teaches us money burns, all I
can say is: Jessica Christ! — garbage in, garbage out, rest assured; fluid
can be a deterrent. Little more than words; self makes meaning —
fatter than margarine, I gave you an F — violations appear to invert the
power of the king; examples are there to deter —
nationalism just means delegate somebody else's self-importance.

1992

Species Means Guilt

Species means guilt. Slave ship somatism grease their wings wrencher
little pat miss dominatrix papal bull
is particularly unseemly for the FBI, negligibly robust video druids.
That's the thing about your poems, nothing but sex — sex sex sex reach
for wall same vista ugh trash lockout cloning derby. My structuralist
easter egg, prostrate angels — machines owl.
Stalin invented crisco. Argue better
chocolate makes us urban, spins of the spine — Arsenio, Chappotin,

truck rumbles into danger meister bed: are 'make it new' & 'make it even' compatible? If you can't get a stiff, get a foreign leader. Laser bugs, get it?
Endurance of eggs, so, whose leisure time isn't depoliticized enough? Let's rerecap. Make your first orgasm a demo tape. Well, don't malice shown; only the bold choose liver, ass what gender — can you pee while you're laughing? Helmets always fascism;
classical means what, fake sense of order? — give up the ghost as a rental property, blood gravy monarch: ballast
not strong suit. Or: who cares?

Marathon your mother; invalid baton. Pinochet fumbles on the side-lines, a voluntary hormone —
farce width, brittle thrusts, impatience is not an achievement
hell was less philosophical smiling kotex reconstruction; Flintstone burnouts. Tintype into the commodity form plans zigzag into blessings, meat cleaners in a house of ho. Lipread chevrons sheen-deep & unable to press the shift-key; I've got a little mood on.
You call off your dogs & we'll call off our talk bleach popular leak, to transform counterfeit objects into things. Do I have to be an adult in this garbage? Listen, the pink stains are heroic; arrogant obedient
remained as pure as Virginia ham clubbing and punching the marchers.

Suds down the dick in the outfield —
to get to the top, step on yourself. They blindfold you & toys come out: unquote
worming comma incest dunce, my coherence chained to the grass: Cuba will annex us — seminal chow, our body socket twists valve doth plead euthanasia mishaps. Diderot with a hard-on
buck crunch — no human has a history. Nobody accepts your excuses.
Eureka, the bond-holders — prefabricated
the decision to vacate the intestines, o islam semen trumps witch, grav-ity let them eat stock
face the squeegee modestly: midgets torch the lavatory. I haven't got anything specifically against Jung, stretch marks no authenticity
below which is. Me worry!

I was castrated for seducing the local tax collector's wife, including the First Crusade, girls' tailored kitchens vend our trash spoon accultur-ation, this clot goes crabwise. Don't eat your friends, dollies regret to creek; men were the first typewriters — apoplectic chickens . . .
let's fuck, or let's fuck with it
cipher banks on truth slump worse shit waterproofed horn guys
notice girls' goons ply the spit your lather litter funk. We face each other across the ballistic trajectory of the Arctic waste. Tripodless zoo direc-tors who look'd as if they'd walked out of an . . .
Abuse's buddy.
Banality jolts
duty rinse; pink brink can't beat much by the, fence walking with Mary

Magdalene — happy new yield! This is disingenuous twaddle. As raw as
bazooka invade the cake imagination feasts on spam.

I made an offering to the king's dead cod-piece, tunnel dogs choke;
heckling makes us prone to Republican . . . waste that self
defense budget drag queens, nice slow ham vacancy attracts a fuse.
Blue sprint humid as the lips are prone to non sequiturs, whiskey fits the
snorkel
low motion phonemes store our millennium adrenalin gaseous gravity
zero sum pop tarts
. . . delicate apartheid happenstance glee to pee force syrian weapons
we need: men are capital, women are the baby labor factory? Squirrels
are happy without our help.

1992

Bomb Then, Bomb Now

Bomb then, bomb now — doing the breathing arsenic job, we want
mouth-sized suburbs; yale locks running hot round-robin stillbirths —
politics attracts, income remainders. Resilver that hired fold — to make
sense out of, and its incoherence — is that too much to ask, 120 years
after we abolished slavery as a felony? That's a lot of crap, didn't have
the balls to dedicate
unfertilized ova are not responsible
so why don't we get going — we have a well-financed sense of our own
lack of self-importance — crystalline aerial grease being wounded: clo-
verleaf are obvious fictional Jesus locust, skeptical scabs put those na-
chos to work. Heart's career
is over.

Worm at random
& even noise
hot spit!, it was bootwhip — your spoon makes my sauce go run; bruise
to alert to the busboy disowning to be famous extraparliamentary scar
tissue
of the Marxist star, sick to me fat
that reannointed playpen, protozoas of literacy —
extra duck sauce. I'm not your jimmies factory; I pursue the vinylette —
my mouth noodle constitutive magnets to nauseate organized crime
brain's mediocre subsidiary, jugular respect — raw! Those widows
would *defoliate* your redemption — gene pool became our dessert — do
you want an interpreter? Rust never sips. We will die in sphincters with
primates
they believe in muff ornaments — elaborate what you can cannot swal-
low.
If you want content, you have to pay extra.

   Labial pesto — popeye less of a man
lizards better-equipped beefcake phosphated determinism carried to
the Nth degree: how many of them are junkies? — aristocrats in pam-
pers
voodooized hit list, preppies sink. Intellectuals learn to make their own
beds; dent of insolvency
as a debris aficionado, plump unionism to advertise toy airplanes hang-
ing from the ceiling — this is not the poetry project, wheelchair back-
pedalling into our prehistory as a drain — the lips will have to work over
time. Did you get sanctified enough? Gabby drool how it's effective, this
grotesque totalitarian mediocrity: probate courtroom be so brief, sterile
spinsters are making us clean our plates in a pieta position. A saint
that wets its turnkey; putting things in your mouth is postmodern? Cli-
ented doubt — cannibalism's larynx, osteopathic gutter why crabs pre-
fer jockey shorts — can a man beget pure oil? — those that walk their
food by patrol dogs rest on someone else's diseased laurels. Box-
spring'd tomb just sit in the sandbox until all thought peels away, bald
to prove a point to petrify the eggs be a bigger basket funk
of wet suit a spore to spur
baile, baile, baile, sweet marijuana smell gives the lie to this republic.
Little handbags of the lord
talent = expired coupons damaged sponsor; you speak so soft you know
they heteros — he stopped calling when the phone didn't make his dick
hard.

   Gratuitous nonviolence
else dust, black stuff goes on what exercises power, so? — suspect suspi-
cion. Combat the automobile
by divided imbeciles
which is obviously these squatters are motorvatin'
what is it? The influence of envy in secretarial work, nutrition's affec-
tion for the body swallows these expectations, my name is on high.
Monster goo urbanism that spurts a valet; my epoch's not up yet —
some deft tuck no longer setting out for the hacienda, then the single
women get tied up to watch the divorcees. There is no such thing as an
emergency in the world, resuscitation won't work — & yet bodies keep
swarm, that's gangland slang, hypnosis surveillance kill a crustacean for
Christ's criminology a nobody treachery hope. We must reject into ac-
count; true, not truth — resumes for Reagan. Castigate masters — can't
a man flout a goat? At last, a chewing gum for the bellybuttons of the
rich; couple talk is coop talk
mirandized him — pump iron to be bright
her usual spinster tourist spitfire *fantasy causes stress:* the universe is
perfect.

                                                                    1992

BARRETT WATTEN ■ ■ ■ ■ ■ ■ ■ ■ ■ ■ ■ ■ ■

b. 1948

Born in Berkeley, California, where he now lives, Barrett Watten was educated at MIT, the University of California at Berkeley, and the University of Iowa. Founder of *This* magazine with Robert Grenier and publisher since 1974 of This Press, Watten is a leading proponent of language poetry.

Among his books of poetry are *Opera—Works* (1975), *Decay* (1977), *1–10* (1980), *Complete Thought* (1982), the book-length poem *Progress* (1985), *Conduit* (1988), *Under Erasure* (1991), and a book of collected poems, *Frame: 1971–1990* (1994). He is also the author of a book of essays, *Total Syntax* (1984), and the collaborative account *Leningrad: American Writers in the Soviet Union* (1991). With Lyn Hejinian, he edits *Poetics Journal*, a magazine devoted to theory.

Watten is opposed to a poetry of narrative unity and ease of communication; his work calls instead for "the resistance between writer and reader, speaker and hearer."[1] A radical formalist, Watten writes, "The detachment necessary for a valid work can be anticipated only on the level of form; De Kooning's 'I keep painting until I've painted myself out of the picture . . .' indicates both the conditions of the work and its social fact."[2] Thus the purpose of a work of art is not self-expression, but rather an "anarchy of production" that makes for more democratic relations between author and reader.

Watten currently works as Associate Editor of the academic journal *Representations*.

1. Barrett Watten, "The XYZ of Reading: Negativity (&)," *Poetics Journal*, No. 6, 1986, p. 3.   2. The same, p. 4.   3. The same.

Statistics

There is no language but "reconstructed" imaged parentheses back into person "emphasizing constant" explanation "the current to run both ways." The ocean he sees when as "sour frowns of the ancients" 'signifier' " that person jumps in. We are at liberty "to take 'the' out of 'us,' " to have selves "not here" in the machinery of dramatic monologue to "smash, interrupt." To focus primarily "using examples of work" produces "difficulty": "you" in indeterminate distance "building a tower" as the circumstance of writing "to look over 'with concern' the bones of 'speech.' " Machines are "metal" words where "crystallization slipping" is "that tongue spoke" dissolved into "not it" located in constraints. "Causing 'them' to freeze and perish" has no bearing on "stumbling block" of facts "embodied" in old meanings "understood" to be "suffering 'circumstantial' distortions." "It" makes itself "by definition" into "word," missing the point "writing," wanting as "further" point "a persona" clearly named. Biochemistry adds to "average" warmth "lightly voiced" if painfully limited "rhyming with" individual "he." Those "automatons" exist who have by "progress into ground" lost use of "the raised surface" of writing. He becomes you, as "retrograde hero 'having nothing to say' " can't tell what "it" is. But a person smiles "the allowed" look at "examples of" words in front "when present." He speaks "to study inner silence" as absolute: "normally we think 'we think "we have seen 'in writing' what we have seen." ' " The figure "lightbulb turns on" of mind is not the "separate from hearing" talk in the speaker's "much more complicated" brain. One thinks hard "how to read" what "won't read autobiography" thinks "destroys no one" but invokes instants of fear "to say what 'it' wants." Remove "privilege of manifestation" to make words "active and passive" for thousands never met who might yet "passionately react." Circumstances of this writing assume "a recording" will disappear, that "self" cannot be identified as "preoccupation with voice" or "replaced with words." But "pyramids, tombs, chariots 'of personal experience' " want confusion of "schoolboy torn in half" in an odd, "theoretical" way. Transcription stood, the "8-year-old sentient gone": "speaking" twelve feet from the water, its "audience" on the rock. He wanted "baleful 'all-knowing' distance" out of this borrowed substance "often more personal than he." Disregarding if "citizens worth not one cent" listening can't speak for us "circuits not all there" themselves, he "whatever may be 'wanted' " loves to talk. "Let me in" pushed between "to have intelligibility" hopeless repetition "which takes you away."

1980

Radio

Conviction fills the body
The presence of dead souls
flute-like at the base of the ear.
A particle enters the soundings
   suddenly open, a door
   separating bright from careless
patterning, forcing a language
memory designs from sleep.
   The body is more primitive
   attached to the ground.
A frame lights up horizons
to lead forward, larger than life.

   Animals eat words,
exorcize this great and glassy news.
The end of the road a walking flower
   as in any direction, another.
   Peripheries meet, a syntactic
forecast through hostile centuries
a slow drawing out of detail
   reflecting greys.
   To confirm the ear catches
is measured until it disappears.

Breaking code, no one recalls
    appeal to the surface of fact.

    The flames are sponges
    in smoke-blackened hour
Blighted fruits words can't grasp.
Among stations immeasurable across fields
    a flashing sign
    fixes only certainty
Two eyes blinking through a door.
The missing head must be seen whole
    where one word leads
    clouds to accident of end.
The machine never tires.
Edges of stations start to come in.

    The head of a king's son
    multiplies at cross-roads
an immutable exchange. You are the world
wings of oblivion and endless drilling
    a shadow of things to come
    the wind on their heels.
In pursuit of a ship in harbor
the voices of towns without body
    stars without voice in space.
    A night for the blind.
Passing through his fingers
the short black branches of the eye.

                                        1980

FROM *Progress*

Relax,
        stand at attention, and.
        Purple snake stands out on
        Porcelain tiles. The idea
Is the thing. Skewed by design. . . .

One way contradictory use is to
        Specify empty.
                Basis, its
        Cover operates under insist on,
Delineate. Stalin as a linguist. . . .

I trust replication.
                Gives,
        Surface. Lights string

The court reporter, distances.
That only depth is perfect. . . .

Comes to the history of words.
    The thought to eradicate
    In him. The poetry,
        by
Making him think certain ways. . . .

White, to each of these cancels
    Shadow,
        fog. Collapses self,
    And invading enemy wins.
The argument itself, disassembling. . . .

Objection. Of essence is the
    Time falls apart in his hands.
    Hatred, under the engine,
Of daily events.
        I trust wheat. . . .

And doubt it, to control by dis-
    Orientation.
        Eisenhower
    Did not come to power.
Terms for the period, state. . . .

Figure. State is severed from
    States of affairs? You
    Speak for themselves,
Materials,
        the voice comes out. . . .

Only I trust the materials. The
    Offspring are in relation
    By chain of command to
Inculcate extremes.
        Uttermost. . . .

Oxymoronic logic in his fears,
    Such.
        Canned corn, peas.
    Fixation on these things
Leads only to isolate a few. . . .

Mexico and Canada. Remembering,
    She sends the package
    And finally,
        dies. The one
Image. I trust the thing itself. . . .

To speak, and be struck down
    By remorse. Pure relation
    That, given the time, an
Assailant,
        in training films. . . .

In the media of their claims.
    The language is a trope,
    Turning metal into assimilation
Of burns itself,
        the forehead. . . .

Some breathe loudly. I parse
    Doubts, replacement.
                Music
    Is a cause of disease, no
Picture *wants* to be taken. . . .

But there *are* firsts, cultural
    And literary norms,
           a carved
    Wooden bust of Will Rogers,
Storehouses of information. . . .

A hand of bridge,
           predicated on
    The classicism of means.
    Into the missing center of
Detail, a circumambulation. . . .

Impression, the total support
    Of the body.
           I print money
    To pay my bills, construed as
The ground is covered with rain. . . .

Like ramparts, the industrial
    Approaches,
           diagonal signs
    Empty the heart in Korea
Of parallels, a situation. . . .

Ineffective, the curse returns.
    I write, as in a mirror,
    This present.
           The weather is
Fiction, surrounding the whole. . . .

Fog lifts, to be chained down
    In warehouses.

Some men's
Codes are locally inversed.
Subtract an idea from thinking. . . .

But he is leaving this place.
Los Angeles, the city of
Numbers still alive in
The brain.
Mutual hands wave. . . .

And a valuable object results.
The work ends.
Saturday
Afternoon on the sidewalk,
Soldiers removing their shirts. . . .

Then I erupt my articulation.
Down through history, sand
Scratching at entrances,
A private hospital,
steps. . . .

A disposition that unlike of
Ethics speaks.
Concert for
Precisionist, with broken
Glass, the Northern Lights. . . .

Cars bursting into the light.
The cargo is a critique.
A flexible schema for trees,
Strings,
output signals to both. . . .

To multicolored opaque rings.
Thinking on the planes
Of a building,
but in verse.
The rest is faster, speech. . . .

Aggressive neutrality.
Haig,
On the disposition of needs.
Suppose I cancel this, and
What is left are my mistakes. . . .

Clash of symbols, doors close.
Lighthouse for the blind,
I want to say to your eyes.
Difficult,
completely inert. . . .

Piranesi's interiors,
                caught
Up in the middle of things.
An airplane descends into
Voltaic arcs, patches of space. . . .

Pressed into certain relief.
The copy is an addition
Drawn into unstable motifs,
The grids vertical,
                lifting up. . . .

                                        1985

DAVID LEHMAN ■ ■ ■ ■ ■ ■ ■ ■ ■ ■ ■ ■ ■ ■ ■
b. 1948

David Lehman grew up in the Inwood section of Manhattan and attended Columbia and Oxford universities. At Columbia, his professors included Kenneth Koch, who encouraged his study of experimental poetry. After a brief teaching stint at Hamilton College, Lehman worked for a number of years as a book critic for *Newsweek*.

He now makes his living as a free-lance literary journalist and author; he edits the series *The Best American Poetry* and is the author of *Signs of the Times: Deconstruction and the Fall of Paul de Man* (1991) and *The Line Forms Here* (1992), a collection of his critical writings.

In his two full-length collections of poetry, *An Alternative to Speech* (1986) and *Operation Memory* (1990), Lehman reveals a playful fascination with formal gamesmanship and received poetic forms such as the villanelle and sestina. His disposition as a poet is essentially ironic. "Irony," Lehman says, "is the accomplice of complexity . . . the attitude of mind best suited to the presentation of an internal conflict. Irony is the literary mode of intense ambivalence. Irony also suggests a certain kind of literary structure in which oppositions coexist and paradoxes can prevail."[1]

Lehman lives in Ithaca, New York.

1. "Twenty Questions," an interview conducted by Nin Andrews, in *The Line Forms Here*, Ann Arbor, 1992, p. 240.

The Difference Between Pepsi and Coke

Can't swim; uses credit cards and pills to combat
    intolerable feelings of inadequacy;
Won't admit his dread of boredom, chief impulse behind
    numerous marital infidelities;
Looks fat in jeans, mouths clichés with confidence,
    breaks mother's plates in fights;
Buys when the market is too high, and panics during
    the inevitable descent;

Still, Pop can always tell the subtle difference
    between Pepsi and Coke,
Has defined the darkness of red at dawn, memorized
    the splash of poppies along
Deserted railway tracks, and opposed the war in Vietnam
    months before the students,
Years before the politicians and press; give him
    a minute with a road map
And he will solve the mystery of bloodshot eyes;
    transport him to mountaintop
And watch him calculate the heaviness and height
    of the local heavens;
Needs no prompting to give money to his kids; speaks
    French fluently, and tourist German;
Sings Schubert in the shower; plays pinball in Paris;
    knows the new maid steals, and forgives her.

1986

Toward the Vanishing Point

VARIOUS nostalgias: rock, scissor, and paper:
Cardinals and opposing orioles in the April rain:
No pain: a brain perfectly in tune with the newspaper,
Like a commuter in love with a computer, and with the paper
On which he neatly jots down, in blue
Ballpoint ink, opposing arguments on the burning issue of paper
Money and the inflationary rate. Alas, what good are paper
Airplanes for traveling down streets longer than the cities
Of which they are a part? Yet we elect to live in these cities,
Our faces greeted by windswept pieces of paper,
Fragments of flowers: a life in which to pause
Is both a luxury and a defeat, and not to pause

Unthinkable, for it makes resumption possible, though each pause
Requires its own first cause. All newspapers
Are plausible; therefore none are. (Pause.)
As he wiped the dirt off him, he paused
Momentarily, in a daze: it had begun to rain,
But he did not feel a drop. The pause
Brought no applause in its wake, like the pause
Of a parenthesis, bracketing blank space, or like the parting blue
Sea of the biblical tale, emptiness between blue
Walls, held back in an eternal pause.
What happens next? Up the twisting alleys of these
    mountainous cities,
Motorcycles murder sleep. "Who runs our cities?

I mean, who really runs them? Not that all our cities
Have turned into mortuaries and airports, but. . . ." A pause
With the grace of sleep ensued, bringing relief to the cities
Of our discontent, our cities
On and off the plain, committed on paper
To the building of sanitary new cities
On the same old sites, only cleansed now of the truth that can
    poison our cities
With the truth, lovely as roses in a light rain
Or the migration of starlings on a day made quiet by rain.
Paris and Florence are examples of cities
That know but one moment of ignition, when the blue
Of collars and stockings is erased, replaced by the blue

Of a hero's bruised skin, until everything is as blue
As what you see out of plane windows blurred by rain.
There are those who regard Picasso's blue
Period as anomalous, but the chronic push-and-pull of blue
Clouds and a chameleon sky, during a thunderous pause
In a storm, delights even implacable critics of blue,
Who prefer the red of berries and blood to the icier sheen of blue.
Adrift, marooned, yet equipped with sufficient paper
For the task, we experience the familiar white of the paper
As an invitation to a lifetime of urges for the blue:
The sea receives us as it does the rain:
Our tears are made superfluous by the rain.

We remember them fondly: fog equals snow plus rain:
Evening in the city equals blue sky minus blue:
If dirges and laments could put off death, it would rain:
If laughter could cure insomnia, it would rain:
You could share in the malevolent joy of cities
As enemy clouds drop their payload of rain:
On the battlefields of Waterloo it would rain
And on the apartment houses of Watergate, rain without pause:
It would rain forty days and forty nights without pause:
And after it stopped, nostalgia for the rain
Would set in, and editorials in our daily papers
Would recommend that we set fire to the paper

And no longer write poems on paper
But on a surface like water, during a pause
Between waves. We would live in unfamiliar cities,
Our pleasure the promise of babies in blue,
Our weather the invention of rain.

1986

First Offense

I'm sorry, officer. I didn't see the sign
Because, in fact, there wasn't any. I tell you
The light was green. How much is the fine?

Will the tumor turn out malignant or benign?
Will the doctor tell us? He said he knew.
I'm sorry, officer. I didn't see the sign.

Not every madman is an agent of the divine,
Not all who pass are allowed to come through.
The light was green. How much is the fine?

Which is worse, the rush or the wait? The line
Interminable, or fear of coming late? His anxiety grew.
I'm sorry, officer. I didn't see the sign.

I'm cold sober. All I had was one glass of wine.
Was anyone hurt? Is there anything I can do?
The light was green. How much is the fine?

Will we make our excuses like so many clever lines,
Awkwardly delivered? Never to win, always to woo?
I'm sorry, officer. I didn't see the sign.
The light was green. How much is the fine?

1986

GEORGE EVANS ▪ ▪ ▪ ▪ ▪ ▪ ▪ ▪ ▪ ▪ ▪ ▪ ▪
b. 1948

George Evans was born and raised in Pittsburgh, where he began writing in early adolescence. A chronic runaway, he left home permanently at fourteen to live on the streets. At age eighteen, he joined the U.S. Air Force and served in Vietnam as the crew chief of an emergency and triage unit. While in Vietnam, he was unsuccessfully court-martialed for disobeying orders, but the actual reasons for his trial, Evans claims, were rooted in war protest activities forbidden by the U.S. government. After completing high school through a GED test taken in Vietnam, he went on to receive degrees from Carnegie-Mellon and Johns Hopkins.

Evans's first three poetry books, *Nightvision* (1983), *Wrecking* (1988), and *Eye Blade* (1988), were published in Great Britain. *Sudden Dreams: New & Selected Poems* (1991) was his first book published in the United States.

Influenced by Black Mountain and Objectivist poetics, Evans shares with Denise Levertov and Hilda Morley the lyrical use of William Carlos Williams's "variable foot." Perhaps his closest associations, however, have been with poet Cid Corman, who edited the poetry journal *Origin*. Evans is editor of *Charles Olson & Cid Corman: Complete Correspondence, 1950–1964* and *Streetfare Journal*, a program that puts poetry and art on posters in buses nationwide.

He lives in San Francisco.

A Renaissance Drunk

They never read their Hedylos, nor could,
where he sings how sweet was Sokles
in his cups, how he wrote better for it,

or the sot Santōka:

The leaves drop   (horohoro)
weaving down drunk
from their trees

           Beauty.
           I am the leaves.

The shape of the traveler
in the puddle is the traveler

                   or in the wine,

walking, balancing a dragonfly
on his hat,

threading, stepping lightly
over shadows in the pines.

                             1983

Revelation in the Mother Lode

I walk into the vineyard at night, into acres of cordoned vines
   against their stakes at pruning time, but see, stretching
   off through tule fog, only cross-marked graves.

How did it come to be that my generation would be stiff
   under hoarfrost, and that I should come across them
   twenty years after watching them die to remember and feel
   I've truly wasted my time, have left no mark upon the earth
   in their name, have left only the small craters of a boot
   sucking vineyard mud.

And is this guilt, or the product of being swept up
   in a time on human earth when few do more than raise
   the cause of their own names—and am I one, or is all this
   death just sloth which one pretends
   to work against the belly of
   but which in fact
   controls?

You who return to me as vines in the deep night under fog
   have come at a bad time, a time when the world is obsessed
   with rubbing you smooth, and its concentration
   on ceremony brings you to nothing.

Somewhere, mixed in with all the rest I'd meant to get to
   which is receding, is a day floating above jungle, flak
   exploding in small fists from the trees, rocking
   the chopper where I sit in shock and blood and urine
   staring into patchwork fields.

I stand behind bamboo shaking, thinking of Nguyet
   in a Saigon bar, worried how willingly we forget,
   bombs dropping like hair straight down   a shadow
   a black sheet   everything about us muscle   hot
   prick and resolve   and have no idea where I am
   but am everywhere   and she   wobbling on spiked heels
   around the bar stools and smoke has everything I cannot
   not the least of which is a reason
                   which makes her more beautiful
   than possible, but also quite a bit like the ragged edge
   of a ruined wall, and like the crisp brown bamboo leaves
   dropping after terrible heat, dripping with an ache I love
   which is more for youth than anything   certainly not war,
   which also feels like dropping.

How tired I am of hearing about that war,
   which one should struggle
   to keep the nightmare of, suffer from rather than forget.
   I don't want to heal, and am sick of those who do.
   Such things end in license.

Back here it turns out newspapers
   and monuments are taxidermy;
   there is little retribution, little learning; what is lost
   is forgotten; sometimes it gets so bad I'm not sure
   I'm the one who lived . . . then come upon you in a field
   —a one-time soldier with a trick knee, flagging humor,
   monsoon debt—and find you enfolded by fog as if by spirits,
   and become the visage of all that's been
   thrown from the world.
                              1991

Horse on a Fence

We might have died by now
could be among the dead
where the numbers are greater

but for courage   course
or luck,

meeting like roads
only to divide like roads,
or regenerate,

wild,
performing the act
out loud, in the open

forgetting what
made us want to kill
made us kill
ever

believing ourselves invisible

though passion makes us
visible
even
strangely out of place
the way the present always is,
our hold on it four hooves of a horse
stopped mid-flight in a leap

standing now on a fence
between two worlds

1/1/90
Big Sur

1991

AUGUST KLEINZAHLER ▪ ▪ ▪ ▪ ▪ ▪ ▪ ▪ ▪ ▪ ▪
b. 1949

Born in Jersey City, New Jersey, August Kleinzahler studied at the University of Wisconsin and with Basil Bunting at the University of Victoria in British Columbia. Kleinzahler's skilled use of American speech and the everyday occasion links him to a tradition derived from William Carlos Williams; unlike Williams, however, his poetry is characteristically sardonic. The poem "A Case in Point," for instance, is a trenchant critique of language poetry and related deconstructive strategies that take "refuge in a text / of a text."

In a related comment, Kleinzahler writes, "The language and movement of poetry have become disconnected from the body, away from physical expression—breath, mouth, muscle, and pulse—to lexical meaning. Because of this break, the poetic line has lost its structural integrity."[1] A firm believer in the value of craft, Kleinzahler insists that, "for a poet, the handling of time becomes a very intimate, *hands-on* business. Each word is a *shape carved in time*. . . .

Vowels have their varying durations and pitches: *eek! what a weird moon.*"[2]

Kleinzahler's first collection, *Storm Over Hackensack* (1985), won wide acceptance. His second, *Earthquake Weather* (1989), was nominated for the National Book Critics Circle Award. A volume of new and selected poems, *Like Cities, Like Storms,* was published by Picador in Australia in 1992. He is the recipient of a 1990 Guggenheim Fellowship and a former Holloway Lecturer at the University of California at Berkeley.

Kleinzahler lives in San Francisco.

1. "Poetry's Decay," *Harper's*, May 1992, pp. 35–36.   2. Review of *The Well-Tempered Sentence* by Karen Elizabeth Gordon, *Sulfur*, No. 8, 1983, p. 172.

An Autumnal Sketch

What to make of them, the professors
in their little cars,
the sensitive men paunchy with drink
parked at the fence
where the field begins and the suburb ends?

If there is a mallard in the reeds
they will take it.
They will take it and make it their own,
something both more than a duck
and less.

They so badly want a poem,
these cagey and disheartened men
at the edge of the field.
And before they turn back for supper
they shall have one.

                                                            1985

Hamburger

They come to resemble Buddhas,
these old fucks,
with their *hamburgeronly15¢/lb.
andgoodmeat,too.*

They're out there on the street
like undercover cops,
short-brim and necktie,
watching it all go to hell.

                Vestigial,
dead in the pants . . .

—Miami before the war,
you should have seen it:
paradise.

A lemon tree in every yard.

1985

Poetics

I have loved the air outside Shop-Rite Liquor
on summer evenings
better than the Marin hills at dusk
lavender and gold
stretching miles to the sea.

At the junction, up from the synagogue
a weeknight, necessarily
and with my father—
a sale on German beer.

Air full of living dust:
bus exhaust, air-borne grains of pizza crust
wounded crystals
appearing, disappearing
among streetlights and unsuccessful neon.

1985

Spleen

The night Ottawa brought down the budget
Mrs. Mooney's pals sat shit-faced in the bar
next to three Québecois, brilliantly scarved.
Around the block streetlamps intruded
on clusters of branch—

                    et voilà:
catkins dripping from ash.

A hundred million was spent to make jobs.
Bronchial trouble was in every house.
March had been wet. Dark women looked pale;
fair women, sallow. All that day
the skin doctor lanced eruptions.

Bankers were generally pleased.
The last traces of black snow became air
and that air trailed a slow Greyhound

to the Dairy Queen in Plattsburg.
It was a budget without surprises.
The dead were dead. The rest of us on call.

1985

The Lunatic of Lindley Meadow

At nightfall, when the inquisitive elves in elf-pants
wander over the ridge with chummy screed,
the snaps of the beak your hand becomes cease,

and evening's last fungo dwindles
high over the spruce, for an instant getting lost
in one band of sky turning dark under another,

falling back into view falling
out of the sky, *pop*, a dead wren in his mitt.   *Let's
get home*, the big boy says, *Mom'll holler.*

The car horns along Fulton subside with the dark,
the big felt-lined dark: bright little logos and cars
set in black felt while still pulsing light,

a lid on top.   And see, here he comes now,
Conga Lad, pleasing the elves who come close but not too,
making the birds go way.   Time to start home,

so clean it up nice and blow germs off your pouch—
the nice warm room, the smell in the wool.

1989

Ebenezer Californicus

Don't make me go out eat goose
be nice get a headache
all right?
because the sun's so strong
so warm delish the back of my neck
making mutinous the wee city-states
that dot it—
goosebumps of intrigue, of the possible

Terrible people
up&down the street terrible people
smiling
    the smiles of greed

the mooncalf's grin
 the Bob Hope Holiday Leer of Delight
the smile of the broken,
hurt
 pullulating:
 not six weeks out of the can
 like drunk at 8 A.M.

 that smile

—Maddy crifsmuss, brudder
Stare shhange?
 O Christ
O
 Merry WhackWhack, Mrs QuackQuack

 Write soon

 Love

 Baby Teapot

 1989

A Case in Point

Because he's lost the way to his pulse
and doesn't know how to get back.
He bips when he ought to bop,
so now can't do any better than that.

Because even if he knew how
there's nothing in his head or heart
to drive it down the track,
just the corrosive white noise of anxiety,

a sort of ether
coursing through rancor and cunning.

Because he is flummoxed by the world,
the crush of it, the variety.
Too daunted to field what he might,
takes refuge in a text
of a text,
 finding *tickle points of nyceness*
there to stay him.

Because he is a team player, a flak
for the ward boss, the whiffling panjandrums,

backing off from the authentic
like a jackal from the lion's scent.

Because he honors not the made thing
nor can he recognize it when coming upon it.

And yet, should it declare itself
with such force as to penetrate even this,

he averts his eyes and hurries off.

1992

EILEEN MYLES ▪ ▪ ▪ ▪ ▪ ▪ ▪ ▪ ▪ ▪ ▪ ▪ ▪ ▪

b. 1949

Born and raised in Cambridge, Massachusetts, Eileen Myles attended the University of Massachusetts in Boston. In 1974, she moved to New York City, where she now resides. Myles's offhandedly personal and lyrical poetry has an affinity with the work of James Schuyler; this is most evident in her diaristic style of composition, narrative ease, and use of short, enjambed lines.

For Myles, the performance of a poem occurs more at the moment of its composition than during its enactment before an audience. Referring to the creation of one of her poems, "Hot Nights," she writes, "The process of the poem . . . is central to an impression I have that life is a rehearsal for the poem, or the final moment of spiritual revelation. I literally stepped out of my house that night, feeling a poem coming on. . . . I went over to Yaffa [a restaurant] and wrote it looking out the window."[1] In Myles's view, "going out to get a poem" is like hunting: "I felt '. . . erotic, oddly / magnetic . . .' like photographic paper. As I walked I was recording the details, I was the details, I was the poem."[2]

Myles's poetry collections include *Not Me* (1991) and *Maxfield Parrish* (1994). She has also published the story collections *Bread & Water* (1987), *1969* (1989), and *Chelsea Girls* (1994). A frequent contributor to *The Village Voice* and *Art in America*, Myles was a write-in candidate for president of the United States in 1992.

1. "How I Wrote Certain of My Poems," in *Not Me*, New York, 1991, p. 201.   2. The same, p. 202.

December 9th

I have the same
birthday as John
Milton. Did
you know that?
So I don't have to
write long poems about
heaven & hell—everything's
been lost in my lifetime

& I'm usually blind drunk
and not so serious
either. However . . .
when I am nearly dead
will you read to me
in bed? Will you pre-
tend to be my daughter
or my wife, Whoever,
will you crawl in
& die with Me?

1982   1991

New England Wind

Remember me this summer
under the eaves again
stretched out against
the sky again
like Orion's moon

when a breeze crawls
down a screen, pip, zing
or is that a cat
crawling up

Oh was I alone in the
first room I ever
had or who would've
writ this then? Me too
when I am mad.

O leave me alone with
my aching head,
panicky panicky
no where to go
pretty north & silly

the other night
under the eaves
in a rain at 4 o'clock
I woke up it was
so sexy; listened so
careful in the world
the next day
for who also heard it
dreamy-eyed, who could've

come up or I come down
for once from
the sky
to be what
fell.

1982   1991

The Sadness of Leaving

Everything's
    so far away—
my jacket's
    over there. I'm terrified
        to go & you
won't miss me
        I'm terrified by the
bright blues of
        the subway
        other days I'm
            so happy &
prepared to believe
        that everyone walking
down the street is
            someone I know.
The oldness of Macy's
        impresses me. The
        wooden escalators
            as you get
higher up to the furniture,
        credit, lampshades—
            You shopped here
            as a kid. Oh,
you deserve me! In
        a movie called
        Close Up—once in
a while the wiggly
bars, notice
    the wiggly blue
        bars of
            subway entrances,
the grainy beauty,
        the smudge. I won't
kill myself today. It's
        too beautiful. My heart
            breaking down 23rd
St. To share this

with you, the
sweetness of the
        frame. My body
in perfect shape
    for nothing but
        death. I want
to show you this.
        On St. Mark's Place
        a madman screams:
my footsteps, the
        drumbeats of Armageddon.
        Oh yes bring me
        closer to you Lord.
I want to die
        Close Up. A handful
of bouncing yellow
        tulips for David.   I
    admit I love tulips
        because they
        die so beautifully.
                            I
        see salvation in
their hanging heads.
A beautiful exit. How do
    they get to
        feel so free? I am
    trapped by love—
        over french fries
    my eyes wander to
        The Hue Bar. A blue
sign. Across the
life. On my way to
    making a point,
        to making
        logic, to not
falling in love to-
        night and
    let my pain remain
        unwrapped—to push
the machine—Paul's
staying in touch, but
oh remember Jessica
Lange, she looked so
        beautiful all
        doped up, on her
way to meet King
Kong. I sit
on my little red
    couch in February
how do they get

> to feel so free
> 1,000,000 women
>   not me moving through
> the street tonight
> of this filmy
>   city & I
>   crown myself
>   again & again
>   and there
>   can't be
>   two kings.

1987   1991

VICTOR HERNÁNDEZ CRUZ ▪ ▪ ▪ ▪ ▪ ▪ ▪ ▪ ▪
b. 1949

Victor Hernández Cruz was born in Aguas Buenas, Puerto Rico, and moved to the Lower East Side of Manhattan with his parents at the age of six. At the age of seventeen, he wrote his first book of poetry, *Papo Got His Gun* (1966), which he published himself on a mimeograph machine under the Calle Once (Eleventh Street) imprint. Cruz dropped out of high school in his senior year to co-found the East Harlem Gut Theatre, a Puerto Rican collective of writers and actors. In 1967, he became an editor of *Umbra*, the literary magazine associated with the Umbra Workshop, a black writer's group on the Lower East Side. In 1968, he moved to Berkeley, California, and has since alternated his residence between New York, Puerto Rico, and the West Coast.

Of Cruz's collection *Red Beans* (1991), critic Julio Ortega writes, "Victor Hernández Cruz's writing is the first major realization of the Spanish language as English poetry" as well as a source of a new "migratory poetics" and "cultural pluralingualism." According to Cruz, "The Caribbean is a place of great convergence; it mixes and uniforms diversities; it is a march of rhythm and style." Thus, the mixture of Spanish and English in Cruz's poetry, which he calls "linguistic stereo," reflects the migratory, and inherently political, nature of the Caribbean and modern culture in general: "The earth is migration, everything is moving, changing interchanging, appearing disappearing. National languages melt, sail into each other."[1]

Influenced by the Latin American poets Ernesto Cardenal and Octavio Paz and the musical rhythms of Tito Puente, the impulse of Cruz's work is toward orality and jazz improvisation in performance. As the poet Tom Clark describes it, the pace of Cruz's work "is modern, post-bop, post-rock, post-salsa—not a 'minuet slow' but a '*mambo* of much more haste.' "[2]

Cruz's first four books, *Snaps* (1968), *Mainland* (1973), *Tropicalization* (1976), and *By Lingual Wholes* (1982), have been collected, along with newer work, in *Rhythm, Content & Flavor* (1988).

1. "Mountains in the North: Hispanic Writing in the U.S.A.," in *Red Beans*, St. Paul, 1991, p. 87.   2. "These Tropics Aren't Triste," in *The Poetry Beat: Reviewing the 80s*, Ann Arbor, 1990, p. 9.

Areyto

My empire of flamboyans
Through boulevards made of mountains
Dressed green to the heavens
As voices circulate the hymns
of our history
From the dancers of the round
serpent formed at the center of
Life
This is Americas Areyto
This is Americas Areyto

In cities mountains of flying metallic
cars and consumer junk/
Nerves piled up upon horizons
of progress
That whisper inside/
Mira look
Look mira that whisper inside
Is the old calendar ticking
The Areyto is still swinging:
The Gods said they would take
us back and deliver us from
Plush media inventions
From racket and industrial tension
From textbooks that are lying
tongues of pretensions
The river on the other side
of English is carrying the message
Yukiyu has not abandoned you
The quetzals are still flying
Quetzalcóatl is on the phone
Be cool Roberto and José
Carmen and María
Just go horizontal into the circle
Areyto
The current will take you

America that Betances, José Martí
That Hostos wanted all together as
ONE
Vasconcelos said RAZA CÓSMICA
Seeing red mixed with black
And black with white
Rhythms united married in history
This is the greatest flavor
The earth has to offer

Marimba tango samba
Danza Mambo bolero

Linda America just rise and take
off your clothes
Your age is so old that
Giants appear out of trees as tobacco
smoke takes photographs of the wind
Directing itself into a voice
Where salt pebbles dance guaguancó
Something so good that it became
blueprint for legs
That moved with such precision
That ten thousand appear to be one
In the Areyto where you hear the drum
As the knees and the legs
describe an area between two stars

Old fire of agricultural guitar
spreading North
Trio Los Diamantes sunrise moving
through silk on slow tropical wind
Johnny Albino Trio San Juan
Making an escalator of sound
Into your hearts that grow feathers
To fly towards the desert to enter
The la'uds invasion of Iberian perfume
To land upon the shoulders of Gypsies
and Mayas as a fan from Granada cools
our Amerindian features of the love
That comes of the love that goes

America is our belly
Our abdomen of spirit
We grew out of the plants
It knows who we are
Linda America that Betances
José Martí to Hostos us up UNIDOS
As único one (JUAN)

America sur south
America norte
Juan America
Two America Juan
Juan America one
Then America blend
Give the idea roots of
harmonious peace serene/
Sí and yes it is possible for the

Snake of heart and mind to
grow quetzal feathers and fly
Out of the Areyto circle
Areyto circle
Areyto dance

Possible to be possible
Possible to be
A whole unto one
A nation with lots of fish to
eat
And fruit that offers itself
it is possible to be
it is possible to
Struggle against blocks
of inertia
Against conquistadors' wishes
lurking in blood nervous system
Nightmaring dreams/
Dogs that come bark at the
beautiful dance
It is possible to be
pure fresh river water
We are bird that sings
Free

Areyto
Maraca güiro and drum
Quicharo maraca y tambor
Who we are
Printed in rhythm and song

Areyto south
Areyto North
Two America Juan
One America One
America that Bolívar Betances
to José Martí Us to Hostos who wanted
us to be one único Unidos

Areyto güiro and drum
Quicharo maraca y tambor

Areyto song
Areyto song
AREYTO.

1991

An Essay on William Carlos Williams

I love the quality of the
spoken thought
As it happens immediately
uttered into the air
Not held inside and rolled
around for some properly
schemed moment
Not sent to circulate a cane
field
Or on a stroll that would include
the desert and Mecca
Spoken while it happens
Direct and pure
As the art of salutation
of mountain campesinos come to
the plaza
The grasp of the handshake upon
encounter and departure
A gesture unveiling the occult
behind the wooden boards of
your old house
Remarks show no hesitation
to be expressed
The tongue itself carries
the mind
Pure and sure
Sudden and direct
like the appearance
of a green mountain
Overlooking a town.

1991

Problems with Hurricanes

A campesino looked at the air
And told me:
With hurricanes it's not the wind
or the noise or the water.
I'll tell you he said:
it's the mangoes, avocados
Green plantains and bananas
flying into town like projectiles.

How would your family
feel if they had to tell

The generations that you
got killed by a flying
Banana.

Death by drowning has honor
If the wind picked you up
and slammed you
Against a mountain boulder
This would not carry shame
But
to suffer a mango smashing
Your skull
or a plantain hitting your
Temple at 70 miles per hour
is the ultimate disgrace.

The campesino takes off his hat—
As a sign of respect
towards the fury of the wind
And says:
Don't worry about the noise
Don't worry about the water
Don't worry about the wind—
If you are going out
beware of mangoes
And all such beautiful
sweet things.

1991

JESSICA HAGEDORN ■ ■ ■ ■ ■ ■ ■ ■ ■ ■ ■

b. 1949

Born and raised in the Philippines, Jessica Hagedorn moved to the United States in her teens and studied theater arts at the American Conservatory Theater in San Francisco. From 1975 to 1985, she performed her poetry with jazz musicians and her own band, the West Coast Gangster Choir.

Hagedorn sees the traditional poetry reading as "young women wearing tweed suits and tortoise-shell glasses, clearing their throats and 'reading' about their anima rising and libidos pulsating in trembling, Sarah Lawrence–type voices."[1] Instead Hagedorn wants poetry performances to go in the direction of "an extravaganza of voices and moving bodies playing instruments that would hypnotize an audience numbed by the pomp and circumstance of academia, forgetting that the origins of poetry are oral and physical."[2]

The concept of the Gangster Choir was to include "shades of the old 'Doo-wop' school, Smokey Robinson, the Flamingoes, some Hector Lavoe chanting, always the tropics lurking in the background, the way we sing . . . the message in the music. The poetics of our lives, that's what I'm interested in."[3]

Hagedorn has published the poetry volume *Dangerous Music* (1975); *Petfood & Tropical Apparitions* (1981), a collection of poetry and short prose; a much-heralded novel about the Philippines, *The Dogeaters* (1990); and a collection of new and selected poems, *Danger and Beauty* (1993).

Hagedorn lives in New York City.

1. "Makebelieve Music," in *The Poetry Reading*, eds. Stephen Vincent and Ellen Zweig, San Francisco, 1981, p. 140.   2. The same.   3. The same.

Latin Music in New York

made me dance with you
tito   eddie   n ray
somewhere with plumjam eyelids
i danced with you
in a roomful of mirrors
in miss harlow's house

the white girl's in town
and i smell death
the poet dying in a bar
body shaking in time
to lady day's song
   he's dying in a nod
   in a lullaby
   of ambulance haze
   and chloral hydrate
   they burned his brain

somewhere
i saw the white girl smiling
la cucaracha was up all night
hiding her spoons   her mirrors   her revolutions
in the morning
   the trace of vampires
   still there
   in the blood   even after a bath

you can't wash it away
you can't hide it
again and again
i looked under my bed
  inside a perfume box
   in the argentinian dagger
    the baby wolf gave me
     in your eyes
      in a furtive smile
      in a good fuck
       in the boogaloo i do
there's no escaping it

somewhere   with plumjam eyelids

i danced the tasty freeze shuffle with you
the reds   the blues   the tango con tu madre
it's there
in town for the night
a guest appearance   a quick solo
death gets hyped
and i'm in love again

latin music in new york
made me dance with you
azucar y chocolaté
the alligator dream
of a tropical night

death makes a quick run
to las vegas
trying to take the poet
with him

latin music in new york
made me dance with you
tito   eddie   n ray

revolutions are creeping out
from under my bed!

and i sing a song for you
and you
and
you

1975

Something About You

this is for ntozake
of the painted sacred monkeys
on the beaches of the caribbean
the chinese ladies weep
into their ivory fans
as she dances the bomba

and this is for pedro
in brooklyn and puerto rico
and the beautiful blueness
of the water of my voices

the music will save you
from madness
if you listen

and this is for rose who is dead

and thulani with the moon in her hair

this is for the cartoon lady ifa
of the planet venus with the green eyes
and the darkness of her
that all new orleans weeps
as she dances for lena horne
and dorothy dandridge
who is dead

and this is for the wizard
who swallows his tears
like diamonds
lost in the caves
of his gentle throat
the music will consume your sadness
if you keep singing

this is for the one whose aura was silver

and this is for the man
who chases butterflies and alcoholics
in latin nightclub dreams
and kisses me with zoom lenses
on the beaches of the hollywood freeway
all the hibiscus bloom
as you devour iguanas

and this is for the men who loved me

and the one i love

and the child who is a mirror

this is for the one who bears light
who is the color of egypt
the cuban drummers are joyous
when nashira moves across the floor
of crying laughter

something about you
all of us
with songs inside

knifing the air of sorrow
with our dance
a carnival of spirits
shredded blossoms
in the water

1975

CHARLES BERNSTEIN ▪ ▪ ▪ ▪ ▪ ▪ ▪ ▪ ▪ ▪ ▪ ▪
b. 1950

Born and raised in New York City, Charles Bernstein attended Harvard University, where he studied with the philosopher Stanley Cavell.

The leading theorist of language poetry, Bernstein was co-editor with Bruce Andrews of the journal $L=A=N=G=U=A=G=E$ as well as The $L=A=N=G=U=A=G=E$ Book (1984), a collection of essays. Bernstein's own essays are collected in Content's Dream: Essays 1975–1984 (1986) and A Poetics (1992). His numerous poetry books include Poetic Justice (1979), Controlling Interests (1980), Islets/Irritations (1983), The Sophist (1987), and Rough Trades (1991).

In "Artifice of Absorption," an essay in verse, Bernstein makes a distinction between the terms absorption ("rhapsodic, spellbinding, / mesmerizing, hypnotic, total, riveting, / enthralling") and impermeability ("artifice, boredom, / exaggeration, attention scattering, distraction, digression, interruptive, transgressive"[1]). Absorptive literature depends on realism, transparency, and continuity, while the antiabsorptive, which Bernstein prefers, is comparatively artificial, opaque, and discontinuous in character.

"In my poems," he writes, "I / frequently use opaque & nonabsorbable / elements, digressions & / interruptions, as part of a technological arsenal to create a more powerful ('souped up') absorption than possible with traditional, / & blander, absorptive techniques." Ultimately, the project of "impermeable" writing is "to wake / us from the hypnosis of absorption."[2] Rather than be held captive by the text, the reader is required "to be actively involved in the process of constituting its meaning."[3] Despite the difficulties presented by Bernstein's poetry, it frequently displays an antic sense of humor.

Bernstein is currently David Gray Professor of Poetry and Letters at the State University of New York, Buffalo.

1. A Poetics, Cambridge, MA, 1992, p. 29.   2. The same, pp. 52–54.   3. Charles Bernstein, "Writing and Method," in Content's Dream, Los Angeles, 1986, p. 233.

The Klupzy Girl

Poetry is like a swoon, with this difference:
it brings you to your senses. Yet his
parables are not singular. The smoke from
the boat causes the men to joke. Not
gymnastic: pyrotechnic. The continuousness

of a smile—wry, perfume scented. No this
would go fruity with all these changes
around. Sense of variety: panic. Like
my eye takes over from the front
yard, three pace. Idle gaze—years
right down the window. Not clairvoyance,
predictions, deciphering—enacting. Analytically,
i.e., thoughtlessly. Begin to push and cue
together. Or I originate out of this
occurrence, stoop down, bend on. The
Protest-ant's voice within, calling for
this to be shepherded, for moment's
expression's enthroning. Able to be
alibied (contiguity of vacuity). Or
do you think you can communicate
telepathetically? Verena read the epistle
with much deliberateness. If we are
not to be phrasemongers, we must
sit down and take the steps that will
give these policies life. I fumbled clumsily
with the others—the evocations, explanations,
glossings of "reality" seemed like stretching
it to cover ground rather than make
or name or push something through.
"But the most beautiful
of all doubts is when the downtrodden
and despairing raise their heads and
stop believing in the strength of their oppressors."
To be slayed by such sighs: a noble figure
in a removed entranceway.
"This is just a little note
to say that it was nice working with
all of you. It has been a rewarding
experience in many ways. Although I
am looking forward to my new position with
great anticipation, I shall never forget
the days I spent here. It was like
a home-away-from-home, everyone was
just so warm and friendly. I shall ever
remember you in my prayers, and I
wish you the best for the future." Preoccupations
immediately launch: to set straight, to glean
from her glance. Terrifically bored
on the bus. Any really you want
go to mixed on me. Sumptuous slump.
As it becomes apparent. Just that I thought.
Contraction that to you perhaps an
idealization. Have I kept. But that
point is—such repair as roads no

joint, what?, these few years must
admit to not expecting, as if the
silent rudeness might separate us out. &
maybe anger would be better than explaining.
When in tents or families in comparative.
Which sums digest. Disclaimer
alights what with begin. That's
maybe the first pace, the particular. I mean
I feel I've got to and a few while
I can just look to see unrelenting
amount of canny criticism whatever
occasions overriding for comparison
spin for the sake of intrinsic in that
or that I've already made although
against reaction's consequent proceeding.
But it's to the point that you've
begun to broach like you could almost
fault me on as if you were going to
use could become primarily propulsion
to affinity have itself so. She
gets nutty. Oh she settles in, she
settles the curdles, unhooks the latches,
but I, preferring hatches . . .
When batters, benumbs, the lights
in a basket, portable. Potted & make
believe—your rudeness amounts to not
noticing, i.e., I'm on a different
scale of jags. To be in replacement
for a number of linings. Tubes of turmoil.
To stroll on the beach is to be in
the company of the wage-earner and
the unemployed on the public way, but
to command a view of it from a vantage
both recessed and elevated is to enter
the bourgeois space; here vantage and view
become consumable. I can't describe
how insulted I felt, it's a ruthlessness
not so much I didn't know you possessed
as that I didn't think you'd turn
on me. When you stop acting in good
faith any residue of the relationship
gets really unpleasant and the gratuitous
discounting severs what I can't necessarily
define the circumferences of. "There are a
number of calls in the June bill
which I have been unable to document. We
believe these calls were made by S———
O—— who is no longer employed by

this project. We presume these calls
to be program related although she
did not keep a log of long distance
calls as requested in the memo
circulated March 11, 1980." It has
more to me than please to note acquits
defiant spawn. But your letter does
not scan its view nor serve our
own resolve. Little noticing sectored
demonstration, or flail with inheld
throng. Content to meet or not to meet
what inlays subsequent flustered
adjustment. "The Good *is*
for the fact that I will it, and apart
from willing it, it has no existence."
"There is no document of civilization
that is not at the same time a
document of barbarism." Blue suede pestilence.
Binds bins. History and civilization
represented as aura—piles
of debris founded on a law and mythology
whose bases are in violence, the release
from which a Messianic moment
in which history itself is vanquished.
That's why I'm perplexed
at your startlement, though obviously
it's startling to see contexts changed on you
to have that done to you and
delivered unbeknownst. The Ideal
swoops, and reascends. "With real
struggle, genuine tax relief
can be won." A manic
state of careless grace. Mylar juggernauts
zig-zag penuriously. Car smashed into;
camera stolen; hat lost; run out of
money, write for money, money doesn't come.
Long interruption as I talk to woman
most of the way back—a runner,
very pleasant. Get off in Boston and everything
seems to go crazy.

> All of gets where
> Round dog-eared head
> The clear to trying
> Forgets issues of trembles
> Address vestiges to remain
> These years after all
> Fog commends in discourse

1983

Whose Language

Who's on first? The dust descends as
the skylight caves in. The door
closes on a dream of default and
denunciation (go get those piazzas),
hankering after frozen (prose) ambiance
(ambivalence). Doors to fall in, bells
to dust, nuances to circumscribe.
Only the real is real: the little
girl who cries out "Baby! Baby!"
but forgets to look in the mirror
—of a . . . It doesn't really
matter whose, only the appointment
of a skewed and derelict parade.
My face turns to glass, at last.

1991

Of Time and the Line

George Burns likes to insist that he always
takes the straight lines; the cigar in his mouth
is a way of leaving space between the
lines for a laugh. He weaves lines together
by means of a picaresque narrative;
not so Hennie Youngman, whose lines are strict-
ly paratactic. My father pushed a
line of ladies' dresses—not down the street
in a pushcart but upstairs in a fact'ry
office. My mother has been more concerned
with her hemline. Chairman Mao put forward
Maoist lines, but that's been abandoned (most-
ly) for the East-West line of malarkey
so popular in these parts. The prestige
of the iambic line has recently
suffered decline, since it's no longer so
clear who "I" am, much less who *you* are. When
making a line, better be double sure
what you're lining in & what you're lining
out & which side of the line you're on; the
world is made up so (Adam didn't so much
name as delineate). Every poem's got
a prosodic lining, some of which will
unzip for summer wear. The lines of an
imaginary are inscribed on the
social flesh by the knifepoint of history.
Nowadays, you can often spot a work

of poetry by whether it's in lines
or no; if it's in prose, there's a good chance
it's a poem. While there is no lesson in
the line more useful than that of the pick-
et line, the line that has caused the most ad-
versity is the bloodline. In Russia
everyone is worried about long lines;
back in the USA, it's strictly soup-
lines. "Take a chisel to write," but for an
actor a line's got to be cued. Or, as
they say in math, it takes two lines to make
an angle but only one lime to make
a Margarita.

1991

Wait

This is the way to start a sentence about startling a sentence. Here is the
tense that has not heart, that tramples beyond its own infirmity. O! how
exquisite is the loss of all that we have shared, all that we might better
have hoped only to have lived for. Pleased, said I, who cares so little
about such things, who'd rather be a mast on a plumb of piddle than
underlit by dunks . . .

At this point dive into second. Soon I will try to correct a foil trivial to
all but those who see behind a wet-pressed fin. Or would this mean that
all was tossed in this here twirl? What am I to do sayeth the elderly
man. I will goes into these houses that you have made for me and will
tell you all I slate.

So it crawls off far into the sky that never answers
Where daylight falls but knows neither you or ye
        Fall into my arms of twilight
        As I kiss the pit that stomachs not its pith
And in this return to faithful sentience, gaze but have not
Fear for all I try will bring to nought this pail of peers.

To say again.
To say it here/
Only this
can I know, that where I fly together will you warp that
abode embrace my flight.
        Or shall it only be that here do swim upon the grace of all
that has o'ercome this vault of
        sceptres. Steeped in vain revamp
or put upon
        at reason's heap.

Not to say or not to
As

with this gaze upon failed Mystery
or in the giving go, the living loss
strikes against these bows
            ˌ
Which only says to this that will go variously to bay for noisesome
        sleep.
                           Stern

among the frolicsome pompadors.
                                    1991

JOHN YAU ▪ ▪ ▪ ▪ ▪ ▪ ▪ ▪ ▪ ▪ ▪ ▪ ▪ ▪ ▪ ▪ ▪ ▪ ▪
b. 1950

John Yau was born in Lynn, Massachusetts, a year after his parents emigrated from China. He was educated at Bard College and Brooklyn College, where he studied with John Ashbery.

Since 1978, he has written art criticism for *Art in America*, *Artforum*, *ARTnews*, and *Vogue*, among other magazines. His publications include *The Sleepless Night of Eugene Delacroix* (1980), *Broken Off by the Music* (1981), *Corpse and Mirror* (1983), *Radiant Silhouette: New & Selected Work 1974–1988* (1989), and *Edificio Sayonara* (1992).

Despite the cool surfaces and uncommitted tone of his work, which suggest Ashbery's influence, Yau's work is not associated with the New York School sensibility. In the mid-1970s, Yau composed poems using word-substitution games suggested by the work of French novelist Raymond Roussel.[1] By the late 1970s, he had turned to more narrative forms of poetry that also communicate a dreamlike sense of discontinuity.

Yau's use of narrative draws on film techniques. "I'm also influenced by movies," Yau claims, "that kind of *speed* of seeing, the seamless jumps, the echoes, and the way something dissolves something else." Although he often uses the materials of memory, Yau believes that "to write about one's life in terms of a subjective 'I' . . . is to fulfill the terms of the oppressor. I suppose I don't know who this 'I' would or could speak for. Myself, what for?"[2]

A contributing editor to the literary magazine *Sulfur*, Yau lives in Brooklyn.

1. Edward Foster, "An Interview with John Yau," *Talisman*, No. 5, Fall 1990, p. 43.
2. The same, pp. 48, 49.

Chinese Villanelle

I have been with you, and I have thought of you
Once the air was dry and drenched with light
I was like a lute filling the room with description

We watched glum clouds reject their shape
We dawdled near a fountain, and listened
I have been with you, and I have thought of you

Like a river worthy of its gown
And like a mountain worthy of its insolence . . .
Why am I like a lute left with only description

How does one cut an axe handle with an axe
What shall I do to tell you all my thoughts
When I have been with you, and thought of you

A pelican sits on a dam, while a duck
Folds its wings again; the song does not melt
I remember you looking at me without description

Perhaps a king's business is never finished,
Though "perhaps" implies a different beginning
I have been with you, and I have thought of you
Now I am a lute filled with this wandering description

1979

Cenotaph

I

The clues to what they remembered had been pasted into an album.
Photographs of her family and friends, snapshots he had taken during
the war. The album was packed neatly in a trunk, which was then
stored in the ship's hold. It was nearly spring when they sailed from
Shanghai to San Francisco.

II

The album was not, as the word suggests, white. Its pages were black—
the time inside the camera before light casts its shadows on the wall.
What were white were the words, the laconic summations printed
along the bottom of every page.

III

The album was divided into two parts, his and hers. In the second part,
his part, someone (most likely her) had carefully removed the snap-
shots. It was here I always slowed down and inspected the pages. The
place where the words were lined up beneath black rectangles.

IV

What had reflected the light was gone. Only the rows of white letters remained. Only the faded rectangles framing empty black spaces.

V

I would spin in my room until I was too dizzy to stand. Then, lying on the bed with my eyes closed, I would pretend the plane was about to crash.

VI

Those black rectangles surrounded by faded black almost blue frames. The words were arranged neatly along the bottom of every page. My father was an accountant, this was his ledger.

VII

I understood someone had tried to erase this history of excerpts. The words continued echoing long after I returned the album to its place on the shelf.

VIII

The hospital was next to the jail. From the roof I could see the inmates playing basketball, the interns practicing their serves.

IX

I tried imagining the pictures the black rectangles once held. *Mound of Heads, Shanghai, 1946* was my favorite. Movies showed me everything but this.

X

At the beach I saw the words transformed by the sun. Saw them become hills of bleached skulls. Now they were smooth and round, white as the words describing them.

XI

Lying beside the sagging castles, watching the sand trickle through my fingers. Tiny examples of what I read. All afternoon I played beneath the sun with the skulls, molding them into little mountains.

1984

Engines of Gloom and Affection

The sky is green, and there is no book to tell us what it means. It has never stopped raining. Three men, four of them speaking. A woman carries a photograph of worms under her tongue. I have spoken out of turn. The proportions are awkward, the details coarse.

The sky is green, and there is no book to tell us the names of our children. Have you noticed the dead man hugging a doll? Have you thought about why she found it necessary to laugh so loudly? And why, for example, the heads of the statues were removed and stored in a vault beneath the hospital?

The sky is green, and there is no book to show us the route. Once a week, he forgets where he parked his car and must return to his apartment. A set of instructions has been placed on the kitchen table. Since his breathing apparatus is so poorly developed, he is confined to driving beside the wall of stucco clouds circling the plaza. The sky is gray mixed with green. Someone claims to be your friend.

1989

JIM CARROLL ▪ ▪ ▪ ▪ ▪ ▪ ▪ ▪ ▪ ▪ ▪ ▪ ▪ ▪ ▪ ▪
b. 1951

Born and raised in New York City, where he now lives, Jim Carroll was an All-City basketball star at Trinity High School in Manhattan. This period of his life, which also included drug use and homosexual hustling, is described in his book *The Basketball Diaries* (1978). For many years Carroll struggled with and ultimately overcame heroin addiction, though addiction has remained a concern of his poems.

His books of poetry include *Living at the Movies* (1973) and *The Book of Nods* (1986). They reflect Carroll's poetic stance of outsider and bohemian in the tradition of Arthur Rimbaud. But for a rock-and-roll poet—his group, the Jim Carroll Band, issued a popular album, *Catholic Boy* (1981)—Carroll's work is markedly literary; his influences include poets of the New York School, especially Ted Berrigan, whose list poem "People Who Died" provided the inspiration for Carroll's celebrated song of the same title. As a singer and songwriter, Carroll has been compared to Lou Reed and Patti Smith.

Recently, he has turned to writing monologues for performance and for "spoken word" recordings on compact disk.

Withdrawal Letter

Wild geese waking in the March wind

it's morning
I don't think much about March

though the weather disturbs me
and
the geese, they disappear eventually
with enormous groans of lost possibilities

I am truly a fragment of your secret worlds
though this eludes me. I think
all day about the likeness of heroin
to skindiving, how sharks never sleep
are marked from Southampton to Japan in three days

and how pure the waves are
no matter what the professors say,
in their motion . . . a gull glows in my sweat

                              Eastward

simple, yet the pain of remembering
so much before, so many gulls
seen and jammed into poems
this one just glided onto the reef
it was easy to include, and I trust it.

and horses, count the horses
in this poem and that
I saw a palomino once in Kansas and wept
the eye ring froze from each touch,
truck drivers passing on the highway
shouting with their fingers

though I nodded mostly through Kansas
treating someone I love badly, though
confusion results, and from there one realizes
it is not alone, anything
in the end, and one loves again
in this marvelous hollow decoration
each moves slowly within

you want to whisper, mainly of fear,
"Who are they?"

it is daylight now

the truth is you lost your willow
for me to find, for each muse to dance
why not joy to change pace
under these weeping leaves, only nature's gimmick

and "They," well, they surround you in N.Y.C.
on subways and park entrances near the plaza

but can you turn your head to the fountain?
I sit with my long hair breathing spray

and can I bear all those other scenes
so many other words might shoot up?

I want my hands and neck to be free and clear
no crucifixes and no rings.

these hands that hold the blood that rises
to a level where joy is pumped
visually to one's heart
in the serpent red dawn

1981

Maybe I'm Amazed

Just because there is music
piped into the most false of revolutions

it cannot clean these senses
of slow wireless death crawling
from a slick mirror
1/8th its normal size . . .

Marty was found dead by the man literally
blue 12 hours after falling out
at the foot of the Cloisters
with its millions in rare tapestry
and its clear view of the Hudson

and even testing your blue pills
over and over to reverse
my slow situations
I wind up stretched across the couch
still nodding with Sherlock Holmes
examining our crushed veins

Richard Brautigan,
I don't care who you are fucking
in your clean california air

I just don't care

though mine are more beautiful anyway
          (though more complex perhaps)

and we have white flowers too
right over our window on 10th St.
like hands that mark tiny x's
across infinity day by day

but even this crumb of life
I eventually surface toward
continues to nod as if I see you all
thoughtlessly
through a carefully inverted piece
of tainted glass

shattered in heaven
and found on these streets

1981

Paregoric Babies

Clocks blue seconds fold over me
slow as swamp dreams I feel
heavy like metal shade pre-dawn thickness

I sit

in my chair of nods shivering
from a sickness I took years to perfect

dark paddling in the wave membrane
the monkey woman's dream streams
are places of shy creatures, head infants
I had born on a whim and abandoned . . . my eye

drips the strain in the sweet March air, frozen
pure as my blood refuses to flow . . .
stilled, sweat that shines the breath of my poem

1981

CARLA HARRYMAN ■ ■ ■ ■ ■ ■ ■ ■ ■ ■ ■ ■ ■
b. 1952

Born and raised in Orange, California, Carla Harryman was educated at the
University of California at Santa Barbara and San Francisco State University.
    Author of *Percentage* (1979), *Under the Bridge* (1980), *Property* (1982), *The
Middle* (1983), *Vice* (1987), *Animal Instincts* (1989), and *In the Mode of* (1991),
Harryman likes to blend fictive and essayistic elements in her prose poems. "I

prefer to distribute narrative rather than deny it," she writes. "Narrative exists, and arguments either for or against it are false."[1]

In Harryman's view, "narrative might be thought to be a character," the defects of which lie in the " 'potential to observe his own practice of making falsehoods.' If this narrative is imitating anything, it's the intention to convince the audience to enjoy its imitation, whatever the lack of truth or reasonableness."[2] Harryman's narratives are intentionally marked by interruptions so that, as she writes in *The Middle*, "Causality is dimmed." Her work is self-reflexive, often humorously erotic: "Since I am often forced to write in the nude, I often fantasize wearing beautiful clothes," she writes. "In this way I never suffer from abuse, since my characterlessness is not perceived."[3]

A playwright and co-founder of the Poets' Theater, which produced experimental plays in San Francisco from 1978 to 1984, Harryman lives in Berkeley, California.

1. "Toy Boats," *Poetics Journal*, No. 5, May 1985, p. 104.   2. The same.   3. San Francisco, 1983, p. 4.

My Story

Speaking in a state of fidelity to the subject, living flesh though it may be, is similar to assuming one has acquired the song of birth through the ritual repeating of the names and gestures of newborn infants. This makes me want to cry. But I can't lie: no way am I going to disguise myself in the habit of that body, the one that isn't mine.

My story will never turn out because of the mass surrounding its small and devious posturings. Assuming the tone of reverence, an author describes a woman climbing a hill.

This is a braggart's tale. It starts in the endless heartlands of a dull plain when looked at from the point of view of a small animal. Perhaps a snail travels along the borders ceaselessly making the visible world the token of some larger obliteration.

I was born but do not understand that phenomenon any better than whatever creature may never think about it. I, however, am not perplexed. Incognito striplings suspend the rapidly changing paths of life. Their job is to curtail the disappearance of whatever has failed to be held up for observation, to keep potential beasts from jumping into deep and invisible water before they have been judiciously examined by Expertise, that changeling hanging supine over the town of Nemole, the farthest point from the border. In the interest of the flesh, the striplings dine out every so often, showing their teeth, their raunchy ways, and heckling anyone who offers to serve them by rippling the fur on their necks.

Childhood doesn't exist. Infancy is out of the question. I mastered the things I have forgotten. Aggrieved, I lose jokes to the stepping-stone mentality employed by one's associates and so on. The striplings kept to their course and I to mine. I couldn't console them. They couldn't show me my face.

1989

Realism

When I'm eating this I want food. I mean what I say because . . .

I act it all out. Everything is perfumed: the assurance that knowledge will pick it up. It is real. The I expands. The individual is caught in a devouring machine, but she shines like the lone star on the horizon when we enter her thoughts, when she expounds on the immensity of her condition, the subject of the problem which interests nature.

What I think I want to eat is going to be food—this is the intuitive sense. Not to be discredited but glorified in the face of/faced with the bald-faced bold bleak wall of descriptive intonations otherwise known as information. But what the unconditional tone of exactitude promises is the reverse image: the mind and body are understood to be eunuchs hunted by the darkness of the human condition. The unconditional exactitude wants us to believe in this darkness and partialness. Find a passage (vocabulary) which glorifies the subtle conditions in which we find ourselves approached from the outside in.

Yes, I am a realist. In other words, the point of focus is distorted by the enormity of the objects surrounding the particular thing or the individual word. We talk about the subject of our conversation in an ideal setting while giants expound around us. Trees promote the ground. The world is going to seed, if that. Can I extend my imagination into an unknown habitation in which I can't live? If I were a realist would I say something else instead?

1989

The Male

Would you prefer the examples? The pancakes? Or the words?

Oh, I have been used as an example so many times, said the Male. I think I . . . Do I? Do I think? said the Male.

Pancakes are good, I reminded him.

If, said the Male, I say anything, I reveal something of myself: my stupidity, or arrogance, or inability to make selections. I can't speak . . .

If you could only make a choice, I could say, for example, well the Male prefers pancakes and that must mean something. Words pain the Male, I could say. And then I would attempt to apply that information as an example. Everybody would be able to make sense out of the expression *the male's pancakes.* When in the galleries, I could point to the portrait of an ancestor and say "the male's pancakes," and everyone would laugh from the pleasure that words and things can so transform each other they make the most sense when used in tandem.

I have always liked the word *tandem,* said the Male, seemingly inspired or abstracted by a distant shadow creeping slowly over his brow.

You are not concentrating!

Con-cen-tra-ting? said the Male. The pressure to concentrate is very heavy, I imagine.

You imagine? I asked.

I can't quite make it out, so I would say I do imagine . . .

The Male stood next to a rock in a large bed of rocks at the top of the near-bald hill. Some sheep ran up the hill, pulled at turf, and descended to richer pastures.

We climbed side by side to an old fort where the Welsh had defended themselves from the Vikings. The wind was so strong, I had to climb on my hands and knees because I was pregnant. I would rest against a mound on the hillside and the Male would disappear in a trough in the hill. I could look down to an empty swimming pool behind a farmhouse. The pool had probably been out of use since the renovation of the Roman canals where boatloads of people now traveled along a steamy strip of water above the town, unseen by the people in the town below. One person from the town stuck out in my reflections, a woman with pruning shears standing in a driveway arguing with a man whose car she had had towed.

A lot more heavy breathing on the part of jealous neighbors and the Male asked me, Is a poet a poet all the time? I don't like riddles and didn't want to answer the question. The Male, however, was desperately serious, singing out the following verse:

> *These loud birds*
> *Flying above the cathedral*
> *Counter the politeness*
> *That keeps me anonymous*
> *Noise makes drama*
> *Out of ruins*
> *The trees develop in the ruins*
> *An authoritative base for birds*

Was this the poetry of prose? The Male by nature prosaic, moving from one place to the next in an unrhapsodic way, thinking hard perhaps but communicating little, allowing his motions to speak for him, so that he was followed by a trail of his own making? Would others follow this trail, each having their own experience of it, each wondering what it was like for anyone else to have been there? (For instance, what was it like for Orphan Annie? The cranky-looking filling station out the window? The hoses on the pumps having lost their resilience? The attendant limp as grease? The comic-strip reader in a sunlit, airy place?) Life is like a book, any book, even technical manuals.

On the other hand, there is the body, a form, and who knows what goes on in the Male's mind? The Male would exhibit a deep, ponderous blank. And yet, *I* do not have a verse in any of my thoughts. Is a landowner a landowner *all* the time? The landowner would either say "yes" or "no, I'm just a person."

I am just a person, I said to the Male, but you are not just a male. I don't know why I chose to present myself in this way to the creature.

What can you tell me about the *faux-naif*? asked the Male.

There is something in your question that reminds me of masturbating while reading Wordsworth. The reader effaces the merits of the poet's journey at the same time as she follows it with enthusiasm. A great inarticulateness has overcome her as she encounters the high rhetoric.

We were standing against the crumbling wall of the fort as I spoke. The wind was taking my words away from me. The Male was still watching the sheep race back to richer pastures long after they had reached that destination. It is possible to become very fond of a trace, a story that is always the same.

Epilogue

Rituals are like ducks in pink water, says the Male. Like everything else he says, this is from out of the blue. In the background Baudelaire imitates an orator: If I am not decorated for having done my duty, I will cease to do it . . . Words come to the Male. They are not willed into being. There is a sinking feeling at the end of any utterance. The last word may by accident use up the potential of all the others. Then the pitch downward will be into the eternity of the Male's mind, his endless spontaneity and lack of preference. When I drink pink water out of the bowl shaped from his head, he looks at my throat. Bolus, says the Male. This seems to cover up some kind of disparity. The desire to be touched is overwhelming. But whose desire is it? This relates to our initial conversation, where one word could be taken to the land of many.

1989

MAXINE CHERNOFF ▪ ▪ ▪ ▪ ▪ ▪ ▪ ▪ ▪ ▪ ▪
b. 1952

Born and raised in Chicago, Maxine Chernoff is author of five books of poetry including *Utopia TV Store* (1979), *New Faces of 1952* (1985), and *Leap Year Day: New and Selected Poems* (1990). A leading prose poet, Chernoff writes, "In writing prose poems, I am indebted to the work of Henri Michaux and Julio Cortazar, among others, who create alternate universes that are as surprising, banal, stupid, and true as our own."[1] Prose poems, she believes, "may be a contemporary equivalent of metaphysical poetry, since in both cases metaphor can expand to become the central concept (conceit) of the writing."[2] In their "yoking of disparate elements," Chernoff's poems also resemble the surrealist collage.

In her essay "The Fence of Character," Chernoff states that "character" in many of her prose poems "exists so that language can occur."[3] That is, there is a limit, or fence, beyond which the elements of narrative, including the use of fictional characters, cannot pass. The work contained in the abecedarium *Japan* (1987) breaks with normal sentence structure and explores the acoustic relations of words rather than their imagistic properties.

Author of two books of short stories, *Bop* (1986) and *Signs of Devotion* (1993), and a novel, *Plain Grief* (1991), Chernoff lives in Chicago.

1. Author's note to *Ecstatic Occasions, Expedient Forms,* New York, 1987, p. 28. 2. The same, p. 29. 3. *Poetics Journal*, No. 5, 1985, p. 88.

The Man Struck Twenty Times by Lightning

I've known him so long I've almost forgotten the first photo he showed me. The helpless orphan in the cloudlike bonnet abandoned in a rainstorm. And the scrapbook: "Boy Struck by Lightning on Little League Field." "Teen Struck by Lightning at Graduation Exercise." "Bride and Groom Struck by Lightning at Altar. One Dies."

Extraordinary, yes, but his relationship with lightning, which seems the most personal in nature, no longer astounds me. I sometimes think of lightning as his pushy employer. At other times *he* is the master, lightning the recalcitrant servant. He is the ship, lightning the challenging sea. His favorite is him as countryside, lightning the endless white fence.

Often I wonder whether he's contrived the danger to make his attachments more tender. I must admit I can't think of the speed of lightning without some tears. In this way I'm like the mother of the baby born with a full set of teeth. Night after night she lies awake, examining the record book, imagining its dubious future.

"Charlatan," I say on rainy nights, for he's never been struck in my presence. Yet with every weather forecast I fear his loss, knowing I'd miss those singed greetings, those thunderous goodbyes.

1979

Lost and Found

I am looking for the photo that would make all the difference in my life. It's very small and subject to fits of amnesia, turning up in poker hands, grocery carts, under the unturned stone. The photo shows me at the lost and found looking for an earlier photo, the one that would have made all the difference then. My past evades me like a politician. Wielding a fly-swatter, it destroys my collection of cereal boxes, my childhood lived close to the breakfast table. Only that photo can help me locate my fourteen lost children, who look just like me. When I call the Bureau of Missing Persons, they say, "Try the Bureau of Missing Photos." They have a fine collection. Here's one of Calvin Coolidge's seventh wedding. Here's one of a man going over a cliff on a dogsled. Here's my Uncle Arthur the night he bought a peacock. O photo! End your tour of the world in a hot air balloon. Resign your job at the mirror-testing laboratory. Come home to me, you little fool, before I find I can live without you.

1985

Breasts

If I were French, I'd write
about breasts, structuralist treatments
of breasts, deconstructionist breasts,
Gertrude Stein's breasts in Père-Lachaise
under stately marble. Film noire breasts
no larger than olives, Edith Piaf's breasts
shadowed under a song, mad breasts raving
in the bird market on Sunday.
Tanguy breasts softening the landscape,
the politics of nipples (we're all equal).
A friend remembers nursing,
his twin a menacing blur. But wait,
we're in America, where breasts
were pointy until 1968. I once invented
a Busby Berkeley musical with naked women
underwater sitting at a counter
where David Bowie soda-jerked them
ice cream glaciers. It sounds so sexual
but had a Platonic airbrushed air.
Beckett calls them dugs, which makes me think
of potatoes, but who calls breasts potatoes?
Bolshoi dancers strap down their breasts
while practicing at the bar.
You guess they're thinking of sailing,
but probably it's bread, dinner,
and the *Igor Zlotik Show* (their
Phil Donahue). There's a photo of me
getting dressed where I'm surprised
by Paul and try to hide my breasts, and another
this year, posed on a pier, with my breasts
reflected in silver sunglasses. I blame
it on summer when flowers overcome gardens
and breasts point at the stars. Cats
have eight of them, and Colette tells
of a cat nursing its young while
being nursed by its mother. Imagine the scene
rendered human. And then there's the Russian
story about the woman . . . but wait,
they've turned the lights down, and Humphrey
Bogart is staring at Lauren Bacall's breasts
as if they might start speaking.

1985

FROM *Japan*

Amble

Shotgun
      blossoming
outward
      ranting rangle
smoky
   entrance
      evidence
   aspen
pent-up   tenderly
    lying
fulsome
      mentor
miscue
   julep jitters
sisterly
    sub-strata
das ich is
  "or delicate surgery"
mental
     trappings
hair and
      tangents
fruited
    fingered
lily
  alley
alabaster

Black

Sixty second
     August
"a bruised tenderness"
    kitsch operatic
  clucking
certainty
    fulsome
vulgate
    I Ching
  eggplant

```
question
            native vacancy
      recant
            panic
        bodily
                  orbit
      if
            then
      freon
            tempest
   whatnot
            treeline
        languor
            listed
                  vested
      savvy
            really
```

1987

How Lies Grow

The first time I lied to my baby, I told him that it was his face on the baby food jar. The second time I lied to my baby, I told him that he was the best baby in the world, that I hoped he'd never leave me. Of course I want him to leave me someday. I don't want him to become one of those fat shadows who live in their mother's houses watching game shows all day. The third time I lied to my baby I said, "Isn't she nice?" of the woman who'd caressed him in his carriage. She was old and ugly and had a disease. The fourth time I lied to my baby, I told him the truth, I thought. I told him how he'd have to leave me someday or risk becoming a man in a bow tie who eats macaroni on Fridays. I told him it was for the best, but then I thought, I want him to live with me forever. Someday he'll leave me: then what will I do?

1990

ART LANGE ▪ ▪ ▪ ▪ ▪ ▪ ▪ ▪ ▪ ▪ ▪ ▪ ▪ ▪ ▪ ▪ ▪ ▪ ▪
b. 1952

Art Lange was born and raised in Chicago, and studied with Ted Berrigan at Northeastern Illinois University in the 1970s. A music critic of international reputation, he was editor of *Downbeat*, the leading jazz journal, from 1981 to 1987. He is now a free-lance music and literary critic.

Editor of the magazine *Brilliant Corners*, which appeared from 1975 to 1979, he has published the poetry books *Glee: Song* (1977), *The Monk Poems* (1977), *Evidence* (1981), and *Needles at Midnight* (1986). With Nathaniel Mackey, he is co-editor of the anthology *Moment's Notice: Jazz in Poetry and Prose* (1993).

Lange is influenced by William Carlos Williams, Louis Zukofsky, and Robert Creeley in his musical use of the short poetic line; he also admires the introspective nature of James Schuyler's poetry. The spare phrasing of Lange's poetry is reminiscent of Thelonious Monk's jazz compositions, but his influences also include classical music, which in his opinion has, along with jazz, trained his ear for poetry.

Awarded a National Endowment for the Arts Fellowship in poetry in 1980, Lange lives in Chicago.

Sonnet for the Season

The wistful vistas are living in objects
without fuss, a lovely talent, fur-lined with
impudent grace, evidence an old-fashioned notion
though modest, walking while longing
to levitate, to get some air, a trace
like pulling teeth out of the wind or lighting
an expatriate's cigar; though never nudge you
with their face, some information
we digest, a Callas nostalgia, oboe blunder,
orgy of casual haltingly hovering through space,
over weather, simplifying and acknowledging
the distances we keep from each other, red
and green something bulging with wonders lent:
wet, crouched, beautifully recalcitrant.

1981

Perugia

Awoke in this
aged space
apprehensive,

throb-
bing, the language,
can't place

it, cadences
like
warm creme in

cappuccino, curdling—
who
drinks it?

Who speaks
it? The summer
sky so

high, so
blue, the few
clouds

seem
an intrusion. Lewd
landscape

lousy
with figures, none
of them

ghosts, none of them
you. Centuries
of sun

fade
sour brick to white
wash; confused,

hours
eyeing an embarrassed
road worn

by the wear
and tear of Roman
legions? Often

comes someone who
looks
like someone, but

isn't. One woman,
completely
copper, another,

thin
as sin, sinister—
a photo-

journalist? Apparitions
shiver
in the heat, thick

as thieves,
extravagant, un-
zipped,

in light
so
specific a rude

remark slits
the Campari-colored
air—

a smudge
on the mirror, blues
blur

the tightening
in the chest. To the
West,

a monstrous
cathedral
crouches and clenches

its teeth, an orange
moon
punishes the black

bruised sky. Birds
drown
out traffic. Time fries.

1989

JIMMY SANTIAGO BACA ▪ ▪ ▪ ▪ ▪ ▪ ▪ ▪ ▪ ▪

b. 1952

Half Chicano and half Apache, Jimmy Santiago Baca was born in Santa Fe, New Mexico. His parents divorced when he was two and left him in the care of a grandparent and friends of the family. At five, Baca lived at St. Anthony's Home for Boys in Albuquerque; at eleven, he ran away to live on the streets. At twenty, Baca was in prison for drug possession; it was there that he stole a book on English Romantic poetry from an attendant and began his education as a poet. He was still in prison when his first poems were published in *Mother Jones* magazine by the poetry editor Denise Levertov.

Baca's narratives about Chicano, Mestizo, and Indio people of the American Southwest—especially the impoverished South Valley area outside Albuquerque, where Baca settled to raise his own family—mix autobiography with devices of fiction. Gary Soto has written of the two long narrative poems that comprise *Martin & Meditations on the South Valley* (1987), "What makes this story succeed is its honesty, a brutal honesty, as well as Baca's original imagery and the passion of his writing. Moreover, a history is being written of a culture of poverty, which, except for a few poets . . . is absent in American poetry."[1]

Baca has also written *Immigrants in Our Own Land* (1979), *Black Mesa Poems* (1989), *Immigrants in Our Own Land and Earlier Selected Poems* (1990), a collection of essays, *Working in the Dark* (1992), and the filmscript for *Bound by Honor* (1993).

In a glossary appended to *Black Mesa Poems*, Baca indicates that a matanza is "a barrio social event where people gather to talk and eat, involving butchering and dressing an animal, and, usually, but not always, focusing on an event," such as Cinco de Mayo or a baptism.[2] "Matanza to Welcome Spring" is therefore ritual invocation for the arrival of that season.

Baca now lives in a hundred-year-old adobe house atop Black Mesa, south of Albuquerque.

1. Review of *Martin & Meditations on the South Valley* in the *San Francisco Chronicle*, January 24, 1988.   2. New York, 1989, p. 126.

Voz de la Gente

I went to river last night,
sat on a sandbar, crosslegged,
played my drum. My third hour,
tum—tum-tum, I noticed four young boys
waist-high in water, quarter mile down river,
staring at me. Tum—tum-tum. . . .
I stared, tum'd louder, stronger,
pads of my hands stung with each slap
on deerskin drum,
sound radiating ancient tribal rap
into night, an ancient heartbeat.
        Where the shore doglegs
        to the middle of the river,
        group of men and women stood.
Their silhouettes
defined in metallic moonlight,
gleaming in brown murky water.
I slapped harder, faster,
wild weed doctor covering night with my cure,
with *matachines* handstep, slow, then fast,
brown notes smoked and misted
close to sleeping children's lips,
curled in their hair, in adobe houses
along La Vega, Vito Romero road, and Atrisco.
        There would be no tomorrow,
        no mountains, no *llano*,
        no me,
and my drum softened its speech to whisper
sleeping to the shores,
singing us all together.
        I heard rattling branches
        crackle

as thousands of *la gente* pushed through the bosque,
    lining the Río Grande shore.
Standing knee high in water, crowds swooped
out into the shallows,
drawn by the ancient voice of their beginnings.

        Then I awoke.
And now this morning I run five miles
to Bridge street and back,
the dream clings to my ankles like leg-irons
a prisoner drags, and there is a pain
in the pads of my hands
that will not subside,
        until I play the drum.

        1989

Mi Tío Baca el Poeta de Socorro

Antonio Ce De Baca
chiseled on stone chunk gravemarker,
propped against a white wooden cross.
Dust storms faded the birth and death numbers.
Poet de Socorro,
whose poems roused *la gente*
to demand their land rights back,
'til one night—that terrible night,
hooves shook your earthen-floor
one-room adobe, lantern flame
flickered shadowy omens on walls,
and you scrawled across the page,
"*¡Aquí vienen! ¡Aquí vienen!*
Here they come!"
Hooves clawed your front yard,
guns glimmering blue
angrily beating at your door.
        You rose.
Black boots scurried round four adobe walls,
trampling flower beds.
They burst through the door.
It was a warm night, and carried the scent
of their tobacco, sulphur, and leather.
Faces masked in dusty hankies,
men wearing remnants of Rinche uniforms,
arms pitchforked you out,
where arrogant young boys on horses
held torches and shouted,
"Shoot the Mexican! Shoot him!"

Saliva flew from bits
as horses reared from you,
while red-knuckled recruits held reins tight,
drunkenly pouring whiskey over you,
kicking you up the hill by the yucca,
where you turned, and met the scream
of rifles with your silence.

            Your house still stands.
Black burnt tin covers window openings,
weeds grow on the dirt roof
that leans like an old man's hand
on a cane *viga*. . . .
I walk to the church a mile away,
a prayer on my lips bridges
years of disaster between us.
Maybe things will get better.
Maybe our struggle to speak and be
as we are, will come about.
For now, I drink in your spirit, Antonio,
to nourish me as I descend
into dangerous abysses of the future.
I came here this morning
at 4:30 to walk over my history.
Sat by the yucca, and then imagined you again,
walking up to me
face sour with tortuous hooks
pulling your brow down in wrinkles,
cheeks weary with defeat,
face steady with implacable dignity.
The softness in your brown eyes
said you could take no more.
You will speak with the angels now.
I followed behind you to the church,
your great bulky field-working shoulders
lean forward in haste
as if angels really did await us.
Your remorseful footsteps
in crackly weeds
sound the last time
I will hear and see you. Resolve is engraved
in each step. I want to believe
whatever problems we have, time will take
its course, they'll be endured and consumed.
Church slumps on a hill, somber and elegant.
After you, I firmly pull the solid core door back.
You kneel before La Virgen De Guadalupe,
bloody lips moving slightly,
your great gray head poised in listening,

old jacket perforated with bloody bullet holes.
I close the door, and search the prairie,
considering the words *faith, prayer* and *forgiveness,*
wishing, like you, I could believe them.

1989

Matanza to Welcome Spring

for Pat and Victorio

Spread eagle sheep legs wide,
wire hooves to shed beams,
and sink blade in neck wool,
'til the gray eyes drain of life
like cold pure water
from a tin pail.
>   (It kicked, choking on nasal blood,
>   liquid gasping coughs
>   spattered blood over me.)

Slit down belly, scalp rug-wool
skin away, pinch wool back
with blade to pink flesh, ssst ssst ssst
inch by inch, then I sling
whole carcass in bloody spray over fence.
>   (Close to its face, I swear
>   it gift-heaved a last breath
>   from its soft black nose
>   and warmed my nostril hairs
>   as I sniffed the dark smell
>   of its death.)

Mesquite in hole
boils water in the iron cauldron
which steam-cooks
hind quarter
on grill across cauldron.

>   Tonight I invite men and women
>   *con duende,*
>   who take a night in life
>   and forge it into iron
>   in the fire of their vision.

Aragon has gone
to the river to play his drum.
I hear the deep pom pom pom.
Round bonfire
Alicia squats, ruffles sheaf of poems,
while Alejandro tunes guitar.

Shadows dance round
stones that edge the fire.
          (In Alejandro's boot
          a knife hilt glimmers.)
Their teeth gleam grease juice
          (as do those of the children, who play
          in the dark behind us).
There is fear
in the horse's eye
corralled nearby.
          (Hear the drum on the Río Grande.
          Boom pom boom pom. . . .)
Blood sizzles,
moist alfalfa in the air,
bats flit above the flames.
I toss a gleaming bone to spirits
in the orchard,
and Gonzales yells,
with his old earthen voice,
"Play, *hombre, ¡Canta, mujer!* Sing!
Sing the way the old ones sang!"

        Tonight life is
        lust
        death
        hunger
        violence
        innocence
        sweetness
        honor
        hard work
        and tomorrow I will go
        to church.
        But tonight
        I leap into
        impulse, instinct,
        into the burning
        of
                this moment.

        (I commit myself! One moment to the next
        I am chasm jumper and silence is
        a blue fire on my papery soul. I construct
        out of nothing. I am air, am labyrinth,
        place with no entry or exit,
        am a smoking mirror.

        Commit myself! Storms stroke my heart
        and destroy its neat furrows.
        My words are mule teams,

       that loosen, pound, hurl, out and up,
       and leave me standing in the open, naked,
       with star flame roar, life opening. . . .

       Commit myself!)

Hear the two hands
bleed along the river beating
drumskins,
deep sounds of thu-uba,
of magic, despair, joy,
       emotions trance-weave through sound,
          thumba, thumba, thumba.
Follow drum,
     thumba thumba thumba,
     umba umba umba
     ba-ba ba-ba
     thumba thumba thumba,
hear hearts mate with earth
in song,
spiral toward death
       in its long thuuumbaa,
toward life again
     in ba-ba ba-ba.

The sound is stain on purity,
is cry of broken thing,
drum does not wither beneath bed,
but rises heart
     into newness around us,
all around us,
     come follow   Follow the drum,
     thumba thumba thumba
            ba—ba—ba
     thumba thumba thumba
            ba—ba—ba,

    of living!

                1989

DAVID TRINIDAD ▪ ▪ ▪ ▪ ▪ ▪ ▪ ▪ ▪ ▪ ▪ ▪ ▪
b. 1953

Born and raised in Southern California, David Trinidad has published six books of poetry, among them *Pavane* (1981), *Monday, Monday* (1985), *November* (1987), and *Hand Over Heart: Poems 1981–1988* (1991).
    Trinidad is associated with a group of poets, including Amy Gerstler and Dennis Cooper, who gave readings at Beyond Baroque, a poetry center in Ven-

ice, California, in the 1980s; he also published the work of Gerstler and Cooper as the editor of Sherwood Press.

Like the poet Frank O'Hara, Trinidad likes to take his materials from everyday life, especially the mass media. Thus he insistently focuses on the blander elements of 1960s popular culture such as "The Patty Duke Show," which featured the "identical cousins" Cathy and Patty, the simultaneous speakers of "Double Trouble." In using dual speakers, Trinidad employs the technique of John Ashbery's long poem *Litany*, in which both columns are intended to be read as simultaneous but independent monologues. Trinidad's "Movin' with Nancy" makes use of the pantoum, a Malaysian form in which the first and third lines of each succeeding quatrain repeat the second and fourth lines of the previous stanza.

Now living in New York City, Trinidad teaches poetry workshops at the Writer's Voice at the Sixty-third Street YMCA and serves as poetry editor of *OutWeek* magazine.

Movin' with Nancy

It is almost time to grow up
I eat my TV dinner and watch
Nancy Sinatra in 1966
All boots and thick blonde hair

I eat my TV dinner and watch
The daughter of Frank Sinatra
All boots and thick blonde hair
She appears on "The Ed Sullivan Show"

The daughter of Frank Sinatra
She sings "These Boots Are Made For Walkin' "
She appears on "The Ed Sullivan Show"
The song becomes a number one hit

She sings "These Boots Are Made For Walkin' "
She sings "Somethin' Stupid" with her father
The song becomes a number one hit
She marries and divorces singer/actor Tommy Sands

She sings "Somethin' Stupid" with her father
She sings "The Last Of The Secret Agents"
She marries and divorces singer/actor Tommy Sands
She sings "How Does That Grab You, Darlin'?"

She sings "The Last Of The Secret Agents"
She sings "Lightning's Girl" and "Friday's Child"
She sings "How Does That Grab You, Darlin'?"
She sings "Love Eyes" and "Sugar Town"

She sings "Lightning's Girl" and "Friday's Child"
She puts herself in the hands of writer/producer Lee Hazelwood

She sings "Love Eyes" and "Sugar Town"
She co-stars with Elvis Presley in *Speedway*

She puts herself in the hands of writer/producer Lee Hazelwood
Three gold records later
She co-stars with Elvis Presley in *Speedway*
She rides on Peter Fonda's motorcycle

Three gold records later
She has developed an identity of her own
She rides on Peter Fonda's motorcycle
The wild angels roar into town

She has developed an identity of her own
Nancy Sinatra in 1966
The wild angels roar into town
It is almost time to grow up

1991

Double Trouble

Patty:

"Hi, Mom! I'm home!"
I shouted as I burst
through the front door.
"Hello, dear." I dashed
upstairs, threw my books
on the floor, tossed
on a stack of singles
and flopped down on
the bed. Chad & Jeremy
sent me instantly to
Dreamsville. I rolled
over and reached for
my princess phone. "Hi,
Sue Ellen." "HI! Oh,
Patty!" she gushed,
"You're absolutely the
talk of the campus! I
mean you're practically
a celebrity!" We gig-
gled about how I'd
been dragged to the
principal's office
for cutting my geome-
try class and spying
on Richard in the
boys' locker room.

Cathy:

From the beginning, I
was opposed to Patty's
"wild" idea. It just
didn't seem feasible.
Her enthusiasm, how-
ever, was dizzying.
After listening to her
plan, she persuaded
me to exchange clothes
with her. Frantically,
she threw on my white
blouse, plaid skirt,
knee socks and oxfords
while, reluctantly, I
slipped into her sweat
shirt, blue jeans and
scruffy tennis shoes.
Next, she brushed her
flip into a pageboy
and wiped the makeup
off her face, then
spun around, brushed
my pageboy into a flip
and applied her fa-
vorite Yardley shade
(Liverpool Pink) to my

"Have you told your
dad yet?" "And miss
my date with Richard
tonight? Not on your
life! I'm meeting him
at the Shake Shop at
eight." There was a
knock on my door. "I
gotta run, Sue Ellen.
See you tomorrow." We
hung up. "Come in!"
It was Dad. I'd never
seen him look so mad.
"I received a call
from the principal
of your school today,"
he said. My heart just
about stopped. "Gosh,
Pop-O ..." "Don't 'Gosh,
Pop-O' me, young lady.
You are grounded. For
the next two weeks,
you're to stay home
and study every night.
You're to be in bed
by nine o'clock. No
phone privileges." "OH!"
I cried. "No music." He
switched off the phono-
graph. "And clean up
this mess!" The door
slammed behind him. I
moaned and buried my
head in the pillow. My
whole life was ruined!
What about my date???
How in the world could
I be in two places at
once? Just then, Cathy
came into the room.
"Hello, Patty," she
smiled. I stared at
her. She blinked back.
"Anything wrong?" "Yes!
No! I mean LIKE WOW!"
I yelled as I jumped
up and down. "I have
the *wildest* idea!!!"

pursed lips. We stood
back and looked at each
other in the mirror. It
was perfectly uncanny:
I couldn't even tell us
apart. Patty squealed
with delight and grabbed
my hands. "Now, Cath,"
she coached, "Try not
to act so brainy, or
we'll never pull this
off!" She picked up a
few library books and
said "Bye-eee," then
glided out the door. I
sat down and studied
for my geometry mid-
term. At one point,
Ross stuck his head
in the room. "What's
up, Sis?" he asked. I
took a deep breath,
turned around and
said "Scram, brat!"
in the harshest tone
of voice I could mus-
ter. He made a nasty
face and stomped off.
The real test came at
nine o'clock, when
Uncle Martin stopped
by to turn out the
lights. "I hope you
understand this is for
your own good," he said.
"I dig, Pop-O," I uttered
with a weak smile. He
didn't seem the least
bit suspicious, so I
slid into Patty's bed
and blew a goodnight
kiss at him. Then, for
a convincing finishing
touch, I blew another
kiss across the room,
at Patty's heart-shaped
framed photograph
of Frankie Avalon.

1991

ELAINE EQUI ■ ■ ■ ■ ■ ■ ■ ■ ■ ■ ■ ■ ■ ■ ■ ■
b. 1953

Elaine Equi was born and raised in the suburbs of Chicago, and received her B.A. and M.A. in creative writing from Columbia College, Chicago.

A minimalist and ironist, Equi's work reflects "deep image" and surrealist influences in its surprising juxtaposition of objects such as "pendants / and bracelets of soot." Her poetry also makes use of the serial organization, or catalogues, common to surrealist poetry. Equi's work draws playfully on complex forms, as in the pantoum "A Date with Robbe-Grillet," and metaphysical concepts; the unifying conceit of "In a Monotonous Dream" is that the language consists of only one word.

In a review of her work, Tom Clark refers to her "post-punk, Dorothy Parkerish kit of weapons: arched eyebrow barbs, nervy, catchy hooks of pop-conscious metaphor, and double meanings stitched in light-handedly."[1]

Equi's gentle use of irony is evident in the titles of her books, the wryly turned *The Corners of the Mouth* (1986) and *Surface Tension* (1989); other collections include *Federal Woman* (1978), *Rose of Lima* (1978), *Shrewcrazy* (1981), and *Accessories* (1988).

Equi now lives in New York City, where she teaches poetry workshops and has directed the reading series at the Ear Inn.

1. "Pop Hooks," in *The Poetry Beat*, Ann Arbor, 1990, p. 194.

A Bouquet of Objects

Lovely to be
like a racehorse surrounded by flowers

but it is also lovely
to be surrounded by air and own pendants

and bracelets of soot.
Here is a factory made fresh by broken windows

and there is my muse
returning home with a pail of milk.

He brings me
down to earth where all poetry begins

with such beautiful hands
that I am forever doing nothing but thinking

of objects
and asking him to hold them.

1988

Puritans

There are no small ones.
All big-boned

men and women
without a hint of child's play.

They creak
as they walk

like doors left open
to bang in the wind.

One imagines from their gait
that years from now

they will make adroit bowlers.
Meanwhile, they whisper

careful not to sound rhythmic.
Dovegray, lavender and eggshell

are the only colors
and even these must be bleached, muted,

in order for their profiles
to emerge on cold cash

as if doodled there
with invisible ink.

If not optimistic,
they are eternally democratic

and can be handled
without contamination.

That word
has no meaning for them.

Touch them
as much as you like,

wherever you please.
They have never felt

the desire to reciprocate
and for that they are grateful.

1988

In a Monotonous Dream

The language
created the landscape

and there was only
one word

which meant
at various times

depending on
the inflection

motherdeath
cabbagefangs

ominous headwaiter
sinister whirring

bad joke
rude uncle

song that is stuck
half-open window

lecturing priest and
bride that was never a virgin.

1989

A Date with Robbe-Grillet

What I remember didn't happen.
Birds stuttering.
Torches huddled together.
The cafe empty, with no place to sit.

Birds stuttering.
On our ride in the country
the cafe empty, with no place to sit.
Your hair was like a doll's.

On our ride in the country
it was winter.
Your hair was like a doll's
and when we met it was as children.

It was winter
when it rained

and when we met it was as children.
You, for example, made a lovely girl.

When it rained
the sky turned the color of Pernod.
You, for example, made a lovely girl.
Birds strutted.

The sky turned the color of Pernod.
Within the forest
birds strutted
and we came upon a second forest

within the forest
identical to the first.
And we came upon a second forest
where I was alone

identical to the first
only smaller and without music
where I was alone
where I alone could tell the story.

1989

DENNIS COOPER ■ ■ ■ ■ ■ ■ ■ ■ ■ ■ ■ ■ ■ ■
b. 1953

Born in Pasadena, California, Dennis Cooper is one of the writers of the so-called blank generation of the 1980s, as well as an important writer of the Queer fiction movement. His books of poetry include *Idols* (1979), *The Tenderness of the Wolves* (1982), and *He Cried* (1984).

In his introduction to *The Tenderness of the Wolves*, the novelist Edmund White wrote, "In one sense the refinement of the blank generation consists in not selling anything. No moral lesson, no message, no political outcry, no artistic slogan—nothing is insisted on and the voice is never raised. Indeed, this is a world governed by style alone and that style's greatest injunction is: Never say or do anything embarrassing."[1]

Author of two novels, *Closer* (1989) and *Frisk* (1991), and a collection of short stories, *Wrong* (1992), Cooper was editor and publisher of the now defunct *Little Caesar*, a literary magazine, and Little Caesar Press. He also helped establish a lively Los Angeles poetry scene in the early 1980s through his coordination of the reading series at Beyond Baroque Poetry Center in Venice, California.

After living in New York City and Amsterdam in the mid to late 1980s, Cooper returned to Los Angeles, where he is pursuing his career as a novelist.

1. Trumansburg, NY, 1981, p. ix.

Being Aware

Men are drawn to my ass by
my death-trance blue eyes
and black hair, tiny outfit,
while my father is home with
a girl, moved by the things
I could never think clearly.

Men smudge me onto a bed,
drug me stupid, gossip and
photograph me till I'm famous
in alleys, like one of those
jerk offs who stare from
the porno I sort of admire.

I'm fifteen. Screwing means
more to the men than to me.
I daydream right through it
while money puts chills on
my arms, from this to that
grip. I was meant to be naked.

Hey, Dad, it's been like this
for decades. I was always
approached by your type, given
dollars for hours. I took a
deep breath, stripped and they
never forgot how I trembled.

It means tons to me. Aside
from the obvious heaven
when cumming, there's times
I'm with them that I'm happy
or know what the other guy
feels, which is progress.

Or, nights when I'm angry,
if in a man's arms moving
slowly to the quietest music—
his hands on my arms, in my
hands, in the small of my back
take me back before everything.

1982

No God

for Michael Silverblatt

Sometimes I go to the pornos,
look through films for a face
I remember from youth, grow
distracted, drive the street
till I find it drawn in shadow

over another, open my car door
and swipe love. My Mercedes
still smells empty seven years
later. The dust from a thousand
big hiking boots, tennies and

sandals blurs softly into the
fur at the foot of the seat
nearest my side, where guys have
enthroned themselves for long
drives, slouched in the vinyl,

having gazed inside from the
sidewalk, like into a wishing
well. I parted the traffic
tonight, prowled for a young
man who looked like a shadow,

saw this guy staring straight
through me, swaying downtown
in loose jeans, with something
vague on his mind. He'll go
with me, do what I do. Nothing

else interests him this side
of death. Like me he's just
moving farther away. I can give
him a ride there, because my
route takes me over his haunt

like a man who, so long ago,
gathered livestock lost in the
snow, ran out of gas and froze
going home. We touch in a black
car, on a back road, until numb.

1982

Drugs

A friend dies one night,
swallows too many pills
on his way to a party
and grows pale as dust
in a shaft of moonlight.
You long to reach him
again, all your life.
A priest says you'll
find him in the future
under cover of death;
you will stand and sing
near his glowing side.
We tell you to join us,
get loaded, forget him.
One day you shoot so
much stuff you fall over.
You hope to see him but
only grow clammy, more
stupid, like someone on
quaaludes. Now you and
he walk the same clouds
only when we've been
stoned and think back
on our lives, full of
dead bodies, and bright
now as heaven behind us.

1982

AMY GERSTLER ▪ ▪ ▪ ▪ ▪ ▪ ▪ ▪ ▪ ▪ ▪ ▪ ▪ ▪ ▪ ▪

b. 1956

Amy Gerstler was born in San Diego and attended Pitzer College in Claremont, California, before moving to Los Angeles, where she now lives.

Reviewing her collection *The True Bride* (1986), the poet Tom Clark writes that Gerstler's "most salient gift is her awesome capacity for surrendering authorial identification with the voicing of the work."[1] This distancing of authorial ego is achieved by narrative devices such as the creation of fictional characters; in "The True Bride," the narrator is the male suitor of a woman named Elaine, "the prettiest invalid I've ever seen." It is also achieved by a compression of language that suggests the influence of Emily Dickinson; however, the poet Eileen Myles refers to "Gerstler's knowing voiceovers" as a form of "deep TV" which "by using simple American surfaces in a voyeuristic, Hitchcockian way . . . explores the deeper resonances lurking there."[2]

The force of Gerstler's poetry comes from its impulse to locate and sound these resonances. Commenting on Gerstler's *Bitter Angel* (1990), winner of the National Book Critics Circle Award, critic Sarah Gorham writes that Gerstler's poems "strip down all basic assumptions about beauty and truth and holiness," and begin a struggle for redemption from the gutter. . . . Because of this, the drive for ascension in Gerstler's work becomes that much more valiant, and comic."[3]

Gerstler's other books include *Yonder* (1981), *Christy's Alpine Inn* (1982), *Early Heaven* (1984), *Primitive Man* (1987), and *Nerve Storm* (1993).

A frequent contributor of reviews to *Artforum* magazine, she has provided the text for the dance performances of her sister, choreographer Tina Gerstler, and collaborated with visual artist Alexis Smith in the 1989 installation *Past Lives*.

1. "Creating Paradise," in *The Poetry Beat*, Ann Arbor, 1990, p. 151.   2. Review of *Bitter Angel* in VLS (*Voice Literary Supplement*), No. 82, February 1990, pp. 7–8.   3. "Drive for Ascension," *The American Book Review*, January–March 1991, pp. 27, 29.

The True Bride

Elaine sleeps most of the day. She's the prettiest invalid I've ever seen, and I collect them. Her name means *illumination,* which I think refers to her skin: luminous and unused as a newborn's. Her breath smells lofty as an attic with cedar beam ceiling, ancient papers, forgotten bottles that once held medicine or scent. Limp Raggedy Ann dolls, and old bath toys.

I've always been attracted to crippled women. I'm convinced that if they were pruned in early girlhood, the beauty of what survives (face, neck, hands) is intensified. My potted palm grows greener and puts forth new shoots after I nip off a few ailing fronds.

Elaine's legs are all that's wrong with her. Her mother was rushed one day when Elaine was three, and prepared her salad carelessly. Germs on the unwashed romaine lettuce gave Elaine polio. Earmarked her for me. The outdoors are still myth to her. She doesn't completely believe weather or landscape. Phonograph records, stains, telegrams, TV, calendars—these are her dear flat realities. Her mother tongue. Trees, golf courses, airplanes, and hail she distrusts as too good to be true . . .

She braves perpetual headaches, brought on by harsh and ruinous daylight. Invalids are experts in bed. Bed and bath are their habitats. When I stroked her shoulder through her nightgown for the first time, Elaine was silent for a while. Then she said "Please go now. I'm praying." I love her odd remarks and mind, formed in confinement. These days, I move my hands closer, to sculpt her muscles and she says "oh yes," then later, impatient, her hair all unbraided, she says "Hurry up." Her bed's my pillow-piled shrine. After our long phone conversations, I know she hangs up a black receiver that's taken on the smell of her unwashed hair, and the receiver feels slightly greasy.

Once I held her hand while she napped. She murmured the word "Africa." Her favorite desert, the Sahara, is a melted margarine color on her Atlas map. *That's why she liked it.* She's exquisite. One piece of zwieback for breakfast. Her luncheon is lemonade. At dinner my true bride sniffs and nibbles my wrist. She insists her strong foreign coffee be bitter, and smiles as she tastes that it is, through her red chapped lips.

She must stand up. We must travel. She'll learn to fry eggs and wear sandals. She'll tan, feel bee stings and slaps. I want to slobber on her neck, then lap her wet hem. Her thirst for suffering quenched, now she's famished for a better destiny.

An army of true brides like her, hobbling women, are crossing a desert. The sand is yellow. They limp and crawl over the dunes, making new ripples and waves on the soft desert floor. They're not afraid of snakes. They're hunting for husbands. Their backpacks are filled with thick sandwiches. Bait. Pyjamas and open robes flutter in the hot breeze. Occasionally one stumbles, loses her shirt, but it's like falling into a pit of raw sugar, it doesn't hurt. She brushes herself off and gets up again. These crippled women don't wear sunglasses, their eyes glint like diamonds. Their gaze could cut glass, or fuse the sand they're knee deep in. I tell Elaine that this dream of so many making a pilgrimage towards us, through her Sahara and mine, a handful of scorching sand sprinkled on a bland map, is my ideal pornography.

1986

BZZZZZZZ

There's a certain beekeeper I've fallen in love with. His hair smells disheveled and fragrant as chaff. His bees are neither captives nor slaves. They're capricious. I'll follow their example. When he leads me into the cool green woods, I'll soothe and rule him. I'll open to reveal the complicated maze of my patiences, stored up since I was a tiny child. Beekeepers constitute a brotherhood. Their urine smells of pinenuts and justice. Each keeper is kept with his head in a cloud like a choirloft. Nectar-fed music is disclosed to him, coded in so many notes he feels handfuls of soot are being thrown in his face and he blinks like a simpleton. But soon the bees mold their keepers into sharp-eyed disciples. Honeybees swarm but cannot be sent out on missions. They dance and form first an anvil, then a breastplate of chain mail, then tornadoes and ancient sayings in the air. At last they serve as my wreath and veil. My love harvests their collective spirit made syrup. He bows to the murmured vernacular of pollen and wax. The sonata hovering over his head, that constant hum, is his promise to me: he'll bind us together with wild zigzag stitches and stings, since nothing but the bees can keep him.

1990

Bitter Angel

You appear in a tinny, nickel-and-dime light. The light of turned milk and gloved insults. It could be a gray light you're bathed in; at any rate, it isn't quite white. It's possible you show up coated with a finite layer of the dust that rubs off moths' wings onto kids' grubby fingers. Or you arrive cloaked in a toothache's smoldering glow. Or you stand wrapped like a maypole in rumpled streamers of light torn from threadbare bed-sheets. Your gaze flickers like a silent film. You make me lose track. Which dim, deluded light did I last see you in? The light of extinction, most likely, where there are no more primitive tribesmen who worship clumps of human hair. No more roads that turn into snakes, or ribbons. There's no nightlife or lion's share, none of the black-and-red roulette wheels of methedrine that would-be seers like me dream of. You alone exist: eyes like locomotives. A terrible succession of images buffets you: human faces pile up in your sight, like heaps of some flunky's smudged, undone paperwork.

1990

Marriage

Romance is a world, tiny and curved, reflected in a spoon. Perilous as a clean sheet of paper. Why begin? Why sully and crumple a perfectly good surface? Lots of reasons. Sensuality, need for relief, curiosity. Or it's your mission. You could blame the mating instinct: a squat little god carved from shit-colored wood. NO NO NO. It's not dirty. The plight of desire, a longing to consort, to dally, bend over, lose yourself . . . be rubbed till you're shiny as a new minted utensil. A monogrammed but-terknife, modern pattern or heirloom? It's a time of plagues and lapses, rips in the ozone layer's bridal veil. One must take comfort in whatever lap one can. He wanted her to bite him, lightly. She wanted to drink a quart of water and get to bed early. Now that's what I call an exciting date. In the voodoun religion, believers can marry their gods. Some nuns wed Jesus, but they have to cut off all their hair first. He's afraid he'll tangle in it, trip and fall. Be laid low. Get lost. Your face: lovely and rough as a gravestone. I kiss it. I do.

In a more pragmatic age many brides' veils later served as their burying shrouds. After they'd paid their dues to mother nature, they com-manded last respects. Wreaths, incense, and satin in crypts. In India, marriage of children is common. An army of those who died young marches through your studio this afternoon to rebuke you for closing your eyes to the fullness of the world. But when they get close enough to read what's written on your forehead, they realize you only did what was necessary. They hurriedly skip outside to bless your car, your mangy lawn, and the silver floss tree which bows down in your front yard.

His waiting room is full of pious heathens and the pastor calls them into his office for counseling, two by two. Once you caressed me in a restau-rant by poking me with a fork. In those days, any embrace was a strain. In the picture in this encyclopedia, the oriental bride's headdress looks like a paper boat. The caption says: "Marriage in Japan is a formal, solemn ceremony." O bride, fed and bedded down on a sea of Dexatrim, tea, rice, and quinine, can you guide me? Is the current swift? Is there a bridge? What does this old fraction add up to: you over me? Mr. Numerator on top of Miss Denominator? The two of us divided by a line from a psalm, a differing line of thinking, the thin bloodless line of your lips pressed together. At the end of the service, guests often toss rice or old shoes. You had a close shave, handsome. Almost knocked unconscious by a flying army boot, while your friends continued to converse nonchalantly under a canopy of mosquito netting. You never recognized me darling, but I knew you right away. I know my fate when I see it. But it's bad luck to lay eyes on each other before the appropriate moment. So look away. Even from this distance, and the chasm is widening (the room grows huge), I kiss your old and new wounds. I kiss you. I do.

1990

DIANE WARD ▪ ▪ ▪ ▪ ▪ ▪ ▪ ▪ ▪ ▪ ▪ ▪ ▪ ▪ ▪

b. 1956

Associated with language poetry, Diane Ward is the author of *On Duke Ellington's Birthday* (1977), *Trop-i-dom* (1977), *The Light American* (1979), *Theory of Emotion* (1979), *Never Without One* (1984), *Relation* (1989), and *Imaginary Movie* (1992).

Ward's poetry shows an intense awareness of the relationships between men and women, as well as the charged emotions that lie beneath seemingly casual social events. Like Virginia Woolf, Ward gives precedence to the state or "mood" of a work over its story: "It's the *story* of a detective novel that keeps you reading but also prevents you from reading intimately. Virginia Woolf told stories but rearranged the priorities and made real-time events recede behind the sea (the rhythms)."[1] Rejecting, however, the "automatic connection between women and a preoccupation with emotion," Ward sees emotion as the result of deliberate use of form: "I believe that mood can convey a thought as it moves in and out, around, as if on a string. . . . I can put things side by side that wouldn't make sense in another context, or I can contrast two disparate objects or events thereby creating a third feeling (state) of perception."[2]

Ward was born in Washington, D.C., and studied for a time at the Corcoran School of Art, with an emphasis on studio art, before moving to New York City in 1979. Since 1987, she has lived in Los Angeles, where she works as a staff member of the Urban Planning Department at UCLA.

1. "The Narration," *Poetics Journal*, No. 5, May 1985, pp. 94–95.   2. The same, p. 95.

Immediate Content Recognition

Looking at the post love world
where no one's corroding themselves, but each other
the lesson, as an arm extends with another

the lovers are looking at each other and the world
through vitamin capsuled eyes
where we appear obvious but secretly involved
with cloudy stares of two times a million feet
being felt by it instead of feeling it
in Montana there's a monument that looks like my memory
made up of well-marketed cigarette packs
and 6-foot intellects
remember everything to do and to do with you
our hands are superimposed on well-lighted glossy magazine ads and each
    crack and unkept cuticle is revealed
with tears in your eyes on a tiny ocean in a floating device that carried
    you away by the scenery
not green or red or blue but all of those implied sentiments make
    up our cloudy outlook
the final person proposes nothing and doing it is satisfying
mirrors were nonexistent to keep life simple and cerebral
these thoughts that occur simultaneously are without any
    immediate content recognition
minds race down narrow streets thinking one, two, three more
    to get there
there, the billboard is too small to survive on the big highways
    but here where it's reflected in the windows and caressing
    the giant lobby inside
a few little micros escape from your mind you refer to them as emotions
no jokes. Three minutes pass messing up the concept of time.
beautiful people with blue face
concealing cathode ray guns
giving up meat but smoking believing that bad habits enhance
    your personality
lost in the hours of education and fingering despair and silk
you're panhandling
life in the panhandle is routinely one of pain and suffering
light that's suspended above the peaks
light that's blinding the river
light that exists brilliantly but seems to come from nowhere
a sunburned prune of a hand is tying knots and squeezing juices
    from ominous berries
a conditioned imagination is jetting from the hot summer apartment
    from the east all the way across to the blue pacific
taking it all in and turning out stupid romanticisms
propped up with boredom and longing to be struck down in disbelief
no more of that
just real furs and real jade rings as real
as disappointments and refusals that you want to leave behind
unlike furs that you should hold onto and put into
special storage in the summer
unless you're someone who doesn't have furs but keeps
misfortunes in cold storage and doesn't forget

the times I used you without mentioning you to decline invitations
were a sort of on-call improvised emotional flow
an aura surrounds each phrase stumbled through
not like bubbles around words in comic strips
or even thought bubbles
or static on the radio
more of a disembodied mouth making perfect choreographed words
    without sounds and each twitch
twist and frown composed for the moment

1984

Glass House

The hand   reaches for the cocktail, it's in darkness
imbalanced money, freedom, no need for reflection,
high positron count shakes crt generated thoughts
black glass tux impassive beneath white eyes pinpoints
of intense halation imagination or after image after
lips have curled around the clean rim where liquid
defies gravity graceful suction victim settles back
calculated subreption that's tension a sweeping gesture
of arm attentive to each still his mind his control
tower over-manned by chronoscope controllers. Noted
on white in a tiny jerky hand with the purple inky expression
of her lactescent gaze.

The hand   that caresses the thigh is the instrument of
possibility philosophy monogenesis the basic theory
an absolute comfort factor and she a fact that object
of her own dream she sips arrack sweet coconut of
terrible infanta delusions daddy can never take back
or go back to the voice of attempted torment
the man hired to roil by hips and guitar rouse a
roomful of over-controlleds *en masse* to heightened
convolving. The random thudding glasses of sweet
liqueur on horizontal surfaces his monotonous
color of thirst.

1984

Lovely Stuff

Columns constructed from delirious dust
forgotten under the rug. One lovely
part is the confusion of this dust
with the slime of a thousand other
places, an infinite number of footprints

can be made but not remade. I'm a liar
and fact maker; a monster and
an incredibly benevolent soul.
My words aren't new, these thoughts, too,
are old. The time we're allowed to spend
here is lovely: as if two wires, one red,
the other blue, joined at their tips
by a jewel-like drop of solder were holding
it up. If this were a room I'd lie down,
my body growing and folding comfortably
into the four corners, into each crack
of the floorboards. Because I care
to try this, I'm an integral part of the
coarse connoisseurship of life. This
is lovely, size isn't the question, this
is a tiny thing. The didactic food that feeds
it is controllable. Its lust is more
than machine slots or catch phrases.
Not silly enough to say that anything
is permanent, fearless enough to admit,
in this context, the lovely stuff staring,
couldn't be made to order. A tall order
that wasn't ever dreamed or duplicated,
traced in perfect peeks
beneath frantic erasures.

1984

Poetics

CHARLES OLSON ▪ ▪ ▪ ▪ ▪ ▪ ▪ ▪ ▪ ▪ ▪ ▪ ▪ ▪

PROJECTIVE   VERSE

(projectile   (percussive   (prospective

vs.

The NON-Projective

*(or what a French critic calls "closed" verse, that verse which
print bred and which is pretty much what we have had, in English
& American, and have still got, despite the work of Pound &
Williams:*

*it led Keats, already a hundred years ago, to see it (Wordsworth's,
Milton's) in the light of "the Egotistical Sublime"; and it persists,
at this latter day, as what you might call the private-soul-at-any-
public-wall)*

Verse now, 1950, if it is to go ahead, if it is to be of *essential* use, must,
I take it, catch up and put into itself certain laws and possibilities of the
breath, of the breathing of the man who writes as well as of his listen-
ings. (The revolution of the ear, 1910, the trochee's heave, asks it of the
younger poets.)

I want to do two things: first, try to show what projective or OPEN
verse is, what it involves, in its act of composition, how, in distinction
from the non-projective, it is accomplished; and II, suggest a few ideas
about what stance toward reality brings such verse into being, what
that stance does, both to the poet and to his reader. (The stance in-
volves, for example, a change beyond, and larger than, the technical,
and may, the way things look, lead to new poetics and to new concepts
from which some sort of drama, say, or of epic, perhaps, may emerge.)

FROM *Charles Olson: Selected Writings*, 1966. First published in *Poetry New York*, No. 3,
1950.

I

First, some simplicities that a man learns, if he works in OPEN, or what can also be called COMPOSITION BY FIELD, as opposed to inherited line, stanza, over-all form, what is the "old" base of the non-projective.

(1) the *kinetics* of the thing. A poem is energy transferred from where the poet got it (he will have some several causations), by way of the poem itself to, all the way over to, the reader. Okay. Then the poem itself must, at all points, be a high energy-construct and, at all points, an energy-discharge. So: how is the poet to accomplish same energy, how is he, what is the process by which a poet gets in, at all points energy at least the equivalent of the energy which propelled him in the first place, yet an energy which is peculiar to verse alone and which will be, obviously, also different from the energy which the reader, because he is a third term, will take away?

This is the problem which any poet who departs from closed form is specially confronted by. And it involves a whole series of new recognitions. From the moment he ventures into FIELD COMPOSITION— put himself in the open—he can go by no track other than the one the poem under hand declares, for itself. Thus he has to behave, and be, instant by instant, aware of some several forces just now beginning to be examined. (It is much more, for example, this push, than simply such a one as Pound put, so wisely, to get us started: "the musical phrase," go by it, boys, rather than by, the metronome.)

(2) is the *principle*, the law which presides conspicuously over such composition, and, when obeyed, is the reason why a projective poem can come into being. It is this: FORM IS NEVER MORE THAN AN EXTENSION OF CONTENT. (Or so it got phrased by one, R. Creeley, and it makes absolute sense to me, with this possible corollary, that right form, in any given poem, is the only and exclusively possible extension of content under hand.) There it is, brothers, sitting there, for USE.

Now (3) the *process* of the thing, how the principle can be made so to shape the energies that the form is accomplished. And I think it can be boiled down to one statement (first pounded into my head by Edward Dahlberg): ONE PERCEPTION MUST IMMEDIATELY AND DIRECTLY LEAD TO A FURTHER PERCEPTION. It means exactly what it says, is a matter of, at *all* points (even, I should say, of our management of daily reality as of the daily work) get on with it, keep moving, keep in, speed, the nerves, their speed, the perceptions, theirs, the acts, the split second acts, the whole business, keep it moving as fast as you can, citizen. And if you also set up as a poet, USE USE USE the process at all points, in any given poem always, always one perception must must must MOVE, INSTANTER, ON ANOTHER!

So there we are, fast, there's the dogma. And its excuse, its usableness, in practice. Which gets us, it ought to get us, inside the machinery, now, 1950, of how projective verse is made.

If I hammer, if I recall in, and keep calling in, the breath, the breathing as distinguished from the hearing, it is for cause, it is to insist upon a part that breath plays in verse which has not (due, I think, to the smothering of the power of the line by too set a concept of foot) has not been sufficiently observed or practiced, but which has to be if verse is to advance to its proper force and place in the day, now, and ahead. I take it that PROJECTIVE VERSE teaches, is, this lesson, that that verse will only do in which a poet manages to register both the acquisitions of his ear *and* the pressures of his breath.

Let's start from the smallest particle of all, the syllable. It is the king and pin of versification, what rules and holds together the lines, the larger forms, of a poem. I would suggest that verse here and in England dropped this secret from the late Elizabethans to Ezra Pound, lost it, in the sweetness of meter and rime, in a honey-head. (The syllable is one way to distinguish the original success of blank verse, and its falling off, with Milton.)

It is by their syllables that words juxtapose in beauty, by these particles of sound as clearly as by the sense of the words which they compose. In any given instance, because there is a choice of words, the choice, if a man is in there, will be, spontaneously, the obedience of his ear to the syllables. The fineness, and the practice, lie here, at the minimum and source of speech.

> O western wynd, when wilt thou blow
> And the small rain down shall rain
> O Christ that my love were in my arms
> And I in my bed again

It would do no harm, as an act of correction to both prose and verse as now written, if both rime and meter, and, in the quantity words, both sense and sound, were less in the forefront of the mind than the syllable, if the syllable, that fine creature, were more allowed to lead the harmony on. With this warning, to those who would try: to step back here to this place of the elements and minims of language, is to engage speech where it is least careless—and least logical. Listening for the syllables must be so constant and so scrupulous, the exaction must be so complete, that the assurance of the ear is purchased at the highest—40 hours a day—price. For from the root out, from all over the place, the syllable comes, the figures of, the dance:

> "Is" comes from the Aryan root, *as*, to breathe. The English "not" equals the Sanscrit *na*, which may come from the root *na*, to be lost, to perish. "Be" is from *bhu*, to grow.

I say the syllable, king, and that it is spontaneous, this way: the ear, the ear which has collected, which has listened, the ear, which is so close to the mind that it is the mind's, that it has the mind's speed . . .

it is close, another way: the mind is brother to this sister and is, because it is so close, is the drying force, the incest, the sharpener . . .

it is from the union of the mind and the ear that the syllable is born.

But the syllable is only the first child of the incest of verse (always, that Egyptian thing, it produces twins!). The other child is the LINE. And together, these two, the syllable *and* the line, they make a poem, they make that thing, the—what shall we call it, the Boss of all, the "Single Intelligence." And the line comes (I swear it) from the breath, from the breathing of the man who writes, at the moment that he writes, and thus is, it is here that, the daily work, the WORK, gets in, for only he, the man who writes, can declare, at every moment, the line its metric and its ending—where its breathing, shall come to, termination.

The trouble with most work, to my taking, since the breaking away from traditional lines and stanzas, and from such wholes as, say, Chaucer's *Troilus* or S's *Lear*, is: contemporary workers go lazy RIGHT HERE WHERE THE LINE IS BORN.

Let me put it baldly: The two halves are:
the HEAD, by way of the EAR, to the SYLLABLE
the HEART, by way of the BREATH, to the LINE
And the joker? that it is in the 1st half of the proposition that, in composing, one lets-it-rip; and that it is in the 2nd half, surprise, it is the LINE that's the baby that gets, as the poem is getting made, the attention, the control, that it is right here, in the line, that the shaping takes place, each moment of the going.

I am dogmatic, that the head shows in the syllable. The dance of the intellect is there, among them, prose or verse. Consider the best minds you know in this here business: where does the head show, is it not, precise, here, in the swift currents of the syllable? can't you tell a brain when you see what it does, just there? It is true, what the master says he picked up from Confusion: all the thots men are capable of can be entered on the back of a postage stamp. So, is it not the PLAY of a mind we are after, is not that that shows whether a mind is there at all?

And the threshing floor for the dance? Is it anything but the LINE? And when the line has, is, a deadness, is it not a heart which has gone lazy, is it not, suddenly, slow things, similes, say, adjectives, or such, that we are bored by?

For there is a whole flock of rhetorical devices which have now to be brought under a new bead, now that we sight with the line. Simile is only one bird who comes down, too easily. The descriptive functions generally have to be watched, every second, in projective verse, because of their easiness, and thus their drain on the energy which composition by field allows into a poem. *Any* slackness takes off attention, that crucial thing, from the job in hand, from the *push* of the line under hand at the moment, under the reader's eye, in his moment. Observation of any kind is, like argument in prose, properly previous to the act of the poem, and, if allowed in, must be so juxtaposed, apposed, set in, that it does not, for an instant, sap the going energy of the content toward its form.

It comes to this, this whole aspect of the newer problems. (We now enter, actually, the large area of the whole poem, into the FIELD, if you like, where all the syllables and all the lines must be managed in their relations to each other.) It is a matter, finally, of OBJECTS, what they are, what they are inside a poem, how they got there, and, once there, how they are to be used. This is something I want to get to in another way in Part II, but, for the moment, let me indicate this, that every element in an open poem (the syllable, the line, as well as the image, the sound, the sense) must be taken up as participants in the kinetic of the poem just as solidly as we are accustomed to take what we call the objects of reality; and that these elements are to be seen as creating the tensions of a poem just as totally as do those other objects create what we know as the world.

The objects which occur at every given moment of composition (of recognition, we can call it) are, can be, must be treated exactly as they do occur therein and not by any ideas or preconceptions from outside the poem, must be handled as a series of objects in field in such a way that a series of tensions (which they also are) are made to *hold*, and to hold exactly inside the content and the context of the poem which has forced itself, through the poet and them, into being.

Because breath allows *all* the speech-force of language back in (speech is the "solid" of verse, is the secret of a poem's energy), because, now, a poem has, by speech, solidity, everything in it can now be treated as solids, objects, things; and, though insisting upon the absolute difference of the reality of verse from that other dispersed and distributed thing, yet each of these elements of a poem can be allowed to have the play of their separate energies and can be allowed, once the poem is well composed, to keep, as those other objects do, their proper confusions.

Which brings us up, immediately, bang, against tenses, in fact against syntax, in fact against grammar generally, that is, as we have inherited it. Do not tenses, must they not also be kicked around anew, in order that time, that other governing absolute, may be kept, as must the space-tensions of a poem, immediate, contemporary to the acting-on-you of the poem? I would argue that here, too, the LAW OF THE LINE, which projective verse creates, must be hewn to, obeyed, and that the conventions which logic has forced on syntax must be broken open as quietly as must the too set feet of the old line. But an analysis of how far a new poet can stretch the very conventions on which communication by language rests, is too big for these notes, which are meant, I hope it is obvious, merely to get things started.

Let me just throw in this. It is my impression that *all* parts of speech suddenly, in composition by field, are fresh for both sound and percussive use, spring up like unknown, unnamed vegetables in the patch, when you work it, come spring. Now take Hart Crane. What strikes me in him is the singleness of the push to the nominative, his push along that one arc of freshness, the attempt to get back to word as handle. (If logos is word as thought, what is word as noun, as, pass me that, as Newman Shea used to ask, at the galley table, put a jib on the blood, will ya.) But there is a loss in Crane of what Fenollosa is so right about, in syntax, the sentence as first act of nature, as lightning, as passage of force from subject to object, quick, in this case, from Hart to me, in every case, from me to you, the VERB, between two nouns. Does not Hart miss the advantages, by such an isolated push, miss the point of the whole front of syllable, line, field, and what happened to all language, and to the poem, as a result?

I return you now to London, to beginnings, to the syllable, for the pleasures of it, to intermit:

> If music be the food of love, play on,
> give me excess of it, that, surfeiting,
> the appetite may sicken, and so die.
> That strain again. It had a dying fall,
> o, it came over my ear like the sweet sound
> that breathes upon a bank of violets,
> stealing and giving odour.

What we have suffered from, is manuscript, press, the removal of verse from its producer and its reproducer, the voice, a removal by one, by two removes from its place of origin *and* its destination. For the breath has a double meaning which latin had not yet lost.

The irony is, from the machine has come one gain not yet sufficiently observed or used, but which leads directly on toward projective verse and its consequences. It is the advantage of the typewriter that, due to its rigidity and its space precisions, it can, for a poet, indicate exactly the breath, the pauses, the suspensions even of syllables, the juxtapositions even of parts of phrases, which he intends. For the first time the poet has the stave and the bar a musician has had. For the first time he can, without the convention of rime and meter, record the listening he has done to his own speech and by that one act indicate how he would want any reader, silently or otherwise, to voice his work.

It is time we picked the fruits of the experiments of Cummings, Pound, Williams, each of whom has, after his way, already used the machine as a scoring to his composing, as a script to its vocalization. It is now only a matter of the recognition of the conventions of composition by field for us to bring into being an open verse as formal as the closed, with all its traditional advantages.

If a contemporary poet leaves a space as long as the phrase before it, he means that space to be held, by the breath, an equal length of time. If he suspends a word or syllable at the end of a line (this was most Cummings' addition) he means that time to pass that it takes the eye—that hair of time suspended—to pick up the next line. If he wishes a pause so light it hardly separates the words, yet does not want a comma—which is an interruption of the meaning rather than the sounding of the line—follow him when he uses a symbol the typewriter has ready to hand:

"What does not change / is the will to change"

Observe him, when he takes advantage of the machine's multiple margins, to juxtapose:

"Sd he:
    to dream takes no effort
    to think is easy
        to act is more difficult

    but for a man to act after he has taken thought, this!
is the most difficult thing of all"

Each of these lines is a progressing of both the meaning and the breath-
ing forward, and then a backing up, without a progress or any kind of
movement outside the unit of time local to the idea.

There is more to be said in order that this convention be recognized,
especially in order that the revolution out of which it came may be so
forwarded that work will get published to offset the reaction now afoot
to return verse to inherited forms of cadence and rime. But what I want
to emphasize here, by this emphasis on the typewriter as the personal
and instantaneous recorder of the poet's work, is the already projective
nature of verse as the sons of Pound and Williams are practicing it.
Already they are composing as though verse was to have the reading its
writing involved, as though not the eye but the ear was to be its mea-
surer, as though the intervals of its composition could be so carefully put
down as to be precisely the intervals of its registration. For the ear,
which once had the burden of memory to quicken it (rime & regular
cadence were its aids and have merely lived on in print after the oral
necessities were ended) can now again, that the poet has his means, be
the threshold of projective verse.

II

Which gets us to what I promised, the degree to which the projective
involves a stance toward reality outside a poem as well as a new stance
towards the reality of a poem itself. It is a matter of content, the content
of Homer or of Euripides or of Seami as distinct from that which I might
call the more "literary" masters. From the moment the projective pur-
pose of the act of verse is recognized, the content does—it will—
change. If the beginning and the end is breath, voice in its largest sense,
then the material of verse shifts. It has to. It starts with the composer.
The dimension of his line itself changes, not to speak of the change in his
conceiving, of the matter he will turn to, of the scale in which he imag-
ines that matter's use. I myself would pose the difference by a physical
image. It is no accident that Pound and Williams both were involved
variously in a movement which got called "objectivism." But that word
was then used in some sort of a necessary quarrel, I take it, with "sub-
jectivism." It is now too late to be bothered with the latter. It has
excellently done itself to death, even though we are all caught in its
dying. What seems to me a more valid formulation for present use is
"objectism," a word to be taken to stand for the kind of relation of man
to experience which a poet might state as the necessity of a line or a
work to be as wood is, to be as clean as wood is as it issues from the hand

of nature, to be shaped as wood can be when a man has had his hand to it. Objectism is the getting rid of the lyrical interference of the individual as ego, of the "subject" and his soul, that peculiar presumption by which western man has interposed himself between what he is as a creature of nature (with certain instructions to carry out) and those other creations of nature which we may, with no derogation, call objects. For a man is himself an object, whatever he may take to be his advantages, the more likely to recognize himself as such the greater his advantages, particularly at that moment that he achieves an humilitas sufficient to make him of use.

It comes to this: the use of a man, by himself and thus by others, lies in how he conceives his relation to nature, that force to which he owes his somewhat small existence. If he sprawl, he shall find little to sing but himself, and shall sing, nature has such paradoxical ways, by way of artificial forms outside himself. But if he stays inside himself, if he is contained within his nature as he is participant in the larger force, he will be able to listen, and his hearing through himself will give him secrets objects share. And by an inverse law his shapes will make their own way. It is in this sense that the projective act, which is the artist's act in the larger field of objects, leads to dimensions larger than the man. For a man's problem, the moment he takes speech up in all its fullness, is to give his work his seriousness, a seriousness sufficient to cause the thing he makes to try to take its place alongside the things of nature. This is not easy. Nature works from reverence, even in her destructions (species go down with a crash). But breath is man's special qualification as animal. Sound is a dimension he has extended. Language is one of his proudest acts. And when a poet rests in these as they are in himself (in his physiology, if you like, but the life in him, for all that) then he, if he chooses to speak from these roots, works in that area where nature has given him size, projective size.

It is projective size that the play, *The Trojan Women*, possesses, for it is able to stand, is it not, as its people do, beside the Aegean—and neither Andromache or the sea suffer diminution. In a less "heroic" but equally "natural" dimension Seami causes the Fisherman and the Angel to stand clear in *Hagoromo*. And Homer, who is such an unexamined cliche that I do not think I need to press home in what scale Nausicaa's girls wash their clothes.

Such works, I should argue—and I use them simply because their equivalents are yet to be done—could not issue from men who conceived verse without the full relevance of human voice, without reference to where lines come from, in the individual who writes. Nor do I think it accident that, at this end point of the argument, I should use, for examples, two dramatists and an epic poet. For I would hazard the guess that, if projective verse is practiced long enough, is driven ahead hard enough along the course I think it dictates, verse again can carry much larger material than it has carried in our language since the Elizabethans. But it can't be jumped. We are only at its beginnings, and if I think that the *Cantos* make more "dramatic" sense than do the plays of Mr. Eliot, it is not because I think they have solved the problem but because the methodology of the verse in them points a way by which, one day, the problem of larger content and of larger forms may be solved. Eliot is, in fact, a proof of a present danger, of "too easy" a going on the practice of verse as it has been, rather than as it must be, practiced. There is no question, for example, that Eliot's line, from "Prufrock" on down, has speech-force, is "dramatic," is, in fact, one of the most notable lines since Dryden. I suppose it stemmed immediately to him from Browning, as did so many of Pound's early things. In any case Eliot's line has obvious relations backward to the Elizabethans, especially to the soliloquy. Yet O. M. Eliot is *not* projective. It could even be argued (and I say this carefully, as I have said all things about the non-projective, having considered how each of us must save himself after his own fashion and how much, for that matter, each of us owes to the non-projective, and will continue to owe, as both go alongside each other) but it could be argued that it is because Eliot has stayed inside the non-projective that he fails as a dramatist—that his root is the mind alone, and a scholastic mind at that (no high *intelletto* despite his apparent clarities)—and that, in his listenings he has stayed there where the ear and the mind are, has only gone from his fine ear outward rather than, as I say a projective poet will, down through the workings of his own throat to that place where breath comes from, where breath has its beginnings, where drama has to come from, where, the coincidence is, all act springs.

JOHN CAGE ▪ ▪ ▪ ▪ ▪ ▪ ▪ ▪ ▪ ▪ ▪ ▪ ▪ ▪ ▪ ▪ ▪

FROM *Themes & Variations*

Nonintention (the acceptance of silence) leading to nature; renunciation of control; let sounds be sounds.

Each activity is centered in itself, i.e., composition, performance, and listening are different activities.

(Music is) instantaneous and unpredictable; nothing is accomplished by writing, hearing, or playing a piece of music; our ears are now in excellent condition.

A need for poetry.

Joyce: "Comedy is the greatest of arts because the joy of comedy is freest from desire and loathing."

Affirmation of life.

FROM the Introduction to *Themes & Variations*, 1982.

Purposeful purposelessness.

Art = imitation of nature in her manner of operation.

Coexistence of dissimilars; multiplicity; plurality of centers; "Split the stick, and there is Jesus."

Anonymity or selflessness of work (i.e., not self-expression).

A work should include its environment, is always experimental (unknown in advance).

Fluent, pregnant, related, obscure (nature of sound).

Empty mind.

No ideas of order.

No beginning, middle, or end (process, not object).

Unimpededness and interpenetration; no cause and effect.

Indeterminacy.

Opposites = parts of oneness.

To thicken the plot (Ramakrishna); his answer to the question: Why, if God is good, is there evil in the world?

Adventure (newness) necessary to creative action.

If the mind is disciplined (body too), the heart turns quickly from fear towards love (Eckhart).

Anything can follow anything else (providing nothing is taken as the basis).

Influence derives from one's own work (not from outside it).

Chance operations are a useful means; moksha.

Being led by a person, not a book; artha.

Love.

Right and wrong.

Non-measured time.

Process instead of object.

America has a climate for experimentation.

World is one world.

History is the story of original actions.

Move from zero.

All audible phenomena = material for music.

Impossibility of errorless work.

Spring, Summer, Fall, Winter (Creation, Preservation, Destruction, Quiescence).

Possibility of helping by doing nothing.

Music is not music until it is heard.

Music and dance together (and then other togethers).

Men are men; mountains are mountains before studying Zen. While studying Zen, things become confused. After studying Zen, men are men; mountains are mountains. What is the difference between before and after? No difference. Just the feet are a little off the ground (Suzuki).

If structure, rhythmic structure.

Boredom plus attention = becoming interested.

Principle underlying all of the solutions = question we ask.

Activity, not communication.

The nine permanent emotions (the heroic, the mirthful, the wondrous, the erotic; tranquillity; sorrow, fear, anger, the odious).

The practicality of changing society derives from the possibility of changing the mind.

The giver of gifts (returning to the village having experienced no-mind-edness).

Studying being interrupted.

Nothing-in-between.

Object is fact not symbol (no ideas).

Poetry is having nothing to say and saying it; we possess nothing.

Uncertainty of future.

Noises (underdog); changing music and society.

Not working = knowing. Working = not knowing.

Distrust of effectiveness of education.

HCE

It is, is cause for joy.

Earth has no escape from Heaven (Eckhart).

Mobility, immobility.

Highest purpose = no purpose. Vision = no vision. (In accord with nature.)

We are the oldest at having our airway of knowing nowness (Gertrude Stein).

Fluency in and out.

No split between spirit and matter.

Importance of being perplexed. Unpredictability.

Not being interrupted by shadows (by environment).

Theatre is closer to life than art or music.

Devotion.

Enlightened = not enlightened. Learning = learning we're not learning.

Breaking rules.

No use for value judgments.

We are all going in different directions.

Importance of no rules.

Going to extremes (Yuji Takahashi).

Absence of boredom.

Anarchy.

Meaninglessness as ultimate meaning.

Mind can change.

To do more rather than less.

To sober and quiet the mind thus making it susceptible to divine influences.

The means of thinking are exterior to the mind.

Art is criminal action.

Love = leaving space around loved one.

Utilities, not politics (intelligence; problem solving). Anarchy in a place that works.

Not just self- but social-realization.

Unemployment (cf. artists).

Giving up ownership, substituting use.

Whole society (including, e.g., the mad: they speak the truth).

Religious attitude (George Herbert Mead); world consciousness.

More with less.

Music is permanent; only listening is intermittent (Thoreau).

Invention.

Not things, but minds.

Dealing with 1, not 2.

To make a garden empty-minded.

Music = no music.

Inclusive, not exclusive: aperiodic; no vision, etc.

Objective within; going in all directions.

Demilitarization of language (no government).

A music that needs no rehearsal.

Feet on the ground.

To set all well afloat (Thoreau: Yes and No are lies. The only true answer will set all well afloat.).

Art's self-alteration.

Impossibility of repeated actions; loss of memory. To reach these two's a goal (Duchamp).

Complexity of nature; giving up simplicity of soul, vision, etc.

Constellation of ideas (five as a minimum).

Problems of music (vision) only solved when silence (non-vision) is taken as the basis.

Giving unto others what they wish to be given, not what you would wish to be given (alteration of the Golden Rule).

Use all solutions; do everything!

Inactivity (the camera).

Goal is not to have a goal.

ROBERT DUNCAN ▪ ▪ ▪ ▪ ▪ ▪ ▪ ▪ ▪ ▪ ▪ ▪ ▪ ▪

Equilibrations

I'd like to leave somewhere in this book the statement that the real "we" is the company of the living, of all the forms Life Itself, the primal wave of it, writing itself out in evolution, proposes. Needs, as our poetry does, all the variety of what poets have projected poetry to be.

"They" can be differentiated into "he" and "she." "We" is made up of "I"'s, pronounced "eyes," as Zukofsky reminds us, and "you," in whom the word "thee" has been hidden away.

Where "he" becomes "He" and "she," "She," a second power of person comes into play. As the lastness and firstness of every phrase is a second power.

Pound sought coherence in *The Cantos* and comes in Canto 116 to

FROM the Introduction to *Bending the Bow*, 1968.

lament *"and I cannot make it cohere."* But the *"SPLENDOUR, IT ALL COHERES"* of the poet's Herakles in *The Women of Trachis* is a key or recognition of a double meaning that turns in the lock of the Nessus shirt.

Hermes, god of poets and thieves, lock-picker then, invented the bow and the lyre to confound Apollo, god of poetry. *"They do not apprehend how being at variance it agrees with itself,"* Heraklitus observes: *"there is a connexion working in both directions."*

The part in its fitting does not lock but unlocks; what was closed is opend. Once, in the scale of Mozart, a tone on the piano key-board could be discordant; then, in Schönberg's scale, the configuration uses all the keys, only the tone row is set. But the harmony, the method of stringing, in which conflicts are transformd in their being taken as contrasts, I mean to take in the largesse of meanings. It is in the movement of the particles of meaning before ideas that our ratios arise. In the confrontation, had we danced, taking the advance of the soldiers by the number in ranks into the choreography of the day, or, members of the dance, sat where we were, tensing the strings between the horns for the music's sake, the event the poem seeks might have emerged. The poet of the event senses the play of its moralities belongs to the configuration he cannot see but feels in terms of fittings that fix and fittings that release the design out of itself as he works to bring the necessary image to sight. Had the blue of the sky and the delite eyes have in trees been preserved in the battle; had the lives of the victims been preserved in the victory, as the notes of the song come alive in its tune . . . Life demands sight, and writes at the boundaries of light and dark, black upon white, then color in which the universe appears, chemical information in which Argus eyes of the poem strive. War now is a monstrosity in the hands of militarists who have taken no deep thought of the art of war and its nature.

Working in words I am an escapist; as if I could step out of my clothes and move naked as the wind in a world of words. But I want every part of the actual world involved in my escape. I bring the laws that bound me into an aerial structure in which they are unbound as outlines of a prison unfolding.

The ground is compounded of negative and positive areas in which we see shapes defined. In the immediate work, puns appear. The line of the poem is articulated into phrases so that phases of its happening resonate where they will. Or lines stand as stanzas in themselves of our intention. The sentence remains. But related to a multitude of laws.

Two sonnets belonging to a series of five belong in turn to the larger configuration of the book, and their content, that concludes at this point the series, initiates a theme of Love that moves in other poems. Passages of a poem larger than the book in which they appear follow a sentence read out of Julian. I number the first to come *one*, but they belong to a series that extends in an area larger than my work in them. I enter the poem as I entered my own life, moving between an initiation and a terminus I cannot name.

This is not a field of the irrational; but a field of ratios in which events appear in language. Our science presumes that the universe is faithful to itself: this is its ultimate rationality. And we had begun to see that language is faithful to itself. Wherever we learned to read, the seemingly irrational yielded meaning to our reason. But here *language* does not mean what the tongue sounds and no more. A sign is written on the wall. The blind and deaf may read a language in shapes felt and forces inscribed. Let crowds or clouds enter at this stage; they tell us something. Olson in *Maximus*, "Letter, May 2, 1959," paces off boundary lines; and yet a poet has told me this ceases to be proper to poetry. But surely, everywhere, from whatever poem, choreographies extend into actual space. In my imagination I go through the steps the poet takes so that the area of a township appears in my reading; were I to go to the place and enact the text, I would come into another dimension of the poetry in which Gloucester would speak to me. I am talking here about the fact that if a man set his heart against falling in love, he will find the poetry of falling in love empty and vain. Must I reiterate the fact that the boundary lines in the poem belong to the poem and not to the town?

The poem is not a stream of consciousness, but an area of composition in which I work with whatever comes into it. Only words come into it. Sounds and ideas. The tone leading of vowels, the various percussions of consonants. The play of numbers in stresses and syllables. In which meanings and ideas, themes and things seen, arise. So that there is not only a melody of sounds but of images. Rimes, the reiteration of formations in the design, even puns, lead into complexities of the field. But now the poet works with a sense of parts fitting in relation to a design that is larger than the poem. The commune of Poetry becomes so real that he sounds each particle in relation to parts of a great story that he knows will never be completed. A word has the weight of an actual stone in his hand. The tone of a vowel has the color of a wing. "Dont mess up the perception of one sense by trying to define it in terms of another," Pound warnd. But we reflect that the ear is the organ not only of hearing but of our equilibrations.

DENISE LEVERTOV ■ ■ ■ ■ ■ ■ ■ ■ ■ ■ ■ ■ ■

Some Notes on Organic Form

For me, back of the idea of organic form is the concept that there is a form in all things (and in our experience) which the poet can discover and reveal. There are no doubt temperamental differences between poets who use prescribed forms and those who look for new ones—people who need a tight schedule to get anything done, and people who have to have a free hand—but the difference in their conception of

FROM *The Poet in the World*, 1973. First published in *Poetry*, Vol. 106, No. 6, September 1965.

"content" or "reality" is functionally more important. On the one hand is the idea that content, reality, experience, is essentially fluid and must be given form; on the other, this sense of seeking out inherent, though not immediately apparent, form. Gerard Manley Hopkins invented the word "inscape" to denote intrinsic form, the pattern of essential characteristics both in single objects and (what is more interesting) in objects in a state of relation to each other, and the word "instress" to denote the experiencing of the perception of inscape, the apperception of inscape. In thinking of the process of poetry as I know it, I extend the use of these words, which he seems to have used mainly in reference to sensory phenomena, to include intellectual and emotional experience as well; I would speak of the inscape of an experience (which might be composed of any and all of these elements, including the sensory) or of the inscape of a sequence or constellation of experiences.

A partial definition, then, of organic poetry might be that it is a method of apperception, i.e., of recognizing what we perceive, and is based on an intuition of an order, a form beyond forms, in which forms partake, and of which man's creative works are analogies, resemblances, natural allegories. Such poetry is exploratory.

How does one go about such a poetry? I think it's like this: first there must be an experience, a sequence or constellation of perceptions of sufficient interest, felt by the poet intensely enough to demand of him their equivalence in words: he is *brought to speech*. Suppose there's the sight of the sky through a dusty window, birds and clouds and bits of paper flying through the sky, the sound of music from his radio, feelings of anger and love and amusement roused by a letter just received, the memory of some long-past thought or event associated with what's seen or heard or felt, and an idea, a concept, he has been pondering, each qualifying the other; together with what he knows about history; and what he has been dreaming—whether or not he remembers it—working in him. This is only a rough outline of a possible moment in a life. But the condition of being a poet is that periodically such a cross section, or constellation, of experiences (in which one or another element may predominate) demands, or wakes in him this demand: the poem. The beginning of the fulfillment of this demand is to contemplate, to meditate; words which connote a state in which the heat of feeling warms the intellect. To contemplate comes from *"templum*, temple, a place, a space for observation, marked out by the augur." It means, not simply to observe, to regard, but to do these things in the presence of a god. And to meditate is "to keep the mind in a state of contemplation"; its synonym is "to muse," and to muse comes from a word meaning "to stand with open mouth"—not so comical if we think of "inspiration"—to breathe in.

So—as the poet stands openmouthed in the temple of life, contemplating his experience, there come to him the first words of the poem: the words which are to be his way in to the poem, if there is to be a poem. The pressure of demand and the meditation on its elements culminate in a moment of vision, of crystallization, in which some inkling of the correspondence between those elements occurs; and it occurs as words. If he forces a beginning before this point, it won't work. These words sometimes remain the first, sometimes in the completed poem their eventual place may be elsewhere, or they may turn out to have been only forerunners, which fulfilled their function in bringing him to the words which are the actual beginning of the poem. It is faithful attention to the experience from the first moment of crystallization that allows those first or those forerunning words to rise to the surface: and with that same fidelity of attention the poet, from that moment of being let in to the possibility of the poem, must follow through, letting the experience lead him through the world of the poem, its unique inscape revealing itself as he goes.

During the writing of a poem the various elements of the poet's being are in communion with each other, and heightened. Ear and eye, intellect and passion, interrelate more subtly than at other times; and the "checking for accuracy," for precision of language, that must take place throughout the writing is not a matter of one element supervising the others but of intuitive interaction between all the elements involved.

In the same way, content and form are in a state of dynamic interaction; the understanding of whether an experience is a linear sequence or a constellation raying out from and into a central focus or axis, for instance, is discoverable only in the work, not before it.

Rhyme, chime, echo, reiteration: they not only serve to knit the elements of an experience but often are the very means, the sole means, by which the density of texture and the returning or circling of perception can be transmuted into language, apperceived. A may lead to E directly through B, C, and D: but if then there is the sharp remembrance or revisioning of A, this return must find its metric counterpart. It could do so by actual repetition of the words that spoke of A the first time (and if this return occurs more than once, one finds oneself with a refrain—not put there because one decided to write something with a refrain at the end of each stanza, but directly because of the demand of the content). Or it may be that since the return to A is now conditioned by the journey through B, C, and D, its words will not be a simple repetition but a variation . . . Again, if B and D are of a complementary nature, then their thought- or feeling-rhyme may find its corresponding word-rhyme. Corresponding images are a kind of nonaural rhyme. It usually happens that within the whole, that is between the point of crystallization that marks the beginning or onset of a poem and the point at which the intensity of contemplation has ceased, there are distinct units of awareness; and it is—for me anyway—these that indicate the duration of stanzas. Sometimes these units are of such equal duration that one gets a whole poem of, say, three-line stanzas, a regularity of pattern that looks, but is not, predetermined.

When my son was eight or nine I watched him make a crayon drawing of a tournament. He was not interested in the forms as such, but was grappling with the need to speak in graphic terms, to say, "And a great crowd of people were watching the jousting knights." There was a need to show the tiers of seats, all those people sitting in them. And out of the need arose a formal design that was beautiful—composed of the rows of shoulders and heads. It is in very much the same way that there can arise, out of fidelity to instress, a design that is the form of the poem—both its total form, its length and pace and tone, and the form of its parts (e.g., the rhythmic relationships of syllables within the line, and of line to line; the sonic relationships of vowels and consonants; the recurrence of images, the play of associations, etc.). "Form follows function" (Louis Sullivan).

Frank Lloyd Wright in his autobiography wrote that the idea of organic architecture is that "the reality of the building lies in the space within it, to be lived in." And he quotes Coleridge: "Such as the life is, such is the form." (Emerson says in his essay "Poetry and Imagination," "Ask the fact for the form.") The *Oxford English Dictionary* quotes Huxley (Thomas, presumably) as stating that he used the word organic "almost as an equivalent for the word 'living.' "

In organic poetry the metric movement, the measure, is the direct expression of the movement of perception. And the sounds, acting together with the measure, are a kind of extended onomatopoeia—i.e., they imitate not the sounds of an experience (which may well be soundless, or to which sounds contribute only incidentally)—but the feeling of an experience, its emotional tone, its texture. The varying speed and gait of different strands of perception within an experience (I think of strands of seaweed moving within a wave) result in counterpointed measures.

Thinking about how organic poetry differs from free verse, I wrote that "most free verse is failed organic poetry, that is, organic poetry from which the attention of the writer had been switched off too soon, before the intrinsic form of the experience had been revealed." But Robert Duncan pointed out to me that there is a "free verse" of which this is not true, because it is written not with any desire to seek a form, indeed perhaps with the longing to avoid form (if that were possible) and to express inchoate emotion as purely as possible.[1] There is a contradiction here, however, because if, as I suppose, there is an inscape of emotion, of feeling, it is impossible to avoid presenting something of it if the rhythm or tone of the feeling is given voice in the poem. But perhaps the difference is this: that free verse isolates the "rightness" of each line or cadence—if it seems expressive, o.k., never mind the relation of it to the next; while in organic poetry the peculiar rhythms of the parts are in some degree modified, if necessary, in order to discover the rhythm of the whole.

But doesn't the character of the whole depend on, arise out of, the character of the parts? It does; but it is like painting from nature: suppose you absolutely imitate, on the palette, the separate colors of the various objects you are going to paint; yet when they are closely juxtaposed in the actual painting, you may have to lighten, darken, cloud, or sharpen each color in order to produce an effect equivalent to what you

---

[1]See, for instance, some of the forgotten poets of the early 20's—also, some of Amy Lowell—Sandburg—John Gould Fletcher. Some Imagist poems were written in "free verse" in this sense, but by no means all. [Levertov's note.]

see in nature. Air, light, dust, shadow, and distance have to be taken into account.

Or one could put it this way: in organic poetry the form sense or "traffic sense," as Stefan Wolpe speaks of it, is ever present along with (yes, paradoxically) fidelity to the revelations of meditation. The form sense is a sort of Stanislavsky of the imagination: putting a chair two feet downstage there, thickening a knot of bystanders upstage left, getting this actor to raise his voice a little and that actress to enter more slowly; all in the interest of a total form he intuits. Or it is a sort of helicopter scout flying over the field of the poem, taking aerial photos and reporting on the state of the forest and its creatures—or over the sea to watch for the schools of herring and direct the fishing fleet toward them.

A manifestation of form sense is the sense the poet's ear has of some rhythmic norm peculiar to a particular poem, from which the individual lines depart and to which they return. I heard Henry Cowell tell that the drone in Indian music is known as the horizon note. Al Kresch, the painter, sent me a quotation from Emerson: "The health of the eye demands a horizon." This sense of the beat or pulse underlying the whole I think of as the horizon note of the poem. It interacts with the nuances or forces of feeling which determine emphasis on one word or another, and decides to a great extent what belongs to a given line. It relates the needs of that feeling-force which dominates the cadence to the needs of the surrounding parts and so to the whole.

Duncan also pointed to what is perhaps a variety of organic poetry: the poetry of linguistic impulse. It seems to me that the absorption in language itself, the awareness of the world of multiple meaning revealed in sound, word, syntax, and the entering into this world in the poem, is as much an experience or constellation of perceptions as the instress of nonverbal sensuous and psychic events. What might make the poet of linguistic impetus appear to be on another tack entirely is that the demands of his realization may seem in opposition to truth as we think of it; that is, in terms of sensual logic. But the apparent distortion of experience in such a poem for the sake of verbal effects is actually a precise adherence to truth, since the experience itself was a verbal one.

Form is never more than a *revelation* of content.

"The law—one perception must immediately and directly lead to a further perception."[2] I've always taken this to mean, "no loading of the rifts with ore," because there are to be no rifts. Yet alongside this truth is another truth (that I've learned from Duncan more than from anyone else)—that there must be a place in the poem for rifts too—(never to be stuffed with imported ore). Great gaps between perception and perception which must be leapt across if they are to be crossed at all.

The X-factor, the magic, is when we come to those rifts and make

[2]Edward Dahlberg, as quoted by Charles Olson in "Projective Verse," *Selected Writings* (New York, New Directions, 1966). [Levertov's note.]

those leaps. A religious devotion to the truth, to the splendor of the authentic, involves the writer in a process rewarding in itself; but when that devotion brings us to undreamed abysses and we find ourselves sailing slowly over them and landing on the other side—that's ecstasy.

FRANK O'HARA ▪ ▪ ▪ ▪ ▪ ▪ ▪ ▪ ▪ ▪ ▪ ▪ ▪ ▪

Personism: A Manifesto

Everything is in the poems, but at the risk of sounding like the poor wealthy man's Allen Ginsberg I will write to you because I just heard that one of my fellow poets thinks that a poem of mine that can't be got at one reading is because I was confused too. Now, come on. I don't believe in god, so I don't have to make elaborately sounded structures. I hate Vachel Lindsay, always have, I don't even like rhythm, assonance, all that stuff. You just go on your nerve. If someone's chasing you down the street with a knife you just run, you don't turn around and shout, "Give it up! I was a track star for Mineola Prep."

That's for the writing poems part. As for their reception, suppose you're in love and someone's mistreating *(mal aimé)* you, you don't say, "Hey, you can't hurt me this way, I *care!*" you just let all the different bodies fall where they may, and they always do may after a few months. But that's not why you fell in love in the first place, just to hang onto life, so you have to take your chances and try to avoid being logical. Pain always produces logic, which is very bad for you.

I'm not saying that I don't have practically the most lofty ideas of anyone writing today, but what difference does that make? they're just ideas. The only good thing about it is that when I get lofty enough I've stopped thinking and that's when refreshment arrives.

But how can you really care if anybody gets it, or gets what it means, or if it improves them. Improves them for what? for death? Why hurry them along? Too many poets act like a middle-aged mother trying to get her kids to eat too much cooked meat, and potatoes with drippings (tears). I don't give a damn whether they eat or not. Forced feeding leads to excessive thinness (effete). Nobody should experience anything they don't need to, if they don't need poetry bully for them, I like the movies too. And after all, only Whitman and Crane and Williams, of the American poets, are better than the movies. As for measure and other

FROM *The Collected Poems of Frank O'Hara*, 1972. First published in *Yugen*, No. 7, 1961, where its date of composition was given as September 3, 1959. According to critic Marjorie Perloff in *Frank O'Hara: Poet Among Painters* (1977), this essay was written in response to an essay by Allen Ginsberg, "Abstraction in Poetry," which appeared in the journal *It Is*, No. 3, Winter/Spring, 1959. O'Hara's essay also parodies Charles Olson's "Projective Verse."

technical apparatus, that's just common sense: if you're going to buy a pair of pants you want them to be tight enough so everyone will want to go to bed with you. There's nothing metaphysical about it. Unless, of course, you flatter yourself into thinking that what you're experiencing is "yearning."

Abstraction in poetry, which Allen recently commented on in *It is*, is intriguing. I think it appears mostly in the minute particulars where decision is necessary. Abstraction (in poetry, not in painting) involves personal removal by the poet. For instance, the decision involved in the choice between "the nostalgia of the infinite" and "the nostalgia *for* the infinite" defines an attitude towards degree of abstraction. The nostalgia *of* the infinite representing the greater degree of abstraction, removal, and negative capability (as in Keats and Mallarmé). Personism, a movement which I recently founded and which nobody yet knows about, interests me a great deal, being so totally opposed to this kind of abstract removal that it is verging on a true abstraction for the first time, really, in the history of poetry. Personism is to Wallace Stevens what *la poésie pure* was to Béranger. Personism has nothing to do with philosophy, it's all art. It does not have to do with personality or intimacy, far from it! But to give you a vague idea, one of its minimal aspects is to address itself to one person (other than the poet himself), thus evoking overtones of love without destroying love's life-giving vulgarity, and sustaining the poet's feelings towards the poem while preventing love from distracting him into feeling about the person. That's part of personism. It was founded by me after lunch with LeRoi Jones on August 27, 1959, a day in which I was in love with someone (not Roi, by the way, a blond). I went back to work and wrote a poem for this person. While I was writing it I was realizing that if I wanted to I could use the telephone instead of writing the poem, and so Personism was born. It's a very exciting movement which will undoubtedly have lots of adherents. It puts the poem squarely between the poet and the person, Lucky Pierre style, and the poem is correspondingly gratified. The poem is at last between two persons instead of two pages. In all modesty, I confess that it may be the death of literature as we know it. While I have certain regrets, I am still glad I got there before Alain Robbe-Grillet did. Poetry being quicker and surer than prose, it is only just that poetry finish literature off. For a time people thought that Artaud was going to accomplish this, but actually, for all their magnificence, his polemical writings are not more outside literature than Bear Mountain is outside New York State. His relation is no more astounding than Dubuffet's to painting.

What can we expect of Personism? (This is getting good, isn't it?) Everything, but we won't get it. It is too new, too vital a movement to promise anything. But it, like Africa, is on the way. The recent propagandists for technique on the one hand, and for content on the other, had better watch out.

ALLEN GINSBERG ▪ ▪ ▪ ▪ ▪ ▪ ▪ ▪ ▪ ▪ ▪ ▪ ▪

Notes for *Howl and Other Poems*

By 1955 I wrote poetry adapted from prose seeds, journals, scratchings, arranged by phrasing or breath groups into little short-line patterns according to ideas of measure of American speech I'd picked up from W. C. Williams' imagist preoccupations. I suddenly turned aside in San Francisco, unemployment compensation leisure, to follow my romantic inspiration—Hebraic-Melvillian bardic breath. I thought I wouldn't write a *poem*, but just write what I wanted to without fear, let my imagination go, open secrecy, and scribble magic lines from my real mind—sum up my life—something I wouldn't be able to show anybody, write for my own soul's ear and a few other golden ears. So the first line of *Howl*, "I saw the best minds," etc. the whole first section typed out madly in one afternoon, a huge sad comedy of wild phrasing, meaningless images for the beauty of abstract poetry of mind running along making awkward combinations like Charlie Chaplin's walk, long saxophone-like chorus lines I knew Kerouac would hear the *sound* of—taking off from his own inspired prose line really a new poetry.

I depended on the word "who" to keep the beat, a base to keep measure, return to and take off from again onto another streak of invention: "who lit cigarettes in boxcars boxcars boxcars," continuing to prophesy what I really knew despite the drear consciousness of the world: "who were visionary indian angels." Have I really been attacked for this sort of joy? So the poem got serious, I went on to what my imagination believed true to Eternity (for I'd had a beatific illumination years before during which I'd heard Blake's ancient voice & saw the universe unfold in my brain), & what my memory could reconstitute of the data of celestial experience.

But how sustain a long line of poetry (lest it lapse into prosaic)? It's natural inspiration of the moment that keeps it moving, disparate thinks put down together, shorthand notations of visual imagery, juxtapositions of hydrogen juke-box—abstract haikus sustain the mystery & put iron poetry back into the line: the last line of "Sunflower Sutra" is the extreme, one stream of single word associations, summing up. Mind is shapely, Art is shapely. Meaning Mind practiced in spontaneity invents forms in its own image & gets to Last Thoughts. Loose ghosts wailing for body try to invade the bodies of living men. I hear ghostly Academics in Limbo screeching about form.

Ideally each line of *Howl* is a single breath unit. Tho in this recording it's not pronounced so, I was exhausted at climax of 3 hour Chicago reading with Corso & Orlovsky. My breath is long—that's the Measure, one physical-mental inspiration of thought contained in the elastic of a

FROM *The New American Poetry: 1945–1960*, 1960. First published as the liner note to the recording of *Howl and Other Poems* issued in 1959 by the Fantasy record label (Fantasy 7006), where its date of composition was given as Independence Day 1959.

breath. It probably bugs Williams now, but it's a natural consequence, my own heightened conversation, not cooler average-dailytalk short breath. I got to mouth more madly this way.

So these poems are a series of experiments with the formal organization of the long line. Explanations follow. I realized at the time that Whitman's form had rarely been further explored (improved on even) in the U.S. Whitman always a mountain too vast to be seen. Everybody assumes (with Pound?) (except Jeffers) that his line is a big freakish uncontrollable necessary prosaic goof. No attempt's been made to use it in the light of early XX Century organization of new speech-rhythm prosody to *build up* large organic structures.

I had an apt on Nob Hill, got high on Peyote, & saw an image of the robot skullface of Moloch in the upper stories of a big hotel glaring into my window; got high weeks later again, the Visage was still there in red smokey downtown Metropolis, I wandered down Powell Street muttering, "Moloch Moloch" all night & wrote *Howl* II nearly intact in cafeteria at foot of Drake Hotel, deep in the hellish vale. Here the long line is used as a stanza form broken within into exclamatory units punctuated by a base repetition, Moloch.

The rhythmic paradigm for Part III was conceived & half-written same day as the beginning of *Howl*, I went back later & filled it out. Part I, a lament for the Lamb in America with instances of remarkable lamblike youths; Part II names the monster of mental consciousness that preys on the Lamb; Part III a litany of affirmation of the Lamb in its glory: "O starry spangled shock of Mercy." The structure of Part III, pyramidal, with a graduated longer response to the fixed base.

A lot of these forms developed out of an extreme rhapsodic wail I once heard in a madhouse. Later I wondered if short quiet lyrical poems could be written using the long line. "Cottage in Berkeley" & "Supermarket in California" (written same day) fell in place later that year. Not purposely, I simply followed my Angel in the course of compositions.

What if I just simply wrote, in long units & broken short lines, spontaneously noting prosaic realities mixed with emotional upsurges, solitaries? "Transcription of Organ Music" (sensual data), strange writing which passes from prose to poetry & back, like the mind.

What about poem with rhythmic buildup power equal to *Howl* without use of repeated base to sustain it? "The Sunflower Sutra" (composition time 20 minutes, me at desk scribbling, Kerouac at cottage door waiting for me to finish so we could go off somewhere party) did that, it surprised me, one long Who . . .

Last, the Proem to *Kaddish* (NY 1959 work)—finally, completely free composition, the long line breaking up within itself into short staccato breath units—notations of one spontaneous phrase after another linked within the line by dashes mostly: the long line now perhaps a variable stanzaic unit, measuring groups of related ideas, marking them—a method of notation. Ending with a hymn in rhythm similar to the synagogue death lament. Passing into dactyllic? says Williams? Perhaps not: at least the ear hears itself in Promethian natural measure, not in mechanical count of accent.

I used Chicago Big Table readings (Jan. 1959) of *Howl*, "Sunflower" and *Kaddish* on this record because they're the best I can find. Though the tapes were coarse. And hope the reproduction of that reading will permanently give lie to much philistine slander by the capitalist press and various brain-washed academies. And convince the Lamb. I tried recording *Howl* under better mechanical conditions in studio but the spirit wasn't in me by then. I'm not in control. The rest of the poems were recorded in June '59 Fantasy Studios in SF. "Footnote to *Howl*" may seem sick and strange, I've included it because I trust it will be heard in Heaven, though some cruel ear in U.S. may mock. Let it be raw, there is beauty. These are recorded as best I can now, though with scared love, imperfect to an angelic trumpet in mind, I quit reading in front of live audiences for while. I began in obscurity to communicate a live poetry, it's become more a trap and duty than the spontaneous ball it was first.

A word on Academies; poetry has been attacked by an ignorant & frightened bunch of bores who don't understand how it's made, & the trouble with these creeps is they wouldn't know Poetry if it came up and buggered them in broad daylight.

A word on the Politicians: my poetry is Angelical Ravings, & has nothing to do with dull materialistic vagaries about who should shoot who. The secrets of individual imagination—which are transconceptual & non-verbal—I mean unconditioned Spirit—are not for sale to this consciousness, are of no use to this world, except perhaps to make it shut its trap & listen to the music of the Spheres. Who denies the music of the spheres denies poetry, denies man, & spits on Blake, Shelley, Christ & Buddha. Meanwhile have a ball. The universe is a new flower. America will be discovered. Who wants a war against roses will have it. Fate tells big lies, & the gay Creator dances on his own body in Eternity.

ROBERT CREELEY ▪ ▪ ▪ ▪ ▪ ▪ ▪ ▪ ▪ ▪ ▪ ▪

To Define

The process of definition is the intent of the poem, or is to that sense— "Peace comes of communication." Poetry stands in no need of any sympathy, or even goodwill. One acts from bottom, the root is the purpose quite beyond any kindness.

A poetry can act on this: "A poem is energy transferred from where the poet got it (he will have some several causations), by way of the poem itself to, all the way over to, the reader." One breaks the line of aesthetics, or that outcrop of a general division of knowledge. A sense of the KINETIC impels recognition of force. Force is, and therefore stays.

FROM *The Collected Essays of Robert Creeley*, 1989. First published in *Nine American Poets*, Liverpool, 1953.

The means of a poetry are, perhaps, related to Pound's sense of the *increment of association;* usage coheres value. Tradition is an aspect of what anyone is now thinking—not what someone once thought. We make with what we have, and in this way anything is worth looking at. A tradition becomes inept when it blocks the necessary conclusion; it says we have felt nothing, it implies others have felt more.

A poetry denies its end in any *descriptive* act, I mean any act which leaves the attention outside the poem. Our anger cannot exist usefully without its objects, but a description of them is also a perpetuation. There is that confusion—one wants the thing to act on, and yet hates it. *Description* does nothing, it includes the object—it neither hates nor loves.

If one can junk these things, of the content which relates only to denial, the negative, the impact of dissolution—act otherwise, on other things. There is no country. Speech is an assertion of one man, by one man. "Therefore each speech having its own character the poetry it engenders will be peculiar to that speech also in its own intrinsic form."

Form

The Whip

I spent a night turning in bed,
my love was a feather, a flat

sleeping thing. She was
very white

and quiet, and above us on
the roof, there was another woman I

also loved, had
addressed myself to in

a fit she
returned. That

encompasses it. But now I was
lonely, I yelled,

but what is that? Ugh,
she said, beside me, she put

FROM *The Collected Essays of Robert Creeley,* 1989. First published in *Ecstatic Occasions, Expedient Forms,* 1987, in which poets were asked to comment on the formal decisions that went into the making of one of their poems. "The Whip," the poem Creeley chose for comment, was first published in *For Love: Poems, 1950–1960,* 1962.

> her hand on
> my back, for which act
>
> I think to say this
> wrongly.

Form has such a diversity of associations and it seems obvious enough that it would have—like *like*. Like a girl of my generation used to get a formal for the big dance, or else it could be someone's formalizing the situation, which was a little more serious. Form a circle, etc.

It was something one intended, clearly, that came of defined terms. But in what respect, of course, made a great difference. As advice for editing a magazine, Pound wrote, "Verse consists of a constant and a variant . . ." His point was that any element might be made the stable, recurrent event, and that any other might be let to go "hog wild," as he put it, and such a form could prove "a center around which, not a box within which, every item . . ."

Pound was of great use to me as a young writer, as were also Williams and Stevens. I recall the latter's saying there were those who thought of form as a variant of plastic shape. Pound's point was that poetry is a form cut in time as sculpture is a form cut in space. Williams' introduction to *The Wedge* (1944) I took as absolute credo.

"The Whip" was written in the middle fifties, and now reading it I can vividly remember the bleak confusion from which it moves emotionally. There is a parallel, a story called "The Musicians," and if one wants to know more of the implied narrative of the poem, it's in this sad story. The title is to the point, because it is music, specifically jazz, that informs the poem's manner in large part. Not that it's jazzy, or about jazz—rather, it's trying to use a rhythmic base much as jazz of this time would—or what was especially characteristic of Charlie Parker's playing, or Miles Davis', Thelonious Monk's, or Milt Jackson's. That is, the beat is used to delay, detail, prompt, define the content of the statement or, more aptly, the emotional field of the statement. It's trying to do this while moving in time to a set periodicity—durational units, call them. It will say as much as it can, or as little, in the "time" given. So each line is figured as taking the same time, like they say, and each line ending works as a distinct pause. I used to listen to Parker's endless variations on "I Got Rhythm" and all the various times in which he'd play it, all the tempi, up, down, you name it. What fascinated me was that he'd write silences as actively as sounds, which of course they were. Just so in poetry.

So it isn't writing like jazz, trying to be some curious social edge of that imagined permission. It's a time one's keeping, which could be the variations of hopscotch, or clapping, or just traffic's blurred racket. It was what you could do with what you got, or words to that effect.

Being shy as a young man, I was very formal, and still am. I make my moves fast but very self-consciously. I would say that from "Ugh . . ." on the poem moves as cannily and as solidly as whatever. "Listen to the sound that it makes," said Pound. Fair enough.

JEROME ROTHENBERG ■ ■ ■ ■ ■ ■ ■ ■ ■ ■ ■

New Models, New Visions: Some Notes
Toward a Poetics of Performance

The fact of performance now runs through all our arts, and the arts themselves begin to merge and lose their old distinctions, till it's apparent that we're no longer where we were to start with. The Renaissance is over or it begins again with us. Yet the origins we seek—the frame that bounds our past, that's set against an open-ended future—are no longer Greek, nor even Indo-European, but take in all times and places. To say this isn't to deny history, for we're in fact involved with history, with the sense of ourselves "in time" and in relation to other forms of human experience besides our own. The model—or better, the vision— has shifted: away from a "great tradition" centered in a single stream of art and literature in the West, to a *greater* tradition that includes, sometimes as its central fact, preliterate and oral cultures throughout the world, with a sense of their connection to subterranean but literate traditions in civilizations both East and West. "Thought is made in the mouth," said Tristan Tzara, and Edmond Jabès: "The book is as old as fire and water"—and both, we know, are right.

The change of view, for those who have experienced it, is by now virtually paradigmatic. We live with it in practice and find it more and more difficult to communicate with those who still work with the older paradigm. Thus, what appears to us as essentially creative—how can we doubt it?—carries for others the threat that was inherent when Tzara, as arch Dadaist, called *circa* 1917, for "a great negative work of destruction" against a late, overly textualized derivation from the Renaissance paradigm of culture and history. No longer viable, that great Western thesis was already synthesizing, setting the stage for its own disappearance. The other side of Tzara's work—and increasingly that of other artists within the several avant-gardes, the different, often conflicted sides of "modernism"—was, we now see clearly, a great positive work of construction/synthesis. With Tzara it took the form of a projected anthology, *Poèmes nègres*, a gathering of African and Oceanic poems culled from existing ethnographies and chanted at Dada performances in Zurich's Cabaret Voltaire. To the older brokers of taste— the bearers of Western values in an age of chaos—this may have looked like yet another Dada gag, but seeing it now in its actual publication six decades after the fact, it reads like a first, almost too serious attempt at a new classic anthology. In circulation orally, it formed with Tzara's own poetry—the process of a life and its emergence as performance in the soundworks and simultaneities of the dada soirées, etc.—one of the prophetic statements of where our work was to go.

FROM *Pre-faces & Other Writings*, 1981. First published in *Performance in Postmodern Culture*, 1977, as a version of an essay presented at the symposium "Cultural Frames & Reflections: Ritual, Drama & Spectacle" held in Burg Wartenstein, Austria, August 27 to September 5, 1977.

Sixty years after Dada, a wide range of artists have been making deliberate and increasing use of ritual models for performance, have swept up arts like painting, sculpture, poetry (if those terms still apply) long separated from their origins in performance. (Traditional performance arts—music, theater, dance—have undergone similarly extreme transformations: often, like the others, toward a virtual liberation from the dominance of text.) The principal function here may be viewed as that of mapping and exploration, but however defined or simplified (text, e.g., doesn't vanish but is revitalized; so, likewise, the Greco-European past itself), the performance/ritual impulse seems clear throughout: in "happenings" and related event pieces (particularly those that involve participatory performance), in meditative works (often on an explicitly mantric model), in earthworks (derived from monumental American Indian structures), in dreamworks that play off trance and ecstasy, in bodyworks (including acts of self-mutilation and endurance that seem to test the model), in a range of healing events as literal explorations of the shamanistic premise, in animal language pieces related to the new ethology, etc.°

•

While a likely characteristic of the new paradigm is an overt disdain for paradigms *per se*, it seems altogether possible to state a number of going assumptions as these relate to performance. I won't try to sort them out but will simply present them for consideration in the order in which they come to mind.

(1) There is a strong sense of continuities, already alluded to, within the total range of human cultures and arts, and a sense as well that the drive toward performance goes back to our pre-human biological inheritance—that performance and culture, even language, precede the actual emergence of the species: hence an ethological continuity as well. With this comes a rejection of the idea of artistic "progress" and a tendency to link avant-garde and "traditional" performance (tribal/oral, archaic, etc.) as forms of what Richard Schechner calls *transformational* theater and art—in opposition to the "mimetic/re-actualizing" art of the older paradigm.

(2) There is an unquestionable and far-reaching breakdown of boundaries and genres: between "art and life" (Cage, Kaprow), between various conventionally defined arts (intermedia and performance art, concrete poetry), and between arts and non-arts (*musique concrete*, found art, etc.). The consequences here are immense, and I'll only give a few, perhaps too obvious, examples (ideas of this kind do in fact relate to much else that is stated in these pages):

—that social conflicts are a form of theater (V. Turner) and that

°When I made a similar point in *Technicians of the Sacred* ten years earlier, I attributed the relation between "primitive" ritual and contemporary art and performance to an implicit coincidence of attitudes, where today the relation seems up-front, explicit, and increasingly comparable to the Greek and Roman model in Renaissance Europe, the Chinese model in medieval Japan, the Toltec model among the Aztecs, etc.: i.e., an overt influence but alive enough to work a series of distortions conditioned by the later culture and symptomatic of the obvious differences between the two. [Rothenberg's note.]

organized theater may be an arena for the projection and/or stimulation of social conflict;

—that art has again recognized itself as visionary, and that there may be no useful distinction between vision-as-vision and vision-as-art (thus, too, the idea in common between Freud and the Surrealists, that the dream is a dream-*work*, i.e., a work-of-art);

—that there is a continuum, rather than a barrier, between music and noise; between poetry and prose (the language of inspiration and the language of common and special discourse); between dance and normal locomotion (walking, running, jumping), etc.;

—that there is no hierarchy of media in the visual arts, no hierarchy of instrumentation in music, and that qualitative distinctions between high and low genres and modes (opera and vaudeville, high rhetoric and slang) are no longer operational;

—that neither advanced technology (electronically produced sound and image, etc.) nor hypothetically primitive devices (pulse and breath, the sound of rock on rock, of hand on water) are closed off to the artist willing to employ them.

The action hereafter is "between" and "among," the forms hybrid and vigorous and pushing always toward an actual and new completeness. Here is the surfacing, resurfacing in fact of that "liminality" that Victor Turner recognizes rightly as the place of "fruitful chaos" and possibility—but no less "here" than "there." It is, to say it quickly, the consequence in art-and-life of the freeing-up of the "dialectical imagination."

(3) There is a move away from the idea of "masterpiece" to one of the transientness and self-obsolescence of the art-work. The work past its moment becomes a document (mere history), and the artist becomes, increasingly, the surviving non-specialist in an age of technocracy.

(4) From this there follows a new sense of function in art, in which the value of a work isn't inherent in its formal or aesthetic characteristics— its shape or its complexity or simplicity as an object—but in what it does, or what the artist or his surrogate does with it, how he performs it in a given context. This is different in turn from the other, equally functional concept of art as propaganda, at least insofar as the latter forces the artist to repeat "truths" already known, etc., in the service of the total state. As an example of a non-formal, functional approach to the art object as instrument-of-power, take the following, from my conversations with the Seneca Indian sculptor/carver, Avery Jimerson:

> I told him that I thought Floyd John's mask was very beautiful, but he said it wasn't because it didn't have real power [the power, for example, to handle burning coals while wearing it]. His own father had had a mask that did, until there was a fire in his house and it was burnt to ashes. But his father could still see the features of the mask and so, before it crumbled, he hurried out and carved a second mask. And that second mask looked like the first in every detail. Only it had no power. (J. R., *A Seneca Journal*)

(5) There follows further, in the contemporary instance, a stress on action and/or process. Accordingly the performance or ritual model in-

cludes the act of composition itself: the artist's life as an unfolding through his performance of it. (The consideration of this private or closed side of performance is a little like Richard Schechner's discovery that rehearsal/preparation is a theatrical/ritual event as important as the showing it precedes.) Signs of the artist's or poet's presence are demanded in the published work, and in our own time this has come increasingly to take the form of his or her performance of that work, unfolding it or testifying to it in a public place. The personal presence is an instance as well of localization, of a growing concern with particular and local definitions; for what, asks David Antin, can be more local than the person?

(6) Along with the artist, the audience enters the performance arena as participant—or, the audience "disappears" as the distinction between doer and viewer, like the other distinctions mentioned herein, begins to blur. For this the tribal/oral is a particularly clear model, often referred to by the creators of 1960s happenings and the theatrical pieces that invited, even coerced, audience participation toward an ultimate democratizing of the arts. In a more general way, many artists have come to see themselves as essentially the initiators of the work ("makers of the plot but not of everything that enters into the plot"—Jackson Mac Low), expanding the art process by inviting the audience to join them in an act of "co-creation" or to respond with a new work in which the one-time viewer/listener himself becomes the maker. The response-as-creation thus supersedes the response-as-criticism, just as the maker/particularizer comes to be viewed (or to view himself) as the superior of the interpreter/generalizer. It is this which Charles Olson had in mind when he saw us emerging from a "generalizing time," etc., to regain a sense of the poem "as the act of the instant . . . not the act of thought about the instant." More dramatically, as a contrast between the involved participant and the objective observer, it turns up in Gary Snyder's story of Alfred Kroeber and his Mojave informant, *circa* 1902, in which Kroeber sits through six days of intense oral narration, the story of the world from its beginnings, and then writes:

> When our sixth day ended he still again said another day would see us through. But by then I was overdue at Berkeley. And as the prospective day might once more have stretched into several, I reluctantly broke off, promising him and myself that I would return to Needles when I could, not later than next winter, to conclude recording the tale. By next winter Inyo-Kutavere had died, and the tale thus remains unfinished. . . . He was stone blind. He was below the average of Mojave tallness, slight in figure, spare, almost frail with age, his gray hair long and unkempt, his features sharp, delicate, sensitive. . . . He sat indoors on the loose sand floor of the house for the whole of the six days that I was with him in the frequent posture of Mojave men, his feet beneath him or behind him to the side, not with legs crossed. He sat still but smoked all the Sweet Caporal cigarettes I provided. His house mates sat around and listened or went and came as they had things to do.

To which Snyder adds the single sentence: "That old man sitting in the sand house telling his story is who we must become—not A. L. Kroeber, as fine as he was."

The model switch is here apparent. But in addition the poet-as-informant stands in the same relation to those who speak of poetry or art from outside the sphere of its making as do any of the world's aboriginals. The antagonism to literature and to criticism is, for the poet and artist, no different from that to anthropology, say, on the part of the Native American militant. It is a question in short of the right to self-definition.

(7) There is an increasing use of real time, extended time, etc., and/or a blurring of the distinction between those and theatrical time, in line with the transformative view of the "work" as a process that's really happening. (Analogues to this, as alternative modes of narration, performance, etc., are again sought in tribal/oral rituals.) In addition an area of performance using similarly extended time techniques toward actual transformations (of the self, of consciousness, etc.) parallels that of traditional meditation (*mantra, yantra,* in the Tantric context), thus an exploration of the boundaries of mind that Snyder offers as the central work of contemporary man, or Duchamp from a perspective not all that different: "to put art again at the service of mind."

●

For all of this recognition of cultural origins and particularities, the crunch, the paradox, is that the place, if not the stance, of the artist and poet is increasingly beyond culture—a characteristic, inevitably, of biospheric societies. Imperialistic in their earlier forms and based on a paradigm of "the dominant culture" (principally the noble/imperial myths of "Western civilization" and of "progress," etc. on a Western or European model), these have in their *avant-garde* phase been turning to the "symposium of the whole" projected by Robert Duncan. More strongly felt in the industrial and capitalist west, this may be the last move of its kind still to be initiated by the Euro-Americans: a recognition of the new/old order in which the whole is equal to but no greater than the works of all its parts.

AMIRI BARAKA ■ ■ ■ ■ ■ ■ ■ ■ ■ ■ ■ ■ ■ ■

How You Sound??

"HOW YOU SOUND??" is what we recent fellows are up to. How *we* sound; our peculiar grasp on, say: a. Melican speech, b. Poetries of the world, c. Our selves (which is attitudes, logics, theories, jumbles of our lives, & all that), d. And the final . . . The Totality Of Mind: Spiritual . . . God?? (or you name it): Social (zeitgeist): or Heideggerian *umwelt.*

MY POETRY is whatever I think I am. (Can I be light and weightless as a sail?? Heavy & clunking like 8 black boots.) I CAN BE ANYTHING I CAN. I make a poetry with what I feel is useful & can be saved out of all the garbage of our lives. What I see, am touched by (CAN HEAR) . . . wives, gardens, jobs, cement yards where cats pee, all my interminable artifacts . . . ALL are a poetry, & nothing moves (with any grace) pried apart from these things. There cannot be closet poetry. Unless the closet be wide as God's eye.

And all that means that I *must* be completely free to do just what I want, in the poem. "All is permitted": Ivan's crucial concept. There cannot be anything I must *fit* the poem into. Everything must be made to fit into the poem. There must not be any preconceived notion or *design* for what the poem *ought* to be. "Who knows what a poem ought to sound like? Until it's thar." Says Charles Olson . . . & I follow closely with that. I'm not interested in writing sonnets, sestinas or anything . . . only poems. If the poem has got to be a sonnet (unlikely tho) or whatever, it'll certainly let me know. The only "recognizable tradition" a poet need follow is himself . . . & with that, say, all those things out of tradition he can use, adapt, work over, into something for himself. To broaden his *own* voice with. (You have to start and finish there . . . your own voice . . . how you sound.)

For me, Lorca, Williams, Pound and Charles Olson have had the greatest influence. Eliot, earlier (rhetoric can be so lovely, for a time . . . but only remains so for the rhetorician). And there are so many young wizards around now doing great things that everybody calling himself poet can learn from . . . Whalen, Snyder, McClure, O'Hara, Loewinsohn, Wieners, Creeley, Ginsberg &c. &c. &c.

Also, all this means that we want to go into a quantitative verse . . . the "irregular foot" of Williams . . . the "Projective Verse" of Olson. Accentual verse, the regular metric of rumbling iambics, is dry as slivers of sand. Nothing happens in that frame anymore. We can get nothing from England. And the diluted formalism of the academy (the formal culture of the U.S.) is anaemic & fraught with incompetence & unreality.

FROM *The LeRoi Jones/Amiri Baraka Reader*, 1991. First published in *The New American Poetry: 1945–1960*, 1960.

SUSAN HOWE ■ ■ ■ ■ ■ ■ ■ ■ ■ ■ ■ ■ ■ ■ ■ ■

There Are Not Leaves Enough to Crown
to Cover to Crown to Cover

For me there was no silence before armies. I was born in Boston Massachusetts on June 10th, 1937, to an Irish mother and an American father. My mother had come to Boston on a short visit two years earlier. My father had never been to Europe. She is a wit and he was a scholar. They met at a dinner party when her earring dropped into his soup.

By 1937 the Nazi dictatorship was well-established in Germany. All dissenting political parties had been liquidated and Concentration camps had already been set up to hold political prisoners. The Berlin-Rome axis was a year old. So was the Spanish Civil War. On April 25th Franco's Lufftwaffe pilots bombed the village of Guernica. That November Hitler and the leaders of his armed forces made secret plans to invade Austria, Czechoslovakia, Poland, and Russia.

In the summer of 1938 my mother and I were staying with my grandmother, uncle, aunt, great-aunts, cousins, and friends in Ireland, and I had just learned to walk, when Czechoslovakia was dismembered by Hitler, Ribbentrop, Mussolini, Chamberlin, and Daladier, during the Conference and Agreement at Munich. That October we sailed home on a ship crowded with refugees fleeing various countries in Europe.

When I was two the German army invaded Poland and World War II began in the West.

The fledgling Republic of Ireland distrusted England with good reason, and remained neutral during the struggle. But there was the Battle of the Atlantic to be won, so we couldn't cross the sea again until after 1945. That half of the family was temporarily cut off.

In Buffalo New York, where we lived at first, we seemed to be safe. We were there when my sister was born and the Japanese bombed Pearl Harbor.

Now there were armies in the west called East.

American fathers marched off into the hot Chronicle of global struggle but mothers were left. Our law-professor father, a man of pure principles, quickly included violence in his principles, put on a soldier suit and disappeared with the others into the thick of the threat to the east called West.

> B u f f a l o
> 12. 7. 41

FROM *The Europe of Trusts*, 1990.

(Late afternoon light.)
(Going to meet him in snow.)
HE
(Comes through the hall door.)
The research of scholars, lawyers, investigators, judges
Demands!

    SHE

       (With her arms around his neck
       whispers.)

Herod had all the little children murdered!

It is dark
The floor is ice

they stand on the edge of a hole singing—

In Rama
Rachel weeping for her children

refuses
to be comforted

because they *are* not.

Malice dominates the history of Power and Progress. History is the record of winners. Documents were written by the Masters. But fright is formed by what we see not by what they say.

From 1939 until 1946 in news photographs, day after day I saw signs of culture exploding into murder. Shots of children being herded into trucks by hideous helmeted conquerors—shots of children who were orphaned and lost—shots of the emaciated bodies of Jews dumped into mass graves on top of more emaciated bodies—nameless numberless men women and children, uprooted in a world almost demented. God had abandoned them to history's sovereign Necessity.

If to see is to *have* at a distance, I had so many dead Innocents distance was abolished. Substance broke loose from the domain of time and obedient intention. I became part of the ruin. In the blank skies over Europe I was Strife represented.

Things overlap in space and are hidden. Those black and white picture shots—moving or fixed—were a subversive generation. "The hawk, with his long claws / Pulled down the stones. / The dove, with her rough bill / Brought me them home."

    Buffalo roam in herds
    up the broad streets connected by boulevards

and fences

their eyes are ancient and a thousand years
too old

hear murder throng their muting

Old as time in the center of a room
doubt is spun

and measured

Throned wrath
I know your worth

a chain of parks encircles the city

Pain is nailed to the landscape in time. Bombs are seeds of Science and
the sun.

2,000 years ago the dictator Creon said to Antigone who was the daugh-
ter of Oedipus and Jocasta: "Go to the dead and love them."

Life opens into conceptless perspectives. Language surrounds Chaos.

During World War II my father's letters were a sign he was safe. A
miniature photographic negative of his handwritten message was re-
produced by the army and a microfilm copy forwarded to us. In the top
left-hand corner someone always stamped PASSED BY EXAMINER.

This is my historical consciousness. I have no choice in it. In my poetry,
time and again, questions of assigning *the cause* of history dictate the
sound of what is thought.

Summary of fleeting summary
Pseudonym cast across empty

Peak proud heart

Majestic caparisoned cloud cumuli
East sweeps hewn flank

Scion on a ledge of Constitution
Wedged sequences of system

Causeway of faint famed city
Human ferocity

Dim mirror Naught formula

archaic hallucinatory laughter

Kneel to intellect in our work
Chaos cast cold intellect back

Poetry brings similitude and representation to configurations waiting from forever to be spoken. North Americans have tended to confuse human fate with their own salvation. In this I am North American. "We are coming Father Abraham, three hundred thousand more," sang the Union troops at Gettysburg.

I write to break out into perfect primeval Consent. I wish I could tenderly lift from the dark side of history, voices that are anonymous, slighted—inarticulate.

CLARK COOLIDGE ▪ ▪ ▪ ▪ ▪ ▪ ▪ ▪ ▪ ▪ ▪ ▪ ▪

Words

Words, what to say about these things. Not things exactly, but what. As a subject? But am I not the subject of all things. You start with a tangle, put any head at all on it, it runs. About, in words. What to say. They obsess me? That they want out? They light and sculpt their own particular spaces. Such spaces that Gogol can have a man lose his nose and the nose walks about in the streets without feet of explanation; Beckett can watch himself giving himself the words, a special anxiety and delight inherited from our age of thought. Whole edifices of philosophy rising and falling on the momentary basis of what one has said. Word space, a marvelous and terrible and most friable condition. What I mean to say, pointed indications of an unconscious. Which, as Duncan says, we can never contact, whatever in mind already conscious. Transformation. How it all changes from what you thought to anymore think. *Moby Dick*, a distressing mess—the essentials of madness in a structure of whales?! Months of tracking the Pacific scratching on paper in a northlit room of Berkshire hills. Who is in there now. Lies, how. A space in which Guy Davenport can dispense with the painter Van Gogh, point for point an invention of Lautrec, Gaugin and brother Theo. Beckett begins Molloy's second section: "It is midnight. The rain is beating on the windows." and end it: "Then I went back into the house and wrote, It is midnight. The rain is beating on the windows. It was not midnight. It was not raining." Alright, obvious gaps, and naturally finally of time also. Otherwise how go any words. Sometimes it feels like Wittgenstein has written the armature of this century in his quicksand notebooks. Melville having already given us too much size. His pyramid of a whale still the vastest scale thing in any book. And Beckett pulled back to so few things that there is no end to the words arriving. The mind seizing

FROM *Friction*, No. 7, 1984. Originally given as a talk at Naropa Institute in Boulder, Colorado, July 1977.

on whatever, the motor then seized. Writing as a process of the freeze
and thaw. Rules? There are none. But forms, movements, flashes and
residua. What is a cat. Say, what? And having said that, how do you like
your cat now? Cat placed in such a situation is no longer a question. A
cat what is. What cat is a. The word is always initial. Zukofsky inhabit-
ing the first position for a lifetime, finds he must add all the other letters
quickly at the other end, to make an end. "For it is the end gives the
meaning to words"—Beckett. But my work will never be completed.
And habitually thinking of the title after the work, I realize too late
there will never be a title to this one, this lifetime. "Frequently there
must be a beverage"—Woody Allen. Rule, form the Latin: "model"
and "to direct." To direct a model? Sounds like photography. Plenty of
instruction, turn your head, again, just a little that way, but no cer-
tainty. Muybridge's stop-frames of a naked man on the run (1880's).
Then how come anyone could have mistaken "Breathless" (1959). It
seems relativity means it. Melville on himself writing *Moby Dick:* "He
has assassinated the natural day." Nothing if not the slamming together
of times and their spaces. Condensations and deformations of the book
"like a vast lumbering planet, revolves in his aching head. And all the
outside coming upon that becomes in it squeezed and transformed into
the final irreducible unrecognizability."—*Pierre.* Or is it all but that
rock on the window ledge, glowing in the grey light of this particular
spot of day? The words don't say. Though at least they move on. Move
on what. What I in the midst of this am trying to say. Yes, the midst, that
of this am trying. Then what I in this midst? The I picks up again, I was
waiting for it?, at this am that's trying to say. To say back again to the
initial what. The what not circular, but demanding yet another comple-
tion. In what I am trying to say of this midst. For "everything comes to
him from the middle of his field"—Wallace Stevens. In New Haven
where all evenings are ordinary (they move in succession): "The eye's
plain version of a thing apart . . . Of this, a few words, an and yet, and
yet, and yet—as part of the neverending meditation . . . these houses,
these difficult objects, dilapidate appearances of what appearances,
words, lines, not meaning, not communications, dark things without a
double, after all . . ." and on and on for thirty pages. Thus, the common-
place. A mountain covered with cats. "The catalogue is too commodi-
ous." So much for Whitman, Williams so much wanted to take the
measure of. And now the well-known plethora, our land with its car
stops. The "mess"—Beckett. And the accompanying desire to have it
all, but particularly (Uccello's battles). Can it be the language now
contains more words than there are things. Thus precipitates additional
things out of solution back into the universe. What a revolting develop-
ment that is. Human mind on the move (running scared?). "There
seemed to be an endless stream of things"—Dashiell Hammett, *The
Tenth Clew.* Surrounded and breathing. In my own words, what do
they want out of me. And I only own them in the very act of releasing
them. More than I know. "More than I could"—Beckett. And there's
another one, a little known form of peanut? But, looking closer, it's an

agate. "Indeed the whole visible world is perhaps nothing other than a motivation of man's wish to rest for a moment"—Franz Kafka, a writer of few satisfactions. But perhaps the reason one can never do what one feels oneself able to do is that one's ability is actually limitless?

Bring it all back down and in to the singular, the specific, the one. The unique, as one feels oneself to be in any strong act of focus. From the many the one. And then the next one. Not quite still, but as if just moved or about to move. And the absolutely still? Too impossibly mysterious, as every thing seems in motion, if only at the edge. Stillness of that order, perhaps a node peculiar to the mind alone. "To restore stillness is the role of objects"—Beckett. His desire? But for any radiance there must be motion. The pyramids in a noon sun. As Pound mis-had it from Confucius (and later Zukofsky in the annals of the Objective), the precise definition of the word *sincerity:* "pictorially the sun's lance coming to rest on the precise spot verbally." Some conundrum. To Zukofsky there is the motion of incompleteness in this sincerity ("which does not attain rested totality"). Next to this he places Objectification (rested totality): "distinct from print which records action and existence and incites the mind to further suggestion, there exists, though it may not be harbored as solidity in the crook of an elbow, writing (audibility in two-dimensional print) which is an object or affects the mind as such." This conglomerate stillness, the highest order to a man who lived his life in a house of music. Who later kept a regular count of the words in his lines, the barest possible ground for his variables? We merely count.

It is a field now. And the figures (of one possible figure) are oppositely Olson and Cage. Follow your nose, and follow your no's. Olson wants to possess it all, to will it all into definition ("I compel Gloucester/to yield, to/change"—Letter #27), Cage to get out of its way. What they leave us with is The Field. And pictures of possible activity. To Go, or To Let Go. All, or Nothing At All. One wants to Have, the other to Receive (Leave). Olson loved Melville because he was full, took on the largest things, and quantity became the prime term; Cage Zen because it holds everything as empty, no weight and not waiting. Both men of large ego, different techniques to divert or still them. Olson to heap up his will on things to make form, Cage to counter his will to allow forms he would otherwise have missed. They make a curious figure for art in our time. They seem mirrored opposites, but can be seen also to mix. Olson often to hazard a guess. Cage to will his indeterminacies into workable existence. Both inclined toward the pedagogic and the quest for social solutions. They only seem to have come together once, at Black Mountain, Olson reading from a stepladder, Cage arranging all other matters so that he could not be heard. They do seem to present an interference figure, but only if one follows them as dogmas. Instead, see the matter they are pointing out: The Field, of things and forces and absences. And the uses that can be made (transformations/syntheses) of their separate stands. As, one example, Godard's "The immediate is chance. At the same time it is definitive. What I want is the definitive by chance."

Olson's much-quoted statement, via Creeley (Form is never more than an extension of content), reposes the old scholastic separation, though seeking to close the gap by a more active mechanism. But there is no separation. Things are. No avoidance. And no scholarly equational rhymes (To be content with form one must form the content, etc.). To the working artist there is no such state as Form. or Content. Only forms. (Zukofsky's "we are words, horses, manes, words"—end of A-7.) Olson knows this in his quoting of Melville ("By visible truth we mean the apprehension of the absolute condition of present things"). But rather than accenting the necessary plural, he seems to come down harder on the *absolute* there (an unpublished Maximus, the single word: "Absoluteness"). One might say, we live intruded by a world of absolute plurals. The plethoran mode. Varying like and dis-likenesses. The heavy every, the noted nothing. Olson, Cage.

Put it all together, it spells "other," the "m" having been lost in the fray. I find myself very close in spirit and work to the Yes, But dialectics of the painter Philip Guston. You never have one thing but you have another, and they are never alike. They push, and recede, and blend, and advance, and refuse. But never stand long, except in the flash of a pause, having just moved, and/or being about to move once again. This seems the kinetics of thought/action: growth, destruction, transformation. An endless working of matters and forms. And it reveals doubt as active, if it forces on to move. As the scientists say, a negative result is after all also a result. What is it? Where is it? And what's next?

I have the sensation that the most honest man in the world is the artist when he is saying I don't know. At such moments he knows that, to the questions that truly interest him, only the *work* will give answers, which usually turn out further questions. This should be an instruction to any possible audience. I am reminded by this memory picture: a guy in my highschool class of such quick imaginative wit he could transform any happening into what it had not been a second before, thus making us all laugh, one day called on in physics class to answer a question stood up and gazing fiercely into space yelled "I DON'T KNOW!" Amazing. Obdurate as hell. And sametime a most apt correction of all his surroundings.

Cage: We're not going to go on playing games, even if the rules are downright fascinating. We require a situation more like it really is—no rules at all. Only when we make them do it in our labs do crystals win our games. Do they then? I wonder.

LYN HEJINIAN ▪ ▪ ▪ ▪ ▪ ▪ ▪ ▪ ▪ ▪ ▪ ▪ ▪

FROM The Rejection of Closure

✿   ✿   ✿

My title, "The Rejection of Closure," sounds judgmental, which is a little misleading—though only a little—since I am a happy reader of detective novels and an admiring, a very admiring, reader of Charles Dickens' novels.

Nevertheless, whatever the pleasures, in a fundamental way closure is a fiction—one of the amenities that fantasy or falsehood provides.

What then is the fundamental necessity for openness? Or, rather, what is there in language itself that compels and implements the rejection of closure?

I perceive the world as vast and overwhelming; each moment stands under an enormous vertical and horizontal pressure of information, potent with ambiguity, meaning-full, unfixed, and certainly incomplete. What saves this from becoming a vast undifferentiated mass of data and situation is one's ability to make distinctions. Each written text may act as a distinction, may be a distinction. The experience of feeling overwhelmed by undifferentiated material is like claustrophobia. One feels panicky, closed in. The open text is one which both acknowledges the vastness of the world and is formally differentiating. It is the form that opens it, in that case.

✿   ✿   ✿

Two dangers never cease threatening in the world: order and disorder.

Language discovers what one might know. Therefore, the limits of language are the limits of what we might know. We discover the limits of language early, as children. Anything with limits can be imagined (correctly or incorrectly) as an object, by analogy with other objects—balls and rivers. Children objectify language when they render it their plaything, in jokes, puns, and riddles, or in glossolaliac chants and rhymes. They discover that words are not equal to the world, that a shift, analogous to parallax in photography, occurs between things (events, ideas, objects) and the words for them—a displacement that leaves a gap. Among the most prevalent and persistent category of joke is that which identifies and makes use of the fallacious comparison of words to the world and delights in the ambiguity resulting from the discrepancy:

> Why did the moron eat hay?
> To feed his hoarse voice.

FROM *Writing/Talks*, ed. Bob Perelman, Carbondale, Ill., 1985. First given as a talk at 544 Natoma Street, San Francisco, on April 17, 1983. The essay was also published, in a different form, in *Poetics Journal*, No. 4, May 1984.

Because we have language we find ourselves in a peculiar relationship to the objects, events, and situations which constitute what we imagine of the world. Language generates its own characteristics in the human psychological and spiritual condition. This psychology is generated by the struggle between language and that which it claims to depict or express, by our overwhelming experience of the vastness and uncertainty of the world and by what often seems to be the inadequacy of the imagination that longs to know it, and, for the poet, the even greater inadequacy of the language that appears to describe, discuss, or disclose it.

This inadequacy, however, is merely a disguise for other virtues.

"What mind worthy of the name," said Flaubert, "ever reached a conclusion?"

Language is one of the principal forms our curiosity takes. It makes us restless. As Francis Ponge puts it, "Man is a curious body whose center of gravity is not in himself." Instead it seems to be located in language, by virtue of which we negotiate our mentalities and the world; off-balance, heavy at the mouth, we are pulled forward.

> She is lying on her stomach with one eye closed, driving a toy truck along the road she has cleared with her fingers. Then the tantrum broke out, blue, without a breath of air. . . . You could increase the height by making lateral additions and building over them a sequence of steps, leaving tunnels, or windows, between the blocks, and I did. I made signs to them to be as quiet as possible. But a word is a bottomless pit. It became magically pregnant and one day split open, giving birth to a stone egg, about as big as a football.
>
> —My Life

Language itself is never in a state of rest. And the experience of using it, which includes the experience of understanding it, either as speech or as writing, is inevitably active. I mean both intellectually and emotionally active.

The progress of a line or sentence, or a series of lines or sentences, has spatial properties as well as temporal properties. The spatial density is both vertical and horizontal. The meaning of a word in its place derives both from the word's lateral reach, its contacts with its neighbors in a statement, and from its reach through and out of the text into the other world, the matrix of its contemporary and historical reference. The very idea of reference is spatial: over here is word, over there is thing at which word is shooting amiable love-arrows.

                    ०   ०   ०

Writing develops subjects that mean the words we have for them.

Even words in storage, in the dictionary, seem frenetic with activity, as each individual entry attracts to itself other words as definition, example, and amplification. Thus, to open the dictionary at random, mastoid attracts nipplelike, temporal, bone, ear, and behind. Then turning to temporal we find that the definition includes time, space, life, world, transitory, and near the temples, but, significantly, not mastoid. There is no entry for nipplelike, but the definition for nipple brings protuberance, breast, udder, the female, milk, discharge, mouthpiece, and nursing bottle, and not mastoid, nor temporal, nor time, bone, ear, space, or world, etc. It is relevant that the exchanges are incompletely reciprocal.

> and how did this happen like an excerpt
>   beginning in a square white boat abob on a gray sea
>   tootling of another message by the hacking lark
> as a child to the rescue and its spring
>   many comedies emerge and in particular a group of girls
>   in a great lock of letters
>   like knock look
> a restless storage of a thousand boastings
> but cow dull bulge clump
>   slippage thinks random patterns through wishes
>   I intend greed as I intend pride
>   patterns of roll extend over the wish
>   —*Writing is an Aid to Memory*

The "rage to know" is one expression of restlessness produced by language.

> As long as man keeps hearing words
> He's sure that there's a meaning somewhere

says Mephistopheles in Goethe's *Faust*.

It's in the nature of language to encourage, and in part to justify, such Faustian longings. The notion that language is the means and medium for attaining knowledge, and, concomitantly, power, is old, of course. The knowledge towards which we seem to be driven by language, or which language seems to promise, is inherently sacred as well as secular, redemptive as well as satisfying. The *nomina sint numina* position (i.e., that there is an essential identity between name and thing, that the real nature of a thing is immanent and present in its name, that nouns are numinous) suggests that it is possible to find a language which will meet its object with perfect identity. If this were the case, we could, in speaking or in writing, achieve the at-oneness with the universe, at least in its particulars, that is the condition of paradise, or complete and perfect knowing—or of perfect mental health.

But if in the Edenic scenarios we acquired knowledge of the animals by naming them, it was not by virtue of any numinous immanence in the name but because Adam was a taxonomist. He distinguished the individual animals, discovered the concept of categories, and then organized the species according to their functions and relationships in a system.

What the naming provides is structure, not individual words.

As Benjamin Lee Whorf points out, ". . . every language is a vast pattern-system, different from others, in which are culturally ordained the forms and categories by which the personality not only communicates, but also analyzes nature, notices or neglects types of relationships and phenomena, channels his reasoning, and builds the house of his consciousness."

In this same essay, which appears to be the last he ever wrote (1941), entitled "Language, Mind, Reality," Whorf goes on to express what seems to be stirrings of a religious motivation: ". . . what I have called patterns are basic in a really cosmic sense." There is a "PREMONI-TION IN LANGUAGE of the unknown vaster world." The idea

> is too drastic to be penned up in a catch phrase. I would rather leave it unnamed. It is the view that a noumenal world—a world of hyperspace, of higher dimension—awaits discovery by all the sciences [linguistics being one of them], which it will unite and unify, awaits discovery under its first aspect of a realm of PATTERNED RELATIONS, inconceivably manifold and yet bearing a recognizable affinity to the rich and systematic organization of LANGUAGE.

It is as if what I've been calling, from *Faust,* the "rage to know," which is in some respects a libidinous drive, seeks also a redemptive value from language. Both are appropriate to the Faustian legend.

Both also seem in many respects appropriate to psychoanalytic theory, if one can say that in the psychoanalytic vision the "cure" is social and cultural as well as personal.

Coming in part out of Freudian psychoanalytic theory, especially in France, is a body of feminist thought that is even more explicit in its identification of language with power and knowledge—a power and knowledge that is political, psychological, and aesthetic—and that is identified specifically with desire.

The project for these French feminist writers is to direct their attention to "language and the unconscious, not as separate entities, but language as a passageway, and the only one, to the unconscious, to that which has been repressed and which would, if allowed to rise, disrupt the established symbolic order, which Jacques Lacan has dubbed the Law of the Father" (Elaine Marks, *Signs,* Summer 1978).

If the established symbolic order is the "Law of the Father," and it is discovered to be repressive and incomplete, then the new symbolic order is to be a "woman's language," corresponding to a woman's desire.

Luce Irigaray:

> But woman has sex organs just about everywhere. She experiences pleasure almost everywhere. Even without speaking of the hysterization of her entire body, one can say that the geography of her pleasure is much more diversified, more multiple in its differences, more complex, more subtle, than is imagined. . . . "She" is indefinitely other in herself. That is undoubtedly the reason she is called temperamental, perturbed, capricious—not to mention her language in which "she" goes off in all directions. . . .
>
> —*New French Feminisms*

I find myself in disagreement with the too narrow definition of desire, with the identification of desire solely with sexuality, and with the literalness of the genital model of women's language that some of these writers insist on.

But what was striking to me in reading the collection of essays from which the above quote was taken was that the kinds of language that many of these writers advocate seem very close to, if not identical with, what I think of as characteristic of many contemporary avant-garde texts—including an interest in syntactic disjunctures and realignments, in montage and pastiche as structural devices, in the fragmentation and explosion of subject, etc., as well as an antagonism to closed structures of meaning. Yet of the writers from this area whom I have read to date, only Julia Kristeva is exploring this connection.

For me, too, the desire that is stirred by language seems to be located more interestingly within language, and hence it is androgynous. It is a desire to say, a desire to create the subject by saying, and even a feeling of doubt very like jealousy that springs from the impossibility of satisfying this desire.

This desire is like Wordsworth's "underthirst / Of vigor seldom utterly allayed."

Carla Harryman:

> When I'm eating I want food. . . . The I expands. The individual is caught in a devouring machine, but she shines like the lone star on the horizon when we enter her thoughts, when she expounds on the immensity of her condition, the subject of the problem which interests nature.
>
> —"Realisms"

If language induces a yearning for comprehension, for perfect and complete expression, it also guards against it. Hence the title of my poem "The Guard."

> Windows closed on wind in rows
> Night lights, unrumorlike, the reserve for events
> All day our postures were the same
> Next day the gentleman was very depressed and had a
>   headache; so much laughing had upset him he thought
> The urge to tell the truth is strong
> Delightful, being somewhere else so much the moment of
>   equivalence
> To be lucky a mediation
> To look like life in the face
> The definition quotes happiness
> The egg is peafowl
> The kitchen: everyone eats in different cycles—yeh,
>   the dishes are all over the counter. . . . yeh, food's
>   left out, things are on the stove. . . . yeh, the floor's
> filthy—that's amazing! have you been there?
> Like the wind that by its bulk inspires confidence
> Red and yellow surefire reflect on the breakdown
> The forest is a vehicle of tremors
> When mad, aged nine, and dressed in calico
> Confusion is good for signs of generosity
> Each sentence replaces an hallucination
> But these distractions can't safeguard my privacy
> During its absence, my presence

> Every hour demonstrates time's porosity
> The ghosts that blend with daylight come out like stars
>   in the dark longing to have their feet fit in boots
> And finish in Eden.

Faust complains:

> It is written: "In the beginning was the Word!"
> Already I have to stop! Who'll help me on?
> It is impossible to put such trust in the
> Word!

Such is a recurrent element in the argument of the lyric:

> Alack, what poverty my Muse brings forth. . . .

> Those lines that I before have writ do lie. . . .

> For we / Have eyes to wonder but lack tongues to praise. . . .

In the gap between what one wants to say (or what one perceives there is to say) and what one can say (what is sayable), words provide for a collaboration and a desertion. We delight in our sensuous involvement with the materials of language, we long to join words to the world—to close the gap between ourselves and things, and we suffer from doubt and anxiety as to our capacity to do so because of the limits of language itself.

Yet the very incapacity of language to match the world allows it to do service as a medium of differentiation. The undifferentiated is one mass, the differentiated is multiple. The (unimaginable) complete text, the text that contains everything, would be in fact a closed text. It would be insufferable.

For me, a central activity of poetic language is formal. In being formal, in making form distinct, it opens—makes variousness and multiplicity and possibility articulate and clear. While failing in the attempt to match the world, we discover structure, distinction, the integrity and separateness of things.

BERNADETTE MAYER ▪ ▪ ▪ ▪ ▪ ▪ ▪ ▪ ▪ ▪ ▪

The Obfuscated Poem

The poem may have to mean nothing for a while or reflect in its meaning just the image of meaning. As a method of learning how to write, the obfuscated poem must still cover to hide a real energy in training. The obfuscated poem leads nowhere on its own, it is a study, it is occasionally a political nothingness text, it is an experiment conducted by a

FROM *Code of Signals: Recent Writings in Poetics*, ed. Michael Palmer, Berkeley, 1983.

person (who may have something to hide). There's something that isn't learned or even known yet. The best obfuscation bewilders old meanings while reflecting or imitating or creating a structure of a beauty that we know. So something can be perceived and it's that. This is the talent of the poet who is studying to learn and who feels or thinks a certain way today. Under an influence, swayed or swaying, obfuscation could become a profession or addiction (there is always the danger of making a statement). Then at best hints of great illumination in the medium mix with now erudite structure which betrays an inimitable synchronicity with the workings of the mind and its psychology.

Abdication of feeling in life or in the mind creates a liverish potential for dead issues.

The idea that real change—and its consequent repellent revolution where your best friend's suddenly the prison warden in the rigid stumbling of professional belief—is not at the heart of experiment in which lies the chance for liberation, is the kind of scam where you might find the book you are reading grabbed from your hands.

Your new friends say structure is complex but we must leave out a part of everything not to see what happens like we used to think but to just not see. Therefore you've committed a felony.

Like a vogue for resuscitation abdication of feeling makes the scene of the dying man protected from the doctor by the experimenting crowd.

To change without belief is anarchistic as instinct pricks from the Latin (stinguere), no law but that the absence of law is the resistance of love instinct with tact like the expression of this thought.

Poetry's not a business; it was not her business or his to remake the world.

Holding to a course with the forbidden sublime, love of beauty originally obfuscates or sublimates to refine what is unclear to be unscrambled later from its perception of perfection by that continuing. Which is to change the world. As it does which is why, nothing individually lost, there's a difference to be told.

RON SILLIMAN ▪ ▪ ▪ ▪ ▪ ▪ ▪ ▪ ▪ ▪ ▪ ▪ ▪ ▪ ▪ ▪ ▪

Of Theory, To Practice

> To write poetry after Auschwitz is barbaric.
> —THEODOR ADORNO

Lenin's comment that "Thought, rising from the concrete to the abstract, does not get farther away *from* the truth, but gets closer to it"[1] stands in sharp contrast to the stated beliefs of many, perhaps most, 20th century American poets, expressed succinctly by Williams' "no ideas but in things." Such a self-containment would seem to preclude any "rising from the concrete to the abstract." Robert Creeley states the case for this confinement:

> A poetry denies its end in any *descriptive* act, I mean any act which leaves its attention outside the poem. Our anger cannot exist usefully without its objects, but a description of them is also a perpetuation. There is that confusion—one wants the thing to act on, and yet hates it. *Description* does nothing, it includes the object—it neither hates nor loves.[2]

He carries this to a logical conclusion, one that apparently manifests itself in the early poems of Clark Coolidge: "poems are not referential, or at least not importantly so."[3]

Yet the work of both Creeley and Williams is actively concerned with theory. *Words, Pieces* and *Spring & All* explicitly address issues of writing without ceasing to be literature. Both poets have written reviews, theoretical essays and prefaces. Each has been associated with at least one semi-organized literary movement. If a contradiction is perceived between their practice and their discourse about it, this is due only to a misconception of the function of theory, and to the sort of degeneration which occurs when any idea is generalized through popular usage (such as that which has rendered "no ideas but in things" the battle cry of anti-intellectualism in verse).

The goal of poetry can never be the proof of theory, although it is inevitably a test of the poet's beliefs. Such beliefs are themselves the writer's perceptions of *already-written* poems (by others as well as oneself), combined with a sense of a desired direction: "this is where I want my poem to go."

Not surprisingly for a society based on capitalism and its ideology of individualism, these perceptions often consist of unorganized intuitions. Intuition is, for me, the critical term in this discussion. It is the raw

FROM *The New Sentence*, 1987. A different version of this essay was first published in *Paper Air*, Vol. 2, No. 2, 1979, under the title "Notes on the Relation of Theory to Practice."

1. Cited in Ferruccio Rossi-Landi, *Linguistics and Economics* (Mouton, 1975), p. 5. [Silliman's note.] 2. "To Define," *A Quick Graph: Collected Notes & Essays* (Four Seasons Foundation, 1970), p. 23. [Silliman's note.] 3. "Poems are a complex," *A Quick Graph*, p. 54. [Silliman's note.]

material of what Lukács terms "proletarian consciousness." In its unorganized state, it can only *react* "spontaneously" to the undigested phenomenological data of everyday life. Reaction, in this sense, is always the inverse of action: it is the kind of intuition that recognizes the objective existence of a large mass of permanently unemployed black males in this society, without perceiving why or how such a fact has come to be, thus apt to blame individuals for a lifestyle they were born and literally tracked into. Organized intuition would transfer one's anger to the appropriate causes of this condition. One rises from the concrete person to the abstract politics of labor.

This has everything to do with poetry, but not in the way of justifying propaganda. The writer cannot organize her desires for writing without some vision of the world toward which one hopes to work, and without having some concept of how literature might participate in such a future. Unorganized reactive intuition is incapable of achieving any vision beyond the current fact, although it is quite able to psychologically block much of what makes the present unpleasant. Dozens of happy love poems are written every day.

As the organization of intuition and critical perception, theory functions in poetic practice through the selection of goals and strategies. This specifically implies the *rejection* of some in favor of others. To the degree that these methods differ visibly from those of the past (a shift which may rightly be interpreted as a rejection of the present), their result will be works of art which appear new. The production of novelty, of art objects that could not have been predicted, and cannot be accounted for, by previous critical theory, is the most problematic area in aesthetics. Like a record in sports, made only to be broken, a poetics is articulated in order to be transcended.

Yet there is something about American poetry in the 20th century which is generating an increasingly rapid evolution of form(s). The formal distance between Dryden and Yeats is less than between Pound and Warren. Just as *Personae* now reeks of an epoch from which it was once thought to be a radical break, any poet writing today is assured a future conventionality beyond their control. No doubt the pressure of this acceleration in literary historicity contributes to confusion, doubt and defensiveness on the part of poets and likewise sets the stage for works whose sole redeeming value is some vague commitment to Make It Different, if not new.

Heretofore, discussion of this "heating up" of forms has been in the terms of commodification, which seems generally correct, as far as it goes. But poetry is only partly a commodity in the strict sense of that term, in that to become a commodity a product must specifically be created with the purpose of exchange within a market. All books and magazines are commodities, but not all poems, a fact which complicates literature, creating numerous levels of bastard cases.

There is, however, a second factor, one first noted by Laura Riding,[4] contributing to this disease of newness in poetics, related to the poem

---

4. "T.E. Hulme, the New Barbarians, & Gertrude Stein," in *Contemporaries and Snobs*, (Cape, 1928), pp. 123–99. [Silliman's note.]

as product, not commodity. This is a shift in perception of the role of form in modern life, specifically as an *index of labor*. The more any product looks like its predecessors, the less work appears to have gone into it.

This is true for many cases. The less modification one must make from one generation of a product to the next, the less capital an owner, corporate or otherwise, must expend in design and "modernization" of manufacturing equipment. The capitalist is thus permitted to either carry these unexpended costs forward in the price of the product as pure surplus value, or else to amortize them over a longer period of time, lowering the price in order to expand the potential market. Consider the history of the Volkswagen "bug."

An object's life as product is fused with its career as commodity. The origin of style, as Riding sensed and Walter Benjamin stated explicitly, is the transference of the perception of the *labor : form* relation away from structure towards packaging. Most automobiles just look new. So too the poem.

It is a loaded question whether less labor need be put into a sonnet than into the prosoid works of contemporary poets. Certainly the disjuncture between the regularities of the sonnet form and the discordances of contemporary life renders any good one a monument of productive work. But in the case of the loosely written, speech-like free verse dramatic monolog concerning the small travails of daily existence—in short *most poems now being written*—the conclusion is painfully evident. Half of the graduate students in any creative writing program can turn these out with no more effort than it takes to bake bread.

But is labor a value in itself for poetry? Among the several social functions of poetry is that of posing a model of unalienated work: it stands in relation to the rest of society both as utopian possibility and constant reminder of just how bad things are. But here too the situation of the poem is undergoing change. Once this template of useful activity was predicated upon the image of the poem as individual craft of the artisan type, while now the collective literature of the community, an ensemble of "scenes," is gradually emerging as more vital than the production of single authors. In either situation, maximum productivity is going to be a critical quality of labor. In the poem this means a maximum of effort.

This does not mean that good poetry should, prima facie, be difficult or obscure. Modernism has been no less immune to the shift in emphasis from production to consumption than other domains of life, and much literature can be reduced to the consumption of effort, in which the opposite of difficulty is thought to be trash. *Spring & All,* "A" 9 and *Pieces* might have cured us of that, but obviously they haven't. Once reading strategies catch up to those of writing, a lot of complexity is going to dissolve. Ease awes. For good reason.

All these issues have crucial analogs at the level of writing itself. For example, the recognition that the very presence of the line is the predominant current signifier of The Poetic will cause some poets to discard, at least for a time, its use. This, in turn, requires a new organizational strategy constructed around a different primary unit. Two alternative candidates have recently been proposed: (1) prose works built around investigations of the sentence (although Watten and Hejinian's approach to paragraph and stanza are interesting variations); (2) the page itself as spatial unit filled with "desyntaxed" words or phrases, as in the work of Bruce Andrews. Either road is going to determine the kinds of language which the resulting poem can incorporate and that means restricting to some degree the domains of life which can be presented.

In the *sentence-centered* poem, a major problematic surrounds the use of long sentences. Unless one is specifically seeking the ironic tonality of an Ashbery, long hypotactic sentences cannot be strung together so as to hold a reader's attention without highly convoluted internal syntax to break them down into phrase clusters. Even more difficult is the long sentence taken from a class-specific professional jargon with a minimal use of clear "technical" terms. The special, oppressive meanings of these words (an important area of language to investigate) tend to disappear when removed from originating contexts.

Andrews' *page-as-field* presents different problems. The polysemic quality of words at the bottom or top of the paper is lost when a work is presented on two (or more) pages. Print alters the invariant em of the typewriter. Syntax, that lineating element, also has a habit of reinserting itself in even the smallest of phrases. As Robert Grenier has shown, the organization of letters into a single word already presumes the presence of a line.

Are these examples of poetry made subservient to (or, in Creeley's words, "describing") theory? No more than the sonnet. Every mode of poem is the manifestation of some set of assumptions. It's no more foolish to be conscious of them—and their implications extending into the daily life of the real world—than it is to actually have some idea how to drive before getting behind the wheel of a car.

NATHANIEL MACKEY ▪ ▪ ▪ ▪ ▪ ▪ ▪ ▪ ▪ ▪ ▪

FROM Sound and Sentiment, Sound and Symbol

Senses of music in a number of texts is what I'd like to address—ways of regarding and responding to music in a few instances of writings which bear on the subject. This essay owes its title to two such texts, Steven Feld's *Sound and Sentiment: Birds, Weeping, Poetics and Song in*

FROM *The Politics of Poetic Form: Poetry and Public Policy*, 1990. Originally presented on April 26, 1985, as part of the St. Mark's Talks series and first published in *Callaloo*, Vol. 10, No. 1, 1987. This excerpt is Part 1 of a five-part essay.

Kaluli Expression and Victor Zuckerkandl's *Sound and Symbol: Music and the External World.* These two contribute to the paradigm I bring to my reading of the reading of music in the literary works I wish to address.

Steven Feld is a musician as well as an anthropologist and he dedicates *Sound and Sentiment* to the memory of Charlie Parker, John Coltrane, and Charles Mingus. His book, as the subtitle tells us, discusses the way in which the Kaluli of Papua New Guinea conceptualize music and poetic language. These the Kaluli associate with birds and weeping. They arise from a breach in human solidarity, a violation of kinship, community, connection. *Gisalo*, the quintessential Kaluli song form (the only one of the five varieties they sing that they claim to have invented rather than borrowed from a neighboring people), provokes and crosses over into weeping—weeping which has to do with some such breach, usually death. *Gisalo* songs are sung at funerals and during spirit-medium seances and have the melodic contour of the cry of a kind of fruitdove, the *muni* bird.[1] This reflects and is founded on the myth regarding the origin of music, the myth of the boy who became a *muni* bird. The myth tells of a boy who goes to catch crayfish with his older sister. He catches none and repeatedly begs for those caught by his sister, who again and again refuses his request. Finally he catches a shrimp and puts it over his nose, causing it to turn a bright purple red, the color of a *muni* bird's beak. His hands turn into wings and when he opens his mouth to speak the falsetto cry of a *muni* bird comes out. As he flies away his sister begs him to come back and have some of the crayfish but his cries continue and become a song, semiwept, semisung: "Your crayfish you didn't give me. I have no sister. I'm hungry. . . ." For the Kaluli, then, the quintessential source of music is the orphan's ordeal—an orphan being anyone denied kinship, social sustenance, anyone who suffers, to use Orlando Patterson's phrase, "social death,"[2] the prototype for which is the boy who becomes a *muni* bird. Song is both a complaint and a consolation dialectically tied to that ordeal, where in back of "orphan" one hears echoes of "orphic," a music which turns on abandonment, absence, loss. Think of the black spiritual "Motherless Child." Music is wounded kinship's last resort.

In *Sound and Symbol*, whose title Feld alludes to and echoes, Victor Zuckerkandl offers "a musical concept of the external world," something he also calls "a critique of our concept of reality from the point of view of music." He goes to great lengths to assert that music bears witness to what's left out of that concept of reality, or, if not exactly what, to the fact that something *is* left out. The world, music reminds us, inhabits while extending beyond what meets the eye, resides in but rises above what's apprehensible to the senses. This coinherence of immanence and transcendence the Kaluli attribute to and symbolize through birds, which for them are both the spirits of the dead and the

1. Examples of *gisalo* and other varieties of Kaluli song can be heard on the album *The Kaluli of Papua Niugini: Weeping and Song* (Musicaphon BM 30 SL 2702). [Mackey's note.]   2. *Slavery and Social Death: A Comparative Study* (Cambridge, 1982). [Mackey's note.]

major source of the everyday sounds they listen to as indicators of time, location and distance in their physical environment. In Zuckerkandl's analysis, immanence and transcendence meet in what the terms "the dynamic quality of tones," the relational valence or vectorial give and take bestowed on tones by their musical context. He takes great pains to show that "no material process can be co-ordinated with it," which allows him to conclude:

> Certainly, music transcends the physical; but it does not therefore transcend tones. Music rather helps the thing "tone" to transcend its own physical constituent, to break through into a nonphysical mode of being, and there to develop in a life of unexpected fullness. Nothing but tones! As if tone were not the point where the world that our senses encounter becomes transparent to the action of nonphysical forces, where we as perceivers find ourselves eye to eye, as it were, with a purely dynamic reality—the point where the external world gives up its secret and manifests itself, immediately, *as symbol*. To be sure, tones say, signify, point to—what? Not to something lying "beyond tones." Nor would it suffice to say that tones point to other tones—as if we had first tones, and then pointing as their attribute. No—in musical tones, being, existence, is indistinguishable from, *is*, pointing-beyond-itself, meaning, saying.[3]

One easily sees the compatibility of this musical concept of the world, this assertion of the intrinsic symbolicity of the world, with poetry. Yeats' view that the artist "belongs to the invisible life" or Rilke's notion of poets as "bees of the invisible" sits agreeably beside Zuckerkandl's assertion that "because music exists, the tangible and visible cannot be the whole of the given world. The intangible and invisible is itself a part of this world, something we encounter, something to which we respond." His analysis lends itself to more recent formulations as well. His explanation of dynamic tonal events in terms of a "field concept," to give an example, isn't far from Charles Olson's "composition by field." And one commentator, to give another, has brought *Sound and Symbol* to bear on Jack Spicer's work.[4]

The analogy between tone-pointing and word-pointing isn't lost on Zuckerkandl, who, having observed that "in musical tones, being, existence, is indistinguishable from, *is*, pointing-beyond-itself, meaning, saying," immediately adds: "Certainly, the being of words could be characterized the same way." He goes on to distinguish tone-pointing from word-pointing on the basis of the conventionally agreed-upon referentiality of the latter, a referentiality writers have repeatedly called into question, frequently doing so by way of "aspiring to the condition of music." "Thus poetry," Louis Zukofsky notes, "may be defined as an order of words that as movement and tone (rhythm and pitch) approaches in varying degrees the wordless art of music as a kind of mathematical limit."[5] Music encourages us to see that the symbolic is the orphic, that the symbolic realm is the realm of the orphan. Music is

3. *Sound and Symbol: Music and the External World* (Princeton, 1956), 371. Subsequent citations are incorporated into the text. [Mackey's note.]   4. Stephanie A. Judy, "The Grand Concord of What': Preliminary Thoughts on Musical Composition and Poetry," *Boundary 2*, VI, 1 (Fall 1977): 267–85. [Mackey's note.]   5. *Prepositions* (Berkeley, 1981), 19. [Mackey's note.]

prod and precedent for a recognition that the linguistic realm is also the realm of the orphan, as in Octavio Paz's characterization of language as an orphan severed from the presence to which it refers and which presumably gave it birth. This recognition troubles, complicates, and contends with the unequivocal referentiality taken for granted in ordinary language:

> Each time we are served by words, we mutilate them. But the poet is not served by words. He is their servant. In serving them, he returns them to the plenitude of their nature, makes them recover their being. Thanks to poetry, language reconquers its original state. First, its plastic and sonorous values, generally disdained by thought; next, the affective values; and, finally, the expressive ones. To purify language, the poet's task, means to give it back its original nature. And here we come to one of the central themes of this reflection. The word, in itself, is a plurality of meanings.[6]

Paz is only one of many who have noted the ascendancy of musicality and multivocal meaning in poetic language. (Julia Kristeva: "The poet . . . wants to turn rhythm into a dominant element . . . wants to make language perceive what it doesn't want to say, provide it with its matter independently of the sign, and free it from denotation."[7])

Poetic language is language owning up to being an orphan, to its tenuous kinship with the things it ostensibly refers to. This is why in the Kaluli myth the origin of music is also the origin of poetic language. The words of the song the boy who becomes a *muni* bird resorts to are different from those of ordinary speech. Song language, "amplifies, multiplies, or intensifies the relationship of the word to its referent," as Feld explains:

> In song, text is not primarily a proxy for a denoted subject but self-consciously multiplies the intent of the word.
> . . . Song poetry goes beyond pragmatic referential communication because it is explicitly organized by canons of reflexiveness and self-consciousness that are not found in ordinary talk.
> The uniqueness of poetic language is unveiled in the story of "the boy who became a *muni* bird." Once the boy has exhausted the speech codes for begging, he must resort to another communication frame. Conversational talk, what the Kaluli call *to halaido*, "hard words," is useless once the boy has become a bird; now he resorts to talk from a bird's point of view . . . Poetic language is bird language.[8]

It bears emphasizing that this break with conventional language is brought about by a breach of expected behavior. In saying no to her brother's request for food the older sister violates kinship etiquette.

What I wish to do is work *Sound and Sentiment* together with *Sound and Symbol* in such a way that the latter's metaphysical accent aids and is in turn abetted by the former's emphasis on the social meaning of sound. What I'm after is a range of implication which will stretch, to quote Stanley Crouch, "from the cottonfields to the cosmos." You notice again that it's black music I'm talking about, a music whose "critique of

6. *The Bow and the Lyre* (New York, 1973), 37. [Mackey's note.]   7. *Desire in Language: A Semiotic Approach to Literature and Art* (New York, 1980), 31. [Mackey's note.]
8. *Sound and Sentiment: Birds, Weeping, Poetics and Song in Kaluli Expression* (Philadelphia, 1982), 34. [Mackey's note.]

our concept of reality" is notoriously a critique of social reality, a critique of social arrangements in which, because of racism, one finds oneself deprived of community and kinship, cut off. The two modes of this critique which I'll be emphasizing Robert Farris Thompson notes among the "ancient African organizing principles of song and dance":

> *suspended accentuation patterning* (offbeat phrasing of melodic and choreographic accents); and, at a slightly different but equally recurrent level of exposition, *songs and dances of social allusion* (music which, however danceable and "swinging," remorselessly contrasts social imperfections against implied criteria for perfect living).[9]

Still, the social isn't all of it. One needs to hear alongside Amiri Baraka listening to Jay McNeeley, that "the horn spat enraged sociologies,"[1] but not without noting a simultaneous mystic thrust. Immanence and transcendence meet, making the music social as well as cosmic, political and metaphysical as well. The composer of "Fables of Faubus" asks Fats Navarro, "What's *outside* the universe?"[2]

This meeting of transcendence and immanence I evoke, in my own work, through the figure of the phantom limb. In the letter which opens *From a Broken Bottle Traces of Perfume Still Emanate* N. begins:

> You should've heard me in the dream last night. I found myself walking down a sidewalk and came upon an open manhole off to the right out of which came (or strewn around which lay) the disassembled parts of a bass clarinet. Only the funny thing was that, except for the bell of the horn, all the parts looked more like plumbing fixtures than like parts of a bass clarinet. Anyway, I picked up a particularly long piece of "pipe" and proceeded to play. I don't recall seeing anyone around but somehow I knew the "crowd" wanted to hear "Naima." I decided I'd give it a try. In any event, I blew into heaven knows what but instead of "Naima" what came out was Shepp's solo on his version of "Cousin Mary" on the *Four for Trane* album—only infinitely more gruffly resonant and varied and warm. (I even threw in a few licks of my own.) The last thing I remember is coming to the realization that what I was playing already existed on a record. I could hear scratches coming from somewhere in back and to the left of me. This realization turned out, of course, to be what woke me up.
> Perhaps Wilson Harris is right. There are musics which haunt us like a phantom limb. Thus the abrupt breaking off. Therefore the "of course." No more than the ache of some such would-be extension.[3]

I'll say more about Wilson Harris later. For now, let me simply say that the phantom limb is a felt recovery, a felt advance beyond severance and limitation which contends with and questions conventional reality, that it's a feeling for what's not there which reaches beyond as it calls into question what is. Music as phantom limb arises from a capacity for feeling which holds itself apart from numb contingency. The phantom limb haunts or critiques a condition in which feeling, consciousness itself, would seem to have been cut off. It's this condition, the non-objective character of reality, to which Michael Taussig applies the expression "phantom objectivity," by which he means the veil by way

9. *Flash of the Spirit: African and Afro-American Art and Philosophy* (New York, 1984), xiii. [Mackey's note.]   1. *Tales* (New York, 1967), 77. [Mackey's note.]   2. Charles Mingus, *Beneath the Underdog* (New York, 1980), 262. [Mackey's note.]   3. *Bedouin Hornbook* (Charlottesville, 1986), 1. [Mackey's note.]

of which a social order renders its role in the construction of reality invisible: "a commodity-based society produces such phantom objectivity, and in so doing it obscures its roots—the relations between people. This amounts to a socially instituted paradox with bewildering manifestations, the chief of which is the denial by the society's members of the social construction of reality."[4] "Phantom," then, is a relative, relativizing term which cuts both ways, occasioning a shift in perspective between real and unreal, an exchange of attributes between the two. So the narrator in Josef Skvorecky's *The Bass Saxophone* says of the band he's inducted into: "They were no longer a vision, a fantasy, it was rather the sticky-sweet panorama of the town square that was unreal."[5] The phantom limb reveals the illusory rule of the world it haunts.

BRUCE ANDREWS ▪ ▪ ▪ ▪ ▪ ▪ ▪ ▪ ▪ ▪ ▪ ▪ ▪

FROM Poetry as Explanation, Poetry as Praxis

> O, the vilest are destined for rewards
> and the best stand gaping
> mouths wide before an empty simalcrum,
> The narrative alone makes me gloomy,
> and the rich conduct their business on their heads.
> — MARCABRU, Provencal 12th century, tr. Blackburn

I'll use as the fulcrum of my remarks on politics & radicalism in recent literary work the two book-length anthologies of the kind of poetry Charles Bernstein & I focussed on in editing $L = A = N = G = U = A = G = E$ and *The $L = A = N = G = U = A = G = E$ Book* (1984): Douglas Messerli, ed., *"Language" Poetries* (1987), & Ron Silliman, ed., *In the American Tree* (1986).

I'm always trying to reorganize my life. And I'm always trying to reorganize the world — words writing writing politics. Incomprehension is the subtitle.

I GET IMPATIENT

Conventionally, radical dissent & 'politics' in writing would be measured in terms of communication & concrete effects on an audience. Which means either a direct effort at empowering or mobilizing — aimed at existing identities — or at the representation of outside conditions, usually in an issue-oriented way. So-called 'progressive lit.' The

4. *The Devil and Commodity Fetishism in South America* (Chapel Hill, 1980), 4. [Mackey's note.]   5. *The Bass Saxophone* (London, 1980), 109. [Mackey's note.]

FROM *The Politics of Poetic Form: Poetry and Public Policy*, 1990. Originally presented as a talk in the fall of 1988 at the Wolfson Center for National Affairs at the New School for Social Research. "I Get Impatient" and "Method" are parts one and five of a five-part essay.

usual assumptions about unmediated communication, giving 'voice' to 'individual' 'experience,' the transparency of the medium (language), the instrumentalizing of language, pluralism, etc. bedevil this project. But more basically: such conventionally progressive literature fails to self-examine writing & its medium, language. Yet in an era where the reproduction of the social status quo is more & more dependent upon ideology & language (language in ideology & ideology in language), that means that it can't really make claims to comprehend and/or challenge the nature of the social whole; it can't be political in that crucial way.

A desire for a social, political dimension in writing — embracing concern for a public, for community goods, for overall comprehension & transformation — intersects an overall concern for language as a medium: for the conditions of its makings of meaning, significance or value, & sense. Technicians of the Social — the need to see society as a whole. That has meant, in recent years with this work, a conception of writing *as* politics, not writing *about* politics. Asking: what is the *politics* inside the work, inside *its* work? Instead of instrumentalized or instrumentalizing, this is a poetic writing more actively *explanatory*. One that explores the *possibilities* of meaning, of 'seeing through': works that foreground the process by which language 'works,' implicating the history & context that are needed to allow the writing to be more comprehensively understood, bringing those building blocks & limits of meaning & sense back *inside* the writing, giving you greater distance by putting them within the internal circuitry.

Explanation embeds itself in the writing itself — *locating* work in relation to its social materials: to what it handles, resists, characterizes. It reads the outside, it doesn't just read itself. It doesn't try to be self-explanatory in a formalist, process-oriented way, enclosed within its own separate realm. It is itself an interpretation. It is a response, a production that takes place within a larger context of reproduction. And this is the reflexivity which we should be on the look-out for — a social kind, that comes through *method* (of writing & of reading) — not (just) 'content.' Method as Prescription — posing problems, eliciting reading.

Nothing passes unalarmed. Limits aren't located until they're pushed. Rewriting the social body — as a body to body transaction: to write *into operation* a 'reading body' which is more & more self-avowedly *social*. Lay bare the device, spurn the facts as not self-evident. A V-effect, to combat the obvious; to stand out = to rebel; counter-embodiment, with our "paper bullets of the brain." All this points to a look at language as medium — in two respects: first, as a sign system; second, as discourse or ideology. Concentric circles, one inside the other. In both cases, though, the same concern: stop repressing the active construction, the *making* of meaning, the *making* of sense — social sense.

What we face first is the language seen in formal terms: the *sign*. There is no 'direct treatment' of the thing possible, except of the 'things' of language. Crystalline purity — or transparency — will not be found in words. That classical ideal is an illusion — one which recommends that we repress the process of production or cast our glance away from it. An alternative would face the medium of language — through which we might get a poetry that is a reading which acknowledges, or faces up to, its material base as a rewriting of the language. To cast doubt on each & every 'natural' construction of reality. Not just by articulating the gap between the sign & the referent — or theatricalizing that gap by avoiding meaning altogether — but to show off a more systematic idea of language as a system & play of differences, with its own rules of functioning. Radical praxis — at this level, at this level, or within this first concentric circle — here involves the rigors of formal celebration, a playful infidelity, a certain illegibility *within* the legible: an infinitizing, a wide-open exuberance, a perpetual motion machine, a transgression.

o   o   o

METHOD

In editing $L=A=N=G=U=A=G=E$, we said we were "emphasizing a spectrum of writing that places attention primarily on language and ways of making meaning, that takes for granted neither vocabulary, grammar, process, shape, syntax, program, or subject matter." And that refusal to take things for granted can in turn pose a direct challenge to *social norms* about vocabulary, grammar, process, shape, syntax, program & subject-matter.

The method of the writing confronts the *scale & method* by which established sense & meaning reign: an allegory — (or will we be called 'the Methodist Poets' now?). Form & content unfold within — that is to say, are choices within — *method*, on a total scale. And writing's (social) method is its politics, its explanation, since 'the future' is implicated one way or another by how reading reconvenes conventions. By obedience or disobedience to authority. By the way writing might be prefigurative in its *constructedness* at different levels, within different arenas: semiosis, dialogue, hegemonic struggles. To widen the realm of social possibility: not just by embodying dreams but by mapping limits — the possible rerouted through the impossible — by disruptiveness, by restaging the methods of how significance & value in language do rest upon the *arbitrary* workings of the sign yet also on the *systematic* shaping work of ideology & power. An encompassing method.

Faced with rules or patterns of constraint — the negative face of ideology — writing can respond with a drastic openness. Here, an open horizon gets defined, dynamically, by failures of immediate sense — surrenders, even — which are failures in the workings of this *negative power*. To look for — & make — problems. To open up new relationships by crazed collision — laying bare the device, but this time it's a more social device, the Emperor wearing no clothes.

It's as if the established order tries to sew itself up — into permanent stability — & to sew us & our meanings up inside it. Yet if the social order both constructs & disrupts us, we both construct & disrupt that social order. And if there was romanticism in celebrating the barely sustained cohesion of the sign, the same may be true socially. Writing's method, in other words, can suggest a *social* undecidability, a lack of successful *suture*. Tiny cuts: syntacted glare, facts *en bloc,* circuit breaking in which a break *renders,* syntax as demolition derby. This displacement or social unbalancing has more than nuisance value. It's more than an invitation to an ego trip for righteous poets. Instead, it offers a guide by which matters outside *do not* hang together — an unsuturable condition: where norms are contradicted & where you can recognize that therefore they *can* be contradicted, the space for reading blossoms.

But ideology also works in a positive way, as a form of *positive power:* constructing our identities, soliciting our identification, our pledges of allegiance. If identification is built into the subject form — so that its positive meanings are already overproduced — then 'subjects speaking their minds' 'authentically' will not be enough. The overall shape of making sense needs to be reframed, restaged, put back into a context of 'pre-sense' — to reveal its constructed character; to reveal by critique, by demythologizing. Otherwise, its apparent immediacy dupes us: the lack of distance is a kind of closure.

An active dramatizing of this socialization — by what the writing does with its own reading & its own readability — shows off this process. By detonating this identifying impulse, we get closer to a full social reflexiveness. Questions & doubt subvert an exterior which has now insinuated itself inside. For the only immediacy possible is an immediacy of address, of *readers* 'talking back,' where the distances writing creates appear as hospitality.

What is called for is writing as a *counter*-reading — that is, as a counter-socialization. To put in motion this *social* productivity: the process by which significance is constructed for others (& for ourselves as others). To remotivate & politicize, for the reader, the identity-making process; to make it possible to become *less* of an exile in our own words — the words we read by writing. Both negatively (confronting the restrictions of constraining rules) — & positively (by remotivating the desires produced by positive or constitutive rules). [Provisionally — if we use the distinction between metonymy & metaphor — it looks like surprises of constraint & the skirting of negative power would be most visible at the metonymic level; while excitements of desire — 'deep content,' verticality, metaphor — would appear as recastings of *motive,* of the 'why for' of positive power. A notion of an *allegory of method* would offer a way to think about radical poetry's work *on this* positive, metaphoric front.]

Not only the workings of the sign but also the workings of sense & ideology are part of the social order's way of defining itself. And these can both be questioned — within a counterculture or counter-hegemony embracing reader & writer — so that a different & more global mode of address is suggested: by poetry's social scale & social method as it rematerializes & reconstructs the language (both as sign & context). Writing that in this way public-izes, publicizing its way into the public sphere, can foster this recognition of the system, of what we're up against: a recognition that's at the basis of *social literacy;* a social comprehension or total encompassing & *maximizing* that we need to orient our praxis & re-envision the social contract. This is the method of 'intelligence,' as Bakhtin defined it: "a dialog with one's own future and an address to the external world." And if writing can imply such a future, that future will serve as its radical prescription.

VICTOR HERNÁNDEZ CRUZ ■ ■ ■ ■ ■ ■ ■ ■ ■

Mountains in the North: Hispanic Writing in the U.S.A.

The earth is migration, everything is moving, changing interchanging, appearing, disappearing. National languages melt, sail into each other; languages are made of fragments, like bodies are made of fragments of something in the something. Who'd want to stand still, go to the edges where you see clear the horizon, explore the shape of the coast? Are poets not the antennas of the race? Then tune into the chatter, the murmur that arises from the collection. Add and subtract, submit it to your mathematics. Take and give. Enlarge, diminish. The Romans ate everything up and now we dance Latin to African music, so we don't exactly fall into the things through the words. Columbus thought he came to the land of India and he even mistook Cuba for Japan. Language is clarification of the inner, of the part that does not rot. Moving through a terrain, languages would sound out gradation scale—Italian, Spanish, Portuguese—and so move through the whole planet making a tapestry. Old geography lingers in the language of the conquistadores: names of rivers and fruits. Our Spanish—which has Latin and Italian—has Taino, Siboney, Chichimeca. It has sounds coming out of it that amaze it and over the years it has been spiced, making it a rich instrument full of our history, our adventures, our desires, ourselves. The Caribbean is a place of great convergence; it mixes and uniforms diversities; it is a march of rhythm and style.

Those of us who have ventured off into writing should be in awe of the possibilities inherent in our tradition. Writing is behind the scenes; it is not like music and dance which engulf the masses. Poetry gets to the people in the form of lyrics within a bolero or a salsa tune. It is a valid form of expression, for it contains image and story line; it places old proverbs at the entrance of our contemporary ears. Poetry also lives in the oral tradition known as declamation. There is a warehouse of poems from the Spanish which are memorized and bellowed from the various

FROM *Red Beans,* 1991.

corners of balconies and colors. The moon is in the tongue between the cheeks, the troubadours move between ceiba trees and plazas, their poetry full of the battles of love, romance, lost love, what to do within the pain of departure. Conversation, spontaneous chitchat constantly interchanging, is a poetry that arises all around us; it is poetry in flight, it is the magic of words bouncing off the pueblos, off the trees into the vines, it comes through the floor like an anaconda, it darts like lizards, it soars like garzas: this language of the Caribbean, this criollo incarnation. Full of passion and opinions, this is the language of our parents. We are the sons and daughters of campesinos, fishermen, farmers who cultivated café and tobacco, cutters of cane whose eyes contain the memory of ardent green vistas out of wooden windows within the hottest tropicality. They have pictures of the ocean tongues and the vibrant hugging of the coast upon a sofa within their retinas. They were spiritual mediums and santeros who worshiped natural forces tapped since time immemorial by African and indigenous societies.

As the children of these immigrants, we are at the center of a world debate; we can speak of the shift from agriculture to industry to technology and the toll it has taken upon the human equilibrium. Let us look at it with clear eyes in our trajectory from one language (Spanish) to another (English). What have we lost or gained? Claro, there is the beautiful lyricism, rhyming and blending of that great romance language, exemplified even in the reading of books on mechanical operations in which the words are still sonorous despite the subject. Is there an inner flower which passions its fragrance despite its being clothed in English words? I believe that this is happening in much U.S. Hispanic literature; the syntax of the English is being changed. This can be seen very prominently within the work of Alurista, a Chicano poet. In his recent work, the subject is the language itself; it is not that he merely plays with the language as some Anglo language experimenters do, for his poetry still contains social meanings directed towards personal and political change and awareness. We also find in the prose work of Rudolfo Anaya a natural Spanish pastoral style resounding through his English, a very relaxed, unharsh sentence. In both the English and the Spanish the poets and writers uphold a sensibility of Hispanitude.

We battle the sterility of Anglo culture, of television clichés; we labor at being ourselves in a land of weirdos, electric freaks who sit mesmerized in front of screens and buttons, only stopping to eat the farthest reaches of junk or to jerk off about some personal need to be understood, barking about having the freedom to do whatever nauseous things their lifestyles call for. You know that a pastime of the North American middle class now is to go out to fields and dress up in military fatigues and play war, shoot the commies or, better yet, shoot third-world guerrillas—shoot real guerrillas—and after that get back in the pickup and go down to Burger King and eat whatever that is. Meanwhile, the ozone layer is disappearing and, what's that song sung by Richie Havens, "Here Comes the Sun"? Then they have that thing where they eat until they almost explode and then stick their fingers down their throat and vomit, solely to start the process again. It's an image culture: what you see is all there is. Jane Fonda in *Barbarella* was offering body; now that she has gained consciousness she is offering more body and even better build.

Did Richard Rodriguez fall down hard? Well there are those who jump quickly to attack him because he seemed to say the opposite of what was being fought for. Of course we must strive for an English that is standard and universal, a language that can be understood by as many people as possible, but why lose the Spanish in the process? We should change the English and give it spice, Hispanic mobility, all this can be done within the framework of understanding, whether the reader is Anglo or Latino.

U.S. Hispanics have not blended into Northern Americana because our roots stay fresh. Due to the close proximity of the Americas, rushes of tropical electricity keep coming up to inform the work and transform the North American literary landscape. The location and atmosphere of stories and poetry have been taken to places that until now North American authors were only able to write about from the position of tourists. The literature is full of border towns, farm workers, the lives of salsa musicians blowing through northern cities. The racial and cultural mixing of our cultures keeps us jumping through a huge spectrum of styles and philosophies. In terms of history, we can walk the planet with our genes, imagine ourselves in the Sevilla of the Arabs holding court with ibn 'Arabi and al-Ghazálí, quickly switch over to the halls of Tenochtitlán, then once again wake up in our contemporary reality dancing Yoruba choreography in some club in Manhattan near a subway train. You can change the content and mix into the infinite. Worlds exist simultaneously, flashes of scenarios, linguistic stereo; they conflict, they debate, Spanish and English constantly breaking into each other like ocean waves. Your head scatters with adverbs over the horizon.

All art forms borrow from each other for the purpose of enrichment. Architects can draw from ancient and colonial styles to arrive at their contemporary geometries—structures which improve human living. Musicians are constantly blending and mixing the rhythms of the earth; Caribbean music is like Andalucía and the Ivory Coast. In New York's Latin-Jazz fusion in the forties and fifties there are cuts where Tito Puente jams with Charlie Parker; this is like a toning of temperaments, or adjusting reality to get the most out of it. It seems to be the center of the musician to translate, rearrange, to give personal flavor to a variety of rhythms and melodies.

There are some words, so personal, so locked up in the oral and geographic area of a certain people that puns and stories have to be translated first into the standard language in order for them to be understood by speakers of the same language from another country, and passing them into another language is a labor of losing flavor, for there are things which remain within the mountains and can never be put into the textbook. If I said *un maflon* next to a Spaniard, he might look at me with a certain degree of curiosity and wonder what space I was coming from. Latinos speaking to each other have to constantly stop and review certain words. Sometimes when a word jumps over to the next country, it takes on an opposite meaning, or a word which you can yell in the plaza at the top of your voice, like *popusa* in El Salvador, moonlights as the private part of a woman in Guatemala. Anglos have difficulty grasping the variety of our world and have a tendency to slip us all under the same blanket in a careless act of generalizing, which upholds their manner: "Oh," they might say, "if you've read one Latino novel, you've read them all." In a system that works on quotas, this dispatches a lot of talented voices. Latin American writers publish with a lot more facility than U.S.-born Hispanics writing in English or Spanish. It is the habit of the establishment to enjoy things at a distance; package it with ease, throw the label "magic realism" on it—it's gotta be magic, unreal sells well as exotica. Now, we know who these writers are and I for one have great respect for them and their work, but because the Anglos work on quotas, the tremendous visibility of the Latin American writers obscures the chances for U.S. Hispanics of getting published by the same presses. It isn't the fault of these brilliant Latin American writers, but of the publicity machinery they get attached to. The society of the Americas is probably the most complex and diverse experiment in culture upon this earth and a full picture can only be obtained by allowing writers from many angles and countries to be exposed.

Unlike other groups who have had to erase their own cultural memories, Hispanics are moving forward, maintaining their own tradition and language. We will be the first group that does not melt; our ingredients are raw and the Anglo fire is not hot enough to dissolve them.

In the North of America it is a constant job just keeping ourselves from going looney-tunes, for this is a place where every stupidity is made available for the purpose of jamming the circuits. Explore, for example, the limited capacity of many in this electric culture to remember details of events: they are not able to tell stories. Computer screens have everybody dizzy, seeing dots in the air. Food preservatives are destroying taste buds. With all this going on, one must be on the watch: you gotta watch out that the next person doesn't jump and start acting out something he saw on television the previous night. It is the job of writers to perceive and explain the truth. To get to the essence of things in this society is a monumental task of awareness.

CHARLES BERNSTEIN ▪ ▪ ▪ ▪ ▪ ▪ ▪ ▪ ▪ ▪ ▪ ▪

Semblance

> It's as if each of these things has a life of its own.
> You can stretch them, deform them and even
> break them apart, and they still have an inner
> cohesion that keeps them together.

Not "death" of the referent—rather a recharged use of the multivalent referential vectors that any word has, how words in combination tone and modify the associations made for each of them, how 'reference' then is not a one-on-one relation to an 'object' but a perceptual dimension that closes in to pinpoint, nail down (*this* word), sputters omnitropically (the in in the which of who where what wells), refuses the build up of image track/projection while, pointillistically, fixing a reference at each turn (fills vats ago lodges spire), or, that much rarer case (Peter Inman's *Platin* and David Melnick's *Pcoet* two recent examples) of "zaum" (so-called transrational, pervasively neologistic)—"ig ok aberflappi"—in which reference, deprived of its automatic reflex reaction of word/stimulus image/response roams over the range of associations suggested by the word, word shooting off referential vectors like the energy field in a Kirillian photograph.

All of which are ways of releasing the energy inherent in the referential dimension of language, that these dimensions are the material of which the writing is made, define its medium. Making the structures of meaning in language more tangible and in that way allowing for the maximum resonance for the medium—the traditional power that writing has always had to make experience palpable not by simply pointing to it but by (re)creating its conditions. °

Point then, at first instance, to see the medium of writing—our area of operation—as maximally open in vocabulary, forms, shapes, phoneme/morpheme/word/phrase/sentence order, etc., so that possible

FROM *Content's Dream: Essays 1975–1984*, 1986. First published in *Reality Studios*, Vol. 2, No. 4, 1980, as part of a symposium, "Death of the Referent?"

° Alan Davies has objected that language and experience are separate realms and that the separation should be maximized in writing, in this way questioning the value of using language to make experience palpable.—But I don't mean 'experience' in the sense of a picture/image/representation that is calling back to an already constituted experience. Rather, language itself constitutes experience at every moment (in reading and otherwise). Experience, then, is not tied into representation exclusively but is a separate 'perception'-like category. (& perception not necessarily as in perception onto a physical/preconstituted world, as "eyes" in the Olson sense, that is, not just onto a matrix-qua-the-world but as operating/projecting/composing activity.) The point is, then, that experience is a dimension necessarily built into language—that far from being avoidable, or a choice, it is a property. So this view attempts to rethink representational or pictorial or behaviorist notions of what 'experience' is, i.e., experience is not inextricably linked to representation, normative syntax, images, but rather, the other way around, is a synthetic, generative activity—"in the beginning was the word" & so on, or that's our 'limit' of beginnings. [Bernstein's note.]

areas covered, ranges of things depicted, suggested, critiqued, considered, etc., have an outer limit (asymptotic) of what can be thought, what can (might) be. But then, taking that as zero degree, not to gesturalize the possibility of poetry to operate in this 'hyperspace,' but to create works (poems) within it.

The order of the words, the syntax, creates possibilities for images, pictures, representations, descriptions, invocation, ideation, critique, relation, projection, etc. Sentences that follow standard grammatical patterns allow the accumulating references to enthrall the reader by diminishing diversions from a constructed representation. In this way, each word's references work in harmony by reinforcing a spatiotemporal order conventionalized by the bulk of writing practice that creates the 'standard.' "The lamp sits atop the table in the study"—each word narrowing down the possibilities of each other, limiting the interpretation of each word's meaning by creating an ever more specific context. In a similar way, associations with sentences are narrowed down by conventional expository or narrational paragraph structure, which directs attention away from the sentence as meaning generating event and onto the 'content' depicted. By shifting the contexts in which even a fairly 'standard' sentence finds itself, as in some of the prose-format work of Barrett Watten, the seriality of the ordering of sentences within a paragraph displaces from its habitual surrounding the projected representational fixation that the sentence conveys. "Words elect us. The lamp sits atop the table in the study. The tower is burnt orange. . . ." By rotating sentences within a paragraph (a process analogous to jump cutting in film) according to principles generated by and unfolding in the work (rather than in accordance with representational construction patterns) a perceptual vividness is intensified for each sentence since the abruptness of the cuts induces a greater desire to savor the tangibility of each sentence before it is lost to the next, determinately other, sentence. Juxtapositions not only suggest unsuspected relations but induce reading along ectoskeletal and citational lines. As a result, the operant mechanisms of meaning are multiplied and patterns of projection in reading are less restricted. The patterns of projection are not, however, undetermined. The text operates at a level that not only provokes projections by each sentence but by the sequencing of the sentences suggests lines or paths for them to proceed along. At the same time, circumspection about the nature and meaning of the projections is called forth. The result is both a self-reflectiveness and an intensification of the items/conventions of the social world projected/suggested/provoked. A similar process can also take place within sentences and phrases and not only intersententially. Syntactic patterns are composed which allow for this combination of projection and reflection in the movement from word to word. "For as much as, within the because, tools their annoyance, tip to toward."—But, again, to acknowledge this as the space of the text, and still to leave open what is to be said, what projections desire these reflections.

The sense of music in poetry: the music of meaning—emerging, fogging, contrasting, etc. Tune attunement in understanding—the meaning sounds. It's impossible to separate prosody from the structure (the form and content seen as an interlocking figure) of a given poem. You can talk about strategies of meaning generation, shape, the kinds of sounds accented, the varieties of measurement (of scale, of number, of line length, of syllable order, of word length, of phrase length, or measure as punctuation, of punctuation as metrics). But no one has primacy—the music is the orchestrating of these into the poem, the angles one plays against another, the shading. In much of my own work: working at angles to the strong tidal pull of an expected sequence of a sentence—or by cutting off a sentence or phrase midway and counting on the mind to complete where the poem goes off in another direction, giving two vectors at once—the anticipated projection underneath and the actual wording above.

My interest in not conceptualizing the field of the poem as a unitary plane, and so also not using overall structural programs: that any prior principle of composition violates the priority I want to give to the inherence of surface, to the total necessity in the durational space of the poem for every moment to *count*. The moment not subsumed into a schematic structure, hence instance of it, but at every juncture creating (synthesizing) the structure. So not to have the work resolve at the level of the "field" if this is to mean a uniplanar surface within which the poem operates. Structure that can't be separated from decisions made within it, constantly poking through the expected parameters. Rather than having a single form or shape or idea of the work pop out as you read, the structure itself is pulled into a moebius-like twisting momentum. In this process, the language takes on a centrifugal force that seems to trip it out of the poem, turn it out from itself, exteriorizing it. Textures, vocabularies, discourses, constructivist modes of radically different character are not integrated into a field as part of a predetermined planar architecture; the gaps and jumps compose a space within shifting parameters, types and styles of discourse constantly crisscrossing, interacting, creating new gels. (Intertextual, interstructural . . .) (Bruce Andrews has suggested the image of a relief map for the varying kinds of referential vectors—reference to different domains of discourse, references made by different processes—in some of his work in which words and phrases are visually spaced out over the surface of the page. However, the structural dissonance in these works is counterbalanced by the perspicacious poise of the overall design, which tends to even-out the surface tension.)

Writing as a process of pushing whatever way, or making the piece cohere as far as can: stretching my mind—to where I know it makes sense but not quite why—suspecting relations that I understand, that make the sense of the ready-to-hand—i.e., pushing the composition to the very limits of sense, meaning, to that razor's edge where judgment/aesthetic sense is all I can go on (know-how). (Maybe what's to get beyond in Olson's field theory is just the idea of form as a single web, a unified field, one matrix, with its implicit idea of 'perception' onto a given world rather than, as well, onto the language through which the world is constituted.) So that the form, the structure, that, finally, is the poem, has emerged, is come upon, is made.

Credits

Bruce Andrews: "I Get Impatient" and "Method" from "Poetry as Explanation, Poetry as Praxis" in *The Politics of Poetic Form* (Roof Books, 1989). Copyright © 1989 by Bruce Andrews. Reprinted by permission of the author.

Angel Hair Books. **Hannah Weiner**: "3/10," "3/15," and "Fri May 17" from *Clairvoyant Journal* (Angel Hair Books, 1978). Copyright © 1978 by Hannah Weiner. Reprinted by permission of the publisher.

Another Chicago Press. **Maxine Chernoff**: "The Man Struck Twenty Times by Lightning," "Lost and Found," "How Lies Grow," and "Breasts" from *Leap Year Day: New and Selected Poems* (Another Chicago Press, 1990). Copyright © 1990 by Maxine Chernoff. Reprinted by permission of Another Chicago Press.

Arte Publico Press. **Miguel Algarín**: "Tato—Reading at the Nuyorican Poets' Cafe," "Nudo de claridad," and "San Francisco" from *On Call* (Arte Publico Press–University of Houston, 1980). Reprinted by permission of Arte Publico Press.

Art Lange: "Perugia" and "Sonnet for the Season" from *Evidence* (The Yellow Press, 1981). Copyright © 1981 by Art Lange. Reprinted by permission of the author.

Avenue B. **Maxine Chernoff**: "Amble" and "Black" from *Japan* (Avenue B Press, 1987). Copyright © 1987 by Maxine Chernoff. Reprinted by permission of the publisher. **Michael Davidson**: "The Form of Chiasmus; The Chiasmus of Forms" and "Thinking the Alps" from *Post Hoc* (Avenue B, 1990). Copyright © 1990 by Michael Davidson. Reprinted by permission of the publisher.

Awede. **Keith Waldrop**: *A Shipwreck in Haven*, Part 1, from *A Shipwreck in Haven: Transcendental Studies* (Awede, 1989). Copyright © 1989 by Keith Waldrop. Reprinted by permission of the publisher.

Bill Berkson: "Russian New Year" and "Rebecca Cutlet" from *Blue Is the Hero: Poems 1960–1975* (L Publications, 1976). Copyright © 1976 by Bill Berkson. "Melting Milk" from *New American Writing* (No. 1, 1987). Copyright © 1987 by Bill Berkson. Reprinted by permission of the author.

Charles Bernstein: "The Klupzy Girl" from *Islets/Irritations* (Roof Books, 1992). Copyright © 1983, 1992 by Charles Bernstein. Reprinted by permission of the author.

Black Sparrow Press. **Charles Bukowski**: "crucifix in a deathhand," "startled into life like fire," and "i am dead but i know the dead are not like this," from *Burning in Water, Drowning in Flame: Selected Poems 1955–1973*, © 1974; "my old man" from *Love Is a Dog from Hell: Poems 1974–1977*, © 1977; "the mockingbird" from *Mockingbird Wish Me Luck*, © 1972. Reprinted with the permission of Black Sparrow Press. **Tom Clark**: "You (I)," "You (III)," and "Baseball and Classicism" from *When Things Get Tough on Easy Street: Selected Poems 1963–1978*; "Suicide with Squirtgun" from *Disordered Ideas*, © 1987; "Society" from *Fractured Karma*, © 1990. "Like musical instruments . . ." from *Sleepwalker's Fate: New and Selected Poems 1965–1991*, © 1992. Reprinted with permission of Black Sparrow Press. **Wanda Coleman**: "Essay on Language" and "Brute Strength" from *Heavy Daughter Blues: Poems & Stories 1968–1986*, © 1987. "the ISM" from *Imagoes*, © 1983. "African Sleeping Sickness" from *African Sleeping Sickness: Stories & Poems*, © 1990. Reprinted with permission of Black Sparrow Press. **Larry Eigner**: "trees green the quiet sun," "how it comes about," "open air where," "Wholes," "a temporary language" from *The World and Its Streets, Places*, © 1977. Reprinted with permission of Black Sparrow Press. **Clayton Eshleman**: "The Lich Gate" from *Hades in Manganese*, © 1981. "Notes on a Visit to Le Tuc d'Audoubert" from *The Name Encanyoned River: Selected Poems 1960–1985*, © 1986. Reprinted with permission of Black Sparrow Press. **Robert Kelly**: "Coming" from *The Mill of Particulars*, © 1973. "The Rainmakers," "Bittersweet growing up the

Schuyler: "A Man in Blue," "The Crystal Lithium," "Letter to a Friend: Who Is Nancy Daum?," and "Korean Mums" from *Selected Poems*. Copyright © 1988 by James Schuyler. Reprinted by permission of Farrar, Straus and Giroux, Inc. **Gary Snyder:** "Riprap" from *Riprap and Cold Mountain Poems*. Copyright © 1959, 1965 by Gary Snyder. "Axe Handles" from *Axe Handles*. Copyright © 1983 by Gary Snyder. Published by North Point Press and reprinted by permission of Farrar, Straus & Giroux, Inc.

The Figures. **Clark Coolidge:** *At Egypt*, Part I, from *At Egypt* (The Figures, 1988). Reprinted by permission of the publisher. **Stephen Rodefer:** "Pretext," "Codex," and sections from *Plane Debris* from *Four Lectures* (The Figures, 1982). Copyright © 1982 by Stephen Rodefer. Reprinted by permission of the publisher.

Four Seasons Foundation. **Edward Dorn:** "The Rick of Green Wood," "Geranium," "From Gloucester Out," and "An Idle Visitation" from *Collected Poems 1956–1974*. Copyright © 1975, 1983 by Edward Dorn. Reprinted by permission of the Four Seasons Foundation.

Kathleen Fraser: "re:searches (fragments after Anakreon, for Emily Dickinson)" from *Notes Preceding Trust* (The Lapis Press, 1987). Copyright © 1987 by Kathleen Fraser. Reprinted by permission of the author.

Amy Gerstler: "The True Bride" from *The True Bride* (The Lapis Press, 1986). Copyright © 1986 by Amy Gerstler. Reprinted by permission of the author.

Allen Ginsberg: Part I of *Howl* from *Howl*, edited by Barry Miles (Harper & Row, 1986). Copyright © 1986 by Allen Ginsberg. "Notes for *Howl and Other Poems*" from *The Poetics of the New American Poetry* (Grove Press, 1973). Copyright © 1973 by Allen Ginsberg. "A Supermarket in California," "To Aunt Rose," "America," the Proem section of *Kaddish*, "First Party at Ken Kesey's with Hell's Angels," and "On Neal's Ashes" from *Collected Poems 1947–1980* (Harper & Row, 1984). Copyright © 1984 by Allen Ginsberg. The above are reprinted by permission of the author.

John Giorno: "Scum & Slime" and "Life Is a Killer" from *You Got to Burn to Shine* (Serpents Tail Press, 1993). Reprinted by permission of the author.

John Godfrey: "Our Lady" and "Wings" from *Dabble: Poems 1966–1980* (Full Court Press, 1982). Copyright © 1982 by John Godfrey. "So Let's Look at It Another Way" and "Where the Weather Suits My Clothes" from *Where the Weather Suits My Clothes* (Z Press, 1984). Copyright © 1984 by John Godfrey. Reprinted by permission of the author.

Robert Grenier: "Has Faded in Part but Magnificent Also Late," "Crow," "Wrath to Sadness," and "Sunday Morning" from *Phantom Anthems* (O Books, 1986). Copyright © 1986 by Robert Grenier. Reprinted by permission of the author.

Grove Press. **Jack Kerouac:** Choruses from *Mexico City Blues*. Copyright © 1959 by Jack Kerouac; copyright renewed in 1987 by Jan Kerouac. Used by permission of Grove Press, Inc. **Frank O'Hara:** "Poem" ("The eager note on my door . . .") and "Poem" ("At night Chinamen . . .") from *Meditations in an Emergency*. Copyright © 1957 by Frank O'Hara. Reprinted with permission of Grove Press.

Barbara Guest: "Red Lilies" from *Moscow Mansions* (Viking/Compass, 1973). Reprinted by permission of the author.

Hanging Loose Press. **Charles North:** "A Note to Tony Towle (After WS)" from *The Year of the Olive Oil* (Hanging Loose Press, 1989). Copyright © 1989 by Charles North. Reprinted by permission of the publisher. **Tony Towle:** "Random (Rearrangeable) Study for *Views*" from *Some Musical Episodes* (Hanging Loose Press, 1992). Copyright © 1992 by Tony Towle. Reprinted by permission of the publisher. **Paul Violi:** "When to Slap a Woman" from *Likewise* (Hanging Loose Press, 1988). Copyright © 1988 by Paul Violi. Reprinted by permission of the publisher.

Carla Harryman: "My Story," "Realism," and "The Male" from *Animal Instincts* (This, 1989). Copyright © 1989 by Carla Harryman. Reprinted by permission of the author.

Anselm Hollo: "Godlike," "Italics," and "Wild West Workshop Poem" from *Near Miss Haiku* (The Yellow Press, 1990). Reprinted by permission of the author.

Paul Hoover: "Poems We Can Understand" and "Heart's Ease" from *Somebody Talks a Lot* (The Yellow Press, 1983). Copyright © 1983 by Paul Hoover. "Desire"

Index